C‹

F‹ ... ,

TEMPLE

LONDON EC4Y 9 DH

01-583-3335

Butterworths
Medico-legal
Encyclopaedia

Butterworths Medico-legal Encyclopaedia

J K Mason, CBE, MD, FRCPath, DMJ
Regius Professor (Emeritus) of Forensic Medicine,
University of Edinburgh

R A McCall Smith, LLB, PhD
Associate Dean, Faculty of Law,
University of Edinburgh

Butterworths
London Boston Durban Singapore Sydney Toronto Wellington

First published 1987

© **Butterworth & Co. (Publishers) Ltd, 1987**

British Library Cataloguing in Publication Data

Mason, J.K.
    Butterworths medico-legal encyclopaedia.
    1. Medical laws and legislation – Great
Britain – Dictionaries
    I. Title   II. McCall Smith, R.A.
    344.104'41   KD3395

    ISBN 0-407-00374-6

Library of Congress Cataloging in Publication Data

Mason, J.K. (John Kenyon)
    Butterworths medico-legal encyclopaedia.

    1. Medical laws and legislation–Great Britain–
Dictionaries.   2. Medical jurisprudence–Great Britain–
Dictionaries.   3. Medical laws and legislation–
Dictionaries.   4. Medical jurisprudence–Dictionaries.
I. McCall Smith, R. A.   II. Title.   III. Title:
Medico-legal encyclopaedia. [DNLM: 1. Forensic Medicine
–encyclopedias.   2. Jurisprudence–Great Britain–
encyclopedias.   W 13 M399b]
KD3395.A68M37   1987   344'.041'03   86-24446

    ISBN 0-407-00374-6   342.44103

Photoset by Unwin Brothers Ltd, Old Woking, Surrey
Printed and bound by Robert Hartnoll (1985) Ltd, Bodmin, Cornwall

Preface

The purpose of this volume is to define the terms and concepts which arise commonly in medico-legal practice. In particular, the book, firstly, gives lawyers a guide to the interpretation of medical terms which they are likely to find in reports provided in both criminal and civil proceedings. It also provides doctors and other health professionals with an outline of how the law affects not only the practice of medicine but also their patients – either within or without the doctor/patient relationship. Finally, we were especially hopeful of a product which would be helpful to Procurators Fiscal and Coroners.

When we were asked to undertake the task, we had little idea of its daunting nature. Among the many difficulties subsequently encountered, we draw particular attention to the constraints of space. There is clearly no way in which whole textbooks of, say, criminal law, family law, obstetrics and gynaecology and forensic medicine can be combined in a handlable volume and most entries represent no more than outlines of the subjects covered. We anticipate up to 600 experts each seeking his specialist subject and declaring its treatment to be superficial – but we have attempted no more; we hope, however, that the citations given at the end of each entry will serve to guide the reader who requires more in-depth knowledge. The very large number of topics covered has also posed problems of immediacy; something relevant has changed almost daily during preparation and it may well be that some sections are more 'dated' than are others. We believe, however, that our law is correct as at April 1986.

We have made no attempt at a comprehensive comparative assessment of United States and Commonwealth law and practice. Strong leadership from both sources is, however, a feature of modern legal medicine and it has been our intention to include such material when it indicates trends likely to be followed or avoided in the United Kingdom. Within the United Kingdom, we have concentrated mainly on English law but hope that we have given due regard to Scottish practice and, in less detail, to that in Northern Ireland.

One or other of us has contributed the overwhelming majority of entries. Very occasionally, friends have composed an item for us and, among these, we would like to thank Professor Ian McCallum, Mr D.W. Crosthwaite and Ms Sophie Barrowcliffe. Similarly, a few colleagues have not shied away at the sight of our typescripts and have read and commented most helpfully on some entries; we are especially grateful in this respect to Professor Alan Emery, Ms Elaine Sutherland

and Ms Sheila McLean. Once again, we record our gratitude to our secretary, Mrs E.A. MacDonald, without whose unswerving determination and loyalty completion would have been impossible. Finally, we thank our publishers, particularly in the person of Ms Sue Deeley, for their sympathetic handling of a more than average measure of creative caprice.

J.K.M.
R.A.M.S.

Contents

A

Abdominal Cavity

The abdominal cavity, which is bounded by the diaphragm above and the pelvic floor below, is lined by a fibrous membrane — the peritoneum; inflammation within the cavity is therefore known as peritonitis.

The major contents include the digestive tract comprising the stomach, duodenum, small intestine and large intestine or colon, which includes the caecum and its attached vermiform appendix. The duodenum and, to a great extent, the colon are tied down behind the peritoneum and, being immobile, are vulnerable to blunt injury. The small intestine and the stomach are suspended by membranes known as mesenteries; the stomach, being fixed at either end, is only partially mobile but the intestine can move freely. The small bowel will therefore be injured by blunt force only occasionally, as when it is caught transversely by a lap belt. The contents of the stomach and small intestine are sterile but the colon contains a mass of bacteria; rupture of the colon is therefore likely to result in peritonitis.

Other major organs associated with the digestive tract include the liver, with its associated gall bladder, and the pancreas. The liver is a massive solid organ which lies anteriorly beneath the lower right ribs; on all counts, therefore, it is susceptible to injuries of all sorts, including the vibratory injury of sudden deceleration. The pancreas is fixed behind the peritoneum and is, again, susceptible to crushing injury although it does lie posteriorly and is, to an extent, protected. The spleen, which is mainly associated with red blood cell destruction, lies under the left ribs and is frequently lacerated in accidents; it is not, however, essential to life.

The kidneys, with their associated adrenal glands, lie behind the peritoneum on each side of the spinal column. Although they are partially protected by the large muscles of the back, they are susceptible to kicking injuries and, for somewhat obscure reasons, appear to be particularly vulnerable in road traffic accidents. They are often involved in stab wounds from behind.

The lower part of the abdominal cavity, the pelvic cavity, contains the urinary bladder and the female reproductive organs. It is protected by the pelvic bones but fracture of these may lead to distortion of the rigid element of the birth canal and, perhaps, permanent difficulties with childbirth.

See also: Kicking injuries; Lap belts; Road traffic accidents; Stab wounds

Abortifacients

It is difficult to dislodge a normally implanted fetus from the womb of a normal woman; the majority of successful attempts to achieve this by the use of drugs taken orally can be attributed as much to the toxic effects on the mother as to those on the fetus.

Large numbers of substances were once used illegally in such attempts; these ranged from gin to pharmacologically active drugs such as ergot which were often available to paramedical or medical abortionists. The remainder, including so-called emmenagogues (potions designed to increase the menstrual flow) are now of historic interest only, although a surprising number are still sold as 'female remedies'. Ecbolics (drugs capable of promoting uterine contractions) were also in use and included preparations of lead and of quinine, both of which are dangerous if taken in overdose. Compounds containing lead are controlled both as Schedule 1 poisons and as Prescription Only medicines (*see* 'Poisons Act 1972' and 'Medicines Act 1968'); quinine is, however, still available as a Pharmacy medicine, or General Sale List medicine if present in the preparation in a concentration which is below a maximum dose.

Drugs given by mouth are so fickle in their action that they would not be used for legal abortion under the Abortion Act 1967; most such abortions are performed in the first trimester using surgical methods. In mid-trimester, however, drugs are used by intra-amniotic injection. This includes the use of strong saline solutions, solutions of urea and solutions of different forms of the hormone prostaglandin, sometimes used in combination; prostaglandin can be given as a vaginal suppository. Intravenous infusions of the potent hormone oxytocin, which stimulates uterine contraction, are also employed either alone or in combination with intra-amniotic treatment. It is a sad reflection that saline infusions, which are more toxic to the mother than are prostaglandins, are often advised as preferable in late abortions because the moral complications of producing a living abortus are, thereby, largely eliminated.

See also: Abortion; Abortion Act 1967; Hormones; Living abortus; Medicines Act 1968; Poisons Act 1972

Abortion

Abortion may be defined as the separation of the non-viable fetus from the mother. The legal presumption that the fetus is capable of being born alive is statutorily defined in England and Wales as being reached after 28 weeks' gestation[1]; separation of the fetus after this is not, therefore, strictly speaking an abortion and may result in premature birth, still-birth or child destruction.

Abortion may be natural or induced. Natural spontaneous abortion — due mainly to disease in either the mother or the fetus — can be seen to occur in some 10 per cent of pregnancies. Modern research indicates that occult abortion is probably very common in the early stages of pregnancy, many embryos being chromosomally abnormal and being rejected at the time of implantation in the endometrium. Induced abortion may be criminal or legal. The criminal law in England and Wales is contained in the Offences Against the Person Act 1861, s.58, which defines the offence of intending to procure a miscarriage by the administration of any poison or other noxious thing or by the unlawful use of any instrument; s.59 makes it illegal to supply or procure any poison or thing knowing that it is intended to be used for the purpose of procuring a miscarriage. An offence under s.58 may be committed by the woman herself, provided she is pregnant, or by an outsider; in the latter case, it is the intention which is paramount and the offence under both sections is committed whether or not the woman is 'with child'. Abortion is a crime at common law in Scotland but no offence is committed in the absence of pregnancy.

The criminal abortionist uses many methods to achieve his end, including direct violence, piercing instruments to kill the fetus, dilators to open the cervix uteri, enemas to separate the placenta, and many drugs, few of which, other than those with a known pharmacological effect on the uterus, have an ill-effect which is greater on the fetus than on the mother. Criminal abortion, particularly that which is self-induced, thus carries with it distressing morbidity and mortality rates which increase with inexperience of the practitioner; abortionists may range from the woman's partner, through paramedical persons to unregistered physicians or surgeons. The 1861 Act makes no allowance for therapeutic abortion. It was not until 1929[1] that limited, and indirect, relief was given to the medical profession; the Act stated that no offence was committed if the fetus was destroyed 'for the purpose only of preserving the mother's life'. The abortion laws were first openly challenged in 1938[2], when the concept of preserving the mother's life was effectively extended to preserving her mental and physical health. Even so, an uneasy relationship existed between the law and good medical practice until the passing of the Abortion Act 1967 which statutorily defined conditions in which no offence is committed.

The Abortion Act 1967 is discussed in a separate entry where it will be seen that the provisions are very liberal — and many would say that the safeguards in the Act have been grossly eroded in practice[3]. Thus, organisations such as the Society for the Protection of Unborn Children have evolved and have expressed great hostility to what is regarded as the wholesale taking of human life. Moreover, the widespread performance of abortions strikes at a fundamental Hippocratic principle expressed in the Declaration of Geneva as 'I will maintain the utmost respect for human life from the time of conception' — despite the modifications introduced by the Declaration of Oslo 1970, the acceptance of the Abortion Act by the medical profession represents a watershed in medical ethics. The situation is further complicated by the extension of the debate into such fields as postcoital contraception and, at the other extreme, neonaticide.

See also: Abortion Act 1967; Child destruction; Contraception; Declarations; Neonaticide; Viability

1. Infant Life (Preservation) Act 1929 (not applicable to Scotland).
2. *R v Bourne* [1939] 1 KB 687. There are significant differences between the Law Report and the version in [1938] 3 All ER 615. *See also R v Newton and Stungo* [1958] Crim LR 469.

3. Gardner RFR 'A new ethical approach to abortion and its implications for the euthanasia dispute' (1975) 1 J Med Ethics 127.

Abortion Act 1967

The Abortion Act 1967 was passed against the background of mounting public disquiet at the prevalence of illegal abortions together with concern for the care of large numbers of unwanted children. It is an enabling Act which lays down the conditions under which the performance of an abortion does not contravene either the Offences Against the Person Act 1861, ss.58 and 59, or the common law of Scotland. The 1967 Act states (s.1(1)):

> '... a person shall not be guilty of an offence under the law relating to abortion when a pregnancy is terminated by a registered medical practitioner if two registered medical practitioners are of the opinion, formed in good faith —
>
> (a) that the continuance of the pregnancy would involve risk to the life of the pregnant woman, or of injury to the physical or mental health of the pregnant woman or any existing children of her family, greater than if the pregnancy were terminated; or
> (b) that there is a substantial risk that if the child were born it would suffer from such physical or mental abnormalities as to be seriously handicapped.'

There are, thus, effectively four reasons which justify a legal abortion: (a) life saving, (b) relating to preventive medicine, (c) societal, and (d) eugenic.

In practice, it is the preventive aspect which is most commonly invoked. In 1984 there were 169,993 legal abortions performed in England and Wales; of these, 596 were life saving, 149,674 were related to the future physical or mental health of the mother, 17,487 were societal and 2,219 were concerned with fetal abnormality. In the same year, 17 emergency operations were carried out for the purpose of saving the life of or preventing grave permanent injury to the mother on the authority of a single medical practitioner (s.1(4)).

The terms of the 1967 Act are very wide and it has been argued that any properly conducted operation is legal because the risks of pregnancy itself are greater than are those of termination. Whether this is true or not may depend not only upon the gestational age of the fetus but also on the age and parity of the mother[1]; nevertheless, the demand for abortions is so great that the main limiting factors are those of the staff and space available for the purpose. One of the most unfortunate aspects of the operation of the Act has been the need to utilise to the full the authority to carry out terminations in places approved for the purpose by the Minister of Health or the Secretary of State in addition to hospitals operating under the National Health Service Acts[2] (s.1(3)); specific financial rewards are thereby introduced into an already complex ethical field. At one time, advertisements for abortion services to women from overseas were not uncommon[3] but only one action by the General Medical Council in this respect appears to have reached the Courts[4]. It is of some interest to note that, in 1984, only 103 of 33,605 legal abortions on non-residents in England and Wales were performed in NHS hospitals. So far as has been discovered, however, only one doctor has been prosecuted criminally under the 1967 Act and this appears to have been more because of the way the operation was performed than on the basis of lack of good faith[5].

It has been suggested[6] that any shortcomings, and consequent opportunities for abuse, in the operation of the Act are due mainly to lack of facilities in the National Health Service rather than to any deliberate disregard of the spirit of the legislation, and this view was supported by the Lane Committee[7]. The figures for England and Wales and for Scotland, again using 1984 as a model, are interesting reading in this connection — in brief, 47.5 per cent of 'residents' abortions were performed in NHS hospitals in England and Wales while 98 per cent were so treated in Scotland. It could be argued that, as a result, Scots women were forced to go to England or Wales for their terminations but, in fact, only 781 'non-resident' operations, comprising less than 8 per cent of total Scottish abortions, were performed in England or Wales on women with Scottish addresses.

Acceptance of the Act represents a very great change in the medical ethos and, as a result, a 'conscience clause' is included in the Act (s.4) which relieves any person who has a conscientious objection to abortion of a duty to participate in any treatment authorised by the Act. This concession specifically does not apply if the life of the woman is in danger or if there is a possibility of grave permanent injury to her health (s.4(2)); there is no doubt, in addition, that every doctor must advise a patient correctly and is further bound to treat, say, any complications of a legal termination. The Declaration of Geneva has been modified, as regards the ethics of abortion, by the Declaration of Oslo; nevertheless, it is a practical fact that the profession of gynaecologist is now virtually closed to those with a strong Hippocratic or religious objection to abortion.

The 1967 Act is constrained by the Infant Life (Preservation) Act 1929 in that nothing in the former shall affect the provisions of the latter (s.5(1)). The effect, although probably not in Scotland where the 1929 Act does not apply, is that an abortion after the 28th week of gestation can be legal only if done for the purpose of preserving the life of the mother. In practice, this is no limitation because termination as an abortion would be very unlikely to be advised at that stage of pregnancy. Rather, the concern is that, with increasing medical skills, live births and viable fetuses can be anticipated at ever-shortening periods of gestation. In view of the growing possibility of producing living abortuses, there have been frequent attempts to modify the 1929 Act and these have generally been opposed by the medical profession; there is, however, some evidence of a change of attitude and the limiting gestational age for the purposes of the 1967 Act may be reduced to 24 weeks[8].

A legal abortion must be reported to the relevant Chief Medical Officer within seven days of the operation. The report must be on a statutory form[9] which contains a great deal of information as to the circumstances and the extent of the operation. These details are confidential save for certain stipulated purposes[10]; the latest of these authorises information to be given to the President of the General Medical Council if he so requests when a doctor is charged with serious professional misconduct in relation to the Act[11].

The Abortion Act 1967 does not run to Northern Ireland.

See also: Abortion; Declarations; Eugenics; General Medical Council; Viability

1. Myerscough PR (1975) 1 J Med Ethics 130.
2. National Health Service Act 1977; National Health Service (Scotland) Act 1978.
3. See, for example, *Faridian v GMC* [1970] 3 WLR 1065 PC.
4. *Tarnesby v Kensington, Chelsea and Westminster Area Health Authority* [1980] ICR 475, CA; [1981] IRLR 369, HL.
5. *R v Smith (John)* [1973] 1 WLR 1510, CA.
6. 'No case for an abortion Bill' [1979] 2 Br Med J 230.
7. Lane Justice (chairman) *Report of the Committee on the Working of the Abortion Act* (Cmnd 5579) (1974) HMSO, London.
8. 'Abortions too late', (1984) *The Times*, 19 January, p.11.
9. Abortion (Amendment) Regulations 1980 (SI 1980/1724); Abortion (Scotland) Amendment Regulations 1980 (SI 1980/1864 (S.169)).
10. Abortion Regulations 1968 (SI 1968/390), r.5; Abortion (Scotland) Regulations 1968 (SI 1968/505 (S.49)), r.5. .
11. Abortion (Amendment) Regulations 1976 (SI 1976/15); Abortion (Scotland) Amendment Regulations 1976 (SI 1976/127 (S.8)).

Abrasions

An abrasion is an injury which does not penetrate the full thickness of the skin. It may be so superficial as to do little more than raise an imprint — as in a handslap — or it may be deep enough to allow the exudation of tissue fluid which, when dry, gives rise to a typical scabbed or parchmented appearance. In any event, the superficial nature of the injury prevents its spread and the result is often a remarkably faithful representation of the way in which the abrasion was caused.

Impact by a solid object may give rise to abrasions at the periphery where the skin is forced downwards. The inner contour of the resultant abrasion may thus represent the external contour of the object; a heelmark may be clearly delineated and damage from a strong stick generally appears as 'tramlines'. The direction of an abrasion may be gauged by the 'piling up' of the epithelium at its forward edge relative to the movement of the causative object. Abrasions can be inflicted easily *post mortem*, a fact which often complicates the interpretation of findings at a second postmortem dissection undertaken, say, for the defence.

Two specific types of abrasion are worth mention because of their diagnostic importance. The fingermark abrasion is often superficial, long and curved, and some 1–2 mm in breadth; parallel abrasions of this type are very specific. The 'knifepoint' abrasion (*see* 'Knife wounds') is narrower and is usually quite deep and scabbed. Other specific types of abrasion include those made by ligatures — especially around the neck as in hanging; the combination of ligature abrasions and fingernail abrasions is very suggestive of an assault.

Abrasions may contain trace evidence of their cause — fibres from cloth, gravel dirt, etc.

See also: Fingernail marks; Hanging; Knife wounds; Rape; Road traffic accidents; Strangulation

Accidental Death

Accidental death comprises the second largest category — after sudden natural death — of cases reported to the medico-legal authority. The subject is thus extremely wide and most facets are discussed individually within this work.

In general, death by accident is markedly age dependent. It is very rare in the post-neonatal stage because of the immobility of the subject; occasional reports that a large proportion of deaths which would be attributed by most pathologists to the sudden infant death syndrome are, in fact, due to accidental suffocation are almost certainly without foundation. Accidental death in the 'toddler' stage is largely a matter of inquisitiveness — in particular, severe scalds or burns may be cited, as may accidental poisoning which is sometimes associated with the use of parents' pills[1]. Death due to accident in childhood was once seriously associated with alighting of clothing but recent legislation has greatly reduced this cause[2]. Most accidental deaths in young adulthood occur in road trafffic accidents or in industry, both of which are discussed separately.

It is, however, to be noted that, over all, as many accidental deaths occur in the home as are attributable to the use of vehicles. The reason why the latter attract so much attention by comparison is largely a matter of economics; whereas vehicular accidents mainly involve males in their most productive phase of life, the typical victim of an accident in the home is an elderly person. Even so, increasing legislative pressure on building and safety standards has resulted in a dramatic decrease in the number of fatalities in the home and, whilst this is certainly true of the elderly, it is even more pronounced in the case of child fatalities.

As might be anticipated, there is a strong association between alcohol and accidental death even when road traffic fatalities are excluded; there is increasing agreement that such an association does not extend to suicide[1,3]. It is of very considerable forensic importance that the *post mortem* body alcohol content be estimated in every accidental death occurring other than in children; the very word 'accident' implies potential fault and the finding of excess alcohol in a cadaver may indicate contributory negligence.

Accidental deaths of many types raise the problem of differential diagnosis from homicide or suicide and this may not be easy. Death due to accidental discharge of a shotgun may, for example, be distinguishable from homicide only on the basis of probability; non-accidental injury in children may end in death which appears, at first sight, to have no criminal connotations; a case of carbon monoxide poisoning in a garage is not always what it seems; and determining the cause of a person's fatal fall from a window may become an almost intractable problem[4]. In addition, any accidental death is likely to result in civil controversy if not litigation and, finally, the satisfactory investigation of an accidental death is rewarding for the pathologist in that every such death opens up opportunities for the practice of preventive medicine[5]. For all these reasons, it is important that the accident autopsy is not regarded as a necessary chore to be completed as rapidly as possible but rather as a particularly important part of the medico-legal service to the community.

See also: Alcohol; Burning; Contributory negligence; Industrial injury; Non-accidental injury in children; Poisoning; Road traffic accidents; Sudden infant death syndrome

1. Although, in one of the authors' studies, only one such case was discovered in 275 fatal ingestions: Campbell S and Mason JK 'Fatal ingestions in Edinburgh 1974–78' (1981) 21 Med Sci Law 159.
2. Heating Appliances (Fireguards) Regulations 1973 (SI 73/2106 made under the Consumer Protection Act 1961).
3. Crompton MR 'Alcohol and violent accidental and suicidal death' (1985) 25 Med Sci Law 59.
4. *See,* for example, the notorious case of *R v West Yorkshire Coroner, ex parte Smith* [1982] 3 WLR 920.
5. For elaboration of this theme, *see* Mason JK 'Medicolegal aspects of fatal aircraft accident investigation' (1970) 2 Community Hlth 36.

Accomplices

An accomplice or accessory is a secondary party to a criminal offence defined as one who aids, abets, counsels or procures the commission of the offence[1]. To abet means to encourage or invite the commission of an offence but, in general, the words 'aid', 'abet', 'counsel' and 'procure' are given their ordinary meaning in everyday language[2]; moreover, in deciding whether or not an offence has been committed, it is preferable to consider the phrase as a whole[3]. An accomplice is distinguished from a principal in the first degree who is the person directly and most immediately responsible for the commission of the act — the one who, for example, pulls the trigger when a victim is shot. Where, however, the actual offence is that of abetting, the accessory is the principal offender, who can therefore also be guilty of an attempt. There is no distinction between principal and accessory when it comes to punishment; for example, both will be sentenced to life imprisonment following a conviction for murder. Moreover, a person can be guilty of being an accessory to a crime which he or she is incapable of committing as a principal and be punished accordingly; thus, whilst a woman cannot commit rape, she can be an accessory to rape.

Mens rea, or actual intention, is required on the part of a secondary party even when the offence is one of strict liability[4]. However, no liability is imposed on the secondary party for an unforeseeable consequence of criminal activity. The test of *mens rea* in the circumstances is subjective; it is what the individual accused contemplated which matters — that is, did he contemplate that, in carrying out a common unlawful purpose, one of the parties might, say, use a loaded gun[5].

1. Accessories and Abettors Act 1861, as amended.
2. *Attorney General's Reference* (No. 1 of 1975) [1975] QB 773.
3. *Attorney General v Able and others* (1983) Times, 29 April.
4. *See* Smith JC and Hogan B *Criminal Law* (5th ed, 1983) p.129, Butterworths, London.
5. *Chan Wing-Sin and others v The Queen* [1984] 3 WLR 677.

Acquired Immune Deficiency Syndrome

The acquired immune deficiency syndrome (AIDS) was first reported in 1981 and is an example of a seemingly new disease appearing suddenly as human ecology is affected by changes and advances in social and medical science. The condition is of minor forensic interest in so far as it appears to be associated with sexual practices and with blood transfusion therapy.

The disease process essentially consists of an inadequate cellular immune response with consequent susceptibility to opportunistic infections (*see* 'Pathogenic organisms'), to lymphomas (or malignancy of the lymphatic system) and to an unusual form of malignant growth known as Kaposi's sarcoma. Some 8,000 cases have been reported, with just under 200 occurring in the UK; at the time of writing, the five-year mortality of the diagnosed disease is 100 per cent but there are an uncertain number of subclinical cases. Although the overwhelming association is with homosexual activity, cases are not infrequent in haemophiliacs and others who have received blood transfusions, drug addicts, heterosexual partners of victims and even in babies born to affected women[1]. This distribution strongly suggests an infecting organism as the cause — almost certainly a virus which is not, as yet, fully identified but which may be that known as HTLV-III/LAV — and rebuts the sometimes seriously held suggestion that the disease is an example of divine wrath. There is a curious association with Haiti, and an interesting and widely held view is that the disease is endemic in and has spread from Central Africa[2]; as has happened before, such a disease only becomes virulent and epidemic when it is introduced into an unexposed and unresistant population.

AIDS is not notifiable under the Public Health (Control of Disease) Act 1984 but the Secretary of State can order hospitalisation and, if necessary, detention of sufferers (ss.35, 37, 38)[3].

See also: Blood transfusion; Haemophilia; Homosexuality; Immune reaction; Notifiable diseases; Pathogenic organisms

1. Of the large number of articles on the subject, a recent, easily understood example is Gracie JA et al 'Acquired immune deficiency syndrome — an overview' (1985) 30 Scott Med J 1.
2. De Cock KM 'AIDS: an old disease from Africa?' (1984) 289 Br Med J 306.
3. Public Health (Infectious Diseases) Regulations 1985 (SI 1985/434).

Actus Reus

There are two basic requirements of criminal liability: an *actus reus* (a criminal act) and *mens rea* (a criminal state of mind). There can be no conviction in the absence of either of these features.

An *actus reus* exists when a person has, by his conduct, created a state of affairs proscribed by the criminal law. What constitutes the *actus reus* of a particular offence will be defined in each case, either by statute or through case law. The *actus reus* of each offence is therefore unique to that offence. That of theft, for example, is the unlawful removal of another's property; sexual intercourse with a girl under the age of 16 is the *actus reus* of an offence under s.6 of the Sexual Offences Act 1956. Positive conduct is not always required; an omission to act when the law imposes a positive duty of action can constitute the *actus reus* of an offence, as when a parent omits to provide the necessities of life for his child. An attempt may constitute the *actus reus* of an offence; an unsuccessful attempt to kill is the *actus reus* of the offence of attempted murder.

In the case of the so-called 'status offences', it is being in a certain situation rather than conduct which constitutes the *actus reus* of the offence. The case of *Larsonneur*[1], when the relevant offence was that of being in the UK after permission to land had been denied, is an example.

An *actus reus* may consist of an act by itself or of an act together with its consequences. The term 'conduct crime' is sometimes applied when an act only is required, the crime of assault being an example; the term 'result crime' may be used when an act together with its consequences constitute the *actus reus* [2]. The *actus reus* in murder, which is a resultant crime, consists of the infliction of physical harm upon the victim together with the consequence — the victim's death.

It is an important requirement of an *actus reus* that there be a voluntary act on the part of the accused; there is, for example, no *actus reus* if the driver of a car is attacked by a swarm of bees and is consequently prevented from controlling the car properly[3]. Automatic action likewise involves no *actus reus* as the actor has no control of his movements and no proper awareness of them. However, not every involuntary act need exclude an *actus reus*. In *Ryan v the Queen*[4] it was held that an involuntary pulling of a trigger could be viewed as only one part of a longer sequence of events making up the overall *actus reus*.

The use of 'bad Latin' has been criticised in the courts; it has been suggested that the use of the term *actus reus* is likely to mislead since it suggests, wrongly, that some positive act on the part of the accused is needed to make him guilty of a crime — the English phrase 'conduct of the accused' is to be preferred[5].

See also: Automatism; Criminal responsibility

1. (1933) 24 Crim App R 74.
2. For a discussion of this distinction, *see* Gordon G *The Criminal Law of Scotland* (2nd ed, 1978) p.63, W. Green, Edinburgh.
3. *Hill v Baxter* [1958] 1 QB 227.
4. (1967) 40 ALJR 488.
5. *R v Miller* [1983] 2 AC 161 per Lord Diplock at 174.

Acupuncture

Acupuncture has its origins in China, where it has been practised as a system of preventive and curative medicine for over 5,000 years. Its classic, the *Nei Ching*, is considered the oldest extant medical textbook.

In traditional acupuncture, any symptom is considered to be associated with imbalance in that person's vital energy (known as ch'i energy) — hence, literally, lack of harmony and dis-ease. The ch'i energy runs along pathways (meridians) and can be specifically contacted at precise points. The acupuncturist aims to help restore flow and balance within the energy; to do this, fine needles are inserted into these points and are carefully manipulated. The site of the energy within the meridians is reflected in each of twelve pulses; these are felt on the radial artery of each wrist.

Many types of acupuncture are now practised in the West; these range from what was called 'barefoot doctor' in China — acupuncture which aims only to alleviate symptoms — to more holistic forms which seek to identify and treat the underlying cause of disease.

The types of training given vary greatly. In Britain, it can be anything from a weekend course (often for doctors who are using the method as an adjunct to western medicine) to three years' training in the more traditional forms of acupuncture. Three- and six-month courses are also given especially for foreigners in China.

There is no legal bar to setting up as an acupuncturist and there are now three major professional bodies represeting over 500 practitioners. These are the British Acupuncture Association and Register (BAAR), the Register of Traditional Chinese Medicine (RTCM) and the Traditional Acupuncture Society (TAS). These all come under the Council for Acupuncture (CFA) which works towards a common educational standard and a joint code of practice and of ethics. There is also a British Medical Acupuncture Society (BMAS), the membership of which is confined to registered medical practitioners. This society believes that only practitioners with an orthodox medical training should be allowed to practise acupuncture.

The three main professional bodies are working towards registration at national level and, eventually, to legal recognition. The aim over all is to ensure that all practitioners have adequate training in acupuncture irrespective of their expertise in other areas.

Adipocere

The fatty tissues may be converted to adipocere if a dead body lies in wet or moist conditions; the change is most often seen in drowned bodies or in those exhumed from wet coffins. Adipocere consists in the main of fatty acids and presents as grey–white, greasy material giving the impression of waxy fat. The presence of a high concentration of fatty acids prevents putrefaction and the material may persist for years. Particular anatomical areas of body fat are generally involved rather than that of all the body; the cheeks are often affected and may provide recognisable features long after death. There is often enough moisture in the body to promote the formation of adipocere in a relatively dry environment; adipocere will burn when heated, a fact which might explain some of the rare authenticated cases of spontaneous combustion of dead bodies.

See also: Changes after death; Putrefaction

Admissibility of Evidence

Admissible evidence is that which may be used by the court to determine the issues before it. Only relevant evidence is admitted; that which is irrelevant will only cause confusion and is therefore excluded. Relevant evidence will be admitted unless it is subject to an exclusionary rule based on policy or procedural considerations. Policy factors prevent the admission of confidential matters of state[1] but do not necessarily exclude evidence which is improperly or illegally obtained.

Evidence obtained as a result of an illegal search is admissible[2], as is that obtained by eavesdropping or even by illegal telephone tapping[3]. The whole question of the admissibility of improperly-obtained evidence was given a thorough airing in the House of Lords in the important case of *R v Sang* [4]. The effect of the decision is that, while the judge has power to exclude evidence, the probative value of which is outweighed by its prejudicial effect on the defendant's case, the way by which that evidence is obtained is generally irrelevant[5]. This, of course, does not apply to confessions. The means by which breath samples are obtained in drinking and driving cases will be of concern to the courts only if impropriety such as inducements or threats is involved. The fact that a suspect has been unlawfully arrested is irrelevant to the question[6].

Hearsay evidence is inadmissible, as is evidence which a party seeks to adduce without first having observed specific legal prerequisites. There are problems specific to confessions which are discussed under that heading.

As a general rule, statements made by a witness on occasions other than particular to the matter under consideration will not be admissible as evidence and will not provide confirmation of that witness's immediate testimony. A major exception of medico-legal significance is, however, provided by recent complaints in sexual cases. Statements made in complaint do not provide evidence of the facts on which the complaint is based but they can be taken to indicate consistency. This rule has been applied in cases of rape[7], indecent assault against a female[8] and indecent assault against a male[9]. The complaint must be made at the first reasonable opportunity. In *R v Ingrey*[10] the offence was committed on the Saturday and the complaint made on a Tuesday. In this particular case, the interval was regarded by the court as being too long although there have been decisions in which a more liberal view has been taken.

See also: Confessions; Hearsay rule; Indecent assault; Rape; Road Traffic Act 1972

1. *Conway v Rimmer* [1968] AC 910; [1968] 1 All ER 874, HL.
2. *Jeffrey v Blank* [1978] 1 All ER 555.
3. *R v Ali and Hussain* [1965] 2 All ER 464; *R v Senat* (1968) 52 Crim App R 282.
4. [1979] 2 All ER 1222, HL.
5. *See* Dawson JB 'Exclusion of unlawfully obtained evidence: a comparative study' (1982) 31 ICLQ 513; Yeo H 'Discretion to exclude illegally and improperly obtained evidence' (1981) 13 Melb ULR 31.
6. *Fox v Gwent Chief Constable* [1985] 1 WLR 1126, HL; *Bunyard v Hayes* (1984) Times, 3 November.
7. *R v Lillyman* [1896] 2 QB 167.
8. *R v Osborne* [1905] 1 KB 551.
9. *R v Camelleri* [1922] 2 KB 122.
10. (1900) 64 JP 106.

Adoption

Adoption of a child in the United Kingdom is strictly regulated by statute. The making of private arrangements to transfer custody of a child is illegal save in very particular circumstances[1]; thus, surrogacy contracts, even if entered into privately without illegal commercial intervention, can be effective only if associated with legal adoption or with a direction of the court in wardship proceedings[2]. The legal intricacies of adoption are forbidding and only the outlines can be given here[3]. The time taken to implement legislation is, however, a remarkable feature: the Adoption Act 1976, which was intended to consolidate previous legislation, including the

Children Act 1975[4], is only partially in force as yet, and the Adoption (Scotland) Act 1978 has only very recently been applied. Meantime, the scope for adoption has markedly declined, due in no small part to the impact of the Abortion Act 1967.

Adoptions must be arranged through an adoption agency which may be run by the local authority or exist as a non-profit making voluntary organisation; the intention is that a comprehensive adoption service, which includes counselling, will be available through either agency, the ultimate responsibility resting on the local authority[5].

In making arrangements for adoption, both the adoption agency and the court must take into account the sensibilities of the child, whose welfare must be a first consideration[6]. A child who is aged over 18 years cannot be adopted, and an adopter must be aged over 21 years — there is a *de facto* bias against elderly adopters and against married couples who are distanced in age. An order for adoption may be made in favour of a single unmarried person or to a married couple, but permanent separation renders a married person 'single' for this purpose. Adoption by one natural parent — which, in this case, probably includes the father of an illegitimate child[7] — by step-parents or by other relatives is possible but, for reasons which are obscure, at least to us, considerable difficulties are put in the way. This is particularly so when an adoption order is sought as an alternative to other arrangements available in the law relating to divorce, such as custodianship; the evidence is, however, that the courts are more sympathetic to step-parent adoption than was previously the case[8], especially when the child's wishes point in that direction.

Adoption of a child younger than 19 weeks old is not permissible and a mother cannot agree to an adoption of her child within six weeks of its birth. The child must have lived with its prospective adopters for at least 13 continuous weeks and the adoption agency must see the child in the total family environment; this period is extended to one year if the child is with the applicant for reasons other than being placed by an adoption agency — e.g. living with foster parents, when the local authority must also be informed of an intention to apply for an adoption order.

Many of the major unfairnesses to prospective adopting parents or to foster parents inherent in the earlier legislation have been removed by the Children Act 1975[9]. Foremost among the changes is the process of freeing for adoption which enables the court, on the application of the adoption agency, to make an order for adoption without any later evidence of parental consent. Such freedom can be granted only if each parent or guardian of a child has already freely consented or if the court has reasons for dispensing with such agreement. The Adoption Act 1976, s.16, gives six possible reasons why such dispensation can be made, including an unreasonable withholding of agreement[10]. The imbalance between the parents and the adopters during the compulsory observation period is thus reduced and the child is freed for adoption 'unconditionally' — e.g. without stipulation as to religious upbringing. An adoption agency may, however, still arrange for a specific adoption, in which case parental powers of revocation of agreement are retained but final agreement must still be unconditional. A parent may apply for revocation of a freedom declaration if a child has not been adopted within a year of being freed for the purpose.

The court cannot make an order for adoption if illegal payments have been made[11]; this, in itself, might make commercial surrogacy impossible[12]. Otherwise, there is a wide discretion. Subject to appeal, the making of an adoption order is irrevocable. Normally, there is anonymity between the parents and the adopters but this may be waived; an adopted child is, however, entitled to obtain his birth certificate at the age of 18 or on marriage if younger and may also obtain counselling on the subject (Adoption Act 1976, s.51).

The effects of adoption are far reaching. The adopted child becomes the legitimate child of the adopting parents and has succession and citizenship rights accordingly. There are, however, some curious anomalies as to marriage. An adopting parent cannot marry an adopted child but an adopted child may marry the natural child of his adopting parents; similarly, marriage prohibitions remain as to an adopted child and his natural relations. As an extension of this, there can be no incest between adopting parents and adopted children[13] but incest is still possible within the child's natural 'family'.

The law on adoption in Scotland is broadly similar to that in England and Wales[14].

See also: Abortion Act 1967; Divorce; Illegitimacy; Surrogate motherhood; Wardship proceedings

1. As, for example, when the proposed adopter is a relative (Adoption Act 1976, s.72).
2. *In re a Baby* (1985) Times, 15 January.
3. For a full description, *see* Cretney SM *Principles of Family Law* (4th ed, 1984) Chap. 18, Sweet & Maxwell, London.
4. The Children Act 1975 has, itself, been amended in minor detail by the Health and Social Services and Social Security Adjudications Act 1983. But since the regulations will probably be in force by the time this book is published, references are made to the Adoption Act 1976.
5. Adoption Agencies Regulations 1983 (SI 1983/1964).
6. This contrasts with the paramount consideration in wardship proceedings and other court decisions subject to the Guardianship of Minors Acts 1971–1973. The parents and the adopters also have rights in adoption cases.
7. But, otherwise, the father of an illegitimate child is not a 'parent' — e.g. his consent to adoption is not required unless he is an appointed guardian (*Re M* [1955] 2 QB 479).
8. *Re D (minors)* (1980) 2 FLR 102.
9. Consolidated in Adoption Act 1976, ss.18 and 28. *See also* Adoption (Scotland) Act 1978, s.18.
10. When the balance of the parental rights (*Re D (an infant)* [1977] AC 602) against the welfare of the child (*Re P (an infant)* [1977] Fam 25) is not easy to preserve (*see Re W (an infant)* [1971] AC 682).
11. Adoption Act 1976, s.24.
12. A matter which was not considered in *In Re a Baby* (n.2 above), which was essentially a matter of wardship.
13. Sexual Offences Act 1956, ss.10, 11; *HM Adv v RM* 1969 JC 52.
14. *See* P.M. 'The Adoption (Scotland) Act 1978' 1985 SLT 1.

Adulteration of Food

Two principal statutes govern the adulteration of food and drugs in Britain: the Food Act 1984 and the Medicines Act 1968. There are many regulations made to ensure the safety of food reaching the public and the subject is discussed in some detail under 'Food legislation'. It is also a common law offence knowingly to supply food which is injurious to the health of the consumer[1].

There is also an increasing volume of EEC regulations aimed at achieving uniformity in the standard of foodstuffs and their labelling by manufacturers[2].

See also: Food legislation; Medicines Act 1968

1. *Shillito v Thompson* (1875) 1 QBD 12.
2. Section 123A(1) of the Food and Drugs Act 1955, inserted in 1972, empowered the Ministry of Agriculture, Fisheries and Food and the Secretary of State to make regulations to comply with EEC provisions.

Adultery

Divorce may be granted if the respondent has committed adultery and the petitioner finds it intolerable to live with him[1] — the two phrases are, however, independent[2].

Adultery may be defined as an act of consensual sexual intercourse between a married person and a person of the opposite sex other than the spouse[3]. A married woman does not commit adultery if she is raped[4] and the courts may, in certain circumstances, hold that there is no adultery if the act of intercourse took place while the respondent was intoxicated[5]. Some penetration is required and forms of sexual contact other than intercourse per vaginam, including masturbation[6], will not amount to adultery. An unsuccessful attempt to achieve penetration will be viewed similarly by the law[7]. Instances of general indecency between the parties may, however, give rise to the inference that adultery has occurred on other occasions[8].

The question of whether artificial insemination by donor to which the husband has not consented constitutes adultery was considered in the Scottish case of *MacLennan v MacLennan*[9] in which it was affirmed that there could be no adultery in the absence of penetration by the male organ. A different view was taken in a very much earlier Canadian case[10] but it has been ruled more recently in South Africa that consensual AID does not involve adultery[11].

A woman denying adultery may produce expert evidence of the fact that she is *virgo intacta*[12]. Such evidence does not, of course, exclude partial penetration but it will have the effect of placing a heavy burden of proof on the petitioner[13].

Medical evidence may also be invoked to prove adultery. The fact that venereal disease has been contracted during the marriage from somebody other than the spouse is indicative. Adultery will normally be established where blood tests or other medical evidence indicate that a child born to a wife could not be the child of the husband.

It is to be noted, as a particular medico-legal circumstance, that adultery by a doctor with one of his or her patients — or even with a member of the patient's family — will be regarded most severely by the General Medical Council. The Council is, however, not concerned with a doctor's relationship with those not in his or her medical care.

See also: Artificial insemination by donor; Divorce; General Medical Council; Parentage testing

1. Matrimonial Causes Act 1973; Divorce (Scotland) Act 1976.
2. *Cleary v Cleary* [1974] 1 ALL ER 498; Divorce (Scotland) Act 1976, s.1(2)(a).
3. Jackson, J (ed) *Rayden's Law and Practice in Divorce and Family Matters in All Courts* (14th ed, 1983) Vol.1, p.196, Butterworths, London.

4. *Clarkson v Clarkson* [1930] TLR 623.
5. *Goshawk v Goshawk* (1965) 109 SJ 290; *see* Bromley P *Family Law* (6th ed, 1981) p.196, Butterworths, London. For the effect of insanity, *see S v S* [1962] P 133; [1961] 3 All ER 133.
6. *Sapsford v Sapsford and Furtado* [1954] P 394; [1954] 2 All ER 373.
7. *Dennis v Dennis* [1955] P 153; [1955] 2 All ER 51.
8. *Rayden*, n.3 above, p.198.
9. 1958 SC 105.
10. *Orford v Orford* 58 DLR 251 (1921).
11. *V v R* (1979) 3 SA 1007.
12. *Rutherford v Richardson* [1922] P 144, CA; [1923] AC 1, HL.
13. *Christian v Christian* (1962) 106 SJ 430, CA.

Advertising by Doctors

As a general rule, doctors are not allowed by the General Medical Council to advertise their availability or their expertise. Essentially, this is a matter of medical etiquette, a main purpose of which is to prevent doctors competing against one another and using commercial methods to attract custom — even the size and content of doorplates are subject to review by the Standards Committee of the GMC. The original purpose of medical registration was to enable 'persons requiring medical aid to distinguish qualified from unqualified practitioners'[1] and it is clearly right that the public should have factual information about their doctors; moreover, it would be supposed that the near elimination of remuneration by fees has removed the main incentive towards unethical advertising. Nevertheless, advertising or canvassing constitutes the most rapidly increasing type of case reported to the GMC[2]. One particular reason for this lies in doctors' relationship with the several types of commercial organisation which offer medical or paramedical services — e.g. cosmetic surgery, vasectomy clinics or clinics for the termination of pregnancy; relationships with the pharmaceutical industry may also sometimes involve the doctor in advertising — perhaps unwittingly.

A very great change has come over the GMC's attitude to lay press writing and broadcasting by doctors. It is now accepted that the public has a legitimate interest in medical science and that, as a corollary, the public are entitled to know the standing of the person providing them with information. The important distinction lies between, on the one hand, suggesting in the article or broadcast that the author has an expertise superior to his colleagues and, on the other, providing informed discussion of the general principles of medical practice[3].

See also: Abortion Act 1967; General Medical Council

1. Medical Act 1858 (repealed).
2. General Medical Council *Annual Report for 1982* (1983) GMC, London.
3. General Medical Council *Professional Conduct and Discipline: Fitness to Practise* (August 1983) GMC, London.

Age of a Body at Death

Methods for the assessment of the age of a body at the time of death differ according to the circumstances. The matter may be one of common observation if the body is well preserved and of an age between infancy and senility. More sophisticated observations are needed if the body is of fetal age or is decomposed, incinerated or skeletonised.

Fetal age estimation is a matter of assessing its size and the stage of development of centres of ossification in the bones. A simple size rule is that the gestational age in weeks is twice the fetal length in inches. A good estimate can also be made from the weight — an infant weighing more than 1.5 kg will be of more than 28 weeks' gestation. Recourse must be had to anthropomorphic tables to find the age of appearance of the many centres of ossification[1]. The more important in medico-legal terms are those which appear at about the 28th week of pregnancy — in the talus bone of the ankle and in the first segment of the breast bone — and the centres for the lower end of the femur and for the cuboid bone of the foot which are present at full term.

Centres of ossification continue to appear in infancy and adolescence but, from childhood until early adult life, the union of these centres becomes the most significant indication of age. Such unions occur with reasonable regularity but the more centres which can be examined, the narrower will be the band of probability as to accuracy. The female skeleton is commonly about one year more advanced developmentally than is that of the male.

The evidential value of skeletal changes greatly diminishes after the age of 25. From the age of 40, however, the skull sutures begin to close and this, together with some changes in the shape of the bones, especially the jaw bone, will help distinguish the skeleton of an elderly person from a youth — but little more than that.

Over all, by far the most useful indication of age is to be found in the development of the teeth. This is particularly so in infancy when both the deciduous and permanent dentition are available for assessment; children separated by as little as three months in age can be identified by this means[2]. The permanent teeth, apart from the wisdom teeth, are generally erupted by the age of 13, and the presence of wisdom teeth is good evidence that the body was aged more than 21 years at the time of death. Again, the teeth mature rather more quickly in girls than in boys. Changes of fair wear and tear continue with age and, in skilled hands, can lead to an estimation of age within a bracket of a decade[3]; certainly, the dentist's estimation of age is likely to be more reliable than that of the pathologist in the face of severe burning or putrefaction.

See also: Odontology; Ossification centres; Union of epiphyses; Viability

1. The main monograph on the subject is Krogman WM *The Human Skeleton in Forensic Medicine* (1962) CC Thomas, Springfield Ill.
2. Ashley KF 'Identification of children in a mass disaster by estimation of dental age' (1970) 129 Br Dent J 167.
3. Classically described by Gustafson G *Forensic Odontology* (1966), p.118 et seq, Elsevier, New York.

Age of Consent to Sexual Practices

Consent to touching or injury is regulated either by common law or by statute. Sexual contact is in the latter category, the concern of the law being to protect young persons against exploitation and against their own inclinations or desires which cannot be based on experienced judgement[1].

It is commonly said that the age of legal consent to sexual intercourse by a girl is 16, the girl having reached that age at the first moment of the day preceding her 16th birthday; it is more correct to say that 16 is the age of a girl below which a man cannot lawfully have sexual intercourse with her[2]. It is certain that many girls do have sexual intercourse below the legal age and there is a sizeable body of opinion which regards it as being put unnecessarily high in these days of sexual liberation and enlightenment[3]. There is some *de facto* support for this view in that less than a quarter of instances of having intercourse with a girl between the ages of 13 and 16 which are known to the police are prosecuted, and custodial sentences are rare in the event of conviction. The rule must be framed mainly to protect young girls against exploitation by older men, and the National Council for Civil Liberties has proposed that the age of consent should be lowered to 14 and that an 'overlap' of two years on either side should be accepted in law; love play including actual sexual intercourse between adolescents aged between 12 and 16 would, accordingly, not be an offence[4]. Again, this just about represents the state of the law in practice — a custodial sentence in such circumstances would be unthinkable[5]. The fact that the legal age of marriage is also 16[6] is immaterial to the act of sexual intercourse. It is true that 16 is the age of consent to sexual intercourse in many EEC countries but the main justification for retention of the age limit may well be that it corresponds to the school-leaving age.

No person under the age of 16, whether a boy or a girl, can consent to an indecent assault — and this is irrespective of its being in a homosexual or a heterosexual situation[7]. It is impossible to consent legally to incestuous intercourse but no offence is committed by a girl below the age of 16 years who does so[8].

Adult males above the age of 21 years may consent to homosexual practices in private[9]. There seems no reason why the age of 21 should be retained now that the age of majority has been reduced to 18 other than that there is probably greater public resistance to exposing the young to homosexual activity than there is in the case of orthodox sexuality. A case might be made, however, for decriminalising homosexual experimentation between young boys of comparable age. In fact, a boy below the age of 14 cannot be found guilty of buggery[10]. This limitation, including the fact that a boy below the age of 14 cannot commit incest, derives from the curious presumption in criminal law that such a boy is incapable of sexual intercourse; such credulity does not exist in Scotland.

The age of consent to lesbian activity is governed by consent to indecent assault.

See also: Age of majority; Consent to injury; Homosexual offences; Incest; Indecent assault; Lesbianism; Marriage; Unlawful sexual intercourse

1. The basic law is contained in the Sexual Offences Act 1956 and the Sexual Offences (Scotland) Act 1976.
2. *Gillick v West Norfolk and Wisbech AHA and the Department of Health and Social Security* [1985] 3 WLR 830, HL, per Lord Brandon.

3. *See* the remarks as to other judgments by Lawton LJ in *R v Taylor, R v Simons, R v Roberts* [1977] 1 WLR 612 at 616.
4. National Council for Civil Liberties *Sexual Offences*, Report No.13 (1976) NCCL, London.
5. *John O'Grady* (1978) 66 Crim App R 279.
6. Marriage Act 1949; Marriage (Scotland) Act 1977.
7. Sexual Offences Act 1956, s.14(2); s.15(2).
8. Sexual Offences Act 1956, s.11.
9. Sexual Offences Act 1967; Criminal Justice (Scotland) Act 1980, s.80.
10. *R v Allen* (1848) 1 Den 364. *See* Mitchell S (ed) *Archbold Pleading, Evidence and Practice in Criminal Cases* (42nd ed, 1985), p.1617, Sweet & Maxwell, London.

Age of Legal Responsibility

Children can perform destructive acts; their moral and legal responsibility for such acts is, however, another matter. The point at which criminal responsibililty could be imputed in common law was placed at the age of 7. This age was raised to 8 by the Children and Young Persons Act 1933, s.50, and to 10 by the Children and Young Persons Act 1963, s.11(1). A presumption exists that a child cannot be found guilty of an offence between the ages of 10 and 14 but this is rebuttable if evidence is adduced of a malignant disposition. This rule is expressed in the adage *malitia supplet aetatem* (malice makes up for age). Evidence of background, experience and even of relevant previous convictions[1] may be brought by the prosecution to show that the child knew the difference between right and wrong, the test being whether or not it was appreciated that some wrong was being done[2]. Evidence of a good background may act to the child's detriment as tending to indicate the benefits of a sound moral training[3].

A boy under the age of 14 is presumed to be incapable of sexual intercourse and, therefore, of committing rape[4]. He may, however, be convicted of an offence of this nature if he participates as a principal in the second degree, and he may also be convicted of indecent assault[5]. By extension of this rule, a boy under 14 cannot be guilty of buggery. A boy under the age of 14 who submits to buggery is unlikely to be considered an accomplice[6]. There is no similar presumption as to age and sexual incapacity in Scots law.

There is no arbitrary age at which a child will be held liable for tortious conduct. A child is generally expected to conform to the standards of behaviour anticipated in the age group to which he belongs. Accordingly, the standard of care will be based in each case on what a reasonable child of the dependant's age would have done in the circumstances[7]. It is a concomitant of this rule that a child of tender years will be held incapable of committing a tortious act[8].

See also: Buggery; Homosexual Offences; Torts

1. *R v B, R v A* [1979] 3 All ER 460.
2. *McC v Runickles* (1984) Times, 5 May.
3. James TE 'The age of criminal responsibility' [1959] Crim LR 497.
4. This absurd, though irrebuttable, presumption applies only to the criminal law; a boy below the age of 14 may be liable to an affiliation order (*L v K* [1985] 1 All ER 961).
5. *R v Williams* [1983] 1 QB 320.
6. *R v Tatam* (1921) 15 Crim App R 132; *R v Cratchley* (1914) 9 Crim App R 232.

7. *McHale v Watson* (1966) 115 Crim LR 119.

8. Black R 'The tort liability of children under the laws of England and France' (1973) 6 Comp Int LJ Southern Africa 365; Smith TB 'The age of innocence' (1974) Tul LR 311. For the South African standard, *see Roxa v Mtshayi* 1975 (3) SA 761 (AD); American law: Gray OS 'The standard of care for children revisited' (1980) 45 Miss LR 597.

Age of Majority

A minor becomes a person of full age for legal purposes on achieving the age of 18[1]. The passing of this milestone has a number of significant legal effects — an adult can vote in elections, can hold a legal estate in land and has full contractual capacity.

The age of majority does not necessarily coincide with other legally significant birthdays. The age of consent to heterosexual sexual activity comes two years earlier, at the age of 16, as does the age at which statute recognises that consent may be given to medical treatment. The legal age of consent to homosexual practices occurs later, remaining at the traditional majority age of 21, and there are other interesting concessions to age — e.g. a person aged 17 may give consent to fingerprinting. Such anomalies are noted under the relevant headings.

See also: Age of legal responsibility; Consent to medical treatment; Fingerprints; Sexual offences

1. Family Law Reform Act 1969, s.1(1). In Scotland, the age of majority was also set at 18 by the Age of Majority (Scotland) Act 1969.

Agonal Period

The agonal period is the time elapsed between a lethal occurrence and death. The term is hardly applicable to natural disease — if it has any meaning, it will imply the period of confinement to bed before death. Its real medico-legal significance is in those cases in which a finite moment of onset can be ascribed to the process of dying and this, effectively, implies an unnatural injury. The assessment of the agonal period becomes crucial to the application of the commorientes rules in the event of two related persons being injured at the same time. Since it is the relative time, irrespective of its absolute value, which is important, the pathologist may be faced with a difficult task if neither the injuries nor the deaths were witnessed; establishing the mode of death and adducing more subtle evidence[1] may become essential. The precise length of the agonal period may be impossible to estimate in persons whose existence is maintained artificially.

See also: Burning; Commorientes; Fat embolism; Ventilator support

1. This may be very difficult to apply in practice. *See* Buchanan D and Mason JK 'Occurrence of pulmonary fat and bone marrow embolism' (1982) 3 Am J Forens Med Path 73.

Air Embolism

The presence of air or of any undissolved gas in the blood stream is incompatible with an efficient circulation and may rapidly cause sudden death due to cerebral or myocardial anoxia.

The causation of air embolism has altered markedly in the last few decades. Prior to the Abortion Act 1967 it was a fairly common cause of death following illegal abortion. Air was inadvertently pumped into open uterine vessels while using an enema syringe to separate the placenta; such occurrences are now virtually unknown but orogenital sex play in pregnant women has achieved the same result[1]. Simultaneous cutting of the larynx and the adjacent jugular vein in cut throat results in air being sucked into the latter; cut throats are now rare but the condition remains an improbable hazard of any surgical operation on the neck. Other therapeutic procedures which could cause air embolism included the induction of pneumothorax but this is no longer a treatment for tuberculosis. Theoretically, air embolism could be provoked if a transfusion system is allowed to run dry but, in practice, this can occur only if positive pressure is being used.

The trade which is now mainly at hazard is that of divers in whom air embolism may result from rupture of the lung during over-rapid ascent from a pressurised environment. This condition is to be distinguished from decompression sickness which occurs in similar conditions but results from intravascular bubble formation.

The amount of injected gas which can be tolerated by the body is extremely variable but it is generally agreed that 60 ml of air is the minimum lethal intravenous dose and this is probably an underestimate. However, death may result from a very much smaller quantity if this is introduced into a major artery. Thus, some of the newer investigative techniques such as coronary or carotid angiography carry such a risk which can be regarded as virtually non-existent in competent hands.

Death from air embolism is characteristically rapid. Occasional cases of survival for up to 20 minutes are reported but these must be extremely rare. The demonstration of air embolism as a cause of death requires special pathological expertise[2].

See also: Abortion; Cut throat; Decompression sickness; Diving hazards

1. Fatteh A et al 'Fatal air embolism in pregnancy resulting from oro-genital sex play' (1973) 2 Forensic Sci 247.
2. *See* Hendry WT et al 'The offshore scene and its hazards' in Mason JK (ed) *The Pathology of Violent Injury* (1978) Chap.17, Edward Arnold, London.

Aircraft Accidents

Aircraft accidents tend to be either wholly fatal or non-fatal. As might be expected, accidents occurring at airfields, in the circumstances of take-off or landing, provide the majority of the rarer instances where there are both survivors and fatalities. Such accidents are the most difficult to deal with in immediate practical terms.

Aircraft accidents are a heterogeneous group. Military accidents, which tend to be of great severity, are of major interest in relation to inflight escape (*see* 'Parachuting injuries'); many light aircraft accidents are potentially survivable and pose problems of safety provisions and of the relatively unfit and unselected pilot; commercial accidents raise fascinating questions as to causation but also involve many medico-legal problems related to the identification of victims and to the precise relationship between the accident and the cause of death (*see* 'Commorientes').

Whilst commercial disasters get maximum publicity, it is worth noting that more persons are killed in light aircraft in the USA alone than are killed in commercial operations on a world-wide basis; travel in the latter is now safer than it has ever been and has a mortality comparable to that on the British railways[1]. Alcohol is not a causative feature of fatal military or commercial aviation accidents but some 15 per cent of fatal light aircraft accidents are associated with alcohol in the USA[2]; comparable figures are found elsewhere. The introduction of a minimum alcohol-free period before piloting in the USA resulted in a reduction in the total alcohol-related accidents but an increase in the proportion of those associated with very high levels of body alcohol — the implication being that, as in road traffic accidents, there is a core of alcoholics who are not amenable to regulation and propaganda[3]. Curiously, there is no legislation comparable to the Road Traffic Act 1972 to permit breath analyses of pilots involved in non-fatal accidents.

Disease as a cause of aircraft accidents is considered in more detail under 'Trauma and disease'. As might be expected, it is more common in private pilots than in the highly selected military and commercial aircrew. The incidence of disease-related commercial accidents is certainly less than 1 per cent of all accidents but its recognition in fatal aircraft accidents is complicated by the very severe bodily injuries sustained[4].

It is now mandatory in the majority of countries for the occupants of front seats of light aircraft to be restrained by upper torso harnesses; previous to such regulation, it was shown that some 40 per cent of fatalities in private aviation were preventable by the use of adequate harness and of protective helmets — there is still no legislation as to the latter[5].

The injuries sustained in aircraft accidents are almost unique in combining severe horizontal with vertical deceleration forces. The number of subjects to be examined in commercial disasters provides a major opportunity, when correlated with an examination of the wreckage, for the pathologist to give evidence as to the type of the accident[6]. Burning is, unfortunately, a common cause of death in accidents occurring at take-off or undershooting the airfield; this is largely due to the difficulty rescue services often encounter in reaching the disaster (cf. 'Road traffic accidents') but the speed of evolution and the intensity of the fire play a very important role[7]. The pattern of injuries, supported by intensive radiological investigation, may enable the pathologist to diagnose hijacking or other types of sabotage as a cause of an accident, which is then likely to have been of maximum ferocity.

All aircraft accidents occurring in the UK are reportable to the Chief Inspector of Accidents, who is responsible for their investigation[8]. On an international scale, the country in which the aircraft crashes is responsible for the accident investigation but may, if it is so desired, delegate this to the country in which the aircraft was registered. The country in which the aircraft was registered is, in any event, entitled to send accredited representatives to the investigation, as is the country of manufacture in the case of large aircraft; the co-operation of the operator is usually also sought and any country of which a major proportion of the passengers were citizens also has limited rights of participation. Recommended standards and practices in accident investigation are laid down in the Convention on International Civil Aviation, to which the UK is a signatory.

Aircraft accidents are, of course, subject to the normal considerations of negligence, and massive damages have been awarded against the operators of commercial airliners. No-fault liability for personal injuries or death is, however, admitted under the Warsaw Convention[9] in respect of international travel and is then limited to $75,000 per passenger when the flight is to, from or includes an agreed stopping place in the USA; the limitation is more severe in relation to other flights. The Carriage by Air Act 1961 applies to flights which are wholly within the UK. In the event of sabotage being found to be the cause of an aircraft accident, responsibility for insurance passes from the 'all risks' insurers to those underwriting 'war risks'.

See also: Alcohol; Commorientes; Deceleration injuries; Hijacking; No-fault compensation; Parachuting injuries; Patterns of injury; Protective helmets; Road Traffic Act 1972; Seat belts; Trauma and disease

1. Mason, JK 'Accidents and travel' (1982) 82B Proc R Soc Ed 63. This statement may need modification in the light of experience in 1985.
2. Ryan LC and Mohler SR 'Current role of alcohol as a factor in civil aircraft accidents' (1979) 50 Aviat Space Environ Med 275.
3. Ryan LC and Mohler SR 'Intoxicating liquor and the general aviation pilot in 1971' (1972) 43 Aerospace Med 1024.
4. *See*, for example, *Report of the Public Inquiry into the cause and circumstances of the accident near Staines on 18 June 1972* (CAAR 4/73, 1973).
5. Cullen SA 'Death in general aviation accidents and its prevention' in JK Mason and WJ Reals (eds) *Aerospace Pathology* (1973) Chap.12, College of American Pathologists Foundation, Chicago.
6. Mason JK 'Passenger tie-down failure: injuries and accident reconstruction' (1970) 41 Aerospace Med 781.
7. Escape from burning commercial aircraft is a cause for concern; at the time of writing, the investigation into the deaths of 55 persons in what should have been a wholly survivable accident at Manchester Airport in 1985 is continuing.
8. Civil Aviation (Investigation of Accidents) Regulations 1983 (SI 1983/551) made under the Civil Aviation Act 1982.
9. Convention for the Unification of Certain Rules Relating to International Carriage by Air 1929 [Warsaw Convention] as amended 1955 [Hague Protocol].

Airgun Injuries

Injuries due to pellets fired from air weapons are seldom given much space in works on forensic pathology yet it has been said that more than 60 per cent of all firearm injuries in England and Wales are so caused[1].

Any lethal effect of an airgun pellet depends upon the muzzle energy of the weapon and upon the format of the pellet. The muzzle energy will vary very considerably and, in normal circumstances, penetration of the skull occurs only in children or adolescents. Whilst involvement of a vital soft structure such as the eye is virtually independent of muzzle velocity or energy, a pellet fired from close range could cause head injury even in an adult; for this reason, a pump action air rifle with a muzzle energy in excess of 16 J (12 ft lbf) or an air pistol of more than 8 J (6 ft lbf) is classified as a specially dangerous air weapon[2] and is subject to firearm restrictions.

The pellet may be specially softened when powerful airguns are used for target practice, and such pellets have a very low power of penetration[3]. On the other hand, an interesting phenomenon known as 'dieseling' may occur — oil in the barrel is combusted by heat generated as the pellet passes down the barrel and acts as an explosive charge, thus greatly increasing the apparent power of the gun[4].

Significant airgun injuries, other than those of the eye, are largely confined to the brain although an unfortunate shot in the trunk could penetrate a major artery. As stated above, all injuries are more likely in a child than in an adult. Children under the age of 14 are not allowed to use airguns except in private when in the care of an adult aged more than 21 or in a shooting gallery; a gift or loan of an air weapon to a minor aged between 14 and 17 years is allowable but sale of air weapons is limited to persons over the age of 17 years[5].

See also: Firearms

1. Green MA 'Injury and sudden death in sport' in Mason JK (ed) *The Pathology of Violent Injury* (1978) p.272, Edward Arnold, London.
2. Firearms (Dangerous Air Weapons) Rules 1969 (SI 1969/47).
3. Steindler RA 'Air gun pellet penetration' (1980) 20 Med Sci Law 93.
4. Buchanan JD '"Dieseling" — a potentially lethal phenomenon in air weapons' (1982) 22 Med Sci Law 107.
5. Firearms Act 1968, s. 24.

Alcohol

Alcohol, which is regarded for the purposes of this entry in its popular meaning (i.e. ethyl alcohol) is primarily a cerebral depressant; its apparent stimulant effect results from a selective depression of the higher, socially discriminant activities of the human brain. It is an effective drug for the treatment of anxiety but one which has adverse side effects and which certainly induces a degree of dependence — the condition of alcoholism. Increased tolerance is also a feature of persistent drinking although it is possible that much of this apparent result is more in the nature of habituation and adaptation — the pharmacological effect is still present but is repressed.

Alcohol is absorbed in the main from the small intestine; thus the effects appear more rapidly when the stomach is emptied quickly or when the stomach has been removed surgically. Once absorbed, alcohol is distributed through the blood to the tissues where its quantitative distribution will depend very largely on the water content. Thus its concentration in the blood, which has a major solid component, will always be lower than in, say, the cerebrospinal fluid. Some 90 per cent of the absorbed alcohol is broken down in the liver, the remainder being excreted in the urine, sweat and breath. It is therefore possible to assess the degree of intoxication by reference to the concentration of alcohol in these excretions. The precise rate at which alcohol is eliminated from the body is particular to the individual but varies around a mean of 8 g per hour. Put another way, this implies a reduction in the blood alcohol concentration of between 11 and 19 mg alcohol/100 ml blood per hour for social drinkers[1].

The best measure of the effective alcohol concentration in the body would be that in the brain but, since this is clearly impossible to measure in life, the alcohol in the blood which is supplying the brain provides a reasonable quantification. The taking of blood is not always easy and involves inflicting a wound, albeit minimal. For these reasons, it is often useful, as in the application of road traffic legislation, to use breath as an admittedly indirect measure of the effective body alcohol concentration. Urine may also be used although, since the bladder contains urine which results from the continuous filtration of the blood, its content is a poor measure of the body alcohol at a given moment; the nearest possible approach is to empty the bladder and then test the earliest specimen it is possible to void — but this is still open to considerable criticism in the case of urinary retention due, say, to prostatism.

The pharmacological action of alcohol is such that it will have a profound effect on social behaviour, homicidal intent and accidental death, these last two aspects being of such importance that they are discussed under separate entries. Since the higher cerebral control may be diminished in an individual who is depressed, the possibility of suicide is also affected by alcohol. Alcohol may cause or potentiate disease and its effects may be passed on to the fetus. It is apparent that alcohol is a potent drug which is unique in that its distribution is controlled only by the general licensing laws[2].

The consequences of alcohol consumption may be important in relation to accidental injury or death. In the first place, it will be contributory negligence to place oneself in the hands of someone who is known to be drunk and, therefore, likely to be negligent[3]. Further, being under the influence of alcohol may well invalidate the terms of a personal accident insurance policy[4]. For this purpose, the term 'while under the influence of intoxicating liquor' is interpreted in a temporal sense — there is no need to show a causative relationship between the injury and the state of acute alcoholism[5]; there is a general impression that insurers would, now, pragmatically, accept the prescribed limits of the Road Traffic Act 1972 (as amended) as distinguishing 'being under the influence'.

Considerable importance may therefore attach to the validity of any laboratory results, and this applies particularly to alcohol estimations made on *post mortem* specimens of blood. There is evidence that putrefactive organisms may themselves produce alcohol, and this is especially so if there are multiple injuries facilitating bacterial growth and if the autopsy has been delayed without refrigeration of the body[6]; there are sound arguments in favour of always checking the blood alcohol in such circumstances by an examination of the urine or vitreous humour of the eye, neither of which is subject to putrefactive changes to the same extent.

See also: Accidental death; Alcoholism; Drunkenness; Intoxication and criminal responsibility; Putrefaction; Road Traffic Act 1972; Suicide

1. Winek CL and Murphy KL 'The rate and kinetic order of ethanol elimination' (1984) 25 Forens Sci Int 159. The authors suggest that alcoholics may eliminate alcohol twice as fast.
2. The most important medico-legally is the Licencing Act 1964, s.169, which prohibits the sale of alcoholic liquor to minors.
3. *Owens v Brimmell* [1976] 3 All ER 765.
4. *Louden v British Merchants Insurance Co* [1961] 1 All ER 705.
5. *See also Givens v Baloise Marine* (1959) 17 DLR 2d 7.
6. For a very full resumé of the problems, *see* Corry JEL 'Possible sources of ethanol ante-

and post-mortem: its relationship to the biochemistry and microbiology of decomposition' (1978) 44 J Appl Bact 1. For a practical example of the importance, *see* Railway Inspectorate *Report on the Accident that occurred on 28th February 1975 at Moorgate Station* (1976) HMSO, London.

Alcoholism

The term 'alcoholism' is necessarily vague because it embraces so many different kinds of harm — medical, social and financial — in many different kinds of person. Alcohol dependence, which refers to only one aspect of the problem, is rather easier to define and can be regarded as excessive drinking by persons who have become so psychologically dependent on alcohol that it interferes with their health, social functioning and interpersonal relationships. There may be an element of addiction in some cases which is exemplified by withdrawal symptoms and signs, some of which may be both serious and distressing (*see* 'Delirium tremens').

Even so, the incidence of alcoholism as a disease is difficult to assess as there are wide variations available within the definition given above; 'labelling' is, to an extent, a subjective exercise which depends upon the attitudes of the labeller. The most objective attempt, introduced some 30 years ago, depends on a complex relationship between the number of chronic alcoholics, the incidence of cirrhosis of the liver and the number of deaths due to cirrhosis[1]; these parameters all have their pitfalls and depend very much upon the accuracy of the observations made and how they are recorded. An example of how estimates can vary is provided by the fact that, based on formal indices of harm (e.g. cirrhosis) it has been widely believed that alcoholism is a greater problem in Scotland than it is in the rest of Great Britain; new research, based on a study of hospital admissions and community drinking habits, has, however, suggested that this may be wrong[2]. The problems of subjective labelling are circumvented by using a specified intake as satisfying the criterion of dependence; this is often regarded as 15 cl absolute alcohol per day — which corresponds to drinking half a standard bottle of spirits.

There is a strong suggestion that, whilst there may be a constitutional, or even genetic, basis for alcoholism — particularly of the addictive type — the greater motivation towards a high alcoholic intake derives, firstly, from learning and, secondly, from the fact that alcohol is an effective drug for the treatment of mild anxiety states and is available subject only to minimal control. The sale of alcohol to persons under the age of 18 is an offence in the UK[3] and, whilst there are restricted hours for drinking on licenced premises, there is no limitation on the far more economical form of drinking in the home. Heavy drinking may well be related to societal practices but societies of very different types have a high level of alcohol consumption — it would seem to be a common link between the moneyed classes of southern England and the workers in the totalitarian states of eastern Europe.

These considerations confirm the need to confine the concept of alcoholism as a disease to that of compulsive drug dependence. There then seem to be two relevant populations — the social drinker who steadily becomes addicted and the inadequate or abnormal personality who takes to alcohol as the most easily available drug to assist him with his problems[4].

The true alcoholic then provides the nucleus of the group of offenders who can be categorised as 'criminal alcoholics'. Many offences by such persons will be of a natural consequential type — breaches of the peace, drunkenness and disorderliness; others, however, will stem from the dilemma that the alcoholic has no money and yet requires it in order to obtain alcohol — such offences will be mainly of theft and of others against property. At the same time, the severe alcoholic will be forced to resort to cheaper forms of drink and will take to methylated spirit, skin lotions and the like. It is said that such persons constitute a minority of alcoholics but, again, such a statement depends upon one's definition of the condition. The 'criminal alcoholic' is to be distinguished from the 'alcoholic criminal' — that is, the person who commits crime, often of a serious nature including violence against the person, when his normal societal inhibitions are removed by the cerebral depressant effect of alcohol.

It is not to be denied that heavy drinking is both physically and societally harmful — particularly, perhaps, in employment — and every effort should be made to reduce its incidence. It is, however, difficult to see this as likely when most governments other than those of Moslem states regard alcoholic consumption as an essential source of revenue[5].

Alcohol has many physical effects on the body. Chronic alcohol abuse almost certainly induces some cerebral neuronal deficit and, ultimately, a frank organic psychosis; the well-known association between alcohol and disease of the liver is discussed under 'Cirrhosis'; alcoholic cardiomyopathy is a well-established entity; carcinoma of the oesophagus is more common in alcoholics than in the general population; and there are a number of other relatively dangerous effects — including a well-documented effect on the fetus. It is to be noted that deaths associated with alcoholism are automatically reportable to the coroner — but not necessarily to the Scottish procurator fiscal. The coroner is, however, now disbarred from returning a conclusion that death was due to chronic alcoholism[6].

See also: Alcohol; Cardiomyopathy; Cirrhosis; Coroner; Delirium tremens; Methyl alcohol

1. Jellinek EM 'Estimating the prevalence of alcoholism' (1959) 20 Quart J Studies Alcohol 261.
2. Latcham RW et al 'Regional variations in British alcohol morbidity rates: a myth uncovered?' (1984) 289 Br Med J 1341, 1343.
3. Licensing Act 1964, s.169.
4. A rather similar approach is adopted in seeking a genetic basis for alcoholism. *See* Saunders JB 'Alcoholism: new evidence for a genetic contribution' (1982) 284 Br Med J 1137.
5. Kendell RE 'Alcoholism: a medical or political problem?' [1979] 1 Br Med J 367; Paton R 'The politics of alcohol' (1985) 290 Br Med J 1.
6. Coroners Rules 1984 (SI 1984/552) Sch.4.

Allergy

Allergy is essentially an excessive expression of the immune reaction — the response to the foreign protein becomes positively disadvantageous to the body. A naturally occurring allergy may be inborn or may be acquired through exposure to the 'allergen'. Common examples of allergens in nature are the pollens of certain flowers or, more seriously, the venoms of bees and wasps. The body is usually able to cope with the result of such insults but severe reactions may arise if the subject is exceptionally sensitive or if the dose of allergen is particularly large. The anaphylactic response is generally manifested by a shift of the intravascular fluid to the extra-vascular spaces, with the production of oedema; occasionally the shock may be so severe as to cause sudden collapse and death due to reduction in the blood pressure. The adverse mechanical effect of oedema is twofold. Occurring in the lungs, the outpouring of fluid may be so severe as to fill so many air sacs that uptake of oxygen is compromised (*see* 'Pulmonary oedema'). Alternatively, swelling of the tissues may cause secondary blockage of the tubes they surround — the most important area is the glottis, oedema of which may result in fatal blockage of the airway.

Allergic reactions to cosmetics, toiletries and the like do occasionally result in actions against manufacturers or suppliers[1]. The most important medical aspect of allergy, however, relates to drug hypersensitivity and, particularly, to allergy to antibiotics.

An appreciable number of deaths do, in fact, result from hypersensitivity to penicillin — especially if this is rapidly absorbed following injection — and this occurs world wide. It would certainly now be regarded as negligent not to take precautions against such a mishap[2]. The nature of such precautions is a matter for some debate. The ideal is to employ an intradermal test dose to exclude sensitivity, the possibility of a severe reaction to the test being countered by the ready availability of antidotes of the adrenaline type. Cases have, however, been recorded of fatal reactions occurring despite the use of test doses[3]; moreover, it is logistically impossible to test dose every person before administering an antibiotic. The alternative approach is to ask routinely if there is any history of sensitivity; unfortunately, this puts an onus on the patient to solve a question to which he may well not know the answer. The pragmatic solution is probably to make a routine inquiry and to test dose in any case which gives rise to doubt; it is essential that the patient's notes are prominently marked if allergy to a drug is established and that this fact is positively included in any communication between caring physicians.

See also: Immune reaction; Pulmonary oedema

1. *Ingham and another v Emes* [1955] 3 **WLR** 245.
2. *Chin Keow v Government of Malaysia and another* [1967] 1 **WLR** 813.
3. *See* Denning LJ n.1 above at 247.

Amnesia

Memory is the ability to call to consciousness information which has been registered in the mind at some previous time. The absence of memory is amnesia, which may be complete or partial. The memory of the events of entire days, months or years may be lost permanently; alternatively, there may be merely loss of ability to recall certain minor incidents or facts which have been learned. Amnesia may be emotional in origin or it may be caused by some organic factor such as cerebral trauma or arteriosclerotic disease. Other defects in memory include hypermnesia, which involves excessive retention of information and is a feature of paranoia; paramnesia, which involves falsification in recall; and confabulation, in which there is unconscious filling in of gaps by 'memories' which are untrue.

Hysterical amnesia is of particular medico-legal interest. The condition is characterised by the selective loss of memory in respect of events which are of particularly emotional significance. Memory of criminal conduct, such as a serious assault, may thus be lost by both the victim and the offender[1]. The unpleasant nature of the experience or the sense of guilt may serve to blot the event from the subject's consciousness. It is not rare to find that those involved in accidents lose the ability to recollect not only what happened some hours before the incident but also the incident itself and its aftermath. The duration of post-traumatic amnesia correlates fairly well with the severity of diffuse injury to the brain[2]. Recollection may return in many cases, particularly if the subject's memory is triggered in some way.

Loss of memory may also occur in the so-called 'alcoholic blackout'[3]. This may result in the loss of memory of a period during a drinking spell or, in some cases, the inability to recall what happened over a period of days. Alcoholic amnesia can be fragmentary or total. In the latter case, it is unlikely that memory will return in respect of the 'lost time'. Alcoholic blackouts are a relatively late manifestation of alcoholism.

Amnesia is not a defence to a criminal charge and it will not be accepted as the basis for a plea of unfitness to be tried[4]. There is a strong case for a contrary view because it is difficult to see how a defendant can give proper instructions to counsel in respect of incidents of which he may have no recollection. Were it, however, to be accepted, difficulties would no doubt be experienced in distinguishing the genuine from the false claim of amnesia.

See also: Alcoholism; Psychoses

1. Gudjonsson G 'A specific recognition deficit in a case of homicide' (1983) 23 Med Sci Law 37; O'Connell BA 'Amnesia and homicide' (1960) 10 Br J Delinq 262.
2. Lishman WA 'Psychiatric sequelae of head injuries: problems in diagnosis' (1978) 71 Ir Med J 306.
3. Goodwin DW, Crane JB and Guze SB 'Phenomenological aspects of the alcoholic blackout' (1969) 115 Br J Psychiat 1033.
4. *R v Podola* [1959] 3 All ER 418; *Russell v HM Adv* 1946 JC 37.

Amniocentesis

Amniocentesis involves inserting a needle in the sac which surrounds the fetus in the uterus (the amnion) and withdrawing some of the contained amniotic fluid. This fluid contains metabolites and excretions of the fetus together with shed fetal cells; it is thus possible to study the biochemistry of the fetus and also, by culturing the cells, to ascertain both their chromosomal pattern and their enzymatic activity. The procedure therefore has a great potential for antenatal diagnosis and for providing the genetic counsellor with scientific data on which to base his discussion with prospective parents.

The most important biochemical test is that for the presence of alpha-fetoprotein, a raised level of which indicates an open neural tube defect in the fetus — spina bifida being of the greatest practical significance. Chromosomal abnormalities — of which Down's syndrome is pre-eminent — can be diagnosed, as may many of the group of diseases known as inborn errors of metabolism, some of which are associated with mental impairment.

The disadvantages of amniocentesis include the facts that adequate fluid cannot be obtained until approximately the 14th week of pregnancy and, even then, no fluid is obtained in about 1 per cent of attempts. It has been suggested that the process may cause miscarriage in some 0.5 per cent of cases; it is problematical whether there is any risk of induced fetal abnormality. Irrespective of negligence, some false positive and false negative tests are inevitable. Taken all round, it has been suggested that amniocentesis should be reserved for mothers who have absorbed alpha-fetoprotein into their own blood, for those who exhibit a family history of neural tube defect and for those who are aged over 35 years[1]. Fully informed consent is essential, particularly as to the extent of the study — the parents may not wish to know of genetic abnormalities which are of uncertain significance.

There are other limitations of amniocentesis. For example, the degree of impairment in a downsian infant cannot be prejudged, nor can the degree of neural tube defect — although some of these criticisms may be overcome by the concurrent use of modern techniques such as ultrasound screening, fetoscopy or fetal blood sampling. Moreover, culture of the cells for chromosomal diagnosis takes some 20 days whilst the provision of adequate material for enzymatic assay may take up to six weeks. It is apparent that such delays increase the chances of a live birth in the event of termination of pregnancy under the Abortion Act 1967, s.1(1)(b), being indicated. The technique of chorionic villus sampling (*see* 'Prenatal diagnosis') may obviate many of these objections. The related problems of negligence are discussed under the heading of 'Wrongful life'.

See also: Abortion Act 1967; Chromosomal disease; Consent to medical treatment; Down's syndrome; Fetoscopy; Inborn errors of metabolism; Living abortus; Neural tube defects; Prenatal diagnosis; Spina bifida; Wrongful life

1. Brock, DJH 'Impact of maternal serum alpha-fetoprotein screening on ante natal diagnosis' (1982) 285 Br Med J 365.

Amphetamines

The amphetamines comprise a group of drugs which stimulate the brain and depress the appetite. They give a spurious impression of self-confidence but excessive use leads to impairment of judgement; delusions and hallucinations may occur, giving rise to a frankly psychotic state. Not all the effects of amphetamines are enjoyable and they are often taken in conjunction with barbiturates — a combination once known as 'purple hearts'. Psychological dependence occurs and severe withdrawal symptoms may be precipitated.

Amphetamines are controlled under the Misuse of Drugs Act 1971 as Class B drugs. They were at one time widely used for the treatment of obesity and as a means to maintain wakefulness, although mental agility was not always simultaneously preserved; they have also been used as illegal adjuvants to sporting prowess, including a veterinary application. The medical use of amphetamines has been greatly reduced by voluntary action on the part of the profession and, currently, only two central nervous system stimulants including amphetamines are listed in the *Monthly Index of Medical Specialities (MIMS)*.

See also: Drug addiction; Barbiturates; Controlled drugs; Psychoses

Anaemia

Although literally translatable as 'no blood', anaemia in practice means a reduction in the haemoglobin content of the blood and, thus, of its capacity to transport oxygen.

The causes of anaemia are many. Some, particularly those associated with deficiency of vitamin B_{12} which leads to the metabolic condition of pernicious anaemia, are of no immediate medico-legal significance. Anaemia due to blood loss may, however, be of practical importance.

Such anaemia may be of chronic or acute type. The former is always due to some medical condition. Acute blood loss may also be natural — in the form of ruptured aneurysm, perforating stomach ulcer, etc. — but anaemia will also be a frequent concomitant of traumatic haemorrhage due to wounding or accidental injury. The immediate results of oxygen starvation in the tissues will be those of surgical shock which may require urgent treatment by transfusion of blood and other fluids; persistent shock may lead to acute kidney failure. Blood restoration following acute traumatic anaemia is relatively rapid in an otherwise healthy person and in the absence of shock.

Haemolytic anaemia results from an abnormal destruction of the red cells within the body. Some forms of the disorder may be of forensic interest in being precipitated by sensitivity to drugs whilst others (e.g. the disease known as march haemoglobinuria) may be occupational in origin. Others, known as haemoglobinopathies, are distributed on ethnic and genetic bases.

All forms of acute or subacute anaemia have it in common medico-legal interest that an anaemic person is more susceptible to induced oxygen lack than is a normal subject. This must influence considerations of foreseeability in civil negligence and special sensitivity in the criminal sphere.

See also: Blood transfusion; Foreseeability; Haemoglobinopathy; Haemorrhage; Kidney failure; Shock; Special sensitivity

Anaesthesia

Anaesthesia — the abolition of sensation — involves a highly skilled medical specialty which can only be touched upon in a work of this nature. Basically, the techniques involved can be divided into local anaesthesia, which produces absence of sensation in specific body areas while maintaining consciousness in the patient, and general anaesthesia in which sensation is depressed by virtue of rendering the whole patient unconscious. Local anaesthesia includes spinal anaesthesia; both have many specific problems and are discussed separately. General anaesthesia can be divided into inhalation and intravenous types. Any substance which depresses cortical function can operate as an anaesthetic — ethyl alcohol was for long used in an inadequate attempt to alleviate the pain of surgery — but modern surgical practice was made possible only by the introduction of controlled inhalation anaesthetics.

Any inhalation of anaesthetic involves the replacement of a proportion of the atmosphere by the active gas and the resulting oxygen deficiency must be compensated for in the technique; the possibility of hypoxia, although extremely rare in skilled hands, remains and hypoxic cerebral damage is still the commonest cause of personal injury resulting from a negligently given anaesthetic[1]. Other general hazards include those associated with unconsciousness (*see* 'Inhalation of gastric contents') and the risk of explosion or fire — but ether and cyclopropane, which are the most combustible agents, would scarcely be used today. Disease of the liver is a complication generally associated with volatile hydrocarbons and even the most useful general anaesthetic — halothane — may sensitise the liver to toxic effects[2]. Other anaesthetic agents have their own particular hazards. Those that are especially toxic rapidly become obsolete — eg. chloroform and cyclopropane.

It is now possible to offer major surgery to patients who would be unlikely to withstand the effects of the deep anaesthesia necessary to produce muscle relaxation. This may be achieved by supplementation with relaxant drugs of the curare type. Since all the muscles are paralysed, forced respiration must be given during the operation; relaxant drugs introduce the hazard of inadequate postoperative recovery of muscle function — respiratory failure may occur or, since the throat muscles are affected, there may be postoperative aspiration of gastric contents or other secretions.

Intravenous anaesthesia, which is generally achieved by the use of extra-fast-acting barbiturates, is extremely useful, particularly for inducing anaesthesia — not a pleasant matter if left entirely to inhalation. All the barbiturate group of drugs are cardiorespiratory depressants and all intravenous anaesthetics carry the hazard that they cannot be removed once they have been injected. There is an attraction in the technique in that it is easy to perform but there is an inherent danger that the inexperienced anaesthetist will concentrate on the injection site and fail to notice an airway incompetence and resultant hypoxia. Tragedies of this sort are at their least uncommon in dental practice where comparatively long intravenous anaesthetics are sometimes given in order to facilitate access to the mouth. It is often logistically convenient for the dentist to both anaesthetise and operate single handedly but this practice has been condemned by the profession. The seriousness with which it is regarded was shown in the case of *Abrol v General Dental Council*[3] where, despite the fact that a conviction for manslaughter as a result of such practice was quashed at review, the dentist concerned was still found guilty of serious professional misconduct by the General Dental Council and his name was erased from the Register; the decision was upheld by the Privy Council.

See also: Barbiturates; Hypoxia; Inhalation of gastric contents; Local anaesthesia; Spinal anaesthesia

1. And is the source of some of the largest damages awarded in Britain — e.g. *Lim Poh Choo v Camden and Islington Area Health Authority* [1979] 2 All ER 910, HL.
2. Walton B et al 'Unexplained hepatitis following halothane' [1976] 1 Br Med J 1171.
3. (1984) 156 Br Dent J 369.

Analgesic Poisoning

Analgesic poisoning has been singled out for specific comment because the majority of mild analgesics are available as General Sale List medicines and they are a potent source of both parasuicide and suicide — approximately one-fifth of all fatal ingestions are associated with analgesics. Acetylsalicylic acid, generally known as aspirin, is available without restriction but is not without danger even in therapeutic doses in so far as, in sensitive persons, it may cause gastric erosion and serious bleeding — the drug is certainly contraindicated in any person with pre-existing gastric ulceration. It enhances the effects of anticoagulants and, at the time of writing, a wide ranging research programme is in progress testing the value of aspirin as a prophylactic of myocardial infarction. Aspirin is often combined with other drugs, some of which are potent, and this may convert its legal category into that of a Pharmacy or Prescription Only medicine. Prominent among these additives is codeine, which is a controlled drug but which is released from control when present in small quantities by virtue of the Misuse of Drugs Regulations 1985, Sch.5. Overdosage of aspirin causes severe biochemical disturbance — in particular, acidosis — and death is essentially due to electrolyte imbalance. Containers of preparations which include aspirin must be clearly labelled as doing so.

Phenacetin was once commonly used as an analgesic but has serious effects on the kidney and on the blood; its use is now effectively prohibited[1].

The analgesic which has caused greatest concern in recent years is paracetamol. It is obtainable as a Pharmacy medicine — and containers must clearly indicate its presence — but, taken in overdose, it may result in delayed severe liver disease; the importance of this has somewhat diminished since the introduction of a prophylactic treatment but it remains a serious potential hazard. As with aspirin, paracetamol is often coupled with other drugs, the most important of which is dextropropoxyphene — the combination occurs in proprietary preparations of which the best known in the UK is Distalgesic. Dextropropoxyphene is a powerful depressant of the central nervous system; it is now a Class B controlled drug but is exempted from restriction as to possession when present in low concentration. Distalgesic accounted for 11 per cent of fatal ingestions in Scotland in 1978 but it has become less of a problem now that its dangers have been well publicised[2].

The great majority of newer analgesics are now restricted as prescription only medicines and present less of a problem than do aspirin and paracetamol.

See also: Controlled drugs; Electrolytes; General Sale List medicines; Parasuicide; Pharmacy medicines; Prescription Only medicines; Suicide

1. Medicines (Phenacetin Prohibition) Order 1979 (SI 1979/1181).
2. Young RJ and Lawson AAH 'Distalgesic poisoning — cause for concern' [1980] 280 Br Med J 1045.

Anatomy Act 1984

The Anatomy Act 1984 repeals the Acts of 1832 and 1871 together with some minor sections of the Human Tissue Act 1961.

Section 1 defines anatomical examination as dissection of the body for purposes of teaching or studying or researching into morphology; diagnostic postmortem examinations are specifically excluded and the scope of the Act as a whole is clearly more limited than is that of the Human Tissue Act 1961.

A system of control is maintained — both the premises in which the dissection is carried out and the dissector must be licenced (s.3(1)) and the dissector must be authorised to make the examination and to be in possession of the body (s.3(3) and 3(4)).

The authorisation of anatomical dissection is now much closer to that made under the Human Tissue Act 1961. Thus, if a person has properly expressed the request that his body be used for anatomical dissection, the person in lawful possession of the body may authorise such use of the body so long as he has no reason to believe that the request had been withdrawn (s.4(2)). The veto of the spouse or nearest relative and the absolute duty to act which obtained in the 1832 Act have been removed. In the absence of 'contracting in', a person in lawful possession of the body may authorise its use provided the deceased has not objected during life and provided that the spouse and any surviving relative do not object (s.4(3)). Again, he must now make such reasonable enquiry as may be practicable — the old circumstance in which the relative objecting had to intervene positively[1] no longer holds. Section 4(9), in speaking of delegation of power, makes it clear that the manager or controller of a hospital, nursing home or other institution is the person lawfully in possession of the body; undertakers and controllers of burial grounds or crematoria are specifically excluded from giving authority for dissection. Currently, any authority given expires after three years and this is not negotiable by the authoriser (s.4(8)). No authority can be given when there is reason to believe that the coroner will hold an inquest or that the procurator fiscal will wish to inquire into the death.

Possession of the body or of parts of the body after dissection is subject to licence and to authorisation on terms similar to those for the actual dissection (s.6).

The appointment of inspectors of anatomy is continued by s.9, and the inspectors have powers of entry at a reasonable time in order to inspect premises; they may also require the production of records.

See also: Human Tissue Act 1961

1. *R v Feist* (1858) Dears and Bell 590.

Aneurysm

An aneurysm is a dilatation of the arterial wall without concomitant growth of tissue; the wall is therefore weakened and is liable to rupture. Aneurysms may results from a congenital abnormality of the vessel wall, when they are most often saccular in type; fusiform aneurysms may be due to degeneration of the vessel wall through atheromatous change or to infections of which syphilis was once an important variety but which has now been largely eliminated. Traumatic aneurysms are of a different character and are due to venous dilatation which occurs when an arteriovenous communication is established through injury to the area. So-called dissecting aneurysms are not true dilatations but arise when the vessel wall is damaged or diseased and the blood tracks within the medial or muscular coat; rupture may result from the consequent disorganisation of the structure of the vessel wall.

Medico-legally, the most important aneurysms are those which cause sudden death. The congenital or berry aneurysm of the arteries at the base of the brain (circle of Willis) are pre-eminent in young adulthood; the aneurysms are small and the blood loss may not be great but the location within the rigid skull makes the resulting subarachnoid haemorrhage especially dangerous. The aneurysmal sac may, indeed, not be demonstrable at autopsy. A raised pressure due to exertion may precipitate rupture; the possible result in the event of an accusation of homicide is discussed under the heading of causation.

An atheromatous aneurysm may occur in any vessel but is particularly associated with the abdominal aorta; massive bleeding from rupture in this situation is particularly common in elderly males. Atheromatous aneurysms also occur in the circle of Willis[1].

A dissecting aneurysm of the ascending aorta may result in a backflow of haemorrhage into the pericardium — the sac surrounding the heart; death from this cause, which is known as cardiac tamponade, is very rapid and the condition occurs predominantly in middle-aged women[2].

See also: Cardiac tamponade; Cardiovascular system; Causation; Haemorrhage; Sudden natural death

1. Crompton MR 'The coroners' cerebral aneurysm: a changing animal' (1975) 15 J Forens Sci Soc 57.
2. Fothergill DF et al 'Dissecting and atherosclerotic aneurysms: a survey of post-mortem examinations, 1968–77' (1979) 19 Med Sci Law 253.

Angiography

Angiography allows the visualisation of blood vessels by X-ray; it may also demonstrate the size and shape of organs supplied by vessels and may show displacement of vessels by extraneous tissue. The procedure involves injection of a radiopaque dye at a site which depends to some extent on the position of the part to be visualised. Most penetrations are made through the femoral artery but the brachial and carotid arteries can be used; a catheter is then passed from the point of penetration to the artery which is to be specifically examined and the drug is injected. The process can be long and commonly involves some pain and subjective feelings of heat.

Angiography offers a most useful means of diagnosis and guide to treatment — it has, for example, revolutionised the treatment of coronary artery disease. Nevertheless, it is not without risk; the incidence of significant risk depends to a large extent on the part to be catheterised but, in general, is less than 1 per cent of investigations — the incidence decreasing with the experience of the unit. Ill-effects may be due to irritation and spasm of the vessel but the most serious are those due to embolism — whether this be of a dislodged atheromatous plaque or of a thrombus which may form at the tip of the catheter; thus, a stroke or coronary heart attack may be precipitated. The catheter may damage the wall of or even penetrate the vessel under examination. Very occasionally, there may be severe neurological complications[1]. Despite improvements in both technique and contrast media, it is doubtful if angiography could be acceptable simply in the role of, say, a screening test.

One use of angiography of particular medico-legal interest is in the diagnosis of brain death; this physical test is required either in conjunction with or as an alternative to electroencephalography in several European countries as proof of brain death. The test depends on the fact that no blood flow occurs in the brain once the intracranial pressure rises to the level of the diastolic blood pressure. Death is indicated by the absence of flow in the cerebral arteries or of a circulation time exceeding 15 seconds.

See also: Atheroma; Brain stem death; Coronary disease; Embolism; Thrombosis

1. For a general review, *see* Herlinger H 'Aortography and peripheral arteriography' in Ansell G (ed) *Complications in Diagnostic Radiology* (1976), Chap.2, Blackwell Scientific, Oxford.

Anoxia

Anoxia is, literally, the absolute absence of oxygen. As such, it must be extremely rare in terrestrial conditions. It is the extreme of hypoxia, which would probably be a more correct term whenever 'anoxia' is used in a medical context other than in considering death — one definition of which is 'a permanent state of tissue anoxia'.

See also: Death; Hypoxia

Antenatal Injury

A plaintiff who suffers injury while he is within the womb may subsequently bring an action in tort against the person who caused the injury. Until recently, there was doubt as to the competence of such actions, the view being expressed that the fetus is not a person for the purposes of legal protection. This approach was not followed in the pioneering Australian case of *Watt v Rama*[1] in which the plaintiff's mother had been rendered quadriplegic in a traffic accident. It was alleged that this led to the plaintiff's being born with brain damage. The court had no difficulty in holding that damage to an unborn child was foreseeable in the circumstances and that the duty of care therefore owed to the fetus 'crystallised' on his birth.

The issue arose dramatically in the UK following the discovery of the teratogenic effect on the fetus of the drug thalidomide. Although the manufacturers of the drug and the victims of injury reached a settlement, there were considerable political implications in the affair[2]. The Law Commission examined the problem in detail[3] and legislation reached the statute books in the form of the Congenital Disabilities (Civil Liability) Act 1976. Under the terms of the Act, a person who is injured antenatally through an occurrence affecting either parent, or directly during the course of birth, is given a right of action against the person whose negligence caused the injury. This right does not exist against the plaintiff's mother except where the injury is caused as a result of the mother's negligent driving (this exception being, presumably, introduced for insurance reasons). No damages are recoverable unless the child lives for at least 48 hours (s.4(4)). The Act provides a remedy not only where the plaintiff was injured *in utero* but also where the wrongful act, committed prior to conception, affected the ability of either parent to have a normal, healthy child. In the latter case, a defendant will not be answerable if the parents knew of the risk of a child being born disabled but proceeded, none the less, to conceive the child (s.1(4)). No legislation was thought to be necessary for Scotland where there is no objection in principle to an action for antenatal injury being brought at common law[4]; indeed, it has been suggested that the common law would have developed similarly in England and Wales without legislation[5]. It is to be noted that the Act specifically protects the doctor or genetic counsellor as regards allegations of negligence. The normal rules of 'standard of care' apply and the wording suggests that allowance may be made for innovative forms of treatment or advice (s.1(5)).

An obvious difficulty in any case of antenatal injury will be that of establishing a causal link between the defendant's act and the eventual disability suffered by the plaintiff[6]. There may be doubt as to the causal link between traumatic injury to the mother and defects in the fetus[7] although the court in *Watt v Rama* seemed to be satisfied in just such a case. Similarly, it may not always be easy to satisfy the court as to factual causation where damage is alleged to have been caused by maternal ingestion of drugs. Damage to the fetus may, of course, be caused also by illness in the mother (for example, rubella or syphilis) or by medical procedures connected in some way with the pregnancy (such as exposure to ionising radiation or amniocentesis).

See also: Causation; Foreseeability; Genetic counselling; Negligence; Pharmaceutical liability

1. [1972] VR 353. Followed by the Ontario Court of Appeal in *Duval v Seguin* (1973) 40 DLR (3d) 666. For general discussion, *see* Lovell P and Griffith-Jones R 'The sins of their fathers — tort liability for pre-natal injuries' (1974) 90 LQR 531.
2. *See* Teff H and Munro C *Thalidomide: The Legal Aftermath* (1977), esp. p.40 et seq, Saxon House, Farnborough, Hants.
3. Law Commission *Report on Injuries to Unborn Children* (Law Com No. 60) (Cmnd 5709) (1974), HMSO, London.
4. *Liability for Ante-natal Injury* (Scot Law Com No. 30) (Cmnd 5371) (1973) HMSO, London.
5. Pace PJ 'Civil liability for pre-natal injuries' (1977) 40 MLR 141. Common law liability was accepted by the defendant in *Williams and another v Luff* (1978) 122 SJ 164 in which the relevant injury occurred before the 1976 Act.
6. Anonymous 'The impact of medical knowledge on the law relating to pre-natal injuries' (1962) 110 U Pa LR 554.
7. There is a useful discussion of medical aspects of antenatal injury in the Law Commission's Report (n.3 above) paras. 18–31. An excellent survey is to be found in Gordon D 'The unborn plaintiff' (1965) 63 Mich LR 579.

Antibody

Antibodies are substances provoked by antigens with which they can be shown to react specifically. Antibodies may form part of the circulating plasma proteins (immunoglobulins or humoral antibodies) or be bound to the white blood cells (cellular). The function of antibodies is essentially a matter of recognition of non-self. A foreign antigen will provoke an antibody response and the buildup of antibody will eventually form one component of the process of removal or destruction of the invader. More importantly, the invader is remembered, the template of antibody response is retained and, in the event of a second attack, the antibody defence mechanism will come into action immediately and before invasive damage can be done.

Put simply, humoral antibodies react physico-chemically with their corresponding antigens: they will precipitate them if they are particulate or agglutinate or lyse them if they are cellular — this is the general response to, say, bacterial invasion. The cellular reaction is, by contrast, a matter of attack and destruction — the most apposite example of which is the rejection of transplanted tissue.

Antibodies can be deliberately provoked — a form of biological manufacture — or be recovered from the natural state; they can then be used to test for the presence of antigens, this being the method of parentage testing in practice. In the same way, antibodies may be used to ensure that degree of antigenic similarity which is essential to successful transplantation of tissues — whether it be a transfusion of blood or donation of an organ. Alternatively, manufactured antigens may be used to detect the presence of antibodies from which the diagnosis of a disease can be inferred — tests for syphilis, for example, depend upon this principle; previous disease, or asymptomatic disease, can also be identified in this way.

See also: Antigen; Blood transfusion; Immune reaction; Immunisation; Transplantation of organs

Antigen

An antigen is a substance, generally protein in nature, which, when introduced into the tissues of a person who does not possess it, will initiate the production of an antibody with which it can be shown to react specifically. Thus, whilst all of us contain large numbers of potential antigens, these do not normally become antigenic until introduced into another person. Since our protein makeup is determined genetically, the antigens can be used to distinguish between individuals and to identify those who could or could not have passed on to us our genetic pattern. This is the basis of testing for parentage.

Chemically appropriate non-human substances will always be antigenic when introduced parenterally into the human body and will provoke antibody formation. The resulting reaction may destroy the antigen if it is in living form; this is the basis of natural immunity and of processes inducing active immunisation such as vaccination.

Not all substances are equally antigenic. Whilst some (e.g. the virus of smallpox) will stimulate antibody formation rapidly and intensely, other 'weakly antigenic' substances will produce antibodies only after repeated challenge. This principle is of major medico-legal importance in blood transfusion but it is also applied in immunisation in which repeated doses of vaccine may be used.

See also: Allergy; Antibody; Blood groups; Blood transfusion; Immune reaction; Immunisation; Parentage testing

Anxiety States

Anxiety states may be no more than an exaggerated reaction to a hostile environment. On the other hand, they may present as a true neurosis with impairment of physiological function and lowered efficiency at work. Anxiety states are usually divided into acute and chronic variants, the latter being, in effect, a persistence of the former in a lower key; the anxiety may become fixed on a specific cause or target organ. The acute anxiety state is characterised by hyperactivity of the autonomic nervous system and is, thus, an amplified 'flight or fight' reaction to stress. The latter is a valuable defence mechanism and the distinction between the good and the bad becomes blurred — at what point, for example, does the prudent taking of precautions become a fixed neurosis as to the possibility of burglary?.

The distinction must, however, be made sometimes. The precipitation of an acute anxiety reaction through a negligent act would be an injury for which damages could be recovered; a simple reaction of distress or disgust would not be[1]. Of greater importance is the distinction of a chronic anxiety state from physical disease — particularly associated with overactivity of the thyroid gland — and also the recognition that an anxiety state can co-exist with a psychosis, particularly of depressive type.

See also: Autonomic nervous system; Nervous shock; Psychoses

1. For example, *Hinz v Berry* [1970] 1 All ER 1074.

Aorta

The aorta is the major artery of the body from which all other systemic arteries derive. It arises from the left ventricle of the heart and ascends for a short distance before arching downwards; it then descends in the posterior thoracic and abdominal cavities and ends by dividing into the common iliac arteries which are destined to supply blood to the legs.

Aortic injury is common in road traffic and aircraft accidents. Much of this injury is associated with differential movement. The heart, being free, can move downwards as a result of vertical deceleration of the body and can thus be torn from the aorta at its origin; alternatively, the aorta may rupture where the relatively free ascending portion meets the tethered arch. Traumatic rupture of the descending aorta generally occurs only in association with severe spinal injury. Sometimes, the vessel is only partially torn and the victim survives for a short time in a state of shock; delayed rupture of the aorta may occur when the blood pressure increases to normal. Stab wounds of the aorta are not uncommon; a clean incision of such a major artery leads to massive haemorrhage and rapid death.

Natural disease of the aorta is a cause of sudden unexplained death resulting from aneurysm formation and subsequent rupture. The aneurysm is usually of dissecting type in the ascending aorta where, in addition, syphilitic aneurysms were once frequent; ruptured atheromatous aneurysm of the abdominal aorta is a common cause of sudden natural death in elderly males.

The blood pumped into the aorta is prevented from returning to the heart by the aortic valve. Disease of the valve — whether resulting in stenosis or incompetence —

puts great strain on the heart and causes hypertrophic cardiomyopathy which, again, is a potent cause of sudden death.

See also: Aircraft accidents; Aneurysm; Atheroma; Cardiomyopathy; Road traffic accidents; Surgical shock.

Arson

Arson is the offence of deliberately setting fire to the property of others. The offence is now charged under the Criminal Damage Act 1971, s.1(3). Setting fire to property with the intention of endangering life or in a state of recklessness as to whether life is endangered is a separate offence under s.1(2)[1]. Arson is not committed if property is destroyed by fire as a result of a destructive act but in which there was no intention to cause such destruction[2]. Unintentionally causing a fire can lead to a charge of arson if the defendant takes no action to extinguish the fire and the court holds that he had such a duty[3]. The offence is known as fire raising in Scotland where it is considered to be the most serious form of criminal damage to property[4].

The setting of the fire is seen by some psychoanalysts as a sexual act aimed at resolving sexual conflicts[5]. Recent psychiatric reviews of arson have focused more on identification of the overall personality of the fire setter, and, although such persons are frequently sexually maladjusted or inadequate, other important personality defects tend to be revealed[6]. Fire setting by children is not infrequent[7]. Many young fire setters are boys who come from homes in which the father is either absent or fails in other ways to provide a satisfactory model for the psychosexual development of his son.

Although many acts of arson are 'motiveless' in so far as the fire is created for its own sake, there are other specific circumstances in which a fire may be started deliberately[8]; it may be in order to conceal evidence of a crime, to make a political point, it may be suicidal or result simply from confusion or hallucination. There is often an association with alcoholic intoxication; in these circumstances, the psychiatric background of the fire setter is likely to be relatively normal.

1. *See R v Caldwell* [1982] AC 341, HL. To cause death in this way is also culpable homicide in Scotland: *Mathieson v HM Adv* 1981 SCCR 196.
2. Smith J and Hogan B *Criminal Law* (5th ed, 1983) p.649, Butterworths, London.
3. *R v Miller* [1983] 1 All ER 978, HL.
4. Gordon GH *The Criminal Law of Scotland* (2nd ed, 1978) p.719, W Green, Edinburgh.
5. Arson is discussed by Freud in 'Fragment of an analysis of a case of hysteria' (1905). The connection between enuresis and fire setting is often stressed; *see* Wax DE and Haddox VG 'Sexual aberrance in male adolescents manifesting a behavioural triad considered predictive of extreme violence: some clinical observations' (1974) 19 J Forens Sci 102.
6. Vandersall TA and Wiener JM 'Children who set fires' (1970) 22 Arch Gen Psychiat 63. *See also* Bloomberg NH 'Arson update: a review of the literature on fire setting' (1981) 9 Bull Am Acad Psychiat Law 255.
7. Strachan JG 'Conspicuous fire setting in children' (1981) 138 Br J Psychiat 26.
8. *See* the classification suggested by Scott D in 'The problems of malicious fire raising' (1978) 19 Br J Hosp Med 259. *See also*, by the same author, *Fire and Fire Raisers* (1974) Duckworth, London.

Art and Part

Art and part guilt arises in Scots law when a person is involved in the commission
of an offence in a subordinate role[1]. This involvement may take the form of counselling
or instigating the commission of the offence, supplying the means or assisting in
some way at the time the offence is committed. It is not possible to be art and part
guilty after an offence has been committed. Thus, no such guilt for murder can be
attributed to a person who, say, conceals the murder weapon.

Difficulties have arisen over the question of art and part guilt for the unintended
consequences of a plot. Modern Scots law invokes notions of foreseeability to tackle
this problem[2], although the precise circumstances in which a consequence will be
treated as foreseeable are difficult to define[3]. Art and part offenders in English law
are known as accomplices and are discussed under that heading.

See also: Accomplices; Foreseeability

1. *See*, in general, Gordon GH *The Criminal Law of Scotland* (2nd ed, 1978) p.129 et seq,
W Green, Edinburgh.
2. *Docherty v HM Adv* 1945 JC 89, per Lord Moncrieff at pp.95–96.
3. *See* the discussion of three important modern unreported cases in Gordon (n.1) at p.156.

Artefacts

In the context of forensic pathology, an artefact can be defined as a spurious *post
mortem* presentation which simulates a finding which would be significant in the
course of *ante mortem* events.

Many such artefacts are associated with burning. Thus, the pugilistic attitude in
which many burnt bodies are found does not represent an *ante mortem* defensive
state but is simply the result of heat contraction of the muscles. More importantly,
heat may fracture bone and may boil the body fluids. The pathologist may therefore
be presented with a burnt body showing fracture of the skull and extradural
haemorrhage. He must then distinguish an artefact due to burning from *ante mortem*
head injury associated with later incineration.

Other examples include *post mortem* injury by, say, the propellers of ships
simulating *ante mortem* lacerations. The common thread of all artefacts lies in the
importance of experience in their recognition.

See also: Burning; Extradural haemorrhage; Fractures; Lacerations

Arteries

The arteries carry the blood from the heart to the tissues where they end as capillaries.
Two main arteries leave the heart — the aorta, which carries oxygenated blood to
the periphery, and the pulmonary artery, which transports the returning blood to
the lungs for reoxygenation.

The bore of arteries decreases by a process of division of the trunks as the
peripheral tissues are approached; transport of blood therefore requires pressure

which is supplied principally by the pumping action of the heart but also by the thick, muscular walls of the arteries themselves. Haemorrhage from an artery is therefore likely to be profuse and difficult to control.

The pressure in the arteries is now measured in kPa (kilopascals) — although many clinicians will still use millimetres of mercury (mmHg). As measured in a vessel of medium size in a normal person, it is approximately 16–19 kPa (120–145 mmHg) during the contraction of the heart (systolic pressure) and 10–11 kPa (75–85mmHg) while the heart is relaxed (diastolic pressure), the limits depending upon the age of the person. The blood pressure may be raised by virtue of abnormal activity of the autonomic nervous system (essential hypertension), through disease or abnormality of kidney function or as a result of the disease process of atheroma which leads, in particular, to constriction of the bore of moderate-sized vessels. A raised blood pressure puts increasing strain on the heart; the arterial blood pressure is, accordingly, a fair measure of life expectancy. An unacceptably low blood pressure will, by contrast, lead to poor oxygenation of the tissues, this being a typical feature of surgical shock.

Apart from the slow process of atheroma, arteries may be blocked by thrombosis or embolism; the tissues supplied by the blocked vessels are suddenly deprived of oxygen and will die unless an alternative supply is available. Such an alternative or emergency network is known as a collateral circulation; this provides a major defence against arterial disease and also accounts for, say, the survival of a limb when a major vessel has been severed or ligated.

See also: Aneurysm; Aorta; Atheroma; Embolism; Haemorrhage; Heart disease; Hypertensive disease; Infarction; Kidney failure; Shock; Thrombosis

Artificial Insemination by Donor

Artificial insemination by donor (AID) involves the instrumental insemination of a woman with sperm derived from a man other than her husband. Some 5 per cent of marriages are unwittingly childless by reason of the husband's infertility and AID may be the preferred route to a family. The procedure should entail counselling of the parties and careful genetic selection of the donor; potential issues of liability for negligence in this area have yet to be tested in the courts. There is no illegality attached to the procedure, although it is possible that a woman who resorts to AID without her husband's consent might be viewed as behaving unreasonably for divorce purposes[1]. The husband is not, however, considered to be the father of the child and, should the legal presumption of legitimacy be rebutted, parental rights will be vested solely in the mother[2]. The husband, not being the father of the child, would be unlikely to be awarded custody in the event of divorce.

The husband's duties are not correspondingly limited. By virtue of his acceptance of the AID-conceived child as a child of the family, he takes on an obligation to support the child during the marriage and, possibly, after its dissolution. Should the child establish the identity of the donor, it could theoretically claim his support as its natural father and, since one cannot contractually surrender parental rights and obligations, it is unlikely that any such liability of the donor could be excluded by agreement[3]. For this reason, anonymity of the donor is strongly supported, taking precedence over any other considerations. The prospects of success for a donor seeking access to his child would probably be slight, although the only available indicative precedent involved additional policy considerations[4]. AID also raises certain problems of registration of birth. Although most husbands register themselves as the father of the child, this contravenes the Births and Deaths Registration Act 1953 and the Registration of Births, Deaths and Marriages (Scotland) Act 1965. Strictly speaking, the birth certificate of an AID-conceived child should state that the father is unknown. The frequently made suggestion that it should also disclose the mode of conception is aimed at avoiding the admittedly slight risk of marriage between closely related children but this might, at the same time, entail the child hearing of its mode of conception. In spite of the adopted child's right to discover the facts of his parentage, there is a strong case for denying a similar right to the AID child; the confidentiality essential to donors would be compromised and this would discourage what is a useful medical treatment. The Warnock Committee nevertheless recommended limited access to a knowledge of fatherhood at the age of 18[5].

The legal difficulties to which AID gives rise are best solved by legislation. In some jurisdictions in the USA, statutes provide for the legitimisation *in utero* of the child conceived through AID[6] (provided there is consent on the part of the husband); this solution has received strong medico-legal support in the UK including that of the Warnock Committee[5]. The same conclusion has statutory approval in New South Wales[7], where the legitimacy of a child born as a result of consensual AID is an irrebuttable presumption; similar legislation exists in Victoria[8]. In the absence of such measures, the adoption of a child by the couple would seem to be an acceptable alternative to what is, in effect, a deception. The problems surrounding the insemination of unmarried or lesbian women are several; it would seem that the interests of the child should take precedence over what might be seen as women's rights.

See also: Adoption; Infertility; Lesbianism

1. In *MacLennan v MacLennan* 1958 SC 105 it was held that AID without the husband's consent was not adultery.
2. Children Act 1975, s.85(7).
3. Ibid, s.2.
4. *A v C* (1978) 8 Fam Law; Parker DC 'Legal aspects of artificial insemination and embryo transfer' (1982) 12 Fam Law 103.
5. Warnock Mary (chairman) *Report of the Committee of Inquiry into Human Fertilisation and Embryology* (Cmnd 9314) (1984) para.4.17, HMSO, London.
6. *See* the Model Uniform Parentage Act 1974, s.5(a).
7. Artifical Conception Act 1984.
8. Status of Children (Amendment) Act 1984. For further discussion, *see*: Cusine D 'AID and the law' (1975) 1 J Med Ethics 39; Whelan D 'The law and artificial insemination with donor semen (AID)' [1978] 1 Med J Austral 56; Shaman JM 'Legal aspects of artificial insemination' (1979) 18 J Fam Law 331.

Artificial Insemination by Husband

Artificial insemination by a husband (AIH) may be indicated as a result of impotence on the part of the man or of an aversion to sexual intercourse amounting to impotence in the woman. Moral objections to the practice can be held only if there is objection to *any* interference with the course of nature. The practical and legal problems associated with AID have no relevance to AIH save in two respects.

The first of these involves nullity and the prospect of a marriage being voidable by virtue of non-consummation despite the existence of admittedly genetic offspring of the couple. The legal position would seem to be that the existence of such a child would be no bar to nullity *per se* but that the approbation inevitably associated with the process would constitute a bar[1]. The child, having been conceived within wedlock, would, in any event, remain legitimate.

The second question involves cryopreservation or 'banking' of the husband's semen — which is a not uncommon accompaniment to sterilisation by vasectomy — and its use subsequent to his death. Such a practice leads to almost insurmountable problems of inheritance, succession and the like[2]. Whilst it is true that, the husband being dead, there is no marriage and that any children then born would be illegitimate[3], it is equally true that many of the advantages of legitimate children are now applicable to a man's illegitimate children and the '*post mortem* AIH' child is certainly the child of the husband. It is clearly impracticable to delay the winding up of an estate until a widow remarries or has passed the child-bearing age. The Law Society of Scotland have, therefore, recommended[4] that AIH after the husband's death should be regarded as being AID by an innominate donor without consent, the resulting child being the illegitimate offspring of its mother only. The Warnock Committee themselves recommended that legislation be introduced to provide that any child born by AIH who was not *in utero* at the date of the death of its father shall be disregarded for the purposes of succession to and inheritance from its father[5]. Neither suggestion covers the eventuality of the husband being missing, death not being presumed, at which time the relict might be particularly minded to use the sperm bank. Such cases might be contested (e.g. by a pensions fund), and it is suggested that each would have to be decided on its own particular facts.

See also: Artificial insemination by donor; Non-consummation of marriage; Nullity of marriage; Sterilisation

1. *L v L* [1949] P 211; *G v G* 1961 SLT 324.
2. *See* Cusine DJ 'Artificial inseminsation with the husband's semen after the husband's death' (1977) 3 J Med Ethics 163 for discussion.
3. Family Law Reform Act 1969, ss.14–19: Law Reform (Miscellaneous Provisions) (Scotland) Act 1968, ss.1–4.
4. In evidence to the Warnock Committee, n.5, below.
5. Warnock Mary (chairman) *Report of the Committee of Inquiry into Human Fertilisation and Embryology* (Cmnd 9314) (1984) para.10.9, HMSO, London.

Asbestosis

Asbestos occurs as two main types — chrysotile and amphiboles. The former consists of long fibres which are used in the main for the manufacture of fireproof clothing; the fibres of the latter are needle shaped and the material is used for roofing, insulation and the like. There are three variants of amphiboles — crocidolite (blue asbestos), amosite and anthophyllite.

Asbestosis is a prescribed disease and, whilst exposure to the mineral at work is always hazardous, the main risks come from asbestos in its purified form or while it is being purified; in these circumstances, large numbers of particles can be inhaled from the 'asbestos cloud' which forms most dangerously when the material is very dry.

Asbestosis is a form of pneumoconiosis and therefore results in fibrosis of the lung which may be finely nodular or massive in type. The offending particles are, however, indestructible and continue to act after the individual is removed from the dangerous environment. Asbestosis is distinguished from most other forms of pneumoconiosis by its incontrovertible association with malignant disease of the lungs and pleura — a relationship which was only appreciated in the mid twentieth century[1]. An indication of exposure to asbestos is given by the finding of asbestos bodies (pigmented deposits on asbestos fibres) in the sputum or in lung tissue; the mere finding of asbestos bodies does not prove the presence of the disease asbestosis, but the association of such bodies with proven carcinoma of the lung would strongly suggest a causal association. The appearance of clinical asbestosis is dose dependent, both the magnitude and the length of time of exposure being significant. Carcinoma associated with asbestos may take years to develop; smoking also causes lung cancer and the two conditions appear to act in multiplicative manner — the risk of lung cancer in smokers exposed to asbestos is some eight times that of the risk for smokers who are not so exposed, but the risk increases to 90 times when compared with those who have neither smoked nor been exposed to asbestos[2]. The most interesting malignancy associated with asbestos exposure is the tumour of the pleura or peritoneum known as mesothelioma. This tumour is very largely associated with inhalation of crocidolite and may take from 20 to 40 years to develop clinically; proof of causation may then be difficult if only for want of memory but, on the other side of the coin, it has been pointed out that those relatively few mesotheliomas which develop in a short time are probably not asbestos related — differentiation may involve a fine judgement[3]. Diffuse mesothelioma is a prescribed disease of itself.

Perhaps the most burning medico-legal issue as regards asbestosis is whether the disease can be contracted by those whose only contact with the mineral is by chance. Large numbers of asbestos fibres are found in a high proportion of lungs examined at random and this is particularly so in the larger cities where absolute freedom from contamination is rare. Taking the dose/response relationship into account, it seems unlikely that the community at large is exposed to a perceptible risk[4]; clearly, however, much depends upon limiting the total dose to the population and this must include stringent regulations as to the use and disposal of asbestos[5].

See also: Cancer; Causation; Pneumoconioses; Prescribed diseases and occupations

1. For an early review, *see* Hughes DTD 'Lung disease related to exposure to asbestos' (1974) 14 Med Sci Law 147.
2. Jones JSP 'Pathological and environmental aspects of absestos-associated diseases' (1974) 14 Med Sci Law 152. *See also* Leading Article 'Smoking, coal, asbestos, and the lungs' (1981) 283 Br Med J 457.
3. Davies D 'Are all mesotheliomas due to asbestos?' (1984) 289 Br Med J 1164.
4. Leading Article 'Risks of environmental exposure to asbestos' [1978] 1 Br Med J 1164.
5. Asbestos (Prohibition) Regulations 1985 (SI 1985/910); the importation and use of crocidolite and amosite is now prohibited in the UK.

Asphyxia

The body's need for oxygen is urgent; the most sensitive cells — those of the brain — may well be damaged if deprived of oxygen for more than five minutes. Asphyxia can be defined as a means of preventing oxygenation of the tissues — or as a method of rendering the tissues hypoxic.

The most important forms of asphyxia from the point of view of forensic medicine are those which are unnatural. Mechanical means of this type can be summarised as:

obstruction at:

the nose and mouth	suffocation
the larynx	choking; throttling; strangulation (garotting); or hanging
the trachea	aspiration (inhalation) of foreign substances; including drowning
or of inhibition of chest movements	traumatic asphyxia

These conditions are discussed under their appropriate headings. An interesting variation was practised by the notorious Edinburghians Burke and Hare who combined manual suffocation with pressure on the victims' chests — a process which has become known as 'burking'.

Other unnatural forms of asphyxia are toxic in origin. The best known toxic agent, carbon monoxide, acts mainly by substitution at the oxygen receptor locus in the haemoglobin molecule. Other poisons have an asphyxiant effect by inhibiting the enzymes responsible for transferring oxygen to the tissues. Cyanide is the most dramatic example but narcotics in overdose, including barbiturates, have a similar action.

A decrease in the available respirable atmospheric oxygen occurs as one ascends in the atmosphere. Unnatural environmental hypoxia can occur when a subject is confined in an airproof space or if an artificial atmosphere which is being breathed is exhausted (e.g. in scuba diving). In such circumstances, poisoning by carbon dioxide may also play a part in mortality. Hypoxia is equally a hazard of poorly administered anaesthesia.

The transfer of atmospheric oxygen to the tissues will be affected by such naturally occurring conditions as disease of the lungs — in particular, fibrosis and emphysema, which are common accompaniments of the industrial pneumoconioses — incompetence of the respiratory muscles, anaemia and heart disease. None of these conditions is likely to asphyxiate by itself but their effects may be synergistic or additive. Of greater importance is their cumulative interaction with unnatural forms of asphyxia. Thus, an anaemic subject will be more susceptible to carbon monoxide poisoning than is the normal person whilst one with impaired cardiac function will suffocate correspondingly more easily. Such conditions are of particular relevance to special sensitivity in victims.

See also: Anaemia; Anaesthesia; Aspiration; Barbiturates; Carbon dioxide; Carbon monoxide poisoning; Choking; Cyanide; Drowning; Emphysema; Garotting; Hanging; Heart disease; Hypoxia; Narcotic drugs; Pneumoconioses; Special sensitivity; Strangulation; Suffocation; Throttling; Traumatic asphyxia

Aspiration

Medico-legally, aspiration implies the inspiration of foreign material into the tracheobronchial system and/or into the alveoli (*see* 'Respiratory system').

The aspirated substance may be a single solid particle such as a peanut accidentally inspired by a child or a tooth inhaled during dental extraction. The object may lodge in a bronchus or bronchiole and the segment of lung thus deprived of air collapses; the danger is then of inflammatory disease developing in the immobile tissue.

Inhalation of gastric contents is a subject of sufficient importance in forensic pathology to merit separate consideration under that heading. Aspiration of blood arises in much the same circumstances but is of less significance because blood is not so irritant as are the gastric juices.

Aspiration of water occurs in all cases of near-drowning. The presence of a non sterile, osmotically incompatible fluid in the pulmonary tree often results in post immersion pneumonitis which may cause death even though the original drowning episode has been successfully treated.

See also: Drowning; Inhalation of gastric contents; Respiratory system

Assault and Battery

Assault and battery are closely related criminal offences. Strictly speaking, an assault is an act which causes another to apprehend 'immediate and unlawful personal violence'[1] whilst the actual application of violence to the person is the crime of battery. In common usage, however, assault has become a broad term and is frequently used in both statute and court decisions to describe the unlawful application of force to another person. There is much to be said for abandoning the distinction between assault and battery and, instead, treating both the threat of violence and its application as assault. The approach adopted by Glanville Williams — referring to battery as 'physical assault' — is useful[2].

It should be noted that there does not need to have been physical contact between the accused and his victim for assault to occur. A gesture, such as the pointing of a gun at another, can be an assault, even though the gun is unloaded; the victim may still have cause to apprehend violence. The use of threatening words probably does not constitute an assault although the matter is not beyond dispute[3].

Battery requires the application of some degree of force, no matter how slight. There need not have been direct contact between the person of the accused and that of the victim; this may have taken place, say, through the medium of a weapon. Alternatively, the physical damage to the victim may be caused by another agency — e.g. the setting of a dog onto him[4].

The *mens rea* requirement of assault and battery is that there should have been intention or recklessness on the part of the accused[5]. Accident is a defence[6], as may be consent, particularly in relation to such activities as contact sports or surgical treatment; consent may also be appropriate in other less obvious circumstances[7]. The infliction of violence may also be acceptable on the grounds that it is legally justified as in the defence of person or property or in the making of a lawful arrest.

Assault and battery are common law crimes. Legislation has created a number o specific categories of assault or other offences involving violence to the person (note that 'assault' in this context includes battery). The most commonly charged of these offences are defined in the Offences Against the Person Act 1861 and include:.

(a) assaulting a constable in the execution of his duty (s.38) (*see also* Police Act 1964, s.51).
(b) assault occasioning actual bodily harm (s.47).
(c) wounding or causing grievous bodily harm with intent *inter alia* to do grievous bodily harm (s.18).
(d) unlawful wounding (s.20).

Statutory sexual offences are discussed under that heading.

See also: Bodily harm; Consent to injury; Consent to medical treatment; *Mens rea*; Offences Against the Person Act 1861; Sexual offences; *Volenti non fit injuria*

1. *Fagan v Metropolitan Police Commissioner* [1969] 1 QB 439; [1968] 3 All ER 442; Smith JC and Hogan B *Criminal Law* (5th ed, 1983) p.351, Butterworths, London.
2. *Textbook of Criminal Law* (2nd ed, 1983) p.173, Stevens, London.
3. *Mead v Belt* (1823) 1 Lew CC 184; *David Springfield* (1969) 53 Crim App R 608; Glanville Williams, n.2 above, p.140; Smith and Hogan, n.1 above, p.352.
4. *Plunkett v Matchell* [1958] Crim LR 252.
5. *R v Venna* [1975] 3 All ER 788 CA.
6. *Stanley v Powell* [1891] 1 QB 86.
7. *Attorney General's Reference (No.6 of 1980)* [1981] QB 715.

Atheroma

In atheroma, fatty tissue is deposited beneath the lining of arteries (in the subintima). The fatty material becomes fibrous over a period of years and may ultimately calcify, leading to rigidity of the normally muscular wall. The process in the important coronary vessels is typically eccentric and patchy in distribution, which leads to the formation of atheromatous plaques. Disease based on atheroma constitutes a major cause of death in western society and, in the UK, is responsible for over 80 per cent of sudden unexpected deaths reported to the coroner or procurator fiscal. Atheroma appears early in life, and significant involvement of the coronary arteries is present in about 20 per cent of apparently fit young men[1]. Its precise cause is unknown and its distribution varies both ethnically and anatomically. Numerous attempts have been made to incriminate diet but lowering the cholesterol level in the blood is of proven benefit only in those persons who appear to be at greatest risk of death[2]. The aetiology is complex and is related to life style and genetic influence; some very definite factors predictive of death or severe handicap from the results of atheroma can be defined (e.g. a raised blood cholesterol, hypertension, obesity and smoking) but these must be distinguished from causal conditions[3]. The process is generally more advanced in men than in women but the sex difference is very much less in the case of cerebral atheroma than it is in cardiac disease. The extent of atheroma in a given vessel is best seen radiologically through the technique of angiography, but it does not necessarily equate with the risk of sudden ischaemia or death. The subject is discussed in greater detail under 'Coronary disease'.

The disease underlies several conditions predisposing to sudden death and which are, therefore, of major medico-legal significance. These include the following:

(a) Vascular insufficiency. This may be slowly developing and counterbalanced by the formation of a collateral circulation. Alternatively, a haemorrhage into the atheromatous plaque may cause sudden restriction of the bore or an increased demand for oxygenated blood by, say, the heart may not be met because of the rigid nature of the atheromatous wall. Generalised reduction in blood flow may lead to chronic dysfunction of the tissue supplied — e.g. dementia due to cerebral atheroma. Constrictive atheromatous disease is often referred to as atherosclerosis or arteriosclerosis.

(b) Thrombosis. Changes in blood flow and the deposition of platelets on a plaque may lead to thrombosis. A thrombus may also form within an atheromatous plaque.

(c) Embolism. Fragments of atheroma may break off and suddenly obstruct a smaller, more distal artery.

(d) Aneurysm. Involvement of the wall of the artery may result in dilatation and consequent weakness with a possibility of rupture.

(e) Hypertension. The increase in peripheral resistance may result in a raised blood pressure with consequent strain on the heart. Increased pressure will also predispose to haemorrhage from already damaged vessels — e.g. those within the brain.

Perhaps the main medico-legal problem posed by the finding of severe atheroma at autopsy is to distinguish disease which is compatible with good function from that which has caused incapacity or death; the circumstantial evidence is then essential to intelligent interpretation.

See also: Aneurysm; Angiography; Arteries; Coronary disease; Embolism; Hypertensive disease; Thrombosis

1. Underwood Ground KEA 'Prevalence of coronary atherosclerosis in healthy United Kingdom aviators' (1981) 52 J Aviat Space Environ Med 696.
2. Oliver MF 'Hypercholesterolaemia and coronary heart disease: an answer' (1984) 288 Br Med J 423.
3. For an example of the debate, *see* McMichael J 'Fats and atheroma: an inquest' [1979] 1 Br Med J 173 and Mann JI 'Fats and atheroma: a retrial' [1979] 1 Br Med J 732.

Autoeroticism

The greater part of forensic interest in autoerotic behaviour lies in the sexual asphyxias, which generally involve bonding, transvestism and some mechanism for inducing hypoxia.

Other forms of the deviance often involve some instrumentation and many such appliances are worked by electricity. So long as this is provided by a transformer or battery — as, for example, in the case of vaginal stimulators — there is little danger other than the occasional loss of a large foreign body into the rectum. There is, however, an understandable tendency to use home-made appliances which may be attached to the mains supply; since the medium in which they are used is ideal for the passage of an electric shock, death from electrocution is not uncommon. Any number of bizarre arrangements have been reported as having caused death[1].

See also: Electricity; Sexual asphyxia

1. For example, Sivaloganathan S 'Curiosum eroticum — a case of fatal electrocution during auto erotic practices' (1981) 21 Med Sci Law 47; Tan CTT and Chao TC 'A case of fatal electrocution during an unusual auto erotic practice' (1983) 23 Med Sci Law 92.

Automatism

Conduct is automatic when the actor's consciousness is impaired to such a degree that he is unaware of what he is doing. The automatic actor is unable to control his actions and generally he will have no subsequent recollection of what was done during the period of automatism[1].

Automatism may be the product of disease, both organic and non-organic, of external factors (as with a blow to the head leading to concussion) or of psychological states (as in a case where stress produces dissociation). Automatic behaviour may range from simple acts — twitches or spasmodic movements of the limbs — to complex and purposeful action. It is possible that acts of criminal violence may be committed while the actor is in a state of automatism, although automatic conduct is by no means always violent[2].

The law recognizes automatism as a defence to a criminal charge. Since there is no consciousness, there can be no *mens rea* and therefore no criminal responsibility. English law now divides the condition into insane and non-insane automatism[3]. Insane automatism is present where the condition results from a disease of the mind; non-insane automatism occurs where the factor producing the condition is an external one acting upon the mind. In the event of insane automatism, the accused will be disposed of as an insane offender whereas complete acquittal should result in the case of non-insane automatism.

The question of what constitutes a disease of the mind for these purposes has caused some difficulty. The term 'disease of the mind' is one of legal art, and is discussed under that heading. For present purposes it is noted that automatism resulting from an epileptic seizure will consequently be treated as insane automatism[3], as will that due to cerebral atherosclerosis[4]. Automatic behaviour during a dissociative state has been dealt with similarly by Canadian courts[5] and this approach might be followed in England. Generalised diseases which may act on the mind, such as diabetes, may or may not be regarded legally as causing non-insane automatism and, in this respect, cases associated with the use of insulin have been both instructive and confusing. In *Quick*[6], where a mental nurse attacked a patient while allegedly in a state of hypoglycaemic automatism, the condition was regarded as non-insane because the abnormality of mind was attributable to an outside influence — insulin; the inescapable inference to be drawn was that insanity, and consequent admission to a mental hospital, would have been the correct interpretation had the automatism been due to diabetes *per se*[7]. However, the Court of Appeal in *R v Bailey (John)*[8] took the view that the correct basis for the decision in *Quick* lay in the question of recklessness — failing to take food in the knowledge that violence was likely as a sequel to hypoglycaemia. The court distinguished the knowledge in such a case from that involved in taking alcohol or drugs and made it clear that a defence of automatism would be available — success or failure would depend on the absence or presence of recklessness. This view was reaffirmed in *R v Sullivan*[9].

There can be no doubt that, although the law has been stated without equivocation[3], it is not ideal from the point of view of the accused. It cannot be satisfactory when doctors attempt to define 'disease' in terms of the duration of symptoms and signs[10] nor when 'insanity' is diagnosed in terms of public danger[11]. The consequences of compulsory admission to a mental hospital for an unspecified time are severe and, clear though the law may be, it is questionable whether it is right that a person who pleads not guilty due to non-insane automatism should run the risk of a verdict of not guilty by reason of insanity and, thus, be forced to plead guilty to a lesser charge. This occurred in the case of *Sullivan*, where such a plea was accepted in the interests of natural justice.

Scots law does not accept the concept of non-insane automatism[12]; attempts to reverse this principle have met with stiff opposition[13].

See also: Concussion; Diabetes; Disease of the mind; Epilepsy; Insanity and criminal responsibility; Insulin; *Mens rea*

1. Blair D 'The medicolegal aspects of automatism' (1977) 17 Med Sci Law 167.
2. *Bratty v AG for Northern Ireland* [1961] 3 All ER 523; [1963] AC 386.
3. *R v Sullivan* [1983] 2 All ER 673, HL.
4. *R v Kemp* [1956] 3 All ER 249; [1957] 1 QB 399.
5. *R v Isitt* (1977) 67 Crim App R 44; *Rabey v The Queen* (1981) 114 DLR (3d) 193.
6. *R v Quick, R v Paddison* [1973] 3 All ER 347.
7. Maher G, Pearson J and Frier BM 'Diabetes mellitus and criminal responsibility' (1984) 24 Med Sci Law 95.
8. *R v Bailey (John)* [1983] 1 WLR 760. *See* Maher G 'Automatism and diabetes' (1983) 99 LQR 511 for discussion.
9. As n.3, above per Lord Diplock at 678.
10. As occurred in *Sullivan's* trial. *See* Medicolegal 'Insanity at law' (1983) 287 Br Med J 694.
11. As suggested by Lord Denning in *Bratty* (n.2, above). *See* Clements LM 'Epilepsy, insanity and automatism' (1983) 133 NLJ 949 for an analysis.
12. Since *HM Adv v Cunningham* 1963 JC 80 in which it was held that the law recognised no state between insanity and full responsibility other than in a case of murder.
13. *Carmichael v Boyd* 1985 SLT 399. For review of Scots decisions, *see* 'Automatism and responsibility' 1985 SLT 308.

Autonomic Nervous System

The autonomic nervous sytem activates those functions of the body which are not under voluntary control. Many such parts, however, have a dual innervation — e.g. we are not usually conscious of our breathing but we can control it volitionally when required. The autonomic system consists of the sympathetic and parasympathetic systems which are, to an extent, antagonistic.

The sympathetic chains lie on each side of the spinal column and consist of a number of interconnected ganglia related to the thoracic and upper lumbar spinal nerves. Sensory sympathetic nerves form junctions within the spinal cord, and motor elements run outwards with the spinal nerves to the tissues. In addition, there are a number of outlying ganglia which supply, *inter alia*, the heart, the lungs and the bowel. These ganglia, which include the carotid sinus in the neck and the solar plexus in the upper abdomen, are of great medico-legal importance as their abnormal stimulation may initiate the phenomenon of vagal inhibition of the heart. The function of the sympathetic nervous system is essentially to 'tone up' the body — it increases the heart rate, maintains the tone of the blood vessels and, in general, reduces those activities which are not required in an emergency such as bowel and bladder movements.

The parasympathetic system consists of fibres within the vagus nerve and, at the lower end of the body, the sacral nerves which combine to form the pelvic nerves. The most important action of the vagus nerve from the medico-legal aspect is that it slows the heart.

See also: Vagal inhibition of the heart

Autonomy

The principle of rational beings having a unique capacity to choose for themselves is central to the kantian theory of moral philosophy[1]. The individual is self-legislating or autonomous and it is morally impermissible to deprive that individual of a capacity to choose.

The concept of autonomy can be seen as regulating the doctor/patient relationship. On the one hand, the doctor has the power to choose whether he will take part in a particular treatment and, on the other, the prerogative of the patient must, in the modern moral climate, be to retain the right to decide what is to be done with his body. Autonomy is therefore at the heart of the doctrine of informed consent. The concept may be regarded as the antithesis of paternalism; nevertheless, the two are not wholly incompatible if autonomy is regarded as a relative rather than an absolute concept[2].

See also: Informed consent; Paternalism

1. A very simple guide to moral philosophy and medicine is to be found in Campbell AV *Moral Dilemmas in Medicine* (3rd ed, 1984) Churchill Livingstone, Edinburgh.
2. Brody H 'Autonomy revisited — progress in medical ethics: discussion paper' (1985) 78 J Roy Soc Med 380.

Autopsy

Autopsy, sometimes known as necropsy or postmortem dissection, is the dissection of the body after death, primarily to establish or confirm the cause of death or to investigate the nature and spread of disease and its response to treatment. The law regulating autopsy is contained in the Human Tissue Act 1961, s.2 (as amended by the Anatomy Act 1984), which stipulates that the examination can be authorised only by the person lawfully in possession of the body after consultation with surviving relatives or by the competent medico-legal authority; the dissection may be carried out only by a fully registered medical practitioner or in accordance with his instructions. Postmortem dissections can thus be regarded as either 'hospital or clinical autopsies' or 'medico-legal or forensic autopsies'.

Hospital autopsies have undoubtedly been decreasing in numbers in recent years and are unlikely to be carried out in more than 20–30 per cent of deaths occurring in major hospitals[1]. There is strong pressure that this proportion should be increased mainly on the grounds that surveys which included a high autopsy rate have shown clinically significant diagnostic discrepancies between clinical and autopsy findings[2]; autopsy should therefore be regarded as a form of medical audit. Whether or not there is resistance to autopsy on the part of near relatives and whether such resistance, if present, could be overcome by such measures as improving the general mortuary setting are matters for argument.

The main purpose of the medico-legal autopsy in England and Wales is to ensure the validity of the mortality statistics. As a consequence, a very high proportion of deaths reported to the coroner — some 98 per cent or more — are subjected to autopsy; even so, the academic pathologist would criticise the system in that a thorough review of the case as a whole is usually lacking and that, as a consequence, approximately 25 per cent of the total deaths are diverted from centres of intensive study. The Scottish procurator fiscal's main concern is to establish or eliminate criminality or negligence associated with the death; thus, less than 25 per cent of fiscal cases are dissected after death. The resultant of these variables is that, whereas, proportionately, nearly twice as many autopsies are carried out in England and Wales as compared with Scotland, the Scottish rate for hospital autopsies is three times that for England and Wales.

In the event of the pathological evidence being likely to be used in criminal proceedings, the dissection must be carried out by two doctors in Scotland; no such corroboration is needed in England and Wales. A second — or 'defence' — postmortem may be carried out under both jurisdictions but the displacement of organs and the artefacts introduced render this a particularly difficult and often frustrating examination; close co-operation between the experts of the two sides is, now, almost invariable.

Attention is also drawn to the importance of the autopsy in accidental death for the purpose of demonstrating the cause of the accident and the cause of the fatality; accidental deaths also pose problems such as those of life expectancy which can only be resolved satisfactorily by postmortem dissection.

The autopsy presents something of a hazard to the pathologist and his technicians from the point of view of spread of infectious disease, including opportunistic infection by organisms responsible for putrefaction of the body. Dangerous pathogenic organisms have been classified in categories A and B[3]. Postmortem examination must never be made on cases suspected of infection with category A pathogens — viruses of intense pathogenicity which are not normally encountered in routine clinical laboratories — except under conditions approved by the Dangerous Pathogens Advisory Group. Category B1 pathogens include the organisms responsible for tuberculosis and the typhoid fever group whilst category B2 includes all specimens known to be or potentially positive for the virus of serum hepatitis. Special precautions for dealing with such cases at autopsy are laid down in the Howie Report[4] in addition to general recommendations for the operation of mortuaries. Although not binding under the Health and Safety at Work etc. Act 1974, there is no doubt that inspectors approved under the Act would expect the code of practice to be implemented. The medico-legal autopsy, in which the presence or absence of infectious disease cannot be anticipated, may be particularly hazardous.

See also: Accidental death; Coroner; Health and Safety at Work etc. Act 1974; Hepatitis; Human Tissue Act 1961; Pathogenic organisms; Procurator fiscal; Registered medical practitioner

1. Black D (chairman) 'Report on medical aspects of death certification' (1982) 16 J Roy Coll Phys Lond 3.
2. Cameron HM, McGoogan E and Watson H 'Necropsy: a yardstick for clinical diagnoses' (1980) 281 Br Med J 985.
3. Godber G (chairman) *Report of the Working Party on the Laboratory Use of Dangerous Pathogens* (1975) (Cmnd 6054).
4. Howie J (chairman) *Report of the Working Party to formulate a Code of Practice for the prevention of infection in clinical laboratories* (1978), HMSO, London.

B

Bacteria

Bacteria are unicellular organisms characterised by having no nucleus. They are omnipresent and form an essential component of the earth's ecology. Some forms, however, cause disease in man, and at one time bacterial disease was the most widespread and lethal form of infectious disease. Bacteria are, however, very sensitive to the antibiotic group of drugs; the control of bacterial disease is, essentially, a running battle between the development of resistance in the organisms and the production of new antibiotics.

Bacteria are commonly classified as to their shape when seen under the microscope. Thus, one speaks of, among others, cocci (round), bacilli (rod shaped) or spirochaetes (spiral) and these can be subdivided according to their staining properties. Most bacteria can be isolated, grown and identified in the laboratory — some only with difficulty — and most are destroyed by antiseptics, heat or ionising radiation. Some, however, develop spores which are relatively resistant to physical agents, and among these are the important organisms responsible for tetanus and gas gangrene.

Bacteria which are parasites of man are generally spread in human tissue or secretions — e.g. the bacillus of tuberculosis is spread in the sputum whilst that causing dysentery is passed in the faeces and on the hands. Some, however, survive well in dust, and among these the most significant are the staphylococci which are responsible for much of the wound infection which occurs occasionally in wards and especially in medical units dealing with burns. The spread of bacteria from man to man is a complex subject which is discussed under 'Communicable disease'. Much depends on the capacity of bacteria to survive in, for example, water or sewage.

Clinically, it should be possible to divide bacteria into those which are pathogenic (i.e. cause disease in man) and those which are non-pathogenic but the practical situation is not so simple. Some non-pathogenic bacteria become pathogenic when displaced (*see* 'Pathogenic organisms'); other pathogens may infect man without causing symptoms — this results in the 'carrier state' which is so important in the spread of, say, staphylococcal infection and typhoid fever. Other relatively innocuous bacteria become virulent when given a suitable medium — e.g. a burnt area or the lungs of the debilitated and the bed ridden. It is the latter example which explains the frequent appearance of bronchopneumonia as a cause of death.

The symptoms of disease due to many bacteria depend upon the production of toxins. These may be excreted by the bacterium (exotoxins) or retained within the cell (endotoxins). It is apparent that the latter are liberated on the death of the organism and this is the basis of one serious form of surgical shock. Both bacteria and their toxins may be potently antigenic; the diseases they cause are, accordingly, amenable to control by vaccination or immunisation. Many bacterial diseases — of which diphtheria is a main example — have been virtually eliminated by this means.

See also: Communicable disease; Gangrene; Immunisation; Pathogenic organisms; Pneumonia; Surgical shock; Vaccination

Barbiturates

The barbiturate group of drugs are synthetic compounds which have a profound depressant or hypnotic effect. They may be injected intravenously or taken by mouth. In the former case, they can be ultra-short acting and very valuable as anaesthetic agents — methohexitone is a good example. Taken by mouth, they may be short (quinalbarbitone or Seconal), medium (amylobarbitone or Amytal) or long (phenobarbitone or Luminal) acting. The first two types are used, often in combination (Seconal + Amytal = Tuinal), for inducing sleep; the last are particularly valuable in the treatment of epilepsy.

Barbiturates are drugs of dependence; increasing tolerance is a feature and severe symptoms may result from withdrawal. They have been widely misused by addicts either alone or, often, in combination with stimulants ('purple hearts'); the confirmed addict may crush tablets designed for oral use and inject them intravenously with consequent anatomical damage in the lungs additional to the toxicological effects. Barbiturates constitute a major objective of theft from pharmacies.

Insomnia being a frequent symptom of depression, it is not surprising that barbiturates are commonly used as suicidal agents. In Scotland, 43 per cent of suicidal poisonings were due to barbiturates in 1974; this proportion had fallen to 20 per cent in 1978[1]. The availability of the drugs was clearly due to their prescription and the general decline in barbiturate deaths was attributable to a voluntary limitation on prescription by many practitioners. It is probable that equally effective and less addictive drugs are available as substitutes for barbiturates for all but anaesthetic and antiepileptic use but a ban on their use is unlikely to be accepted by the medical profession as a whole.

The barbiturates are now categorised as Class B controlled drugs[2] and are likely to become less readily available to the public. The only barbiturates which can be dispensed by a pharmacist in an emergency without prescription are those used for the treatment of epilepsy[3].

See also: Anaesthesia; Epilepsy; Misuse of Drugs Act 1971; Prescription Only medicines; Suicide

1. Campbell S and Mason JK 'Fatal ingestions in Edinburgh 1974–78' (1981) 21 Med Sci Law 159.
2. Misuse of Drugs Act 1971 (Modification) Order 1984 (SI 1984/859).

3. Medicines (Products other than Veterinary Drugs) (Prescription Only) Order 1983 (SI 1983/1212), Sch.3.

Battered Babies

This term was coined by Kempe[1] in a deliberately emotional attempt to draw attention to the existence of cruelty to children in the family environment. It has been established that 'battering', as such, is only one aspect of the infliction of injury on children; moreover, cruelty may be of diverse kinds[2]. The term 'battered babies' is now generally replaced by 'non-accidental injury in children' and is discussed under that heading. The law is described under 'child abuse'.

See also: Child abuse; Non-accidental injury in children

1. Kempe CH et al 'The battered child syndrome' (1962) 181 JAMA 17.
2. Macaulay RAA and Mason JK 'Violence in the home' in Mason JK (ed) *The Pathology of Violent Injury* (1978) Chap.13, Edward Arnold, London.

Battery

A battery is the unlawful touching of another person (*see* 'Assault and battery').

In addition to the possibility of a criminal offence, a civil action may be brought for battery and, indeed, this is open to a patient who has undergone medical treatment without consenting. The bringing of such actions in battery has, however, been discouraged recently[1] and it would be appropriate to do so only in circumstances where there has been no consent at all to the treatment undertaken. In *Schweizer v Central Hospital*[2], for example, a surgeon who operated on a patient's back when permission had been given only for an operation on the toe was held liable for damages for battery.

An action in battery has certain advantages for the plaintiff over an action in negligence in that the plaintiff neither has to establish a causal link between the wrongful action and any specific damage nor, indeed, the occurrence of damage[3]. Moreover, in an action for battery, the patient has only to prove lack of consent; what decision would have been taken in the presence of consent is relevant only to an action in negligence.

See also: Assault and battery; Consent to medical treatment

1. *Hills v Potter and another* [1984] 1 WLR 641. *See also Freeman v Home Office* (1983) 127 SJ 825 QBD; (No.2) [1984] 2 WLR 802, CA.
2. (1975) 53 DLR (3d) 494.
3. Brazier M 'Informed consent to surgery' (1979) 19 Med Sci Law 49.

Beating Heart Donor

Excluding the donation of biological material which is readily replaceable, such as bone marrow, blood or skin, the use of live organ donors is virtually confined to the removal of a kidney, a procedure which is not without legal and moral difficulties. At the same time, the use of cadaver tissue is limited technically by the interposition of a 'warm anoxic time' during which the organs will deteriorate. The diagnosis of brain stem death, however, allows for the recognition of the cadaver state while the heart is still beating. The use of the brain stem dead cadaver as a 'beating heart donor' then presents a nearly ideal mode of transplantation therapy; it has, in fact, been stated that the transplantation of tissues less perfect than those obtained in this way could be regarded as medical malpractice in the USA[1].

There is, however, something of an emotional 'block' to the use of beating heart donors, and in some countries the practice is not permitted despite the acceptance of the principle of brain stem death[2]. The use of beating heart donors is common in the UK although there are some grounds for legalistic disquiet. It is widely agreed[3] that the transplant team should be dissociated from the practical diagnosis of brain stem death. At the same time, the Human Tissue Act 1961, s.1(4), lays it down that the surgeon must have satisfied himself that life is extinct by personal examination of the body before removing any organs from the cadaver; whilst it is highly probable that it does do so, it has never been decided in law whether reading another doctor's notes to this effect satisfies the wording of the Act. To obviate any difficulty, many surgeons disconnect the ventilator in the theatre and wait until a flat electrocardiogram is registered; the warm anoxic time is limited, thereby, to not more than a few minutes. The philosophical objection to such a practice is that it detracts from the absolute concept of brain stem death which is so essential to its acceptance. A more logical device would be to ensure that a death certificate is provided before any donor operation is undertaken; there is currently no legal requirement for this to be done.

See also: Brain stem death; Death certification; Human Tissue Act 1961; Transplantation of organs

1. Leading Article 'Brain death' [1975] 1 Br Med J 356.
2. Pallis C *ABC of Brain Stem Death* (1983) p.27 (British Medical Association, London) records this as the position in Sweden and in Poland.
3. *Code of Practice including the Diagnosis of Brain Death* (Lord Smith, Chairman) (1983) para.29.

Best Evidence Rule

The proposition that it is necessary to produce in court the best evidence of a fact in issue is no longer applied in the law of evidence. It is now the general case that all admissible evidence is given equal consideration although there may be certain circumstances in which failure to produce the best evidence may affect the weight given to such as is produced. In general, however, direct evidence will be preferable to circumstantial or secondary evidence, as it will increase the prospects of acceptance[1].

See also: Evidential burden

1. For discussion, *see* Buzzard JH, May R and Howard MN *Phipson on Evidence* (13th ed, 1982) p.69 et seq, Sweet & Maxwell, London.

Bestiality

Bestiality is a form of buggery in England and Wales[1] but is a distinct common law crime in Scotland. The offence consists of vaginal or anal intercourse with an animal[2] and can be committed by a man or by a woman. Whether a woman can be guilty of bestiality in Scotland is uncertain but it is unlikely that any such charge would be brought[3].

The nature of the offence makes it unlikely that many cases will present for medical examination save when the act is performed under duress. In such a case, spermatozoa of an animal type might be discovered in the female vagina but emission is unnecessary for completion of the offence in either an active or a passive role; other generalised injury might also be found.

Bestiality is a frequent subject for 'hard' pornography, in which context it is closely associated with sadism. Even so, strong reasons can be adduced for removing the offence as such from the statute book[4].

See also: Buggery; Sadomasochism

1. Proscribed under Sexual Offences Act 1956, s.12(1).
2. *R v Bourne* (1952) 36 Crim App R 125.
3. Gordon GH *The Criminal Law of Scotland* (2nd ed, 1978) p.895, W Green, Edinburgh.
4. Honoré T *Sex Law* (1978) p.176, Duckworth, London.

Biomedical Experimentation

The relatively acceptable concept of experimentation using humans as subjects was given a savage jolt during the Second World War. The discovery of grossly unethical practices led to the rapid production of the Nuremburg Code. This was followed in 1964 by the World Medical Association's Declaration of Helsinki, which was revised in 1975. Many national bodies have produced their own codes to amplify or extend the international guidelines[1]. The conceptual difficulty involved in human research work is to equate the need for such research with the inevitable appropriation of some of the subjects' rights to autonomy. It has been held that experiments or research on humans must conflict with the Declaration of Geneva that 'the health of my patient will be my first consideration'; on the other hand, there are those who would contend that human experimentation for the benefit of humans is less immoral than is animal experimentation to the same end.

Human research or experimentation can be rationalised by its division into clinical research, when the aim is to benefit a specific patient or patients as a whole, and scientific research, when the aim is orientated towards a search for knowledge for its own sake. It follows that research subjects may be patients or healthy volunteers. Both groups may involve 'captive populations' but the legal and ethical constraints surrounding their use must be very different. A major criticism of the Declaration of Helsinki must be, however, that it envisages the use of patients for non-therapeutic research[2].

The most important research relationship for the medical doctor must be that which involves a therapeutic trial of different methods of treatment for the same condition or of a comparison between a form of treatment and none at all. The latter generally involves the use of placebos and is a sufficiently important aspect of biomedical research to merit a separate entry under that heading.

The ethical dilemma of the controlled trial can be summed up as being that, no matter how the researchers may wish to minimise it, there is an in-built probability that one of the forms of treatment is, or is likely to be, preferred to the others. Since this is a subjective assessment, it follows that research teams should be independent of the treating physicians and that consent of these physicians to 'randomisation' of their patients is a prerequisite; such consent must depend to a large extent on the assurance that the trial will be undertaken as rapidly as possible and that it will be terminated if any direct or side effect becomes apparent. The time such trials may take to reach a conclusion can give the counselling doctor cause for grave concern.

One would have thought it to be axiomatic that the patient also consents and, indeed, the criteria for consent to participation in a controlled trial or research of any sort have generally been set very high[3]. It is surprising to read of cases in which consent has deliberately not been sought in instances where the alternative treatments are markedly different as to risk; coroners are placed in a difficult position if death occurs in such circumstances[4]. In fact, many commentators tend to doubt that it is possible for the ordinary patient to give true consent to a trial of the treatment of complicated diseases such as cancer; if the doctors do not know the role of an intact lymphoid system in the prevention of spread of the disease, it is difficult to see how the patient can choose between, say, conservative and radical treatment. Cancer trials do tend, in practice, to have a relatively poor accrual rate, which is due to reactions on the part of both patients and their medical advisers. But the principle of informed consent appears now to dominate the philosophy of the most responsible research bodies[6]. There is no doubt that the role of ethical committees in the overseeing of therapeutic research and experimentation will increase in importance.

Scientific research involves the doctor/patient relationship far less in so far as the subjects concerned are mainly healthy volunteers or the researchers themselves. The doctor is concerned ethically only when patients are used simply for their accessibility — a practice which is, at best, to be discouraged — when it becomes the duty of the caring physician to ensure that no adverse effects are introduced by the research. The use of healthy populations is a matter for the researchers' ethical conscience and this deserves some scrutiny in the case of special populations such as prisoners. The motives of the apparently truest 'volunteers' are often suspect and care must be taken that the health of a repetitive volunteer is not being affected by research. Every effort must be made to avoid injury to the experimental subjects when they themselves can derive no benefit from the research project, and it is important that the potential benefit greatly exceeds any inherent risks of the research protocol. As the risk of research increases, the obligation on the researchers to involve only themselves also grows; even then, no research can be either ethical or legal if serious injury to the subjects can be anticipated. Nevertheless, some remarkable advances have been made in scientific research by physiologists acting with great gallantry. The onus for ensuring a controlled and well-monitored series of experiments then rests squarely on the shoulders of the departmental head.

In the event of mishap, compensation for personal injury sustained in a research programme presents some difficulties. The normal framework of actions in negligence is clearly inadequate and the Pearson Commission were in favour of strict liability in these circumstances[7]; others believe that no-fault compensation is the only equitable way of recompensing those injured in research[8] but, in the absence of legislation, it must be left to tort law at present.

Research involving children, fetal experimentation and the recent possibilities of embryonic research all pose problems of somewhat different dimensions and are discussed under separate headings.

See also: Child experimentation; Compensation; Embryonic experimentation; Ethical committees; Fetal experimentation; Human experimentation; Informed consent; No-fault compensation; Placebo; Prisoners; Strict liability

1. *See*, for example, Committee of Privy Council for Medical Research *Responsibility in Investigations on Human Subjects*, Report of the Medical Research Council of 1962–63 (Cmnd 2382) (1964) HMSO, London.
2. Belsey A 'Patients, doctors and experimentation: doubts about the Declaration of Helsinki' (1978) 4 J Med Ethics 182.
3. *Halushka v University of Saskatchewan* (1966) 53 DLR (2d) 436.
4. *See* the extraordinary case reported by Brahams D 'Clinical trials and consent of the patient' (1982) 226 Practitioner 1829; a coroner's conclusion that death was due to misadventure was reached. For further discussion of the case, *see* Editorial 'Secret randomised clinical trials' [1982] 2 Lancet 78.
5. Taub S 'Cancer and the law of informed consent' (1982) 10 Law Med Hlth Care 61.
6. Cancer Research Campaign Working Party in Breast Conservation 'Informed consent: ethical, legal, and medical implications for doctors and patients who participate in randomised clinical trials' (1983) 286 Br Med J 1117; Dudley HAF 'Informed consent in surgical trials' (1984) 289 Br Med J 937.
7. Pearson CH (chairman) *Report of Royal Commission on Civil Liability and Compensation for Personal Injury* (Cmnd 7054) (1978) HMSO, London.
8. Ciba Foundation Study Group 'Medical research: civil liability and compensation for personal injury — a discussion paper' [1980] 1 Br Med J 1172.

Further reading

For an overall critical view of randomised research, *see* Burkhardt R and Kienle G 'Basic problems in controlled trials' (1983) 9 J Med Ethics 80.

Birth Injuries

It was, at one time, thought that up to 50 per cent of all deaths which occurred in the first two weeks of life were attributable to birth injuries; such a figure is now regarded as a gross exaggeration and birth trauma probably accounts for about 5 per cent of deaths in a well-conducted obstetric practice. The infant is subject to major hazards during birth — trauma to the head due to the moulding which is necessary and hypoxia due to interference with the function of the placenta or umbilical cord. Both processes can produce intracranial haemorrhage — that due to hypoxia being commonly subarachnoid whilst that due to injury is subdural which can sometimes be related to tears in the venous sinuses of the cranial cavity. A number of birth injuries — some of which might be misinterpreted as attempts at infanticide[1] — were at one time due to the use of forceps; modern obstetric practice, however, severely limits the use of forceps to assist delivery, caesarian section being preferred[2].

Routine scanning of the head in infants who are suspected of injury allows for quick treatment but, even so, cases of residual morbidity still occur. The most important of these are the cerebral palsies or spastic paralyses, which may be of various types, and these will be accompanied by general mental retardation. Epilepsy may develop later as an occasional complication of birth injury. Such cerebral complications may be due to injury or to hypoxia during a prolonged labour; it is also to be noted that brain damage can occur *in utero* as a result, say, of viral infection or of haemolytic disease of the newborn. The arm may be paralysed due to traction injury of the nerves during delivery and this may be particularly so in breach deliveries. Damage to the facial nerve occurs both as a complication of forceps delivery and during normal birth. The majority of peripheral nerve lesions of this type recover under treatment.

Spinal cord injury is a rare complication of breach delivery; a lesion in the region of the neck may result in stillbirth.

Subdural haemorrhage is related to prematurity, as the immature infant's head is particularly susceptible to injury. It is clearly more likely to occur in unsupervised conditions and when labour is precipitate; these are just the circumstances in which infanticide may be considered — it is often impossible to make the diagnosis with certainty and the benefit of any doubt must be given to the mother.

See also: Infanticide; Paralysis; Subarachnoid haemorrhage; Subdural haemorrhage

1. Nuijeu S and Hausman R 'Fatal forceps' (1983) 23 Med Sci Law 254.
2. See the decision in *Whitehouse v Jordan* [1980] 1 All ER 650, CA; [1981] 1 WLR 246, HL.

Bite Marks

Identification of the origin of human bite marks depends on the fact that the teeth may leave impressions of various types which may be later matched to the biter. Leaving aside remarkable stories such as those of bites in wax intended as signatures to documents[1], identifiable matter may be found in foodstuffs or in the human skin.

It is astonishing how often burglars, vandals and the like will eat at the locus and leave bitten material behind. Many bite marks are found which can be matched with comparative ease — particularly in chocolate, cheese and apples — but foods, and especially those with a high water content, alter shape and also contract as they age. The investigation of such bite marks should therefore be expeditious. It involves accurate photography, saliva testing, the making of impressions and, with less urgency, the preparation of plaster moulds for subsequent matching with impressions taken from suspects' teeth. Following this, the material should be preserved for future court presentation in formalin solution; this preserves the shape best.

Human-to-human bite marks are generally of two types — the love bite and the aggressive bite — although the two sometimes overlap. Whilst it is seldom necessary to identify the former, they have certain characteristics, being generally of suckling type. Thus, frank tooth marks are relatively uncommon; more often there is a peripheral area of bruising due to lip pressure and a central 'bulls-eye' appearance of bruising or petechial haemorrhage due to tongue pressure. Tooth marks may be present and are then usually of clear appearance as compared with the abrasions or lacerations associated with aggressive bites. These may be found in life following sexual assault or at postmortem examination of homicides with sexual overtones. Aggressive bites may be inflicted by the victim of an assault as a defensive attempt; bites of intermediate appearance are a feature of the child abuse syndrome in which self-inflicted bites are sometimes seen — often as a way of self-preservation against crying out and consequent secondary assault. Whether they be discovered in life or after death, bite marks change rapidly with time — the appearance alters as part of the process of bruising and the shape is affected by changes in skin elasticity.

In the investigation of bite marks, the most urgent need is to test for saliva because this disappears rapidly with time and manipulation. The simplest way of recovering saliva is by means of moistened cigarette paper[2] which may be preserved between glass slides. Group-specific antigens may be present in the victim's sweat; thus, a control specimen, conveniently taken from the contralateral portion of the body, is essential, as is a simple moistened paper to exclude any suggestion that the investigator's own sweat may be involved. Specimens of boiled saliva (*see* 'Saliva testing') and blood from the victim and from any suspects will be required by the laboratory.

Photography, often repeated because of changing appearances, with an included linear scale, is essential for court presentation where the major difficulty lies in presenting the evidence in a way comprehensible by and acceptable to the jury. Such evidence is essentially a matter of comparing the mark with the dentition of any suspect. Dental impressions are 'non-intimate samples' as defined in the Police and Criminal Evidence Act 1984, and obtaining them is subject to consent or to the authority of a senior police officer (s.63) (*see* 'Detention by the police'); specimens obtained through the medium of a sheriff's warrant would be admissible in evidence in Scotland[3]. Rather than attempt a full matching, it is often better to concentrate on a number of obvious points of similarity or dissimilarity; these may be demonstrated by transparent overlays[4] or other suitable highlighting techniques[5].

The difficulty with bite mark evidence is that, although the appearances may convince the expert, they are often of such a type that the jury can be persuaded into reasonable doubt as to their positive significance; it may well be that the evidence is of maximal use in excluding a suspect. Some remarkable convictions have, however, been obtained as a result of bite mark identification[6]. The controversy which such cases have often generated confirms the difficulty confronting the expert witnesses.

See also: Abrasions; Bruises; Child abuse; Detention by the police; Saliva testing

1. Holt JK 'Identification from bitemarks' (1980) 20 J Forens Sci Soc 243.
2. Clift A and Lamont CM 'Saliva in forensic odontology' in Harvey W (ed) *Dental Identification and Forensic Odontology* (1976) Chap.18, Kimpton, London.
3. *Hay v HM Adv* 1968 JC 40.
4. Rentoul E and Smith H *Glaister's Medical Jurisprudence and Toxicology* (13th ed, 1973) p.65 et seq, Churchill Livingstone, Edinburgh.
5. Furness J 'A new method for the identification of bite marks in cases of assault and homicide' (1968) 124 Br Dent J 261.
6. Harvey W et al 'The Biggar murder' (1968) 8 J Forens Sci Soc 156.

Blast Injuries

The results of an explosion are several: there are the injuries sustained from the displacement of the body, impact injuries from flying missiles of many types and the physiological effects of the blast wave. These last were extensively studied during the Second World War and the conclusions remain true today[1].

The major effect of blast itself operates through the impact of a pressure wave on the body. The determining prognostic feature is the effect on the lungs in which the concussive wave produces patchy but often massive haemorrhage, this being the result of movement and recoil in tissues containing multiple gas/fluid interfaces. The result is a dramatic fall in blood pressure which, in company with respiratory embarrassment, may be rapidly fatal. It is to be noted that these findings are difficult to distinguish from those of deceleration of the lungs following, say, a fall from a height — the force is positive in one instance and negative in the other[2].

Similar interfaces exist in the hollow organs of the abdomen, in which blast may cause severe injury. This will be particularly so in a watery environment in which the body is held relatively rigidly. The bodies of dead persons exposed to underwater blast may appear uninjured externally but will be found at autopsy to have sustained extensive internal disruption. Further evidence of blast effects may be obtained from the eardrums which, for similar reasons, are also often ruptured.

It is to be noted that homogeneous organs, without distinct physical interfaces such as muscle, are relatively unaffected by blast.

See also: Bomb injuries; Explosions

1. *See*, for example, Krohn PL, Whitteridge D and Zuckerman S 'Physiological effects of blast' [1942] 1 Lancet 252.
2. *See* the practical and experimental results reported in Armstrong JA et al 'Investigation of injuries in the Comet aircraft disasters' [1955] 1 Lancet 1135.

Blood Groups

The blood cells, of both the red and the white series, have surface antigens which are genetically determined. These antigens exist as two or more alleles, or alternates (*see* 'Genetic disease') which are segregated as blood group systems; each system is genetically distinct from the other. The antigens which are present within each system can be determined by the use of antibodies, many of which appear, and are obtained, naturally as a result of multiple transfusions. Discovery of the 'full blood group profile' of a person depends, therefore, on the availability of antibodies and this availability in turn reflects the strength of the antigens within the various systems.

The 'strongest' system is the ABO system. Each member of the allelic pair may be one of these three antigens but the antigen O is 'silent' — its presence cannot be determined except as an inference from the absence of both A and B. We can therefore identify four 'ABO groups' — A, B, AB and O. Group A could be either AA or AO and group B could be BB or BO; an uncertain genetic profile of this type is known as a *phenotype*. Both alleles are, however, demonstrable in group AB whilst group O must, in fact, be group OO; in these cases, we know the full profile or the *genotype*. In practice, the genotypes AA, AO, BB and BO can often be derived through family investigations (*see* 'Parentage testing'). The distribution of the ABO groups is very dependent upon geography and ethnology. Thus, the antigen B is common in Asia but relatively rare in the Americas, whilst O is especially common in the more closed island communities. Variations occur even in such a small area as the UK where 43 per cent of those in southern England are of group A as compared with only 34 per cent of Scots. The distribution as a whole in Great Britain is approximately 42 per cent group A, 8 per cent B, 3 per cent AB and 47 per cent O. The ABO system is complicated by the fact that the antigen A exists in a modified form A_2 in about 20 per cent of those who are of groups A or AB.

The rhesus (Rh) system has considerable clinical importance; it is also complicated to explain. For these reasons, it is discussed in a separate entry.

The MNS system was the second to be discovered and merits special mention because it is the most useful single system in parentage testing. The main alternate alleles are designated M and N, and, since antibodies are available to both, the three genotypes MM (28 per cent), NN (22 per cent) and MN (50 per cent) can be demonstrated. The system shows, in addition, the phenomenon of 'linkage' (also present in the rhesus system) by which genes and their resultant antigens are transmitted 'true' in a stable combination or complex. In this system, the genetically derived antigens M and N are 'linked' to one of the alleles S or s; as a result, ten genotypes can be identified in the system. As with most systems, variants on the basic antigens occur and may cause some difficulty, even if no more than theoretical, for the parentage tester.

Many other blood group systems have been discovered. Some are of importance in blood transfusion and some in parentage testing, but often the distribution of the alleles is so disparate that their usefulness is slight. Some of the lesser systems are known by the names of the persons through whom they were discovered — Kell, Duffy and Kidd systems are routinely tested for in most parentage testing laboratories; a feature of these systems is their frequently distinct ethnic distribution. The lawyer may occasionally see references to the P, Lewis and Lutheran systems, among others, but a detailed description is not called for here; the Lewis system has a close relationship with secretion of blood group substances (*see* 'Saliva testing').

Although they are not antigens of the type discussed above, mention must be made of serum protein groups and red cell enzymatic systems which are inherited according to mendelian laws. These are of importance in parentage testing and in the examination of blood stains.

There is also the secretor group in which the dominant gene *Se* is responsible for the secretion of A, B and H (equivalent to O) substances in the tissue fluids of persons of the similar ABO blood group. About 24 per cent of the UK population (genetically *se se*) fail to secrete in this way. Secretion of ABH substances is of profound importance in the investigation of, say, stains — particularly seminal — or bite marks.

White cell, or human leucocyte, antigens (HLA), which occur in other tissue cells besides leucocytes, are also inherited on mendelian principles. They are of major significance in the phenomenon of rejection of transplants and their use increases the exclusion of falsely accused parentage to approximately 100 per cent. There are, however, very many more alternate antigens available as alleles; the intricacies of the system have not been fully explored and the techniques involved in their determination are complex. 'Tissue matching' is therefore a matter for the specialist, and only the practical aspects are discussed under 'Transplantation of organs'.

See also: Bite marks; Blood stains; Blood transfusion; Genetic disease; Parentage testing; Rhesus system; Saliva testing; Transplantation of organs

Further reading
The major work on blood groups is Race RR and Sanger R *Blood Groups in Man* (6th ed, 1975) (Blackwell Scientific, Oxford) but this is essentially for the expert. A short, easily understood summary is to be found in Dodd BE and Lincoln PJ *Blood Group Topics* (1975) Edward Arnold, London.

Blood Stains

The examination of blood stains follows much the same lines, as does the determination of blood groups with the proviso that the specimens available are strictly limited in quantity and are irreplaceable; they may well also be of poor quality. It is not, however, essential that recognisable cells are present for the contained antigens to be demonstrated. Using sensitive and technically somewhat complicated methods, some 17 antigens can be identified in a piece of cloth 0.5 cm² in area[1]. It is also possible to demonstrate serum protein and red cell enzyme systems.

A major purpose of identifying blood stains is to exclude their origin from a person suspected of having left them. Nevertheless, following the principles involved in parentage testing, it is possible to estimate the probability of positive identification of a suspect — figures such as a potential incidence of 1 in 17,000 of the population have been quoted[2]. Other valuable uses include the demonstration of contact — especially effective if only two or three persons are candidates for involvement — proof of the previous presence of a person or body at a particular locus, corroborating an account of movements of the body or person and confirming the use of a particular object to inflict a wound[3]. It may, of course, sometimes be necessary to establish that the blood is human.

Blood stains deteriorate with age but ABO antigens can be identified years after the blood has been shed if the stain dried rapidly. Rhesus antigens will persist certainly for months but the weaker antigens are more labile. The blood cell enzyme systems seldom persist for more than one month but generalisations are, in all cases, difficult to make — much depends on the conditions in which the stain was preserved.

See also: Blood groups; Parentage testing; Rhesus system

1. Lincoln PJ and Dodd BE 'The application of a micro-elution technique' (1975) 15 Med Sci Law 94.
2. But the statistical considerations may be very complex. *See*, for example, Evett IW 'What is the probability that this blood came from that person? A meaningful question?' (1983) 23 J Forens Sci Soc 35.
3. Lincoln PJ 'Blood group evidence for the defence' (1980) 20 Med Sci Law 239. This paper gives an interesting view of the evidential value of blood stain examinations in practice.

Blood Transfusion

Blood transfusion is the simplest and oldest established form of transplantation of organs; it is virtually free of risk to the donor, as 600 ml of blood is replaced in a normal person within a few days. The only ethical problem involved relates to the sale of biological material. In the UK, blood is obtained and distributed through the National Blood Transfusion Service; a few rare blood components may have to be obtained commercially but the only charges are those which are made to cover the administrative costs of supply to private patients. Blood is widely bought and sold in the USA. This practice may be detrimental unless closely controlled, as the economic pressures to sell a readily available commodity may bear hardest on those whose life styles is conducive to the transmission of blood-borne disease (*see* 'Acquired immune deficiency syndrome' and 'Hepatitis').

The practical problems relate, firstly, to those of compatibility of donor and recipient. The blood group antigens in the donor will, by definition, stimulate antibodies in the recipient if they are foreign to the recipient. Equally, any antibodies present in the recipient will react with transfused antigens for which they are specific. By contrast, the antigens in the recipient, being part of 'self', are of no concern whilst antibodies in the donor plasma are rapidly diluted in the recipient and normally cause no difficulty. An 'incompatible' transfusion may therefore result in an immediate reaction between transfused blood and antibodies already present in the recipient or it may provoke the formation of antibodies which will react with the next transfusion or, indeed, the next pregnancy — during which blood and antibodies cross the placental barrier.

The ABO system is unique in that antibodies to the alternative antigens other than O, which is, immunologically speaking, inert, are naturally present in the plasma from the first few weeks of infant life — probably because A and B substances are widely distributed in nature apart from the red blood cells. A person of group A contains anti-B in the plasma, group B contains anti-A, group O both anti-A and anti-B whilst group AB can contain no such antibodies. The transfusion of group A blood into a group B person would result in an immediate reaction which could be severe and possibly fatal in view of the 'strength' of the antigens and antibodies involved. Thus, the first essential in transfusion is to select a donor of the same ABO group as the recipient. It will, however, be seen that an AB person could accept blood from any group — the universal recipient — and, because AB donors are in short supply, this is often done in practice. Conversely, persons of group O can be regarded as universal donors. Their use as such is not acceptable as a routine, firstly because it places an unfair logistical burden on such donors and also because the contained antibodies may be of such strength that dilution is not immediate and minor reactions may occur. Transfusion of ABO blood which is apparently of a compatible group must not be done without further testing save in a dire emergency. There are other difficulties quite apart from administrative errors (*see* below) — persons who are of subgroups of A (e.g. A_2 or A_3) may possess naturally occurring antibodies to the main antigen A_1.

The rhesus system is of sufficient importance to be discussed separately. It is enough to say here that blood should be chosen so as to be compatible with D+ (rhesus positive) or D− (rhesus negative) recipients; the use of D− blood when it was unnecessary would be a waste of scarce resources.

It is, in practice, impossible to test for compatibility of all the other systems; indeed, it would become extremely difficult to find donors for individual patients. The practical solution is to make sure that no *immediate* reaction will occur — i.e. that no relevant antibodies are already present in the recipient. This is a matter of 'cross-matching': the cells to be donated are tested against the actual recipient's plasma. Such testing for antibodies, some of which can be demonstrated only by special techniques, is now an essential part of a transfusion. It is clear that the more transfusions given, the more likely is the presence of antibodies; should one appear, it must be identified and blood of the group appropriate to that system be substituted. Very occasionally, minor reactions are due to antibodies to white cells or to platelets.

Compatibility testing is now thoroughly understood by laboratories and a 'mis-matched' transfusion is far more likely to be due to administrative error — misreading of labels, errors due to telephoned rather than written messages, etc. Blood must be stored at optimum temperature which is carefully monitored, and even then it has a limited life; electrolytes leaching from ageing cells may give a toxic reaction. Several diseases can be transmitted by transfused blood. Of these, the most important is hepatitis (the role of blood transfusion in the transmission of AIDS is currently under review) although syphilis was once very significant as is malaria in the areas in which the disease occurs; all such conditions must be eliminated before the product is issued for use.

Packed red cells, rather than whole blood, are often the appropriate treatment for cases requiring transfusion. As a result, it is possible to retain the plasma and extract from it many of the elements required to treat specific deficiency diseases — e.g. haemophilia. The 'overloading' of the circulation by excess intravenous fluid is unlikely in the case of blood by virtue of its economic restriction; blood substitutes, which might include simple solutions of electrolytes, are, however, a different matter. In fact, there appears to be only one recorded instance of a successful plea of *nova causa interveniens* in the criminal courts by reason of overtransfusion and the case posed several unusual features[1]. Surprisingly, the plea has been rejected in cases when an apparently indicated blood transfusion was not given by the medical authorities following a criminal assault[2] and also when the patient herself refused the transfusion[3].

The small religious group of Jehovah's Witnesses is conscientiously opposed to blood transfusion. They raise a number of medico-legal problems which are discussed as a separate entity.

See also: Acquired immune deficiency syndrome; Antibody; Antigen; Blood groups; Causation; Hepatitis; Immune reaction; Jehovah's Witnesses; *Nova causa interveniens*; Pregnancy; Rhesus system

1. *James Clinton Jordan* (1956) 40 Crim App R 152.
2. *R v Smith* [1959] 2 QB 35.
3. *R v Blaue* [1975] 1 WLR 1411.

Further reading

Mollison PL *Blood Transfusion in Clinical Medicine* (5th ed, 1972) (Blackwell Scientific, Oxford) is the classic work. Adequate summaries are available in most textbooks of forensic medicine; e.g. Mason JK *Forensic Medicine for Lawyers* (2nd ed, 1983) Chap.31, Butterworths, London.

Blunt Injury

Blunt injury can be regarded as injury which does not cut the skin. Nevertheless, the skin can be split and lacerations are characteristically caused by blunt instruments.

The most frequent result of blunt injury is a bruise; in certain circumstances involving major force (e.g. injuries due to kicking) bruising may be far more obvious in the deep tissue than it is superficially. This is a good example of the rule that damage due to blunt injury is essentially a matter of compression of the tissues.

See also: Bruises; Lacerations

Bodily Harm

The Offences Against the Person Act 1861 designates two degrees of bodily harm — actual and grievous.

Actual bodily harm simply means harm. There must be some recognisable injury but the only limiting definition would seem to be that a minor abrasion and a bruise went 'to the very margin of what was meant by actual bodily harm'[1]. The distinction of actual bodily harm is important in practice — the maximum penalty for assault rises from one year to five years in the presence of acceptable injury. Bodily harm can also include an injury to the state of mind[2].

Grievous bodily harm is said to mean no more than really serious bodily harm[3] and the decision is thus one for the jury. The Criminal Law Revision Committee[4] have, in fact, recommended that grievous bodily harm be replaced by severe injury, a term which is to be contrasted with injury. The distinction between actual and grievous or between simple and serious must, in either case, be blurred and there is much to be said for the Scottish practice of recognising only an offence of assault, the seriousness of the particular offence depending on its own general circumstances; even so, there are certain recognised aggravations of an assault which must be specified in the charge in Scotland and which must be left to the jury to decide upon — e.g. assault to the danger of life[5].

See also: Offences Against the Person Act 1861; Wounds

1. *Christopher Jones* [1981] Crim LR 119.
2. *R v Miller* [1954] 2 QB 282.
3. *DPP v Smith* [1961] AC 290.
4. Criminal Law Revision Committee, Report 14, *Offences against the Person* (Cmnd 7844) (1980) HMSO, London.
5. Gordon GH *The Criminal Law of Scotland* (2nd ed, 1978) p.816, W Green, Edinburgh.

Bomb Injuries

Bomb injuries have been vividly described by Marshall[1] whose experience of terrorist activities must be unique. He has described six categories of injury:

(a)   Complete disruption. This is uncommon unless the bomb is in contact with the body.

(b)   Explosive injury. In those close to the bomb, this consists of amputations and evisceration of the thorax and abdomen but, in general, of a triad of punctate bruises, abrasions and small punctate lacerations occurring in those located within a few metres of the bomb.

(c)   Injury by separate fragments. The peppering type of injury is not seen in those at some distance from the explosion and is replaced by specific injuries due to large fragments of metal or masonry striking the body with great force.

(d)   Injury by falling masonry. Some persons die from injuries due to this cause whilst others die later from crush asphyxia.

(e)   Blast injury. This is not a great feature of terrorist bombings due to the relatively small charges involved.

(f)   Burns. These may be of flash type when a bomb factory explodes but, otherwise, burns directly due to the bomb are of only a minor nature; severe burning may result from the conflagration which can follow a bombing.

Marshall also points out that occasional fatalities in bombing incidents are so little injured that their death can only be attributed to 'lethal reflexes' — something akin to vagal inhibition of the heart.

The presence of punctate injury combined with unusual injuries suggestive of blast may, on occasion, lead to the diagnosis of a bombing incident when it is not to be anticipated[2]. X-ray examination is ideal for searching for bomb fragments in such circumstances but, as Marshall points out, the radiologists and radiographers must be particularly dedicated to the task.

See also: Aircraft accidents; Blast injuries; Burns; Crush injury; Vagal inhibition of the heart

1. Marshall TK 'Violence and Civil Disturbance' in Mason JK (ed) *The Pathology of Violent Injury* (1978) Chap.5, Edward Arnold, London.
2. *See*, for example, Mason JK and Tarlton SW 'Medical investigation of the loss of the Comet 4B aircraft, 1967' [1969] 1 Lancet 431.

Boxing

Boxing is something of a medico-legal maverick for two main reasons. The first relates to whether it should be banned on medical grounds and the second to the legality of a sport in which the intention is to render another unconscious, a matter which can scarcely be anything other than inflicting bodily harm.

The medical case against boxing rests almost entirely on its long-term effects. Death in the boxing ring is surprisingly rare but this is almost entirely due to the stringent measures taken by the organisers (*see* below). The major long-term effect is termed traumatic encephalopathy or 'punch drunkenness'; the precise mechanism of this is uncertain but is probably associated with multiple episodes of concussion.

The ill-effects of boxing were heavily underscored in 1969[1] and the sport has recently come under renewed medical attack[2]. Boxing has been subjected to many voluntary restrictions in the meantime; equally, methods for identifying minor alterations in the function of the living brain have been greatly improved. Nevertheless, the British Medical Association intensified its campaign for the abolition of boxing as a result of the report of its Working Party.

A medical code has been enforced in professional British boxing since 1953 and this involves, *inter alia*, annual examination of licenced boxers as well as immediate pre-fight check-ups. The number of bouts is controlled by the Medical Commission of the British Board of Boxing Control who can also withdraw a licence on the grounds of ill-health. Appointed doctors are present at the ringside and, while they cannot stop a fight, they will advise on fitness to continue. An injured boxer must be suspended until declared fit for another bout and an investigation is undertaken if a professional boxer loses four fights in a row.

There is some evidence that it is the length of a bout rather than the number of bouts which predisposes to permanent brain damage. Amateur boxing is, in practice, limited to three rounds but the professional game still persists with bouts of up to 15 rounds. There is, thus, a great difference between the two sports. Professional boxing is 'big business' and a surprising number of people enjoy it as a spectator sport; the chances of a ban of boxing on medical grounds seem remote and such a ban could lead to a return of clandestine prizefighting. Amateur boxing has already lost much of its attraction and boxing in schools is now a rarity; it is, however, at least arguable that a little more closely supervised amateur boxing on a club basis might lead to less violence on the football terraces and less overall injury.

The legality of boxing was undoubtedly confirmed in the Court of Appeal opinion in 1981[3] but this depends upon its being a properly conducted sport. Deliberately permitting bouts outside the Queensberry Rules, obvious mismatches, the use of boxers who were clearly ill and the like would almost certainly elide the concept of what is proper control; charges of inflicting bodily harm or even of manslaughter could be brought against the principals, with additional charges of abettment against the organisers, in such circumstances. The legality of boxing in Scots law probably rests on the absence of evil intent[4].

See also: Assault; Bodily harm; Concussion; Punch drunkenness; Sports injuries

1. Royal College of Physicians *Report on the Medical Aspects of Boxing* (1969) RCP, London. This report dealt only with injuries sustained between 1929 and 1955.
2. British Medical Association *Report of the Board of Science and Education Working Party on Boxing* (1984) BMA, London.
3. *Attorney General's Reference (No.6 of 1980)* [1981] QB 715.
4. *Smart v HM Adv* 1975 SLT 65.

Brain

The brain lies within the skull and is protected by a thick outer lining membrane — the dura mater — and by an inner thin arachnoid membrane; the brain tissue itself is held in shape by a thin membrane known as the pia mater which is so closely applied to its surface as to leave no space. The space between the dura and the arachnoid is known as the subdural space and that between the arachnoid and the pia is the subarachnoid space; a protective water cushion — the cerebrospinal fluid — lies in the latter space, which also contains the major arteries supplying the brain substance and which are known collectively as the circle of Willis as they encircle the brain stem.

Developmentally, the brain can be regarded as having a central core which runs upwards from the spinal cord forming, from below upwards, the medulla, which contains the vital centres, and the pons, the short midbrain and the thalamus which, for ease of description, can be regarded as being responsible for our animal existence. Major bilateral symmetrical extensions are grafted onto the core and form the cerebellum in the hindbrain and the massive cerebrum in the forebrain. The cerebellum is essentially responsible for our muscular co-ordination and balance. The cerebrum, which dictates our human existence, is divided into bilateral lobes: the frontal, responsible anteriorly for intellect and posteriorly for motor action and speech; the parietal, which is mainly taken up with sensation; the occipital which lies posteriorly and is concerned with vision; and the temporal, which lies beneath the parietal and controls hearing, taste and smell together with equilibrium. Co-ordination of movement, instinct, perception, etc. within the brain is achieved through a complex system of intercommunicating fibres. The motor area of the posterior frontal lobe can be 'mapped' for responsibility for different areas of the body; in general, the more intricate the function, the greater is the cortical surface devoted to that area. The fibres which connect the cerebrum to the spinal cord cross over — an injury to the right cerebrum will therefore affect the movements of the left side of the body. When looked at in section, the brain consists of grey and white matter — the former being composed of nerve cells and the latter of tracts of fibres. Grey matter covers the cerebrum — the cerebral cortex — and also forms important nuclei within its depths.

Generalised damage to the brain results either from deprivation of oxygen from whatever cause or from abnormally increased intracranial pressure which blocks the arterial supply. In either event, the fundamental lesion is due to hypoxia of the brain cells; not only are the cells extremely sensitive to oxygen lack but they cannot be replaced once they are dead. Recovery from a generalised cerebral insult therefore results in a degree of brain damage which, in turn, relates to the relative hypoxic sensitivity of the various areas; thus the cerebral cortex is the most susceptible area and the brain stem the least. Localised damage in the form of mechanical injury or of haemorrhage, thrombosis or embolism — the so-called cerebrovascular accident — will lead to permanent loss of relatively specific function. A proportion of this loss will, however, have been due to secondary effects; thus there may be some functional recovery as oedema, haemorrhage, etc. resolve — moreover, the brain may learn to adapt to minor defect by reason of its intricate network of intercommunication.

It has been said that the rest of the body exists in order to support the brain; alternatively, that the intrinsic quality of life is the ability of the brain to support the body[1]. As a consequence, the anatomy, physiology and pharmacology of the brain impinge on virtually every aspect of medico-legal practice.

See also: Brain stem death; Central nervous system; Dura mater; Hypoxia; Intracranial haemorrhage

1. Kennedy IM 'The legal definition of death' (1973) 41 Med-Leg J 36.

Brain Stem Death

It has long been the custom to define death in terms of irreversible failure of the cardiorespiratory system which leads to 'a permanent state of tissue anoxia'. It is, however, possible to override failure of both the cardiovascular and the respiratory systems by mechanical means, the commonest relevant procedure being the provision of ventilator support in intensive care units; the heart is thereby adequately supplied with oxygen and will continue to beat normally. To decide whether a patient who is being artificially maintained in this way is dead, it is necessary to go back and assess the status of the controller of respiration — the brain and, in particular, the brain stem where the respiratory centre lies. The diagnosis of death by means of brain stem function is, effectively, diagnosing the impossibility of autonomous cardiorespiratory life. Something less than 1 per cent of all deaths fall to be so diagnosed[1] and the concept is now accepted on a world-wide basis. The only controversy relates to whether physicians should speak in terms of whole brain death or of brain stem death.

Much of the confusion could be dissembled if it were to be clearly understood that death is an absolute — there should be no attempt to relate life to a sapient state[2]. The various parts of the brain differ in their sensitivity to oxygen lack. The brain stem is the least sensitive and, since the majority of lesions resulting in destruction of brain cells are accompanied by cerebral hypoxia, it is very nearly impossible to conceive of brain stem death occurring in the presence of a functioning higher brain — primary brain stem haemorrhage might present difficulties but one is driven to thinking in terms of judicial hanging or beheading to provide examples. But, as Pallis has pointed out[3], massive localised lesions in the brain stem must result in respiratory failure — could one conceive of a greater hell for a patient showing some activity in the higher brain to be ventilated with the express and only purpose of perpetuating helpless awareness for the few days before the heart irrevocably stopped? Such a concept might, of itself, be sufficient to deflect those who argue that whole brain death should be proved by means of a negative electroencephalographic tracing before death is pronounced; in fact, there are additional physiological and technical reasons why such tests are unnecessary[4].

It has been stated firmly in the UK that, medically speaking, death of the brain stem constitutes death of the person as a whole[5]. The principle that the diagnosis can be made clinically has also been laid down[6]. It is very important to note that the UK criteria, in addition to proving an absence of brain stem reflexes (which includes an inability to maintain spontaneous respiration) interpose some essential pre-conditions; these include the presence of apnoeic coma due to a brain disorder of the type which can lead to brain death and the exclusion of reversible causes of apnoeic coma such as hypothermia, metabolic disease (eg. diabetes) or drug overdose. All diagnoses are dependent upon the passage of time for observation and on the repetition of the specific tests of function.

Much has been said as to a need to legislate the definition of death[7] but it may be felt to be illogical to insist on statutory regulation in the use of the brain as an indicator of death when none has ever been required in the case of cardiorespiratory function. In practice, British judges have been at pains to recognise good medical practice while, at the same time, refusing to make their own definitions[8]. No apposite civil cases have been reported in the UK but there may be difficulties which are related not so much to the fact of death as to the time of death. It is clear that death must actually have occurred some time before the diagnosis is made, the precise time being unascertainable. Moreover, the time at which the diagnosis itself is made is, to some extent, arbitrary. It is possible, therefore, that the operation of time bars or time exclusion clauses in insurance policies and the like could raise problems; one apparently insoluble question relates to the application of the commorientes rules to brain stem death.

It is, perhaps, not widely understood that the main advantage in accepting the principle of brain stem death is to the patient and to the relatives, death thereby being allowed to take its natural place in the pattern of irremediable brain damage. At the same time, it offers great help to independent parties in opening the way to the provision of high quality organs for transplantation through the medium of the beating heart donor. *Post mortem* viability of individual tissues cannot, however, be maintained indefinitely. The heart will cease to beat within a few days of brain stem death occurring[9].

See also: Anoxia; Beating heart donor; Commorientes; Electroencephalogram; Persistent vegetative state; Transplantation of organs; Ventilator support

1. Jennett B and Hessett C 'Brain death in Britain as reflected in renal donors' (1981) 283 Br Med J 359.
2. But legal minds often appear ambivalent on the point. *See* Scarman Lord 'Legal liability in medicine' (1981) 74 J Roy Soc Med 11; Skegg PDG 'Irreversibly comatose individuals: alive or dead?' (1974) 33 Camb LJ 130; Williams G 'Euthanasia' (1977) 41 Med-Leg J 14.
3. Pallis C *ABC of brain stem death* (1983) BMA, London. This pamphlet gives an excellent overview of the subject.
4. For the early US view, *see* Beecher HK 'After the "definition of irreversible coma"' (1969) 281 New Engl J Med 1070; Mohandas A and Chou SN 'Brain death — a clinical and pathological study' (1971) 35 J Neurosurg 211. For an opposing view, *see*, for example, Van Till-d'Aulnis de Bourouill A 'How dead can you be?' (1975) 15 Med Sci Law 133; Evans DW and Lum LC 'Cardiac transplantation' [1980] 1 Lancet 933.
5. Conference of Royal Medical Colleges and their Faculties in the United Kingdom 'Diagnosis of death' [1979] 1 Br Med J 332.
6. Conference of Royal Medical Colleges and their Faculties in the United Kingdom 'Diagnosis of brain death' [1976] 2 Br Med J 1187.
7. For opposing opinions, *see* Skegg PDG 'The case for a statutory "definition of death"' (1976) 2 J Med Ethics 190; Kennedy I 'The definition of death' (1977) 3 J Med Ethics 5.
8. *Finlayson v HM Adv* 1978 SLT (Notes) 60; *R v Malcherek, R v Steel* [1981] 2 All ER 422.
9. Jennett B, Gleave J and Wilson P 'Brain death in three neurosurgical units' (1981) 282 Br Med J 533.

Further reading
Molinari GF 'Brain death, irreversible coma, and words doctors use' (1982) 32 Neurology 400.

Brain Swelling

Generalised swelling of the brain is a most dangerous complication of head injury, particularly in the young, and may occur in the absence of fracture or of more specific intracranial lesions. Somewhat similar but asymmetric swelling sometimes occurs in association with localised injury.

The accumulated fluid acts, in effect, as a space-occupying lesion and the whole brain, including the brain stem, may be rendered hypoxic. The accumulation of fluid is at cellular level and it cannot therefore be simply aspirated. It follows that post-traumatic brain swelling is difficult to treat and decompression is often attempted through burr holes or skull flaps; the fact that this may result in further localised brain damage is a price which must be paid for alleviating the major lesion.

See also: Head injury

Breathalysers

Breath testing provides the definitive evidence relating to charges under the Road Traffic Act 1972, s.6(1) since the passing of the Transport Act 1981; this is subject only to the availability and satisfactory operation of an approved apparatus. It is now an offence to be driving or to be in charge of a vehicle while having a breath alcohol concentration in excess of 35 μg/100 ml (s.12(2)).

Breath analysis machines in current use in the UK operate on the principle that alcohol absorbs radiation in the infrared region of the spectrum and that the amount of infrared light absorbed by a vapour is proportional to the concentration of alcohol in that vapour[1]. Breath analysis machines are self-calibrated so as to eliminate the influence of any alcohol in the surrounding atmosphere. The process of operation is to record automatically the zero state, to record a control simulated breath specimen and to estimate, in relation to these, the alcohol content of a specimen of breath passed into the machine. Acetone, which is produced in the blood of diabetics, is the only volatile substance likely to be present in the breath and the machines are designed, by including a special detector cell, to eliminate false positives due to this substance.

Infrared breathalysers are not, however, specific for ethyl alcohol (ethanol) which is the alcohol in social use. Methyl alcohol (methanol), glycol and several other volatile hydrocarbons — contained, for example, in petrol — will be recognised by the machine. Such substances are, however, either highly toxic and unlikely to be present in significant quantities in a conscious subject or are not absorbed into the blood stream and therefore do not appear in the breath. It is possible that, say, petroleum fumes — or, indeed, ethanol fumes — could be regurgitated if 'belched' from the stomach during breath testing but, to guard against this, the Act requires the provision of two breath specimens; the lower result is that which is presented in evidence (s.8(6)).

The basic problem presented by breath analysis as a definitive test of driving with a body alcohol in excess of the prescribed limit is that the accused is unable to make a concurrent test using an analyst independent of the police. As some acceptance of this criticism, the Road Traffic Act 1972, s.8(6) as amended, allows that a blood or urine test may be substituted if the breath analysis gives a result between 35 μg and 50 μg alcohol/100 ml breath. Nevertheless, it was inevitable that defences would be built around inadequacies in the technology and, at the time of writing, an interim period has been declared in England and Wales whereby an accused motorist who is dissatisfied with his breath analysis can demand a blood analysis with the consequent provision of a specimen for his own use[2]. No such obligation upon the police exists in Scotland but, in practice, the machine is declared 'out of order' if there is a discrepancy of more than 20 per cent in the values of the two mandatory breath specimens; the constable may then demand a blood or urine specimen under the terms of the Act (s.8(3)).

See also: Alcohol; Road Traffic Act 1972

1. For a very thorough analysis of the efficiency of breath alcohol analysers, *see* Emmerson VJ et al 'The measurement of breath alcohol' (1980) 20 J Forens Sci Soc 3.
2. For an example of the potential physiological hazards of breath analysis, *see* Gatt JA 'The effect of temperature and blood:breath ratio on the interpretation of breath alcohol results' (1984) 134 NLJ 249. The possibilities as to mechanical breakdown are beyond the scope of this entry.

Bruises

A bruise is an extravasation of blood into the tissues. It always results from blunt force; the presence of bruising is inversely proportional to the sharpness of an object which causes injury to the skin. The extent of bruising is limited by the surrounding tissues. Thus, for the same force, it will be greater in lax tissues, such as in the eyelid, than it will in fibrous areas such as the outer side of the thigh. Bruising is more severe in the elderly and in children than in young adults; a bleeding diathesis, such as haemophilia, will grossly exacerbate a bruise in any subject. Permeation of blood through the tissues will be affected by gravity — a bruise which has its origin in the deep tissues of the face may appear as a collection of blood in the soft tissues of the neck. Bruising of the deep tissues may be extensive and show no evidence on the skin; this is particularly true of blunt injury to the abdominal wall. The extravasation of blood and movement within the tissue may continue for some time; in cases of assault it is therefore always worthwhile to re-examine the subject, say, 24 hours after the supposed offence.

A bruise, being a result of forcible pressure, may be maximal on the inside of the tissues if there is bone beneath. Thus, severe bruising of the scalp may be present on the inner surface yet be invisible from the outside; similarly, bruising of the lips may not be seen unless the inside of the mouth is examined.

Whilst bruises are, as a result, uncertain indicators of their cause, 'fingertip' bruising is generally diagnostic in appearance. This consists of a series of two to three bruises, each approximately 1 cm in diameter, and results from gripping. It is very common in cases of sexual assault and child abuse (*see* 'Non-accidental injury in children').

During resolution of a bruise, the haemoglobin is converted to bile pigments. This process shows as a colour change — generally from the purple–blue of the original to brown, to green, then yellow before fading finally. A bruise can subsist for some 7–14 days but the time is so dependent upon variables such as extent and depth that it is extremely difficult to 'date' a single bruise with any precision. It may be useful to be able to say a bruise is 'not recent' but the most important aspect of ageing bruises lies in their comparison as this may be the key to the recognition of repetitive injury. Bruises may undergo repair — particularly if they lie in a fibrous space rather than in the tissues — in which case microscopic changes with time may be found which are similar to those seen in wounds.

Bruises become very much more prominent when the body is exsanguinated; as a result, there may be marked discrepancies between the reports of consecutive postmortem dissections in this respect[1]. They may be produced *post mortem* although they then do not spread so obviously.

See also: Assault and battery; Non-accidental injury in children; Rape; Wounds

1. *See*, for example, Foot, P *The Helen Smith Story* (1983) Fontana, London.

Buggery

Buggery is proscribed under the Sexual Offences Act 1956, s.12. In England and Wales it may be either sodomy or bestiality; both are described under separate headings. There is no comparable statute law in Scotland where both sodomy and bestiality are offences at common law. The term 'buggery' has not been used since 1570 in Scotland where it is doubtful if having anal intercourse with a consenting adult woman constitutes a crime as such[1].

See also: Bestiality; Sodomy

1. Gordon, GH *The Criminal Law of Scotland* (2nd ed, 1978) p.894, W Green, Edinburgh.

Bullets

Bullets, in general, consist of a lead core which is cased in copper alloy. They may be composite, most rifle bullets having a leading cone of aluminium. The nose is either sharply pointed or relatively gently rounded but the stability of the bullet in flight is maintained by rotation which is imparted by the rifling of the barrel — the bullet is fractionally larger than the barrel and is gripped by the spiral grooving of the latter which is imparted during manufacture. The bullet will therefore be marked by the grooves or rifling as it passes down the barrel but the 'lands', or barrel surface between the grooves, will also have minor irregularities which will be reflected on the surface of the bullet. Bullets fired from the same weapon will be similarly and specifically marked; recovery of bullets from a shooting incident is therefore essential so that comparisons of patterns can be made after tests using suspect weapons. The destructive energy of a bullet is proportional to its mass but also to the square of its velocity; modern weapons are therefore designed to increase the muzzle velocity which allows for reduction of mass and, as a result, an increased capacity for fire. The 0.223 calibre Armalite bullet has a muzzle velocity of some 990 m/s as compared with the 0.22 short rifle bullet's speed of 275 m/s which is, even so, described as high velocity.

The bullet is held in a cartridge which is a metal cylinder adapted at its base to any ejection mechanism — thus, it is 'rimmed' for use with non-automatic weapons such as revolvers and rimless in automatics. The base of the cartridge case contains the detonator, which is activated by the firing pin of the weapon, and the propellant powder. The cartridge case will be marked by the firing pin, the ejection mechanism and by insertion and extraction; this will, again, be specific to the weapon, and comparative examination of spent cartridge cases may be as informative to identification, or even more so, than is the examination of bullets[1].

See also: Rifled weapon injuries

1. For a thorough and easily read description of ballistics see Bradford LW and McCafferty J 'Firearms evidence' in Camps FE and Lucas BGB (eds) *Gradwohl's Legal Medicine* (3rd ed, 1976) Chap.13, Wright, Bristol.

Burden of Proof

The legal burden of proof is the burden which falls on a party to prove those facts which will justify a decision in his or her favour. This burden usually falls on the party who initiates the action; in a civil case this will be the plaintiff, and the prosecution will have to discharge the burden of proof in a criminal matter. The burden in criminal proceedings is that of establishing the defendant's guilt beyond a reasonable doubt, whilst in civil matters it is that of proving facts on the balance of probabilities. The latter burden is clearly the easier to discharge. The defendant in the criminal case is entitled to an acquittal if a jury has a doubt such as a reasonable man would hold as to his guilt[1].

See also: Evidential burden

1. *Woolmington v DPP* [1935] AC 462; *R v Bentley* [1960] Crim LR 777.

Burial

The law regarding burial of dead bodies was rationalised in the Local Government Act 1972. The provision and maintenance of cemeteries is now the responsibility of Burial Authorities (s.214(1)).

Detailed regulations as to how the body is to be interred are given in the Local Authorities' Cemeteries Order 1974. The overriding concerns are for public decency and public health. The registrar must inform the local community physician if he has received no notice of disposal within 14 days of the issue of his certificate for disposal; a magistrate may order the burial of a body if its retention above ground constitutes a danger to health[1]. The general laws distancing a cemetery from houses and public places have been repealed and the siting of burial grounds is now a matter of regulation by byelaw.

There is a common law obligation resting on persons in possession of a dead body to dispose of it in 'a manner suitable to the estate'[2] and this obligation cannot be evaded by the provisions of a will[3]; directions made in a will as to the precise methods of disposal cannot, however, be binding on the executors[4].

There is a common law right to be buried in one's parish churchyard[5]; the local authority must take the responsibility when no other arrangements have been made[6].

Burial of a body which has been returned to England or Wales is subject to the issue by the local registrar of a certificate of non-liability to register and the fact of disposal must be notified to the registrar; burial of a body returned to Scotland is simply controlled by the local cemetery authority.

See also: Coroner; Disposal of the dead; Procurator fiscal; Registrar of births, deaths and marriages

1. Public Health Act 1936, s.162; Public Health (Scotland) Act 1897, s.69.
2. *Rees v Hughes* [1946] 1KB 517.
3. Administration of Estates Act 1925, ss.32–34.
4. *Williams v Williams* (1882) 20 ChD 659.
5. *Preston Corporation v Pyke* [1929] 2 ChD 338.
6. National Assistance Act 1948, s.50 as amended.

Further reading
Russell Davies MR *The Law of Burial, Cremation and Exhumation* (5th ed, 1982) Shaw, London.

Burning

Death from burning may be immediate or delayed. Immediate death can, in some instances, be ascribed to pain and physical destruction of tissue. More often, a raised carboxyhaemoglobin (COHb) is discovered, when the question arises as to whether this represents no more than an indication of survival in fire or whether death was, in fact, due to carbon monoxide poisoning; it seems doubtful if the latter can be accepted unless the COHb value exceeds 60 per cent. There is increasing evidence that some deaths may be due to poisoning by cyanide or other rapid asphyxiants derived from polymeric furnishing materials[1].

Severe burning may produce artefacts including, in particular, fracture of the long bones and of the skull and extradural haemorrhage. The distinction between death from burning and *post mortem* burning following death from injury may thus be difficult to make in the context of accident investigation. For some reason, the two parameters most likely to assist — a raised carboxyhaemoglobin and the discovery of soot in the air passages — do not always run true to expectation but they will not be discovered unless they are sought; post-mortem dissection is essential to the accurate certification of the cause of death in those dying in conflagrations. The result may be of particular importance in the solution of problems relating to commorientes. It is to be noted, however, that a comparison of raised COHb levels cannot be used to assess the relative speeds of dying in fire.

The occurrence and causation of burning vary particularly with age and with the society concerned. Thus, in the UK burning from fire and hot fluids is common in children and in the aged — the latter often being associated with locomotor or cerebral disability. The serious association between open fires and alighting of clothing has been greatly reduced by manufacturing practice and by legislation[2]. Suicide by burning is rare other than as an occasional political act, suttee in India having been outlawed for many years. Accidental burning is, however, extremely common in countries such as India where much open stove cooking is done. Homicidal burning must be very rare save as a concomitant of arson although, again, some societies provide remarkable exceptions — 500 brides were reported as having been 'done to death' by burning in Delhi in 1981 as part of the pattern of 'dowry deaths'[3]. Burning is, of course, a major form of injury in war time, the crews of tanks being particularly susceptible[4].

Delayed death from burning is most often due to infection or surgical shock resulting from loss of fluids or from a combination of both[5]; recovery from shock still leaves the patient at risk from kidney failure of a type which is particularly resistant to treatment. The delayed mortality from burning depends mainly on the age of the patient and on the extent of the body area involved. Thus, with modern treatment, a 20-year-old person may well survive a burn involving 60 per cent of the body surface; a 60-year-old is likely to die if only 25 per cent of the body is affected. The openness of burn wounds renders them particularly liable to invasion by bacteria which may be very resistant to antibiotics; the success of a burns treatment unit depends to a large extent on the measures taken to combat cross-infection between patients.

See also: Agonal period; Burns; Carbon monoxide poisoning; Carboxyhaemoglobin; Commorientes; Cyanide; Kidney failure

1. Anderson RA, Watson AA and Harland WA 'Fire deaths in the Glasgow area: II. The role of carbon monoxide' (1981) 21 Med Sci Law 288.
2. For example, Heating Appliances (Fireguards) Act 1952; Children's Nightwear Regulations 1964 (SI 173/64).
3. Das Gupta SM and Tripathi CB 'Burnt wife syndrome' (1984) 13 Ann Acad Med Singapore 37.
4. Ben-Hur N and Soroff H 'Combat burns in the 1973 October war and the anti-tank missile burn syndrome' (1975) 1 Burns 217.
5. An excellent overview is to be found in Brown RF 'Injury by burning' in Mason JK (ed) *The Pathology of Violent Injury* (1978) Chap.7, Edward Arnold, London.

Burns

Burns may be of thermal or chemical type; in either case, the resultant injury is destruction of the skin, the integrity of which is essential for many physiological processes including the regulation of temperature and the preservation of the fluid component of the tissues. The best known type of burn is due to fire and it is this type which will be discussed. Burns due to scalding by liquids are, however, frequent in children and in industry which is also the most common source of chemical burns.

The external application of heat or corrosive fluids may cause anything from reddening of the skin to charring of the deep tissues but, for practical purposes, it is convenient to classify burns as being of partial skin thickness — when the skin may regenerate itself, full thickness — which will require skin grafting for healing to take place — and deep — which will cause extensive destruction of the subcutaneous tissues and muscles and which will involve not only major surgical treatment but also consequent severe disability and deformity. The skin proteins coagulate and full thickness burns result if the deepest layers of the skin reach a temperature of 45°C.

Burnt skin dies and forms an eschar (scab) beneath which granulation tissue, containing fibrous elements, forms. The healing severe burn thus forms scar tissue which is not only disfiguring but also contracts leading to serious physical deformity; the prevention of such conditions is the essence of good treatment. Scarring following deep partial thickness burns may become hypertrophic or excessive; such relatively common scars tend to improve with time and are to be distinguished from the rare keloid scar — this is a variation which is progressive and recurrent when excised. The development of carcinoma in burn scars is well documented and causation is generally not difficult to prove despite the very considerable time lapse which is frequently seen.

Post mortem burns may be distinguished from those occurring in life in that they show no vital reaction. Coagulation and contraction of the skin and muscle proteins may occur, leading to the common pugilistic attitude of charred bodies. The stiffness of coagulated muscles must not be confused with rigor mortis.

See also: Burning; Causation; Rigor mortis; Scars; Vital reaction

C

Cadaveric Spasm

In this condition, the muscles go into spasm in such a way that sustained muscular contraction just before death is maintained after death. It is a very rare phenomenon which appears to be associated with high emotional tension at the time of death. Its medico-legal importance is that it accurately records the deceased's last living state. It most commonly presents as the hand gripping some 'life line' — as in a drowning person clutching at reeds — but bizarre instances of whole body spasm have been reported in battle conditions. Cadaveric spasm of the hand around the firing mechanism of a firearm is virtually diagnostic of suicide. The condition must be distinguished from rigor mortis but true cadaveric spasm cannot be simulated by rigor which is non-specific and of less intensity.

See also: Changes after death; Rigor mortis

Cancer

'Cancer' is a vernacular term which covers all malignant tumours. Medically, malignant tumours can be divided into carcinomas — which derive from epithelium such as the skin or the gut lining — and sarcomas — which arise in connective tissue such as bone and muscle. Cancer of the blood-forming organs is rather different; most forms are associated with the white cells of the blood and are known as leukaemias. Malignant tumours are distinguished from benign tumours in that they invade the surrounding tissues (local malignancy) and, most importantly, they metastasise — which is to say that they are distributed to distant parts of the body by a process of embolisation. In general, although not absolutely, carcinomas metastasise through the lymphatic system and sarcomas through the blood stream.

The fundamental nature of cancer is unknown but it clearly stems from a genetic abnormality arising in a single cell or a group of cells which can be passed from cell to cell as division occurs. The general preventive medical problem of cancer lies in distinguishing those factors which precipitate such a genetic change, and the specific medico-legal importance rests on the fact that many of these derive from theoretically preventable causes; the forensic issue is therefore one of causation.

The precise mode of action of most carcinogenic (cancer-producing) agents is not known and the probability is that there is interaction of several factors of various types. Pragmatically, it can be said that ionising radiation sustained in moderate dosage will increase the risk of certain cancers — indeed, non-ionising radiation in the form of ultraviolet light also predisposes to cancer of the skin. The same can be said of some chemicals, of which the most important are the anthracene group of hydrocarbons. This may have very important associations with industrial causation; the potentiating effects of the hydrocarbons of tobacco smoke with the inflammatory reaction in the lungs provoked by the presence of asbestos bodies is a good example of the multifactorial nature of carcinogenesis. Cancer is also more likely to occur in tissues which are actively growing — this includes those which are being repaired and would account for the increased incidence of cancer in scars, particularly those due to burning. Any form of chronic irritation may 'promote' a cancer in cells which have achieved the potential for malignant change; in this connection, the role of viruses is a nagging consideration — particularly exemplified in the possible causation of carcinoma of the female uterine cervix (see 'Sexually transmitted diseases').

In summary, proof of causation of a cancer as a result of a single incident or type of exposure can seldom be absolute. Moreover, not everyone exposed to an identical agent will develop cancer and similar tumours will always be found in persons who have not been so exposed. At the end of the day, a cause and effect can, as in all civil actions, be decided or refuted only on the basis of probability; the sad feature is that this is not a basis on which it is possible to satisfy all interested parties.

See also: Asbestosis; Causation; Embolism; Radiation hazards; Sexually transmitted disease; Smoking; Wounds

Cannabis and Its Aliases

The use by many ethnic cultures of extracts of the plant *Cannabis sativa* as mild inebriants or hallucinogens is as old as man. The British adopted the general term 'hashish' to describe the drug in India; this name became associated with the word assassin and, accordingly, with crime. A committee of inquiry appointed by the British Indian government in the late nineteenth century[1] found — strongly against the prevailing opinion — that there was no relationship between hemp and either insanity or crime save when it was used to excess. Its effect was, therefore, to be compared with alcohol or, even, with tobacco.

Similar extracts are known in the USA as marihuana[2]. A major effect of smoking or otherwise absorbing the drug is a sensation of timelessness — it was therefore much used by musicians of the inter-war years and it is probable that the use of a commercial crop as a source of psychotropic drugs spread from that cult. Although it was at one time used to a minor extent in medicine in the USA, it was abandoned as a therapeutic drug owing to its unpredictability as to action. Marihuana was accorded the same status as narcotics in the federal Marihuana Act 1937. Subsequent inquiries — notably those set up by the Mayor of New York[3] and by President Nixon[4] — also failed to trace an association between the moderate use of marihuana and physical or mental deterioration or with crime. The great majority of modern reports[5,6] are either ambivalent as to its adverse properties or come to the firm conclusion that it is harmless when used in moderation[7]. The impression is that official attitudes in the USA are changing and that little notice is now taken of the possession of small quantities of the substance. However, as with the chewing of coca leaves in South America, there is no certainty that the use of a single derivative of the natural substance — in that case, cocaine — will have the same effect as is found in the social use of the natural substance, and much depends on the motivation of the user.

The drug is known generically as cannabis in the UK — although being referred to more commonly in the vernacular as 'pot' or 'grass'. The leaves and flowers of the plant may be smoked in 'joints' or may be added to a tobacco cigarette. Cannabis itself is classified as a Class B controlled drug under the Misuse of Drugs Act 1971; its active ingredient, tetrahydrocannabinol (THC) is placed in Class A.

The typical psychological effect of cannabinol is to enhance the user's sense of well-being and to distort his spatial relationships. Those who regard the use of cannabis as socially unacceptable point to the fact that the user may feel disinclined to work; the association of the use of cannabis by young people with personal irresponsibility and lack of motivation has caused particular concern[8].

Cannabis is not an addictive drug in the accepted sense but there may be considerable psychological dependence. There is no necessary progression from the use of a 'soft' drug such as cannabis to the use of 'hard' drugs such as heroin but there is some evidence that many addicts with a serious drug problem have used cannabis in the earlier stages of their drug abuse[9].

A more serious view is taken of being in possession with intention to supply cannabis than of the simple offence of being in possession[10]; the defence of ignorance that the substance possessed was cannabis is now allowed[11] but the burden of proving ignorance rests on the defendant[12]. Moreover, in *Peregrine Boyesen*[13], the Court of Appeal held that conviction should result only when usable quantities of the drug were possessed.

See also: Drug addiction; Controlled drugs; Misuse of Drugs Act 1971

1. Young WM (Chairman) *The Indian Hemp Drugs Commission Report 1893–4* (1897).
2. Many other names are used locally — e.g. bhang, daja, ganja, kif.
3. Report of Mayor La Guardia's Committee on Marihuana. *The Marihuana Problem in the City of New York* (1944).
4. US National Commission on Marihuana and Drug Abuse *Marihuana: A Signal of Misunderstanding* (1972) (Shafer Report).
5. Relman AS 'Marijhuana and health' (1982) 306 New Engl J Med 603.
6. Evans MA et al 'Effects of marijhuana smoking on pulmonary function in man' (1984) 3 Med Law 253.
7. Advisory Committee on Drug Dependence *Cannabis* (1965) HMSO, London.
8. Lamanna M 'Marijhuana: implications of use by young people' (1981) 11 J Drug Depend 281.
9. Gordon AM 'Do drug offences matter?' [1978] 2 Br Med J 185.
10. Misuse of Drugs Act 1971, s.5.
11. For a discussion on the legal control of cannabis, *see* Farrier D *Drugs and Intoxication* (1980) p.84 et seq, Sweet & Maxwell, London.
12. *R v Champ* [1982] Crim LR 108.
13. (1980) 72 Crim App R 43. *See also* Bentil JK 'Possession of minute drug quantities' (1982) 126 SJ 388.

Capital Punishment

Capital punishment is still used extensively in world-wide terms. It was, however, abolished in several European countries in the nineteenth century[1] but only ceased to be available as a punishment for homicide in Britain after the passing of the Murder (Abolition of Death Penalty) Act 1965. Technically, sentence of death may still be applied in cases of treason and piracy with violence[2] but it is more than unlikely that it would be carried out today even in such circumstances. Nevertheless, there remains a body of opinion in favour of its reintroduction, especially for terrorism-inspired homicide.

The method of execution in Britain was traditionally hanging whereby, in the modern process, death is brought about by destruction of the upper spinal cord and brain stem. Other methods still in use include electrocution, death by shooting, cyanide gas poisoning and lethal injection. The last provokes particular difficulties for members of the medical profession who cannot, ethically, participate in capital punishment except to confirm the extinction of life. The Royal Commission on Capital Punishment[3], which reported in 1953, concluded that judicial hanging was as quick and as painless a system as could be reasonably required, a conclusion with which not all would agree[4].

The rate of executions in non-abolitionist countries differs greatly. Many countries provide no statistics whilst others reveal the number of people who have been executed by the State and, thereby, attract criticism. South Africa, for example, executed 132 persons in 1978; Pakistan reported the execution of 800 people in the same year.

Capital punishment was not carried out in many of the United States in the 1960s and 1970s, partly as a result of abolitionist pressures and partly because of legal difficulties. The Supreme Court has since opened the way to the reimposition of the death penalty by recognising the validity of certain forms of death sentence statutes, and a number of executions have since followed[5].

Capital punishment can be objected to on the straightforward moral ground that it is intrinsically wrong to take life in any circumstances (other than in self-defence). It can also be attacked on aesthetic grounds — that it is a brutalising process which harms the society which applies it. Most supporters of capital punishment will claim deterrence as a justification but there is no supportive criminological consensus on the point[6].

See also: Brain stem death

1. The Portugese abolition law, for example, dates from 1867. Norway abolished the death penalty in 1905 although there had been no executions in the previous 30 years.
2. Treason Act 1914, s.1; Piracy Act 1837, s.2.
3. Gowers EA (chairman) *Report of the Royal Commission on Capital Punishment*, 1949–1953 (Cmd 8932) (1953) HMSO, London.
4. There are some disturbing associations with the concept of brain stem death — Pallis C *ABC of Brain Stem Death* (1983) p.9, BMA, London.
5. Radin MJ 'The jurisprudence of death: evolving standards for the cruel and unjust punishment clause' (1978) 126 U Pa LR 989.
6. Walker N *Crime and Punishment in Britain* (2nd ed, 1968) p.237 et seq, Edinburgh University Press, Edinburgh; Bowers WJ 'Deterrence or brutalisation: what is the effect of executions?' (1980) 26 Crim Delinq 453.

Carbon Dioxide

Carbon dioxide, together with water, is the product of perfect combustion of hydrocarbons in the presence of oxygen. Thus blood in the veins contains more carbon dioxide in solution, with less oxygen combined with haemoglobin, than does that in the arteries. The presence of carbon dioxide in the blood stimulates respiration; there is, thus, a servo mechanism operating whereby excess carbon dioxide is flushed from the respiratory system as it accumulates in the body.

This delicate balance can be upset in two ways. Firstly, overbreathing will eliminate carbon dioxide; there will thus be no stimulus to breathe and the subject may become dangerously hypoxic — a problem of importance to swimmers and to aviators, both of whom may become comatose in a hostile environment. Secondly, the environment may accumulate carbon dioxide to an unacceptable extent and result in dangerous blood levels. In this case, true carbon dioxide poisoning, as opposed to simple hypoxia, may occur. This is most commonly a hazard of closed circuit diving but may contribute to death in any sealed space; bizarre instances due to the excessive use of nebulisers containing carbon dioxide in enclosed spaces have been reported.

See also: Diving hazards; Hypoxia

Carbon Monoxide Poisoning

In this type of poisoning, carbon monoxide attaches itself to the oxygen-combining sites on the haemoglobin molecule, forming carboxyhaemoglobin. The affected haemoglobin is no longer available for the carriage of oxygen and the tissues are subjected to hypoxia. Since haemoglobin has an affinity for carbon monoxide which is some 300 times its affinity for oxygen and since dissociation is correspondingly reduced, absorption of carbon monoxide is cumulative and is time/concentration related; thus, although equilibrium is eventually established, very small amounts of the gas in inspired air can be injurious or lethal if breathed for sufficiently long, whilst strong concentrations have a rapid effect. The degree of poisoning is usually expressed as the percentage of the haemoglobin which has been converted to carboxyhaemoglobin. Clearly, the respiratory rate will influence absorption. A sitting man breathing 0.07 per cent carbon monoxide in air will achieve a blood carboxyhaemoglobin concentration of 25 per cent in about 1 hour; the same man walking will reach a similar saturation in 30 minutes.

The domestic gas supply was, at one time, an important provider of carbon monoxide as 'town gas' contained 7–10 per cent of the gas. This source has virtually disappeared with the widespread use of natural gas. Gas appliances may, however, still cause intoxication, as the most constant source of carbon monoxide is inefficient combustion of hydrocarbons — inefficient is, in this sense, almost inevitable because production of pure carbon dioxide is achieved only in intense fires such as are produced in military flame throwers. Coke braziers, paraffin and butane gas heaters produce relatively large amounts of carbon monoxide and, since the atmospheric concentration is enhanced by poor ventilation, the watchman's hut, the bathroom and the caravan are frequent sites of accidental poisoning. The internal combustion engine is a potent source and both accidental and suicidal poisoning occur fairly often in garages. Air which is heated by engine exhausts may be contaminated through leaks; the cabin heating air may be a cause of transportation accidents or of deaths in parked cars. Coal miners are exposed to carbon monoxide due to the large number of small fires which occur in underground workings. Atmospheric pollution may give rise to chronic minor poisoning in traffic policemen whilst the majority of heavy smokers maintain a blood carboxyhaemoglobin of up to 8 per cent. Carbon monoxide is produced in nearly all conflagrations; its relationship to death from burning is discussed under the latter heading.

Symptomatic carbon monoxide poisoning may range from headache and impaired cerebral function at a level of 15–25 per cent carboxyhaemoglobin to death in most persons at 60 per cent saturation. Any additional cause of tissue hypoxia — such as pulmonary disease or high altitude — will, of course, accentuate the dangers of carbon monoxide. The cerebral hypoxia induced by carbon monoxide poisoning may result in severe brain damage following recovery. There is also growing evidence that carbon monoxide dissolved in the blood plasma has a direct toxic effect on tissue enzymes.

See also: Accidental death; Burning; Carboxyhaemoglobin; Hypoxia; Suicide

Carboxyhaemoglobin

Carboxyhaemoglobin (COHb) is formed when inspired carbon monoxide combines with the haemoglobin of the red blood cells. The transport of oxygen is thereby inhibited and the tissues are rendered hypoxic to an extent related to the proportion of haemoglobin which is converted to carboxyhaemoglobin — generally expressed as a percentage of the total haemoglobin.

The resultant symptoms vary between individuals but may be summarised:

15–25 per cent:	headache, impairment of higher cerebral functions
25–50 per cent:	increasing dizziness and inco-ordination
50–60 per cent:	unconsciousness
over 60 per cent:	probable death

Carboxyhaemoglobin has a characteristic cherry pink colour which is particularly noticeable in cadaver skin where there is hypostasis; it is also resistant to reduction and may be seen in the formalin solution used to preserve biological tissues. COHb is a stable compound which may be demonstrable in bodies which have been dead for some time[1].

The presence of carboxyhaemoglobin always needs interpreting, particularly in transportation accidental deaths where high values such as are discovered in suicidal carbon monoxide poisoning are unlikely to be achieved — an accident will have been precipitated by the cerebral dysfunction which occurs at relatively low concentrations. Any carboxyhaemoglobin discovered after a fatal vehicular accident may indicate that the driver was significantly intoxicated but it may be no more than a marker of an engine defect without necessarily having produced a physiological effect — a possibility particularly important in aviation accidents. Alternatively, it may make a synergistic contribution to the accident — in conjunction, say, with fatigue or hypoglycaemia — or may be a 'background' value due to smoking or environmental exposure. However, survival in the post crash fire is by far the commonest cause of a raised COHb discovered after a vehicular accident.

The method of analysis of COHb is of some importance. Simple spectrophotometric methods which are suitable for the confirmation of suicidal levels are neither sufficiently accurate nor sufficiently sensitive for use in accident investigation or in environmental studies when a method at least as sensitive as gas chromatography must be used[2].

See also: Accidental death; Aircraft accidents; Burning; Carbon monoxide poisoning; Hypostasis; Hypoxia; Suicide

1. *See*, for example, Camps FE *Medical and Scientific Investigations in the Christie Case* (1953) Medical Publications, London.
2. Blackmore DJ 'The determination of carbon monoxide in blood and tissue' (1970) 95 Analyst 439.

Cardiac Arrest

The most common natural cause of sudden cessation of the heart beat is ischaemia or infarction of a large area of the heart muscle, this being due to blockage or spasm of a main coronary vessel[1]. Vagal inhibition of the heart is the most frequent cause of cardiac arrest in the unnatural situation.

It may well be that the concept of cardiac arrest is false in both instances and that the abnormal electrical activity generated in the muscle leads not so much to complete paralysis of the heart as to ventricular fibrillation in which the heart beat is ineffective. In such circumstances, a further stimulus — whether it be by external cardiac massage or by the passage of a strong electric current — may serve to restore the normal innervation of the heart and, hence, its beat. Emergency treatment for cardiac arrest is now available in all areas where it is likely to occur — as, say, in the postoperative surgical ward — or in specially equipped ambulances designed to take support to the affected patient. A major concern in all such resuscitation attempts must be to avoid the possibility of restoring to life a person who is severely brain damaged following a prolonged period of cerebral hypoxia.

See also: Infarction; Hypoxia; Vagal inhibition of the heart; Ventricular fibrillation

1. Leading Article 'Sudden death' [1978] 2 Br Med J 1734.

Cardiac Tamponade

Cardiac tamponade is the inhibition of the heart action resulting from a sudden buildup of pressure in the pericardial sac. For all practical purposes, blood is the responsible fluid and the underlying condition is known as haemopericardium.

Haemopericardium, and the resultant cardiac tamponade, is the immediate cause of death following rupture of a myocardial infarct; it also commonly occurs following rupture of a dissecting aneurysm of the ascending aorta.

Haemopericardium will also result from bullet or stab wounds of the heart. The former are almost invariably fatal but cardiac tamponade is not inevitable following the latter and some 40 per cent of cardiac stab wounds are survived. This is because the defect in the heart and that in the pericardium may, in ideal circumstances, adjust to each other until natural healing occurs or, more likely, until the defect is treated surgically.

See also: Aneurysm; Aorta; Myocardial infarction

Cardiomyopathy

Cardiomyopathy means abnormality of the cardiac muscle. It is of considerable forensic interest as it is a not uncommon cause of sudden natural death. From this point of view, the most important type is hypertrophic cardiomyopathy and this may be acquired or idiopathic.

In acquired hypertrophic cardiomyopathy, the heart increases in size by virtue of an extra workload. The most common cause is hypertensive disease. Valvular disease used to be common but is now not often seen owing to the conquest of rheumatic disease and the very great reduction in and the treatability of syphilis. The aortic valve is the important structure in the present context. Whether this becomes rigid and reduced in size (stenotic disease) or whether it simply becomes incompetent (regurgitant disease), the left ventricle must work increasingly hard to maintain the volume of blood pumped out on each contraction. In all these cases, the muscle will increase in size (or hypertrophy). The causes of sudden death may then be several but the most commonly held view is that the muscle mass outstrips the coronary arterial supply; death is then due essentially to coronary insufficiency.

Idiopathic hypertrophic cardiomyopathy is an interesting condition in which the heart muscle is anatomically abnormal and the left ventricle becomes greatly enlarged, so much so that the exit paths of the great vessels may become suddenly obliterated[1]. The condition should be picked up at routine medical examinations but often it is not; it is a not infrequent cause of sudden death in young adults — particularly young men while at contact sport.

Of the other forms of cardiomyopathy, that associated with alcohol is the most important medico-legally. The specific connection may be legally significant and it is important that the diagnosis is confirmed microscopically and that the characteristic appearances are proved to be present[2].

Other forms of cardiomyopathy are less well defined although thyrotoxic cardiomyopathy may be invoked occasionally as a cause of sudden death in a person with evidence of overactivity of the thyroid gland. The heart muscle will be involved in any generalised disease of muscle — particularly the muscular dystrophies — but the diagnosis will have been well established in life and the cause of death will be reasonably clear.

See also: Coronary disease; Heart disease; Hypertensive disease; Sudden natural death

1. James TN and Marshall TK 'Asymmetrical hypertrophy of the heart' (1975) 51 Circulation 1149.
2. Stevens PJ 'Unexpected death due to natural disease' in Camps FE and Lucas BGB (eds) *Gradwohl's Legal Medicine* (3rd ed, 1976) p.231, Wright, Bristol.

Cardiovascular System

The cardiovascular system is mainly responsible for harvesting oxygen from the lungs, for distributing it to the tissues and for removing the products of combustion. It also receives foodstuffs processed in the intestines and liver, distributes these to the tissues and removes the waste products through the kidneys. The system circulates hormones elaborated by the endocrine system and is responsible for mobilisation of the body's immune system of both humoral and cellular type — the latter being by means of the white blood cells. The oxygen-carrying function is that of the erythrocytes (red blood cells) which constitute some 45 per cent of the blood volume; the remaining functions are taken over by the plasma or fluid component of the blood.

The system consists essentially of the heart, the arteries, the capillaries and the veins; the circulation is divisible into the pulmonary circulation which relates to the lungs and the systemic circulation which supplies the rest of the body. The heart consists of two thin-walled atria which receive the great veins — those from the lungs, carrying oxygenated blood, entering the left atrium and the venae cavae from the tissues entering the right side. The atria communicate with the ventricles which distribute the blood into the arteries — those exiting from the heart being the pulmonary artery, which transfers used or deoxygenated blood to the lungs, on the right side, and the aorta, which transmits fresh oxygenated blood to the tissues, on the left. The aorta and the arteries are subject to diseases of great medico-legal importance and are described under separate entries. Here it is sufficient to note that considerable pressure is needed to force arterial blood through vessels of steadily diminishing size; the ventricles must therefore be very muscular and this is particularly true of the left ventricle. A system of one-way valves separates the atria from the ventricles and the ventricles from the major arteries; disease of the valves was once an important component of heart disease. The heart is innervated by the autonomic nervous system and is independent of cerebral control. We expect this remarkable organ to contract rhythmically more than two and a half billion times in our lives and, to do so, it must itself be adequately oxygenated. This is achieved through the coronary arteries, which are the first branches of the aorta; disease of the coronary arteries is, therefore, life threatening.

As the arterial branches of the aorta approach the tissues, they divide into smaller vessels until the ultimate blood supply is achieved through the capillaries which are so thin as to allow penetration of gases and metabolites through their walls. The capillaries then collect into veins in which the pressure is low as they have the formation of a river, increasing in size as they are fed by tributaries. The veins also receive fluid from the lymphatic system, which carries the fatty food processed in the intestine and also maintains an extravascular circulation of tissue fluids.

The fetal circulation depends on oxygen obtained from the placenta rather than from the lungs. Two pulmonary bypass mechanisms are present in the fetus — the foramen ovale, which provides a communication between the two atria, and the ductus arteriosus, which diverts blood in the pulmonary artery to the aorta. Both these shunts normally close after birth; failure of the foramen to close is relatively innocuous but a patent ductus may constitute a serious form of congenital heart disease.

The viability of the cardiovascular system is the root of life; it is therefore reasonable to define death as the irreversible failure of the cardiovascular system. It is only when that viability is maintained by extracorporeal support that the definition becomes inadequate.

See also: Aorta; Arteries; Autonomic nervous system; Coronary disease; Death; Endocrine system; Heart disease; Liver disease and injury; Oxygen; Placenta

Care Proceedings

Care proceedings may be used when there is a breakdown in relations between parents and their children. The governing legislation is the Children and Young Persons Act 1969, as amended by the Children Act 1975[1].

Section 1(2) of the 1969 Act lays down several reasons enabling any local authority, policeman or authorised person (who is likely to be an inspector of the NSPCC) to bring a child before the juvenile court. Over half the cases are based on s.1(2)(a), which lays down the condition that the child's proper development is being avoidably prevented or neglected or his health is being avoidably impaired or neglected or he is being ill treated — effectively, a description of child abuse. For an application under this head to succeed, there must be actual impairment or neglect; the probability of such injury is insufficient[2]. This deficiency is, to an extent, covered in s.1(2)(b) which deals with the probability that impairment or neglect will arise but which operates only if there is evidence to that effect from other children in the household. The most important other reasons for action include that the child is exposed to moral danger (s.1(2)(c)) or that, on the other side of the coin, he is beyond the control of his parents or guardian (s.1(2)(d)). In normal circumstances, the child will be brought before the juvenile court but, in an emergency, a policeman can detain a child in a place of safety for eight days if he has reasonable cause to believe a condition of s.1(2)(a–d) to be satisfied and a magistrate may grant a search warrant if an applicant swears that there is reasonable cause for such suspicion; the child may then be taken to a place of safety for a period of 28 days if the constable finds the suspicions justified. An alternative, and far more commonly used emergency procedure, is for a magistrate to make a place of safety order on application, which need not be sworn, from any person if he is satisfied that the applicant has reasonable cause to believe that s.1(2) is being infringed. The place of safety order may last for 28 days and is not subject to appeal. In any case, including one in which the child is already in a place of safety, the court can make an interim care order, which lasts for 28 days, if it is not yet in a position to decide how to dispose of an application. The order may be repeated but, as this is likely to be against the interests of the child, the practice is not well received[3].

Before making an order, the court must hold that one of the conditions of s.1(2) is satisfied and that the child is unlikely to receive the necessary care and control unless the court makes an order. Various options are then open: an order can be made requiring the parents to enter into a recognisance to take proper care of the child; the child can be placed under the supervision of the local authority for a maximum of three years or until the child's eighteenth birthday; a hospital or guardianship order can be made if the child is suffering from specified mental disorder which is likely to be benefited by such an order[4]; or the court may issue a care order which remains in force until the child is aged 18 unless it is previously discharged by the court or the child is adopted. The care order commits the child to the care of the local authority notwithstanding any claim by his parents or guardian[5]. Care orders can be discharged only if there is no risk of the child's being ill treated if returned home; a guardian ad litem must be appointed if the application for discharge is unopposed[6].

Section 28 of the 1969 Act gives rather wider powers to the local authority to obtain a place of safety order whenever it appears that a child may be in danger. In a recent case, such an order was obtained on the grounds that it was believed that an infant had been born to a surrogate mother; it was later considered that this was not the best procedure[7].

The procedures in the juvenile court are cumbersome and have been widely criticised[8]. The proceedings are supposed to be non-party but inevitably assume an adversarial complexion with, as often as not, the parents appearing to be the target. Yet the parents are not parties to the proceedings and cannot obtain legal aid. The parents can bring evidence to refute allegations made against them but, strictly speaking, they have no right of appeal against the court's order. Nevertheless, the court will allow a parent to conduct the case on a child's behalf save in certain circumstances, the most important of which is when the court decides that there is a conflict of interests[7]; a guardian ad litem will then usually be appointed. Moreover, a parent may appeal to the divisional court ostensibly on behalf of the child[9].

The general principles are similar in Scotland but the application is made to the Reporter to the relevant Children's Panel who decides whether to bring the child before a hearing; he will do this only if he considers the child needs compulsory measures of care. A children's hearing is formed by three members of the Children's Panel, which is composed of voluntary members of the local community appointed by the Secretary of State. The child and the parents must usually be present and, although they may be represented, legal aid is not available; the keynote to the hearing is informality. The hearing may decide upon a supervision requirement of varying type[10]; appeal against the decision to the sheriff is available to both the child and the parents.

See also: Child abuse; Non-accidental injury to children

1. And Social Work (Scotland) Act 1968 as amended by the Children Act 1975.
2. *F v Suffolk County Council* (1981) 2 Fam LR 208.
3. *Re S (A minor), Re P (A minor)* (1983) Times, 15 November.
4. Mental Health Act 1983.
5. Child Care Act 1980, s.10.
6. Children and Young Persons Act 1969, s.32A(2) inserted by Children Act 1975, s.64.
7. *In re a Baby* (1985) Times, 15 January.
8. *See*, for example, Medicolegal 'Bringing care proceedings' (1980) 280 Br Med J 1024; Ellison J 'Care proceedings in the juvenile courts' (1984) 134 NLJ 133.
9. *B v Gloucestershire County Council* [1980] 2 All ER 746.
10. Social Work (Scotland) Act 1968 as amended by the Law Reform (Miscellaneous Provisions) (Scotland) Act 1985.

Castration

Castration is clearly indicated and is a lawful operation when there is significant disease of the testes. Castration for non-therapeutic purposes must constitute a maim and is, therefore, to be distinguished from other forms of sterilisation[1]. It is, however, possible to justify the removal of normal testes on more remote therapeutic grounds, the two which cause greatest interest and controversy being the treatment of trans-sexualism and of the sexual offender. The former is now clearly legal subject to approved medical practice; the latter is still problematical and it is to that aspect that this note is directed.

Castration is still regarded as an available method for the treatment of sex offenders or those who are troubled by abnormal sexual desires. The term 'chemical castration' is sometimes applied to non-surgical techniques which involve hormone treatment. Other methods of dealing with such persons include programmes of aversion therapy or other forms of psychotherapy. These methods do not involve significant intervention in the patient's physical integrity but that is not to say that they do not give rise to ethical issues; any attempt to change a person's behaviour through psychotherapy constitutes a radical interference with his autonomy, particularly if the recipient of such treatment is in a weak position to reject it.

Castration has been used for the management of sex offenders in a number of European countries and in the USA. The known schemes have been voluntary, at least in so far as an incarcerated offender can give a true consent. Some of the United States have had eugenic sterilisation laws specifically applicable to criminals but castration was authorised in none of these[1]. Although some evidence has been collated to the effect that the recidivism rate has been reduced amongst those who have been castrated[2], the belief that castration results in the subsequent loss of all sexual drive is naive; the inclination to sexual activity can continue after castration and depends very much on the psychiatric state of the individual. Sexual conduct can run independently of hormonal control, being, to a certain extent, learned behaviour; as Meyers[1] has put it: 'The cause of and answer to the sexual psychopath's abnormal urges lie in his cranium not in his scrotum'.

Psychosurgery, in the form of stereotaxic hypothalamotomy, has been used on sexual offenders and sexual deviants in West Germany in spite of serious misgivings as to the appropriateness of such programmes[3]. The results of these operations have been seriously questioned and it is, in general, an area of which neurosurgeons are extremely wary.

The chemical alternatives to castration involve the administration of antiandrogens, the effect of which is to inhibit the production of male sexual hormones[4]. A reduction in sexual drive may be achieved in this way but there are some unpleasant side effects, such as the development of female secondary sexual characteristics.

The legality of these various methods of dealing with sex offenders is debatable. There must be a strong question mark over the ability of an offender to give a valid consent to such treatment and this applies particularly when the treatment is offered as an alternative to imprisonment; such consent is inherently constrained. It is reported that a rapist was recently offered, and accepted, castration as an alternative to 30 years' imprisonment in South Carolina; no surgeon has been found willing to carry out the operation[5]. The English Mental Health Act 1983 specifically excludes sexual deviancy from the definition of mental disorder; legal consent under the terms of ss.57 and 58 would be particularly difficult in the event of proposed psychosurgery (*see* 'Compulsory medical treatment').

Antiandrogen therapy poses fewer legal problems in that it is reversible. Nevertheless, the implications of such therapy would have to be explained before consent was valid. The success of any therapy depends heavily on the voluntary initiative of the patient[6].

See also: Compulsory medical treatment; Consent to medical treatment; Hormones; Informed consent; Maim; Mental Health Act 1983; Psychosurgery; Trans-sexualism

1. Although it is a somewhat dated monograph, castration as a maim and as a therapy is elegantly discussed in Meyers DW *The Human Body and the Law* (1970) Aldine, Chicago.
2. There is a full survey of the European literature in Heim N and Hursch C 'Castration for sex offenders: treatment or punishment? A review and critique of recent European literature' (1979) 8 Arch Sex Behav 281.
3. Rieber I and Sigusch V 'Psychosurgery on sex offenders and sexual "deviants" in West Germany' (1979) 8 Arch Sex Behav 523.
4. Berlin FS and Meinecke CF 'Treatment of sex offenders with antiandrogenic medication: conceptualization, review of treatment modalities, and preliminary findings' (1981) 138 Am J Psychiat 601. *See also* Halleck SL 'The ethics of antiandrogen therapy' (1981) 138 Am J Psychiat 642.
5. Dunea G 'Sense and senselessness' (1985) 290 Br Med J 776.
6. Chiswick D 'Sex crimes' (1983) 143 Br J Psychiat 236.

Causation

The identification of the cause of an event is important if the law is to attribute responsibility properly in both civil and criminal contexts.

The law recognises factual and legal forms of causation. Questions of factual causation are those of cause in the physical world — whether death results from the infliction of an injury is a scientific question of fact, despite any difficulties there may be of ascertainment. Medical equivocation as to the aetiology of disease need not inhibit the law from reaching conclusions as to what has caused a condition; certainty in this area is not required — it is necessary only that causation be established on the balance of probabilities[1]. A possible test of factual causation is the 'but for' test, which involves calling the question: 'but for the event, would the consequences have occurred?'. Factual causation is established if this is answered in the negative.

Legal causation addresses itself to issues of legal responsibility and, therefore, involves extraneous considerations, frequently of a moral nature. A condition may be factually caused by an act but legal causation may be defeated by other considerations — including those of remoteness or foreseeability. To say that an act is the legal cause of an event is, in effect, to state that the actor should be held legally responsible for that particular consequence.

Several theories of causation have been developed in jurisprudence. These include: (a) direct consequence theories — which aim at the exclusion of indirect consequences and focus on those consequences which are directly traceable to the original act; (b) proximate cause theories — these refer back to the last event of causal significance and identify that as the cause of the consequence; (c) the foreseeability theory — only those consequences which are foreseeable by an actor can be regarded as having been caused by him; and (d) probability theories — an event is caused by an act if that event is one which is usually a consequence of the act in question[2].

Courts have tended to adopt a fairly robust attitude to problems of causation. In short, an act may be identified as a cause if it impresses the court as being significant in the sequence of events; it may, however, be considered causally irrelevant if it is merely a part of the backdrop or setting against which the event in question occurred. A number of decisions stress the importance of common sense, suggesting that too close a dissection of causal links is unnecessary[3]. A remarkable instance of causation interpreted in the 'but for' context is to be found in *Meah v McCreamer* in which the fact that a man was imprisoned for sexual offences was regarded as being due to injuries received as a result of another's negligent driving[4].

There may be situations in which more than one event contributes to the cause of a consequence and it becomes necessary to determine whether one of the events, considered by itself, can be treated as the cause. This issue arises in both civil and criminal contexts. In the former, the rule used to be that a causal contribution to the damage on the part of the plaintiff excluded liability; this rule is now changed and contributory negligence leads merely to a reduction in damages. In the criminal context, responsibility for a concurrent cause can lead to conviction[5]. Thus, if both A and B stab C, each wound contributing to the death of C, both A and B can be treated by the law as having caused C's death equally. The rule is different if there is a subsequent cause which operates to cancel out the first. A will not be regarded as having caused C's death if he pushes C to the ground and then, quite independently, B shoots him as he lies there[6].

It may not be possible to establish the connection between injury and subsequent disability beyond medical doubt, particularly if an injury is suspected of exacerbating or triggering an existing or latent condition (*see* 'Special sensitivity'). Particular difficulty may be experienced in pharmaceutical cases or in those involving exposure to toxic materials. In some, the evidence for a causal link between the noxious substance and injury will be overwhelming — as in the thalidomide cases. In others, the difficulty of establishing a causal link between exposure of substance and a particular injury may be considerable, as when other environmental factors may equally well have produced the condition. Such questions of causation have recently arisen in the USA in the context of actions against the manufacturers of diethylstilb-oestrol (DES)[7] whilst even greater complications have been raised in the claims by US Army veterans to have an increased liability to malignant disease since being exposed to defoliants. In other cases, as when there has been exposure to a high level of radiation, the causal question will be complicated by virtue of a long interval between exposure and the development of disease[8].

Problems of causation have a special place in industrial injury cases. In *Gardiner v Motherwell Machinery and Scrap Company Ltd*[9] (a case of dermatitis) Lord Reid expressed the view that 'when a man who has not previously suffered from a disease contracts that disease after being subjected to conditions likely to cause it, and when he shows that it starts in a way typical of disease caused by such conditions, he establishes a *prima facie* presumption that his disease was caused by those conditions'. This dictum has been criticised as being too strong, it being suggested that there is an *inference* rather than a *presumption* of causation in such circumstances[10].

A causal connection is usually considered to be broken if there is an intervening event of sufficient significance. This question is dealt with under *nova causa interveniens* and refusal of medical treatment.

See also: Contributory negligence; Foreseeability; *Nova causa interveniens*; Pesticides; Pharmaceutical liability; Refusal of medical treatment; Special sensitivity

1. *Ransom v Sir Robert McAlpine and Sons Ltd* (1971) 11 KIR 141.
2. A full account of causation theories is to be found in Hart HLA and Honoré A *Causation in the Law* (2nd ed, 1985) Clarendon, Oxford; *see also* Honoré A 'Causation and Remoteness of Damage' in *The International Encyclopaedia of Comparative Law* (1983) Vol XI, Chap.7, Nijhoff, Dordrecht.
3. *Barty-King v Ministry of Defence* [1979] 2 All ER 80; *R v Criminal Injuries Compensation Board* [1973] 3 All ER 808.
4. *Meah v McCreamer* [1985] 1 All ER 367. But the further extension, that the insurers' liability ran to settlement of a successful action by the women involved, was regarded as too remote to be acceptable (*Meah v McCreamer and another* (1985) Times, 12 December).
5. Smith JC and Hogan B *Criminal Law* (5th ed, 1983) p.278 Butterworths, London.
6. Williams G 'Causation in homicide' [1957] Crim LR 429.
7. There is a useful discussion of this problem in Grant CM 'Establishing causation in chemical exposure cases: the precursor symptoms theory' (1982) 35 Rutgers LR 163. For discussion of some DES cases, *see* 'Selected recent court decisions' (1981) 7 Am J Law Med 213.
8. In *Barty-King* (n.3 above) the court was prepared to accept that a death from cancer in 1967 could be attributed to a war injury received in 1944. The circumstances of this case, however, were special.
9. [1961] 3 All ER 831.
10. Munkman J *Employer's Liability* (10th ed, 1985) p.200, Butterworths, London; *see also Bonnington Castings Ltd v Wardlaw* [1956] AC 613, [1956] 1 All ER 615.

Central Nervous System

The central nervous system consists of the brain and the spinal cord. The latter is divided into segments corresponding to the spinal vertebrae; a major efferent or *motor* nerve root and an afferent or *sensory* root pass through the lateral aspects of each vertebra, connecting the central nervous system to the peripheral nervous system — the latter activating the muscles and receiving sensations which are analysed in the brain. Motor and sensory pathways travel upwards and downwards in the spinal cord to and from the brain. Damage to the spinal cord therefore affects whole regions beneath the point of injury and is of sufficient importance to be discussed separately. The functional cells of the central nervous system are irreplaceable; a child is born with its full complement of nerve cells and the decreasing cerebral capacity of old age is, to some extent, a measure of how these degenerate during life.

Functionally, the central nervous system can be regarded as a core of nervous tissue running from the head to the tail with nerve fibres carrying information and commands in both directions. The brain also has its central core and the organ basically consists of two major masses, the cerebrum and the cerebellum which are 'grafted on' to that core symmetrically.

See also: Brain; Dementia; Nervous system; Spinal cord injuries

Cerebral Injuries

Destruction of the brain substance may be a secondary result of intracerebral haemorrhage. Traumatic lacerations are also usually associated with some degree of bleeding and, as the pia and arachnoid membranes may well be also torn, blood exudes into the subarachnoid or subdural spaces. Direct lacerations can result from fracture of the skull and tearing of the dura mater. But many lacerations are of the contre-coup type associated with movement of the brain, particularly that of rotational type. Severe movement may cause central laceration and division of the two cerebral hemispheres. Particularly dangerous lacerations occur in the brain stem in association with fracture of the base of the skull, and the brain stem may be completely divided when there is fracture or dislocation of the joints of the upper cervical spine.

Healing of lacerations of the brain results in scarring which may provoke post-traumatic epilepsy. Alternatively, the dead tissue is removed by phagocytic cells and a cavity or cyst remains. Lacerations in a small number of survivors are generalised and are visible only under the microscope as diffuse areas of degeneration of the nerve fibres[1,2]; victims of this type of injury often survive in a state akin to the persistent vegetative state.

See also: Contre-coup injuries; Epilepsy; Intracerebral haemorrhage; Persistent vegetative state; Scars

1. Strich SJ 'Shearing of nerve fibres as a cause of brain damage due to head injury' [1961] 2 Lancet 443.
2. Oppenheimer DR 'Microscopic lesions in the brain following head injury' (1968) 31 J Neurol Neurosurg Psychiat 299.

Changes After Death

If death is defined as the irrevocable failure of the cardiorespiratory system, the changes after death can be anticipated on the twin bases of anoxia and lack of a blood circulation.

Anoxia will show itself first by death of the enzyme systems of the body and cessation of heat production. Cooling of the body will therefore be one of the early phenomena and one which is widely used in the timing of death. Temporary survival of the cells by means of their residual but steadily reducing oxygen content will lead to metabolism in an anaerobic environment with the production of and, in the absence of a circulation, the accumulation of abnormal metabolites such as lactic acid; at the same time, there is a failure to replenish essential chemicals such as adenosine triphosphate. These processes manifest themselves in the musculature as rigor mortis, a matter of stiffening of the fibrils which takes some time to appear but which will remain until putrefaction occurs.

In the absence of a circulation, the blood will settle in the vessels under the action of gravity; the skin will therefore become pale where blood has left the vessels and engorged where it has settled. This is hypostasis, or *post mortem* lividity, a process which begins as soon as the circulation ceases but only becomes evident after some 30 minutes.

The lack of a circulation, associated with the absence of any defensive activity on the part of the blood constituents, allows the normal bacteria of the body, or any abnormal organisms which are present, to proliferate and for others to enter from the environment. The resultant activity leads to putrefaction of the tissues with gas formation, liquefaction and, eventually, dissolution of the tissues. In certain circumstances, the process of putrefaction may be replaced or modified by mummification or the formation of adipocere. If the body is exposed, dissolution will be accelerated by the action of carnivores both on the land and in water or by the action of flesh-eating insect larvae.

It is apparent that the basic condition of the body, its specific state at death and the environment in which it lies will greatly affect the appearance of these signs, which are discussed as individual entries. A corollary to the changes already described is that the chemistry of the body will be greatly altered by the processes occurring after death; the biochemical state discovered at autopsy may therefore bear very little relation to conditions in life. It follows that great care must be exercised in making a diagnosis of 'physiological' or 'biochemical' death on the basis of the interpretation of postmortem chemical estimations. Some of the *post mortem* alterations may be sufficiently specific to have a limited use in the timing of death.

See also: Adipocere; Hypostasis; Mummification; Putrefaction; Rigor mortis; Timing of death

Child Abuse

Legislation on flagrant cruelty to children has existed since 1899. However, since the early 1960s, attention has been drawn to the more subtle, but none the less deliberate, injury to children inflicted in the home in such a way as to make its detection difficult[1]. Growing medical sensitivity to the problem, coupled with the development of an interest on the part of lawyers and social workers focused attention on the reasons for parental abuse of children, such behaviour being frequently explained in psychiatric terms. Many parents of 'battered babies' were found to be of low intelligence, immature and aggressive and were thought to be in need of medical treatment[2].

Dealing with child abuse is complicated by the fact that those involved in the problem may define it in different ways. Lawyers tend to be interested only in violence which is comparatively serious and which fits into one of the established categories of criminal offence; social workers and psychologists may take a broader view, sometimes characterising as violence forms of behaviour which do no more than threaten the child's development[3]. Balancing the interest of society in protecting the child against the rights of the parents to bring up their family as they choose can be difficult. At what point does 'cranky' or bizarre parental behaviour become the legitimate object of legal intervention?.

Such protection against abuse is afforded children both by common law and by statute. Under common law, a parent, or other person having a duty to look after a child, who fails to provide the necessities of life, may commit an offence, a conviction for manslaughter being in order if the child dies as a result. A parent may, of course, be prosecuted for a common law assault on his child although not all violence against the child will be regarded as wrongful. English common law affords the parent or one *in loco parentis* the right to inflict corporal punishment provided such punishment is reasonable and moderate[4]; a criminal assault may be committed in going beyond this[5]. In giving this right to the parent, English law is in step with legal systems such as that of the USA where the Supreme Court has held that corporal punishment in schools is constitutional[6]. Other jurisdictions, particularly those in western Europe, have taken an opposite view; Sweden has gone even further, making it a criminal offence for a parent to chastise a child in the home.

The main locus of legislative protection lies in the Children and Young Persons Act 1933, s.1, which provides that an offence is committed by any person 'having custody, charge or care' of a child or young person under the age of 16 who 'wilfully assaults, ill-treats, neglects, abandons or exposes him, or causes or procures him to be assaulted, ill-treated, neglected, abandoned or exposed in a manner likely to cause him unnecessary suffering or injury to health (including injury to or loss of sight, or hearing, or limb or organ of the body, and any mental derangement...)'. Other sections or subsections of the Act create more specific offences: s.1(2)(a) deals with the suffocation of a child in bed with intoxicated adults, and s.11 refers to exposure to a fire hazard.

It is clear that only acts or omissions which cause real injury to health or an appreciable degree of physical or mental suffering will lead to conviction under s.1 of the Act[7]. Refusal to allow the child to undergo medical treatment may amount to neglect or ill-treatment but the test in each case will be the overall circumstances of the parental refusal[8]. Offences under s.1(1) of the 1933 Act are not ones of strict liability. In *R v Sheppard and another*[9] the House of Lords held that parents could not be convicted of wilful neglect unless they had deliberately and recklessly failed to provide the attention needed[10].

Children who are considered to be at risk due to ill-treatment may be removed from the home by virtue of a place of safety order and subsequent care proceedings which may result in their being placed in the care of the local authority[11]; the procedure is important and is discussed as a separate entry.

See also: Care proceedings; Neglect; Non-accidental injury in children; Reasonable force; Refusal of medical treatment

1. Pfhol S 'The discovery of child abuse' (1977) 24 Soc Prob 310; Freeman MDA *The Rights and Wrongs of Children* (1983) p.105, F Pinter, London.
2. Kempe CH et al 'The battered child syndrome' (1962) 181 JAMA 17; Cameron JM et al 'The battered baby syndrome' (1966) 6 Med Sci Law 2; Steele B and Pollock C 'A psychiatric study of parents who abuse infants and small children' in Helfer RW and Kempe CH (eds) *The Battered Child* (1974) Chicago University Press, Chicago.
3. For example, Gil D 'Societal violence and violence in families' in Eekelaar J and Katz S (eds) *Family Violence* (1978) Butterworths, Toronto.
4. *R v Woods* (1921) 85 JP 272.
5. *R v Derriviere* (1969) 53 Crim App R 637.
6. *Ingraham v Wright* 430 US 651 (1977).
7. *R v Whibley* [1938] 3 All ER 777, 26 Crim App R 184, in which it was held that leaving children unattended in a court room was not conduct punishable under s.1.
8. *Oakey v Jackson* [1914] 1 KB 216, prosecution under a similar provision of the Children Act 1908, s.12(1).
9. [1980] 3 All ER 899.
10. Bentil J 'Strict liability offences and wilful neglect' (1982) 126 SJ 39; Waters R 'Absolute liability or not' (1981) 125 SJ 140; Gamble H 'Mens rea of neglect' (1981) 5 Crim LJ 285.

11. The Child Care Act 1980 places a duty on the local authority to take into care a child under 17 years of age if, *inter alia*, the child's welfare requires such intervention.

Child Destruction

The term 'child destruction' is often used loosely but, in fact, refers to a specific offence in English law. The Infant Life (Preservation) Act 1929 states that child destruction is committed when any person, with intent to destroy the life of a child capable of being born alive, by any wilful act causes the child to die before it has an existence independent of its mother. For the purposes of the Act, a woman who has been pregnant for 28 weeks or more is presumed to be pregnant of a child capable of being born alive. The statute further stipulates that no offence is committed unless it is proved that the act was not done in good faith for the purpose only of preserving the life of the mother. From the point of view of the criminal law, the Act closed the gap between criminal abortion — which was impossible once the process of natural separation of the fetus from the mother had begun — and homicide, which depended on a 'separate existence' (i.e. complete extrusion) of the victim. Since, at that time, there was no such thing as a legal therapeutic abortion in England and Wales, it must have been designed also to decriminalise the operation of craniotomy — a now virtually unused procedure whereby the head of a fetus impacted in the pelvis during birth was crushed and thereby liberated.

However, during the trial of Mr Bourne[1], the provisions of the 1929 Act were taken to represent a defence against charges brought under the Offences Against the Person Act 1861, s.58; the two statutes were therefore closely allied and the Abortion Act 1967, s.5(1) stipulates 'nothing in this Act shall affect the provisions of the Infant Life (Preservation) Act 1929 (protecting the life of the viable foetus)'. It follows that the liberal terms of the Abortion Act do not apply to pregnancies extending beyond the 28th week; any such terminations would have to be justified either by the 1929 Act or by the *Bourne* defence.

The 1929 Act presumes a capability of being born alive after 28 weeks' gestation but it does not presume that a less mature fetus is *in*capable of being so born. Some confusion surrounds the allied concepts of live birth and of viability — the latter properly relates to an ability to survive after birth and is therefore a medical rather than a legal condition and one which depends to a large extent on the medical facilities available. It is unfortunate that s.5(1) of the 1967 Act perpetuates the difficulty by referring to 'the viable foetus'. Since it probably means '*a* viable fetus', the distinction between a late legal abortion and child destruction becomes clouded, the quality of viability being a matter between the fetus itself and its medical attendants and, moreover, one which can only be decided with certainty after birth. It follows that, in the event of an aborted fetus surviving outside its mother — or simply being born alive — the gynaecologist could, in theory, be guilty of attempted child destruction and he might, further, be guilty of homicide or of an offence against the Children and Young Persons Act 1933, s.1 (cruelty or wilful neglect) if it were to die without the benefit of supportive measures[2]. There is therefore much to be said in favour of the Lane Committee's[3] proposal for the insertion into the 1967 Act of a stricter time limit; such a change would also eliminate the possibly unintentional discrepancy between the law on therapeutic abortion in England and in Scotland where the 1929 Act does not apply[4].

See also: Abortion; Abortion Act 1967; Homicide; Live birth; Living abortus; Separate existence; Viability

1. *R v Bourne* [1939] 1 KB 687.
2. Tunkel V 'Abortion: how early, how late, and how legal?' [1979] 2 Br Med J 253.
3. Lane Justice (chairman) *Report of the Committee on the Working of the Abortion Act* (Cmnd 5579) (1974). HMSO, London.
4. Where killing a child in the process of birth would be indistinguishable from homicide (*HM Adv v Scott* (1892) 3 White 240) but could be justified by medical necessity.

Further reading
For further discussion, *see* Somerville MA 'Reflections on Canadian abortion law; evacuation and destruction — two separate issues' (1981) 31 U Toronto LJ 1, which gives an excellent overview from the trans-Atlantic aspect.

Child Experimentation

An overcautious approach to the use of children as experimental subjects may result in a dearth of new treatments, making children 'therapeutic orphans'[1]. Nevertheless, research on children poses particular ethical and legal problems. A child cannot consent to a medical procedure in the same way as can an adult and, consequently, the high standard of informed consent required of experimental subjects may not be satisfied. The substitution of parental consent does not solve the problem; the assumption underlying proxy parental consent is that the parents act in the interests of the child and participation in non-therapeutic research may not satisfy that test[2]. The unattractive prospect then arises of disallowing all participation by children in medical research other than in that which is of therapeutic benefit to the subjects.

Counter-arguments to this strict view attempt to refute the implication that the child is incapable of understanding and giving a valid consent to medical procedures. Altruistic behaviour is not impossible in a child, who should be allowed to follow that instinct provided he is protected from exposing himself to any significant risk of harm. Indeed, such freedom would seem positively beneficial to the child's development as a social being. Paralogistic justifications based, for example, on potential benefit to siblings from participation in research, then become superfluous.

It is possible that paediatric research has been hampered in England and Wales by legal uncertainty. The Medical Research Council suggested in 1962 that there was no legal capacity to consent on the part of a young child[3] and this attitude was reflected in guidelines laid down by the Department of Health in 1974; these suggested that non-therapeutic research on children, even with the consent of parents or guardians, must be limited to procedures in which the risk involved is negligible — as, for example, weighing a child or taking a hair sample[4]. This strict interpretation has been questioned and the better view is that non-therapeutic research on children is justified if (a) the child understands the procedure sufficiently so as to be able to give a valid consent or (b) if a parent consents on behalf of a child who is too young to understand the issues involved. In the latter case, the procedure must involve no more than minor risks[5].

See also: Biomedical experimentation; Consent by minors; Consent to medical treatment; Informed consent

1. For full discussion, *see* van Eys J (ed) *Research on Children* (1978) University Park Press, Baltimore MD. An excellent summary of the issues, with an extensive bibliography, is given by Burchell JM 'Non-therapeutic medical research on children' (1978) 95 SALJ 193.
2. Editorial 'Valid parental consent' [1977] 1 Lancet 1346; Dworkin G 'Legality of consent to non-therapeutic medical research on infants and young children' (1978) 53 Arch Dis Childh 443.
3. Committee of Privy Council for Medical Research *Report of the Medical Research Council for 1962–63* (Cmnd 2382) (1964) HMSO, London.
4. Editorial 'Research on children' [1975] 1 Lancet 1369.
5. This is the view put forward by Skegg P 'English law relating to experimentation on children' [1977] 2 Lancet 754; *see also* Skegg PDG *Law, Ethics and Medicine* (1985) p.65 et seq, Oxford University Press, Oxford.

Child Murder

The Infanticide Act 1938 does not run to Scotland. Nevertheless, it is a matter of practice to charge only culpable homicide in Scotland where a mother kills her child in circumstances which would amount to infanticide in England despite the fact that a charge of murder could properly be brought[1]; diminished responsibility is always conceded by the Crown. In order to avoid confusion with the statutory English offence, it is customary to refer to such cases as child murder. It is to be noted, however, that Gordon retains the word 'infanticide' and applies the term 'child murder' to concealment of pregnancy as it was prior to the passing of the Concealment of Birth (Scotland) Act 1809[2].

See also: Concealment of birth; Infanticide

1. Gordon GH *The Criminal Law of Scotland* (1978, 2nd ed), p.764 W Green, Edinburgh.
2. Ibid, p.808.

Choking

Choking is an accident involving impaction of a foreign body in the larynx. Food 'going down the wrong way' in normal adults is generally coughed up. For fatal choking to occur, the normal reflex closure of the glottis during swallowing must have failed. It may, thus, occur in the intoxicated but is most commonly seen in the slightly demented elderly who are 'bolting' their food — the situation is exaggerated if the subject is edentulous; children may be similarly affected.

The larynx is stimulated and death, when it occurs, is almost always due to vagal inhibition of the heart; the signs of asphyxia are, therefore, absent. Sudden death of this type is sufficiently common to be given the misleading title of 'the café coronary'.

See also: Asphyxia; Dementia; Vagal inhibition of the heart

Chromatography

Chromatography is one of the most useful methods in toxicology and depends upon the ability of a solvent to carry a substance with it as it diffuses in a medium which, itself, tends to hold back that substance. The substance will have moved a constant distance after a given time in which the solvent has been allowed to diffuse. The ratio of the distance travelled by the substance to the distance travelled by the solvent is known as the R_f value of the substance for that particular system. Several substances may have the same R_f value in a given set of circumstances but they can be separated by using different systems. Identification of the substance then rests on comparing the discovered R_f values with those which are detailed in reference tables.

The simplest forms of the method are paper chromatography and thin layer chromatography; in the latter process, ultra-thin layers of various absorbents are spread over glass plates. In either form, the presence of the substance sought is shown by developing a colour reaction with a chemical reagent.

In gas chromatography the medium is a coiled column of powder, which may be coated with a wax or grease (gas liquid chromatography), and the solvent is a carrier gas. This technique, which quantifies as well as identifies substances, is of such importance in toxicological analyses that it is discussed separately.

A further refinement, which requires more expensive and complex equipment, is high performance liquid chromatography in which the substances for identification and measurement are injected under high pressure into the column in a liquid medium. The main advantage of high performance liquid chromatography is that it will separate and identify substances which are in liquid or dissolved form whereas gas chromatography requires the substance to be volatile; moreover, liquid injection allows the substance to be recovered and retested if necessary.

See also: Gas chromatography; Toxicological analyses

Chromosomal Disease

The nuclei of the cells of the body contain 46 chromosomes arranged in pairs (homologues); one set of 23 is derived from the mother and the other set from the father. The formation of the sex cells (gametes) results from interchange of parts (or genes) between homologous chromosomes and their subsequent distancing with the formation of two cells each with only 23 chromosomes; these then combine in the fertilised ovum (zygote) to produce a normal 46-chromosome cell. This process usually proceeds uneventfully but mistakes are occasionally made, in which case the nucleus of the zygote contains abnormal chromosomes. Such abnormalities may be associated with the sex chromosomes, in which case X-linked disease may result. Alternatively, the autosomes (non-sex chromosomes) may be affected. X-linked disease is discussed under that heading; here we are concerned only with abnormalities of the autosomes, which may be of numerical or structural type[1].

The common numerical abnormalities result from a failure of the chromosomal pairs to separate completely during the formation of the sex cells. Thus, sex cells with either 24 or 22 chromosomes are produced leading to zygotes containing 47 or 45 chromosomes. The latter state, known as monosomy, is incompatible with life and the zygote dies. The former is known as trisomy — i.e. there are three homologues — and the location of the abnormality determines the resulting chromosomal disease. The most common example is trisomy-21 (or triplication of the chromosome designated 21 by cytogeneticists) which results in Down's syndrome, or mongolism. Multiple trisomies are almost certainly incompatible with life; indeed, probably less than half of the embryos with trisomy-21 live to full term.

Structural alterations in chromosomes are more difficult to understand but, essentially, they may result from loss of a portion of chromosome or from exchange of portions of chromosomes (translocation). It is to be noted that the great majority of chromosomal abnormalities which are compatible with life result in some degree of mental impairment.

The occurrence of chromosomal disease is capricious in the first instance but it is apparent that a sufferer from Down's syndrome has an equal chance of passing on a trisomy to the next generation; although the danger is confined to the mother, male mongols being sterile, the carrier of a translocation abnormality involving chromosome 21 has a one in three chance of producing a Down's syndrome infant (see 'Genetic disease'). On the other hand, whilst the production of a mongol infant by a genetically healthy female cannot be predicted mathematically, the overall chance of producing a trisomy increases with the age of the mother. The incidence rises from about 1 in 2,000 in mothers under the age of 25 to 1 in 50 in mothers over 40 years old. The probable reason is that the ova, which begin to form very early in life, simply get tired by the time of final development and divide inadequately. There is some evidence that old age in the father may also predispose to trisomies.

See also: Down's syndrome; Genetic disease; Sex chromosomes; X-linked disease

1. This difficult subject is expressed in simple language in Emery AEH *Elements of Medical Genetics* (6th ed, 1983) Churchill Livingstone, Edinburgh.

Cirrhosis

Cirrhosis of the liver involves three main changes — death of liver cells, replacement by fibrous tissue and regeneration in the form of nodules. The condition is most commonly associated in the public mind with alcoholism but this is by no means the only potential cause. Amongst others, it can result from inborn errors of metabolism, from obstruction or infection of the biliary system or from cardiac failure. Viral hepatitis constitutes a medico-legally important predisposing cause and the condition may follow recovery from toxic destruction of liver cells (see 'Industrial poisoning').

Nevertheless, an association between chronic alcoholism and cirrhosis is undeniable although by no means all alcoholics become cirrhotic. The alcoholic fatty liver is, in fact, often compatible with good liver function. The relationship is clearly complex and is not fully understood. The suggestion that the condition results from a combination of alcoholism and sub- or malnutrition has its adherents but is certainly not universally true.

Death from cirrhosis is either due to chronic liver failure or due to rupture of venous varices which form at the lower end of the oesophagus as a result of pressure changes within the portal and systemic venous systems; the latter condition is not uncommon as a cause of sudden unexpected death.

See also: Alcoholism; Hepatitis; Inborn errors of metabolism; Industrial poisoning; Liver disease and injury; Sudden natural death

Clandestine Injury to a Woman

Whereas rape is defined in England and Wales in terms of absence of consent to sexual intercourse, Scots law speaks in terms of overcoming a woman's will. An anomaly then arises when a man has intercourse with a woman who is sleeping, drugged or otherwise unable to respond. The act would be rape in England because the woman had not consented; it could not be so classified in Scotland as she had no will to overcome. Nevertheless, it is an offence, which is commonly known as inflicting clandestine injury on a woman[1]. To ply a woman with drugs or alcohol with the express purpose of having intercourse is clearly rape in Scotland because the intention is to overcome the will; but 'softening up' with the offer of excess alcohol in order to modify the woman's will would not satisfy the conditions for rape[2].

See also: Rape

1. *HM Adv v Sweenie* (1838) 3 Irv 109; *HM Adv v Grainger and Rae* 1932 JC 40.
2. *HM Adv v Logan* 1936 JC 100.

Coagulation of the Blood

Coagulation or clotting of the blood is the body's essential defence against loss of blood through haemorrhage. Staunching damaged small vessels *in vivo* is largely a function of the blood platelets, which react with materials released from the damaged vessel wall to form a haemostatic plug. Platelets also play a part in the initiation of coagulation, which is a matter of enzymatic clotting using factors which are mostly present in normal circulating blood. These factors are known by Roman numerals. The enzymatic activity is of what is known as 'cascade' type — activation of a normally inactive factor by another which then, in turn, activates a further link in the chain. There are two 'pathways' to coagulation — the extrinsic pathway begins with activators in damaged tissue juices and the intrinsic is set in motion by contact of the blood with abnormal surfaces or particles; the practical difference between the two is that the intrinsic coagulation system does not depend upon tissue injury and can be provoked within the blood vessels themselves. For ease of description, the intrinsic pathway can be considered as an interaction between Factor X and prothrombin which is synthesised in the liver utilising vitamin K. As a result, thrombin — which does not circulate normally in the blood — is formed and this reacts with the normal plasma protein fibrinogen to form fibrin, which is the essential scaffolding of the coagulum or clot. Factors VIII and IX are two important, normally circulating, blood constituents essential to the 'cascade' by which Factor X is formed. Absence of either of these results in the genetic disease haemophilia.

Failure of the blood-clotting mechanism may therefore have many causes —

disease of the vessels which do not contract when injured, liver disease, abnormalities of platelet production, alterations in the plasma proteins and genetic disease. The elimination of all is essential in the interpretation of what appears to be excessive bruising or haemorrhage due to injury.

Clearly, there must be a mechanism designed to prevent clotting within the blood vessels themselves and the body carries another intrinsic system known as the fibrinolytic enzyme system which acts in a similar, but contrary, fashion. The balance between the clot-forming and the clot-destroying systems is significantly altered following injury and may give rise to the condition known as disseminated intravascular coagulation. Any condition which predisposes to hypercoagulability may give rise to intravascular thrombosis.

The two antagonistic systems continue to operate after death. Although no hard and fast rule can be stated, the tendency is for the blood to clot *post mortem* in those who have died as a result of illness. Exercise and emotional stress tend to enhance fibrinolysis — the blood is therefore commonly found to be fluid in the bodies of healthy persons who have died unnaturally[1].

See also: Disseminated intravascular coagulation; Haemophilia; Haemorrhage; Thrombosis

1. For a very easily understandable account of blood coagulation, *see* Stalker AL 'Haemorrhage, coagulation and thrombosis' in Mason JK (ed) *The Pathology of Violent Injury* (1978) Ch.18, Edward Arnold, London.

Coma

Coma is a state of unconsciousness from which the patient cannot be fully aroused. Consciousness depends upon the interaction between the neurones in the cerebral cortex and that part of the brain, known as the reticular substance, which lies in the brain stem. Coma may therefore result from interference with function or structure at either of these points; the most common causes include direct trauma, a general state of hypoxia including that resulting from drug overdose, pressure due to a space-occupying lesion — including intracranial haemorrhage of all types — or a generalised metabolic disturbance of which diabetes and its complications are the most important but which also include terminal liver or kidney failure. Hypothermia is a rare cause of coma (*see also* 'Encephalopathy and encephalitis').

Brain cells killed by such insults cannot recover but, once the basic cause is removed, there is no necessary progression of dysfunction; as was originally described by writers in France[1], coma can be quantified in degrees rather than stages. The degree achieved will range from death to recovery of function and this is dependent not only on the efficiency of treatment but also, to an extent, on the underlying cause of brain damage; death is commonest in those cases resulting from intracranial haemorrhage or thrombosis but the dreadful end-point of the persistent vegetative state is most likely to occur following generalised hypoxia which selectively affects the cerebral cortex and tends to spare the brain stem[2].

The assessment of prognosis is an essential part of the treatment of coma. It may very well be appropriate to apply a productive/non-productive treatment test, and, indeed, it may be acceptable to withhold treatment if the best result to be anticipated is a vegetative state. This view, which has been widely accepted in the UK, is gaining ground in the courts of the USA[3].

See also: Brain stem death; Diabetes; Hypoxia; Intracranial haemorrhage; Ordinary/ Extraordinary treatment; Persistent vegetative state

1. Mollaret P and Goulon M 'Le Coma dépassé' (1959) 101 Rev Neurol 3.
2. An up-to-date and very readable medical summary is to be found in Bates D 'Predicting recovery from medical coma' (1985) 33 Br J Hosp Med 276.
3. *John F Kennedy Memorial Hospital Inc v Bludworth* 452 So 2d 921 (Fla, 1984).

Commorientes

Literally 'dying together', 'commorientes' can be taken as synonymous with 'simultaneous death'.

Some provision must be made for the disposal of estates in the event that it is uncertain which of two or more persons concerned have survived the others, and this varies from country to country. There are two basic approaches. In one, the presumption is that neither person survived the other; this is the rule in the USA[1], Japan and in many countries of central Europe. In what might be referred to as the 'English rule'[2], the younger person is deemed to have survived the older and it would seem that evidence to the effect that the deaths were, in fact, truly simultaneous is not admissible[3]; this rule is modified in France to allow for extremes of age and for the comparative vulnerability of the female in conditions of equal adversity.

It is clear that the rule in England and Wales raises the strong possibility of inadvertent diversion of the estate to the distaff side of the family and, for this reason, 'spouse commorientes' is considered separately in Scotland where the US practice is adopted in that particular eventuality[4]. New Zealand changed from the English to the US practice when the inequity became apparent and it would seem that, even in England, opportunities are taken when they are available to demit the presumption[5]. The most important aspect from the medico-legal viewpoint, however, is that the presumption in law can be rebutted by the medical evidence which means, in practice, by the results of the postmortem examination. Thus, a person who has died by fire is likely to have survived one who has sustained severe head injury. More subtle methods have been suggested for comparing the agonal period when death is due to similar causes but, in general, these have not produced the clear-cut results which are desirable[6]. Nevertheless, every effort should be made by the pathologist to provide such evidence as may be available whenever close relatives are involved.

In modern times, 'commorientes' problems have become almost specific to aircraft accidents; since a commercial aircraft is likely to contain citizens of several nations, each with different legal presumptions, the importance of the pathological investigation of such cases scarcely needs emphasis. Serious complications are imposed on the application of the commorientes rules when life is is maintained by machine (*see* 'Ventilator support').

See also: Agonal period: Brain stem death: Ventilator support

1. Uniform Simultaneous Death Act, 8 Uniform Laws Annotated 608.

2. Law of Property Act 1925, s.184.
3. *Hickman v Peacey* [1945] AC 304, HL.
4. Succession (Scotland) Act 1964, s.31.
5. Intestates' Estates Act 1952, s.1(4).
6. Buchanan D and Mason JK 'Occurrence of pulmonary fat and bone marrow embolism' (1982) 3 Am J Forens Med Path 73.

Communicable Diseases

Disease which can be communicated from man to man is of medico-legal importance in that it can be controlled to an extent by legislation; it is of interest that the early Chairs of forensic medicine included public health within their discipline.

Spread of human disease may be direct or indirect. The latter is of two types — spread by insects (discussed under 'Insects and disease') and transfer from excretions which may, again, involve insects but also includes contamination of water and food supplies. Direct spread is classically by means of actual contact or by proximity contact which includes spread by coughing and sneezing and also by way of insects which are obligate human parasites — e.g. the body louse.

The most important method whereby disease is spread indirectly through the excretions is via the faeces — it is arguable that the isolation of faeces from the water supply through the provision of an adequate system of sewage was the most important single step taken in the field of human health in an industrialised society. Diseases which may occur in explosive epidemic form when spread in this way include the typhoid group, the dysenteries and cholera. Food handlers harbouring the organisms — the 'carrier state' — may cause local outbreaks. Carriers are a particular problem in the typhoid group of diseases; the local health authorities have power to order a medical examination of a person suspected of being a carrier[1] and to request him to discontinue his work if it is dangerous to the public; the affected person may be compensated for so doing[2]. This type of indirect spread of disease also includes airborne distribution in dust particles and the like; this poses a major problem in hospital wards and also accounts for much of the spread of the common exanthematous (associated with rash) infectious diseases.

Many of the proximity contact diseases have been eliminated or at least reduced in industrialised countries by provision of better housing and of incomes adequate to maintain a heating supply. Those that remain are the relatively innocuous common colds and other virus diseases such as influenza which can be transmitted during short contacts in public transport and the like. Tuberculosis was, without doubt, the most important proximity contact disease but its ultimate conquest has to be attributed to antibiotic therapy — a development over the last 40 years which has been mainly responsible for the massive reduction in all infectious diseases due to bacteria.

The most obvious examples of diseases spread by direct contact are the infectious diseases of the skin and sexually transmitted diseases. On a world-wide scale, leprosy may well be the most important example. The two most important public health measures to control communicable disease which are related to the individual are immunisation — which is discussed separately (*see also* 'Vaccination') — and notification with its consequent powers of examination and isolation of those who are a danger to the public. There is a basic list of statutorily notifiable diseases, and local authorities may add to this whenever the need becomes apparent[3].

See also: Infectious diseases; Insects and disease; Notifiable diseases; Public health; Sexually transmitted diseases; Tuberculosis; Vaccination

1. Public Health (Control of Disease) Act 1984, s.35.
2. Ibid., s.20.
3. Ibid., s.16; National Health Service (Scotland) Act 1972, s.53.

Community Health Councils

The formation of community health councils (CHCs) was authorised in the National Health Service Reorganisation Act 1973[1]. A CHC is established by the regional health authority (RHA) for each health district and its function is, broadly, to represent the views of the consumer. The district health authority (DHA) is now the primary operational organisation within the National Health Service (Health Services Act 1980) and, since such an authority is closer to the public than was the case under the older area health authorities, the structure of the CHCs has been slightly modified. The CHC consists of 30 members, 15 being appointed by local government councils, 10 by non-profit-making organisations who can be expected to speak for the public on health matters and 5 by the RHA.

Community health councils must be consulted by DHAs and relevant family practitioner committees (FPCs) as is prescribed[2]; they are entitled to information from such authorities and committees and may enter and inspect premises controlled by them; they may give advice to the authority and the committee in matters relating to the operation of the health service within the CHC's district; and they will prepare and publish reports on which the DHA and the FPC must comment publicly[3]. The relevance of a FPC to a CHC depends upon the extent to which the council performs its functions in relation to that part of the council's district which is covered by the FPC. Community health councils have no general remit to visit or inspect registered private hospitals or nursing homes but will generally be allowed to do so when NHS patients are receiving such services under contractual arrangements.

In addition to these statutory powers and duties, the CHCs also provide something of a platform from which individuals may mount complaints against the NHS.

See also: Family practitioner committees; National Health Service

1. Now consolidated in the National Health Service Act 1977, s.20.
2. Community Health Council Regulations 1985 (SI 1985/304).
3. National Health Service Act 1977, Sch.5, Part II, s.15 as amended by Health and Social Security Act 1984, Sch.3.

Compensation

The victim of an accident or deliberately inflicted injury may seek compensation from a variety of sources. State compensation is provided in the form of compensation for criminal injury, and social security payments are available to ensure that domestic income is protected from the results of an industrial accident; in addition, a court may make a compensation order in favour of the victim of a crime[1]. Apart from these public funded sources of compensation, the injured person may also be privately insured against such injury or he may pursue an action for damages against the person by whose fault the injury has arisen[2]. Legal interest in Britain has traditionally focused on the last route to compensation but there have been many calls for reform, particularly directed towards a system of no-fault compensation. The possible impact of no-fault compensation on medical actions is discussed under that heading.

See also: Damages; Negligence; No-fault compensation; Torts

1. Powers of Criminal Courts Act 1973, s.35. The Criminal Justice Act 1982, s.27, provides that the parent or guardian of a child may have such an order made against him in respect of criminal damage caused by his minor.
2. The subject is comprehensively treated in Atiyah PS *Accidents, Compensation and the Law* (3rd ed, 1980) Weidenfeld & Nicolson, London.

Compensation Neurosis

This condition is also known as accident neurosis, postconcussional state or post-traumatic syndrome. The symptoms include anxiety, amnesia, intolerance, irritability and unwillingness, or inability, to return to work after an accident for which compensation may be available. The debate as to whether the condition is a true neurosis, or hysteria, or merely a sophisticated form of malingering is still undecided. Miller[1] investigated some 4,000 patients involved in claims following accidents and took the view that compensation neurosis was fundamentally functional in origin. The opposing view is that it may be connected with trauma to the brain and is, consequently, organic[2].

Whatever the aetiology of the condition, psychological or physical, it remains an important feature of the medical history of many accident victims and an extremely difficult one to assess in terms of justice. Symptoms disappear in most cases once the matter is settled but some observers suggest that the fact that recovery may be delayed, or, indeed, that a 'morbid' personality may precede any claim for compensation, serves to distinguish the syndrome from malingering[3].

See also: Compensation; Head injury

1. Miller H 'Accident neurosis' [1961] 1 Br Med J 919, 992; 'Mental after effects of head injury' (1966) 59 Proc R Soc Med 257.
2. Kelly R and Smith BN 'Post-traumatic syndrome: another myth discredited' (1981) 74 J Roy Soc Med 275. *See also* the extensive review by Weller MPI 'Head injury — organic and psychogenic issues in compensation claims' (1985) 25 Med Sci Law 11.
3. *See* discussion in Thomson WAR 'Accident neurosis' (1982) 22 Med Sci Law 143.

Complaints Procedure in the NHS

Complaints as to breach of the terms of service of practitioners under contract to the health authority are made to the family practitioner committee (primary care committee in Scotland), which is responsible for the running of the service.

The process is laid down in regulations[1]. The complaint passes initially to the chairman of the family practitioner committee (FPC) who is empowered to appoint a negotiator as one means of settling any dispute amicably. A formal hearing is undertaken by the medical service committee (or dental, pharmaceutical or ophthalmic as the case may be) which consists of a lay chairman, three lay members from the FPC and three professionals from the relevant local committee; one lay committee member must be a woman if a woman or a child is concerned in the hearing. Complaints must be laid within eight weeks of the matter becoming known to the complainer, or within six months from the treatment in the event of a dental practitioner being involved. Once the *prima facie* case has been established by the chairman of the FPC, the matter is usually dealt with by a hearing in private, although, in theory, it could be conducted by correspondence. No paid legal help is allowed but the parties can take unofficial advice from such persons as are present with them. The hearing is relatively informal but witnesses can be introduced who will be questioned and cross-questioned by members of the committee. The decision to be made is whether the professional man was or was not guilty of breach of the terms of service.

In the event of a finding of guilt, the service committee may recommend to the FPC that the doctor be cautioned or fined; they may also recommend a compulsory reduction in his list of patients or they may call for a tribunal to consider his fitness to continue to practise (*see* 'National Health Service'). The decision of the FPC is transmitted to the parties and to the Secretary of State, who can alter the recommendations. An appeal against financial penalty may be lodged within one month and, unless the Secretary of State acts on documentary evidence, this is heard by a legal officer of the secretariat, a departmental doctor and a doctor from a panel specially appointed for the task. The evidence in front of the Appeal Board is taken on oath and both sides may be legally represented.

It will be seen that the procedure is discreet and is concerned essentially with contractual rather than professional standards of conduct. Nevertheless, the Secretary of State may report the matter to the General Medical Council in appropriate cases and when he sees fit — 21 such referrals were made in 1984.

Complaints against those working in hospital, whose contract of service makes them servants of the hospital, are likely to be directed at the hospital itself, and, indeed, will very probably derive *from* the hospital authorities. The matter then becomes one of discipline and is dealt with on a simple superior/inferior level in minor cases; a small subcommittee is often created for the purpose. An inquiry may be held in cases in which the complaint is against the professional conduct or competence of a doctor and, in such cases, due warning must be given to the doctor concerned. The employing authority then sets up a committee of inquiry. In the event of dispute, the hearing is then delegated to a panel consisting of a legal chairman appointed by the Lord Chancellor (or Lord Advocate) and, normally, two consultants not concerned with the hospital; the hearing is quasi-judicial and representation is allowed. The recommendations of the panel to the committee may include suspension or dismissal and, in the case of senior staff, are subject to appeal to the Secretary of State. These procedures do not apply in the case of personal conduct; in this, and in cases of exceptionally serious professional incompetence, the employing authority can take immediate action.

Patients in NHS hospitals may complain of their conditions. The Secretary of

State must make directions to ensure that the procedures for dealing with such complaints are adequate and that patients are aware of the arrangements[2].

Although it is not, strictly speaking, a complaints procedure the Secretary of State may set up an inquiry under the National Health Service Act 1977, s.84, in exceptional cases of mishap within the NHS or in relation to any other matter arising under the Act if he thinks it advisable.

See also: Family practitioner committees; General Medical Council; National Health Service

1. National Health Service (Service Committees and Tribunals) Regulations 1974 (SI 1974/455).
2. Hospital Complaints Procedure Act 1985, s.1(1).

Further reading
For full details of these complex procedures, *see* Martin CRA *Law Relating to Medical Practice* (2nd ed, 1979) Chaps.2 and 3, Pitman, London/State Mutual Books, New York.

Compulsory Medical Treatment

The normal requirement that the patient should consent to medical treatment is waived if he is admitted compulsorily into a psychiatric hospital under the terms of the Mental Health Act 1983[1]. The formalities involved in securing such admission are discussed under the heading 'Detention in mental hospitals'.

Prior to the passing of the 1983 Act, doubts had been expressed as to the validity of non-consensual treatment[2] but the legislation now simplifies the situation, giving clearly stated but circumscribed rights to the hospital[3]. Medical treatment includes nursing and other general care (s.145(1)) but statutory authority is limited to treatment for the patient's mental disorder, thus excluding treatment for dissociated physical disorders[4].

Certain forms of compulsory treatment are subject to specific controls. Section 57 of the Act provides that psychosurgery or hormone implantation treatment can be given only if a doctor not concerned with the case and two people other than doctors sign a statement to the effect that the patient understands the treatment and has consented to it and if the independent doctor confirms that the treatment is appropriate to the needs of the patient. Such treatments are therefore not available to patients whose capacity for understanding has been grossly affected by their illness.

The other forms of compulsory treatment currently controlled by legislation are electroconvulsive therapy and the administration of drugs during a period of detention when three months have elapsed in that particular period since drugs were first given for the mental illness (s.58). These treatments can be given only if (a) the patient gives his consent and the responsible medical officer or a doctor appointed by the Mental Health Act Commission certifies that an informed consent has been given, or (b) where an independent doctor testifies that consent has not been given but that the treatment is nevertheless necessary for the patient's welfare. The provisions of ss.57 and 58 are qualifed by s.62(1) of the Act which provides that the treatment in question may be given without observance of the laid down formalities if it is necessary to save the patient's life; or, not being an irreversible treatment, it is 'immediately necessary to prevent a serious deterioration of his condition' or to alleviate serious suffering by the patient; or, subject, likewise, to the conditions as to irreversibility and hazardousness, it is immediately necessary and 'represents the minimum interference necessary to prevent the patient from behaving violently or being a danger to himself or others'.

The common law authorises non-consensual or imposed treatment to patients other than those detained under the Mental Health Acts in certain narrow circumstances. A patient who is about to do harm to others may be physically restrained and may be sedated legitimately. Such intervention should, however, be minimal and not go beyond what is needed to counter the threatened harm. The principle of necessity might also be invoked to justify such medical intervention and it could also be put forward as a justifying argument when the intervention has been made in order to save the patient from harming himself.

See also: Consent to medical treatment; Detention in mental hospitals; Electroconvulsive therapy; Mental Health Act 1983; Necessity; Psychosurgery

1. Mental Health Act 1983, s.20(1). Corresponding legislation is to be found in the Mental Health (Scotland) Act 1984.
2. Jacob J 'The right of the mental patient to his psychosis' (1976) 39 MLR 17; Gostin LO 'The merger of incompetency and certification: the illustration of unauthorised medical contact in the psychiatric context' (1979) 2 Int J Law Psychiat 127.
3. Section 63. These powers do not apply to all detained patients: *see* s.56(1) for exceptions.
4. For comment on the difficulties of distinguishing between unrelated physical illness and physical manifestations of mental disorder, *see* Hoggett B *Mental Health Law* (1984) p.208, Sweet & Maxwell, London.

Concealment of Birth

The difficulties involved in the proof of a live birth when the body of an infant is even slightly decomposed are discussed under 'Separate existence' and 'Infanticide'. Since putrefaction will often be present, it is desirable to have an alternative offence to infanticide with which to charge a suspect. The offence of concealment of birth is defined in the Offences Against the Person Act 1861, s.60 — it is an offence to secretly dispose of the body of a child in an endeavour to conceal the birth of the child. It is immaterial whether the child died before, at or after its birth; the question of a separate existence is not, therefore, fundamental although, as a matter of policy, the section does not apply to the concealment of a non-viable fetus. If any person is acquitted of a charge of murder of a neonate, the jury may find that person guilty of concealing the birth. For the purposes of the Act, concealment means disposition of the body in a place to which the public do not normally have access. The baby must be dead but abandonment of a live infant which later dies could, of course, attract a charge of manslaughter or, even, of murder.

The comparable Scottish statute is the Concealment of Birth (Scotland) Act 1809 whereby a woman who 'conceals her being with child during the whole period of pregnancy and does not call for or make use of help or assistance at birth' is guilty of an offence if the child subsequently 'be found dead or amissing'; the presumption is that the child would have survived had it not been concealed. That presumption is rebuttable by evidence to the effect that the child was not viable in the medical sense, and the same probably applies to evidence as to stillbirth. Scots law differs from that in England and Wales in that the offence is essentialy that of concealment of *pregnancy* and that a prosecution can succeed in the absence of a body.

Glanville Williams[1] has pointed out that the concept of concealment of birth is of doubtful justice as there may be social reasons why a woman who bears no responsibility for the death of her child should want to keep the matter secret.

See also: Infanticide; Separate existence; Stillbirth; Viability

1. *Textbook of Criminal Law* (2nd ed, 1983) p.291, Stevens, London.

Concussion

Concussion is a relatively mild result of head injury which is manifested by transient unconsciousness lasting from seconds to days. The cause is probably physiological, perhaps associated with a general vibratory force applied to the neurones, and no specific pathological changes have been found in those few cases which come to postmortem dissection for other reasons.

Complete recovery is the rule but the clinical danger lies in failure to appreciate the possibility of a more serious injury, such as extradural or subdural haemorrhage, developing during the phase of recovered consciousness.

See also: Extradural haemorrhage; Head injury; Subdural haemorrhage

Confessions

A confession made by a defendant prior to his trial is admissible in evidence provided that the Crown can establish that it was made voluntarily. 'It has long been established as a positive rule of English criminal law that no statement by an accused is admissible in evidence against him unless it is shown by the prosecution to have been a voluntary statement in the sense that it has not been obtained from him either by fear or prejudice or hope of advantage extended or held out by a person in authority'[1].

A confession may be held to have been involuntary if it was made in oppressive circumstances. Oppression in this context has been judicially defined as involving 'something which tends to sap and has sapped that free will which must exist before a confession is voluntary. . .'[2]. The general state of the accused will have a bearing on the question; a weakened suspect, held and questioned for long periods without rest, may be considered by the court to have been the victim of oppression.

See also: Admissibility of evidence

1. *Ibrahim v R* [1914] AC 599 per Lord Sumner at 609. This dictum has since been reaffirmed in a long line of cases — *see*, for example, *DPP v Ping Lin* [1975] 3 All ER 175.
2. *R v Priestley* (1965) 51 Crim App R 1. The inadmissibility of confessions so obtained is now defined by statute (Police and Criminal Evidence Act 1984, s.76).

Confidentiality

Medical ethics impose upon the doctor the duty to treat as confidential all information which he receives in the course of his professional practice. This obligation appears in the Hippocratic Oath and in the more modern codes of conduct[1]. The vast majority of the medical profession supports the concept of medical confidentiality although it has been criticised, even from within the profession[2]. The medical profession is, however, subject to the law and bureaucratic and legislative invasions of medical confidence are increasingly being proposed and applied by the State[3]. Moreover, the doctor may still be entitled — some might say have an obligation — to disclose confidential information provided such a disclosure satisfies certain criteria of public interest or of the interest of the patient himself[4].

A doctor may become aware that his patient has committed or is likely to commit a criminal offence. It may be justifiable to provide information to the police in such circumstances if the doctor feels, on balance, that to do so is in the public interest; he should take into account the seriousness of the offence and the potential damage to the public of non-disclosure. There is, however, no general duty to inform the police that a crime has been committed but a specific duty may be imposed by legislation; there are two such circumstances in which a doctor is included in the group of 'any persons' having relevant knowledge[5,6].

The doctor may feel obliged to pass confidential information to the authorities when he suspects that a patient has been the victim of child abuse. There is a legal duty to report child abuse in all States of the USA, in Canada and in four Australian States but this is not the case in the UK. There may be strong reasons for notifying the social workers and others of the existence of a risk to a child and these are discussed under 'Non-accidental injury in children'. The courts have regarded such reporting as sufficiently important to protect the anonymity of informants as a matter of public policy[7].

A spouse has a right to confidentiality in respect of his or her partner when undergoing medical treatment and this right should be respected unless the doctor is satisfied that there are strong grounds for breaking confidence in the interests of his patient; different attitudes may well obtain in the case of non-therapeutic medical procedures (*see* 'Sterilisation'). The patient's specific or implied consent to disclosure is likely to be forthcoming in most marital situations, in which case the obligation of confidence is waived as it is whenever consent is given. The question of whether a child below the age of 16 is entitled to confidentiality as to its parents has been the subject of controversy with, in general, the medical profession and, in particular, the General Medical Council supporting the rights of the child. The important case of *Gillick v West Norfolk and Wisbech Area Health Authority and another* illustrates the dilemma. The court of first instance[8a] found that an intelligent child below the age of 16 might well be able to make up her own mind as regards medical treatment and was entitled to confidentiality; the Court of Appeal[8b], however, stressed the importance of parental rights. The House of Lords, in reverting to the original view, admitted that the parents were the best judges of a child's welfare in the overwhelming majority of cases but, nevertheless, accepted that, 'in exceptional circumstances', the child had a right to, and a need for, confidential treatment; the only practical course was to 'entrust the doctor with a discretion to act in accordance with his view of what was best in the interests of a girl who was his patient'[8c]. As things stand, the controversial decision reached in *General Medical Council v Browne*[9], in which a doctor breached the confidence of a minor and was found not guilty of professional misconduct, might, or might not, be followed today — depending, it is supposed, on whether or not the doctor had followed the guidelines outlined in *Gillick* in the Lords.

There is a statutory obligation on the doctor to notify the names of patients suffering from certain infectious diseases to the local community health officer and, similarly, certain industrial diseases must be notified to the Health and Safety Executive[10]. Provision also exists for the notification of those addicted to certain drugs to the Chief Medical Officer of Health[11]. The important point to note is that, in all these cases, the recipient of information has a 'right to know'.

Rather more difficulty arises in relation to diseases which are not notifiable but which one might well think ought to be; epilepsy, in relation to driving, is a prominent example and the doctor's position in this respect is discussed under that heading.

A doctor cannot claim any privilege in court in respect of confidences imparted to him by his patient[12]. Britain is, to some extent, isolated in this respect and the subject is discussed under 'Privilege'.

Psychiatrists are likely to be in possession of particularly sensitive information but their position in relation to confidential information is no different from that of any other doctor[13]. The question has arisen recently, however, as to his duty to warn third parties of dangers presented to them by his patient. This issue arose in the USA in the controversial case of *Tarasoff v Regents of the University of California*[14], in which a psychotherapist was held liable in negligence for failure to warn a potential victim of homicide of her situation; the decision brings into sharp focus the problems surrounding psychiatric predictions as to dangerousness.

A patient who is in a contractual relationship with his doctor — which is not the normal relationship in the NHS — may raise an action for breach of contract if the doctor wrongfully discloses confidential information[15]. In the absence of contract, an action may be brought based on negligence or on the equitable remedy provided by the law for breaches of confidence in other areas of activity — such as the revelation of a trade secret. An example of negligence-based action is the New Zealand case of *Furniss v Fitchett*[16] in which liability was imposed on a doctor for allowing circulation of a report which was produced in circumstances which caused severe shock to the patient.

The protection of the patient in Britain is, in fact, ill-founded in law. The major constraint on the doctor lies in the power of the General Medical Council, which takes a particularly strong view of professional secrecy. In effect, the doctor who breaches confidentiality for any reason must consider whether he would be able to justify his action in front of his professional peers. Good arguments can be produced for believing that matters are best left that way[17].

See also: Child abuse; Consent by minors; Dangerousness; Epilepsy; General Medical Council; Misuse of Drugs Act 1971; Non-accidental injury in children; Notifiable diseases; Privilege; Sterilisation

1. *See* Mason JK and McCall Smith RA *Law and Medical Ethics* (1983) Apps.A, B and C, Butterworths, London.
2. Siegler M 'Confidentiality in medicine — a decrepit concept' (1982) 307 New Engl J Med 1518.

3. Pheby DFH 'Changing practice on confidentiality: a cause for concern' (1982) 8 J Med Ethics 12.

4. British Medical Association *Handbook of Medical Ethics* (1984) Chap.1, BMA, London. *See also* Thompson IE 'The nature of confidentiality' (1979) 2 J Med Ethics 57.

5. Road Traffic Act 1972, s.168; *Hunter v Mann* [1974] QB 767. For general discussion, *see* Samuels A 'The duty of the doctor to respect the confidence of the patient' (1980) 20 Med Sci Law 58.

6. Prevention of Terrorism (Temporary Provisions) Act 1984, s.11.

7. *D v National Society for the Prevention of Cruelty to Children* [1978] AC 171.

8. (a) [1983] 3 WLR 859 following *Johnston v Wellesley Hospital* (1979) 17 DLR (3d) 139.   (b) [1985] 2 WLR 413.   (c) [1985] 3 WLR 830 per Lord Fraser.

9. (1971) Times, 6 and 8 March; Editorial Comment (1971) 121 NLJ 214.

10. Health Services and Public Health Act 1968, ss.47–58; National Health Service (Scotland) Act 1972, s.53. Reporting of Injuries, Diseases and Dangerous Occurrences Regulations 1985 (SI 1985/2023).

11. Misuse of Drugs (Notification of and Supply to Addicts) Regulations 1973 (SI 1973/799).

12. *Attorney General v Mulholland and Attorney General v Foster* [1963] 2 QB 477 at 489; *C v C* [1946] 1 All ER 562.

13. Bloch S and Chodoff P (eds) *Psychiatric Ethics* (1981) Oxford University Press, Oxford. There is a move in the United States Supreme Court to restrict medical privilege to psychotherapists.

14. (1976) 551 P 2d 334.

15. *AB v CD* (1851) 14 Dunlop 177. Boyle C 'Medical confidence — civil liability for breach' (1973) 24 NILQ 19.

16. [1958] NZLR 396.

17. *See* Jacob JM 'Confidentiality: the dangers of anything weaker than the medical ethic' (1982) 8 J Med Ethics 18.

Congenital Disease

Congenital disease is disease which is present at birth. It may be specifically genetically dictated (*see* 'Genetic disease'); it may result from a cause which is well known and understood and, therefore, to an extent avoidable — such conditions would be exemplifed by disability associated with infections in the mother by, say, German measles, by drug administration or by haemolytic disease of the newborn; there may be a strong suspicion of the aetiological agent but one which is not wholly proven — for example, maternal smoking or alcoholism during pregnancy. A number of congenital defects are thought to be multifactorial in origin — the basic cause being a combination of genetic and environmental factors; neural tube defects are a classic example. Occasionally, congenital defects are accepted as being due to an accident sustained by the mother during pregnancy and, finally, a number of defects occur as random developmental anomalies for which no reason can be discovered and which will not, save by chance, repeat themselves in related pregnancies. It is apparent that the work of the genetic counsellor following the birth of a defective infant is wide ranging and complex.

The intrauterine diagnosis of congenital disease is improving rapidly. Amniocentesis is now supported by ultrasound investigations, and the science of fetoscopy is emerging from the experimental stage. Fetal blood sampling is also being increasingly

undertaken. Discovery of an abnormality inevitably raises questions as to management, the extremes of which are the continuance of the pregnancy and an abortion
under the terms of the Abortion Act 1967, s.1(1)(b). It is important, therefore, that
the pregnant woman be made fully aware of the extent of the tests to be performed,
of the need for decision in the event of a positive finding and, arguably, that she
undertakes not to exclude medical options on non-medical grounds.

The possibility of prevention of congenital disease or of the termination of
pregnancy when indicated has opened the way for actions for negligence which may
include actions for diminished life or for wrongful life. The Congenital Disabilities
(Civil Liability) Act 1976 is said to preclude actions for wrongful life although that
belief has not been tested by the courts. The concept of the preconception tort is well
established, certainly in Scotland where the 1976 Act does not run, but action under
that head is not now available if the parents knew of the risk at the time of conception.
An action can, however, still be taken against a father if he knew of the risk, provided
that the mother was ignorant of it at the time[1].

See also: Alcohol; Amniocentesis; Fetoscopy; Genetic counselling; German measles;
Neural tube defects; Preconception torts; Smoking; Ultrasound; Wrongful life

1. Congenital Disabilities (Civil Liability) Act 1976, s.1(4).

Consent by Minors

In most circumstances, the medical treatment of minors will be performed with the
consent of the parents or guardians. This proxy consent is legally valid and will
cover all procedures calculated to be in the interests of the child; measures which are
not in the child's interests will not be legalised by parental consent, as was indicated
in *Re D (a minor)*[1]. The question of the participation of children in non-therapeutic
experimentation is, consequently, a vexed one.

The Family Law Reform Act 1969 (s.8(1)) provides that a minor who has attained
the age of 16 is able to give a valid consent to surgical, medical or dental treatment;
this consent will clearly be valid irrespective of a refusal to sanction the treatment
on the part of a parent or guardian. The legislation, however, left open the issue of
whether a child *under* 16 years of age could consent to treatment. The case of *Gillick
v West Norfolk and Wisbech Area Health Authority and another* was basically
concerned with confidentiality in relation to contraception but the opinions are
inseparable from the consent dilemma as a whole. Woolf J, in the court of first
instance[2a], expressed the view that whether or not a child under 16 is capable of
consenting to therapy depends on the child's understanding and ability to assess the
advantages and disadvantages of the proposed treatment. The Court of Appeal[2b]
reversed the ruling and, effectively, upheld the doctrine of parental right to control
the manner in which and the place at which a child spends her time. The court drew
on the nullity of consent by a minor female to indecent assault to support their
conclusion that she could not agree to a gynaecological examination without her
parents' consent. The House of Lords, however, reverted to the original opinion and,
while dealing mainly with parental rights, concluded that there was no provision
which compelled them to hold that a girl under 16 lacked the legal capacity to consent

to contraceptive advice, examination and treatment provided that she had sufficient understanding and intelligence to know what they involved[2c]; Lord Scarman emphasised that, whilst statute had intervened in respect of a child's capacity to consent to medical treatment from the age of 16 onwards, neither statute nor case law had ruled on the extent and duration of parental rights in respect of children under 16 — the courts 'should exercise a flexible principle unless and until Parliament thought fit to intervene'. Thus, there seems no reason why the result in the narrow issue of the particular case should not be extended to include the whole question of consent by minors.

There has been no statement of the law in Scotland and the Family Law Reform Act does not apply there. It is likely that a Scottish court would follow the House of Lords in *Gillick* and the comparable Canadian case, *Johnston v Wellesley Hospital*[3], which was approved by Woolf J.

See also: Child experimentation; Consent; Contraception; Genetic disease; Refusal of medical treatment; Sterilisation

1. [1976] 1 All ER 326. The court refused to allow the sterilisation of a mentally subnormal minor which was requested by the parents.
2. (a) [1983] 3 WLR 859 QBD;   (b) [1985] 2 WLR 413 CA;   (c) [1985] 3 WLR 830, HL, per Lord Fraser.
3. (1979) 17 DLR (3d) 139.

Consent to Injury

Any touching of the person can constitute a battery in the criminal law unless there has been consent. But not all forms of physical violence can be made legal by giving consent. It is no defence to murder, nor is consent a defence in the case of certain forms of sexual touching[1]. This is a matter of public policy[2].

It is no simple matter to decide the point at which the criminal law will not allow consent to justify violence. A degree of physical violence is perfectly acceptable in contact sports. Public policy will, however, prevent the consent of the victim being a consideration when violence becomes excessive; the infliction of bodily damage for purposes which are 'injurious to the public' will not be allowed, the test being the intention behind the violence[3]. The degree of physical damage which ensues will also be relevant; whilst moderate violence can probably be inflicted consensually for the purposes of sexual gratification, major violence will not be tolerated[4]. In Scotland, it is the 'evil intention' behind an assault, rather than the degree of violence, which is fundamental[5].

In the medical context, the issue of consent to injury arises in relation to surgical operations. The consent of the patient justifies the invasion of his physical integrity which the surgery involves so long as the procedure is carried out for his benefit. An operation which is mutilating and which is not therapeutic on either physical or psychiatric grounds will not, however, be covered by this rule and could well be considered criminal. A surgical procedure carried out for the benefit of some other person will be justified by the consent of the 'patient' provided that the risk entailed is not excessive and that the benefit to the other person is considerable. Thus, the donation of an organ which is not essential to the continued existence of the donor can be justified by consent but it would undoubtedly be a criminal offence for a doctor to remove the heart from a live, albeit consenting, donor[6].

There is no legal objection to the involvement of consenting subjects in medical experimentation but, here again, the rule against excessive risks applies. It is likely that public policy would act to negate any consent given if a non-therapeutic experiment involved an appreciable risk to the health of the subject.

See also: Biomedical experimentation; Consent to medical treatment; Sexual offences; Transplantation of organs

1. Koh K 'Consent and responsibility in sexual offences' [1968] Crim LR 81, 150.
2. Williams G 'Consent and public policy' [1962] Crim LR 74.
3. Coke Inst 1, 127; *Pallante v Stadiums Property Ltd* [1976] VR 363; *Attorney General's Reference (No.6 of 1980)* [1981] QB 715.
4. *R v Donovan* (1934) 25 Crim App R 1; *see* criticism by Williams G *Textbook of Criminal Law* (2nd ed, 1983) pp.586-589, Stevens, London. *See also* Leigh L 'Sadomasochism, consent and the reform of the criminal law' (1976) 39 MLR 130; Fletcher GP *Rethinking Criminal Law* (1978) pp.770-771, Little, Brown, Boston MA.
5. *Smart v HM Adv* 1975 SLT 65; *see* Gordon GH *The Criminal Law of Scotland* (2nd ed, 1978) p.828, W Green, Edinburgh.
6. For general discussion, *see* Skegg, P 'Medical procedures and the crime of battery' [1974] Crim LR 693.

Consent to Medical Treatment

As a general rule, no medical procedures may be performed without the consent of the patient. Consent makes the patient *volens* and, consequently, no longer able to claim damages for invasion of his physical integrity.

Consent to treatment may be implicit or explicit. Implicit consent is based on the fact that the patient's conduct (e.g. going to the doctor's surgery) is consistent with consent to treatment which can be reasonably anticipated. Explicit consent, by contrast, involves a specific statement by the patient. This may be either written or verbal and the scope of either form may be problematic. A signature on a form which states that the doctor is authorised to perform such therapeutic procedures as he deems necessary does not give the doctor *carte blanche*. Such consent would be construed as relating only to those procedures which are reasonably closely connected with the complaint for which the patient has sought treatment[1].

The patient must be informed of the nature of the proposed treatment if his consent is to be valid. This requirement, however, poses difficulty as to the extent of disclosure. Two main schools of thought have emerged as the Commonwealth and US courts have grappled with the problem.

The majority of English judgments opt for the 'professional' rule which holds that the standard of disclosure is that which the reasonable doctor would have adopted in the circumstances; the view has been endorsed that what the patient should be told is a matter of clinical judgement[2]. In *Chatterton*[2], it was held that the doctor had a duty to disclose real risks to the patient although no guidance was given as to the definition of reality.

In much the same way, it was held in the influential New Zealand decision in

Smith v Auckland Hospital Board that the decision as to what to disclose depends on the patient's overall needs:

'To be taken into account should be the gravity of the condition to be treated, the importance of the benefits expected to flow from the treatment or procedure, the need to encourage him to accept it, the relative significance of its inherent risks, the intellectual and emotional capacity of the patient to accept the information without such distortion as to prevent any rational decision at all and the extent which the patient may seem to have placed himself in his doctor's hands with the invitation that the latter accept on his behalf the responsibility for intricate or technical details. . .'[3].

The Canadian courts have recently abandoned the professional standard of disclosure in favour of a test based on what the prudent patient would wish to know[4]. In the USA, however, the ruling in *Canterbury v Spence*[5] effectively took the decision out of the hands of the medical profession. In the view taken, the patient has a right to know the risks involved in any medical procedure to which he is to be subjected; the extent of this right is for the patient, not the doctor, to determine. This is the basis of the so-called doctrine of informed consent, which is discussed under that heading.

The nature of the consent given affects the possible remedies for breach. An action in battery is available if no consent has been given to a particular treatment, and this will be particularly appropriate if there has been an express contrary instruction[6]. In general, however, the courts deprecate such actions which, it is said, should more properly be brought in negligence[7]; the distinction is discussed further under both 'Negligence' and 'Assault and battery'.

There are, by contrast, a limited number of circumstances in which medical procedures might be carried out without the patient's consent[8] — e.g. if the patient is unconscious and provided that there is no known objection on his part. Recent cases have distinguished urgent procedures from those which it would be merely inconvenient to postpone; this 'unreasonable/inconvenient' test has been generally approved and is discussed further under 'Unconscious patient'.

A patient who is mentally disordered may be treated compulsorily, either on the basis of necessity — when the treatment is urgently required — or under the statutory provisions relating to the treatment of psychiatric patients admitted to hospital (*see* 'Compulsory medical treatment').

See also: Assault and battery; Compulsory medical treatment; Informed consent; Necessity; Negligence; Unconscious patient

1. *Craig v Glasgow Victoria and Leverndale Hospitals Board of Management* (1974) Court of Session, Scotland (unreported).
2. *Hatcher v Black* (1954) Times, 2 July. *Bolam v Friern Hospital Management Committee* [1957] 2 All ER 118; *Chatterton v Gerson* [1981] 1 All ER 257; *Sidaway v Bethlem Royal Hospital Governors and Others* [1985] 2 WLR 480.
3. [1964] NZLR 241 per Woodhouse J at 250; a similar attitude to reasonable disclosure has been taken in the recent British case of *Blyth v Bloomsbury Hospital Authority* (1985) Times, 24 May.
4. *Hopp v Lepp* (1980) 112 DLR (3d) 67; *Reibl v Hughes* (1981) 114 DLR (3d) 1.
5. 464 F 2d 772 (DC Cir, 1972).
6. *See Mulloy v Hop Sang* [1935] 1 WWR 714 (amputation of hand); *Allan v New Mount*

Sinai Hospital (1980) 109 DLR (3d) 634 (injection of anaesthetic into left arm after specific instructions to the contrary from the patient).
7. *Hills v Potter and Another* [1984] 1 WLR 641.
8. Skegg P 'A justification for medical procedures performed without consent' (1974) 90 LQR 512.

Constructive Malice

Constructive malice was a doctrine of English law whereby the malice or *mens rea* implicit in committing a particular crime could be 'transferred' to another unintended event which occurred during the commission of that crime. It applied in two circumstances: killing a police officer while resisting arrest and killing in the course of committing a felony. The latter was known as the felony murder rule. Both of these forms of constructive malice were abolished by the Homicide Act 1957, s.1.

See also: *Mens rea*

Consummation of Marriage

A marriage is consummated once sexual intercourse takes place between the parties. This intercourse must be *vera copula* or 'ordinary and complete intercourse'[1] although emission need not occur[2]. Penetration for a short time, unaccompanied by emission has been held not to amount to ordinary and complete intercourse[3]. An anatomical abnormality in the wife, which has the effect of restricting the degree of penetration possible, will not necessarily be considered as preventing consummation, particularly if corrective surgery is possible[4]. Contraceptive measures do not prevent consummation and infertility is irrelevant to the question[5].

See also: Sexual intercourse

1. *D-E v A-G* (1845) 1 Rob Eccl 279.
2. *R v R* [1952] 1 All ER 1194.
3. *W v W* [1967] 3 All ER 178.
4. *SY v SY* [1963] P 37; [1962] 3 All ER 55.
5. *Baxter v Baxter* [1948] AC 274; *Applin v Race Relations Board* [1974] 2 All ER 73 at 86, HL (use of condoms); *White v White* [1948] P 330, [1948] 2 All ER 151 (coitus interruptus).

Contraception

Conception may be prevented by chemical, mechanical or surgical means. Chemical contraception involves the use of spermicides, which act directly on the ejaculate, or of hormone-based drugs, which inhibit ovulation or interfere with implantation. Mechanical methods are designed to obstruct the passage of sperm and may be used either by the male or by the female; an alternative is the use of the intrauterine device, the effect of which is to intercept the fertilised ovum. Coitus interruptus could be regarded as a form of 'mechanical' contraception. Surgical methods of contraception may range from 'menstrual extraction' to sterilisation.

The supply of contraceptives to a woman is a matter between her and her doctor. There is certainly no legal or ethical obligation to obtain the consent of a husband when the treatment, of whatever type, is given on medical grounds; the use of contraceptives or sterilisation without spouse consent could conceivably lead to divorce proceedings on the grounds of intolerable behaviour, a possibility which might well influence the doctor who is asked to prescribe or act on purely social grounds[1]. The controversy as to the legality and morality of supplying contraceptives to girls below the age of 16 has been settled, at least as to the law, by *Gillick v West Norfolk and Wisbech Area Health Authority and another*[2]. It is now decided that, in exceptional circumstances, and subject to stringent conditions laid down by Lord Fraser in the House of Lords, a doctor may legally provide contraceptive advice and treatment for a girl under the age of 16 without the knowledge or consent of her parents. It was also made clear that the doctor in so doing cannot, save in wholly improbable circumstances, be held guilty of abetting an offence under the Sexual Offences Act 1956, s.6[3]. Further aspects of *Gillick* are discussed under 'Confidentiality', 'Consent by minors' and 'Parental rights'.

The legal question mark still hanging over contraception relates to those methods which prevent implantation of the fertilised ovum and their relationship to abortion. Clearly, a doctor who prescribes a 'morning after pill' is not complying with the terms of the Abortion Act 1967; is he, therefore, guilty under the Offences Against the Person Act 1861, ss.58 and 59, of administering, supplying or procuring a 'noxious thing' with intent to procure the miscarriage of a woman? The pragmatic position must be that it depends upon whether or not implantation has occurred although, strictly speaking, this is irrelevant as the Act states that an offence is committed 'whether [the woman] be or be not with child'. It is, however, difficult to argue that there can be an intent to procure a miscarriage if it is probable that there is no 'carriage'[4] and it would be straining language to suggest that a fertilised but unimplanted ovum is a 'child' or, indeed, a human being[5].

The Director of Public Prosecutions has ruled that the use of the post-coital pill constitutes no offence but the matter has not been pronounced upon by any court[6]. The issue must therefore remain open, and caution should be adopted in prescribing such treatment at a stage at which implantation might well have taken place. Guidelines issued by the Department of Health and Social Security recommend prescription within 72 hours of intercourse, although this may be unduly restrictive. Similar arguments apply, probably with greater force, to the deliberate fitting of intrauterine devices after intercourse. Most people, it is felt, would regret it if legalistic niceties were to prohibit a procedure which, if it *is* abortion, is certainly the least offensive form of termination of pregnancy.

See also: Abortion; Abortion Act 1967; Age of consent to sexual practices; Confidentiality; Consent by minors; Divorce; Menstrual extraction; Miscarriage; Parental rights; Sterilisation

1. *Baxter v Baxter* [1948] AC 274; *White v White* [1948] P 330.
2. (a) [1983] 3 WLR 859, [1984] 1 All ER 365 QBD;   (b) [1985] 2 WLR 413 CA;   (c) [1985] 3 WLR 830, HL.
3. Having intercourse with a girl below the age of 16.

4. Medicolegal 'The postcoital pill: lawful or not?' (1983) 287 Br Med J 64.
5. Williams G 'Human life and post-coital pill' (1983) *The Times*, 13 April, p.11.
6. (1983) *The Times*, 11 May, p.1.

Contre-coup Injuries

Contre-coup injuries to the brain are found as haemorrhages or as lacerations of the brain substance at the side opposite to the main point of impact by the head with a hard object. The contre-coup lesion is often more severe than is the direct injury and probably results from displacement of the brain, which continues to move after the skull is arrested. A potential space is thus formed and the contre-coup lesion is of the nature of a suction injury aggravated by tearing of small vessels and by abrasive injury as the brain moves over the rough surface of the base of the skull; similar movement of the occipital lobes will be across the smooth dura of the tentorium cerebelli and this may account for the rarity of contre-coup lesions in the occipital lobes as opposed to their frequent occurrence in the frontal and temporal lobes[1].

It is apparent from this explanation that contre-coup lesions are associated with decelerative head injuries — the moving head is stopped abruptly; the double lesion discovered when, say, a person has fallen onto the back of the head contrasts with the single 'coup' or direct injury resulting from a blow by a blunt instrument in the same region.

See also: Head injury; Intracerebral haemorrhage

1. *See* Rowbotham GF *Acute Injuries of the Head* (4th ed, 1964) p.72, Livingstone, Edinburgh.

Contributory Negligence

In the past, the contributory negligence of a plaintiff who was at all to blame for the occurrence of damage constituted a complete defence for the defendant. The injustice of this rule was apparent and the principle of apportionment of damages was introduced into English law with the passing of the Law Reform (Contributory Negligence) Act 1945[1]. A plaintiff who deserves to bear some responsibility for his injury is now not barred from claiming damages, but his award will be reduced in accordance with the degree of his failure to protect himself from injury. The reduction of damages to plaintiffs who were not wearing seat belts at the time of a vehicular accident is a good example of the operation of this principle.

The question of whether a plaintiff showed any negligence is determined on the same grounds as is that of the defendant's negligence — that is, by asking whether his conduct was reasonable in the circumstances. The 'agony of the moment' rule is, however, a particular consideration which applies in this context. A plaintiff who finds himself in a dangerous situation which has been created by another will not be expected to behave in a totally calm and competent fashion; doing something ill-advised in the agony of the moment will not, then, necessarily constitute contributory negligence[2].

See also: Negligence; Seat belts

1. For a good general account, *see* Fleming JG *Law of Torts* (6th ed, 1983) p.241 et seq, Sweet & Maxwell, London.
2. *Workers Compensation Board v Schmidt* (1977) 80 DLR 3d 696.

Controlled Drugs

Controlled drugs are defined as those which are controlled under the Misuse of Drugs Act 1971[1]. The group is no longer confined to the old classification of narcotics but includes drugs which, while not apparently addictive, constitute a social danger. Thus, the hallucinogens, certain stimulants and cannabis come within the regulations.

The classification of controlled drugs is subject to the advice of the Advisory Council on the Misuse of Drugs. They are divided into classes A, B and C. The distinction is based on the punishment specified for their unlawful production, supply and possession; since the penalties for unlawful supply are likely to be greatest in the case of drugs with maximum harmful effect, it follows that those drugs considered most dangerous are in Class A whilst those which are little more than a social nuisance are in Class C. Class A drugs include morphine and its derivatives (including heroin), many alternative addictive drugs, the hallucinogens (LSD, mescaline, etc.) and pure cannabis in the form of cannabinol. The most important Class B drugs are the barbiturates, the amphetamines and cannabis itself; the benzodiazepine tranquillisers are now included in Class C[2]. Certain drugs which are not only controlled but also have no medicinal value are subject to further regulation in Sch.1 of the 1985 Regulations; these include the hallucinogens and derivatives of cannabis, which can be lawfully possessed only under licence from the Home Secretary.

Apart from those who possess the drug by virtue of a medical or dental prescription, practitioners, pharmacists, hospital matrons, ward or theatre sisters (under authority), persons in charge of laboratories and masters of ships without a doctor may produce, supply and possess controlled drugs lawfully; broad categories of persons involved in testing for or transportation of drugs are also excluded from the general prohibition on production and supply (1985 Regulations, rr.8, 9 and 10). Midwives may possess a controlled drug for use in their profession provided it has been supplied by the appropriate community health specialist. Registers must be kept of supply and disposal of Class A and B drugs, and no such drug can be destroyed save under the direction of a person authorised to do so by the Secretary of State (r.26).

The prescription for a controlled drug must conform to r.15. In particular, this stipulates that the prescription must be in the practitioner's own handwriting and written in ink or by other indelible means, that the form, strength and total quantity of the drug to be given must be specified in both words and figures and that the patient for whom the drug is intended for treatment must be identified by name and address. Repeat prescriptions are not permitted but prescription of a total quantity by instalment is allowable if the directions specify the amount of each instalment and the intervals to be observed.

Controlled drugs, other than a limited number, including amphetamines in liquid form, must be kept in a locked receptacle which can be opened only by the person authorised to possess the drug or by someone authorised by him to open it[3]. A locked car is not a locked receptacle for the purpose of these regulations[4]; a locked glove compartment within a locked car would probably qualify.

See also: Drug addiction; Amphetamines; Cannabis and its aliases; Hallucinogens; Misuse of Drugs Act 1971

1. And with its associated Misuse of Drugs Regulations 1985 (SI 1985/2066).
2. Misuse of Drugs Act 1971 (Modification) Order 1985 (SI 1985/2066).
3. Misuse of Drugs (Safe Custody) Regulations 1973 (SI 1973/798). *See also* the (Amendment) Regulations 1985 (SI 1985/2067).
4. *Rao v Wyles* [1949] 2 All ER 685.

Cor Pulmonale

This is a form of heart disease which is secondary to disease of the lungs — particularly fibrosing disease (*see* 'Pneumoconioses'). Restriction of the pulmonary capillary bed throws increasing strain on the right ventricle, which is ill equipped to respond to the demand. Progressive right ventricular failure occurs and cor pulmonale may be a cause of acute death in, say, chronic asthmatics.

See also: Heart disease; Pneumoconioses

Coronary Disease

The heart muscle is supplied with oxygenated blood by the coronary arteries, which branch from the aorta close to its origin. The left coronary artery supplies the bulk of the muscle and divides into two major branches — the left anterior descending and the circumflex vessels; the right coronary artery supplies mainly the right and posterior walls of the heart. The left and right vessels anastomose (interlink) freely and this allows for the formation of a collateral circulation in the event that a vessel becomes ineffective. Life depends upon the efficient functioning of the heart muscle and its blood supply is therefore of paramount importance; in practice, disease of the coronary vessels is a major underlying cause of death in general and is the most important single underlying cause of sudden death. Some 60–70 per cent of deaths referred to the coroner are attributable to coronary disease.

With few exceptions — congenital abnormality being one — atheroma constitutes the basis of fatal coronary disease; for reasons which are uncertain, this most commonly affects the left anterior descending vessel which supplies the nervous conducting system of the heart. Atheroma is a slowly developing process which can be compensated for by the formation of a collateral circulation — which forms the rationale for 'jogging'. Unless the disease is very clearly genetically linked, in which case it characteristically affects young persons, atheroma increases with age and is only rarely symptomatic before the age of 40, from which time the probability of the complication of coronary heart disease increases. Coronary heart disease is usually caused by the acute obstruction of the lumen of a vessel. This may result from detachment of an atheromatous flap or bolus, from the formation of a thrombus on the damaged vascular wall or by reason of acute haemorrhage into a plaque — in which case, the *post mortem* appearances are likely to be those of thrombosis. The vessel may also go into spasm — which will not be demonstrable at autopsy[1]. Alternatively, the vasculature may not be able to respond to the increased demands of emotional or physical stress — as when the vessels are fibrosed or calcified — or increase in the size of the heart may outstrip its blood supply (*see* 'Heart disease'). Thus, the well-known coronary thrombosis is but one aspect of the broad condition of coronary insufficiency[2], the effect of which is to induce ischaemia of the heart muscle or coronary heart disease (*see* 'Myocardial infarction').

Coronary atheroma is widespread in western populations but the prevalence of disease of the heart muscle varies very considerably. Thus, although coronary artery disease is almost a pre-condition to coronary heart disease, the predisposing factors to each are not necessarily the same. Nevertheless, there are strong policy reasons for attempting to eliminate arterial disease from high risk occupations such as professional aviation. Unfortunately, electrocardiography will demonstrate specifically only established myocardial disease and is an inaccurate measure of simple atheroma; apart from some very innovative methods such as radionuclide imaging, the only real measure of coronary artery restriction is the invasive technique of angiography which can scarcely be used as a routine screening test. The modern approach to the elimination of significant coronary artery disease relies on probability estimates — based on risk factors and the results of such tests as can reasonably be applied — and concentration on those likely to be at risk of heart disease rather than on the general population[3].

See also: Aircraft accidents; Angiography; Atheroma; Electrocardiogram; Heart disease; Myocardial infarction; Thrombosis

1. *See* Leading Articles 'Coronary artery spasm': [1977] 1 Br Med J 1176; [1979] 1 Br Med J 969.
2. A recent occlusive thrombus will be found in approximately one-third of those dying suddenly from ischaemic heart disease: Davies M J and Popple A 'Sudden unexpected cardiac death — a practical approach to the forensic problem' (1979) 3 Histopathology 255.
3. Epstein SE 'Implications of probability analysis on the strategy used for non-invasive detection of coronary artery disease (1980) 46 Am J Cardiol 491.

Coroner

The office of the coroner dates, at least, from the twelfth century, since when his role and standing has varied. An unfortunate result of this is that the coronial system was transported to the New World at a very unsatisfactory time and has, thus, attracted some distrust in North America.

The modern English coroner, however, bears very little resemblance to his US counterpart who is now largely replaced by the medical examiner. The English coroner is appointed by the local authority under the Local Government Act 1972. He must be a doctor or a lawyer of at least five years' standing in his profession, many coroners being doubly qualified. He is responsible to himself alone and only the High court can give him instructions. His jurisdiction lies only within his own area but there are practical rules to cover such eventualities as two deaths arising from a single incident but occurring in two different districts.

The watershed in legislation, and still the definitive statute, was the Coroners Act 1887 which emphasised the role of the coroner as an investigator of unexpected, unexplained or suspicious deaths occurring within his jurisdiction. Under s.3(1), the coroner was bound in such circumstances to summon a jury 'to inquire as jurors touching the death of such person'. The 1887 Act was greatly modified in the Coroners (Amendment) Act 1926 which enabled the coroner to look into certain types of death without recourse to an open inquest — i.e. those deaths which were shown at postmortem to be natural in origin — and, whilst still insisting on the public nature of an inquest, to dispense with a jury save in specified conditions.

The role of the coroner vis-à-vis those responsible for criminal investigation and prosecution has been under consideration for some time and the Criminal Law Act 1977 strictly limited his functions in relation to cases of murder, manslaughter, infanticide or killing by reckless driving in such cases he must now accede to a request by the Director of Public Prosecutions to adjourn his inquest — and need not reopen after the criminal proceedings are completed — and, in the event of evidence of unlawful killing coming to light during the course of an inquest, the case must be adjourned and the DPP informed of the circumstances. Thus, whilst the coroner may sit with a jury if he thinks it necessary, the only occasions on which he is now obliged to do so are when it is suspected that death:

(a) occurred in prison or in such circumstances as to require an inquest under any Act other than the Coroners Act 1887.

(b) was due to an accident, poisoning or disease that must be notified to any government department or an inspector appointed under the Health and Safety at Work etc. Act 1974, s.19.

(c) occurred in circumstances, the continuance of or possible recurrence of which is likely to be prejudicial to the public[1].

(d) occurred while the deceased was in police custody or resulted from an injury caused by a police officer in the purported execution of his duty[2].

Other duties and responsibilities of the Coroner have been affected by recent legislation. For example, he need not now view the body which is the subject of his inquiry[3]. He cannot, however, evade his statutory responsibilities, which have been interpreted as including a duty to inquire into the suspicious death of any body lying within his jurisdiction notwithstanding the fact that both the death and the cause of death arose abroad[4].

The conduct of the coroner's court and the procedure to be followed are detailed in the Coroners Rules 1984 (SI 1984/552). The power of the coroner or his jury to make recommendations designed to prevent a recurrence of the conditions leading to the inquest has been removed although the coroner may still report a matter of concern to an appropriate authority; no verdict can be framed in such a way as suggests criminal or civil liability on the part of a named person. The conclusions or verdict of a coroner's inquest as to the manner of death are limited to unlawful killing, killed himself, attempted/self-induced abortion, accident/misadventure, execution of sentence of death, lawful killing, natural causes, industrial disease, want of attention at birth, dependence on drugs/non-dependent abuse of drugs, aggravated by lack of care/self-neglect — this last being restricted to being added, when appropriate, to conclusions of natural causes, industrial disease, drug dependence or abuse, or want of attention at birth; an open verdict can be returned.

A general duty rests on 'any person about the deceased' to inform the coroner of circumstances that indicate the need for an inquiry but the only statutory duty to approach the coroner direct lies with the governor of a prison, borstal or detention centre or the like. The registrar of deaths must report to the coroner any deaths which the certificate of cause of death indicates was, *inter alia*, in doubt as to cause, unobserved, unnatural, associated with anaesthesia and/or surgical operation or industrial in origin. In practice, it is far easier for the doctor concerned to report such a death directly; he should then issue a death certificate which indicates that he has done so.

The coroner has various options open to him when he is informed of a death that he considers to lie within his jurisdiction. He can accept the certificate of cause of death rendered by the practitioner and so inform the registrar; he can order a postmortem examination and can certify the death himself if it is shown to be due to natural causes; in any other circumstances, he may hold an inquest and must do so, with or without a jury (*see* above), if the cause is unnatural. He then issues a certificate of death after inquest. The registrar must not issue a certificate for disposal of a dead body which is the subject of a coroner's inquest; in such circumstances, the coroner himself issues either an order for burial or a certificate for cremation.

The Brodrick Committee[5] concluded forcefully that the main function of the modern coroner is to ensure accuracy in the certification of death, which explains the fact that over 98 per cent of cases referred to the coroner are examined by postmortem dissection. Nearly a quarter of all deaths are so referred and, of these, at least 80 per cent will have been due to natural causes.

See also: Autopsy; Burial; Cremation; Death certification; Medical examiner; Registrar of births, deaths and marriages

1. Effectively only if the recurrence can be prevented or safeguarded against as a result of action taken by some authority. *R v HM Coroner for West Hammersmith ex parte B Peach* (No.1) [1980] 2 WLR 496.
2. Administration of Justice Act 1982, s.62.
3. Coroners Act 1980.
4. *R v West Yorkshire Coroner ex parte Smith* [1982] 3 WLR 920.
5. Brodrick NJL (chairman) *Report of the Committee on Death Certification and Coroners* (Cmnd 4810) (1971) HMSO, London.

Cot Deaths

Also known as 'crib deaths' in the USA, cot deaths can in fact occur anywhere a baby is put to sleep. *See* 'Sudden infant death syndrome'.

Court of Protection

The Court of Protection is set up to deal with the property and business concerns of those who cannot deal with their own affairs by reason of mental disorder[1]. The business of the Court is run by a Master and his assistants, the scope of the Court's powers and the procedure it adopts being governed by Part VII of the Mental Health Act 1983[2].

The Court can intervene on the request of any party with an interest, usually a relative, friend or solicitor. A patient must be suffering from some form of mental disorder, which includes mental impairment. Medical evidence must be produced in any application to the effect that the patient is incapable of looking after his own affairs by reason of his mental condition. A patient may object to an application, although the onus is then on him to prove that he is capable.

The Court normally appoints a receiver who is charged with the task of running the day-to-day property and financial affairs of the patient. Although the Court is empowered to conduct legal proceedings concerned with the patient's personal life, neither the receiver nor the Court has power to take decisions relating to his treatment or his person in general; the jurisdiction is essentially property orientated.

No provision is made for the regular review of the Court's control over the patient's affairs and the Court's interest usually continues until the death of the patient. It is possible, however, that the patient may recover and the receiver is, then, completely discharged.

In Scotland, the functions of the Court of Protection are performed by the *curator bonis*.

See also: Curator bonis; Mental Health Act 1983; Mental patients' rights

1. For brief accounts of the work of the Court, *see* Hoggett B *Mental Health Law* (2nd ed, 1984) p.331 et seq, Sweet & Maxwell, London; Whitehead T *Mental Illness and the Law* (1982) p.104 et seq, Blackwell, Oxford. *See also* Heywood NA and Massey A *Court of Protection Practice* (11th ed, 1985) Stevens, London.
2. Court of Protection Rules 1984 (SI 1984/2035).

Cremation

Cremation, the reduction of the dead body to ashes, is statutorily controlled under the Cremation Acts 1902 and 1952[1]. The legal procedure is founded in the Cremation Regulations 1930 as amended in 1952, 1965 and 1985[2]. It is an offence to burn any remains other than in accordance with the regulations (Cremation Act 1902, s.8(1)) — which means that cremation can be carried out only in a certified crematorium. The crematoria must be sited so they do not create a nuisance. The average programme for the reduction of a body to ashes involves exposure to a temperature of 600°C for one hour. The only circumstances in which a body can be cremated prior to registration of the death are when the coroner or procurator fiscal has issued a certificate for cremation before his inquiries are complete or when the registrar of deaths has issued a certificate of non-liability for registration.

The procedure for disposal of a body by cremation is somewhat cumbersome and is best described in relation to the prescribed forms[3]. Form A constitutes an application for cremation which must normally be signed by an executor or the nearest relative — but it may be signed by anyone whose *bona fides* is accepted by the cremation authority. Ten searching questions must be answered — which, strangely, no longer include a note as to the wishes of the deceased[4] — and the application must be countersigned by a householder. Two medical certificates are required save in special circumstances. Form B is completed by the registered medical practitioner who attended the deceased during his or her last illness and who can certify the cause of death with certainty; Form B does not, however, replace the normal certificate of cause of death. Eighteen answers are required (20 in Scotland) amongst which are statements as to the doctor's relationship to the deceased and to any pecuniary interest in the death. Form C is a confirmatory certificate which must be signed by a doctor who has been fully registered for five years or more. He must not be a relative or a partner of the doctor signing Form B although practicalities generally dictate that two doctors working in the same hospital may sign. Effectively, seven questions are asked; these relate in the main to corroborative investigations made. The confirming doctor must have undertaken *some* form of corroborative investigation; the pathologist will normally complete Form C in the event of a postmortem dissection having been carried out. Both certifying doctors must see the body after death and a fee is chargeable in both cases. The forms are then scrutinised by the medical referee, a practitioner of at least five years' standing appointed for this purpose by the Secretary of State on the nomination of the cremation authority. His powers and duties are described in a separate entry. Having satisfied himself that the conditions have been fulfilled, he authorises the superintendent of the crematorium to cremate the body, on Form F. Form G is the register of cremations completed by the superintendent, who must send a notice of cremation to the registrar of deaths within 96 hours of the event.

The circumstances in which the two medical certificates are waived are as follows. Very rarely, the medical referee himself or his appointee performs a postmortem examination, in which case the results are recorded on Form D. In all cases coming under their jurisdiction, the coroner or procurator fiscal will issue a certificate giving permission for cremation, on Form E which, again, does not substitute for the appropriate certificate of cause of death. If the body has been the subject of anatomical dissection, the licensed teacher of anatomy completes Form H. A recent amendment allows for Form C to be waived if the deceased died in hospital and the doctor completing Form B knows that a postmortem dissection has been done by a registered medical practitioner of at least five years' standing and is aware of the result[5]; in practice, this regulation does little more than complicate the work of the medical referee. The medical referee may dispense with the regulations if death was due to infectious disease.

A distinct form of medical certificate signed by one doctor is used when a stillbirth is cremated. The medical referee must still authorise cremation on Form F in all these cases but, rather surprisingly, a body which has been buried for not less than one year can be cremated after exhumation without further documentation. In the event of a body being returned from abroad, an application for cremation is sent to the appropriate Secretary of State who will either issue a licence for cremation or will refer the matter to the medico-legal authority.

Form G is completed by the superintendent of the crematorium and includes details as to disposal of the ashes; these must either be given to the applicant for cremation or be interred or be scattered on ground set aside for that purpose.

The Roman Catholic Church at one time opposed cremation as a means of disposal of the dead but has now relented and priests may officiate at cremation services.

See also: Coroner; Death certification; Exhumation; Medical referee; Procurator fiscal; Registered medical practitioner; Registration of births and deaths; Stillbirth

1. A number of amendments are contained in the Local Government Act 1972.
2. Separate regulations are issued for Scotland but there are no essential differences from the medico-legal aspect (SI 1935/247 as amended).
3. The Report of the Committee on Death Certification and Coroners (Cmnd 4810) (para.27.34) strongly recommended simplification of the procedure. The statutory forms are laid out in the Schedule to the 1930 Regulations.
4. Cremation Regulations 1965 (SI 1965/1146), r.7.
5. Cremation (Amendment) Regulations 1985 (SI 1985/153); Cremation (Scotland) Amendment Regulations 1985 (S.73) (SI 1985/820).

Criminal Responsibility

Criminal responsibility is attributed to those persons who are capable of being held to account for their criminal actions. A person is not criminally responsible if, for some reason, he is exempted from the normal provisions of the criminal law[1].

Children below the age of 14 are considered to have restricted responsibility for criminal acts to a varying extent; the subject is discussed under 'Age of legal responsibility'[2]. Similarly, persons who are mentally abnormal will not be held to be criminally responsible provided that they can satisfy the requirements of the defence of insanity (*see* 'Insanity and criminal responsibility').

The concept of criminal responsibility differs from that of criminal liability in that the emphasis in determining the latter lies not on the status of the defendant as a person who may or may not be called upon to account for his actions but, rather, on the circumstances in which the criminal act is performed — that is, on the motives or objectives of the defendant at the time of the commission of the *actus reus*.

See also: *Actus reus*; Age of legal responsibility; Insanity and criminal responsibility

1. Hart HLA *Punishment and Responsibility* (1968) Clarendon, Oxford. *See also* Gross H *A Theory of Criminal Justice* (1979) Oxford University Press, New York.
2. For general discussion, *see* Freeman MDA *The Rights and Wrongs of Children* (1983) p.66 et seq, F Pinter, London.

Cruelty to Children
See 'Child abuse'.

Crush Injury

The dangers of crush injury stem from a complex biochemical response to muscle damage which results in acute renal failure with secondary effects upon other organs.

The original injury is typically one of crushing of the major muscle masses, especially those of the legs, which occurs particularly in those who are trapped by a fall of earth or who are pinned in a vehicular accident — often in those accidents in which recovery is a long process such as train disasters[1].

Much depends on how firmly and rapidly treatment is begun and there is a strong case for instituting fluid replacement therapy even while the victim is still trapped. Treatment of the kidney failure is by dialysis but, even then, the mortality in those whose kidneys have failed is more than 60 per cent. This is because other organs of the body which cannot be substituted by machine also fail and, at the same time, the patient becomes susceptible to severe septic infection. Although muscles may some-times recover from severe crushing, amputation will be indicated as soon as the tissues are found to be no longer viable.

The condition is to be distinguished from so called 'crush asphyxia' which is discussed under 'Traumatic asphyxia'.

See also: Dialysis; Fluid replacement therapy; Kidney failure; Traumatic asphyxia

1. For example, Brown AA and Nicholls RJ 'Crush syndrome: a report of 2 cases and a review of the literature' (1977) 64 Br J Surg 397.

Culpable Homicide

Culpable homicide is the equivalent in Scottish criminal law of the English offence of manslaughter. Non-justifiable homicide taking place in the absence of the *mens rea* of murder — that is, in the absence of wicked recklessness or intention to kill — falls to be charged as culpable homicide[1]. Homicide committed under provocation may be considered culpable homicide rather than murder, as may killing by an accused who is found to have diminished responsibility. As a matter of practice, a charge of culpable homicide is brought, *inter alia*, when a mother kills her baby in circumstances which would be charged as infanticide in England, in the case of a survivor of a suicide pact and when a soldier on duty kills in excessive execution of his duty; by and large, killing by omission is regarded as culpable homicide rather than murder. The term 'culpable homicide' is also used in the same sense in certain other legal systems such as in the modern Roman–Dutch law of South Africa.

Culpable homicide attracts a discretionary sentence, the determining factor being the seriousness with which the court views the circumstances of the death.

See also: Homicide; Manslaughter; *Mens rea*; Murder

1. Gordon GH *The Criminal Law of Scotland* (2nd ed, 1978) p.727 et seq, W Green, Edinburgh.

Curator Bonis

A mentally incompetent person is known in Scotland as an incapax and a *curator bonis* may be appointed to manage his affairs. This appointment is made by the court after two independent medical advisers have certified that the incapax cannot look after his own affairs. The *curator bonis* has broad powers over the property of the incapax and sues and is sued on his behalf[1]. Power over the person of the incapax may be exercised by a tutor-at-law who may also be appointed by the court[2]. The powers of the tutor and of the *curator bonis* are, however, distinct.

See also: Court of Protection; Incompetence

1. Walker D *Principles of Scottish Private Law* (3rd ed, 1982) p.211, Oxford University Press, Oxford.
2. *Dick v Douglas* 1924 SC 787.

Cut Throat

Cut throats once formed a relatively common method of suicide; they now seem to be rare whether they are self-inflicted or homicidal. Occasional instances do, however, occur and the interpretation of the specific injuries demonstrates well the distinctions to be made in incised wounds in general.

The homicidal cut throat shows evidence of motivation in that, whilst some cuts may be less deep than others because of resistance by or movement in the victim, none will be superficial and of abrasive type. The tendency will be for cuts to be of irregular shape and direction as the victim moves but, because the intention is to kill rapidly, cuts will be deep and the air passage is likely to be severely severed. Struggles by the victim may have resulted in incisions on the chin or face, and defence injuries in the form of cuts in the fingers or palm are diagnostic when present.

Suicidal throat cuts, by contrast, nearly always show tentative knife strokes, the individual cuts are shelving and, until the major thrust which runs from side to side, are likely to run from the side of the neck to the centre. The tendency is then for the jugular vein to take the main thrust of the stroke although the carotid artery often escapes injury. The site of injury is elective and the face is unlikely to be touched. It may be that the suicide has also attacked his wrists and the finding of characteristic injuries at that point is as diagnostic of suicide as defence injuries are of homicidal assault.

Death may be due to suffocation as the air passages become clogged with blood or the open larynx is occluded by tissue. It is as likely to be due to haemorrhage which can be massive if the carotid artery is cut, as may happen in the homicidal attack. Generally, however, haemorrhage is venous in type and comes from the jugular vein; air may be sucked into open veins and death result from air embolism. Occasionally, death may be very rapid due to vagal inhibition of the heart.

See also: Air embolism; Defence injuries; Haemorrhage; Homicide; Incised wounds; Suicide; Vagal inhibition of the heart

Cyanide

The use of cyanide salts is strictly controlled by their classification, save in very dilute concentration, as both Part I and Schedule 1 poisons (*see* 'Poisons Act 1972'). They may, however, be sold other than through a pharmacy to those whose profession or trade requires their use (Poisons Rules 1978, (SI 1978/1) Sch.4). Cyanide poisoning has therefore lost much of its historic homicidal significance and accidental or suicidal deaths are now virtually confined to chemists, photographers and the like. Its use in the fumigation of ships and so on is controlled by the Hydrogen Cyanide (Fumigation) Act 1937.

An individual entry is given here only because cyanide provides a good example of a toxic asphyxiant — the poisonous action is to inactivate cellular enzymes by a process known as molecular substitution and oxygen cannot be transferred for use within the cells. Thus, a high proportion of the blood remains fully oxygenated and the body is seen at autopsy to be brilliantly pink; it is not difficult to confuse this colour with that seen in carbon monoxide poisoning or with that of the similarly high oxygenation of the blood which is found following hypothermia or refrigeration. The diagnosis can be made by those who are not specifically anosmic to the characteristic smell of bitter almonds which arises in cyanide poisoning. The colour change develops over a finite agonal period and is seen only in those poisoned by cyanide salts — hydrogen cyanide itself causes very rapid death and achieved lasting notoriety as a genocidal agent during the Second World War.

Cyanide salts are present in the seeds of some fruits (eg. apricots and cherries) other than almonds but accidental poisoning from this cause must be exceptionally rare and certainly confined to children.

See also: Asphyxia; Carbon monoxide poisoning; Enzymes; Hypothermia; Poisons Act 1972

Cyanosis

Cyanosis is the colour imparted to the tissues by the presence of an excess of deoxygenated blood — characteristically plum coloured or even purple. It may be localised — for example, in the fingers or toes in cases of reduced arterial blood supply to the limbs. From the medico-legal aspect, cyanosis is significant as evidence of death being associated with generalised hypoxia. Thus, the bodies of persons who have died from asphyxia will appear cyanosed. Nevertheless, it has to be remembered that tissue anoxia is the main component of death and it follows that cyanosis can be, and often is, demonstrable following perfectly natural deaths — the cyanosis of the tissues above the clavicles which is so commonly found in death from coronary insufficiency is a particularly vivid example.

See also: Asphyxia; Coronary disease; Death; Hypoxia

D

Damages

The principle underlying an award for damages for personal injury is that of full compensation for the results of that injury. Damages may be general or special. General damages are awarded for the losses which the courts presume to flow from the tortious act[1]; special damages are particular losses (such as lost earnings) which the plaintiff has suffered and which must be specified and proved before payment. The main types of damages of medico-legal interest are medical expenses, pain and suffering, and loss of amenity.

Medical expenses fall into the category of special damages. It is accepted that an injured plaintiff can recover reasonable medical and incidental expenses incurred as a result of his injury. These may include the cost of travelling to obtain medical treatment, the cost of special appliances and fees[2]. The court will not take account of the fact that a patient can obtain treatment from the NHS without charge[3]. The plaintiff's ordinary living expenses, which he would have faced anyway, may be set off against the cost of being in a private nursing home or hospital[4].

Damages for pain and suffering may be awarded in respect of that which has already been experienced and that which can be anticipated. Pain means pain in the ordinary sense of the word; suffering includes fright, humiliation and embarrassment but does not include grief and sorrow[5]. The duration of the pain is an important factor in assessing damages; an unconscious person, who cannot experience pain and suffering, will not be given an award under this head[6]. Damages may also be awarded for nervous shock.

The distinct nature of damages for loss of amenities has now been recognised. They are awarded for the loss of bodily function, which includes the loss of a sense such as taste or smell[7]. The basis of the award is compensation for the inability to enjoy activities which were available before the accident. The loss of a limb will clearly prevent or inhibit the enjoyment of certain sporting activities; physical injury may also prevent the enjoyment of sexual intercourse. The age and condition of the plaintiff at the time of the injury may be taken into account[8]. The principle that an unconscious patient may be given damages for loss of amenities[9] has been subject to some criticism.

Damages may be reduced if there is contributory negligence on the part of the plaintiff or if it is established that there was a pre-existing medical condition which was merely aggravated by the injury[10]. Similarly, failure on the part of the plaintiff to take steps to mitigate his loss may result in a reduction of the award. The plaintiff's refusal to seek or follow medical advice has frequently led to reduction of damages (see 'Refusal of medical treatment' and 'Contributory negligence').

A major difficulty in assessing damages for personal injury lies in calculating the future losses of the plaintiff. Damages must be awarded in a lump sum and, consequently, the court may have to assess the likelihood of future deterioration in the plaintiff's condition. Pressure for the acceptance of interim awards has now resulted in a change in the law which allows for the awarding, at the plaintiff's request, of provisional damages when the medical prognosis is particularly uncertain[11]. Medical predictions as to the plaintiff's future are still, of course, required when a claim is made for damages in respect of loss of future earnings. These damages, known as 'lost years' damages, are intended to compensate the plaintiff for the loss of earnings that he could have expected during the years which he will not now live because of his injury[12].

The death of the injured party does not mean the extinction of all claims. The estate of the deceased victim may carry on an action against the defendant (or his estate) and the dependants of a deceased can bring an action against the person who has wrongfully caused the death of their relative, under the Fatal Accidents Act 1976 or the Damages (Scotland) Act 1976. This action is open to ascendants and descendants and to a spouse, including a person who lived with the deceased as de facto husband or wife[13]. A claim for bereavement is also available in respect of the death of a spouse or of a minor child who is not yet married.

See also: Compensation; Contributory negligence; Limitation of liability; Nervous shock; Refusal of medical treatment; Unconscious plaintiff

1. Dias RW and Markesinis BD *Tort Law* (1984) p.388, Oxford University Press, Oxford.
2. *Oakley v Walker* (1977) 121 SJ 619. The cost of special forms of accommodation may be awarded: *Cunningham v Harrison* [1973] QB 942; cf. *George v Pinnock* [1973] 1 WLR 118. A claim for a convalescent holiday may be reasonable: *Salmon v Newland* (1983) Times, 16 May.
3. Law Reform (Personal Injuries) Act 1948, s.2 (4); *Harris v Brights Asphalt Contractors Ltd* [1953] 1 QB 617 at 675.
4. *Shearman v Folland* [1950] 2 KB 43, CA.
5. McGregor H *Damages* (14th ed, 1980) p.831, Sweet & Maxwell, London.
6. *Wise v Kaye* [1962] 1 QB 638.
7. As in *Cook v JL Kier and Co* [1970] 1 WLR 774.
8. *Bird v Cocking and Sons Ltd* [1951] 2 TLR 1260.
9. *Lim Poh Choo v Camden and Islington Area Health Authority* [1979] 3 WLR 44.
10. Poole L 'Pre-existing medical conditions and the award of damages' (1981) 131 NLJ 696.
11. Supreme Court Act 1981, s.32A, inserted by Administration of Justice Act 1982, ss.6–12, refers in the same way to Scotland.
12. *Pickett v British Rail Engineering Limited* [1979] 1 All ER 774.
13. Administration of Justice Act 1982, s.3.

Dangerousness

The prediction of dangerous behaviour is a controversial subject both in psychiatry and in criminology[1]. The claims of some experts to be able to predict with near accuracy the likelihood of a person behaving in a dangerous fashion are not always accepted[2]; many would argue, particularly, that such predictions should not be taken into account when considering detention or sentencing. Recent research covering a wide variety of disciplines has, however, meant that a far broader range of techniques is now available for the purpose and indicates that future multidisciplinary studies may yield interesting results.

Some psychiatrists are willing to predict future behaviour on the basis that a person having a particular psychiatric history will be predisposed to violent or aggressive behaviour if exposed to stress or provocation[3]. Occasionally, such formulae seem attractively simple, an illustration being the association of enuresis, firesetting and cruelty to animals as a childhood triad linked with violent criminal behaviour in adulthood[4]. Other studies have attempted to correlate parental violence in childhood with later homicidal tendencies[5].

It is the increasing practice of the UK courts, when having regard to the seriousness of a crime and the likelihood of its repetition, to impose restriction orders under the Mental Health Act 1983, s.41 without limit of time. To some extent, this absolves the psychiatrist from making an almost impossible prognosis of the permanence of dangerousness but it imposes additional strains in advising as to discharge. This, again, implies a predictive skill in an area where infallibility is unlikely to be claimed, and most psychiatrists tend, in the wake of some unfortunate errors, to be overcautious.

The practical difficulties confronting psychiatrists or clinical psychologists in relation to the diagnosis and management of dangerous patients has been comprehensively demonstrated in the USA following the decision in *Tarasoff v Regents of the University of California*[6] in which a psychotherapist was found to be negligent in having failed to warn an identifiable person of the possibility of an attack by a discharged, although violent, patient. This decision limited liability to named persons but the ratio was later further extended to include victims who were unidentifiable — 'a physician may have a duty to take whatever steps are reasonably necessary to protect a potential victim of his patient when he determines, or should determine. . .in accordance with the standards of his profession that the patient may present a probability of danger to that person'[7]. One ethical difficulty in this determination is that it breaks the confidential relationship between physician and patient; nevertheless, the Georgia Supreme Court has held that such cases involve a general duty owed by the physician to 'all the world'[8]. It seems improbable that similar assessments of the physician's duty of care will be made in the UK.

The general ethical implications of predictions of dangerousness dictate great caution in their use. Prognoses made in the expectation of a high false positive rate may result in the protection of the public from a certain number of dangerous people but this will be at the cost of penalising many who pose no real threat. The morality of such involvement of psychiatrists must surely reach its most questionable point when they are asked to assess a prisoner's dangerousness in relation to whether or not the death penalty should be imposed — a duty which is being increasingly opposed in the USA[9]; British psychiatrists are, fortunately, unlikely to be called upon in such a capacity.

See also: Mental Health Act 1983; Psychiatric evidence; Restriction orders; Special hospitals

1. For recent discussion, *see* Hinton JW (ed) *Dangerousness: Problems of Assessment and Prediction* (1983), Allen & Unwin, London.
2. Ennis PJ and Literack TR 'Psychiatry and the presumption of expertise: flipping coins in the courtroom' (1974) 62 Cal LR 693.
3. *See* Scott PD 'Assessing dangerousness in criminals' (1977) 131 Br J Psychiat 127.
4. Hellman DS and Blackburn M 'Enuresis, firesetting and cruelty to animals: a triad predictive of adult crime' (1966) 122 Am J Psychiat 1431.
5. Duncan JW and Duncan GM 'Murder in the family: study of some homicidal adolescents' (1971) 127 Am J Psychiat 1498.
6. 131 Cal Rptr 14 (Cal, 1976).
7. *McIntosh v Milano* 403 A 2d 500 (NJ, 1979).
8. *The Bradley Center Inc v Wessner* 296 SE 2d 693 (Ga, 1982).
9. *See* Ewing CP '"Dr Death" and the case for an ethical ban on psychiatric and psychological predictions of dangerousness in capital sentencing proceedings' (1983) 8 Am J Law Med 407.

De Minimis

The adage *de minimis non curat lex* (the law does not concern itself with trifles) plays a valuable role in distinguishing matters of importance from petty issues. The rationale is really one of common sense — it is not worth wasting the courts' time to consider minor infringements of legal rights.

There have been attempts to extend this principle to occasions when the *actus reus* is defined in terms of quantity. Thus, pleas of special reasons for non-disqualification under the old Road Safety Act 1967, s.1 (now Road Traffic Act 1972, s.6), have been made on the grounds that a slight excess of alcohol over the prescribed limit was scarcely worth consideration and punishment; this argument was rejected[1]. There have been similar attempts in relation to the possession of controlled drugs; such actions have, however, also failed, the court deciding that, here at least, a trifle weighing only a few micrograms should be a proper concern of the law[2].

See also: Misuse of Drugs Act 1971; Road Traffic Act 1972

1. *Delaroy-Hall v Tadman (and associated cases)* (1968) Times, 9 November.
2. *Bocking v Roberts* [1974] QB 307.

Death

It is commonly stated that death is a process rather than something which occurs at a moment in time. This is perfectly true in relation to 'cellular death'. Individual cells of the body will 'live' on their residual oxygen for a variable time after the circulation has stopped, this being the basis for transplantation of essential organs such as the heart. Variations in survival depend upon the metabolic activity of the cell — brain cells, for example, are unlikely to survive more than ten minutes in the absence of fresh oxygen whilst the relatively inert cells of the prostate gland would manage for a matter of hours. 'Somatic death' (i.e. death of the human organism) is, however, different in practice. It is astonishing how easy it is when watching a patient die to know precisely the point at which death occurred — the concept of the 'soul leaving the body' can be well appreciated. Instinctively, the observer is noting the respirations, the heart beat and the tone of the body and, on this basis, death can be defined as 'the irrevocable cessation of the cardiorespiratory system' which becomes 'a permanent state of tissue anoxia' when applied at the cellular level. But difficulties arise in a small minority of cases.

Firstly, there are technical difficulties. If death has not been witnessed, it may be difficult to diagnose it with certainty particularly in those conditions which are associated with what might be described as 'suspended animation' — hypothermia, subnutrition and drug overdose; a combination of these has been responsible for a number of cases 'reviving' in the mortuary. These uncertainties are compounded by the possibilities of, secondly, resuscitation — in any circumstance giving rise to ventricular fibrillation, of which the most important is acute coronary insufficiency, it may well be possible to reactivate the heart; the 'irrevocable' aspect of cardiac failure then becomes a relative matter. Thirdly, there are the philosophical problems associated with the definition of death in terms of the cardiorespiratory system and the maintenance of that system by machine; this wide subject is discussed under 'Brain stem death'.

As a result of the modern proliferation of these minority complications, there are those who advocate a statutory definition of death[1] and, in fact, several States of the USA have enacted such legislation[2]. In view of the reluctance of the British courts to attempt to define death[3], it seems unlikely that such legislation will be introduced in the UK. The great majority of statutes or proposals for legislation do no more than codify what is already good medical practice. Indeed, the main justification for legislation might well be to define what is *not* death; death must be regarded as an absolute concept despite the insidious moves to include within its compass conditions which involve loss of humanity such as the persistent vegetative state.

See also: Brain stem death; Persistent vegetative state; Transplantation of organs; Ventilator support

1. Skegg PDG 'The case for a statutory "diagnosis of death"' (1976) 2 J Med Ethics 190 gives a succinct summary.
2. Meyers DW *Medico-legal Implications of Death and Dying* (1983) Chap.4, Lawyers Co-op, Rochester NY. Three types of statute are recognised: those which provide two alternative definitions of death (e.g. Kansas), those which allow for brain death criteria when the heart and respiration are being maintained artificially (e.g. Michigan) and those in which the law is flexible (e.g. California). The Uniform Brain Death Act follows the last course.
3. *Finlayson v HM Adv* 1978 SLT (Notes) 60; *R v Malcherek, R v Steel* [1981] 2 All ER 422.

Death Certification

A death cannot be registered in the UK in the absence of a certificate as to the cause of death which, unless the death has been reported to the coroner, must be completed by a registered medical practitioner. The immediate cause of death is recorded first and this is followed in chronological order by the antecedent causes; spaces are available for the recording of conditions which contributed to death but which would be misplaced in the chronological sequence. The format is that recommended by the World Health Organization. Certifiers are encouraged to use the nomenclature of the International Statistical Classification of Diseases, Injuries and Causes of Death but there is no statutory obligation to do so; a certificate which is too indefinite for classification will be returned by the registrar of deaths for elucidation.

The provision of a certificate of the cause of death is a statutory duty for those able to do so and no fee is chargeable. Only the practitioner who was in medical attendance during the deceased's last illness may complete the certificate in England and Wales[1]. The death must be reported to the coroner if there is no one competent to certify — for example, if the practitioner concerned is on holiday; no such limitation exists in Scotland, where any practitioner who is able to do so may certify, and this accounts, in large part, for the smaller number of deaths which are reported to the procurator fiscal. A further reason for the discrepancy between medico-legal referrals in England and Wales and in Scotland lies in the fact that the English practitioner is required to state when he last saw the deceased alive; the case must be referred to the coroner by the registrar if it appears that the certifying practitioner neither saw the body after death nor attended the deceased during the last 14 days of life[3]. There is no similar duty imposed on the Scottish registrar because the certificate does not carry the information[4].

There are some practical differences in certification between England and Scotland. The English certificate carries a 'Notice to Informant' which must be handed to the informant. Strictly speaking, the practitioner is then required to forward the certificate to the registrar forthwith; in practice, the certificate is more conveniently given to the informant. There is no such notice in the Scottish certificate, which must be sent to the registrar within seven days; again, it is common practice to hand it to the informant. The English certificate has space on the reverse for indicating whether more detailed information is likely to be available later and for notifying that the case has been reported to the coroner. No similar spaces are available in the Scottish certificate but it is customary for the practitioner in both jurisdictions to inform either the coroner or the procurator fiscal personally of any case which is likely to invoke medico-legal investigation. Even so, the *correct* procedure is for a certificate to be provided whenever a practitioner is able to do so despite the certainty that the registrar will refer the matter to the appropriate authority[5].

A major purpose of the death certificate is to produce accurate mortality statistics, and there is some doubt as to whether this is being achieved. Major attention is focused on the role of the autopsy in the process and on the need to provide more information of an epidemiological nature. The Scottish certificate, for example, singles out information relating to maternal deaths whilst many would wish for more emphasis on occupational disease[6]. Some changes in procedure can be anticipated in the near future[7].

See also: Autopsy; Coroner; Procurator fiscal; Registration of births and deaths

1. Births and Deaths Registration Act 1953, s.22(1).
2. Registration of Births, Deaths and Marriages (Scotland) Act 1965, s.24(2).
3. Births and Deaths Registration Act 1953, s.51(1)(c).

4. The effects of the procedural differences are discussed in Mason JK 'Coroners from across the Border' (1983) 23 Med Sci Law 271.
5. Leading Article 'Confusion over death certification' [1979] 1 Br Med J 1662.
6. The Industrial Diseases (Notification) Act 1981 shows a slight statutory move towards this goal.
7. See 'Medical aspects of death certification' (1982) 16 J Roy Coll Phys Lond 4, and Alderson MR et al 'Death Certification' (1983) 287 Br Med J 444.

Death Penalty

This topic is discussed under the heading 'Capital punishment'.

Deceleration Injuries

Deceleration injuries are of two types — those which are associated with the deceleration of the body as a whole and those which are related to secondary contact of parts of the moving body with a rigid object. The latter are the most common and are, to some extent, reducible by vehicular safety engineering techniques.

Pure deceleration injuries are a matter of differential movement of parts and organs of the body when it is subjected to impact loads; the effect will differ according to the direction in which the force is applied. Forces involved in impacts are measured in units of gravity (G) and their direction is described as being in the x-axis when front to back, z-axis when applied vertically and y-axis in a lateral situation. It is often convenient to identify the direction of force in descriptive terms related to the inertial movement of the eyeballs; thus, a sudden stop in a vehicle results in $+G_x$ or 'eyeballs out' acceleration. Factors other than the peak G forces affect the outcome, including the rate of onset (or jolt) and the time for which the force is applied; moreover, it is not always that the direction of force will be in a pure plane.

It is quite impossible to summarise here the vast amount of work which has been done in this field[1]. Suffice it to say that human tolerance to pure deceleration is very high in the x-axis, particularly when the deceleration occurs in the rearward facing position (eyeballs in). Loads far in excess of any reasonable restraining system or structural strength of a car can be survived and there have been some astonishing reports of survival from free fall particularly when landing in the supine position; the fundamentally limiting factor would seem to be the rate of onset of change of acceleration. Deceleration in the vertical direction is less likely to be well tolerated if only for the reason that relative movement of the organs of the body is not limited by, say, the chest wall. Thus, in a vertical deceleration, the heart is free to move downwards and may well tear from its moorings; it is particularly liable to do so if the torso is simultaneously allowed to flex and this may account for the fact that, in the presence of only lap belt restraint, a light aircraft accident is twice as likely to be fatal as to result in severe injury.

The elimination of deceleration injuries due to secondary impact depends on strengthening the environment so that it does not implode on the occupant, maintaining separation of the occupant from the surrounding structure and 'delethalising' the surroundings by removing obvious hazards and fashioning them so that they deform when impacted, thus reducing the peak load on the striking object and reducing its rate of onset.

Much has been done in the last sphere by fitting collapsible steering wheels in cars, attending to the construction of the fascia, removing sharp projections and the like; most motor vehicle manufacturers have shown great public spirit in the context of research in this area. The most important single advance has been in the provision of seat belts including upper torso restraint without which the head, chest and upper abdomen of the driver are at great risk in deceleration accidents. The fracture tolerance of the cheekbones is about 50 G and that of the forehead about 150 G but such figures depend upon cadaver experiments rather than practical considerations. Direct pressure on the heart may displace it and rupture its attachment to the aorta whilst the fact that electrocardiographic changes follow cardiac concussion in experimental animals suggests that a causative association may be traceable between a deceleration accident and subsequent myocardial pathology.

Decelerative impact injuries often affect the arms and legs but, in so far as these are unlikely to cause death, they excite less medico-legal interest.

See also: Aircraft accidents; Cardiovascular system; Falls; Parachuting injuries; Road traffic accidents

1. Unfortunately, the great majority of experimental work in this field is published in relatively private journals. A good review is to be found in Gurdjian ES et al (eds) *Impact Injury and Crash Protection* (1970) CC Thomas, Springfield IL. For a very simple explanation, *see* Mills FJ and Harding RM 'Short duration acceleration' (1983) 286 Br Med J 1630.

Declarations

In addition to the Hippocratic Oath, there are a number of Declarations, prepared under the auspices of the World Medical Association (WMA), which are intended to guide the ethos of the medical profession.

It would be pointless to reproduce them in full here; they are readily available in standard works[1]. The most important are, however, summarised below.

Declaration of Geneva 1948 (amended at Sydney 1968 and Venice 1983) This is essentially a restatement of the Hippocratic Oath, each clause of which is transmuted into modern language. The Declaration forms the basis of an international code of medical ethics.

Declaration of Helsinki 1964 (amended in 1975 and again at Venice 1983) This Declaration is the professional counterpart of the Nuremberg Code, which was drawn up in the light of the horrific experiments conducted during the Second World War. The need for human experimentation is acknowledged and a distinction is made between research orientated to the good of the patient or his fellow sufferers and that which is purely scientific in purpose. The basic principles are laid down followed by specific recommendations for each of the two main classes of research;

the various provisions give satisfactory protection to the experimental subjects if they are adhered to.

Declaration of Tokyo 1975 This concerns torture and other cruel, inhuman or degrading treatment or punishment in relation to detention and imprisonment. The tone of the declaration strongly suggests that it was motivated by the treatment of political detainees. The application of all its clauses to the recalcitrant or violent prisoner or, indeed, to the terrorist, is not always easy.

Declaration of Sydney 1968 (amended 1983) This statement, accepting the concept of brain death, was possibly useful at the time it was drafted. Most of its provisions are now no more than standard medical practice.

Declaration of Oslo 1970 (amended 1983) This was originally titled 'a statement on therapeutic abortion'; however, the original limitation that abortion should be performed only as a therapeutic measure was removed during revision. The Declaration is an attempt to bridge the gap between the Hippocratic Oath and modern concepts of a woman's rights to privacy[2].

Statement on Computers in Medicine 1973 (amended 1983) This short statement recognises the great advantage to be gained from electronic data processing in the field of health and lays down good criteria for the maintenance of confidentiality, most of which have been incorporated in the Data Protection Act 1984 and its associated Codes of Practice.

Declaration of Lisbon 1981 This is a statement on the rights of the patient, only one clause of which, related to confidentiality, is truly directed at the physician; the rest is largely a matter of medical administration.

Declaration of Venice 1983 In dealing with terminal illness, the WMA permits the use of artificial means to maintain a cadaver for transplantation purposes and positively prohibits the use of extraordinary means of treatment which would be of no benefit to the patient. The statement condones passive euthanasia but does not attempt to distinguish between withholding treatment and withholding nutriment. The distinction between incurable and terminal disease might have been made plainer[3].

Declaration of Hawaii 1977 This was prepared by the World Psychiatric Association rather than by the WMA. It applies the principles of good medical practice to the particular conditions of psychiatry and pays special attention to teaching and research. The difficulties of the forensic psychiatrist are acknowledged[4].

Many of these Declarations suffer inevitably from their general nature and must be adapted to different societies and to changing times. In fact, they nearly always include a clause acknowledging the supremacy of local legislation and custom.

See also: Abortion; Biomedical experimentation; Brain stem death; Confidentiality; Euthanasia; Hippocratic Oath; Prisoners; Psychiatric evidence; Punishment and torture

1. For example, British Medical Association *The Handbook of Medical Ethics* (1984) BMA, London; Duncan AS et al (eds) *Dictionary of Medical Ethics* (Revised ed, 1981) Darton, Longman & Todd, London; Mason JK and McCall Smith RA *Law and Medical Ethics* (1983) Butterworths, London.
2. *See*, for example, *Roe v Wade* 93 S Ct 705 (1973) which laid down that it was an invasion of a woman's privacy to limit her access to abortion by statute.
3. For consideration of the importance of this, *see* Meyers DW 'Legal aspects of withdrawing nourishment from an incurably ill patient' (1985) 145 Arch Intern Med 125.
4. *See* Chiswick D 'Use and abuse of psychiatric testimony' (1985) 290 Br Med J 975.

Decomposition of the Body

Decomposition of the body is, in essence, a matter of putrefaction. The putrefactive process is, however, modified by environmental factors and decomposition may take the form of mummification or of a change to adipocere. The bones can be said to decompose only as regards their protein content; they may still retain their shape once this is destroyed — often a matter of years — but, being composed of largely inorganic material, will otherwise crumble rather than decompose. An estimate of the radioactive decay of the remaining mineral bone may give a fair estimate of its age in archaeological terms.

See also: Adipocere; Mummification; Putrefaction

Decompression Sickness

Exposure to a relatively low ambient atmospheric pressure occurs in two ways. In the first, decompression to altitude, the subject ascends in a high flying aircraft or balloon. In the second, he may be subjected to increased pressure, as when working in any circumstances in compressed air, particularly exemplified these days in diving operations, and then ascends to ground level. There are important clinical differences in the two processes. Far greater differential pressures are normally attained in the latter situation. More importantly, return to ground level is theoretically curative of any disease process attributable to subatmospheric decompression; by contrast, the return to normal pressure is causative of pathological conditions in a compressed-air worker. The underlying mechanical and physiological changes are similar in both circumstances but the management is quite different. In order to avoid undue repetition, the dangers of compressed-air working are described under 'Diving hazards'. This entry is concerned only with decompression to altitude.

Subatmospheric decompression is usually a fairly slow process. Mechanical changes in the lungs are easily compensated and the symptoms of decompression sickness are due to the 'soda syphon' effect of release of gases from the blood and tissue fluids as the ambient pressure decreases. Symptoms due to oxygen release have been described but the vast majority are, in practice, the result of escape of nitrogen from the body fluids. The least severe but most common manifestations are pain in the joints ('bends') and itching ('creeps'); both may, however, be severe. Respiratory distress ('chokes') is a far more serious symptom which may make it impossible to remain at altitude. Neurological involvement is rare in altitude cases. The threshhold for the onset of decompression sickness is about 5,500 m (18,000 ft) although age and obesity have an adverse effect. Serious mechanical damage to the lungs is uncommon owing to the free passage of air through the trachea and nasopharynx. Otitic barotrauma provides an exception to the general improvement in symptoms with descent to ground level; since air cannot enter the middle ear during recompression, the eardrums may be imploded during rapid descent unless active steps are taken to prevent the occurrence.

A far more serious complication of ascent to high altitude is so-called postdescent shock in which the subject sustains neurocirculatory collapse either at altitude or some time after return to ground level. The condition has a high mortality and its mechanism is uncertain although it has a close but ill-understood association with fat embolism[1]. Although it is now very rare due to pressurisation of aircraft, there is evidence that a combination of increased pressure as is sustained in sports diving followed by exposure to normally acceptable altitudes may be dangerous and a ban on diving within 24 hours before flying is strongly advised.

Explosive decompression, which may arise if, say, a major defect suddenly arises in the cabin of a high flying aircraft, is a very serious hazard. The dangers arise not so much from the pressure change *per se* but from the turbulence produced and from the subsequent hypoxia in those not receiving supplementary oxygen. Multiple fatalities are probable as the aircraft is likely to be sent out of control[2].

See also: Diving hazards; Fat embolism; Hypoxia

1. A classic monograph on all medical aspects of decompression to altitude is to be found in Fryer DI *Subatmospheric Decompression Sickness in Man* (1969) Technivision Services, Slough, Bucks.
2. A historic forensic investigation of such a case was reported by Armstrong JA et al 'Interpretation of injuries in the Comet aircraft disasters' [1955] 1 Lancet ll35. *See also* Mason JK and Tarlton SW 'Medical investigation of the loss of the Comet 4B aircraft, 1967' [1969] 1 Lancet 431.

Defence Injuries

Defence injuries are sustained in an attempt to ward off an assault; they can often be virtually diagnostic of having been so caused.

The most characteristic are those sustained in an attack by a cutting instrument in which some attempt to hold or deflect the weapon is very common. The lethal effect of a knife is related more to its point, its blade being relatively blunt, and typical defence injuries may be lacking when one is used; but attacks with a razor blade or broken glass result in incised wounds of the palm of the hand which can scarcely be caused in any other way.

Incised defence wounds — including those of stab type — may also be seen on the backs of the hands or on the forearms but 'covering up' is more likely when a blunt instrument is used. The defence injury then sustained presents as a laceration with or without underlying fracture of the radius or ulna. Bruising may also be a feature but such injuries will be less diagnostic than are those due to incisions.

Bruising is the least specific defence injury and may be found also on the upper arms or the legs according to the many manoeuvres which may be adopted to defend against kicking.

See also: Bruises; Cut throat; Incised wounds; Kicking injuries; Knife wounds; Lacerations

Defence Societies

All professional persons can do harm to their clients by way of negligence, and this may be long lasting and wide ranging. It could be disastrous for a patient or client to be negligently injured and yet be unable to recover damages owing to the inability of the responsible professional to meet his obligations; it is, in some ways, surprising that there is no absolute legal obligation on doctors or lawyers to insure against such liability. On the other hand, there are few professionals who would wish to risk penury as the result of a mistake and, in practice, virtually all subscribe to defence societies or, in the case of the legal profession, carry insurance which will indemnify them against damages for negligence.

Doctors employed in hospitals are in a slightly different position in that they are direct employees of the health authority, who are therefore vicariously liable for their actions. Accordingly, membership of a defence society is a prerequisite of obtaining a position in an NHS hospital. Since partners are equally responsible for negligent actions, it is probable that the great majority of professional partnerships have similar arrangements.

The increasingly high level of damages awarded for medical and other professional negligence is, undoubtedly, imposing strains on the British defence societies[1] but they have, thus far, been able to avoid the almost punitive subscriptions and sometimes limited liabilities which have been found necessary in the USA[2]. The annual premium payable by doctors has risen from £13 in 1970 to £240 in 1984 — figures which do not allow for inflation; the defence societies' expenditure is rising at some 14 per cent per annum after inflation. At least part of the currently acceptable position in the UK may be due to the unofficial agreement that the liability is divided equally between the health authority and the doctor concerned in the event of a successful negligence action against a practitioner in a hospital.

The concept of professional defence societies is sometimes attacked on the grounds that they defend the reputation of poor practitioners at the expense of the good; there is some truth in this in that the worst cases of negligence will be settled out of court and the practitioner is spared even the publicity of an action. Nevertheless, this is probably an acceptable price to pay for the certainty that an injured patient or client will be compensated as soon as a case has succeeded. Justice is also served in that defence societies can afford a justifiable appeal which an individual would be unable to risk. A most inequitable aspect of the system lies in the fact that the defence societies are unlikely to be able to recover their costs in the event of a successful defence on behalf of a member; it is often economically preferable to settle out of court rather than to sustain a successful defence.

It is sometimes forgotten that defence societies do more than assist in the defence of actions in negligence. They will represent medical members, and their equivalent in other professions, in the General Medical Council, at tribunals concerned with the Misuse of Drugs Act 1971 and in similar situations where legal representation is allowed. Probably the greater part of their work, however, consists of providing prospective advice to members so that these more dramatic interventions can be avoided. In this way, defence societies are to be distinguished from insurance companies[3] which provide an alternative means of protection in many parts of the world.

See also: Damages; Negligence; Partnerships in medicine

1. Harland WA and Jandoo RS 'The medical negligence crisis' (1984) 24 Med Sci Law 123.
2. Holland RE 'What is happening and what is ahead in medical malpractice' [1984] Advocates Soc J 13 gives a Canadian view.
3. *The Medical Defence Union v The Department of Trade* [1979] 2 WLR 686.

Defensive Medicine

Defensive medicine is something of a catch-phrase used simultaneously by leaders of the medical profession who are concerned lest litigation against doctors should escalate[1] and by the courts which are anxious to preserve a strictly professional standard in testing medical practice[2]. In essence, the phrase implies a practice of patient care which is designed to protect the doctor against allegations of negligence as much as to achieve the best interests of the patient. There is no doubt that the concept derives from an interpretation of the decisions in negligence cases which have been made in the US courts.

The fear of a translation of US legal trends to the UK is very honestly held but there are several reasons for thinking it may well be exaggerated. In general, the American concept of negligence in all walks of life has always been broader than that which holds in Britain. Secondly, the relationship between doctor and patient in a system which provides free medical care for all, and in which doctors, on the whole, receive relatively modest financial return, is bound to be different from that in one where illness can result in a heavy monetary burden. Thirdly, and perhaps most importantly, the contingency fee system of remuneration for lawyers does not apply in the UK.

On the positive side, there are many who would argue that, once the side issue of monetary gain is avoided, so-called defensive medicine may be good medicine in so far as it leads to a more thorough examination and therapeutic regimen for the patient; it is not difficult to cross the boundary between, on the one hand, a sincere desire to protect a system which has worked well and, on the other, to excuse what could be, effectively, less than ideal practice. There are good reasons for holding that the use of the term 'defensive medicine' should be accepted with some reservation.

See also: Negligence

1. *See*, for example, Havard JDJ 'The influence of the law on clinical decisions affecting life and death' (1983) 23 Med Sci law 157.
2. *See*, for example, Lord Denning MR in *Whitehouse v Jordan* [1980] 1 All ER 650 or, more recently, Lord Dunn in *Sidaway v Board of Governors of the Bethlem Royal Hospital and Others* [1984] 2 WLR 778.

Dehydration

Dehydration occurs whenever there is major loss of water from the body. Since there is a minimum physiological loss through insensible sweating and from the excretion of as much urine as is essential if the plasma is to be cleared of poisonous metabolites, depleted fluid intake will lead ultimately to dehydration; the fatal effect of starvation, whether it results from marooning or to hunger striking, is primarily due to dehydration — given adequate fluid, a man can live off his own tissues for several weeks.

Other results of dehydration are seldom due to pure water depletion. Thus, fatalities due to excess sweating, or heat exhaustion, result from a combination of salt and water loss whilst the dehydration due to diarrhoea and vomiting, typical of cholera or severe malaria, is accompanied by loss of sodium and potassium in addition to water.

In the absence of underlying disease, most cases of severe dehydration will respond to fluid given by mouth or by intravenous infusion; drinking sea water achieves nothing as it needs more water than is drunk to excrete the excess electrolytes which are simultaneously ingested.

Dehydration is occasionally due to endocrine imbalance but, in practical medico-legal terms, the combination of blood loss, sweating and decreased intake which occurs during major surgery makes this the commonest potential cause of dehydration although one which is normally anticipated and combated by intravenous infusion.

See also: Heat effects; Surgical shock

Delirium Tremens

This is the classic psychosis associated with withdrawal from alcohol; the attack may be precipitated unintentionally such as when an alcoholic is admitted to hospital following an accident.

As the name implies, tremors are a prominent feature and there may be epileptiform fits. Hallucinations, commonly visual, are frequent and are often of a frightening nature but many sufferers can compensate with antagonistic false perceptions.

Delusions of a paranoid type are also frequent. The physical signs are relieved by further alcohol.

See also: Delusions; Epilepsy; Hallucinations; Paranoia

Delusions

Delusions are beliefs which have no foundation in reality. They are held firmly by the subject and cannot be dispelled by a process of rational argument. An important feature of a delusion is that it is a belief not held by persons of similar cultural background to the subject — morbid jealousy (Othello syndrome) is a good example. Being associated with disorders of both mood and thought, delusions are a feature of affective and schizophrenic psychoses.

The delusions in depressive illness may lead to such a distorted view of the world that suicide is a major risk; moreover, the urge to 'escape' may be transferred to the family and lead to a combination of murder and suicide. Delusions, in general, may provoke danger for anyone who intrudes into the subject's world. He may react violently against a person whom he believes to be a source of persecution — as in the famous *M'Naghten* case where the delusion was one of persecution by a political party[1]. Such paranoid delusions are a feature of schizophrenia, in which condition they may be bizarre in the extreme.

The clinical assessment of apparent delusions is of importance not only when the insanity defence is raised but also, and perhaps particularly, in relation to testamentary capacity.

See also: Hallucinations; M'Naghten Rules; Othello syndrome; Psychoses; Schizophrenia; Suicide; Testamentary capacity

1. *Daniel M'Naghten* (1843) 10 Cl & Fin 200 HL

Dementia

Dementia, literally loss of mind, is the gradual failure of mental capacity. The effect on the brain is widespread with loss of intellect and memory together with disturbance of emotion and of behaviour. The condition is clearly associated with age and affects nearly a quarter of those aged over 80 years. Cerebral atheroma is also related to age and, certainly, a proportion of cases of dementia, say a quarter, can be attributed to vascular disease[1]. In many, however, no obvious cause is present and it is convenient, if unscientific, to regard senile dementia as a matter of exhaustion of the available neurones. The senile dement, or psychogeriatric patient, presents great problems but very considerable advances in management are now being made (*see* 'Geriatric medicine'). It is quite impossible to identify the inner state of mind in an aged and demented person and there would be few, if any, physicians who would regard active euthanasia as a therapeutic option in such cases. The law, both as to murder and as to the legal doctrine of necessity — or philosophical double effect — has been laid down in the case of *R v Adams*[2]. At the same time, it is doubtful if any therapy designed to give a temporary and incomplete restoration of mental facility is useful in the majority of cases; what is needed is an improvement in medical and social support facilities for the psychogeriatric patient and his concerned relatives.

Presenile dementia, which can be regarded as progressive loss of mental function before the age of 65 years, may be due to a variety of organic diseases which include such different causes as vitamin deficiency, alcoholism, cerebral tumour and neurospyhilis (general paralysis of the insane). Presenile dementia of unknown cause is known as Alzheimer's disease in which there are several clinical variations. Recent work has shown that the pathological findings in this condition are very similar to those found in the traumatic dementia exemplified by 'punch drunkenness'[3].

See also: Atheroma; Double effect; Euthanasia; Geriatric medicine; Punch drunkenness; Senility

1. The condition has been accepted as a cause of organic automatism (*R v Kemp* [1957] 1 QB 399).
2. Palmer H 'Dr Adams' trial for murder' [1957] Crim LR 365.
3. *See* Green MA 'Injury and sudden death in sport' in Mason JK (ed) *The Pathology of Violent Injury* (1978) Edward Arnold, London.

Dental Recording

The use of a dental chart in the identification of a dead body is often invaluable but there is no uniformly accepted practice of recording dental treatment. This may cause some difficulty, particularly when many nationals are involved — as in an aircraft accident in which dental identification is particularly useful.

There are many recording systems in use, of which the commonest are the following:

(a) Zsigmondy's classification is semi-pictorial and is therefore difficult to communicate; it is the system generally adopted in the UK. In it, the four quadrants of the mouth are delineated by a St George's cross and the teeth are numbered 1–8 from the anterior midline to the back. The mouth is recorded as viewed from the front. The lower right canine tooth is, thus, demarcated $\overline{3|}$.

(b) Haderup's system involves a somewhat complex arrangement of minus signs to denote the lower jaw and plus to represent the upper. The sign is placed next to the anterior midline and the teeth in each quadrant numbered 1–8. The lower right canine thus becomes 3−.

(c) Parreidt's system is widely used in the USA. In this, the teeth are number consecutively from the posterior right upper tooth along the upper jaw and from the lower left posterior to the lower right posterior tooth. The lower right canine in this system would be annotated 27.

(d) Viohl's system has been strongly recommended for use on an international basis. In this, the quadrants are numbered in circular fashion 1–4 starting with the right upper quadrant. The quadrant number then precedes the tooth number which runs in each quadrant from 1 to 8 starting in the midline. The lower right canine would be 43.

See also: Dentition; Identification of the dead

Dentition

The human dentition exists in two phases — the deciduous dentition of infancy and the permanent dentition. The former consists of 20 and the latter of 32 teeth. Each exists in four symmetrical quadrants, the deciduous teeth in each quadrant being two incisors, one canine and two premolars, whilst the permanent teeth include two incisors, one canine, two premolars and three molar teeth. The third molar or wisdom tooth sometimes fails to erupt.

Formation of the dentition is one of the most accurate guides to age of a skeleton available up to the age about 16 years. The precise chronological details are to be found in larger works[1] but, in general, the deciduous dentition begins to erupt at approximately 6 months and is completely erupted by about 2½ years or less; the permanent teeth begin to erupt at about 7 years and the second molar tooth appears at the age of about 12 years. Eruption is but the visible end-stage of a process which includes mineralisation, crowning and root formation. An X-ray of the young mouth will therefore show both the late deciduous teeth and the early formative stages of the permanent dentition and this may provide a remarkably accurate estimate of age[2].

The degenerative changes, or those due to wear and tear, which occur in the teeth include attrition, loosening and alterations in their roots and rooting. These changes, which need to be evaluated by experts to be of greatest use, are certainly the best guide to the age of a body in late adulthood.

See also: Age of a body at death; Identification of the dead; Odontology

1. For example, Mason JK *Forensic Medicine for Lawyers* (2nd ed, 1983) Chap.29, Butterworths, London.
2. *See* Ashley KF 'Identification of children in a mass disaster by estimation of dental age' (1970) 129 Br Dent J 167 for a practical example.

Detention by the Police

The Police and Criminal Evidence Act 1984 was, arguably, one of the most controversial pieces of legislation introduced in the UK in recent years. It was brought in to stem the apparent increase in crime but, in so doing, was designed to strike a balance between the needs of the community and the rights of the individual; the Act clarifies the powers of the police but, at the same time, regulates them and provides functional curbs. It is a massive Act, much of which has little medico-legal significance; those parts which do so, however, caused a major confrontation between the medical profession and the legislators during the passage of the Bill. This annotation can be no more than a précis — the details, such as the regulations surrounding the exercise of each provision, must be seen in the original by those interested.

In general, the Act gives the police powers to stop and search any person or vehicle in a public place in order to find prohibited articles which are defined as offensive weapons or articles designed to assist in burglary, theft or stealing a vehicle. The police can obtain extensive powers of entry and search for the purposes of investigating crime but the powers of search do not extend to material which is (a) subject to legal privilege or (b) is excluded material. Excluded material (s.11) includes personal records required in the course of trade, business or profession and held in confidence; human tissue and tissue fluids taken for the purposes of medical diagnosis or treatment and held in confidence; and confidential journalistic material. Medical records and material are, thus, protected.

A considerable part of the Act deals with the important matter of taking samples or impressions from the body. The power to fingerprint is detailed in s.61 but, of equal importance, destruction of fingerprints is compulsory if the offence is not proceeded against, and the person concerned can demand to witness their destruction (s.64(6)). Other samples which may be taken are divided into non-intimate and intimate classes.

Non-intimate samples include hair other than pubic hair, nail clippings and scrapings, swabs taken other than from an orifice and footprints or any other print other than that of a hand — dental impressions are included in the last. Such samples may only be taken with consent except that, when the subject is in detention, a senior police officer can authorise the taking of samples if the investigation is one involving a serious arrestable offence (s.63). A serious arrestable offence is defined in Sch.5 as including, *inter alia*, murder, manslaughter, rape, incest with a girl under 13, kidnapping, non-consensual buggery and killing by reckless driving but any offence which involves serious injury or the probability thereof can be so classified; causing explosions, firearm offences, hostage taking and hijacking are also included by virtue of other legislation.

Intimate samples may only be taken with consent when in police detention and then only in relation to serious arrestable offences (s.62). A judge or jury is entitled to draw inferences from refusal of consent (s.62(10)). Intimate samples include samples of blood, semen or any other tissue fluid, urine, saliva, pubic hair or a swab taken from a person's body orifices. Such samples, other than those of saliva and urine, may only be taken by a medical practitioner (s.62(9)). The provisons of s.62 do not affect those of the Road Traffic Act 1972, as amended, ss.5–12.

The general searching of detained persons is regulated by s.54 but the major medico-legal feature of the Act relates to intimate body searches (s.55). The purpose of the search may be to discover objects which might be used to inflict physical injury on the person himself or on others or to disclose the presence of a Class A controlled drug. An intimate search may only be made at a police station, a hospital, a doctor's surgery or some other place used for medical purposes (s.55(8)). A constable may make the search unless it is in connection with a drug offence, in which case it must be performed by a suitably qualified person (s. 55(4)) and cannot be made at a police station. A doctor or a nurse making an intimate body search can be of either sex but a constable must be one of the same sex as the detainee (s. 55(7)). The concept of intimate body searches has come in for criticism from the medical profession and from the police. There is also a suggestion that the whole process is 'degrading treatment' as condemned by the European Convention on Human Rights; s.55 stands a very good chance of being challenged in the European Court.

Persons can be detained in police custody for up to 24 hours without being charged (s.41(1)) and for a further 36 hours on the authority of a senior police officer during the investigation of a serious arrestable offence (s.42). Further than this, a magistrate's warrant can extend the period of detention without charge up to, effectively, a maximum of 96 hours from when the need became relevant (s.44).

A feature of the Act is that much of its implementation depends upon Codes of Practice which are issued by the Secretary of State (s.66). It is, for example, stated only in the Code of Practice that no person who is not a doctor or a nurse may be present at the intimate body search of a person of the opposite sex.

The long Part IX of the Act deals with the regulation of police procedures. The innovation which is of greatest general interest is the setting up of a Police Complaints Authority (s.83) which consists of a chairman appointed by the Crown and eight members appointed by the Secretary of State. The authority has wide powers to investigate complaints against police actions, and no member of the authority may have had previous close association with a police force.

The Act runs only marginally to Scotland where similar, although by no means identical, police powers are contained in the Criminal Justice (Scotland) Act 1980.

See also: Confidentiality; Fingerprints; Misuse of Drugs Act 1971; Offensive weapons; Privilege; Road Traffic Act 1972

Detention in Mental Hospitals

A patient may be detained compulsorily in a mental hospital as a result of civil or criminal commitment (*see* 'Insanity and criminal responsibility' for the latter). It is still possible for civil commitment to be achieved under common law powers which entitle a citizen to restrain another from action which poses an immediate threat to life, this being justified by the principle of necessity[1]. Such situations are exceptionally rare and need not concern us here.

Statutory authority for compulsory admission to a mental hospital is provided under the Mental Health Act 1983[2]. Ordinary admission for assessment is regulated under s.2 and follows application made by the nearest relative of the patient[3], by a person authorised so to act by the court or by an approved social worker. The applicant must have seen the patient within the previous 14 days and there must be a medical recommendation for admission by two medical practitioners. A patient may be detained under this procedure for up to 28 days but may be discharged before that period has elapsed by the responsible medical officer, the hospital authorities or a mental health service tribunal. An admission for assessment cannot be renewed although the patient may choose to stay voluntarily. The grounds for admission for assessment are that the patient is suffering from mental disorder of a nature or degree which warrants his detention in hospital for a limited period and that 'he ought to be so detained in the interests of his own health or safety or with a view to the protection of others'. Mental disorder is defined (s.1) as meaning 'mental illness, arrested or incomplete development of mind, psychopathic disorder and any other disorder or disability of mind'.

Emergency admission for assessment is covered in s.4 of the Act. This requires only one medical recommendation and lasts for up to 72 hours. A second application may be made under this section, two medical recommendations being then required. The applicant in such a case must have seen the patient within the previous 24 hours.

Admissions for observation and assessment are more common than are those which can be arranged for treatment under s.3. The procedures for securing therapeutic admission are essentially the same as those for assessment; the nearest relative is usually consulted although, in the case of admission for treatment, his objections to admission can be overruled if they are unreasonable. The patient can be detained for a period of six months running from the day of admission but may be discharged before this period is completed. He may apply at any one time during that six months for a review of his case by a mental health review tribunal (s.66). Following the expiry of the first period of six months, his detention can be extended for a further period of six months and, thereafter, for periods of one year at a time. The responsible medical officer renewing detention must believe that treatment is appropriate or that the patient would not be able to look after himself if he were to be discharged.

The grounds for admission under s.3 are that the patient is suffering from 'mental illness, severe mental impairment, psychopathic disorder or mental impairment and that his mental disorder is of a nature or degree which makes it appropriate for him to receive medical treatment in a hospital'. In addition, it is necessary in the case of psychopathic disorder or mental impairment that medical treatment is seen as being likely either to alleviate the condition or to prevent a deterioration of the patient's condition; it is required in all cases that the health or safety of the patient or the protection of others can be achieved only through his detention (s.3(2)(a–c)).

The situation in Scotland is regulated by the Mental Health (Scotland) Act 1984. Emergency admission is effected under s.24; although it is initially for the same period as is emergency admission in England and Wales, it is not renewable under the same section but can be continued as a period of short-term detention — 28 days — under s.26. Compulsory admission to hospital will normally be achieved by an application to the sheriff which is supported by two medical recommendations. The sheriff's approval covers detention in hospital for a period of up to six months (s.30) and this is renewable for a further period of six months and, thereafter, for periods of one year at a time. Appeals against detention will be held in the sheriff court. The Mental Welfare Commission is a particular feature of the Scottish system; this body has particularly wide powers in connection with detention and release of involuntary patients (ss.2–5).

See also: Insanity and criminal responsibility; Mental Health Act 1983; Mental Health Act Commission; Mental Welfare Commission

1. Hoggett B *Mental Health Law* (2nd ed, 1984) p.109, Sweet & Maxwell, London.
2. Part II of the Act deals both with the procedures for admission to hospital and to guardianship.
3. For the definition of nearest relative, *see* s.26.

Deviance

Deviance is a term which has been used in the criminological literature over the last three decades to describe certain forms of non-conformist conduct. What constitutes deviance will clearly be a highly charged decision and fashions in this area have changed rapidly. Theories such as labelling, ethnomethodology and of conflict have all enjoyed a period of vogue. The political aspects of deviance have been stressed recently and groups previously labelled as deviants have been able to assert their claim to social acceptability; the homosexual activists provide an example. Such groups maintain that the idea of sexual deviance merely masks political and social oppression and that society should cease to use concepts of sexual deviance[1].

See also: Homosexuality; Sexual offences

1. There is a vast literature on this subject. Important contributions include: Becker HS *Outsiders. Studies in the Sociology of Deviance* (1966) Free Press, New York; Matza D *Becoming Deviant* (1969) Prentice-Hall, Englewood Cliffs, NJ; Lemert EM 'Issues in the study of deviance' (1981) 22 Sociol Q 285.

Diabetes

Diabetes mellitus results from a deficiency of or ineffectiveness of insulin, a hormone which is secreted by the cells of the islets of Langerhans in the pancreas. The incidence of the disease in one form or another may be as high as 1 per cent of the UK population. It can occur at any age but the majority of cases are first diagnosed in middle or old age. There is a definite hereditary tendency but this is of multifactorial genetic type, the genetic influence being most marked in those cases arising in the younger age groups. The action of insulin on carbohydrates, fats and proteins is complex but the essential result of insulin deficiency is that glycogen storage is interfered with so that an increased quantity of glucose circulates in the blood and is lost in the urine. The acute danger of this is the overproduction of so-called ketoacids and the consequent development of diabetic coma; this complication is often triggered by infection. In the long term, there is a widespread disorder of the small blood vessels, those within the retina of the eye, the kidneys and the nervous system being most seriously attacked. Atherosclerotic changes in the larger blood vessels are increased in diabetics, who are therefore more prone to ischaemic diseases such as myocardial infarction and gangrene of the limbs than are those unaffected by the disease.

Diabetes may be treated by diet, by the use of oral hypoglycaemic drugs or by the periodic injection of insulin, the aim being to stabilise the glucose content of the blood within the normal range; dietary management is essential within any therapeutic regimen. There is now some medico-legal significance in the old aphorism that the success of diabetic treatment depends very largely on the understanding and the co-operation of the patient[1]. Treatment with insulin is almost always needed in young diabetics. Hypoglycaemia may be induced and this may lead to coma; more commonly, it causes faintness and mental confusion which may be associated with abnormal behaviour of which the patient is unaware. The well-controlled diabetic learns rapidly to recognise and treat such attacks by taking sugar orally. As a consequence, the legal approach to automatism associated with either diabetic or insulin coma has tended to be couched in terms of irresponsibility. The somewhat complex subject is discussed further under 'Automatism'.

See also: Atheroma; Automatism; Genetic disease; Hypoglycaemia; Insulin; Recklessness

1. Maher G 'Automatism and diabetes' (1983) 99 LQR 511.

Dialysis

The principle of dialysis depends on the fact that substances dissolved in a fluid will pass through a semi-permeable membrane in such a way as to equate the concentrations of the substance on each side of the membrane. A coiled artificial membrane can therefore be used as a substitute for the natural glomerular epithelium, the process of clearing the blood being known as haemodialysis. Such substitution is highly feasible in the context of acute renal failure when success is limited only by the powers of the renal tubules to recover; in certain circumstances, particularly when the kidney failure is due to burning, restoration of function is poor and dialysis often fails as a curative procedure.

Dialysis as a long-term kidney substitute has distinct limitations. These run from a logistic shortage of machines leading to problems of resource allocation, through ultimate rejection of the machine by the body in the form of thrombosis of vessels, to specific conditions such as contamination with the virus of hepatitis — especially significant as the apparatus must be primed with blood before use. To these particular problems must be added the general ones of psychological dependence upon a machine with its influence on absence from home for holidays and the like[1]. It is fortunate that personal finances are scarcely concerned within the confines of a NHS; in the USA, special legislation has had to be introduced to avoid financial ruin in those suffering from chronic renal failure and all sufferers are now treated.

Dialysis may be provided at a central unit on an outpatient basis at some two- to three-day intervals for a total of up to 20 hours per week; alternatively, it can be supplied at home which is more cost effective but much then depends upon the ability of the patient and his family to use it successfully. Whatever method is employed, the dialysis patient can never be as fit as is the person with a normally functioning kidney. Moreover, the cost of transplantation surgery is considerably less than that of indefinite dialysis. Many haemodialysis units accordingly require an undertaking from long-term patients that they will accept a transplant if one becomes available.

An alternative to haemodialysis in the standard 'artificial kidney' is to dialyse using the peritoneum as the membrane; this is expensive, although becoming less so, but greatly eases the strain on resources.

See also: Abdominal cavity; Burning; Hepatitis; Kidney failure; Resource allocation; Transplantation of organs

1. Wing AJ 'Why don't the British treat more patients with kidney failure?' (1983) 287 Br Med J 1157.

Diatoms

The distinction between death from drowning and immersion after death is obviously of major forensic importance but, since about one-third of all such bodies are decomposed to some extent, the differential diagnosis may be difficult to make on naked eye appearances alone. Several tests have been introduced to overcome this difficulty and the 'diatom' test is undoubtedly the most attractive of these.

Diatoms are unicellular organisms which protect themselves by secreting a well-nigh indestructible coat of silica. Their size is generally between 40 and 80 μm but some are exceptionally small (2–5 μm); over 15,000 species are known and their identity is often very specific to the locality in which they are found. They are very widely distributed both in salt and in fresh water but they are also present in the air.

The diatom test depends upon discovery of the organisms within the immersed body, the presumption being that they have been inhaled with the watery medium — the conclusion follows that the deceased has died from drowning. The demonstration of diatoms is not easy but, since they are so resistant to destruction, acid digestion or even incineration, methods may be used to concentrate them from relatively large amounts of tissue[1]. There are, however, many other difficulties associated with the diatom test. Water may enter the lungs *post mortem* and it is therefore suggested that diatoms must be shown to have circulated and to be present in the inner tissues to be of diagnostic significance; bone marrow is the tissue most commonly investigated in this context. On the other hand, diatoms are likely to be present no more than incidentally if the subject has been exposed to air-borne organisms. The interpretation of the findings is therefore fundamental and this is very much a matter of experience[2]. Quantification is important, as is the comparison of any diatoms discovered in the body with those to be found in the water of immersion. The test is by no means foolproof and is of surprisingly little value in unskilled hands.

See also: Drowning

1. *See* Timperman J and Thomas F 'Diatom identification and the diagnosis of drowning' in Perper JA and Wecht CH (eds) *Microscopic Diagnosis in Forensic Pathology* (1980) Chap.7, CC Thomas, Springfield IL.
2. The debate is well summarised in Peabody AJ 'Diatoms and drowning — a review' (1980) 20 Med Sci Law 254. *See also* Calder IM 'An evaluation of the diatom test in deaths of professional divers' (1984) 24 Med Sci Law 41.

Diminished Life

This semantically indefinite term is generally restricted to a reduction in the quality of life due to an antenatal occurrence. Its use can be contrasted to that of 'wrongful life' which implies that death would be a preferable alternative to life. Whereas the concept of wrongful life is hard to accept both ethically and judicially, diminished life resolves into issues of causation and potential negligence. The jurisprudential problem lies in the question of fetal rights.

There seems little doubt in the UK that the fetus, once born alive and, in England and Wales, surviving for 48 hours[1], has a right to an action in negligence. Neither the English statute nor Scots common law places a lower limit on fetal age and it would seem that a mother is under no obligation to undergo an abortion even if she knows that the fetus has been negligently injured[2].

The situation in the USA has been complicated by the viability rule — which implies that, to be tortious, injury must be done to a person and that the fetus has no personality prior to viability[3]; this concept was emphasised in the seminal case of *Roe v Wade*[4]. There is, however, a considerable body of academic opinion both in Canada and the USA which believes that this fiction is being eroded[5] and a number of US decisions have taken the same course[6]. It is doubtful if there is now any greater difficulty in bringing an action for diminished life than there is in any other form of tort litigation.

See also: Abortion; Unborn child; Viability; Wrongful life.

1. Congenital Disabilities (Civil Liability) Act 1976; *Elliot v Joicey* 1935 SC (HL) 57.
2. *Emeh v Kensington and Chelsea and Westminster AHA* [1984] 3 All ER 1044, CA.
3. *Bonbrest v Kotz* 65 F supp 138 (DC 1946).
4. 410 US 113 (1973).
5. For example, Knoppers B 'Physician, liability and pre natal diagnosis' 18 CCLT 169 (1982); Keyserlingk EW 'A right of the unborn child to pre-natal care — the civil law perspective' (1982) 13 Rev de Droit 49; Lenow JL 'The fetus as a patient: emerging rights as a person?' (1983) 9 Am J Law Med 1.
6. For example, *Bennett v Hymers* 147 A 2d 108 (NH, 1958); *Presley v Newport Hospital* 365 A 2d 748 (RI, 1976); *Taft v Taft* 446 NE 2d 395 (Mass, 1983).

Diminished Responsibility

The plea of diminished responsibility is a creation of Scots criminal law[1] which has since found expression in the Homicide Act 1957, s.2. This provides for the reduction of a charge of murder to one of manslaughter where the accused was 'suffering from such abnormality of mind (whether arising from a condition of arrested or retarded development of mind or any inherent causes or induced by disease or injury) as substantially impaired his mental responsibility for his acts and omissions in doing or being a party to the killing'. A plea of guilty to manslaughter by reason of diminished responsibility can be accepted by a judge at his discretion provided that the medical evidence is not challenged[2]. This is comparatively rare; in one study it was found that medical evidence challenging the defence medical witnesses was led by the prosecution in only 13 per cent of cases in which the defence was raised[3]. The plea is often accepted; it succeeded in over 70 per cent of the cases in which it was used in the first two years of the operation of the 1957 Act in England and Wales[4]. A high proportion of such cases are disposed of by means of a hospital order[5].

The wording of the statute is broad and it is not surprising that there has been some debate as to what constitutes diminished responsibility. A classic statement of the concept is provided by the dictum of the Scottish judge, Lord Alness: 'It is very difficult to put it [diminished responsibility] in a phrase, but it has been put in this way: that there must be an aberration or weakness of mind; that there must be some form of mental unsoundness; that there must be a state of mind which is bordering on, though not amounting to, insanity; that there must be a mind so affected that responsibility is diminished from full responsibility to partial responsibility — in other words, the prisoner in question must be only partially accountable for his actions'[6].

Further guidance is found in the decision in *R v Byrne*[7]. In this case, it was held that abnormality of mind in the context of the statute meant 'a state of mind so different from that of ordinary human beings that the reasonable man would term it abnormal. It appears to us to be wide enough to cover the mind's activity in all its aspects, not only the perception of physical acts and matters, and the ability to form a rational judgement as to whether an act is right or wrong, but also the ability to exercise willpower to control physical acts in accordance with that rational judgement'. *Byrne* has, however, been said not to lay down a general rule as to the severity of the necessary degree of mental irresponsibility[8].

In *Vinagre*[9], the Court of Criminal Appeals stressed that pleas of diminished responsibility should be accepted only when there is 'clear evidence of mental imbalance'. In that case, psychiatric evidence that the accused was suffering from the so-called 'Othello syndrome' (extreme jealousy) was given short shrift, the court taking the view that, until modern times, no one would have considered the killing of a wife by a jealous husband as being anything less than murder (but for a later attitude, *see R v Seers*)[8]. A greater degree of sympathy is shown in mercy killing cases where diminished responsibility may be accepted even if there is no evidence of a previous history of mental abnormality and where there may be little or no helpful evidence from medical witnesses[10].

The diminished responsibility plea has been criticised from a number of angles. From the medical viewpoint, the attitude is sometimes taken that the concept is unacceptably vague and that doctors are being called upon to pronounce on a question which is more a moral than a medical one[11]. Lawyers, too, have been critical. It is argued that what is at issue is not the responsibility of the accused (which should be an all-or-nothing question) but his culpability, which is something which clearly can exist in varying degrees. It has also been suggested that it is inappropriate to limit the defence to homicide and that it should be applied to other crimes; it could then possibly result in a verdict of 'guilty but with diminished responsibility' carrying a reduced sentence[12]. The Butler Committee[5] pointed out that the need for a plea of diminished responsibility would disappear if the mandatory life sentence for murder were abolished but, in the event of the fixed penalty being retained, the diminished responsibility plea should be allowed in the presence of a mental disorder as is now defined by the Mental Health Act 1983[13]. This proposal has, in turn, been criticised on the grounds that it would unduly restrict the availability of the plea[14].

See also: Homicide; Hospital orders; Insanity and criminal responsibility; Mental impairment; Mercy killing; Othello syndrome; Psychopathy

1. Gordon GH *The Criminal Law of Scotland* (2nd ed, 1978) p.380, W Green, Edinburgh.
2. *Cox* (1968) 52 Crim App R 130.
3. Dell S 'Diminished responsibility reconsidered' [1982] Crim LR 809.
4. Wootton B 'Diminished responsibility: a layman's view' (1960) 76 LQR 224.
5. Butler Lord (chairman) *Report of the Committee on Mentally Abnormal Offenders* (Cmnd 6244) (1975) p.243, HMSO, London.
6. *HM Adv v Savage* 1923 JC 49 at 50.
7. [1960] 3 WLR 440 (CCA).
8. *Rose v The Queen* [1961] AC 496 PC quoted in *R v Seers* (1984) Times, 5 May.
9. (1979) 69 Crim App R 104.
10. Williams G *Criminal Law: The General Part* (2nd ed, 1961) pp.557–558, Stevens, London.
11. Hamilton JR 'Diminished responsibility' (1981) 138 Br J Psychiat 434.
12. Walker N 'Butler v CLRC and others' [1981] Crim LR 596.
13. *See* n.5, p.247.

14. Criminal Law Revision Committee, 14th Report *Offences Against the Person* (Cmnd 7844) (1980) HMSO, London.

Further reading
  Jacobs FG *Criminal Responsibility* (1971) p.47 et seq, Weidenfeld & Nicolson, London.
  Walker N *Crime and Insanity in England* (1968) Vol.1, Chap.8, Edinburgh University Press, Edinburgh.
  Samuels A 'Mental illness and criminal liability' (1975) 15 Med Sci Law 198.

Discipline in the Medical Profession

The doctor in the UK is given full clinical freedom to practise his art. He is, nevertheless, answerable in several ways should he appear to transgress the norms of practice.

As with any citizen, the doctor is subject to the criminal law and his professional competence is, to a large extent, regulated by the civil law of contract and of tort or delict. Clearly, a major stimulus to excellence lies in the simple functions of any commercial enterprise — the need to attract patients in the small sector of private medicine and the competition for employment in the public sector.

Once employed in the public sector, professional standards are maintained either through the family practitioner committee in the case of primary care physicians or through the appropriate health authority in the case of hospital practitioners (*see* 'Complaints procedure in the NHS'). Disciplinary action against consultants is particularly complex and often distressing as the original complaint very often arises from colleagues[1]. It is to be noted that the doctor has an equivalent right of action for wrongful process on the part of the authority[2]. All doctors are now subject to the disciplinary provisions of the Misuse of Drugs Act 1971 which, again, involves a complex system of hearing and appeal.

The Royal Medical Colleges, which are responsible for certifying the original competence of a consultant, have no disciplinary function in respect of an errant member or fellow other than expulsion. Such a matter would be a purely internal affair and, whilst it is theoretically possible, it is extremely unlikely that such action would be taken in the absence of parallel disciplinary procedures by the health authority or by the General Medical Council.

The GMC is primarily concerned with infringement of the behavioural standards of the professional man. It will take disciplinary action only when a doctor's conduct is bringing the profession into disrepute, and consideration of a practitioner's competence will be given only in that light; the procedure is detailed under 'General Medical Council'. It is often not appreciated that the British Medical Association has no disciplinary function; it is essentially the doctors' 'trade union' without, incidentally, any 'closed shop' arrangement[3].

Again, whilst the officials have no disciplinary power, a doctor's professional conduct and competence is likely to come under severe public scrutiny in the coroner's court or in a public inquiry held under the Fatal Accidents and Sudden Deaths Inquiry (Scotland) Act 1976.

See also: Complaints procedures in the NHS; Coroner; Family practitioner committees; Fatal accident inquiry; General Medical Council; Misuse of Drugs Act 1971; Royal Medical Colleges

1. *See* Dyer C 'The Savage case: disciplining consultants' (1985) 290 Br Med J 1894.
2. *Bliss v South East Thames RHA* (1983) Times, 13 December.
3. In fact, a registered non-affiliated trade union (Trade Union and Labour Relations Act 1974).

Disclosure of Medical Records

Medical records within the NHS remain the property of the Secretary of State and not of the individual doctor or patient. In private practice, they are the property of the doctor treating the patient. The problem of access to such records has been the subject of considerable debate together with legislation.

Under the terms of the Administration of Justice Act, s.31, a person who is likely to be a party to a claim for personal injuries or to a claim in respect of another's death may seek a High Court order for the disclosure and production of documents in the possession of anyone likely to be a party to the proceedings. Section 32 extends this facility when an action has already been raised — in such circumstances, the court may make an order for the production of any relevant documents including those which are held by persons who are not concerned in the action; disclosure may then be initiated by either plaintiff or defendant. 'Fishing expeditions' for evidence are not, however, allowed under s.31; there must be some positive ground on which the plaintiff feels an action is likely[1].

The question as to whom the records should be disclosed has caused some difficulty. It was first held that they should be passed only to medical advisers[2] but the House of Lords later overruled such a restriction[3]. The matter is now resolved by the Supreme Court Act 1981, ss.33 and 34, which gives the court powers to limit production either to the applicant's legal advisers and any other medical or professional advisers or, in the absence of legal advisers, to the applicant's medical or other professional advisers.

An internal hospital report on an incident may not be recovered by a plaintiff if the report was made to the hospital's solicitors for the sole purpose of seeking legal advice as to prospective litigation. Such reports are covered by a general privilege protecting the confidentiality of communications between solicitor and client. The disclosure of a report not made for such purposes can, however, be sought by the plaintiff[4]. A recent decision has confirmed that 'professional legal privilege' applies when the application is made before the action has started in the same way as it does during the course of an action[5].

Scottish courts have always had a broad power to order the disclosure of documents which are relevant to proposed litigation[6]. Such documents can be obtained by the pursuer himself and there can be no limitation as to disclosure to medical advisers only. Scottish health boards have, in fact, developed a practice of disclosing records to independent experts in cases when litigation is contemplated[7].

See also: Confidentiality; Privilege

1. *Shaw v Vauxhall Motors Ltd* [1974] 2 All ER 1185, CA.
2. *Deistung (a minor) v South Western Metropolitan Regional Hospital Board* [1975] 1 WLR 213.
3. *McIvor v Southern Health Board* [1978] 1 WLR 757.
4. *Waugh v British Railways Board* [1980] AC 521. *See* Medicolegal 'Hospital inquiries: evidence and privilege' (1982) 284 Br Med J 519. The precise purpose of a report, even if communication between solicitor and client is included, is critical — *Lask v Gloucester Health Authority* (1985) Times, 13 December.
5. *Lee v South West Thames Regional Health Authority* [1985] 2 All ER 385, discussed in Medicolegal 'Disclosure of documents by doctors' (1985) 290 Br Med J 1973.
6. *See*, now, Administration of Justice (Scotland) Act 1972.
7. *Lunan v Forresterhill and Associated Hospitals* 1975 SLT (notes) 40.

Discretion in Prosecution and Sentencing

The exercise of discretion is essential for the conduct of an enlightened and responsive system of criminal law and operates at virtually every stage of the process of criminal justice[1]. A decision not to enforce the law may result from a deliberate conclusion that prosecution is inappropriate in the particular case or as a consequence of the inadequacies of the system. The latter category may involve the application of a policy decision to seek a more informal disposition such as through social work agencies[2]. Alternatively, police cautioning may prove to be an effective and low key way of dealing with comparatively minor delinquency[3]. A further important area for the exercise of discretion in dealing with offenders is that known as plea bargaining. This entails the acceptance by the prosecution of the plea of guilty to a lesser charge in exchange for the dropping of a more serious indictment. The attraction of such an arrangement from the prosecution's point of view lies in the avoidance of possibly lengthy trial proceedings whilst the defendant becomes liable for a reduced sentence.

The exercise of discretion is of particular medico-legal interest in relation to the prosecution of mentally disordered offenders. The sanction of the criminal courts may be particularly inappropriate in such cases, which may be dealt with through informal referral for psychiatric treatment[4].

Considerable discretion may be exercised in the sentencing of those convicted of all offences except murder and certain offences under the Road Traffic Act 1972. The principle behind the use of discretion is to enable the court to dispose of an offender so as not only to meet the merits of the case but to further the goal of rehabilitation. Thus, the court may use the available options of suspended sentences, probation and supervision or of community service orders — this last being a comparatively recent possibility[5].

Offenders who are thought to have a psychiatric problem may be made the subject of a probation order on condition that they receive psychiatric treatment[6]. This is a useful device, particularly in the case of sex offenders, but its effectiveness may depend on the solution of social problems and the like which could be independent of the offender's psychiatric difficulties.

1. *See* Bottomley AK *Decisions in the Penal Process* (1973) p.35 et seq, AB Rothman, South Hackensack NJ. More recent literature on the subject includes McClintock FH 'Some aspects of discretion in criminal justice' in Adler M and Asquith S (eds) *Discretion and Welfare* (1981) p.185 et seq, Heinemann/Gower, London; McCluskey Lord 'The prosecutor's discretion' (1979) 1 Int J Med Law 5.
2. *See*, in general, Wilcox AF *The Decision to Prosecute* (1972) Butterworths, London.
3. Ditchfield JA Home Office Study No.37 *Police Cautioning in England and Wales* (1976) HMSO, London.
4. Chiswick D, McIsaac MW and McClintock FH *Prosecution of the Mentally Disturbed: Dilemmas in Identification and Discretion* (1984) Aberdeen University Press, Aberdeen.
5. Pease K and McWilliams W *Community Service by Order* (1980) Scottish Academic Press, Edinburgh.
6. Gibbens TCN, Soothill K and Way C 'Psychiatric treatment on probation' (1981) 21 Br J Criminol 324.

Disease of the Mind

The term 'disease of the mind' is rarely encountered in psychiatric writing[1]. The term is, however, crucial for lawyers and has been the subject of considerable judicial analysis which has been concerned largely with determining what particular conditions of impaired consciousness come within the scope of the term as used in the M'Naghten Rules. As a corollary, the issue has become important in the context of automatism.

Two recent decisions have served to clarify the distinction between a disease of the mind and other abnormal mental conditions. In *Rabey v R*[2], the Canadian Supreme Court adopted the statement 'the distinction to be drawn is between a malfunctioning of the mind arising from some cause that is primarily internal to the accused, having its source in his psychological or emotional makeup, or in some organic pathology, as opposed to a malfunctioning of the mind which is the transient effect produced by some specific external factor such as, for example, concussion'. In *R v Sullivan*[3] the House of Lords ruled that a disease of the mind was any disease which had the effect of so severely impairing the mental faculties as to prevent the accused from knowing what he was doing or knowing that it was wrong. It is unimportant whether the impairment is the result of organic factors (as in epilepsy) or whether it is functional. It is also irrelevant whether it is transient or permanent (per Diplock LJ).

The decision in *Sullivan* confirms that, in English law, epilepsy constitutes a disease of the mind. This is in line with a number of authorities in other Commonwealth countries[4]. *Sullivan* also strengthens earlier decisions in which mental conditions produced by organic disease have been classified as diseases of the mind. In *R v Kemp*[5], the accused suffered from arteriosclerosis which interfered with the supply of blood to the brain; it was ruled, as a matter of law, that arteriosclerosis, being capable of affecting the mind, was therefore a disease of the mind in the context of the M'Naghten Rules. A similar conclusion has been reached in Australia[6].

Rabey and *Sullivan* emphasise that abnormal mental conditions produced by external factors will not be so categorised. In *R v Quick*[7], it was held that automatism due to hypoglycaemia in a diabetic was not the result of the underlying disease but, rather, was due to the external factor of injected insulin. Other similar cases have been disposed of in the same way[8]. The somewhat perverse implication to be derived from *Quick* is that diabetes *per se is* a disease of the mind.

Dissociative states (*see* 'Hysteria') have met with a varied fate in the criminal courts. In *Isitt*[9], the Court of Criminal Appeal would not accept that a state of dissociation might lead to non-insane automatism but did not go so far as to say that hysterical dissociation was a disease of the mind. The Canadian courts have, however, ruled that a dissociative state is a disease of the mind for purposes of the insanity defence[2,10]. Hysterical dissociation has been accepted as a disease of the mind in Australia[11].

The Royal Commission on Capital Punishment concluded that the definition of the term 'disease of the mind' should, in future, exclude, *inter alia*, the neuroses and should be used only to describe psychotic disorders[12].

See also: Arteries; Automatism; Diabetes; Epilepsy; Hypoglycaemia; Hysteria; Insanity and criminal responsibility; M'Naghten Rules; Psychoses

1. *See* discussion by Fingarette H 'The concept of mental disease in criminal law insanity tests' (1966) 33 U Chic LR 229.
2. (1981) 114 DLR (3d) 193. For criticism of this approach, *see* MacKay RD 'Non organic automatism — some recent developments' [1980] Crim LR 350 at 359; Fairall P 'Irresistable impulse, automatism and mental disease' [1981] 3 Crim LJ 136 at 154.
3. [1983] 2 All ER 673 HL.
4. *R v Foy* [1960] Qd R 225; *R v O'Brien* (1966) 56 DLR (2d) 65.
5. [1956] 3 All ER 249.
6. *R v Holmes* [1960] WAR 122.
7. [1973] 3 All ER 347; [1973] QB 910.
8. *Martin* [1958] Crim LR 444; *Bentley* [1960] Crim LR 777.
9. (1978) 67 Crim App R 44.
10. *R v MacLeod* (1980) 52 CCC 193.
11. *R v Joyce* [1970] SASR 184; *R v Williams* [1973] 1 ACTR 1.
12. Gowers EA (chairman) *Report of the Royal Commission on Capital Punishment* (Cmd 8932) (1953) p.131, HMSO, London.

Disfigurement

Damages in respect of disfigurement resulting from personal injury fall into the category of those for lost amenities and take into account such factors as the extent of scarring, the obviousness of the disfigurement and the plaintiff's subjective reaction. 'Personal disfigurement', observed a Scottish judge in the late nineteenth century, 'is a different thing from broken bones or any other injury which can be completely recovered. The sufferer has the prospect of going through life disfigured, a thing that will continue to be a source of pain and annoyance to himself and of distress to his friends'[1].

The courts have tended to treat disfigurement in the case of a female as a more serious matter than similar injury in a male plaintiff. Compensation may be given for the consequent reduction in marriage prospects[2] and, in the case of an already married plaintiff, the defendant may be held to be liable for the consequence of marital breakdown if it can be established that this followed directly upon the disfigurement[3].

See also: Damages; Negligence

1. Per Lord McLaren in *McLaurin v NB Railway* (1892) 19 R 346 at 350.
2. Kemp DAM *The Quantum of Damages* (4th ed, 1973) p.100, Sweet & Maxwell, London; Munkman JH *Damage for Personal Injuries and Death* (7th ed, 1985) p.119, Butterworths, London.
3. *Lampert v Eastern National Omnibus Co* [1954] 2 All ER 719.

Disposal of the Dead

Final legal disposal of the dead in the UK is by means of either burial or cremation, both of which are discussed under the relevant headings. Whilst the regulation of burial is surprisingly lax, cremation can only be carried out legally in a recognised crematorium[1].

Burial outside England and Wales of the person who has died therein requires the authority of the coroner[2]. The procurator fiscal must authorise the removal of a body 'firth of Scotland' if the death has been subject to his inquiries — otherwise, the body is simply accompanied by a certificate of registration of death in Scotland.

Following burial or cremation, a notification of such disposal must be delivered to the registrar of deaths within four days of the event. Failing such advice within 14 days of registration of a death, the registrar must, after inquiry, report the matter to the appropriate community physican. No such duty arises in the case of stillbirths.

See also: Burial; Cremation; Stillbirth

1. Cremation Regulations 1930.
2. Births and Deaths Registration Act 1926, s.4.

Disseminated Intravascular Coagulation

This condition has only recently been recognised as a mode of death particularly related to traumatic injury[1]. The basic cause is activation of the coagulation mechanism within the vessels, probably as a result of damage to tissues (such as the brain) which are rich in thromboplastin — the basic substrate for the 'extrinsic' pathway of coagulation; alterations in the blood, such as the presence of bacteria or of fat particles, may predispose to the condition, and the slowing of the circulation which occurs in surgical shock may also contribute to its progress.

The process is one of deposition of fibrin clot in the smaller blood vessels — particularly those of the lungs and kidneys. This may, of itself, have profound effects but the secondary result is an imbalance of the coagulation/fibrinolytic systems with a consequent overaction of the fibrinolytic component; the end-result is a paradoxical bleeding state brought on by a thrombotic process.

The condition is difficult to detect at autopsy and microscopy is essential. Even then, small deposits of fibrin may be hard to find, especially if *post mortem* fibrinolysis has been active; apparently minor findings may therefore be significant. Fibrin degeneration products can be measured biochemically but, again, the results must be interpreted cautiously.

See also: Coagulation of the blood; Fat embolism; Haemorrhage; Shock; Thrombosis

1. A simple explanation of the condition is contained in Stalker AL 'Haemorrhage, coagulation and thrombosis' in Mason JK (ed) *The Pathology of Violent Injury* (1978) Chap.18 Edward Arnold, London.

Diving Hazards

Diving is becoming increasingly important in industry and is also a popular sport. It is a hazardous occupation in either case although the circumstances alter the dangers; in general, these consist of pressure effects, the difficulties associated with an artificial breathing system and the natural or industrial hazards of the external environment.

The pressure increases by 1 atmosphere (101 kPa) with every 10 m (33 ft) of depth. A greater volume of air is therefore needed to fill the lungs at pressure and the gases inspired will be dissolved in the body fluids in increasing amounts which depend upon the partial pressure which they exert. Both oxygen and nitrogen are toxic in such circumstances — the former causing convulsions and the latter a form of narcosis which is very similar to acute alcoholism; disorientation and death may result from intoxication by either gas. Care is taken in industrial operations to monitor the partial pressure of the oxygen supply so that it does not rise for long above the safe level of 80 kPa (600 mmHg), and air diving is not permitted in the North Sea oil fields at depths greater than 50 m (165 ft)[1]; helium, which introduces problems of its own, is substituted for nitrogen at greater depths.

Greater problems arise from the reducing pressure during ascent at which point the dissolved gases — in particular, nitrogen — will effervesce. This may lead to decompression sickness, to pulmonary barotrauma — in which the pulmonary tissue is disrupted by gaseous expansion — and air embolism. All of these may be exceptionally severe in divers, the severity being governed by the depth of dive, the length of time at depth and the speed of ascent. Decompression sickness results from the presence of bubbles in the blood and tissues and may cause rapid death. Involvement of the central nervous system is a major hazard of diving cases of decompression sickness and this may be responsible for delayed death. So-called dysbaric osteonecrosis (localised death of bone) is a particular hazard for those who work at high pressure for any length of time; the condition may cause serious disability, particularly if the bony necrosis is close to a joint. Cases of dysbaric osteonecrosis are not confined to multiple exposures and have been reported following only a single exposure to as little as 300–400 kPa (3–4 atmospheres); the condition may take many years to appear. Decompression sickness is a prescribed disease.

Lesser effects of expansion of trapped air during ascent — barotrauma — include pain in the ears and sinuses which may be intolerable and lead to panic.

Some of the effects of the artificial breathing mixture in use have been described above. The effect of carbon dioxide, whether in increased or decreased amounts, must also be considered; complete chemical removal of carbon dioxide may suppress the stimulus to breathe and result in death from hypoxia. The substitution of helium for nitrogen dictates an increased heat loss; the loss of heat from breathing at depths below 180 m (600 ft) may be greater than the body can produce — heated breathing mixtures are therefore needed at such pressures.

Cold is, in fact, the major hazard of the diver's external environment; unconsciousness and even death from hypothermia are distinct possibilities, particularly as the foam lining of wet suits becomes compressed at depth and conducts heat quite efficiently. The need for suits heated by electricity or by hot water is increasing.

The prevention of decompression sickness is essentially a matter of controlling the rate of decompression. This can be accomplished by a graduated ascent; after severe exposure, however, it is more convenient to transfer the diver to the decompression chamber at sea level (surface orientated diving with surface decompression). The latter process is limited to dives of less than 50 m (165 ft); diving bells or continued living and working under pressure (saturation diving) are used for greater exposures.

In addition to the pressure and associated effects, commercial divers are prone to chronic bacterial infections; the most distressing of these is inflammation of the ear which may be particularly resistant to treatment.

See also: Air embolism; Carbon dioxide; Decompression sickness; Hypothermia; Prescribed diseases and occupations

1. Diving Operations at Work Regulations 1981 (SI 1981/399).

Further reading
For an account of North Sea diving operations, *see* Hendry WT et al 'The off shore scene and its hazards' in Mason JK (ed) *The Pathology of Violent Injury* (1978) Edward Arnold, London. *See also* Bradley ME 'Commercial diving fatalities' (1984) 55 Aerospace Med 721.

Divorce

The law on divorce was reformed by the Divorce Reform Act 1969 and is consolidated in the Matrimonial Causes Act 1973. The sole ground on which a petition for divorce may now be presented is that the marriage has broken down irretrievably. Nevertheless, such irretrievable breakdown must be demonstrated by at least one of five factual findings; conversely, s.1(4) of the 1973 Act indicates that the court need not grant a decree nisi if, despite the existence of one of these grounds, it is shown that the marriage has not broken down irretrievably — a condition which is obviously very difficult to establish in the circumstances[1]. The five relevant facts are:

(a) That the respondent has committed adultery and the petitioner finds it intolerable to live with the respondent[2].
(b) That the respondent has behaved in such a way that the petitioner cannot reasonably be expected to live with respondent.
(c) That the respondent has deserted the petitioner for a continuous period of at least two years immediately preceding the presentation of the petition.

(d) That the parties have lived apart for a continuous period of at least two years and the respondent agrees to a decree being granted.
(e) That the parties have lived apart for a continuous period of at least five years immediately preceeding the presentation of the petition[3].

It is quite impossible in a note of this nature to follow all the intricacies surrounding these factual situations[4] but the following points are of varying medico-legal importance. Adultery must involve sexual intercourse, the definition of which is discussed under that heading. The chances of medical evidence on this point ever being called are negligible but it is to be noted that artificial insemination by donor (AID) would not constitute adultery[5] although non-consensual AID might well might well be considered as behaviour which makes cohabitation unreasonable.

The doctor may, however, be concerned in divorce petitions based on the behaviour of the respondent particularly as the test of reasonable expectation, although related to the conditions of the particular marriage, is objective. Thus, violence towards a peaceable spouse could be positive evidence that it was unreasonable for the parties to live together. Unacceptable behaviour may, however, be of different, passive nature and this may result from illness of both mental and physical type. The granting of a decree in *Thurlow v Thurlow*[6], in which the husband found it impossible to live with a bed-ridden invalid may seem unfair but behaviour which leads to a petition may be blameless and due to no more than misfortune; clearly, however, each case would have to be decided on its particular merits. The law, both in England and Wales and in Scotland, allows for a period of up to six months in which to try to effect a reconciliation without affecting the court's decision. The court cannot, however, entertain petitions for divorce which are presented within a year of marriage[7].

It is now possible for decrees to be obtained in undefended cases without the appearance of the parties or their representatives in court and this is the usual process. Divorces in Scotland may now be granted in the sheriff court. Indeed, the policy of modern divorce legislation is to dissolve marriages which have irretrievably broken down with as little disturbance as possible[8].

See also: Artificial insemination by donor; Domestic violence; Sexual intercourse

1. *Le Marchant v Le Marchant* [1977] 1 WLR 559.
2. But the phrases are probably independent — *Cleary v Cleary* [1974] 1 All ER 498.
3. Similar conditions are laid down in the Divorce (Scotland) Act 1976, s.1(2).
4. *See* Cretney SM *Principles of Family Law* (4th ed, 1984) Chap. 4 (Sweet & Maxwell, London) for an up-to-date account.
5. *MacLennan v MacLennan* 1958 SC 105.
6. [1975] 3 WLR 161, [1976] Fam 32; discussed from the medical aspect in [1975] 2 Br Med J 715.
7. Matrimonial Causes Act 1973, s.3 as amended by Matrimonial and Family Proceedings Act 1984, s.1.
8. *See* Ormrod LJ in *Grenfell v Grenfell* [1978] Fam 128 at 141.

Domestic Violence

The Select Committee on Violence in Marriage[1] defined 'battered wives' as women who have suffered severe or repeated physical injury from the men with whom they live. The committee noted that violence in marriage was a phenomenon which had been accepted for centuries but that there were very few factual reports available. The main reason for this is that, whereas the battered baby has, because of its vulnerability, attracted support from the state and is entitled to the protection of the courts, a woman is supposed to be a rational and consenting adult who can take care of herself — certainly, there is no way in which a doctor can break the confidence of a woman patient without her consent as he may feel able to do when an infant is in his care. Moreover, the police are generally reluctant to interfere in the domestic field.

Gayford's review[2] remains a classic on the subject. He found, *inter alia*, that 32 per cent of wives seeking shelter had sustained fracture and 42 per cent had been attacked with weapons, including belts and buckles; although the assaults had continued for more than a year, few women held a grudge against their husbands. Heavy drinking was associated with about half the cases of wife battering.

The condition has aroused much attention from women's organisations[3] and, largely as a result of their pressure, important legislation, although of a fragmentary nature[4], has been enacted in recent years. The primary legal defence for a woman under threat is to obtain an injunction or order against molestation or to ensure that the husband vacates the family home. An injunction can be made under:

(a) Domestic Violence and Matrimonial Proceedings Act 1976 which is the main avenue to non-molestation orders and to the protection of battered women including co-habiters.
(b) Matrimonial Homes Act 1983 which, by definition, refers only to married couples. This is the route to be taken in attempting to have the spouse ousted from the home[4] but a non-molestation order cannot be made under the same statute.
(c) The Supreme Court Act 1981, s.37, gives the family division of the High Court wide powers but these are subject to the initiation of other proceedings (e.g. divorce) and they are not often used save when the children's protection is the main concern of the injunction.

These injunctions normally require a varying period of notice to the respondent (four days under the 1976 Act and 21 days under the 1983 Act) but, exceptionally, an *ex parte* order can be made in an emergency. The court also has powers to include a power of arrest when the injunction is defied and when actual harm and the likelihood of repeated injury can be shown.

In addition, application for a protection or an exclusion order can be made under the Domestic Proceedings and Magistrates' Courts Act 1978[5]. The grant of such orders is dependent upon actual or anticipated violence against the legal wife or children; the Act allows for arrest and punishment for breach of the order. The same Act (s.1(c)) allows a woman to apply for a financial order, which provides her with some independence[6], if she can establish that the respondent has behaved in such a way that she cannot reasonably be expected to live with him. Save in an emergency, hearings under this statute are conducted in the magistrates' courts sitting as domestic courts (Magistrates' Court Act 1980 s.67(1)) which also have a duty to attempt reconciliation between the parties. A battered woman can obtain compensation from the Criminal Injuries Compensation Scheme even if she is a wife. Despite the increasing legal protection of women, 'women's shelters' are still necessary and are frequently used. Although the wife has been considered as the applicant in the above note, husbands can obtain similar relief in the rare occasions on which it may be needed.

The position of grandparents, 'in-laws' and the like seems very ill protected in law and 'granny bashing' is likely to become more prevalent with the increase in longevity which goes with improved medical practice. No obligation to support one's parents exists in England and Wales and the common law duty to do so in Scotland has now been abolished[7]. The subject is discussed further under 'Geriatric medicine'.

The position in Scotland is covered by the common law remedy of an interdict or, more recently, by the Matrimonial Homes (Family Protection) (Scotland) Act 1981[8]. Under s.4, the court may make an exclusion order if it is necessary for the protection of the applicant or of any child of the family from any conduct or threatened or reasonably apprehended conduct of the non-applicant spouse. The court may make an interim order suspending the occupancy rights of the non-applicant spouse under s.4(6). Power of arrest for breach of an interdict is provided, when requested, with interdicts under the Act (s.15). Some difficulty has arisen as to what constitutes a valid reason for the granting of an exclusion order[9] and as to the evidence which is necessary before this can be given. The provision for victims of domestic violence may be backed up by the Housing (Homeless Persons) Act 1977 in circumstances in which the applicant may want to leave the home.

See also: Alcohol; Battered babies; Confidentiality; Geriatric medicine; Non-accidental injury of adults in the home; Wardship proceedings

1. *Report of the Select Committee on Violence in the Family*, Vols. I–III (1977) HC 329–i,ii,iii.
2. Gayford JJ 'Wife battering: a preliminary survey of 100 cases' [1975] 1 Br Med J 194. *See also* Freeman MDA 'What do we know of the causes of wife battering?' (1977) 7 Fam Law 196.
3. Pizzey E *Scream Quietly or the Neighbours Will Hear* (1974) Penguin, Harmondsworth.
4. See comments in *Richards v Richards* [1984] 1 AC 174, which is arguably the most important case in the field.
5. As amended by the Matrimonial and Family Proceedings Act 1984.
6. Bradley D 'Matrimonial proceedings in Magistrates' Courts' (1977) 40 MLR 450.
7. Family Law (Scotland) Act 1985, s.1.
8. As amended by the Law Reform (Miscellaneous Provisions) (Scotland) Act 1985, s.13.
9. *Bell v Bell* 1983 SLT 224; *Smith v Smith* 1983 SLT 275; *Ward v Ward* 1983 SLT 472; *Cologiacomo v C* 1983 SLT 559.

Double Effect

Double effect is the moral equivalent of the legal doctrine of necessity. It effectively states that, so long as there is no less injurious alternative, an action is permissible where its intended good effect can be obtained only at the expense of a coincidental ill effect. Although the principle can be applied to any form of medical treatment, it is most often invoked in the management of incurable disease and, particularly, in the treatment of the terminally ill. In the latter case, the good effect is the relief of pain whilst the potential ill effect is the shortening of life — an ill effect which is, in fact, far less likely under modern therapeutic regimens. Subject to allowance for the Christian virtue of suffering, the double effect doctrine is approved by the Roman Catholic Church in this context[1]. It has, however, been suggested that there are three additional factors which are essential to the doctrine: the action itself must either be good or be morally indifferent, the good effect must not be produced by means of the evil effect and there must be a proportionate reason for allowing the foreseen evil to occur[2]. The principle of double effect also has the backing of the Church of England[3] although it is doubtful if it is acceptable in Orthodox Jewish teaching[4]. The application of the principle involves a value judgement which can be resolved only on the basis of good clinical practice.

Judicial acceptance of double effect rests on Devlin J in his classic charge to the jury in *R v Adams*: 'The doctor...is entitled to do all that is proper and necessary to relieve pain and suffering even if the measures he takes may incidentally shorten life' — a dictum which emphasises the importance of intent[5]. Criticisms of the Director of Public Prosecutions[6] — who has said more recently, 'Doctors who deliberately speed death could face the prospect of life imprisonment'— fail to take adequate notice of this fundamental point; the use of the word 'deliberately' in the DPP's statement merely serves to reinforce the distinction made by Devlin J.

See also: Euthanasia; Terminal illness

1. Sacred Congregation for the Doctrine of the Faith *Declaration on Euthanasia* (1980) Vatican Polyglot Press. Confirming the statement of Pope Pius XII (1957) 49 Acta Apostolicae Sedis 147.
2. McLean S and Maher G *Medicine, Morals and the Law* (1983) Chap.3, note 12, Gower, Aldershot, Hants.
3. Coggan Rt Rev D 'On dying and dying well — moral and spiritual aspects' (1977) 70 Proc R Soc Med 75.
4. Jakobovits I 'Jewish medical ethics — a brief overview' (1983) 9 J Med Ethics 109.
5. Quoted in Palmer H 'Doctor Adams' trial for murder' [1957] Crim LR 365.
6. Havard JDJ 'The legal threat to medicine' (1982) 284 Br Med J 612.

Down's Syndrome

Down's syndrome is probably the commonest clinically significant chromosol disease which is compatible with life. The affected child's nuclei contain 47 chromosomes, the scientific name for the condition being trisomy-21.

The condition is readily recognisable at birth from the facial appearances — these gave the syndrome its ealier name of 'mongolism'. There is a frequent association with physical anomalies, including congenital heart disease and abnormalities of the bowel, some of which include absence of segments and which are, therefore, incompatible with survival unless corrected surgically. Downsian infants are abnormally susceptible to infection and to acute leukaemia and there is a varying degree of mental defect which cannot be assessed at birth. The expectation of life is substantially reduced.

Other than when some rare and unusual chromosomal abnormalities are present in clinically normal mothers, the abnormality which causes Down's syndrome arises by chance but its occurrence is markedly associated with maternal age; the chances of having an affected baby run to 1 in 50 pregnancies for women over 40 years old. There is also a slight but significant paternal age effect on the incidence of the syndrome[1]. In the unlikely event of a women with Down's syndrome becoming pregnant, there is a theoretical 1 in 2 chance of the baby being affected although this does not apply in practice because a high proportion of trisomy-21 fetuses abort spontaneously. Males with Down's syndrome are sterile.

Fetal trisomy-21 can be diagonosed by amniocentesis and is a fully acceptable ground for abortion under the Abortion Act 1967, s.1(1)(b). But, although there is a substantial risk that the child will be severely handicapped, this may not materialise and, even if there is severe mental retardation, many Down's syndrome infants are very lovable and are loved. Genetic counselling when such a fetus is discovered is therefore complicated and is a very good example of the maxim that such counselling is there for the benefit of particular parents in particular circumstances. A survey of parents who have had a Down's syndrome child showed that, whilst most would favour abortion of such fetuses, opinions on neonaticide were sharply divided; there was a significant shift towards less tolerance of neonatal abnormality in social classes I and II[2]. Since there is no evidence that a Down's syndrome child is in pain or is unhappy in his own limited world, any positive decisions taken in favour of euthanasia must be heavily biased towards the interests of the parents. On the other hand, a mother who is incorrectly informed of the state of her fetus as shown by amniocentesis may be successful in a claim for damages[3].

Equal or greater difficulty surrounds the question of treating the several life-threatening congenital malformations which are liable to be found in neonates with Down's syndrome. The arguments are pursued under 'Neonaticide'. Here it is merely remarked that there has been only one UK court decision and, in that, a life-saving operation was ordered by the court contrary to the parents' wishes. The implication from the judgment was that the court would not have considered the posibility of euthanasia for an uncomplicated Down's sydrome infant[4]; decisions in the USA, however, might well favour the position of the parents[5].

See also: Abortion Act 1967; Amniocentesis; Chromosomal disease; Genetic coun-selling; Genetic disease; Mongolism; Neonaticide

1. For a simple description of the basis of the problem, *see* Emery AEH *Elements of Medical Genetics* (6th ed, 1983) Chap.4, Churchill Livingstone, Edinburgh.
2. Shepperdson B 'Abortion and euthanasia of Down's syndrome children — the parents' view' (1983) 9 J Med Ethics 152.
3. *Rawnsley v Leeds Area Health Authority* (1981) *The Times*, 17 November, p.2.
4. *Re B* [1981] 1 WLR 1421.
5. *See*, for example, *Re Phillip B* App 156 Cal Rptr 48 (1979).

Driving Offences

Of a very large number of offences detailed in the Road Traffic Act 1972, as amended by the Transport Act 1981, only three are of direct medical importance: causing death by reckless or dangerous driving (s.1), driving or being in charge when under the influence of drink or drugs (s.5) and driving or being in charge with an alcohol concentration above the prescribed limit (s.6). It is of marginal interest that it is also an offence to ride a cycle when unfit to ride through drink or drugs (s.19) and also to be drunk while in charge of a carriage in a public place[1]; there is no provision in either of these cases for compulsory analysis of breath or body fluids[2].

The main medico-legal issues in these offences are discussed in detail under 'Reckless driving' and 'Road Traffic Act 1972'. Here it is sufficient to note that the medical and scientific evidence is very much of a clinical nature as regards offences charged under s.5 — charges which are rarely laid these days. The court shall take into account evidence of the proportion of any drug present in the body of the accused (s.10(2)) and a specimen of blood or urine can be demanded at a police station or hospital (s.8(3)(c)). A refusal to supply a specimen without reasonable excuse is an offence but the choice of blood or urine is left to the discretion of the constable subject to the veto of a blood specimen by a medical practitioner for medical reasons.

This procedure is not without difficulty. The choice of blood or urine is very much a medico-scientific affair. Certain drugs are better sought in one or other medium and, even if the constable is provided with a list of drugs and their detection, the chances of his knowing at the time of arrest which drug is to be sought are not high. The analysis of drugs is very much more dependent on laboratory expertise than is that for alcohol and considerable differences may appear between the prosecution and defence analyses. The court may be in some difficulty as to the conclusions to be drawn from the evidence and this is particularly so if the proportion of the drug discovered is apparently so low as to conflict with the clinical medical evidence.

See also: Reckless driving; Road Traffic Act 1972

1. Licensing Act 1872, s.12; Licensing (Scotland) Act 1903, s.70.
2. Nor is there when flying an aircraft while under the influence of drink or drugs (Air Navigation Order 1974 (SI 1974/1114), art. 45(2)).

Drowning

The term 'drowning' is used here in its popular sense. Strictly speaking, death in a fluid medium should be ascribed to immersion; there are, then, several modes to be considered.

It is not uncommon for death to be sudden and to leave no traces; the mechanism in this case is probably through vagal inhibition of the heart, the necessary abnormal stimulus being the sudden impact of water on the nasopharynx. This is so common when children die in the bath that a 'normal' drowning death is almost to be suspect *per se* in such circumstances. An unusual, although equally uncertain, type of death occurs in swimming baths when a swimmer overbreathes in order to swim under water; not infrequently, he fails to surface and is dead when recovered from the water. It is presumed that overbreathing washes the carbon dioxide from the blood stream and there is, then, no stimulus to breathe which would force the subject to the surface. Death is essentially hypoxic.

Most often, however, death from immersion is due to inhalation of the medium when the power to remain afloat is lost — this is correctly referred to as drowning. The mechanism of death then depends upon the osmotic strength of the medium or, in practical terms, whether it is fresh or salt water. In the latter, the hypertonic water in the alveoli draws fluid from the plasma and the lungs become waterlogged;

death is hypoxic in type although petechial haemorrhages are seen surprisingly rarely. Water may be gulped into the stomach and forced into the middle ears during the hypoxic struggles. The inhalation of fresh water, on the other hand, results in the loss of the protective surfactant which lines the alveolar wall, and a mass of froth at the nose and mouth is characteristic. Internal examination generally shows surprisingly dry lungs. This is because the hypotonic fluid is drawn into the blood stream — a process which may continue after death. The plasma itself then becomes hypotonic in relation to the erythrocytes. These swell and burst, leading to an excess of toxic potassium in the plasma (hyperkalaemia). This sensitises the heart muscle and death is then attributable to ventricular fibrillation. Theoretically, therefore, death in fresh water is more rapid than is that in sea water but this, of course, relates only to the time after the struggle to float has ceased.

Ventricular fibrillation may also result from hypothermia if the body is immersed in cold water. The distinction is important in the event of recovery before death because artificial respiration, which is the treatment for water inhalation, may precipitate death in a subject who might, otherwise, recover from hypothermia on warming. Delayed death in those who have apparently been resuscitated from drowning may occur as a result of postimmersion pneumonitis; this condition, which has a high mortality, is, again, probably associated with removal of the protective surfactant.

Immersion and, in particular, drowning may be accidental, suicidal or homicidal. In ordinary conditions, the distinction is often to be made only on the basis of the circumstantial evidence — it is, for example, surprising how frequent is suicidal drowning and how often hats, handbags and the like are left behind on the bank or shore when this is the cause. The most common forensic decision which falls to be made, however, is whether the subject was dead or alive when immersed. This may be difficult in cases of apparent vagal inhibition of the heart — acute myocardial ischaemia may, for example, precipitate a fall into water and produce similar and confusing postmortem findings. Very often, however, the body will be recovered only in a semi-putrefied state and this will greatly complicate postmortem interpretation. Several biochemical tests which depend upon the osmotic gradient between inhaled water and plasma have been elaborated but none is really satisfactory when the diagnosis is seriously in doubt. The most useful differential test depends on the demonstration of diatoms but even this has serious limitations.

Injuries discovered in a body recovered from the water may have been the result of an assault which precipitated immersion; they may have occurred simultaneously with immersion as may happen in deaths from diving boards; or they may have been inflicted after death due to contact with boats or pounding upon rocks, etc. Fish and crustaceans may cause severe *post mortem* damage with great speed. It is apparent that the interpretation of such injuries requires patience and skill.

Injury from carnivorous fish (e.g. sharks) may precede death from drowning and there is a very high incidence of alcohol-associated drowning accidents in warm climates where water sport is a way of life (e.g. in Australia[1]). The frequent occurrence in such areas of accidental drowning of children in open air swimming pools generally leads to stringent fencing regulations; there is none in the UK[2].

See also: Carbon dioxide; Diatoms; Erythrocytes; Hypothermia; Hypoxia; Immersion; Vagal inhibition of the heart

1. Plueckhahn VD 'Alcohol and Drowning — the Geelong experience, 1957-1980' (1981) 21 Med Sci Law 266.
2. *See* a short note: Barry W et al 'Childhood drownings in private swimming pools: an avoidable cause of death' (1982) 285 Br Med J 542.

Drug Abuse

'Drug abuse' is a term which is often used but for which there is no real definition. It involves more than the use of drugs for non-medicinal purposes although that is certainly an important aspect and the one which is most commonly implied by the term.

The most widespread of the other forms of drug abuse is the continued use of excessive amounts of drugs by patients; much of this is associated with iatrogenic abuse — i.e. overprescription. What constitutes drug abuse in this field is therefore very much a matter of opinion — reasonable practice for one doctor/patient relationship is unacceptable to another. A more serious form of iatrogenic drug abuse is irresponsible prescribing either in the form of the prescription of incompatible drugs or by such excessive prescribing as may render the patient drug dependent. It is for this last reason in particular that the issue of repetitive prescriptions without equivalent consultation is dangerous. Doctors have, in the past, combined to outlaw drugs especially likely to cause dependence. The amphetamines, for example, are now prescribed very rarely but the time may be close when the prescription of many tranquillising drugs may have to be scrutinised. True consensus is, however, difficult to achieve; a determined effort in the UK to limit the use of barbiturates, which still constitute the commonest source of drug overdose, failed for lack of universal support.

See also: Drug addiction; Drug overdose; Misuse of Drugs Act 1971

Drug Addiction

A person is defined as a drug addict if, and only if, he has, as a result of repeated administration, become so dependent on the drug that he has an overpowering desire for the administration of it to be continued[1]. The concept of overpowering desire attempts to distinguish addiction from habituation but the dividing line must, at times, be fine. The essence of addiction lies in psychological and physical dependence, on the need to increase the dose to achieve the same satisfaction of desire and on the phenomenon of withdrawal symptoms. Although not all these criteria will always be present, they serve to distinguish those controlled drugs (see 'Misuse of Drugs Act 1971') which are not addictive — in particular, the hallucinogens and cannabis — from those which have this special danger. The narcotics — including the products of opium and their synthetic analogues such as pethidine and methadone (*see* 'Narcotic drugs') — are prominent among addictive drugs although there is no doubt that, of depressant drugs, the barbiturates are also dangerously addictive. Certain stimulants such as cocaine and the amphetamines also have all the necessary attributes of drugs of addiction.

Surprisingly little is known of the root causes of addiction, and sociological studies of the condition are notoriously biased by the necessarily selected populations which are commonly studied. Availability of addictive drugs must have a considerable influence — before 1960, the great majority of addicts were patients who had been overtreated or professional persons with easy access to drugs. The problem becomes acute when availability is combined with a widespread need for psychological escape from reality; the evidence is, however, that the great majority of addicted veterans of the Vietnam war, who were a classic example of such a population, were cured of their addiction relatively easily. Some underlying urge other than escapism must therefore be present. The use of addictive drugs may be group dependent but solitary addicts are common. Social class is no barrier; the picture of the degenerate 'junkie' is matched by the cocaine addict in high society — although this may be a reflection of availability on financial grounds. It has been suggested that the majority of addicts are those of good intelligence who have failed to meet their potential and who are subject to familial stress[2].

It is therefore not surprising that there is conflict as to the treatment of the addict. On one view, the individual should be forced into abstinence and the use of narcotic drugs in medicine should be strictly supervised. The alternative is to attempt to contain the worst aspects of addiction by supplying the drug in a controlled manner while, at the same time, attempting to wean the patient or to substitute the addictive drug by compounds which are less dangerous. This is the compromise adopted in the UK — addicts may be so treated but only under licence while, at the same time, the treatment of organic disease by powerful narcotics is not unduly inhibited.

Evidence as to the relationship between addiction and crime is conflicting. Whilst it is obvious that many addicts must resort to theft to establish their supply, it is likely that criminality in general and addiction are associated only through the abnormal personality of the individual which predisposes to both. There is, however, a high recidivism rate in some groups — particularly in those who come to the notice of the law. It would seem that long-term abstinence is possible only in highly motivated individuals who receive community support.

The main physical hazards of drug addiction are associated with self-injection using dirty apparatus. Local abscesses may occur, as may severe septic thrombosis of peripheral veins; septic emboli may arise from these. Accidental injection of an artery may lead to gangrene of the distal part. The sharing of syringes and needles leads to the transmission of blood-borne disease — in particular, hepatitis and the acquired immune deficiency syndrome. The incidence of hepatitis in drug addicts is so high that they constitute a very severe problem in renal dialysis units and, even, in the postmortem room.

Acute medical problems due to the drug itself are usually associated with accidental overdose; prolonged unconsciousness may, in fact, so alter the cerebral blood flow as to provoke severe hypoxic damage to the brain, including brain death. The long-term systemic effects of the drug, coupled with the life style of the 'junkie', render the addict very susceptible to infections; a greatly diminished life expectancy is compounded by a high rate of suicide. A particularly distressing effect of narcotic drugs is that on the fetus; the child of an addicted mother may, itself, be an addict from birth.

See also: Acquired immune deficiency syndrome; Amphetamines; Cerebral injury; Gangrene; Hepatitis; Misuse of Drugs Act 1971; Narcotic drugs

1. Misuse of Drugs (Notification of and Supply to Addicts) Regulations 1973 (SI 1973/799).
2. There is a mass of literature on drug addiction from which it is invidious to choose. For a useful short summary, *see* Proudfoot AT 'Drug addiction' in Mason JK *Forensic Medicine for Lawyers* (2nd ed, 1983) Chap.24, Butterworths, London.

Drug Interaction

Many drugs affect the function of others when they are given together. Occasionally, the effect may be beneficial but, in general, interactions should be regarded as adverse owing to their unpredictability. Certain drugs are notorious for interacting; with others, an effect may or may not be present or discernible but it is a general rule that the more drugs which are being given, the greater will be the likelihood of interaction. It is also true that elderly patients are more likely to be affected than are the young.

Drug interactions may be chemical in nature and occur before introduction to the patient — such reactions are to be anticipated and are very rare. Alternatively, one drug may alter the activity of the liver enzymes which are responsible for breaking down (or metabolising) another. The effect of the drug will be increased if its enzyme is inhibited; it will generally be reduced if the enzymatic process is stimulated or induced. A third possibility is that the two drugs may potentiate the action of each other, an effect which is particularly noticeable in drugs which act on the central nervous system — which includes alcohol[1]. Drug interactions are generally manifested by an alteration in the effects of one of them and they are likely to be more severe when the therapeutic range of the drug is narrow — it then becomes easier to tip the balance in favour of ineffectiveness or of toxicity. Of the drugs which are well known for their capacity to interact, the barbiturates, phenytoin (which is used for the suppression of epilepsy) and rifampicin (an antituberculous drug) enhance enzymatic breakdown of others in the liver; the effectiveness of oral contraceptives, for example, may be thus limited. Several drugs, including alcohol, inhibit the breakdown of warfarin, a major anticoagulant used in the treatment of thrombotic disease — the effect may therefore be severe bleeding.

The general conclusions as to drug interactions must be, firstly, that the physician should often be able to recognise that such an effect is operating and, secondly, that dangerous prescribing should be excluded by the availability of information as to adverse effects which must now be given in drug data sheets[2]. At the same time, it must be appreciated that many drug interactions are the fault of the patient who may persist in taking stored drugs which the physician has discontinued or who may visit several doctors. The dangers of self-medication have been greatly limited by the terms of the Medicines Act 1968[3].

See also: Alcohol; Contraception; Enzymes; Medicines Act 1968; Thrombosis

1. A very understandable review is to be found in Aronson JK 'Prevention and detection of adverse drug interactions' (1983) 23 Prescribers J 66.
2. Medicines (Data Sheet) Regulations 1972 (SI 1972/2076).
3. Medicines (Products other than Veterinary Drugs)(Prescription Only) Order 1983 (SI 1983/1212).

Drug Overdose

It is probable that many patients are overdosed with drugs in the sense that some may not require drugs at all and some may be taking more than the therapeutic dose. Problems such as whether the unhappy housewife needs a holiday or a course of tranquillisers are widely argued.

The concept of drug overdose is, however, generally taken to refer to suicide or parasuicide and is discussed in greater detail under those headings. Drug overdose is the commonest manifestation of both and is the only form of suicide which is commoner in women than in men.

These two aspects of drug overdose are, therefore, to some extent interdependent — i.e. deliberate overdose would be far more difficult in the absence of overprescription and of its correlate, hoarding of drugs. The logistic difficulties of prescribing with absolute accuracy are, however, formidable and it is, in any case, very likely that those who now deliberately take an overdose of drugs would find another method of achieving the aim if the necessary drugs were not available.

See also: Drug abuse; Parasuicide; Suicide

Drugs

A drug, as far as the 'man in the street' is concerned, is something which is prescribed by the doctor and obtained from the pharmacist — or the American druggist. British legislation is, however, reticent about the use of the term.

The Medicines Act 1968, which would be the expected place for a definition, speaks only of medicinal substances, and earlier legislation, now repealed, speaks, for example, in terms of therapeutic substances. The Poisons Act 1972, as to be expected, refers only to non-medicinal poisons without further amplification. The basic law on criminal poisoning — Offences Against the Person Act 1861, ss.23 and 24, describes the administration of any poison or other noxious thing, again without further definition[1]. The fact that a medicinal substance, or the layman's drug, can be a noxious thing was held in *R v Marcus*[2], a case which dealt with the administration of sleeping pills. The necessary elements in the transformation would seem to include, first and foremost, an intention to use the drug to do anything from endanger life to annoy and, secondly, a component of either foresight or of proximity — in *R v Cato*[3] heroin was consensually administered and caused death; it was upheld on appeal that heroin was a noxious thing.

Reference in the statute law to drugs as such are limited and of interest. The major reference is in the Misuse of Drugs Act 1971, which derives from the control of narcotic drugs. The Sexual Offences Act 1956, s.4 (s.2 of the parallel Sexual Offences (Scotland) Act 1976), refers to the supply or administration of any drug with intent to stupefy or overpower a woman. The Road Traffic Act 1972, s.5, defines the offence of driving or attempting to drive while unfit through drink or drugs, and it is of interest in this context that a solvent has been regarded as a drug for the purposes of an offence[4].

The inference would seem to be that a 'drug' in law must be something which has a pharmacological effect on the brain and, particularly, something which is narcotic. On this interpretation, not all medicinal substances are 'legal' drugs, and whether a 'legal' drug becomes a poison depends upon intention, quantity and method of administration.

See also: Medicines Act 1968; Misuse of Drugs Act 1971; Offences Against the Person Act 1861; Poisons Act 1972; Road Traffic Act 1972; Sexual offences; Solvent abuse

1. The subject is discussed in detail in Williams G *Textbook of Criminal Law* (2nd ed, 1983) p.210 et seq, Stevens, London.
2. [1981] 1 WLR 774.
3. [1976] 1 WLR 110. Williams (n. 1 above) criticises the decision, but similar reasoning presumably affected the Scottish court in *Finlayson v HM Adv* 1978 SLT (notes) 60. The Offences Against the Person Act 1861 does not run to Scotland where such an offence is one at common law (the Criminal Law (Scotland) Act 1829 having been repealed).
4. *Bradford v Wilson* [1983] Crim LR 482; *Duffy v Tudhope* 1983 SCCR 440.

Drunkenness

Drunkenness, or the social result of alcoholic intoxication, can be related only loosely to the blood alcohol concentration. This is because, as is well known, the habituated drinker can maintain acceptable standards under far greater alcoholic loads than can one who takes alcohol only rarely. The reasons for this are not clear but the probability is that the heavy drinker is able to adapt to conditions better despite the fact that the pharmacological effect of a given dose of alcohol on the brain may well be similar irrespective of habituation. Adaptation is, however, markedly affected by the environment; thus, the average person who is found 'drunk and disorderly' is more likely to be an alcoholic without imposed social responsibilities than an inexperienced drinker. Nevertheless, the reaction to increasing quantities of alcohol follows a fairly standard pattern and, within the limits discussed above, the relationship of the blood alcohol level and its effect can be regarded, on average, as:

10–100 mg/100 ml:	loss of self-control, increased self-confidence, talkativeness, alterations in judgement
100–200 mg/100 ml:	distinct loss of skill, slurring of speech and commencing loss of co-ordination
200–300 mg/100 ml:	loss of equilibrium, decrease in pain sense, disturbances in vision
300–400 mg/100 ml:	increasing dissociation, stupor and possibly coma
400+ mg/100 ml:	coma and possible death[1]

Drunkenness in private is one's own affair and the criminal law takes a hand only when the condition becomes a public nuisance. The law is, then, surprisingly rigid and, some might say, old fashioned. Whether the offence be of being drunk in a public place (Licensing Act 1872, s.12) or of being drunk and disorderly (Criminal Justice Act 1967, s.91), 'drunkenness' can refer only to alcohol consumed and not to any other substances or to other volatiles inhaled[2].

Drunken behaviour in the home may result in considerable civil legal activity (*see* 'Domestic violence'); the police are generally disinclined to interfere in what is essentially a private affair unless drunkenness occasions a serious assault.

See also: Alcoholism; Basic intent; Domestic violence; Intoxication and criminal responsibility

1. A classic cartoon illustrative of these effects was reproduced by Muehlberger CW 'Medico legal aspects of alcoholic intoxication' in the original *Legal Medicine*, RBH Gradwohl (1954) p.762, CV Mosby, St Louis MO.
2. *Neale v RMJE (a minor)* (1985) 80 Crim App R 20; *Lanham v Rickwood* (1984) 148 JP 737.

Dura Mater

The dura mater is a tough fibrous envelope which surrounds the spinal cord and brain. It lies in contact with the bones of the vertebrae and with the skull and it is very closely applied to, and, indeed, almost inseparable from, the latter in infancy. A major function of the dura is to 'iron out' the rough contours of bone so that the brain is not damaged when in normal contact with the skull. The dura also contains a number of venous sinuses or drainage tanks which receive the blood returning from the brain. These sinuses may be torn when the fetal head is moulded during childbirth whilst the 'bridging veins', running from the brain to the sinuses, are prone to rupture when there is excessive movement of the brain within the skull.

Potential spaces exist between the dura and the bony skeleton — the extradural space — and between the dura and the arachnoid membrane which forms an inner lining of the brain and spinal cord; this is the subdural space. Haemorrhages into either of these spaces are often associated with violence and are of great forensic significance in other ways (*see* 'Extradural haemorrhage' and 'Subdural haemorrhage').

Spinal nerves pass to and from the spinal cord across the extradural space. Use is made of this anatomical arrangement to produce segmental anaesthesia for surgical operations and for limiting the pain of childbirth (*see* 'Spinal anaesthesia').

See also: Extradural haemorrhage; Spinal anaesthesia; Subdural haemorrhage

Duress

The defence of duress is open to those who have performed criminal acts when under severe pressure. The defence requires that there should have been an immediate threat of serious harm to the defendant's person — or, possibly, to members of his family; that this threat should be one which would have intimidated a reasonable person; and that there should have been no opportunity of escape. The defence of duress may succeed and conviction be avoided if these criteria are met.

There has been some debate over the acceptability of the defence when the resulting charge is one of murder[1]. English courts have been slow to allow this, taking the view that a man is not entitled to prefer his own life to that of another but this interpretation would not necessarily be applied in other countries.

1. *DPP for Northern Ireland v Lynch* [1975] AC 653; *Abbott v The Queen* [1977] AC 755; *R v Graham* [1982] 1 All ER 801.

Dust Diseases

This is a general term for the pneumoconioses (qv).

Dust diseases other than those associated with mineral dust may occur — in particular byssinosis (the results of exposure to cotton dust) and allergic alveolitis, resulting, *inter alia*, from exposure to the dust of mouldy hay (farmer's lung) or bagasse (bagassosis) — and be classified as prescribed diseases[1].

See also: Pneumoconioses; Prescribed diseases and occupations.

1. Social Security (Industrial Benefit) (Prescribed Diseases) Regulations 1985 (SI 1985/967), Sch. 1.

Dying Declarations and Depositions

An exception is made to the rule against heresay evidence in that an oral or written declaration by the victim may be admitted in certain circumstances as evidence in trials for murder or manslaughter. The rationale for the acceptance of such statements is that it may be assumed that the prospect of death has removed any inclination to lie. Such statements may thus be treated as if given under oath. The well-known dictum of Eyre CB illustrates this approach: 'The general principle on which this species of evidence is admitted is that they are declarations made in extremity when the party is at the point of death and when every hope of the world is gone; when every motive to falsehood is silenced and the mind is induced by the most powerful considerations to speak the truth; a situation so solemn and so awful is considered by the law as creating an obligation equal to that which is imposed by a positive oath administered in a court of justice'[1].

The declaration must be made by the victim — i.e. the person whose death is the subject of the charge. It must be made in the full expectation of death, a state of mind which can be inferred from the victim's statements, demeanour or conduct[2]. The statement can be oral or written but signs may be accepted as being the equivalent, as in *Chandrasekera v R*[3] where the victim, who could not speak due to throat injuries, made signs indicating who was responsible for her wounds. The statement itself must deal only with the cause and surrounding circumstances of the death. No corroboration is required[4] but the declarator must die if the evidence is to be admitted.

Scots law on this subject differs in some important respects. A dying deposition in Scotland is admissible evidence in any criminal case and may be made by any person who would have been a competent witness if alive. His life must be in danger but the prospect of death need not be apparent to the deponent. The normal practice is for the deposition to be taken on oath by a sheriff and signed by him and two witnesses although any responsible person can take it in emergency[5].

See also: Hearsay rule

1. In *R v Wooodcock* 1789 1 Leach 500 at 502.
2. Buzzard JH, May R and Howard MN *Phipson on Evidence* (13th ed, 1982) p.498, Sweet & Maxwell, London.
3. [1937] AC 220 PC.

4. *Nembhard v The Queen* [1982] 1 All ER 183.
5. Walker AG and Walker NML *Law of Evidence in Scotland* (1964) p. 429, William Hodge, Edinburgh and Glasgow.

E

Ectopic Pregnancy

Ectopic pregnancy is the implantation of the embryo and its subsequent development outside the body of the uterus. Since fertilisation usually occurs in the fallopian tube, the most common form of ectopic pregnancy is tubal in location; the possibility of this occurring is increased by tubal disease or injury. Ectopic pregnancies occasionally occur in unusual sites such as within the peritoneum.

In a tubal ectopic pregnancy the normal growth of the placenta and fetus result, to all intents, inevitably in rupture of the tube and/or severe haemorrhage. The clinical diagnosis must always be considered in women in the child-bearing age group who present with evidence of an acute abdominal condition. Pathologically, death due to ectopic pregnancy must be distinguished from the results of criminal abortion.

See also: Abortion; Fallopian tube

Electricity

The passage of electrical energy through the body is dangerous but the outcome of an electric shock depends on several factors, including the nature of the discharge and the physiological state of the subject. The fact that there are so few deaths from this cause is a remarkable tribute to safety engineering. The vast majority of deaths are accidental although electricity is sometimes used as a method of suicide and somewhat bizarre instances of homicide by means of, say, dropping the electric fire in the bath have been reported.

The important physical properties of the discharge include the current (amperage), the electromotive force (voltage) and the time over which the discharge is passed (amperes $\times$ seconds [AS] = coulombs). The duration is critical. Very short discharges are unpredictable in so far as their effect depends on the physiological state of the heart at the time; the effect of discharges of less than three seconds depends upon the coulombs transmitted; that of longer applications depends almost entirely on the amperage, although a high current often initiates muscle spasm which thus, also, dictates a prolonged exposure. Direct current is less hazardous than is alternating. Alternating current in excess of a frequency of 1 kHz becomes no more than a source of heat; the most dangerous frequency is at about 50 Hz (cycles per second) which happens to be the frequency of the public supply in Europe.

The significance of voltage relates to the electrical resistance of the subject and this is a matter of the moisture of the skin. The average skin conducts electricity so that voltages above 200 V are likely to be fatal if the current is over 50 mA. Efficient movement of the current depends on earthing and this, again, is largely a matter of dampness of the ground. The dangers of electricity are very much related to body weight, children being more susceptible than adults, whilst all workers in electricity will testify to the fact that preparedness for a shock goes a long way to providing immunity against its effect. It is to be noted that transmission of electricity is likely to be optimal when an electric current is used in conjunction with 'invasive' medical investigations.

Accidents causing electrocution may be wholly fortuitous — as when an instrument carried by a man on a high vehicle touches a supply cable — but most are due to the use of defective domestic appliances. The use of electricity in autoerotic practices is also dangerous. The *post mortem* diagnosis of death from electricity may be difficult — a distinctive mark may not be present. Marks are likely to be small and typically show a central area of necrosis surrounded by a white zone which, in turn, lies within a zone of capillary dilatation; the microscopic appearances are often specific. Prolonged application of the current is likely to produce a deep burn. The shape of the mark may correspond to that of the electrode and similar appearances may be found at the point of exit. Additional traumatic injuries due to falling may, of course, be present.

Death is generally physiological and is due to ventricular fibrillation. It is to be noted that, for this to occur, the current must be applied at a critical value — the passage of a high intensity current is used for the *treatment* of ventricular fibrillation. Ventricular fibrillation due to electric shock may, in fact, be relieved by any counter-shock and it is widely reported that considerable volitional movement is possible between the incident and death; in general, resuscitation of those electrocuted has a high chance of success. Shocks through the head, however, may paralyse the respiratory centre and be resistant to treatment whilst, occasionally, death is due to widespread muscle spasm — in which case the findings will not be unlike those in traumatic asphyxia.

Judicial execution by electricity is still occasionally practised in the USA. Early experience appears to have been disastrous. The present technique is to fit special electrodes to the head and leg. An impulse of 2,000 V at 2.5 A is transmitted for three to five seconds. After a short interval, tension is reduced to 250–500 V and a new impulse is applied. At autopsy, the brain is found to be grossly hyperthermic[1].

See also: Autoeroticism; Burns; Traumatic asphyxia; Ventricular fibrillation

1. This description is given by Somogyi E and Tedeschi CG 'Injury by electrical force' in Tedeschi CG et al (eds) *Forensic Medicine* (1977) Chap. 17, WB Saunders, Philadelphia PA.

Electrocardiogram

The electrocardiogram (ECG) is a tracing which represents the passage of the nervous electrical discharge through the muscle of the heart. The technique, which involves recording from the leads placed on the limbs and on specified parts of the chest wall, has been greatly improved over the years and areas of impaired conductivity can be located anatomically with great accuracy. The main use of the ECG is therefore to follow the progress of a myocardial infarction or to assist in the diagnosis of the acute condition in the event of uncertainty as to diagnosis — indigestion, particularly that associated with herniation of the stomach through the diaphragm, is, for example, notorious for mimicking cardiac disease. The ECG may also be used to screen persons who may be at risk of cardiac arrest and, thus, if abnormal, debar them from particular occupations in which collapse might be dangerous to the public.

The usefulness of the ECG for this purpose is limited by the fact that it is making a retrospective diagnosis of myocardial damage which has occurred previously — and, even then, areas of fibrotic healing may fail to show up. What is needed is a prospective test — that is, one which will indicate dangerous disease of the coronary arteries before the heart muscle has become affected. Attempts have been made to achieve this by combining the ECG tracing with severe exercise, a method which should, theoretically, tend to disclose areas of myocardium at risk from hypoxia due to coronary insufficiency. Taken as whole, such efforts have been unsuccessful; the evidence is equivocal as to both specificity and sensitivity, so much so that the precise relationship between coronary atheroma and myocardial infarction has been questioned[1]. It seems fair to say that a failure to utilise exercise electrocardiography as a routine by employers of high risk personnel could not be regarded as negligence.

See also: Cardiac arrest; Coronary disease; Myocardial infarction

1. Johnson RL and Bungo MW 'The diagnostic accuracy of exercise electrocardiography — a review' (1983) 54 Aviat Space Environ Med 150 gives a very good summary of the present position.

Electroconvulsive Therapy

Electroconvulsive therapy (ECT) is an accepted treatment for, particularly, depressive psychosis. It consists of the passage of an electric current through the frontal lobes of the brain, the charge being of the order of 100 volts for 0.5 second. As the title suggests, the treatment is associated with convulsions and the accepted pattern of treatment includes the use of anticonvulsants in the form of a rapidly acting barbiturate accompanied by a muscle relaxant such as Scoline (suxamethonium bromide). Other particular clinical precautions are taken and it may well be that the patient requires positive pressure oxygenation following the passage of the electric current. Almost inevitably, treatment is followed by a period of memory loss. The aura of suspicion which tends to surround ECT is, perhaps, due mainly to the fact that its mode of action is uncertain. The most likely hypothesis is that a totally abnormal electric discharge in the brain tends to normalise any in-built cerebral electrical dysfunctions. A number of treatments usually need to be given for a therapeutic result — a reasonable regimen being a total of ten treatments being given on a twice weekly, or more frequent, basis.

Problematical ethical issues are raised by the treatment because of its serious nature and the implications of its use. The essential issue is that of consent[1]. The proponents of non-consensual ECT argue that many patients will be incapable of making a rational decision about treatment by virtue of their condition and that concern as to autonomy is therefore misplaced. It is argued that an essential feature of many cases of depressive illness will be an inability to reach any form of decision about even minor day-to-day matters, let alone about complex questions of treatment[2]. ECT is provided for persons compulsorily detained in the UK under conditions laid down in the Mental Health Act 1983 and the Mental Health (Scotland) Act 1984. The precise requirements of this legislation are dealt with in the entry 'Compulsory medical treatment'.

See also: Consent to medical treatment; Manic–depressive psychosis; Psychoses

1. *See* Sherlock R 'Consent, competency and ECT: some critical suggestions' (1983) 9 J Med Ethics 141; Taylor PJ 'Consent, competency and ECT: a psychiatrist's view' (1983) 9 J Med Ethics 146; Culver CM, Ferrell, RB and Green RM 'ECT and special problems of informed consent' (1980) 137 Am J Psychiat 586.
2. The matter was discussed in *Bolam v Friern Hospital Management Committee* [1957] 2 All ER 118, [1957] 1 WLR 582, which has proved to be one of the most significant modern British case relating to consent.

Electroencephalogram

The electroencephalogram (EEG) amplifies and records the electric potentials arising in the cerebral cortex. The potentials are picked up by scalp electrodes which can be so arranged as to give representation from specific cortical areas. The tracings derived are cyclic in type and the various waves recorded are classified according to their frequency.

Normal cyclic activity increases in strength, or voltage, with age and, as a general rule, also increases in frequency; persistence of the slower wave rhythms is a feature of some epileptics and schizophrenics.

Various cerebral abnormalities produce abnormal patterns of differing specificity but the abnormal wave or spike appearances can be accentuated by relatively simple maneouvres such as causing the patient to overbreathe or flashing lights into his eyes. The interpretation of the abnormal waves and spiking activity is a matter for experts but, in general, the EEG is likely to be abnormal in any form of epilepsy, particularly if several readings are made. Abnormalities of the EEG are less constant in other conditions — at least half those with schizophrenia, for example, have normal tracings. Serial tracings may be helpful in the clinical assessment of organic psychoses or in the assessment of hypoxic brain damage.

The most contemporary medico-legal concern as to the use of the EEG relates to the diagnosis of brain stem death. A flat or negative (isoelectric) EEG supposedly indicates no electrical activity in the brain and such a tracing is required in many countries — particularly those of western Europe and in some of the United States — before a diagnosis of brain death can be made[1]. Pallis[2] has made the distinction between 'death of the whole brain', which is what the EEG attempts to show, and 'death of the brain as a whole', which is a clinical concept to which the EEG is irrelevant. He argues that there are both technical and anatomical limits to the use of the EEG in this way and that it is unwarrantable clinical practice to rely on the tracing for diagnosis. Those who are opposed to the use of the EEG in diagnosing death do not deny that there may be occasional cases of clinical 'brain stem death' in which there is residual evidence of cortical electrical activity but maintain that it is extremely improbable that this correlates with residual sentience. There seems no reason, however, why an EEG examination should not be provided if requested by the deceased's next of kin; although this may be bad clinical practice, it may be excellent community medicine.

See also: Brain stem death; Epilepsy; Schizophrenia

1. *See* van Till A 'How dead can you be?' (1975) 15 Med Sci Law 133 for a lawyer's view of criteria for death.
2. Pallis C *ABC of Brain Stem Death* (1983) p.30 et seq, BMA, London.

Electrolytes

Electrolytes are the inorganic ions — either positively (cation) or negatively (anion) charged — which are carried in the body fluids and which constitute a major pathway through which the metabolism of the body is conducted. The most important cations, other than hydrogen, are sodium, potassium and calcium whilst the anions include chloride, phosphate, sulphate and bicarbonate.

There is a marked diference between the composition of the fluid which is intracellular and that which is extracellular (e.g. the plasma). Basically, the main cation of the intracellular fluid is potassium whilst that outside the cells is sodium — an excess of free circulating potassium is frankly poisonous; additionally, the fluid within the cells is more concentrated than is that outside. Since normal osmotic pressure across the cell membrane would seek to equate the concentrations, there is a constant pumping of sodium and of water out of the cells; this requires energy and, hence, an adequate supply of oxygen and substrate fuel in the form of protein and carbohydrate.

Electrolyte imbalance is thus likely to form part of the syndrome of surgical shock, particularly in cases of severe burning. Changes in the cell membranes may occur even in well-treated patients; failure of the 'sodium pump' of this type is known as the 'sick cell syndrome' which contributes materially to the mortality of burning.

Loss of electrolytes can lead to severe metabolic upset. Pure loss of water will cause a general concentration of electrolytes. Potassium and chloride are lost in large quantities in severe diarrhoea, chloride is excreted in vomit and both sodium and chloride are lost in excessive sweating. Conversely, there is retention of sodium and chloride with loss of potassium after injury. Monitoring of electrolytes, and of concomitant alterations in the acid/base balance of the body, is essential in any severe disease process or following any major operation. Electrolyte balance is also heavily dependent upon steroid activity.

See also: Burning; Burns; Drowning; Heat effects; Steroids; Surgical shock

Electromagnetic Radiation

Electromagnetic radiation, or pulsatile energy, exists in a spectrum which is defined by the frequency of the waves. This ranges from what is known as low frequency radiation, running from 1 MHz to 10^7 GHz, to high frequency which ranges from 10^9 GHz upwards[1].

Low frequency radiations are non-ionising and, therefore, not able to alter the chemical constitution of cells; there is, however, increasing evidence that they are not without danger and they are discussed under 'Non-ionising radiation', which includes radio, radar, light and ultraviolet radiation.

High frequency, or ionising, radiation has very great medical importance and potential medico-legal significance; it is discussed under 'Ionising radiation'. The dangerous effect of ionising radiation is proportional to the energy absorbed by the tissues. The measurement of that energy has undergone several changes in the past half century and several different units may be found in reports and other reading. The original measure of energy absorption was the radian (rad) where 1 rad = energy absorbed when 1 roentgen of X-rays is received by 1 gram of tissue. There are, however, variations in reaction to radiation; a unit of biological response is preferable and the original unit was the REM (roentgen equivalent for man). Rads and rems are numerically equivalent save for the action of alpha particles and neutrons for which 1 rad = 10 REM. Modern usage, however, regards these units as unacceptably small. The unit of energy absorption is now the gray (1 Gy = 100 rad); the equivalent biological unit is the sievert (1 Sv = 100 REM).

A radioactive substance produces electromagnetic radiation within the tissues. The unit of radioactivity is the becquerel (1 Bq = 1 atomic disintegration per second).

See also: Ionising radiation; Non-ionising radiation; SI units

1. 1 hertz (Hz) = 1 cycle per second. For a further discussion of modern units of measurement, *see* 'SI units'.

Embolism

Embolism is the distribution of particulate material through the vascular system. It has no significance until an embolus, or particle, becomes impacted in a vessel — and then the effect depends on the tissue which is supplied by that vessel. The process may be venous — in which case the particles become lodged in the pulmonary artery or lungs — or arterial, when they lodge in the small arteries or arterioles supplying the systemic tissues. Embolism may be thrombotic — that is, a separation of blood clots which have formed in the vessels. The most important venous form of this condition terminates as pulmonary embolism, which is discussed under that heading. Arterial thrombotic embolism commonly arises in the heart, especially in cases of valvular disease, or from the larger vessels which are subject to atheroma. The result is infarction of the area supplied by the minor vessel which is plugged. The effect is sudden and the results may be immediate if, as in the brain, the need for oxygen is urgent, or it may be delayed, as in the digits which will take some time to show gangrene.

Probably the most commonly recognised form of embolism is that of particles of malignant tissue, a process known as metastasis. Collections of bacteria may break away from their place of growth and larger parasites, such as the ova of worms, may also embolise thus distributing a localised disease through the tissues.

Other forms of embolism (e.g. of fat particles or air bubbles) are discussed as separate entries.

See also: Air embolism; Atheroma; Fat embolism; Gangrene; Infarction; Malignant disease; Pulmonary embolism; Thrombosis

Embryo Donation

Embryo donation is the end-product of ovum donation. The term is, however, probably best reserved for those cases in which both husband and wife are sterile and an embryo resulting from *in vitro* fertilisation and which is genetically unrelated to either partner is implanted in the woman. This form of treatment for infertility was accepted, somewhat grudgingly, by the Warnock Committee[1], who considered that any resulting child should be regarded as the legitimate offspring of the consenting couple.

Uterine lavage is a unique form of embryo donation in which a donor woman is artifically inseminated at the time of ovulation; the anticipated resultant embryo is then washed out of the uterus, recovered and implanted in the infertile woman. The Warnock Committee recommended that this method should not be used at the present time[2]. They based this on the grounds of dangers, including pregnancy, to the donor; emotional objections would seem to be more cogent — the technique seems to come perilously close to animal husbandry.

See also: Ovum donation; Reproductive technology

1. Warnock M (chairman) *Report of the Committee of Inquiry into Human Fertilisation and Embryology* (Cmnd 9314) (1984) paras.7.4, 7.6, HMSO, London.
2. Ibid, para.7.5.

Embryo Transfer

Although it has been used in a more restrictive sense [1], it is logical to include in the term 'embryo transfer' any process which involves extracorporeal manipulation of the human embryo with subsequent implantation in the womb. Embryo transfer thus encompasses simple *in vitro* fertilisation, ovum donation, embryo donation and womb leasing — but not surrogate motherhood as the term is normally understood. The potential for damage to the embryo, although very small[2], is the important feature which is common to all four processes irrespective of the origin of the gametes (sex cells).

See also: Embryo donation; *In vitro* fertilisation; Ovum donation; Reproductive technology; Surrogate motherhood; Womb leasing

1. For example, Cusine DJ 'Some legal implications of embryo transfer' [1979] 2 Lancet 407.

2. British Medical Association 'Interim report on human in vitro fertilisation and embryo replacement and transfer' (1983) 286 Br Med J 1594, para 5.

Embryonic Experimentation

Superovulation (the stimulation of several ripe ova for simultaneous harvesting) is an integral part of the technique of *in vitro* fertilisation which, at the same time, results in the formation of embryos which are surplus to the requirements of the individual patient; moreover, ova which can be fertilised in the laboratory may be obtained as a 'fringe benefit' from women undergoing sterilisation. Such embryos as are not implanted in a recipient womb may then be destroyed or may be made available for research into, say, the teratogenic effects of drugs, the occurrence of chromosomal disease, etc. Whether such research of experimentation is morally acceptable depends on whether or not the *in vitro* embryo is to be regarded as a human being — there are many reasons why experimentation should be regarded as unethical if the latter be the case.

The arguments are very finely balanced[1] and some commentators take unusual positions; a recent suggestion, for example, is that the embryo is distinguishable from the fetus in that it can be cryopreserved and is, therefore, not yet committed to life[2]. Another approach is to equate humanity with ensoulment and to regard ensoulment as dependent upon a fetal–maternal connection[3] — a concept not far removed from that of St Thomas Aquinas[4]. Under this formula, the *in vitro* embryo would be acceptably available for research up to the time when it had a potential for successful implantation in the womb. This would further justify the recommendation of the Warnock Committee[5], based on anatomical and physiological grounds, that research may be carried out on any embryo resulting from *in vitro* fertilisation up to the end of the 14th day after fertilisation. It does, however, further distinguish embryos from fetuses or living abortuses.

The Warnock Committee further recommended that research on *in vitro* embryos should be permitted only under licence. This may, to some extent, allay the fears of the minority in the Committee who were opposed to embryonic experimentation as a whole but particularly to the deliberate creation of embryos for that purpose; it is probable that most people would object to this last process.

See also: Embryo transfer; *In vitro* fertilisation; Reproductive technology

1. *See*, for example, Singer P and Wells D 'In vitro fertilization: the major issues' (1983) 9 J Med Ethics 192 with comment by Mitchell GD at p.196; Baron CH '"If you prick us, do we not bleed?": of Shylock, fetuses and the concept of person in law' (1983) 11 Law Med Hlth Care 52.
2. Longley C 'Chilling thoughts for test-tube theologians' (1984) *The Times*, 30 July, p.14.
3. Mason JK and McCall Smith RA *Law and Medical Ethics* (1983) p.41, Butterworths, London.
4. *See* Dunstan GR 'The moral status of the human embryo: a tradition recalled' (1984) 10 J Med Ethics 38.
5. Warnock M (chairman) *Report of the Committee of Inquiry into Human Fertilisation and Embryology* (Cmnd 9314) (1984) para.11.30, HMSO, London.

Emergency Medical Care

The main legal questions raised by the provision of emergency medical services are (a) the standard of care expected of the doctor or other providers of treatment and (b) the legitimacy of proceeding without the patient's consent.

The standard of care expected of the doctor in an emergency is that degree of care which would be exercised by a reasonable doctor in the circumstances. The conditions in which the treatment is provided will therefore be relevant; the occurrence of complications if the doctor is required to perform an operation with inadequate facilities would not be as indicative of negligence as might be so in ideal conditions. The urgency of the case would also be taken into account — time for reflection may not be available and, consequently, errors of judgement will be more acceptable than in normal practice. The doctor who stops at the roadside is, however, perhaps to be distinguished from one enrolled in the 'flying squad' type of organisation which is being developed in many areas for use on motorways and the like. The doctor engaged in the latter is positively providing a measure of care and, by virtue of this, would be expected to have available and to use better therapeutic aids than would the casual passer-by.

The standard of care provided by non-doctors will also be determined in the context of the actual circumstances. The absence of skilled medical help might justify intervention by one who has no qualifications for providing assistance; lay intervention is allowable when it is impossible to arrange for skilled assistance in adequate time and the court would assess the conduct of the helper against the standard of the reasonable man in the circumstances. It is difficult to envisage a court finding negligence in the conduct of a well-meaning bystander who comes to the rescue when there is no reasonable prospect of professional attention — this despite the oft-quoted words of Lord Devlin: 'the good Samaritan is a character unesteemed by the English law'[1]. Foolhardy attempts at assistance, however, which are unreasonable and which cause further damage to the injured party, may well attract liability.

The liability which is to be imposed on the person who creates a situation of peril towards his rescuers is an issue which has attracted considerable attention[2]. The general principle here is that a tortfeasor should foresee the possibility of damage to a rescuer; in *Baker v Hopkins*[3] the widow of a doctor succeeded in her claim in respect of the loss of her husband who was killed when giving assistance to men who had run into difficulties.

Claims against doctors who had undertaken to give emergency help to the victims of accidents and to others in dire straits has given rise to the passage of a number of so-called 'Good Samaritan' statutes in the USA[4]. The aim of such statutes is to deny a medical negligence claim to the recipients of emergency help. It has been pointed out that there was no real need for such protection — those attempting to justify such legislation cannot point to instances in which a doctor has been held negligent in such circumstances. There is an interesting contrast in, for example, France where it is a positive offence for a doctor to fail to render emergency aid at an accident[5].

The problem of the patient's consent to emergency help arises only when the patient is unconscious; the normal requirements of consent apply otherwise. The justification of emergency help in such cases rests on the principle of necessity. The subject is considered in rather more detail under 'Unconscious patient'.

See also: Consent to medical treatment; Necessity; Negligence; Unconscious patient

1. Devlin Lord *Samples of Law Making* (1962) Oxford University Press, London.
2. *See*, for example, Linden A 'Rescuers and Good Samaritans' (1971) 34 MLR 241.
3. [1959] 1 WLR 966.
4. For discussion, *see* Comment 'Good Samaritans and liability for medical practice' (1964) 64 Col LR 1301; Sullivan B 'Some thoughts on the constitutionality of good samaritan statutes' (1982) 8 Am J Law Med 27.
5. Decree 79-506 of 28 June 1979, art.4.

Emphysema

One aspect of emphysema which has forensic importance, is quite distinct from what is usually implied by the term and is known as interstitial emphysema. This occurs as a result of severe respiratory obstruction or of injury to the lung. Air escapes from the alveoli and tracks through the root of the lung; from there it may reach the tissues of the neck and of the superficial chest — bubbles in the skin can be felt and heard to crepitate (crackle). Interstitial emphysema also occurs following pulmonary barotrauma sustained during diving (*see* 'Diving hazards').

Generally, however, 'emphysema' refers to an increase in the size of the pulmonary alveoli which is due either to dilatation or to breakdown of the walls; the result is a decrease in their efficiency. The precise cause of emphysema is both uncertain and various but some types are clearly associated with chronic bronchitis which is likely to occur whenever there is persistent irritation of the air passages. Emphysema is also common in pneumoconiosis, particularly that associated with coal mining; the effects of chronic bronchitis and emphysema may be added to the assessment of the dust disease for purposes of benefit provided that the primary disability is not less than 50 per cent.

Emphysema causes many physiological changes in respiration and the sufferer is often very short of breath, even at rest; the symptoms are increased by slight exercise and by exposure to an irritant atmosphere (*see* 'Environmental poisoning'). The main cause of death associated with emphysema lies in the heart. The change in the vasculature of the lungs lays strain on the right ventricle which may hypertrophy but which may also fail. The result is congestive cardiac failure of the type known as 'cor pulmonale'; it is a cause of relatively sudden death in those with chronic lung disease.

See also: Cor pulmonale; Diving hazards; Environmental poisoning; Lung disease and injury; Pneumoconioses

Employment Medical Advisers

Employment medical advisers replaced appointed factory doctors under the Employment Medical Advisory Service Act 1972. This, in turn, was incorporated *in toto* into the Health and Safety at Work etc. Act 1974 and employment medical advisers now form the medical wing of the Health and Safety Executive. The medical advisers have the full powers of inspectors under the Act and they may investigate the cause of death, injury, disease or poisoning in any cases resulting from employment.

The advisers also retain the previous duties of the factory doctors, including the carrying out of statutory medical examinations and examinations of young persons.

See also: Health and Safety at Work etc. Act 1974

Encephalopathy and Encephalitis

'Encephalopathy' means an abnormality of the brain tissue and, hence, of brain function. The symptoms of encephalopathy are those of altered consciousness, coma and, possibly, a permanent dysfunction of the brain ranging from impaired intellect, through general cerebral dysfunction with or without convulsions, to the syndrome of decerebration or the persistent vegetative state. The spectrum is thus very similar to that of differential brain damage as is discussed in the context of brain stem death.

Encephalopathy may be due to infection which results in frank inflammation, in which case an encephalitis is present. Most bacterial involvement of the brain is secondary to inflammation of the meninges (brain coverings) but viral infections (and sometimes tropical infections involving protozoa) often attack the brain tissue as a primary target. Some such viruses — of which the rabies virus is the best known — are among the most lethal organisms known and are classified as dangerous pathogens; the management of patients, laboratory specimens and autopsies is strictly controlled in such cases. Viral infection affects adults as well as children, and several other brain diseases are believed to be virus dependent but have not been proven to be so; very similar precautions are adopted in such cases as a safety measure. Other viruses appear to sensitise the brain which then shows signs of a postinfective encephalopathy. Very occasionally, as in the case of smallpox, immunisation may produce the same result — this outcome is unpredictable, although there may have been premonitory signs of general cerebral vulnerability in the form of infantile fits or convulsions. Greatest interest in this respect has centered in recent years on the role of whooping cough vaccination. The programme of vaccination against this serious disease is in the public interest; it is therefore only right that the public should compensate those who have suffered in the cause, and this is the basis of the Vaccine Damage Payments Act 1979 — the inadequacy of which, in terms of compensation, is currently under review[1].

There are many other causes of encephalopathy and the child's brain is particularly sensitive to the great majority of them. Hypoxic episodes and trauma are obvious causes but intoxications are of equal forensic importance. Several drugs, including alcohol, will cause encephalopathy in children and, very occasionally, these are administered deliberately — a variation on non-accidental injury in children. Solvent abuse is a potent cause in older children, and accidental poisoning by heavy metals (e.g. by mercury or lead) results in a specific form of brain damage.

Finally, a number of disorders of metabolism will cause encephalopathy which, by definition, manifests itself by alteration in consciousness. The best known of these are the comas associated with diabetes and insulin treatment and with kidney failure (uraemia) and hepatic failure. Such states are of major importance in adults in relation to the defence of automatism in criminal law. One form of acute encephalopathy associated with both hepatic and renal failure, known as Reye's syndrome, occurs in children and is worthy of mention as it presents, not infrequently, as an apparent cot death (*see* 'Sudden infant death syndrome')[2].

See also: Automatism; Brain stem death; Hypoxia; Lead poisoning; Non-accidental injury in children; Pathogenic organisms; Persistent vegetative state; Protozoa; Sudden infant death syndrome; Vaccination; Viruses

1. As much as $29 million has been paid to a brain-damaged child in the USA (*Sunday Times*, 11 August 1985, p.4).
2. For a review, *see* Mason JK and Bain AD 'Reye's syndrome presenting as atypical sudden infant death syndrome?' (1982) 20 Forens Sci Int 39.

Endocrine System

Many of the body's functions depend upon the circulation of hormones which are secreted by the endocrine glands. These glands are rarely of medico-legal importance but their state is often referred to in autopsy reports.

The 'mastermind' of the endocrine system is the *pituitary* gland, which lies in a special fossa or concavity in the base of the skull. Fracture of the base of the skull often involves this area, and the consequent dysfunction of the gland may lead to severe disability even though the original injury is survived. The pituitary gland controls growth, the retention of body water and contraction of the uterus during childbirth but its main function is to supervise the activity of the other glands by virtue of a system of servo mechanisms.

The remaining, albeit subservient, glands are, firstly, the *thyroid* gland, which is present in the neck and which controls the metabolic activity of the body. Overactivity of the thyroid may be mistaken for an anxiety state. The gland itself is so situated as to be often bruised during throttling and this may be a valuable sign at postmortem dissection. The *parathyroid* glands are anatomically closely associated with the thyroid and control the distribution of calcium between the bones and the rest of the body.

The *adrenal* glands are closely applied to the kidneys and are of immense importance to the body. The central part of the gland is responsible for the production of catecholamines, of which adrenaline is the main example. Adrenaline is secreted as a response to sudden stress and 'tunes' the body to fighting trim. The outer fraction of the glands, the cortices, control the salt and water balance of the body and are involved in the reaction to chronic stress. Depletion of the adrenal cortices is therefore a common result of infection, burning and other trauma, and 'adrenal exhaustion' may be a potent cause of death in such circumstances. The adrenal glands also have a marked effect on the sexual characteristics and, hence, the gender of the person (*see* 'Steroids').

The *pancreas* secretes insulin through the islets of Langerhans. Insulin is responsible for the maintenance of sugar balance and has considerable medico-legal significance in relation to automatism due either to insufficiency — diabetic coma —

or to overactivity — insulin coma; the latter is usually therapeutic in origin but may be due to the presence of an insulin-secreting tumour.

The *testes* and the *ovaries* also contain endocrine cells which are responsible for the development of sexual characteristics and physique, and for the control of menstruation and of pregnancy.

See also: Anxiety states; Automatism; Diabetes; Gender; Hormones; Hypoglycaemia; Insulin; Steroids

Environmental Asphyxia

Environmental asphyxia is of two types: either the oxygen in the atmosphere is inadequate to sustain life or it is used up in a closed environment and replaced by irrespirable gases.

The former is a matter of rapid ascent to high altitude or sudden exposure to a rarefied atmosphere as may occur if a pressurised aircraft sustains damage so that the cabin air and the ambient environment are equilibrated. The consequent cerebral dysfunction and death are due to hypoxia and are discussed under that heading.

Breathing in a sealed atmosphere results in reduction of the available oxygen and a corresponding increase in the atmospheric carbon dioxide. Death results from a combination of hypoxia and carbon dioxide poisoning and may be surprisingly rapid because the atmospheric carbon dioxide stimulates breathing and a vicious circle is produced. Heat will also have an additive effect. Accidental tragedies occur and particularly vicious forms of homicide involve locking persons in enclosed spaces — the most famous historic example, perhaps, being the 'Black Hole of Calcutta'.

See also: Carbon dioxide; Heat effects; Hypoxia

Environmental Poisoning

The poisoning of the environment is a vast subject and one which arouses considerable emotion, particularly when the term is extended to include mere alteration of the natural order; the present entry is confined to alterations of the atmospheric environment — the effects of pesticides and the like being discussed under appropriate headings.

Atmospheric pollution may result in an accentuation of the natural order. The old London 'pea-soup fog' is a classic example. In the event of a natural fog occurring, a heavy concentration of chimney effluent causes a massive buildup of smoke particles and of sulphur dioxide. Such an atmosphere carries a mortality of its own which is closely related to the concentration of both substances and affects mainly those who are already suffering from cardiorespiratory disease. The hazard has been virtually eliminated from major British cities by the application of the Clean Air Act 1956 which authorises local authorities to control the production of smoke, including the designation of smoke-free zones. The control of sulphur dioxide is complex and depends to a large extent on control of the sulphur content of fossil fuel — a matter which is addressed in the Control of Pollution Act 1974, s. 76. It is doubtful if sulphur dioxide is harmful to humans *per se* but there is a strong suspicion that it acts as a potent herbicide by way of producing so-called 'acid rain'. Such pollution is subject to wide meteorological distribution and it is difficult to establish the extent to which the evidence is scientifically or politically based — the two are currently difficult to disentangle.

A similar, but more obviously a product of modern civilisation, form of pollution resulting from the combustion of fossil fuels stems from the use of the motor vehicle. Vehicle exhausts liberate both carbon monoxide and partially combusted hydrocarbons into the atmosphere. The interaction of these with sunlight produces a high ozone content of the air and results in what is popularly known as 'smog'. The nitrate compounds produced render this dense atmosphere intensely irritating to the nose and throat but, in contrast to the 'pea-soup' fog, it appears to have little permanent effect on humans. Again, however, there is evidence of a herbicidal effect. Powers to control the content of motor fuel have been given under the Control of Pollution Act 1974, s.75.

The most purely man-made aspect of atmospheric pollution consists of the liberation of specific poisonous elements which are not usually present in the atmosphere in dangerous concentration. The metallic poisons are the most significant of such substances, lead being outstanding but beryllium, cadmium and mercury, among others, being important. Such pollutants are almost entirely a product of industry and their release into the atmosphere is controlled rigidly by regulations[1]. The control of ambient ionising radiation is a separate subject and is discussed more specifically under that heading.

Sudden catastrophic accidental pollution of the atmosphere still occurs; witness the release of methyl isocyanate at Bhopal in December 1984 which killed more than 2,000 persons immediately.

See also: Carbon monoxide poisoning; Ionising radiation; Lead poisoning; Pesticides

1. The Alkali & Co Works Regulation Act 1906 was incorporated into the Health and Safety at Work etc. Act 1974, s.1 and Sch. 1.

Enzymes

Every living cell is in a state of turnover, having not only to replace its own components but also to store and release products of metabolism. Enzymes are proteins attached to the cellular membrane which have the property to accelerate such chemical reactions; each cell must manufacture its own enzymes which form an essential part of the cellular function — enzymatic death, whether it be due to hypoxia or to specific poisoning, is the basis of cellular death.

The protein constitution of enzymes is determined genetically and it is therefore possible to use this property in, say, parentage testing. Equally, the genetic code determining the quality of enzymes may be disturbed and the abnormal genes will be passed on and expressed according to the standard genetic principles (*see* 'Genetic disease'). An enzymatic deficiency may result in severe interference with cellular function; such genetic diseases are known as inborn errors of metabolism.

It is to be noted that the pharmacological effects of many modern drugs depend upon their action on the cellular enzymes and, whilst this is specific and intended in drug therapy, a general effect may also result; this is a major cause of adverse drug interactions.

See also: Drug interactions; Genetic disease; Hypoxia; Inborn errors of metabolism; Parentage testing; Poisoning

Epilepsy

About 1 in 200 persons suffers from epilepsy; half of these sustain their first attack as adolescents. The condition may be idiopathic or acquired. Medico-legally speaking, the most important cause of the latter is head injury. Attacks occur early in up to 5 per cent of injured persons; the incidence of late epilepsy, occurring up to four years after the injury, depends upon the severity of the injury but may be as high as 30 per cent in those with depressed fractures[1]. The treatment of the resultant epilepsy may then involve long-term drug therapy, possibly with associated side effects, and also limitation of activity and occupation.

Epilepsy may present as generalised fits which are associated with loss of consciousness; depending largely on their severity, such fits are known as either grand mal or petit mal — loss of consciousness in the latter may be for only a matter of seconds. The symptomatology of partial or focal epilepsy depends upon the area of the brain which is affected but about 30 per cent of all epilepsies are of temporal lobe type. In this, the symptoms are commonly of hallucinatory type but the condition may involve loss of consciousness when the patient is unaware of and has no memory for his behaviour although he may appear to be in control of his actions. Such 'postictal automatism' is seldom associated with an epileptic attack of other than temporal lobe — or 'psychomotor' — type and involves violence only rarely[2]. The use of the electroencephalogram (EEG) in the diagnosis of epilepsy is discussed under that heading.

At one time it was questioned whether there was an 'epileptic personality' prone to criminality; it is now generally agreed that epileptics are no more antisocial than are other groups who are socially disadvantaged.

Medico-legally, the epileptic attack is mainly important as a cause of accidental death and as a factor in the operation of the criminal law. Sufferers may drown, often in only inches of water; they may be involved in industrial accidents — in which case industrial benefit is still payable despite the known risk[3]. But it is as car drivers that epileptics are most seriously concerned with accidental death — nearly half the incidents of unconsciousness which occur at the wheel are epileptic in origin and the condition is undisclosed in over 75 per cent of these; these figures will not include many cases in which the accident was fatal because the condition is only rarely diagnosable at autopsy. A declaration to the effect that the applicant is not suffering from a designated disease[4] is required before a licence to drive is issued, and there are stringent regulations in the case of epilepsy[5]. It may be that a primary epileptic attack could excuse an act of apparent negligent driving[6] but this would certainly not be so in the case of a known but undisclosed epileptic who would, additionally, be guilty of making a false declaration contrary, *inter alia* to the Road Traffic Act 1972, ss.87(1) and 170(1)(a). The doctor's role in this connection is relatively clear; if an epileptic patient persists against advice in driving contrary to the regulations, his duty to the public overrides his confidential relationship and he should report the case to the Chief Medical Officer at the licensing centre — this is particularly so in the case of drivers of public service or of heavy goods vehicles.

The relationship of epilepsy to the legal definition of automatism and its application to the criminal law has been the subject of some confusion. A sudden, unexpected epileptic fit has been regarded as exonerating from the criminal offence of dangerous driving[7]. In such circumstances, any damage done might be said to be due to failure of action on the part of the accused. The situation is, however, different in the event of positive, albeit involuntary, action occurring in the postictal phase of psychomotor epilepsy[8]. The trend of decisions in such cases, although sometimes tinged with policy considerations[9], has been to regard psychomotor epilepsy as a disease of the mind; this has been confirmed in *R v Sullivan*[10] in which the M'Naghten Rules were applied. The effect is that reliance on a temporal lobe epileptic attack as a defence in criminal cases invokes a special verdict of not guilty by reason of insanity — a situation which is open to criticism and which finds little favour in medical circles[11].

See also: Accidental death; Automatism; Confidentiality; Electroencephalogram; Head injury; Insanity and criminal responsibility; M'Naghten Rules; Road traffic accidents; Road Traffic Act 1972

1. *See* Jennett B 'Post traumatic epilepsy' in Laidlaw J and Richens A (eds) *A Textbook of Epilepsy* (2nd ed, 1982) pp.146–154, Churchill Livingstone, Edinburgh.
2. Knox S J 'Epileptic automatism and violence' (1968) 8 Med Sci Law 96.
3. *Tankard v Stone-Platt Engineering Co Ltd* (1946) 174 LT 277.
4. Defined in Motor Vehicle (Driving Licences) Regulations 1981 (SI 1981/952) r.22 (as amended).
5. Motor Vehicle (Driving Licences) (Amendment) (No.3) Regulations 1982 (SI 1982/423).
6. By inference from *Roberts v Ramsbottom* [1980] 1 WLR 823 per Neill J at 832. Compare *Gordon and others v Wallace* (1973) 42 DLR (3d) 342.
7. *R v Spurge* [1961] 2 QB 205 CA at 210 per Salmon J.
8. Radin EA 'Psychomotor epilepsy and aggressive behavior' (1973) 28 Arch Gen Psychiat 210. Compare Delgado-Esqueta AV, Mattson RH and King L 'The nature of aggression during epileptic seizures. Report of an International Workshop on Aggression and Epilepsy' (1981) 305 New Engl J Med 711; this study concludes that aggressive or violent behaviour can occur during epileptic seizure but that complex courses of criminal conduct are unlikely.
9. As in *Bratty v Attorney General for Northern Ireland* [1961] 3 WLR 965. But *see also: HMAdv v Mitchell* 1951 JC 53 in Scotland; *R v O'Brien* (1966) 56 DLR (2d) 65 in Canada; *R v Cottle* [1958] NZLR 999 in New Zealand; and *R v Meddings* [1966] VR 306 in Australia.
10. [1983] 2 All ER 673 HL.
11. Bennun ME and Gardner-Thorpe C 'M'Naghten rules epilepsy — OK?' (1984) MLR 92; Fenwick P 'Epilepsy and the law' (1984) 288 Br Med J 1938. For American discussion, *see* Weinberg CD 'Epilepsy and the alternatives for a criminal defense' (1977) 27 Case Western LR 771.

Erythrocytes

The function of the erythrocytes, or red blood cells, is to transfer oxygen from the alveolar air to the tissues; at either end of the process, transfer takes place in the capillaries which are virtually the thickness of a single red blood cell. The active agent in the transport of oxygen is the haemoglobin contained in the erythrocyte.

There are normally some 5 million erythrocytes to the cubic millimetre of blood. Their shape, that of biconcave buttons, is important in maintaining their integrity, which depends, to a large extent, upon an osmotic equilibrium between the cellular content and the plasma in which the cells float. This equilibrium is altered in fresh water drowning, which leads to bursting of the erythrocytes. The shape of the red cells becomes more spherical in the condition of congenital spherocytosis; the exceptional fragility of the cells results in an anaemia of haemolytic type.

Other forms of haemolytic anaemia depend upon the fact that the red cell antigens are situated in the cellular capsule. Antibodies produced by disease may then cause rupture but, from the forensic medical aspect, the most important type of haemolytic anaemia is that resulting from mismatched blood transfusion; the subject is discussed in greater detail under 'Transfusion reactions'.

See also: Anaemia; Antibody; Antigen; Drowning; Transfusion reactions

Ethanol

Ethanol is an alternative name for ethyl alcohol, which is the form of alcohol involved in social drinking.

In practice, therefore, reference to 'alcohol' in, particularly, road traffic legislation refers to ethanol and it is of some academic interest that this definition has not been clarified by statute. However, ethanol is by far the least toxic of the alcohols which are commonly available — a blood level of alcohol due to ethanol which is no more than mildly disinhibiting could be fatal if it were due to methanol. The distinction is therefore of no practical importance and there can be no question of founding a defence against, say, contravention of the Road Traffic Act 1972, s.6, on such semantic grounds[1].

See also: Methyl alcohol; Road Traffic Act 1972

1. In practice, current breath analysers could not distinguish ethanol from methanol but gas chromatographic analysis of blood could do so with ease.

Ethical Committees

One way of controlling the often controversial area of medical experimentation using human subjects is through the use of ethical committees. It is a characteristic of the UK system that there is no central authority with responsibility for establishing and controlling ethical committees. They may be based in individual hospitals or may be organised at higher level — central committees with responsibility for the ethical assessment of research within health board areas are now established in Scotland[1].

Ethical committees are usually composed of a mixed medical and lay membership, the medical element predominating. Whilst the approval of the committee is required in order for research to proceed within the institutions concerned, there are also indirect external factors which emphasise the importance of such approval. Thus, medical journals may decline to publish the results of research which has not been approved by the appropriate committee, and funding bodies may similarly call for evidence of endorsement by an ethical committee for a project for which help is sought.

The constitution of the committee must be such that it is able to appreciate descriptive shortcomings in the research protocol, and it is a criticism of the system that, having provided a starting point for the project, there is no scope for the committee to monitor its project; the underlying fear is that the less scrupulous researcher may accept the ethical committee as a substitute for his own conscience. Researchers, on the other hand, may criticise ethical committees on the grounds that they constitute an unwarranted interference with the progress of scientific research and that they are insufficiently subtle instruments to deal with the ethical issues which arise in the course of research[2]. In spite of inevitable criticisms, ethical committees provide a useful safeguard for the public conscience and, at the same time, co-operative help for the individual medical researcher. Their importance is likely to grow.

It is important to appreciate that the remit of British ethical committees is distinctly limited. The function of such committees in the USA seems to be far wider and appears to include clinical decisions involving prognosis; at times, the approved ethical committee has been regarded as an extension of the court's authority. Thus, in the well-known case of *Re Quinlan*, the court's decision to allow withdrawal of support to a comatose patient was made subject to the approval of the hospital ethical committee[3]; the emphasis may, however, be changing — the involvement of the hospital ethical committee in deciding a similar case as to cessation of treatment was rejected in a recent Florida case[4].

See also: Biomedical experimentation; Euthanasia

1. For a discussion of the drawbacks of the Scottish system prior to recent reforms, *see* Thompson IE et al 'Research ethical committees in Scotland' (1981) 282 Br Med J 718.
2. Lewis PJ 'The drawbacks of research ethics committees' (1982) 8 J Med Ethics. 61; Allen P and Waters WE 'Attitudes to research ethical commmittees' (1983) 9 J Med Ethics 61.
3. 355 A 2d 664 (NJ, 1976).
4. *John F Kennedy Memorial Hospital Inc v Bludworth* 452 So 2d 921 (Fla, 1984).

Eugenics

The word 'eugenics' was coined in 1883 and was then defined as 'the study of agencies under social control that may improve or impair future generations either physically or mentally'. Put in such general terms, it is clear that the process is open to potential abuse particularly when applied to groups rather than to individuals. Thus, there are compulsory eugenic sterilisation laws relating to the mentally ill, epileptics and criminals which are still extant in a number of the United States and these may extend to punitive treatment of the sex offender[1]. However, despite the apparently leading case of *Buck v Bell*[2], compulsory eugenic sterilisation is increasingly being regarded as unconstitutional. At the extreme limits of the scale, the Nazi German attempts at achieving racial purity and superiority probably sounded the death knell of herd-inspired eugenics while, at the same time, the increased understanding of medical genetics has enhanced the acceptability of eugenic principles as applied to individuals. Thus, the practice of eugenics as a means of improving 'the physical and mental qualities of future generations by control of mating and reproduction'[3] has general approval and is exemplified in the Abortion Act 1967, s.1(b), where the 'eugenic clause' is probably that part of the statute which excites least controversy despite some antipathy to the concept of a 'right to perfection'[4]. The use of abortion as a means of eliminating genetic disease is greatly improved by such procedures as amniocentesis and fetal sampling and, particularly, by modern methods of genetic counselling.

Eugenic control of individuals is relatively straightforward when applied to monogenetic disease and can be assisted by such procedures as contraception, artificial insemination by donor, ovum donation or even surrogate motherhood in addition to the mutilitating procedure of sterilisation. Counselling is far less easy in the context of multifactorial disease; but, in this situation, it is true to say that techniques of preventive and community medicine constitute an aspect of eugenics. Even so, modern reproductive techniques are not without ethical pitfalls when applied to eugenics — among other possibilities one can think of abortion for frivolous reasons, selective donor insemination and cloning (the repetition of identical individuals); the possibility of an extension of parental rejection in the context of neonaticide must also be considered.

See also: Abortion; Amniocentesis; Artificial insemination by donor; Contraception; Genetic counselling; Genetic disease; Neonaticide; Ovum donation; Punishment and torture; Sterilisation; Surrogate motherhood

1. For a very full discussion of the background to the US scene, *see* Meyers DW *The Human Body and the Law* (1970) Chap. 2, Aldine, Chicago. A more recent study is Isaacs SL 'The law of fertility regulation in the United States: a 1980 review' (1980)19 J Fam Law 65.
2. 274 US 200, 47 S Ct 584 (1927).
3. In *Gleitman v Cosgrove* 227 A 2d 689 (NY, 1967) per Francis J at 701.
4. For an American review of the rights involved, *see* Rush CS 'Genetic screening, eugenic abortion and *Roe v Wade*: how viable is *Roe's* viability standard?' (1983) 50 Brook LR 113.

Euthanasia

Defined as 'the act of killing someone painlessly', and alternatively sometimes referred to as 'mercy killing', euthanasia implies an active role for someone other than the patient in the search for an easy death. This interpretation is preferred to the common classification of euthanasia into active and passive or voluntary and involuntary forms. Passive euthanasia, whether it be in the context of a sentient patient (voluntary) or of the incompetent (involuntary), is better regarded as the treatment of terminal illness and is discussed under that heading[1].

Whilst the legal and ethical problems of passive euthanasia are generally clear in the context of terminal illness, there are two situations of major importance in which the issues become clouded — in the withholding of therapeutic aids and in the provision of the means for self-destruction by the patient.

The former is most commonly exemplified by removal from ventilator support but may equally be applied to the removal of feeding tubes or intravenous lines. British courts appear to have been wise in leaving such matters firmly in the hands of good medical practice[2]. The complications induced by legal intervention can be seen in some US decisions — notably in the contrast between *Quinlan*[3], where the removal of ventilator support was regarded as allowing 'expiration from existing natural causes' and *Conroy*[4], where the removal of artificial feeding aids was considered to be causing death from dehydration and starvation and, accordingly, active euthanasia. In the solution of such problems, US courts have developed the concept of 'substituted judgement'[5] and attach very great importance to wishes expressed, no matter how tenuously, during life[6]. Much depends on the distinction of an action from an omission in such circumstances, an argument which Kennedy[7] has described as 'logic chopping'. It does seem absurd to attempt to make a legal and moral distinction between, say, taking down an intravenous line and failing to replace an empty transfusion bag[8]; it is more honest to admit that withdrawal of supportive apparatus is positive activity but of a special kind.

The second area, that of 'assisted suicide', is a somewhat similar attempt at moral evasion (and is discussed under the heading 'Suicide Act 1961'). The discussion is equally, if not more, applicable to the patient in intolerable, but not terminal, illness.

Active euthanasia has never been publicly advocated other than in the terminal illness phase and it is extremely unlikely that the medical profession as a whole would seek the power to accede to a patient's request to be killed. Logically, there is a case for active intervention in the terminal phase but the law is perfectly clear — it 'does not leave the issue in the hands of the doctors; it treats euthanasia as murder'[9]. 'Mercy killing' is generally qualified by the defence of diminished responsibility. There seems every reason to support the view that any change in the law might do little more than inhibit progress in the modern treatment of the terminally ill[10].

See also: Diminished responsibility; Hospices; Suicide; Suicide Act 1961; Terminal illness; Ventilator support

1. Those who have access to a rather obscure source are directed to a most useful article by McCartney JJ 'The development of the doctrine of ordinary and extraordinary means of preserving life in Catholic moral theology before the Karen Quinlan case' (1981) 45 Conn Med 725. The author even suggests that withdrawal of food might be an acceptable form of passive euthanasia. *See* the recent debate in (1985) 145 Arch Intern Med 122–131.
2. *R v Malcherek, R v Steel* [1981] 1 WLR 690; *Finlayson v HM Adv* 1978 SLT (Notes) 60.
3. *Re Quinlan* 355 A 2d 664 (NJ, 1976)
4. *In the matter of Claire C Conroy* Sup Ct NJ App Div, A-2483-82 T1 (1983). This case is to be reviewed by the New Jersey Superior Court.
5. *Superintendent of Belchertown State School v Saikewicz* 370 NE 2d 417 (Mass, 1978).
6. *In re Storar* 438 NYS 2d 266 (NY, 1981) (consolidating *Eichner v Dillon*).
7. Kennedy IM 'Switching off life support machines: the legal implications' [1977] Crim LR 443.
8. Beynon H 'Doctors as murderers' [1982] Crim LR 17. *See also* Husak DN 'Killing, letting die and euthanasia' (1979) 5 J Med Ethics 200.
9. Williams G *Textbook of Criminal Law* (2nd ed, 1983), p.580, Stevens, London.
10. Twycross RG 'Euthanasia — a physician's viewpoint' (1982) 8 J Med Ethics 86.

Evidential Burden

The evidential burden is part of the burden of proof which rests upon parties to a criminal or a civil case. It must be distinguished from the persuasive burden which is that of establishing a case. The evidential burden is that of establishing the facts which are necessary for the persuasive burden to be discharged.

The persuasive burden does not shift during the course of proceedings. In criminal cases it rests with the prosecution to prove guilt; in civil cases it lies on the party 'who asserts the affirmation of the issue'. The evidential burden, however, shifts. A leading textbook summarises this complex issue succinctly in the following terms: 'The *onus probandi* in this sense rests upon the party who would fail if no evidence at all, or no more evidence, as the case may be, were given on either side — i.e. it rests, *before* evidence is gone into, on the party asserting the affirmation of the issue: and it rests, *after* evidence is gone into, upon the party against whom the tribunal, at the time the question arises, would give judgement if no further evidence were adduced'[1].

See also: Burden of proof

1. Buzzard JH, May R and Howard MN *Phipson on Evidence* (13th ed, 1982) pp.44, 47, Sweet & Maxwell, London.

Ewing's Postulates

It has long been debated whether simple physical injury — as opposed to, say, injury by burning or by ionising radiation — can precipitate malignant disease. If it does so, it must be a very rare occurrence and one which demands stringent proof of causation. To this end, Ewing[1] laid down some criteria which should be met before an association is considered. These can be summarised:

(a) The site of the tumour must coincide with the site of injury.
(b) The degree of trauma must be significant.
(c) The part involved must have been normal before injury.
(d) The time interval between injury and appearance of the tumour must be medically acceptable.
(e) The process from injury to tumour must be continuous.
(f) The tumour must have arisen from cells present in the injured part.

These postulates are clearly open to criticism as being vague and unscientific[2] and, in practice, a causal connection between trauma and neoplastic growth is seriously suggested only in relation to intracranial tumours. Most people would fully accept the view of Ewing himself who believed that 'traumas reveal more malignant tumours than they produce'.

See also: Causation; Head injury; Malignant disease

1. Ewing J 'Relation of trauma to malignant tumors' (1926) 40 Am J Surg 30.
2. An old but useful criticism is to be found in Shapiro HA 'Trauma and malignant disease' (1965) 12 J Forens Med 89.

Exhaust Gases

Although exhaust gases could include a wide range of effluents, the term is restricted here to those distributed through the exhaust systems of the ordinary motor vehicle.

Depending upon the efficiency with which the engine is tuned, such gases contain approximately 6 per cent of carbon monoxide. They are therefore of considerable danger to those working in garages. There is scope for both accidental and suicidal death; the subject is discussed further under 'Carbon monoxide poisoning'.

The carbon monoxide discharged into the general atmosphere is also significant but other discharges are also important as environmental poisons. Among these are the unburnt hydrocarbons and nitrogen oxides which, in combination with bright sunlight and a resulting high ozone content of the air, are responsible for the 'smogs' which are such a feature of, say, Athens and Los Angeles. The mineral content of the fuels used remains unburnt and is also discharged into the atmosphere. The overriding example is lead which is deliberately added to petrol so as to allow for simplification of and economy in engine design. Most industrialised countries are now legislating to reduce the quantity of lead in petrol[1]. Lead poisoning is discussed briefly under that heading.

See also: Carbon monoxide poisoning; Environmental poisoning; Lead poisoning

1. Control of Pollution Act 1974, s.75.

Exhumation

The great majority of exhumations are done for the purpose only of removing the body from one piece of consecrated land to another; in this case, a licence is not required but an ecclesiastical faculty — that is, permission from the Anglican bishop — will be needed[1]. Local authorities also have power to exhume and reinter[2] whilst exhumation may be required by an order in council if the burial place is dangerous or injurious to public health[3].

Exhumation for medico-legal purposes is an emotional procedure which is carried out only rarely. It may, however, be required by the State, as in cases of suspected criminality, by insurance companies or by individuals, particularly when identification is disputed. In general, both a licence from the Home Secretary and a faculty are required[1] but a coroner has powers at common law to order an exhumation in order to either open or reopen an inquest. The coroner may so order in connection with criminal proceedings relating to the death of the body exhumed or to the death of another person which is related to the circumstances surrounding the death of the person to be exhumed[4]. Only about two exhumations occur each year in England and Wales but the coroner's warrant would seem to be a less uncommon method than is the Home Secretary's licence.

Petition for an exhumation in Scotland is to the sheriff, who will then notify the next of kin of the deceased. The next of kin may make objection at a hearing; the sheriff's warrant constitutes authority for exhumation.

Identification of the grave by the superintendent of the graveyard, of the coffin and internal wrappings by the funeral director and, whenever possible, of the name plaque by relatives is of great importance. The procedures outlined under

'Identification of the dead' should be followed if the identity of the coffin's contents is in dispute. Very often, however, the possibility of poisoning is raised, in which case the provision of control specimens — including earth from above and below the coffin, the wood of and fluid within the coffin, portions of burial robes and earth from another part of the graveyard — is essential in answer to the possibility of poison having entered the body after death. In making his examination, the pathologist should always bear in mind that the possibility of a second exhumation is remote.

Whether an exhumation will be of value depends to a large extent on the reason for the investigation. Some features (e.g. fractures) will be recognisable many years after death whilst bullets, bomb fragments and the like can be regarded as everlasting. Evidence of poisoning, particularly by metallic poisons, will often be available so long as there are tissues to examine. Even soft tissues may be preserved for, say, up to five years depending on the nature of the burial environment. In general, the value of an exhumation can be accurately assessed only by undertaking the examination.

See also: Changes after death; Coroner; Identification of the dead

1. Burial Act 1857, s.25.
2. Town and Country Planning Act 1971, s. 128(6).
3. Burial Act 1857, s.23.
4. Coroners Act 1980, s.4.

Expert Evidence

The evidence of an expert may be brought before a court by either side in cases involving issues of a scientific or technical nature. An expert is one who has an established competence in a particular field, it being for the judge to decide whether a witness can be so rated. An expert witness is theoretically compellable[1] but, in practice, there are strong reasons why such a witness would not be required to give evidence in a case against his inclinations.

An expert witness may be allowed to be in court before giving his evidence. He may refresh his memory from his statement before going into the witness box and, in Scotland, while in the box; thereafter, any documents to which he wishes to refer must have been made contemporaneously with the facts to which the witness is speaking[2]. Reference may be made to textbooks or other publications while the witness is testifying and he may rely on material which is accepted scientific knowledge without having studied the matter personally[3].

The task of the expert witness is 'to furnish the judge or jury with the necessary scientific criteria for testing the accuracy of their conclusions, so as to enable the judge or jury to form their own independent judgement by the application of those criteria to the facts proved in evidence'[4]. In certain circumstances, it may be unavoidable that the expert gives an opinion as to the ultimate issue involved in a case and it is then for the judge to decide what weight is to be given to that opinion[5].

The question of whether expert evidence must be accepted has caused some difficulty, particularly in criminal cases. It was stated in *R v Lanfear*[6] that a jury should accept such evidence unless there were reasons for its rejection and it was held in one Privy Council decision that a jury should not be told to disregard scientific evidence when it provided the only answer to a question[7]. By contrast, it was decided in *R v Bailey* that a jury is not bound to accept the evidence of an expert but, nevertheless, it should not act on its own intuitions[8].

Unless there is leave of the court or there is agreement between all parties to the action, expert evidence can be adduced only if the party wishing to bring it has made an application to the court. In general, there should be full disclosure. Written reports by experts in personal injury actions will normally be disclosed to the other party[9] although evidence may be withheld from disclosure in such cases if the pleadings contain allegations of medical negligence or if it either makes suggestions as to the way in which the injuries were caused or comments on the genuineness of the party alleging the injury. The Rules of the Supreme Court may now allow for prior disclosure in criminal cases[10].

The evidence of psychiatrists attracts greater controversy than does that of other expert witnesses and is discussed in greater detail under 'Psychiatric evidence'.

There is an underswell of opinion which doubts if the adversarial system is the best method of bringing expert evidence, the fear being that experts in their specialty may become less important than are experts in giving evidence[11]; it would seem that actual training for this latter purpose is given in the United States[12]. Judges tend to censure experts for taking a partisan attitude[13] although it is arguable that such an attitude is acceptable in certain circumstances — for example, when appearing for the defence in a criminal case.

See also: Admissibility of evidence; Confidentiality; Psychiatric evidence

1. *Harmony Shipping Co. SA v Davis and Others* [1979] 3 All ER 177 (expert compellable); *see also* Bizzard JH, May R and Howard MN *Phipson on Evidence* (13th ed, 1982) p.573, Sweet & Maxwell, London.
2. *Attorney General's Ref No. 3 of 1979* (1979) 69 Crim App R 411.
3. *R v Somers* (1964) 48 Crim App R 11; [1963] 3 All ER 808 CA.
4. *Davie v Edinburgh Corporation* 1953 SC 34 per Lord President Cooper.
5. The Criminal Evidence Act 1972, s.3(1), provides that, in criminal matters, the expert witness may testify as to the ultimate issue in a case.
6. [1968] 1 All ER 683 CA.
7. *Anderson v R* [1972] AC 100 PC.
8. (1977) 66 Crim App R 31.
9. Civil Evidence Act 1972, s.2(3).
10. Police and Criminal Evidence Act 1984, s.81.
11. For some useful reviews of the subject, *see* Shaw S 'The law and the expert witness' (1976) 69 Proc R Soc Med 83; Lawton LJ 'The limitations of expert scientific evidence' (1980) J Forens Sci Soc 237; Brownlie R 'The role of the expert witness' (1983) 51 Med-Leg J 85; Kennedy L 'The rectification of miscarriages of justice' (1984) 29 J Law Soc Scot 351.
12. Miller TH 'Nonverbal communication in expert testimony' (1983) 28 J Forens Sci 523.
13. *Hucks v Cole* (1968) 112 SJ 483.

Explosions

Explosions due to the detonation of bombs are described under 'Bomb injuries'.

Explosions in industry are of equal or greater medico-legal importance. They may give rise to a major disaster and can be of many types. Explosions in factories or other above-ground plants will cause blast injuries but are also characteristically associated with burning or scalding of thermal or chemical type. Such injuries, which may well be of extreme severity, are described under 'Burns'.

The underground explosion constitutes a special case and is particularly associated with coal mining. The application of massive safety regulations has fortunately gone a long way to eliminating mining disasters in the UK but they still occur in many parts of the world. There are two major sources of coal mining explosions: methane gas, which is a violent explosive when mixed with air in a concentration of 5–15 per cent, and finely divided coal dust which is present naturally in mines and is augmented by the actual mining operation. A mixture of methane and coal dust is particularly dangerous because the former serves to ignite the latter, the seeds of catastrophe being sown by the rapid spread of a self-igniting fire along the tunnels.

Death may therefore be due to burning with or without carbon monoxide poisoning, to blast or to injury due to falling rock. Miners not actually in the path of the explosion may yet die from hypoxia as the available oxygen is consumed by the fire; others may be trapped and entombed by falls which block the exits[1].

See also: Asphyxia; Blast injuries; Bomb injuries; Burning; Burns; Carbon monoxide poisoning

1. *See* Knight BH 'Injuries sustained in mining and quarrying' in Mason JK (ed) *The Pathology of Violent Injury* (1978) Chap. 8, Edward Arnold, London.

Extradural Haemorrhage

Extradural haemorrhage occurs between the skull and the dura mater. It is a relatively uncommon type of intracranial haemorrhage which is almost always associated with fracture of the skull. The bleeding is occasionally venous in origin but the great majority of instances stem from rupture of a meningeal artery. Despite its arterial origin, the haemorrhage is usually relatively well contained by the close adherence of the dura to the skull. The classic result is therefore a slowly increasing lesion which, unless it is in an unusual position in the posterior fossa, takes some time to produce symptoms of a space-occuping lesion. Clinically, this includes a 'lucid interval' following recovery from an initial period of concussion[1]; the danger is that a patient may be discharged from the hospital accident and emergency department during this phase only to die in bed at home.

Although the uncomplicated lesion is theoretically easy to treat, a large number of cases also sustain contre-coup cerebral lacerations or subdural haemorrhages.

See also: Contre-coup injuries; Intracerebral haemorrhage; Subdural haemorrhage

1. Jamieson KG and Yelland JDN 'Extradural haematoma: report of 167 cases' (1968) 29 J Neurosurg 13.

F

Fallopian Tube

The fallopian tube is a bilateral structure in continuity within the uterine cavity at one end and in close proximity to the ovary at the other. The fimbriae, or tentacles, at the free end attract the discharged ovum and fertilisation takes place in the tube in the event of successful insemination.

The tubes are subject to inflammation, sometimes due to sexually transmitted disease, and, as a result, may become scarred and occluded. Total occlusion of both tubes results in sterility; partial closure sets the scene for ectopic pregnancy.

Elective sterilisation in the female is commonly achieved by partial excision or by ligature of the tubes. The former method is likely to be irreversible but highly effective; potentially reversible sterilization carries a relatively high risk of failure.

See also: Ectopic pregnancy; Infertility; Sexually transmitted diseases; Sterility; Sterilisation; Wrongful pregnancy

Falls

The number of fatal accidents attributable to falls is surprisingly high. The death rate from this cause approaches that due to road traffic accidents and was actually higher in Scotland in 1983 — when it achieved an incidence of 15.4 fatal falls per 100,000 population. As might be expected, the frequency of fatal falls escalates with old age; the remarkable figure of 200.3 per 100,000 population in the age group 75 years and above was reported for the same year in Scotland. Over twice as many women are killed in the home from falls as are men and, again, the discrepancy increases with advancing age. Thus, although the death rate from road accidents and falls are similar, the economic consequences are very different.

Falls are of many and varied types. Death following the average domestic fall down a flight of stairs is commonly due to a fortuitous head injury. Delayed death in elderly women is, however, particularly associated with the very common fracture of the neck of the femur. The consequent necessary major surgical operation followed by a prolonged period of bed rest conduces, especially, to death from pulmonary embolism; many medico-legal authorities insist on deaths being reported to them when there is a recent history of fracture of the femur despite the fact that there is no apparent causative relationship — this is particularly true of the Scottish procurator fiscal.

Falls from windows, while hill climbing and the like provide classic examples of the forensic need to distinguish between accident, suicide and homicide; indeed, one of the longest running sagas in the history of the coroners' service related to the age-old question 'did she fall or was she pushed?'[1]. The distinction can rarely be made other than on the circumstantial evidence. Alcohol is very commonly associated with death from falls but this is of little use in differentiation as to type — a drunken brawl is as likely as is a drunken stagger. Certain areas are notorious for suicidal attempts and many of these are bridges over water; contact with water is as fatal as is contact with the ground once a significant impact speed has been built up.

The body falling from a height accelerates with gravity but is subjected to air resistance. A constant velocity is attained after some 12 seconds' fall during which 400–450 m (440–500 yd) are traversed; the terminal velocity is then about 53 m/s (120 mph). In more practical terms, a person falling 15 m (50 ft) attains a speed of 17 m/s (56 ft/sec). When falling from a high building, the displaced air tends to act as a cushion which drives the body from the wall; a simple fall can therefore result in a body impact some distance from the foot of the building and this is not necessarily evidence of a push or of a deliberate jump.

Injuries sustained following a fall depend upon the configuration at impact and upon the negative acceleration, which is a compound of the speed at impact and the deformation of the structure impacted. Fracture of the head and of the limbs will be common but are surprisingly rare in water. In a series of relatively severe fatal free falls[2], haemothorax was almost universal as were damage to the lungs and laceration of the liver. The most common fatal injury *per se* was rupture of the aorta and this was followed by laceration of the heart, the atria being more sensitive to deceleration than the ventricles. Even so, the distribution of injuries is often unusual and some remarkable survivals of forces which were calculated to be considerably beyond human tolerance have been reported[3].

See also: Accidental death; Alcohol; Aorta; Cardiovascular system; Deceleration injuries; Liver disease and injury; Pulmonary embolism

1. Beginning with *R v West Yorkshire Coroner, ex parte Smith* [1982] 3 WLR 920.
2. Mason JK 'Injuries sustained in fatal aircraft accidents' (1973) 9 Br J Hosp Med 645.
3. An old but outstanding review is Snyder RG 'Human tolerances to extreme impacts in free-fall' (1963) 34 Aerospace Med 695.

Family Practitioner Committees

Family practitioner committees (FPCs) were continued in being under the National Health Service Act 1977, s.10, but their relationship with District Health Authorities (DHAs) was altered so as to allow for overlap by the Health and Social Security Act 1984, s.5[1]; the committees are now autonomous authorities, independent of

DHAs, with whom they collaborate, and are directly accountable to the Department of Health and Social Security. A committee consists of four members appointed by the DHA, four by the local authority, eight by the local medical committee and seven others by the local dental, pharmaceutical and ophthalmic committees; seven further members, one of whom must be a nurse or a midwife, are appointed after consultation with appropriate bodies.

The duties of the committee are to administer, on behalf of the Minister, the arrangements for the provision of general medical, dental, pharmaceutical and ophthalmic services. The FPC is therefore effectively responsible in its locality for the running of the NHS other than within hospitals. General practitioners are under contract for service to the FPCs. Amongst other duties, the FPC is responsible for the establishment of service committees which will consider any complaints against practitioners as to compliance with their terms of service; for its part, the commitee is a 'relevant body' subject to investigation by the Health Service Commissioner.

See also: Complaints procedure in the NHS; Health Service Commissioner

1. Substituting National Health Service Act 1977, s.10: Family Practitioner Committees (Membership and Procedure) Regulations (SI 1985/213); Family Practitioner Committees (Establishment) Order 1985 (SI 1985/301).

Fat Embolism

This condition should be considered in two forms: firstly, as a pathological finding and, secondly, as a frequently fatal clinical syndrome. In either case, the basic condition is the presence of fat emboli — particles of fat — in the small arterioles.

Fat emboli which are of pathological significance only are confined to the lungs. They are seldom of more than arteriolar size and become lodged as the pulmonary vessels narrow in bore. Their frequent association with particles of bone marrow indicates that they come from the fatty marrow of the bones and are released as a result of fracture or other serious bony injury. Pulmonary emboli are found with great frequency in persons killed while sustaining fractures, and the probability is that some degree of embolism occurs in all non-fatal cases of bony injury. Such emboli eventually resolve and are normally harmless. The significance of pulmonary fat embolism discovered at autopsy following accidental death is that it probably reflects a persistence of the circulation for at least a short time after injury; considerable care is, however, needed in using the findings to solve the problems of commorientes[1]. Some degree of pulmonary fat embolism is often found in natural fatalities who have been subjected to external cardiac massage[2]; the reason is that fractures of the ribs or sternum are frequent complications of this maneouvre.

Severe pulmonary fat embolism may be dangerous in the elderly or others with cardiorespiratory disease but the typical clinial syndrome of fat embolism arises only in some 1 per cent of cases involving fracture of a long bone in healthy persons. The patient becomes febrile, petechial haemorrhages occur and there is cerebral involvement which may proceed to coma and death. The symptoms and signs are due to involvement of the small vessels in the systemic circulation and the danger lies in the involvement of the brain. There is some evidence, supported by observations on persons who have been exposed to atmospheric decompression (*see* 'Decompression sickness'), that other mechanisms additional to simple leaking of fat from the marrow may operate in the production of this serious condition and, although the association with fracture is very close, the precise chain of events remains unresolved; some cases may be complicated by disseminated intravascular coagulation. The syndrome of fat embolism is a natural complication of injury and its occurrence is unrelated to medical negligence.

See also: Commorientes; Decompression sickness; Disseminated intravascular coagulation; Fractures; Petechial haemorrhage

1. Buchanan D and Mason JK 'Occurrence of pulmonary fat and bone marrow embolism' (1982) 3 Am J Forens Med Path 73.
2. Jackson CT and Greendyke RM 'Pulmonary and cerebral fat embolism after closed-chest cardiac massage' (1965) 120 Surg Gynecol Obstet 25.

Fatal Accident Inquiry

The fatal accident inquiry is the closest parallel in Scotland to the English public coroner's inquest. There are, however, significant differences.

The inquiry is held under the provisions of the Fatal Accidents and Sudden Deaths Inquiry (Scotland) Act 1976. Under s.1(1)(a), a public inquiry must be held, on the instigation of the procurator fiscal, firstly, whenever it appears that a death has resulted from an accident occurring in Scotland while the person who has died, being an employee, was in the course of his employment or, being an employer or self-employed, was engaged in his occupation as such or, secondly, when the person who has died was, at the time of his death, in legal custody.

Under s.1(1)(b), an inquiry may be held when it appears to the Lord Advocate to be expedient in the public interest on the grounds that the death was sudden, suspicious or unexplained or occurred in circumstances such as to give rise to serious public concern. The inquiry under this subsection may be instigated by the procurator fiscal, Crown Office or the Lord Advocate himself. At the same time, any interested party can represent to the Lord Advocate that there is a need for an inquiry but the Lord Advocate's decision to hold one is entirely discretionary and need not be justified.

The hearing is by the sheriff, who sits without a jury but who may be assisted by an expert assessor appointed at the request of any properly interested party. Evidence is led by the procurator fiscal. Interested parties may have legal representatives who may examine the witnesses but a witness need not answer a question which incriminates him. At the conclusion of the inquiry, the sheriff gives his determination as to when and where the accident and death(s) took place, their cause or causes, reasonable precautions which might have prevented the accident, any defects in the system of working that contributed to the accident and any other relevant factors. The determination is not admissible in evidence in any judicial proceedings arising out of the accidental death but it must, inevitably, provide grounds for making decisions as to further action in the civil or criminal courts.

On the face of things, the fatal accident inquiry provides a good compromise between total privacy and the undue publicity of the coroner's court; nevertheless, it has its critics. In the first place, its selectivity undoubtedly results in some disgruntled applicants. Moreover, its very rarity[1] immediately focuses attention on those cases which are heard. A large proportion of inquiries heard under s.1(1)(b) relate to medical treatment; whether it is right to single out specific medical mishaps for public scrutiny is questionable. Similarly, there are some who doubt the morality of holding a public inquiry largely because there is insufficient evidence on which to base a criminal charge. Finally, supporters of the coroner's inquest would argue that an inquisitorial investigation is a better way of establishing the truth than is the quasi-adversarial atmosphere of the fatal accident inquiry — a criticism which might well apply also to the English public inquiry.

See also: Coroner; Procurator fiscal; Public inquiries

1. In 1983, 1.2 per cent of cases reported to the procurator fiscal came to a fatal accident inquiry; this compares with the 18 per cent of coroners' cases which are the subject of public inquest.

Fault

The concept of fault is an essential element of the law of negligence in most legal systems. While it should be stressed that, in general, the purpose of the law is to compensate the injured party rather than to punish the wrongdoer, liability is imposed on the defendant who has shown fault in his conduct and who has consequently caused wrongful damage to another. The opposite concept is that of no-fault liability.

According to western notions of compensation, conduct must fall below the standards of what is acceptable in the circumstances before we are prepared to impose an obligation to make reparation, and the current movement away from fault as the basis of the law of torts indicates a lack of confidence in its fair application. The main difficulty is that of proving fault in a highly technical world; the problems which a plaintiff has to overcome in order to demonstrate negligence are considerable and are unacceptable to many. There has been a particular attack on fault-based liability for medical negligence on the grounds that it is a cumbersome and perilous system from the point of view of the plaintiff. Pharmaceutical liability has also been identified as an area in which no-fault liability might be appropriate.

See also: Negligence; No-fault compensation; Pharmaceutical liability

Fear

Fear is an emotion which arises when the subject anticipates harm to himself or to another or when he believes that some other threatening event will materialise.

The condition has implications in both the civil and the criminal law. In the civil context, a person who acts in a state of fear may cause damage to the person or property of others[1]. The finding of negligence in such circumstances may be affected by the emergency conditions in which the defendant acted but, whilst the existence of fear will be taken into account, the defendant, to be successful, must have acted as a 'reasonable frightened man' would have done in the circumstances; the fact of fear may not excuse rash or impetuous action if such action could have been reasonably avoided. In the criminal context, the accused who has acted in a state of fear for himself or for those who are close to him may be entitled to claim the defence of duress. The law here makes a concession to 'human frailty' and a successful defence may depend upon the court's disinclination to impose liabililty on one who commits a criminal act in order to prevent significant harm to himself.

The death of a victim through fright or shock may result in criminal liability. Frightening a person to death is certainly possible, albeit rare, and, in principle, there is no reason why a person who causes another to die as a result of putting him in fear of his life should not be guilty of homicide (*see* 'Culpable homicide'). Similarly, the will of a person may be overcome by fear and this may be as potent as is force in the perpetration of rape.

See also: Culpable homicide; Duress; Negligence; Rape; Reasonable man

1. *The Bywell Castle* (1879) 4 PD 219; *SS Singleton Abbey v SS Paludina* [1927] AC 16.

Fellatio

Fellatio consists of orogenital sex involving the penis. It would not, today, be regarded as aberrant sexual practice and it constitutes no offence in a consensual heterosexual configuration other than those associated with affronts to public decency. Homosexual fellatio would, however, constitute gross indecency and, as such, is an offence unless confined to consenting adults acting in private[1]. Neither boys nor girls below the age of 16 years may consent to an indecent assault nor can boys consent to an act of gross indecency. Fellatio involving a woman and a boy or aggressive fellatio with a girl of less than 16 must, therefore, be an offence, as would be a wholly passive act by the man in Scotland[2]; the latter would certainly be criminal in England or Wales if the girl were aged less than 14 years[3] but, in the absence of any form of assault by the man, the interpretation might be different were the girl above that age.

Non-consensual fellatio is an indecent assault but, in the UK, is no more than that. The absurdity of such a situation is recognised in the USA where non-consensual penetration of the mouth by the male organ constitutes rape[4]. Fellatio is included in the definition of sexual intercourse in New South Wales and a non-consensual act is also rape in South Australia and Victoria[5].

Diseases generally regarded as sexually transmitted can be transmitted orally. The practice is sufficiently common in sexual violence to justify the taking of pharyngeal swabs at autopsy following any death appearing to have sexual overtones.

See also: Gross indecency; Indecency with children; Indecent assault; Rape

1. Sexual Offences Act 1956, s.13; Sexual Offences Act 1967, s.1; Criminal Justice (Scotland) Act 1980, s.80.
2. Sexual Offences (Scotland) Act, s.5.
3. Indecency with Children Act 1960.
4. Schiff AF 'Rape: wife vs husband' (1982) 22 J Forens Sci Soc 235.
5. Crimes (Sexual Assault) Amendment Act 1981 (NSW); Criminal Law Consolidation Act 1935-1980 (SA); Crimes (Sexual Offences) Act 1980 (Vict).

Fetal Disposal

A dead fetus is one which has been expelled from the mother before the 28th week of pregnancy and which has at no time breathed or shown any other sign of life after separation. There are no statutory rules concerning the disposal of such dead bodies other than those which govern general public health and public decency[1]. Dead fetuses are commonly incinerated locally, the Cremation Act 1902 having no application to them.

Similarly, the Human Tissue Act 1961 is irrelevant in the context of the dead fetus, which may therefore be retained for scientific purposes subject, perhaps with qualification in relation to the abortus, to the consent of the mother. The issue is discussed further under 'Fetal experimentation'.

Some difficulty arises when parents of a dead fetus request burial in a cemetery under the control of a burial authority. There is no express reason why the body should not be so disposed of but the superintendent has no way of ensuring that he is not being presented with an unregistered stillbirth. There would seem to be a good case for a 'fetal disposal certificate' which could be signed by a registered medical practitioner but there is, of course, no legal precedent for this.

See also: Burial; Cremation; Fetal experimentation; Human Tissue Act 1961

1. This would, it is suggested, include the sale of fetuses for commercial purposes. *See* **Peel J** (chairman) *Report of the Advisory Group on the use of Fetuses and Fetal Material for Research* (1972) para. 44, HMSO, London.

Fetal Experimentation

There is no doubt that fetal experimentation can produce results which are valuable in the improvement of obstetrical practice. The whole field is, however, strewn with ethical and legal hazards, most of which are bound up with the problems of fetal rights and of consent — particularly of consent by minors.

The simplest and most certain approach is that which assumes that the fetus has rights but that these are enforceable only on the attainment of a separate existence. Any experiments performed on the fetus *in utero* must be subject to the mother's consent and it can be accepted that such consent is valid only if the experiment is to the advantage of the fetus. Consensual experimentation which results in the death of or a damaged fetus is therefore in the nature of a contradiction in terms and the experimenter's relationship with the fetus is one which allows him very little scope for avoiding liability in negligence; moreover, there is no indication in British law of any movement comparable to the American concept that viability is a prerequisite to a right of subsequent action — a concept which is, admittedly, being steadily eroded in the USA. It follows, if for no other than practical reasons, that fetal experimentation carried out in the anticipation of a live birth can only be of a nature which involves no risk whatsoever — and it is to be remembered that even the safest-appearing techniques, such as ultrasound imaging, are subject to some uncertainty.

That being so, problems related to intrauterine fetal injury as a result of experimentation or research should be of theoretical interest only. Paradoxically, however, it would seem that the fetus has no remedy if it is killed and the only liability would then be to the parents in negligence on the grounds of stress and inconvenience; whether this would hold in the USA, where actions for wrongful death of the fetus have been successful[1], is less certain. It is also difficult to see that any criminal offence would have been committed because the Offences Against the Person Act 1861, s.58, requires an intent to procure a miscarriage before an offence can be committed. The situation is, as stated, unlikely to arise but, to guard against the wholly unethical experiment, the Peel Committee[2] considered the possibility of reckless injury to the fetus and we would support, say, the introduction of an offence of feticide — other than as permitted by the Abortion Act 1967 — if only to allay public anxiety. Experiments causing the death of a viable fetus should, we suggest, be chargeable as child destruction or as manslaughter depending upon the moment at which death occurred.

There is no law to cover the fetus which is destined for abortion and which might, indeed, be a valuable experimental subject. The mother has effectively abandoned her fetus and would therefore appear to be precluded from giving consent. The problem thus becomes simply one of ethics — is the fetus an expendable moriturus or is it a human being capable of pain and suffering even if only for a limited time?

There remains for consideration the fetus which is in process of miscarriage whether this be natural or by virtue of the Abortion Act 1967. In practice, the mother will be greatly distressed in the former condition and discussion of the possibility of experimentation would be, at least, poor quality medical practice. In the latter case, consent to experimentation would not seem to be essential although, as suggested by the Peel Committee (at para. 42), the parents should be offered the opportunity to declare any special directions as to management of the abortus. Given that there is no objection, any experimentation in this highly sensitive area should be rigidly controlled by an ethical committee. The abortus is, by definition, non-viable and the relevant considerations centre on whether or not there is a competent fetal/maternal connection. If there is, the fetal heart is beating, sensation is presumably present and destructive experimentation or research is morally unacceptable; if there is not, the situation is analogous to the interval between somatic and cellular death, during which time there would not seem to be any legal or moral contraindication to approved research.

In the event of the abortus showing any evidence of viability, the onus is on the physician to assist its fight for life and any projected experimentation must necessarily be abandoned; the Peel Committee recommended the legal limitation of a maximum fetal weight of 300 g as a safety measure above which no experimentation would be permitted — we believe that this recommendation should be followed.

Experimentation on the dead fetus poses few problems subject to the clear right of the mother to express her wishes as to the disposal of a natural abortus. No legal rules govern the disposal of fetal remains — only those of public decency; we suggest that the sale of fetal remains for commercial purposes offends against the latter.

See also: Abortion Act 1967; Child destruction; Consent by minors; Death; Ethical committees; Fetal rights; Living abortus; Offences Against the Person Act 1861; Separate existence; Ultrasound; Viability

1. For example, *Hale v Manion* 368 P 2d 1 (Kan 1962).
2. Peel J (chairman) *Report of the Advisory Group on the Use of Fetuses and Fetal Material for Research* (1972) HMSO, London.

Fetal Materials

Fetal materials are those products of conception and pregnancy which are discarded by both the mother and the fetus at parturition. They include the placenta, the umbilical cord and the amniotic sac.

Fetal materials have a minor but increasing therapeutic use and, having been discarded, have no legal owner. They are not subject to the conditions of the Human Tissue Act 1961 and they can become the property of the first person into whose hands they rightly fall. Such a person should properly harvest useful material for the public benefit but, whilst reasonable recompense might be given for the time and effort involved, it is suggested that, despite their inanimate nature, fetal materials should be subject to the general public rejection of the sale of human biological tissues[1].

See also: Human Tissue Act 1961

1. *See* Peel J (chairman) *Report of the Advisory Group on the Use of Fetuses and Fetal Material for Research* (1972) HMSO, London.

Fetal Rights

The rights of the fetus are extremely limited and do not, in any case, come into being until it has reached such maturity as leads to a legal presumption of viability, at which point it achieves a right not to be killed. This right is statutory in England and Wales[1] but probably exists in only a modified form in Scotland. The comparable situation in the USA is governed by the ruling in *Roe v Wade*[2] under which the State may intervene on behalf of the fetus in any conflict with its mother after viability; this, it was said, probably occurs between the 24th and 28th week of pregnancy but is to be defined medically in each case. Such limited rights are subject to the overriding consideration of a threat to the life of the mother, and the Supreme Court in *Roe* appears to have gone out of its way to emphasise the absence of any rights in the previable fetus. The terms of the Abortion Act 1967 and later decisions[3] also make it clear that abortion in the UK is a matter between the mother and her medical advisers without reference to the wellbeing of a fetus which is of less than 28 weeks' gestation; the interesting possibility has, however, been raised[4] that, in Scots law, it would be possible for a fetus to petition through his tutor (i.e. his father) for interdict of any threatened harm, a possibility which has not yet been explored. As something of a contrasting anomaly, the fetus has no right to death in the event that that would be preferable to the quality of existence he is being offered; it has been stated that 'to impose such a duty towards the child would be to make a further inroad... into the sanctity of human life which would be contrary to public policy'[5] (*see* 'Wrongful life').

There are indications that the concept of fetal rights is changing in favour of the fetus in the USA where, in particular, the viability standard, which had previously limited the rights of the fetus to recover for damage sustained *in utero*, is being eroded[6] — it seems in every way more logical to define the fetus as a legal entity from conception rather than from an indeterminate point of viability. Fetal rights in tort are advancing even further in the USA and damages have, surprisingly, been awarded to stillbirths[7].

This trend in favour of the fetus has also been notable in Canada where, first, a parental action was regarded as premature[8]; a right of action by an unborn child for damages within the womb was then established[9]; and it is confirmed that this right of action can only take effect at birth[10]. A rather similar statutory position has been reached in England and Wales with the passing of the Congenital Disabilities (Civil Liability) Act 1976; this takes no account of viability in allowing an action at the suit of a child which is born disabled[11]. Even so, the rights of the fetus are limited by the fact that the occurrence which precipitated the cause for action must be one which affected the parents; a direct effect on the child is considered only in relation to the actual course of birth (s.1(2)). Additionally, the child must survive for 48 hours before damages can be recovered in respect of any loss of expectation of life. Comparable rights in Scotland are available at common law.

A somewhat stricter approach to the duties of the expectant mother in relation to her fetus is appearing. This is particularly so in regard to drug addiction or abuse during pregnancy. The right of a child to present evidence as to negligence of the mother by taking drugs during the gestation period has been upheld in the USA[12] whilst the Canadian courts have clearly accepted the right of the fetus to protection prior to birth in this respect[13]. A recent British decision has confirmed that 'legal' child abuse can occur in the womb[14]. There are indications, at least in the USA, that the viable fetus is also entitled to a radical invasion of its mother's privacy on its behalf. In *Jefferson*, for example, the court was prepared to order a caesarian section so as to preserve the life of the fetus during birth[15]. The same may not, however, apply to the previable fetus — in *Taft*[16], the Massachusetts Supreme Court was unable to find any precedent requiring a woman to submit to a surgical procedure in order to carry her 4-month-old fetus to term; they reserved judgment, however, in respect of ordering medical treatment.

Subject to live birth the fetus has property rights in that he is, for example, regarded as being alive at the time of the death of a testator who has willed in favour of his descendants[17]. The major British decision, a Scottish case taken in the House of Lords, held that 'an unborn child is taken care of just as much as if it were in existence in any case in which the child's own advantage comes in question'[18] and it has been pointed out that this is the essential rationale of the live birth requirement — there can be no benefit accruing to a stillbirth. This rule was firmly upheld in the important Australian case of *Watt v Rama*[19] and wrongful death actions probably have no place in Commonwealth legal systems[20].

See also: Abortion Act 1967; Alcohol; Drug addiction; Separate existence; Viability; Wrongful death of the fetus; Wrongful life

1. Infant Life (Preservation) Act 1929, s.1.
2. 93 S Ct 705 (1973).
3. For example, *Paton v British Pregnancy Advisory Service Trustees* [1979] QB 276; *Paton v United Kingdom* (1981) 3 EHRR 408.
4. Yorke DM 'The legal personality of the unborn child' 1979 SLT 158. The proposition would, however, seem unlikely in the light of the European decision in *Paton*.
5. *McKay and another v Essex Area Health Authority and another* [1982] 2 WLR 890 per Stephenson LJ at 902.

6. *Bennett v Hymers* 147 A 2d 108 (NH, 1958). For a full discussion, *see* Lenow JL 'The fetus as a patient: emerging rights as a person?' (1983) 9 Am J Law Med 1.

7. For example, *White v Yup* 458 P 2d 617 (1969).

8. *Smith v Fox* [1923] 3 DLR 785.

9. *Montreal Tramways v Leveille* [1933] 4 DLR 337.

10. *Duval v Seguin* (1972) 26 DLR (3d) 418.

11. A common law right to damages in respect of injuries sustained *in utero* appears first to have been acknowledged in the UK in *Williams and another v Luff* (1978) 122 SJ 164.

12. *Grodin v Grodin* 301 NW 2d 869 (Mich, 1981).

13. *Superintendent of Family and Child Service and McDonald* (1982) 135 DLR (3d) 330; *Re Children's Aid Society of Kenora and J L* (1982) 134 DLR (3d) 249. For a detailed review of these and other cases, *see* Knoppers BM 'Modern birth technology and human rights' (1985) Am J Comp Law 1.

14. *Re D (a Minor)* (1986) Times, 24 March.

15. *Jefferson v Griffin Spalding County Hospital Authority* 274 SE 2d 457 (Ga, 1981).

16. *Taft v Taft* 446 NE 2d 395 (Mass, 1983).

17. *Cox's Trustees v Pegg* 1950 SLT 127.

18. *Elliot v Joicey* 1935 SC (HL) 57 quoted by Lord Macmillan; *In re Stern* [1962] 1 Ch 732. *See* Mellows AR *The Law of Succession* (4th ed, 1983) p.137, Butterworths, London.

19. [1972] VR 353 per Gillard J at 376.

20. Pace PJ 'Civil liability for pre-natal injuries' (1977) 40 MLR 141. For a general review of 'fetal rights', *see* Bondeson WB et al *Abortion and the Status of the Fetus* (1983) Reidel, Dordrecht.

Feticide

Abortion has been defined authoritatively as 'feticide — the intentional destruction of the fetus in the womb or any untimely delivery brought about with the intent to cause the death of the fetus'[1]. Yet there seems very little factual support for this view. The Offences Against the Person Act 1861 mentions abortion only in a marginal note; the statutory offence refers to procuring the miscarriage of a woman and it is this which the Abortion Act 1967 legalises in certain circumstances. A miscarriage, say, between the 24th and 28th week of gestation may well result in a live birth and, perhaps, a viable fetus. Strong arguments have been adduced to the effect that abortions performed at this time should involve methods which offer a maximum chance of life to the abortus[2]; in practice, however, the opposite commonly occurs[3]. It seems preferable to regard only those techniques which are designed to ensure a dead abortus as feticide rather than to equate the process with abortion in general[4].

It has been firmly stated[5] that a living abortus is entitled to the administrative and therapeutic privileges of any premature birth. Yet, currently, it is clear that living fetuses which have been legally aborted are being allowed to die without attention[6]. A legal vacuum is thus caused in so far as there is great reluctance to proffer a charge of homicide in such instances despite the fact that this should be the logical conclusion. It might be preferable to regard such action as feticide and to legislate accordingly.

A further anomalous situation provoked by modern reproductive technology is that in which surplus embryos, which have never seen the inside of a womb, are produced as a necessary part of treatment by *in vitro* fertilisation. The killing of such embryos (or embryocide) causes considerable public disquiet[7]. The potential growth of *in vitro* embryos is currently limited but will undoubtedly be capable of extension into the production of *in vitro* fetuses in the foreseeable future. It is difficult to see what current offence would be committed by killing a fetus which has been raised wholly artificially and it may be that this could be, again, designated as a specific act of feticide for which legislation would certainly be needed.

See also: Abortion; Abortion Act 1971; *In vitro* fertilisation; Live birth; Living abortus; Offences Against the Person Act 1861; Viability

1. Williams G *Textbook of Criminal Law* (2nd ed, 1983) p.292, Stevens, London. Gordon adopts a rather similar line in relation to Scots law: 'To destroy a viable foetus *in utero* is abortion', but this must be regarded as an example (*The Criminal Law of Scotland* (2nd ed, 1978) p.813, W Green, Edinburgh).
2. But a Pennsylvania State statute to this effect was ruled unconstitutional by the US Supreme Court (*Colautti v Franklin* (1979) 439 US 379).
3. This has been charged as manslaughter in the USA (*Commonwealth v Edelin* (1976) 371 Mass 497, 359 NE 2d 4). The present legal position there still seems uncertain as the appeal against conviction in this case was upheld on an unrelated point of law.
4. But this would not apply everywhere. The South African Abortion and Sterilization Act 1975, for example, defines abortion as 'the abortion of a live foetus of a woman with intent to kill such foetus'.
5. Lord Wells-Pestel, 355 HL Official Report (5th series) col. 776 (12 December 1974). In the USA this is statutorily ordered in some States (e.g. California Health and Safety Code 25955.9 (1976)).
6. Tunkel V 'Abortion: how early, how late, and how legal?' [1979] 2 Br Med J 253 has quoted two cases which have been the subject of newspaper reports. So far as is known, the coroner has reached a verdict of want of attention at birth in only one case (Inquest in the matter of the death of female child Campbell, Staffordshire (North) Coroner's District, 19 October, 1983).
7. Kennedy, I 'Let the law take on the test-tube' (1984) *The Times*, 26 May, p.6. *See also* the Unborn Children (Protection) Bill 1985.

Fetishism

The fetishist obtains at least part of his sexual pleasure from contact with or other sense-appreciation of non-sexual parts of the preferred sex — such as the feet or long hair — or of inanimate objects, often, but not invariably, associated with the loved one — e.g. shoes, suspender belts, leather coats and the like. This form of sexual deviation is virtually confined to males and the line between fetishism and transvestism may become blurred; the essential sexual satisfaction in the former is, however, often lacking in the latter condition.

The fetish may stimulate a more normal sexual urge or may, itself, precipitate orgasm; in general, fetishism is little more than a harmless aberration. Occasionally, however, it may drive the subject to seek his particular brand of sexual satisfaction through violence or other criminality. Thus, objects may be stolen, including by shoplifting, or, at the extreme, women may be attacked either as part of robbery with violence or because the fetish provides the trigger for rape or indecent assault.

Such fetishists need psychiatric help and may become the subjects of hospital or restriction orders.

See also: Hospital orders; Restriction orders; Shoplifting; Transvestism

Fetoscopy

The direct visualisation of the fetus provides great opportunities for intrauterine diagnosis and treatment; the procedure known as fetoscopy is being rapidly advanced but must still be regarded as something in the nature of an experimental method.

The fetoscope is introduced into the amniotic sac through the abdominal wall. A very limited view of the fetus is obtainable but abnormalities such as neural tube defects can be diagnosed during the second trimester. Perhaps the most important use of fetoscopy, however, is the coincidental ability to take skin biopsies and to sample blood from fetal vessels in the placenta. The opportunity for making a firm diagnosis of significant haemoglobinopathy is thus presented; in skilled hands, sufficient fetal blood may be obtained from which to diagnose males affected by haemophilia. Actual intrauterine treatment of the fetus may be possible in the long term.

Fetoscopy as it now stands is not without risk to both the fetus and the mother. It is therefore essential that there is a genuine risk of abnormality which requires investigation before fetoscopy is undertaken and also that the parents are adequately counselled. The importance of experience and training is shown by one major series — the fetal mortality was 5 per cent in the first 100 attempted samplings of fetal blood; this dropped to 1 per cent in the second hundred[1].

See also: Genetic counselling; Haemoglobinopathy; Haemophilia; Neural tube defects; Sickle cell disease

1. Rodeck CH 'Fetoscopy and fetal blood sampling' in Wald N J (ed) *Antenatal and Neonatal Screening* (1984) p.469, Oxford University Presss, Oxford.

Fingernail Marks

Fingernail marks are of major importance in the interpretation of assaults and, particularly, of sexual assaults.

Classically, they appear as superficial linear abrasions, some 1–2 mm in width, often arranged in parallel and situated on the face or torso. They are strong evidence of resistance on the part of a woman when found on a suspect sexual assailant.

Fingernail marks of a rather different type are associated with throttling or strangulation by ligature. In the former case, they will be those of the assailant, of relatively regular semilunar pattern and, perhaps, associated with bruising from the fingerpads. In the latter, the marks will have been made by the victim in an effort to release the ligature. They will appear as irregular abrasions which are sometimes of considerable depth; in the event of death, evidence of vital reaction will be seen at the edges of the marks at autopsy.

The presence of fingernail marks is a strong indication for taking nail clippings or scrapings from both the victim and any suspected assailant in order to search for identifiable blood or tissue fragments.

See also: Abrasions; Detention by the police; Rape; Strangulation; Throttling; Vital reaction

Fingerprints

Fingerprints are unique to the individual and, by contrast to the teeth, remain fundamentally unchanged from birth to death. The finding of a fingerprint at a given locus is therefore very highly suggestive that the owner of the fingerprint was there; fingerprinting, or dactylography, is a major weapon in the detective's investigative armoury. The basis for the emotional attitude to having one's fingerprints on record is difficult to define. The libertarian USA are unconcerned at the widespread use of fingerprinting as a means of identification in many walks of life; by contrast, the privacy of one's prints is jealously guarded in the UK where, apart from the somewhat unusual exception of merchant seamen, the only known record of fingerprints maintained is that of persons convicted of recordable offences. The legislation surrounding the taking of fingerprints is detailed and is to be found in the Police and Criminal Evidence Act 1984.

Under s.61(1) fingerprints can normally be taken only with consent. Non-consensual printing can, however, be undertaken if authorised by a senior police officer who has reasonable grounds to suspect that the subject has been involved in a criminal offence and that fingerprinting will tend to confirm or disprove his involvement (s.61(4)). A person who is charged with a recordable offence, and who has not been fingerprinted during the investigation of that offence, can be required to submit to fingerprinting (s.61)(3)) as can a person who has been convicted of a recordable offence (s.61(6)). Also, a person who has been convicted of a recordable offence but has not been detained in police custody in regard to that offence and has not had his fingerprints taken at any time during the investigation, can be required to undergo the examination within one month of conviction (s. 27). Any fingerprints taken must be destroyed if the subject is cleared of the offence in question, if he is not to be prosecuted or if he is no longer suspected of the offence (s.64) and, for this purpose, discontinuance of proceedings is to be regarded as their conclusion. A subject is entitled to witness the destruction of his fingerprints (s.64(6)). The distinction between fingerprinting and any form of impression taken from other parts of the body is remarkable — the latter are considered to be the product of non-intimate searches.

The Act also introduces some interesting modifications to the age of consent. A person over the age of 17 years may give appropriate consent to his fingerprints being taken; between the ages of 14 and 16 years, the consent of the subject and of a parent or guardian is required; a parent or guardian may given appropriate consent if the subject is below the age of 14 years.

The comparative identification of fingerprints is very much a matter for the expert. The general types of arrangement of the skin ridges are classified as arches, loops, whorls or composite forms, all of which may be extensively subdivided, whilst, ultimately, the characteristics of such minutiae as sweat pore sites will give a truly personalised pattern; it is commonly stated that two identical prints from two different fingers have never been reported.

It is of interest to compare the usefulness of dactylography and odontology in the identification of a dead body. Fingerprints have it in their favour that they are unchanging, that well-demarcated criteria are laid down for a positive identification and that, given a probable identity, the prints on the body can be compared with those found on the supposed person's belongings — a possibility which compensates to an extent for the limited recording of fingerprints. The teeth have the advantages that they resist fire and putrefaction and that a record is available of most persons' teeth; on the other hand, their composition is always changing and their examination is useless in the absence of records or, indeed, of dental abnormalities or treatment. Comparative dental X-rays are, however, just about as personalised as are fingerprints.

See also: Age of legal responsibility; Detention by the police; Identificaton of the dead; Odontology

Firearm Injuries

Firearm injuries are here interpreted as those caused through the use of weapons defined in the Firearms Act 1968, s.57(1). They will therefore include wounds caused by shot, bullets or other missiles discharged from lethal barrelled weapons, these being due to the use of shotguns, rifled weapons and airguns. Such injuries differ greatly in character and they are described under the relevant headings.

See also: Airgun injuries; Firearms; Rifled weapon injuries; Shotgun injuries

Firearms

The handling and possession of firearms is governed by the Firearms Act 1968. A firearm is defined (s.57) as a lethal barrelled weapon of any description from which any shot, bullet or other missile can be discharged and includes components of or accessories to such weapons.

Possession, purchase or acquisition of all firearms are subject to the requirement of holding a firearm certificate but exemption is allowed (s.1(3)) in respect of shotguns, or smooth-bore guns with a barrel not less than 24 inches in length, and of air weapons other than those declared to be specially dangerous[1]. A shotgun certificate is required for possession, purchase or acquisition of a shotgun (s.2) and it is an offence to shorten the barrrel of a shotgun to a length less than 24 inches (s.4). The purchase of automatic weapons or weapons designed to discharge a noxious gas or fluid is subject to the authority of the Defence Council (s.5).

The use of a firearm or of an imitation firearm to resist arrest is an offence, as is carrying the same with criminal intent. Carrying a loaded shotgun or airgun or carrying any other firearm together with ammunition in a public place is prohibited (s.19).

The regulations regarding acquisition, purchase and supply of firearms to minors are complex. In general, and subject to certain exclusions such as in a shooting gallery, it is an offence for a person under 14 years to possess any firearm covered by s.1 of the Act or to have with him an air weapon; it is also an offence to lend any s.1 firearm or to make a gift of an air weapon to a child under 14 years. Under 15 years, a person may not have with him an assembled shotgun save with supervision nor may he be gifted a shotgun. It is an offence for any person under the age of 17 years to purchase or have a firearm or to have an air weapon with him in a public place unless it is securely covered; it is also an offence to sell or hire a firearm to any person under that age.

A firearm certificate is granted by the chief officer of police if he is satisfied that the applicant has good reason for its possession and that he is of sound mind and temperate habits (s.27). A shotgun certificate is granted unless the applicant is prohibited under the Act from possessing a shotgun or possession would be a danger to the public (s.28).

1. Firearms (Dangerous Air Weapons) Rules 1969 (SI 1969/47); Firearms (Dangerous Air Weapons) (Scotland) 1969 (SI 1969/270).

Flick Knives

Flick knives or 'spring clip knives', are no recent innovation; Dickens refers to them in *Martin Chuzzlewit*[1]. The knife blade is concealed within the handle and emerges when a spring is activated.

Considerable concern over the weapon's use in street fights has led to legislation to prohibit their manufacture, importation and sale[2]. It has now been decided that flick knives are made to causing injury to the person within the terms of the Prevention of Crimes Act 1953, s.1(4) and, consequently, are offensive weapons *per se*. It is therefore only necessary for the prosecution to prove possession of a flick knife in public for a conviction to be secured under this Act[3].

1. *See* Popkess A 'Flick knives' [1959] Crim LR 640.
2. Restriction of Offensive Weapons Acts 1959 and 1961.
3. *Tudhope v O'Neill* 1982 SCCR 45; *R v Simpson* [1983] 3 All ER 789. For a general discussion on the control of offensive weapons, *see* Supperstone M *Brownlie's Law of Public Order and National Security* (2nd ed, 1981) p.148 et seq, Butterworths, London.

Fluid Replacement Therapy

Loss of fluid from the circulation results in hypovolaemic shock (*see* 'Surgical shock'). Treatment will be by blood transfusion if the loss is due to haemorrhage. There are, however, many conditions in which only fluid is lost. Several of these are physiological and difficult to explain but, amongst others, they include surgical operations, severe pain, burning, crushing, hypoxia and the circulation of toxins. Many of these are accompanied by actual concentration of the cellular elements of the blood; treatment is therefore a matter of replacement of the fluid element only.

The choice of fluids is a matter of careful clinical judgement and depends to a large extent on whether protein is being lost simultaneously. In this circumstance, the provision of fluid without addition of protein or osmotically equivalent material will merely lead to further loss into the tissues. In the past, treatment was mainly through the transfusion of plasma but, since this was pooled from many donors, there was a significant transmission of hepatitis due to the virus HB_sAg (*see* 'Hepatitis'). This danger has been almost totally averted as it is now possible to screen all donors for the virus but, additionally, it is equally efficacious to use artificial 'plasma expanders' of which Dextran was the prototype.

The art of this type of treatment depends upon biochemical control with careful assessment of fluid balance — the maintenance of blood pressure through attempted equation of fluid intake and output. Other variables, such as the acidity of the blood, have to be considered. In general, management is by infusion of simple 'crystalloid' solutions to which drugs, nutritional supplements, etc. can be added. The contrasting danger to undertreatment is overhydration, one result of which is pulmonary oedema or the outpouring of fluid into the lungs, leading, effectively, to drowning. This is extremely unlikely in modern hospital practice but one of the very few reported cases in which a defence of *nova causa* has been successful in a criminal prosecution was based on this occurrence; there do, however, appear to have been some policy considerations behind the rehearing and the case is unlikely to provide a precedent[1].

See also: Blood transfusion; Hepatitis; *Nova causa interveniens*; Surgical shock

1. *James Clinton Jordan* (1956) 40 Crim App R 152.

Fluoridation

The case for fluoridation of the water as a prophylactic against dental caries seems to be proved beyond doubt[1]. Fluoride does have some adverse effects but only in very large amounts — at 2 mg/l mottling of the teeth may occur whilst at 5 mg/l there may be changes in the bones and joints. Thus it is important in any fluoridation scheme to keep a careful check on the concentration; the threshold level, which is accepted as 1mg/l, must take into account the possible excess drinking of water which is likely in hot climates.

At the time of writing, the Water (Fluoridation) Act 1985 is in the Bill stage. This allows a health authority to apply for the fluoride content of the water to be increased to 1 mg/l; the source of fluorine must be of a stipulated compound — currently hexafluorosilicic acid and/or disodium hexafluorosilicate. Wide consultation is required before the health authority can make or withdraw an application and the public may be admitted to any relevant meetings (r.4(7)).

So long as the hazards are understood, the main objections to fluoridation are ethical — is it right to compel people to consume a chemical against their will? And, if so, where should it stop — should the water be deliberately hardened with calcium in an attempt to reduce the incidence of arteriosclerotic disease? Fluoride can be added with advantage to toothpaste, to salt, to milk and the like or can be provided in tablet form which the individual can refuse or accept but, for some reason, no other method is comparable to fluoridation of water as a successful public health measure.

The issue was addressed in Scotland in *McColl v Strathclyde Regional Council*[2] in which the judge concluded that fluoride was not mutagenic nor did it cause cancer in any other way; it was also concluded that increasing the fluoride content of the water would be likely to reduce considerably the incidence of caries and that fluoride used in that way was a medicinal substance as defined by the Medicines Act 1968. The judge did, however, find that the addition of fluoride to the water did not serve to render it wholesome and was, therefore, beyond the powers conferred upon the water authority by the Water (Scotland) Act 1980, s.6(1). The 1985 Bill is, presumably, intended to clarify that interpretation by placing the responsibility for fluoridation on the health authorities. The hearing in *McColl* lasted 201 days and it is arguable that it demonstrated yet again the unsuitability of the civil courts as arenas for deciding scientific controversies (*see* 'Pesticides').

See also: Mutation; Pesticides; Threshold limit values

1. *See* Murray J J and Rugg-Gunn A J *Fluorides in Caries Prevention* (2nd ed, 1982) PSG Publishing, Littleton MA.
2. 1983 SLT 616 quoting *Municipality of Metropolitan Toronto v Village of Forest Hill* (1957) 9 DLR (2d) 113 and *Attorney General of New Zealand v Lower Hutt Corporation* [1964] AC 1469.

Food Legislation

The various acts pertaining to the sale of safe foods in the UK are now consolidated in the Food Act 1984. Inevitably, the Act is massive and only a brief review of some of its more apposite contents is attempted here.

In the general provisions, it is an offence to alter any food — which includes drink, chewing gum and ingredients — in a way which is injurious to health intending it to be sold in that state (s.1); the seller is also bound to sell food of the nature and quality demanded by the purchaser (s.2)[1]. In the interests of public health, regulations can be made prohibiting the adulteration of food and the provision of such food to the public (s.4). Selling food which is unfit for human consumption is forbidden under s.8 and an authorised food inspector can examine and, if necessary, seize any food which he considers to be unfit; food which has been slaughtered in a knacker's yard is unfit for human consumption by definition (s.12).

Under s.13, the Minister may make regulations designed to ensure food hygiene; these may include regulations as to the premises in which food is sold or prepared, to the cleanliness of utensils and to the provision of flush lavatories, to habits such as spitting, to the clothing of food handlers and to the inspection of any animals intended for slaughter as human food — shellfish are specifically noted.

Special regulations are made for licencing premises dealing with the sale of ice-cream and the manufacture of sausages (s.16) and these can be extended to any other food for human consumption. Ice-cream comes in for special note in s.28, which enjoins the dealer to notify the occurrence on the premises of certain diseases — these being, at present, the enteric fevers, dysentery, diphtheria, scarlet fever, any acute inflammation of the throat, gastroenteritis and undulant fever; any food which is thought likely to cause food poisoning can be seized and, if necessary, destroyed (s.31).

The control of milk and dairies occupies a special Part II of the Act. The Minister has very similar powers in relation to dairy farms, dairies and the processing of milk as he has with any other food for human consumption (s.33). In particular, it is an offence to sell milk from a cow known to be tuberculous or, indeed, suffering from any of a number of specific and general diseases involving the cow and its udder. It is an offence to sell reconstituted or imitation cream without making its origin clear (s.48).

County and district councils appoint 'authorised officers' as their agents for implementation of the Act, and any food and drug authority (effectively the county or London borough councils) must appoint qualified public analysts. These specialists are supplied with specimens by an authorised officer acting as a sampling officer who has very wide powers; in addition, any person who has bought food may submit a sample to the public analyst on payment of a fee. The sampling officer must give an equivalent sample to the person in control of the food or milk under examination (Sch.7) and the court before whom any proceedings are taken may, on request, send a similar sample to the government chemist (s.99). In the event of offences being committed under s.13, the court has powers, on application by the local authority, to disqualify catering premises for up to two years; alternatively, if the conditions in which the food business is conducted are found to be insanitary, the court can impose a closure order until the local authority declares the danger to health to have passed. There are also powers for the court to make an emergency order which remains in force until the determination of any resulting proceedings or until the danger to health is declared to be over.

There is an increasing volume of EEC regulations aimed at achieving uniformity in the standard of foodstuffs and their labelling by manufacturers[2].

See also: Food poisoning; Poisoning; Public health

1. For example, 'Minced beef' must not contain 10 per cent pork: *Shearer v Rowe* (1985) Times, 8 August.
2. Section 123A of the Food and Drugs Act 1955, inserted in 1972, gave powers to the relevant Ministers to make regulations to comply with EEC provisions.

Food Poisoning

Natural food poisoning has to be differentiated from homicidal poisoning — which is now rare — and has a further medico-legal significance in that actions in negligence may be brought against suppliers of bulk foods or of meals when damage is suffered.

Food poisoning may be caused by bacteria or by toxins. The former will be destroyed by heat unless present in the form of spores; toxins may well be thermostable and can either be a natural product or be derived from the presence of bacteria.

Although, strictly speaking, death or disease of any sort which is spread by mouth (e.g. typhoid fever or cholera) could be described as food poisoning, the term is generally reserved for illness due to those organisms which have an acute effect, in particular the salmonellae, the virulent staphylococci and the clostridia which are also responsible for the severe wound infection known as gas gangrene. Salmonellae are parasites of animals and may be present in the food before processing or be introduced by contamination; the particular danger is that the food appears normal. Staphylococci are almost always introduced into food by a carrier in the manufacturing or preparative process and are most often found in ice-cream, cream cakes and the like — hence the importance attached to ice-cream in the Food Act 1984. Clostridia typically contaminate raw meat, poultry or stews and are a frequent cause of institutional outbreaks of food poisoning; fatalities are not rare because the resistance of the inhabitants — e.g. the senile — is lower than normal.

The classic example of poisoning due to a preformed bacterial toxin is that due to *Clostridium botulinum* which lies in the soil and which, thriving only in the absence of oxygen, proliferates in canned or, particularly, home bottled food stuffs. The normal symptoms of food poisoning — vomiting and diarrhoea — are absent and the toxin acts as a central nervous system paralysant.

Naturally occurring toxins are to be found in fungi — particularly of the genus *Amanita* — which may be mistaken for the edible mushroom. Whilst some such toxins are extremely dangerous, especially to the neuromuscular system, others have a mildly hallucinogenic property and their culture and distribution constitute something of a modern social problem. The liver and roes of many fish also contain natural neurotoxins.

It is to be noted that death due to poisoning of any sort, including natural poisoning, is reportable to the coroner; natural poisoning is, theoretically, reportable to the Scottish procurator fiscal, whose main concern would lie in the identification of negligence.

See also: Coroner; Food legislation; Gangrene; Hallucinogens; Pathogenic organisms; Poisoning

Forced Feeding

The concept of forced feeding of prisoners strikes at the heart of that of autonomy. There is nothing to prohibit a person from committing suicide but, in the context of the hunger striker, the doctor is torn by his commitment to save useful human life on the one hand and a reluctance to interfere in what is essentially a political confrontation on the other.

The legal position in the UK was first laid down in *Leigh v Gladstone*[1] in which the legality of forced feeding was founded in the duty of prison officials to preserve the life and health of their prisoners; this interpretation has, however, been widely criticised[2]. No power exists to protect a man compulsorily from himself and, at best, the direction in *Leigh* can be justified on the basis of necessity[3]. Subsequently, there have been some dramatic turns in political policy as to the forced feeding of prisoners. The Home Secretary ruled in 1974: '[the alternative of endangering the life of the prisoner is one] we have never regarded as being acceptable in this country'. A change of government, however, produced a remarkable *volte face*, the ministerial policy now being that, having been satisfied that the patient's capacity for rational judgement is not impaired, the medical officer should inform the prisoner that no rule of prison policy requires him to resort to artificial feeding and he should 'plainly and categorically [warn] that the consequent and inevitable deterioration in his health may be allowed to continue without medical intervention unless he specifically requests it'[4]. The difficulty of such a political approach is that it gives no *positive* guidance to the doctor; the Home Secretary cannot interfere if the doctor considers his primary function to be the preservation of life[5]. The policy also makes a distinction, which some would regard as inappropriate, between suicide by starvation and suicide by any other means which the prison authorities clearly have a duty to prevent[6].

The medical establishment was not particularly helpful during the debate which continued in the mid-1970s. In an ethical statement[7], the British Medical Association said that the final decision in the absence of consent to treatment must be for the doctor and not for some outside person and quoted the General Medical Council as saying that, whilst lawful forced feeding would not be professional misconduct, neither would a refusal to take part in the procedure. The Declaration of Tokyo is, however, at least categorical in saying (at item 5) that 'where a person refuses treatment. . .he or she shall not be fed artificially'.

Nevertheless, it is difficult for a doctor to stand by and watch a person die, despite the degrading circumstances and slight dangers involved in forced feeding. It may be tempting to rely on the 'capacity for rational judgement on the part of the prisoner' clause and to treat when the hunger striker has lapsed into coma; but such a practice is very reminiscent of the Prisoners (Temporary Discharge for Ill-Health) Act 1913[8] which added so much to the opprobrium surrounding artificial feeding. We would submit that the decision whether or not to feed cannot be a clinical one because the possible extraneous repercussions of a decision either way are unknown to the doctor. There is a good case to be made for a recognisably political decision in each individual circumstance.

It would appear that the reluctance to feed hunger strikers in the UK is not shared by the authorities in Canada or the USA. In a recent decision in the latter, the trial judge ordered forced feeding and, in doing so, distinguished between self-destruction for political reasons and refusal of treatment on moral or religious grounds[9].

The problem of artificial feeding is generally argued in terms of political prisoners. It must, however, be remembered that similar ethical, although not, of course, political, problems are encountered in the treatment of the elderly demented patient. Whether or not to institute artificial feeding is a purely clinical decision[10]; once that course is taken, the problems of discontinuance become acute, and are discussed under 'Euthanasia'.

See also: Autonomy; Declarations; Euthanasia; Geriatric medicine; Prisoners; Suicide

1. (1909) 26 TLR 139.
2. The whole subject is discussed in detail in Zellick G 'The forcible feeding of prisoners: an examination of the legality of enforced therapy' [1976] Public Law 153. *See also* Brazier M 'Prison doctors and their involuntary patients' [1982] Public Law 282.
3. Medicolegal 'The law and force-feeding' [1974] 2 Br Med J 737.
4. 877 HC Debates, col.451 (17 July 1974).
5. 'Force-feeding in prisons' [1974] 2 Br Med J 513.
6. Smith R 'Deaths in prison' (1984) 288 Br Med J 208.
7. 'Artificial feeding of prisoners' [1974] 3 Br Med J 52.
8. Still in force by reason of the Prisons Act 1952, s.28.
9. *In re Ramon Sanchez* 577 F Supp 7 (1983). *See also Von Holden v Chapman* 87 A 2d 66 (NY, 1982).
10. For an interesting account from Sweden, *see* Norberg A, Norberg BO and Bexell G 'Ethical problems in feeding patients with advanced dementia' (1980) 281 Br Med J 847.

Forensic Medicine

Forensic medicine is something of a British Commonwealth term; the same discipline is more commonly known as legal medicine in the USA and in Europe. The term 'medical jurisprudence' is often used as an equivalent but, in our opinion, this should be reserved to describe the study of the impact of the law on medical practice. This is an undoubted and major part of British forensic medicine but it should not be confused with the whole.

Apart from medical jurisprudence, the scope of forensic medicine and, particularly, its relation with forensic science is often misunderstood and some definitions are not out of place. To make such definitions is not, however, easy as, in many parts of the world, and particularly in those countries influenced by Roman law, there is some social resistance to autopsy which is rarely undertaken in the absence of a suspicion of criminality or negligence; in such circumstances, it is reasonable to adopt the common definition of forensic medicine: 'medicine related to the practice of the courts of law'. Forensic medicine under the coroners' system has, however, a far wider obligation to the public, including the performance of autopsy in some 20 per cent of all deaths; it therefore has very close associations with community medicine and it is noteworthy that the early university Chairs in legal medicine were all combined with public health.

Forensic medicine and forensic science can be divided on the premise that the former deals with biological substances and the latter predominantly with inanimate material which will not decompose and which can be examined in centralised science laboratories; such a definition is not, however, clear cut. Forensic medicine, strictly speaking, should relate to the examination of the living body; autopsy work is more correctly referred to as forensic pathology. In either circumstance, the contents of the body may need examination and this is the province of forensic toxicology. The forensic toxicologist will, however, also be required to examine inanimate tablets and the like and will therefore also be involved in forensic science. Whilst the biological examination is, in general, concerned with 'the how and the why' of injury or death, forensic science is attempting more to identify substances, instruments and subjects — the forensic science divisions of police forces are often known as the 'Identification Branch'.

This classification of the forensic services fails to define forensic serology — the study of blood and body fluids — which is clearly scientific and does not need a specifically medical expertise but which is, at the same time, dealing with biological materials. However, such materials can usually be preserved and, in so far as serology departments can be centralised, forensic serology is best looked upon as a branch of forensic science. But it is unique in that both scientifically and medically qualified persons can give equally competent expert evidence in the subject.

In this connection, it is to be noted that there is no obligation on a British forensic pathologist or forensic physician to have specific qualifications in the subject. The Royal College of Pathologists offers membership in forensic pathology but there are good reasons why this is seldom taken. The Society of Apothecaries offers a Diploma in Medical Jurisprudence (a misnomer in our opinion) and this may be taken in the clinical or pathological forensic disciplines — as a measure of experience or competence, it is more useful in the former. Pathological expertise is commonly judged on experience. Forensic pathologists in England and Wales are generally drawn from university departments or from a panel of Home Office appointed pathologists. The coroner has choice of his pathologist but chief constables may indicate whom they would prefer to act in cases of special complexity. The choice of pathologist in Scotland rests with the procurator fiscal but there is increasing concentration of resources on the universities. Northern Ireland is the only part of the UK which has a regularly established State forensic service.

See also: Blood stains; Coroner; Procurator fiscal; Royal Medical Colleges; Toxicological analyses

Foreseeability

Foreseeability plays a major, if controversial, role in questions of both civil and criminal liability. The foreseeability test is used in civil matters to determine responsibility and negligence for damage done. Stated simply, it provides that if a reasonable man would have foreseen the risk of damage occurring, then a duty of care is owing in relation to that eventuality. In addition to providing a positive definition, the test thus operates also in a negative fashion so as to exclude liability for remote damage; discussion of foreseeability consequently tends to lie within the context of causation and remoteness.

The test does not require that the precise nature and mode whereby the damage occurred should have been foreseen. Following *Hughes v Lord Advocate*[1] it has been held in a series of cases that the minimum requirement is that the defendant should have foreseen that damage of some kind would occur; the extent of the damage need not be foreseen.

The foreseeability of an event is an important consideration when assessing causal responsibility within the criminal law. If it was foreseeable that a harmful consequence would result from an action, then criminal liability may be imposed in respect of that consequence. The rule will be of greatest relevance when the question of recklessness is at issue[2].

See also: Causation; Reasonable man; Recklessness; Remoteness of damage

1. [1963] AC 837.
2. The relationship between foreseeability and intent in homicide cases has been particularly addressed in two recent cases — *R v Moloney* [1985] 2 WLR 648; *R v Hancock, R v Shankland* (1985) Times, 1 November.

Further reading
Dias M 'Remoteness of damage and legal policy' [1962] CLJ 178; Green L 'Foreseeability in negligence law' (1961) 61 Col LR 1401; Hart HLA and Honoré A *Causation in the Law* (1959) Clarendon, Oxford.

Fractures

Fractures, or breaks in continuity of the bone, take various forms. The least deforming is the greenstick fracture which occurs in youthful bones and results in bending rather than division of a long bone; somewhat similar cracks may occur in adult bones in which there is no displacement and the injury is partly self-splinting. A clean break in the bone is known as a simple fracture; a comminuted fracture arises when there are several fragments of bone. A fracture is described as compound when it also includes a break in the skin; such fractures are obviously prone to infection.

Efficient healing of fractures depends largely upon adequate immobilisation and maintenance of the blood supply. A blood clot collects at the fracture site and this organises into immature bone known as callus. This is always formed in excess and specialist cells of macrophage type then set about remodelling the bone to its former structure and strength. These changes are readily seen on X-ray, which may give a very good indication of the age of the fracture. Inadequate treatment often gives rise to excess callus or to other forms of abnormal repair; a radiological examination is therefore almost essential to the assessment of a case of non-accidental injury in childhood.

Fragments of bone may die without an adequate blood supply and remain as sequestra; the presence of such foreign bodies will greatly delay healing. The blood supply of certain bony parts is relatively poor and some fractures are notorious for their reluctance to heal — these include fractures of the scaphoid bone of the wrist and of the neck of the femur, the latter being extremely common in women who fall and in which the whole head of the femur may form a sequestrum; this necessitates removal of the necrotic head and, nowadays, replacement by a plastic or metal joint.

Certain fractures, which can arise from minimal or even no injury, are known as pathological fractures. They occur particularly in the osteoporotic (atrophic) bones of old age or through tumours of bone which may be primary or metastatic (see 'Malignant disease'). Congenital abnormal fragility of the bones occurs rarely in children and should be excluded radiologically in suspected non-accidental injury in children.

Apart from the pain and loss of function involved, the dangers of the fracture itself include haemorrhage and the condition of fat embolism. The former may be extensive if large vessels are involved and, since it will be mainly intramuscular, it may well not be apparent to the naked eye. Fat embolism may cause sudden death some 24 hours after a fracture occurring even in a fit young adult. The dangers of overtight plasters used in treatment are such that they represent a substantial proportion of all claims for negligence — gangrene may occur in extreme cases or there may be ischaemic contractures of the muscle; ischaemic damage to nerves may also cause later dysfunction. Such avoidable results are to be distinguished from the arthritic changes which may develop in the best of circumstances when a fracture has penetrated a joint space.

The general dangers of fractures include infection, which should be very rare in normal circumstances. Prolonged immobilisation predisposes to bronchopneumonia and to the development of pulmonary embolism.

Several fractures carry specific complications by virtue of their anatomical position. Any fractured bone may penetrate a neighbouring organ and this is particularly so of the ribs which may penetrate the heart, lungs, liver or stomach; injury to the breast bone may well bruise the heart. Fracture of the spine may be of compression type, but a fracture with displacement is almost certain to involve the spinal cord. Fractures of the skull constitute a special case and are discussed separately.

Somewhat unrealistically, a simple fracture does not constitute a wound in law[1]; it must, however, be regarded as a matter of grievous bodily harm.

See also: Fat embolism; Gangrene; Haemorrhage; Malignant disease; Non-accidental injury in children; Pneumonia; Pulmonary embolism; Skull fracture; Spinal cord injuries; X-rays

1. *JJC (a minor) v Eisenhower* [1983] 3 All ER 230.

Frigidity

Frigidity, or psychological aversion to sexual intercourse by the female, is not quite the counterpart of male impotence; there is nothing to stop a woman who simply does not like the act having sexual intercourse whereas a man with similar distaste might find coitus impossible.

Female frigidity may be due to any number of factors — unsatisfactory parental or religious counselling in childhood, genuine homosexuality or, occasionally, trans-sexualism, or socio-political objection to male dominance. Psychological frigidity becomes impotence when there is a reflex contraction of the perineal muscles and an inability of the genital passage to open — so-called vaginismus. The precipitation of vaginismus may well be associated with an unsympathetic male approach; indeed, female inability to consummate of this type may well extend only to one man — intercourse with others would not, *per se*, be a bar to a decree of nullity if that one man happened to have married her[1]. Therapeutic counselling is an obviously reasonable option in such cases.

Organic causes of inability to consummate in the female may result from genuine structural abnormality, as in vaginal atresia. Incapacity in such cases might be correctable by surgery but it would still be regarded as permanent and incurable for the purposes of nullity if the necessary operation were considered dangerous[2]. Alternatively, the sexual passages may be normal but, for organic reasons — which may include neurological conditions — penetration is so painful that intercourse is impossible. Dyspareunia of this type may be treatable but, again, the severity of the treatment would be taken into consideration in any nullity proceedings.

See also: Consummation of marriage; Genitalia; Impotence; Nullity of marriage; Trans-sexualism

1. *G v G* [1924] AC 349.
2. *S v S* [1963] P 162.

Fungi

Fungi can be fairly defined as plants which have no power of photosynthesis. Their structure varies enormously and extends from unicellular organisms to complex mushroom-type masses.

The pathogenic fungi which attack man are generally of little medico-legal significance despite the fact that some produce very severe disease. They occur in two main forms: those which produce moulds and are composed of branching filaments, and the yeasts which are single-celled organisms; most fungi will, however, adopt either form according to their environmental circumstances.

Branching forms are common parasites of the skin but it is the yeast-like organisms which cause serious systemic disease — indeed, some, such as *Cryptococcus* and *Histoplasma* are classified as Category B1 pathogens. Two factors help to contain the spread of dangerous fungal disease: firstly, an immunity is fairly readily established and, secondly, the organisms are susceptible to innovative forms of antibiotic treatment.

Fungi may adopt the role of opportunistic pathogens (*see* 'Pathogenic organisms') particularly when their growth is free from competition by bacteria. Thus, the yeast *Candida albicans*, which, at most, generally causes no more than inconvenience in the form of oral or vaginal 'thrush', can become dangerously pathogenic if it takes hold in the open wounds of severely burnt persons who are under treatment with antibacterial antibiotics.

Other fungi, which are not usually harmful to man, may become of medico-legal significance in certain circumstances. The major industrial example is farmer's lung, which is a disease of a prescribed occupation; the precise role of the fungus *Aspergillus* in the production of the disease is not entirely clear but an association with mouldy hay or vegetable produce is an essential part of the syndrome.

Somewhat paradoxically, however, it is the higher fungi, which have no parasitic relationship with man, which have the greatest forensic significance. The simplest medico-legal relationship rests on the fact that many fungi are highly toxic when ingested by man — at least one, *Amanita phalloides*, is extremely dangerous even having been cooked; many fungi exert their action through their content of the alkaloid muscarine, which has a profound effect on the neural stimulation of muscle. The danger is that toxic fungi will be eaten accidentally in mistake for, say, the common mushroom *Agaricus* (*see* 'Food poisoning').

The second, and rather more subtle, medico-legal significance of the higher fungi is that many contain alkaloids which are hallucinogenic. The best known of these is *Psilocybe semilanceata* which is a source of psilocin — a drug controlled under the Misuse of Drugs Act 1971. Much legal discussion has centred upon such problems as when a naturally occurring substance becomes a preparation; the subject is discussed further under the heading of the Act.

See also: Burns; Food poisoning; Hallucinogens; Misuse of Drugs Act 1971; Pathogenic organisms; Poisoning; Prescribed diseases and occupations

G

Gagging

Gagging is the obliteration of the mouth with the object of preventing speech. This must very often involve stuffing the mouth with material; the process is unpleasant but is non-lethal so long as the nasopharynx remains clear. Suffocation or choking may, however, supervene if the gag slips backwards; since the subject is likely also to be bound and immobilised, death is probable and this sequence is by no means uncommon in household robberies. The concept of constructive malice has been abolished in English law[1]; death in such circumstances would therefore now be charged as manslaughter rather than murder. In Scotland, the distinction between involuntary murder and culpable homicide is somewhat blurred but a charge of culpable homicide would be probable in the absence of what has been described as 'wicked recklessness'[2].

See also: Choking; Murder; Suffocation

1. Homicide Act 1957, s.1.
2. Gordon GH *The Criminal Law of Scotland* (2nd ed, 1978) p.735 et seq, W Green, Edinburgh.

Gangrene

Gangrene is localised necrosis of tissue, the main cause being ischaemia of the part. It is a common naturally occurring phenomenon particularly in the elderly whose arteries become gradually obliterated and whose circulation is poor. The process very often begins in the toes. The dead tissue may be dry or wet, the latter being fairly typical of gangrene in diabetics, who are particularly prone to the condition. Natural causes of gangrene other than obliterative arterial disease include thrombosis and embolism.

Unnatural causes of medico-legal importance include the occlusion of the arterial supply by a retained tourniquet or by an overtight plaster cast. Local action on the vessels may also cause gangrene — frostbite is a classic example whilst the condition may also complicate 'trench foot', which results from a combination of cold and vascular stasis. Poisoning by ergot, particularly as a contaminant of bread, was once a common cause of gangrene.

Gangrenous tissue is likely to be invaded by bacteria but the ischaemic disease is to be distinguished from gas gangrene, which is due to the action of specific bacteria of the genus *Clostridium*. These organisms live in the soil and are very persistent because they form spores. They thrive in anaerobic conditions and are particularly likely to cause disease when contaminating deep wounds or wounds in which the blood supply is already compromised. The toxin produced by the bacteria causes local tissue necrosis and severe generalised toxic shock. Antisera are available for passive immunisation of those who have been wounded in conditions conducive to the disease.

See also: Embolism; Immunisation; Pathogenic organisms; Surgical shock; Thrombosis

Garotting

Garotting is a form of strangulation by ligature generally performed from behind the victim. It is usually associated with considerable skill and has ritual overtones.

See also: Strangulation

Gas Chromatography

Gas chromatography is that form of chromatographic toxicological analysis in which volatile substances to be identified are passed in a carrier gas through a column which acts as a retaining medium. The substance in the column may be finely granulated powder (gas solid chromatography) or the granules may be coated with different waxes or greases (gas liquid chromatography).

The columns are heated in ovens in order to ensure vaporisation of the substances sought. The volatile substances are held back by the granules in the column as they are taken through in the carrier gas. The degree of retention is specific to the substance for that particular column. Substances in a mixture, therefore, take different times to emerge from the column and can be identified separately; the time taken to emerge is known as the retention time. In order that variations in apparatus and technique between laboratories can be eliminated, a reference substance is put through the machine at the same time; the ratio of the retention time of the unknown substance and the reference substance is known as the relative retention time, and this can be compared with tables prepared for the drugs, chemicals, etc. for which identification is likely to be needed.

Each volatile is detected as it emerges from the column and this is converted to an electrical impulse which is amplified and recorded. Since the strength of the electric impulse will be proportional to the concentration of the drug, gas chromatography has the great advantage, in common with high performance liquid chromatography (*see* 'Chromatography'), that, in addition to its identification, the quantity of the substance present can also be assessed from the area of the graphic record — this area being calculated by a built in computer.

Gas chromatography is sensitive and specific and, given the apparatus, is not particularly difficult to perform; the skill lies in the preparation and selection of appropriate columns. It can be regarded as the standard method of analysis for volatile substances in low concentration and is available in relatively small laboratories. Although the Road Traffic Act 1972 does not specifically say so, there is little doubt that a urine or blood alcohol result which was obtained otherwise than by gas chromatography would be regarded as less than best evidence.

See also: Chromatography; Toxicological analyses

Gas Poisoning

The general title of gas poisoning could include consideration of those gases used in war — in particular the nerve gases of the organophosphorus group which paralyse the autonomic nervous system — or those currently used in the control of civil disturbance. The latter are known generally as sensory irritants and include 1-chloracetophenone (tear gas or CN), *o*-chlorobenzylidinemalononitrile (CS) and dibenzoxazepine (CR). The last is by far the most effective in producing irritant symptoms in the eyes, nose and mouth and is the least toxic; the 'art' of using such agents is, of course, to effect crowd dispersal without morbidity but occasional unfortunate occurrences such as a direct contact of the concentrated substance on the eyes or skin must give rise to greater disability than is intended[1].

More usually, however, 'gas poisoning' is a term used to describe the toxic effects of the domestic gas supply. The old 'town gas' contained some 7–10 per cent of carbon monoxide; leaking apparatus or unlit apparatus activated by coin-meters were potent causes of accidental death whilst suicide through the gas oven was once the most common method of self-destruction in Britain. Gas poisoning of this type has been virtually eliminated with the introduction of natural gas for domestic use although, strangely, gas poisoning remains a cause of death which the Scottish procurator fiscal is bound to report to the Crown Office for further instructions.

See also: Carbon monoxide poisoning

1. *See* Himsworth H (chairman) *Report of the Enquiry into the Medical and Toxicological Aspects of CS (Orthochlorobenzylidine Malanonitrile)* (Cmnd 4173 and Cmnd 4775) (1971) HMSO, London.

Gender

The gender of a person can be regarded as the sex to which he or she belongs socially. It has to be distinguished particularly from the chromosomal sex because the two may be different (*see* 'Sex'). The gender of a person depends on several factors — the appearances of the genitalia, secondary sex characteristics and psychological acceptance. The last of these is largely determined by the first and it is generally on the basis of the genitalia that the gender is conferred at birth. It may well be that an error is brought to light only by the emergence of the secondary characteristics at puberty.

This is, in practice, only likely to present as an acute problem when mistaken sex is the result of a simple congenital anatomical abnormality which arose independently of chromosomal anomalies or of endocrine dysfunction. As such, these can be the most difficult cases to deal with because something more than psychiatric treatment may be needed if the accepted gender is to be maintained. It is now widely accepted that, so far as is possible, a person should have and pass in the gender to which he or she is psychologically attuned. This must be particularly so in the testicular feminisation syndrome where, despite a male chromosomal profile and the presence of inadequate female genitalia, the secondary sex characteristics are overwhelmingly those of the female.

It has been pointed out[1] that the celebrated case of *Corbett v Corbett (otherwise Ashley)*[2] decided the sex of the respondent only for the purpose of marriage and it is certainly true that adherence to a gender which was wrong on a chromosomal basis would be a likely bar to marriage[3]. The same argument is now true as to the Sexual Offences Act 1956[4]. Otherwise, modern public opinion and, indeed, the law seem content to leave people to find their own gender.

See also: Hermaphroditism; Sex; Sex chromosomes; Trans-sexualism

1. Hamilton W and Walker DM 'Gender: quaesto quid juris?' (1975) 15 Med Sci Law 79. Despite its slight outdatedness, this is an outstanding article from both legal and medical aspects.
2. [1971] P 83.
3. But *see* the allusion to the testicular feminisation syndrome under 'Sex'.
4. *R v Tan and others* [1983] 3 WLR 361.

General Dental Council

Control of discipline and education in dentistry was not removed from the medical profession until the passing of the Dentists Act 1957. This Act is now consolidated with its successors in the Dentists Act 1984 and this governs the establishment and function of the General Dental Council. The powers of the GDC are somewhat broader than those of the General Medical Council in that it controls auxiliary dental workers in addition to registered dental practitioners. The dental members of the GDC consist of 18 registered dentists elected by the profession on a geographical basis, 20 nominated by the dental authorities (the universities and Royal Colleges) and the 4 Chief Dental Officers of the UK. The non-dental members consist of 3 persons appointed by the GMC (who participate in educational matters only) and 6 persons representing the public interest appointed by Her Majesty on the advice of the Privy Council. One dental auxiliary is appointed by their committee. There are thus 52 members of the Council, which appoints a President who must be a registered dentist.

The GDC has a duty to maintain the dentists' register. A dentist must therefore be registered with the GDC and possess a qualification that is recognised by the Council before he may practise dentistry in the UK; the Registrar must also be satisfied as to the identity, good character and sound physical and mental health of a dentist applying to have his name placed on the register. This will also apply to those holding recognised overseas diplomas and to those who have had their names removed from the register. The Registrar may erase from the register the names of dentists who have not paid their registration fee or who have failed to answer an inquiry from the Registrar; other and more important reasons for erasure are discussed below.

The 1984 Act established a Health Committee of the Council. This Committee will operate with jurisdiction over dentists whose fitness to practise is seriously impaired due to physical or mental problems. Such a dentist could be suspended from the register for up to 12 months or be subject to conditional registration for up to three years — both of these periods being renewable.

A principal function of the GDC is to promote high standards of professional conduct among dentists. Section 27 of the Dentists Act 1984 provides that a dentist shall be liable to have his name erased from the dentists' register or his registration suspended if either before or after he is registered he has been convicted of a criminal offence or has been found guilty of serious professional misconduct. The Council issues a notice for the guidance of dentists on this subject from time to time. Information concerning convictions is received from the police and as to alleged misconduct from appropriate public authorities — including the results of any inquiries under NHS arrangements which reveal such a need. Complaints to the Council can be made by an individual but must then be supported by one or more statutory declarations/affidavits.

Reports of convictions and complaints relating to conduct are considered in the first instance by the Preliminary Proceedings Committee. This Committee meets to decide whether or not a case should be referrred to the Professional Conduct Committee. It may decide that no action should be taken or that a warning should be issued. A formal 'notice of inquiry' is issued should it be decided that an inquiry is warranted. The Preliminary Proceedings Committee has the power to order an interim suspension if it considers this to be necessary for the protection of the public.

The Professional Conduct Committee has a Legal Assessor to advise on matters of law. The parties may be legally represented and evidence is taken on oath. Any party may subpoena witnesses; so far as is possible, the rules of evidence of procedure are the same as obtain in a court of law. The Committee decides whether or not the dentist is guilty of serious professional misconduct and, if so, if it is necessary in the public interest that the dentist's name be erased from the dentists' register or that his registration be suspended. The Professional Conduct Committee cannot award damages or impose any other penalty. The dentist has the right of appeal to the Judicial Committee of the Privy Council.

The type of conduct which may be regarded as serious professional misconduct is not defined and can vary with the times. However, that which is considered by the Council often involves abuse of professional relationships, misuse of drugs, drink or general anaesthetics, fraud, covering, advertising and canvassing.

The Council also maintains an education committee which appoints visitors to the dental schools, who inspect and report on their curricula, educational facilities and examinations. It has the power to recommend the withdrawal of recognition of a particular qualification.

Dental auxiliaries are also controlled by the GDC. Auxiliaries, who include dental therapists and hygienists, must, at present, be supervised by a registered dentist who is on the premises. Under the terms laid down by the 1984 Act, the scope of their work is restricted and defined by the Dental Auxiliaries Committee. The Council is also required to maintain a roll for each class of auxiliary.

Information for prospective students of dentistry is available from the Council, who may also provide a certain number of loans to dental students who are in financial difficulty. Dental health educational material is produced and is available to interested parties.

See also: General Medical Council

General Medical Council

The role and composition of the General Medical Council, the governing body of the medical profession, are regulated by the Medical Act 1983. The term 'registered medical practitioner' means registered by the Council.

The members of the GMC may be elected, appointed or nominated and the number of elected members must exceed all the others (Sch.1, para.1(2)). Elections are on a regional basis for the four parts of the UK, the Isle of Man and the Channel Islands being considered, for this purpose, as being part of England. Members are appointed by the universities with medical schools, by the Society of Apothecaries and by the Royal Colleges and their Faculties. Up to 11 members, the majority of whom must be lay persons, are nominated by Her Majesty on the advice of the Privy Council.

The GMC supervises medical education, both pre- and postregistration, and its Education Committee must contain more appointed members than elected (Sch.1, para.19(2)). A comparatively recent statutory role includes providing advice for practitioners on medical conduct or ethics (s.35).

Complaints against doctors may be reported to the GMC and arise in two main ways. All convictions of doctors in a criminal court are automatically notified to the GMC and the verdict of the court is irrebuttable in the Council; otherwise, complaints may be made by individuals, by other doctors or by corporate bodies such as the DHSS or the NHS. Such complaints may relate to alleged professional misconduct or to supposed unfitness to practise through ill-health. In either event, after consideration by the Preliminary Screener — who disposes of some 80 per cent of complaints — those which appear to have substance are considered by the Preliminary Proceedings Committee, members of which cannot be members of the Health Committee or of the Professional Conduct Committee. The PPC may suspend a doctor or place conditions on his registration for a period of two months (s.42(6)). The Committee may otherwise reject complaints, admonish the doctor in a warning letter or refer the matter to either the Professional Conduct or the Health Committee.

The mode of operation of the Health Committee is still being evolved but, when the question is of such delicacy as is that of whether a practitioner is seriously impaired by reason of his physical or mental condition, as many safeguards as is possible are built into the system. Thus, in addition to being examined by two independent practitioners, the subject under review may have an examination by a doctor of his own choice. Legal representation is allowed at the hearings, which are private. The Health Committee may order conditional registration or suspend registration for up to 12 months if they find the case proved (s.37(1)).

Some 7 per cent of disciplinary complaints considered by the Preliminary Screener are ultimately referred by the PPC to the PCC which consists of a panel of up to ten members, the majority of whom must be elected. The hearings are conducted as in a court of law and are public although there are now discretionary powers to hear part of the evidence *in camera*. The question to be answered is whether or not a practitioner has been guilty of serious professional misconduct. In the event of being so judged, the PCC may admonish, postpone their decision pending a period of effective probation, stipulate a conditional form of registration for up to three years initially, suspend registration for periods of up to 12 months or they may erase the practitioner's name from the register; in the last eventuality, the subject may apply for restoration after 10 months and thereafter at intervals of 11 months (s.41(2)). Appeal from the decisions of both the Professional Conduct and Health Committees is to the Privy Council although such appeals can be made only on a point of law in the case of Health Committee decisions (s.40(4)(5)).

There is no definition of serious professional misconduct — it is simply an action which would be regarded as disgraceful by medical practitioners of good standing. In 1984, the PPC referred 52 cases to the PCC[1]. Sixteen of these related to dishonesty, 6 to sexual relationships with patients, 20 to disregard of responsibilities for patients and 6 related to drug prescribing. The PPC commented in 1982 that canvassing or advertising, of which there were 6 referrals out of 15 reports in 1984, were the most noticeably increasing complaints. The PCC have drawn particular attention to the principles of professional confidentiality (3 cases); this is a specially significant area of internal discipline as the patient has surprisingly little remedy at law for breaches.

It will be seen that the Council through its PCC is concerned mainly with the conduct of the profession rather than with professional activity. Errors made in good faith which attract actions for negligence in the civil courts are not, normally, the concern of the GMC unless there is evidence that the doctor has evaded his professional responsibilities. There is, however, no doubt that the Council will increasingly take a serious view of repetitive errors in diagnosis or treatment which endanger the welfare of patients[2].

See also: Advertising by doctors; Confidentiality; Negligence; Registered medical practitioner

1. General Medical Council *Annual Report for 1984* (March 1985) p.21, GMC, London.
2. General Medical Council *Annual Report for 1982* (September 1983) p.39, GMC, London.

General Sale List Medicines

The broad rule to be derived from the Medicines Act 1968, Part III, is that medicines intended for human use must be obtained from a registered pharmacy unless they are designated as being for general sale[1].

The list of such medicines is of little consequence, being largely confined to analgesics of the aspirin type — but including paracetamol — antacids, certain vitamin preparations and a number of historically interesting mixtures. Even so, some are not without danger if taken in excess and the analgesics must carry a warning notice. Moreover, medicines for general sale may be sold only from premises from which it is possible to exclude the public; some are further classified as being saleable by automatic machine but, again, such machines cannot be sited in the open.

Medicinal products used as eyedrops or ointments, anthelminthics or those intended for parenteral injection may not be supplied on general sale — distilled water, for example, is excluded if it is to be used by injection.

See also: Medicines Act 1968

1. Medicines (Products other than Veterinary Drugs)(General Sale List) Order 1984 (SI 1984/769).

Genes

Genes are composed of deoxyribonucleic acid (DNA) and are situated in the chromosomes. Specific genes are responsible for the synthesis of specific proteins and enzymes; it follows that the genes dictate our structure in its widest sense. Genes are present as alleles — or alternatives — of which only one is present in the chromosome. One gene of each pair is donated at random to the sex cell, which contains only 23 chromosomes; thus, a genetic mating has four potential permutations which, in practice, result in three combinations or *genotypes* (Fig. 1). If both genes in a

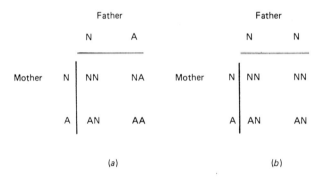

Fig. 1. One gene of an allelic pair is normal (N) and the other abnormal (A). (a) If two heterozygotes mate, the four permutations will result in two heterozygotes and one homozygote of each type. (b) A homozygous and heterozygous mating will result in two heterozygotes and two replicas of the homozygote. The situation may be more complicated if, as often occurs, there are more than two alleles at a particular gene locus (as in the ABO blood group system).

genotype are similar, the person is said to be *homozygous* for that gene; if they are dissimilar, he is *heterozygous*. A gene which can express itself — that is, show up — in the heterozygous state is described as 'dominant'; if it is suppressed by the other it is 'recessive' — but, even though it does not manifest itself it is still present and available for transmission to the next generation. Most genes are passed from parent to offspring independently but some lie so close together on the chromosome that they segregate as a group and are said to be 'linked'; this is particularly evident in the genetics of the rhesus blood group system.

Structurally, genes consist of chains of nucleotides, each nucleotide consisting of a sugar molecule, a phosphate molecule and nitrogenous base. The nucleotide chains exist in what is known as a double helix, which is so disposed that the genetic information is preserved in daughter cells when the parent cell divides. Thus, our genetic makeup is settled in the original zygote from which we are formed and is reproduced in the nuclei of all the cells of the body.

Whilst the normal alleles do no more than provide us with a choice of normal genetic qualities — e.g. whether we have blue or brown eyes — the minutest alteration in the structure of a gene may profoundly affect its function and this may result in an abnormal state of varying severity. A recessive state is expressed only if the abnormality is homozygous; the heterozygote is often no more than a carrier of the trait.

Since genes direct protein synthesis, many express themselves as antigens which may, in turn, stimulate antibodies in what is known as the immune reaction. It is this, which, in particular, complicates tissue transplantation of any type, including blood transfusion.

See also: Antibody; Antigen; Genetic disease; Immune reaction; Transplantation of organs

Genetic Counselling

The function of the genetic counsellor is to consider the particular circumstances of a couple who are at risk of producing a defective child and to lead them to make decisions which are right for them and for their offspring. In doing so, he will assess the risks, which are discussed under 'Genetic disease'; the approach must, however, be orientated to the psychology of the patients.

Parents may seek advice because they already have an abnormal child or because they have received premonitory information from other sources. The latter may be direct — e.g. from relatives — but it may arise as the natural outcome of keeping genetic registers; such registers are almost essential to the preventive control of genetic disease but clearly raise serious problems as to medical confidentiality[1]. The ethical issues of whether it is right to impose knowledge on unsuspecting couples and, if it is, then at what time in relation to pregnancy should that be done, must also be faced. In practice, genetic registers are concerned only with risks in excess of 10 per cent.

The more common presentation is retrospective, following the birth of a defective child. The counsellor can virtually never make a firm statement as to the outcome of further pregnancies; in the end, he is speaking in terms of probabilities and, thus, leading the prospective parents to decide in the light of their own circumstances. No woman can be forced not to have a child[2] but advice as to sterilisation of one or other partner is an open option. Alternatively, the counsellor, if he does not dismiss the risks, can suggest either artificial insemination by donor or ovum donation or he can arrange for a controlled pregnancy. Whether that pregnancy results in an abortion or in a live birth will depend upon the results of maternal or fetal investigations. These may include such well-established procedures as biochemical tests on the mother, ultrasound visualisation of the fetus or amniocentesis; in addition, there are techniques such as fetoscopy, fetal tissue sampling, aspiration of chorionic villi and recombinant DNA technology; some of these are currently in the developmental stage.

The major moral difficulty which then arises is the definition of abnormality. It is possible, for example, to think of parents opting for an abortion simply because the sex of the fetus is unsatisfactory. Whilst this would clearly be frivolous, it is apparent that dangers of misuse in this field are open to escalation.

The legal implications of negligence in relation to genetic counselling are discussed fully under the heading of 'Wrongful life'.

See also: Abortion Act 1967; Amniocentesis; Antenatal injury; Artificial insemination by donor; Confidentiality; Fetoscopy; Genetic disease; Genetic engineering; Neonaticide; Ovum donation; Sterilisation; Wrongful life

1. Emery AEH et al 'A report on genetic registers based on the Report of the Clinical Genetics Society Working Party' (1978) 15 J Med Genet 435.
2. *Re D (a minor)* [1976] 2 WLR 279 per Heilbron J at 286.

Further reading
See Emery AEH 'Prevention of genetic disease' in Wetherall DH (ed) *Advanced Medicine 14* (1978) Pitman, London; Emery AEH and Pullen I *Psychological Aspects of Genetic Counselling* (1984) Academic Press London.

Genetic Disease

The importance of genetic disease increases as the treatment or elimination of infectious disease becomes more effective. Genetic disease is that which is governed by heredity, this being determined by the genes inherited from one's parents (*see* 'Genes').

Genetically dependent diseases are of three main types — chromosomal, monogenetic (or unifactorial) and multifactorial. Chromosomal disease depends upon the presence of an abnormal number or structure of chromosomes and is not necessarily inherited. It is probable that many embryos with such defects die in the uterus. Chromosomal disease, of which Down's syndrome is the outstanding example, is discussed further under that heading.

Monogenetic disease is illustrated in 'Genes' (Fig. 1). If the abnormal — or disease-producing — gene is recessive, it will be clinically evident only in the genotype AA; if it is dominant, it will show up also in the configuration AN. Very deleterious dominant genes will obviously tend to be self-eradicating and they generally persist only if there is some special factor — e.g. in Huntington's chorea, the possession of the gene is not manifested until after the age of marriage and procreation; alternatively, they may arise as a result of spontaneous change, or mutation, a process which is greatly enhanced by exposure to radiation. By contrast, recessive genes will persist in the 'carrier' state and will produce overt disease when they meet as alleles. Many autosomal recessive diseases affect the biochemical mechanisms of the body, phenylketonuria being a good example. The statistical likelihood of monogenetic disease appearing can be determined very simply — clearly, in-breeding will increase the chances of recessive 'carrier' genes meeting.

One other form of recessive disease is that which is X-linked — often spoken of as sex-linked. The expression of such disease arises because there are no genes on the Y chromosome to suppress those present on the X chromosome. As a result, the disease occurs only in the male but is perpetuated through female carriers (Fig. 2). The best known example is haemophilia.

Father

	X	Y
X	XX	XY
x	xX	xY

Mother

Fig. 2. The mother carries an abnormal sex chromosome (x). There are now four possible offspring — a normal female and a normal male (upper line), a female carrier of the disease and a diseased male (lower line).

Multifactorial disease results from a combination of genetic and environmental factors — indeed, it is arguable that virtually every disease involves some degree of genetic predisposition. If the gene — or a combination of genes — is only weakly 'penetrant', the disease will appear only if the environment and/or the combination is particularly propitious; the opportunities for interplay of the various factors are endless. Neural tube defects offer the most impressive example of such a disease mechanism although even such commonplace conditions as coronary heart disease can properly be included in this category.

Some important practical results derive from the above. Monogenetic disease will, in most cases, be untreatable and its control rests in prevention; but, as has been noted, the statistical chance of an affected child can be accurately predicted. Similarly, chromosomal disease, being fixed within the cells, cannot be cured. Multifactorial disease, on the other hand, is open to some form of behavioral or surgical treatment but one cannot predict its appearance or severity with any accuracy; the probabilities can only be derived in an empirical fashion — and such is also the case with chromosomal disease. Thus, taken over all, the control of genetic disease is, to a very large extent, in the hands of the genetic counsellor.

See also: Amniocentesis; Chromosomal disease; Down's syndrome; Genes; Genetic counselling; Mutation; Neural tube defects; Radiation hazards

Genetic Engineering

Genetic engineering, more properly known as recombinant DNA technology, is the process of changing the genetic material of a cell. The techniques, which were largely unknown before 1970, involve the isolation of the specific DNA fragment, coupling this with a vector which will replicate itself and introducing the complex to a host cell which will, itself, multiply so as to produce clones which can later be harvested.

Fragmentation is achieved by enzymatic activity, the vector is generally a simple packet of DNA (plasmid) or a specific virus (phage) or a combination (cosmid); the host is commonly a bacterium — the most widely used being the omnipresent *Escherichia coli*.

Genetic engineering opens new fields in medical research and practice. Current applications include the investigation of gene structure, the control of genetic disease — particularly through antenatal diagnosis, by the detection of carriers and, perhaps, by treatment — and the synthesis of hormones or other proteins which are otherwise obtainable only in their natural state (e.g. insulin and growth hormone[1]).

Such technological advances must arouse some public concern — particularly as to the possibility of producing dangerous bacterial mutants and as to their use as eugenic tools. A Genetic Manipulation Advisory Group was set up following the recommendations of the Williams Committee[2]; the Group must be consulted before any activity involving genetic manipulation is carried out[3]. The main safety measures involve physical containment in specialised laboratories and the manipulation of the host bacteria in such a way that they cannot survive in natural conditions. It is generally agreed that the risks have been exaggerated but it is, nevertheless, clear that the controlled development of genetic engineering depends to a large extent upon the good faith of the scientific professions.

See also: Genetic disease; Genes; Insulin

1. For a review of techniques, *see* Emery AEH 'Recombinant DNA technology' [1981] 2 Lancet 1406. *See also* Leading Article 'Genetic engineering for medicine' (1981) 282 Br Med J 169.
2. Williams R (chairman) *Report of the Working Party on the Practice of Genetic Manipulation* (Cmnd 6600) (1976) HMSO, London.
3. Health and Safety (Genetic Manipulation) Regulations 1978 (SI 1978/752). *See* Emery AEH *An Introduction to Recombinant DNA* (1984) (Wiley, Chichester) for a very wide-ranging analysis of recent developments in the field.

Genitalia

The genitalia are the external attributes by means of which gender is most commonly allocated at birth. The male penis is well developed and the testes are normally descended into the scrotum at birth, at which time the female vulva is also generally obvious in form. Difficulties may arise, however. If both sides of the scrotum and penis are inadequately united and the testes are undescended (hypospadias), the resultant formation may closely simulate a vulva. Conversely, the clitoris may be abnormally developed in the adrenogenital syndrome and can be mistaken for a small penis. An apparently normal vulva but one associated with vaginal atresia (or a vestigial passage) is a feature of the testicular feminisation syndrome but, since the only evidence of maleness in this condition lies in the invisible chromosomal makeup, the gender is seldom questioned. The concept of a sex change occurring in childhood is a false one; evidence of a mistake made at birth may, however, become apparent. In these circumstances, the Registrar in England and Wales may alter the register[1]; the Registrar General for Scotland maintains a separate register of corrections[2].

See also: Gender; Sex

1. Births and Deaths Registration Act 1953, s.29.

2. Births, Deaths and Marriages (Scotland) Act 1965, s.42(5).

Genotype

The genotype of a specific gene pair is its full genetic constitution. In medico-legal genetics, which is largely a matter of the examination of stains and of testing for parentage, the determination of the genotype depends to all intents on the availability of antibodies to the two or more allelic antigens which are gene dependent.

Thus we can identify the blood group genotype AB because we can use both anti-A and anti-B antisera; by contrast, we cannot distinguish the genotype AA from that of AO because the gene O is silent. The blood group A therefore represents an incomplete genotype, or phenotype. Similarly, the 'rhesus positive' individual may have the genotype DD or Dd because, again, d cannot be demonstrated.

See also: Blood groups; Genes; Parentage testing; Phenotype

Geriatric Medicine

The medical treatment of the aged has very different horizons from that of standard clinical care and the differences are such as to justify fully the establishment of geriatric medicine as a distinct specialty. The specialty is, moreover, increasing in importance; something of the order of a quarter of hospital expenditure is related to the geriatric segment and the proportion of old persons in the community is certain to reach 10 per cent in advanced countries[1]. Many old persons suffer from acute disease or from malignancies which are likely to be fatal in the short term and these conditions are best considered under the general title of euthanasia. Here, we are concerned not so much with the actually or potentially terminally ill patient but rather with the incurably ill — because the greater part of geriatric disease is the inevitable result of wearing out of the cardiovascular, locomotor and central nervous systems. The treatment of the geriatric thus becomes mainly a matter of management.

Such management is by no means a simple matter of paternalism and dictation — the right to autonomy does not cease at retiring age. By and large, the law will not condone the treatment of physical disease against the patient's will but the law accepts that the mentally ill may be a source of danger to themselves and to others and that a patient with some degree of dementia may be incapable of forming a rational choice.

Various possibilities exist as to the disposal of what has come to be known as the psychogeriatric case. The patient may be able to continue to live at home assisted by the family and by the provision of home helps, visits from the district nurse, etc[2]. Much here depends upon the mobility of the patient but the situation is also complicated by the fact that there is no legal obligation on children in England and Wales to care for their parents, and the common law duty to do so in Scotland has now been abolished (Family Law (Scotland) Act 1985, s.1). Attempts to force such care may result only in domestic violence; an old person who is subject to such abuse is eligible for priority housing if that is a suitable option[3]. Alternatively, it may be possible to arrange for residential care which the local authority has a duty to provide[4]. Such accommodation may be in short supply and the local authority has no obligation to provide specialist or hospital type medical facilities in such institutions (National Assistance Act 1948, s.21(7)(b)). As a final resort, it may be necessary to admit the patient to hospital either for specific treatment (e.g. orthopaedic) or to a psychogeriatric unit — the number of such units is being slowly increased but their provision is subject to the constraints of the allocation of scarce resources. The correct placement of a psychogeriatric patient is a matter of skill and patience. There is considerable evidence that a system of home visiting by experienced geriatricians may indicate the best options from the points of view of both the patient and the community[5].

Major problems arise when a psychogeriatric patient resists removal from home or treatment. Powers for compulsory removal of an aged or infirm person living in insanitary conditions and unable to look after himself and whose removal is in his interests or is necessary to protect others are vested in the community health officer by virtue of National Assistance Act 1948, s.47 (as amended by the National Assistance (Amendment) Act 1951.) The power of removal is limited and there are strong arguments to be made against the use of such authority[6] but the alternative of compulsory admission to a mental hospital under the terms of Mental Health Act 1983, s.2, may be no less objectionable[7]. In the event of the patient becoming mentally incapable in the legal sense, the court may appoint a receiver or *curator bonis* to safeguard his affairs.

Attitudes to what is the correct management of the demented elderly are tending to polarise as the pressures on the geriatric service grow. At one end of the scale there are those who tend to see dementia as a loss of dignity which is scarcely compatible with a life of adequate quality; others would regard the condition as a challenge to improve society's attitudes to the aged[8]. It is possible to hold either view with great sincerity but there is a danger of a drift from the idea of 'the comfort of death' to that of classes of 'undesirable persons' including the brain damaged — society should be wary of moving from a recognition of an individual's right to die to a climate of enforcing a duty to die[9].

See also: Autonomy; Dementia; Detention in mental hospitals; Domestic violence; Euthanasia; Resource allocation

1. Reiss R 'Moral and ethical issues in geriatric surgery' (1980) 6 J Med Ethics 71.
2. Health Services and Public Health Act 1968, s.13; Social Work (Scotland) Act 1968, s.14. There is a general duty laid on local authorities to promote the welfare of old people (HS and PH Act 1968, s.45).
3. Housing (Homeless Persons) Act 1977.
4. National Assistance Act 1948, s.21(1)(a); Social Work (Scotland) Act 1968, s.49.
5. Arcand M and Williamson J 'An evaluation of home visiting of patients by physicians in geriatric medicine' (1981) 283 Br Med J 718.
6. The ethics are discussed in detail by Gray JAM 'Section 47' (1981) 7 J Med Ethics 146.
7. There is an interesting discussion in 'What to do with a sick elderly woman who refuses to go to hospital' (1984) 289 Br Med J 1435.
8. For an example of the debate, see Robertson GS 'Ethical dilemmas of brain failure in the elderly' (1983) 287 Br Med J 1775, and Murphy E (1984) 288 Br Med J 61.
9. Siegler M and Wiesbard AJ 'Against the emerging stream' (1985) 145 Arch Intern Med 129.

German Measles

German measles is probably the least serious of the common exanthematous infectious diseases for those it affects. The danger of the disease is that an infection of the mother within the first three months of pregnancy is likely to result in congenital disease in the baby — particularly deafness and other affections of the central nervous system. An abortion under the Abortion Act 1967, s.1(1)(b) is clearly legal in such circumstances and much depends upon accurate diagnosis of maternal infection. Actions for 'wrongful life' have been brought on both sides of the Atlantic as a result of failure in this respect but it has been made clear in the only reported British case that any obligation to abort an affected infant is an obligation to the mother and not to the fetus[1]. Actions for diminished life might, however, succeed in the USA[2].

Immunisation against German measles is obviously desirable for all women who have not been affected in childhood but active immunisation in the first trimester of pregnancy carries much the same risk of damaging the fetus as does the disease itself. It is therefore customary to insist on a period of 60 days' contraception after immunising any woman of child-bearing age; this may be accomplished by the coincident injection of a depot-type hormonal contraceptive.

See also: Abortion Act 1967; Diminished life; Immunisation; Wrongful life

1. *McKay and another v Essex Area Health Authority and another* [1982] 2 All ER 771, [1982] 2 WLR 890.
2. *Curlender v Bio-Science Laboratories* 165 Cal Rptr 477 (1980).

Glue Sniffing

The general term 'glue sniffing' should not be used as it implies that all volatile substances inhaled for their psychotropic effects are adhesives, and this is certainly not so; about one-quarter of deaths resulting from this type of abuse are associated with true glue sniffing. 'Solvent abuse' is a less inaccurate term.

See also: Solvent abuse

Gross Indecency

The term 'gross indecency' was introduced in the Sexual Offences Act 1956, s.13, and the Criminal Justice (Scotland) Act 1980, s.80. Although the use of the term suggests that there is a contrast between gross indecency and simple indecency, the former is nowhere defined. It is, perhaps, suggestive that s.13 of the 1956 Act refers to 'an act of gross indecency between men' and nowhere does the Act speak of gross indecency with or between women, the nearest equivalent offence in these circumstances being indecent assault. Unfortunately, the conclusion that the correct legal term is 'gross indecency between men' and that gross indecency by itself is without special meaning is invalidated by the use of the term in the Indecency with Children Act 1960.

Honoré[1] defines gross indecency between men and gross indecency between women but, again, statutory reference to gross indecency with children eliminates the attractive possibility of confining the term to homosexual acts involving either sex. The explanation of the apparent contradiction might be seen as lying between legal and social interpretations. There are many potential sexual acts between women — or, indeed, between men and women — which might be regarded as grossly indecent by large elements of society; legally, however, consenting adult women can behave as they wish provided they do not offend public decency — lesbian activity becomes criminal only when it is non-consensual or when it involves a girl under 16 years of age or one who is mentally subnormal, in which case the offence is indecent assault. Legal gross indecency is, thus, confined to homosexual male acts and to offences against children.

According to Honoré[1] , gross indecency involving males encompasses all forms of sexual activity other than kissing and anal intercourse which may be prosecuted as the offence of buggery. What constitutes gross indecency will be decided by the court but the term clearly includes all forms of sexual contact. Physical contact is, however, not essential to the offence. In *R v Preece*[2], the Court of Appeal took the view that what had to be proved was that the indecent act was 'directed towards another man who willingly participated and co-operated in the indecent exhibition'.

Acts of gross indecency which take place in private and between consenting men over the age of 21 are now not criminal[3]. Age also has a bearing on sentencing. The maximum sentence on conviction of an offence of gross indecency is two years when the accused has committed the act with a man aged 21 or over; the sentence increases to a maximum of five years when the other party is under 21 years old. There is no such differentiation in Scotland where, in fact, imprisonment for such offences is comparatively rare, particularly in the case of first offenders[4].

Gross indecency requires the presence of two persons. Solitary indecent conduct conducted in public can be prosecuted under the common law offence of 'outraging public decency'[5]. It is also an offence to be a party to an act of gross indecency between other men or to procure such an act. An unsuccessful attempt to procure an act of gross indecency can be punished as an attempt to commit the offence. Punishing a person for procuring an act which may, itself, not be a criminal offence, as when the act is between consenting adults in private, would seem to be a legal anomaly. The Scots law on indecency, whether involving one person or more, is similar to the English, the relevant statutory provision being the Sexual Offences (Scotland) Act 1976, s.7. The common law offence of 'shamelessly indecent conduct' also exists in Scotland. This was broadly defined in *McLaughlin v Boyd*[6] when the High Court pronounced that 'all shamelessly indecent conduct is illegal' — this proposition has attracted some criticism[7].

The concept of gross indecency involving females has been discussed above. Honoré[1] describes all genital contact between women as constituting gross indecency but it attracts no criminal sanction save in the context of 'outraging public decency'.

The criminal law prohibits gross indecency with children and, in the case of boys, this protection exists until the age of 21. The topic is dealt with in greater detail under 'Indecency with children'.

See also: Buggery; Homosexuality; Indecency with children; Lesbianism

1. Honoré T *Sex Law* (1978) pp.90, 101, Duckworth, London.
2. [1977] 1 QB 370, CA.

3. Sexual Offences Act 1967, s.1; Criminal Justice (Scotland) Act 1980, s.80; Homosexual Offences (Northern Ireland) Order 1982, s.3.
4. Home Office *Sexual Offences, Consent and Sentencing* (1979) HMSO, London; *R v Clayton* [1981] Crim LR 425.
5. *R v Mayling* [1963] 2 QB 717.
6. 1934 JC 19.
7. Gordon G *The Criminal Law of Scotland* (2nd ed, 1978) p.906, W Green, Edinburgh.

Guardian Ad Litem

A guardian ad litem is appointed by the court for a limited period with the specific purpose of safeguarding the interests of a child. Thus, if proceedings are brought against a child, he must be represented by a guardian ad litem and a parent is usually entitled to act on the child's behalf in this way; in fact, the court must allow the parent to speak on the child's behalf in care proceedings taken under the Children and Young Persons Act 1969[1]. It is, however, apparent that the interest of the child and his parents may be opposed, and it is now possible for the court to order that a parent will not represent the child. Of the four possible reasons for exception stated[2], the most all embracing is that the parent be not treated as representing the child (a separation order) because of a possible or actual conflict of interests. In such circumstances, the court will normally appoint an independent guardian ad litem to look after the child's interests; such a guardian is drawn from a panel of suitably qualified persons[3].

A guardian ad litem may be appointed in wardship proceedings, particularly when there is a dispute either between the ward and the parents or between the parents. In such cases, the position is taken by the official solicitor, who has wide investigative powers on behalf of the court and is also the solicitor acting for the child.

The role of the guardian ad litem in adoption proceedings has been limited by the Children Act 1975, s.20, and he is now appointed only if the parent or guardian disagrees with the adoption order. The guardian ad litem then, again, has an investigative role in protecting the child's interests and may be either the official solicitor or a person selected by the local authority from a panel appointed on the same lines as those in care proceedings.

A guardian ad litem will also be appointed if it is thought that the child should play a part in applications for or appeals against access orders made by parents in relation to children in care[4], and an order may be made for a guardian ad litem to represent a child in divorce proceedings — it is stated that such a power is rarely used other than in cases of disputed paternity[5].

See also: Adoption; Care proceedings; Divorce; Wardship proceedings

1. Magistrates' Courts (Children and Young Persons) Rules 1970 (SI 1970/1792), r.17.
2. Children and Young Persons Act 1969, s.2A, inserted by the Children Act 1975, s.64.
3. Guardians *ad litem* and Reporting Officers (Panels) Regulations 1983 (SI 1983/1908). For an appointment under the Scottish Children's Hearings system, *see* the Social Work (Panels of Persons to Safeguard the Interests of Children) (Scotland) Regulations 1984 (SI 1984/1442).
4. Child Care Act 1980, s.12F.

5. For general discussion of the appointment of the guardian ad litem, *see* Cretney SM *Principles of Family Law* (4th ed, 1984) Sweet & Maxwell, London.

Gunshot Injuries

For all practical purposes, gunshot injuries can be regarded as synonymous with firearm injuries and are, therefore, injuries caused by shot, bullets or other missiles discharged from lethal barrelled weapons[1]. Injuries causes by these weapons differ very much in character and they are described under the appropriate headings.

See also: Airgun injuries; Firearm injuries; Rifled weapon injuries; Shotgun injuries

1. Firearms Act 1968, s.57(1).

H

Habeas Corpus

The prerogative writ of *habeas corpus ad subjuciendum* is a historical means of protecting the liberty of the subject. The writ provides for the production of the person before the High Court in order that the judges may satisfy themselves as to whether or not the subject of the writ is unlawfully detained. The writ may be used in both a civil and a criminal context. In the former, it is often used in arguments as to the proper custody of minors.

Further reading

There is a succinct explanation of the writ of *habeas corpus* in *Halsbury's Laws of England* (4th ed, 1976) Vol.11, 768. *See also* Bradley AW and Bates TStJN (eds) *Wade and Phillips' Constitutional and Administrative Law* (10th ed, 1985) Chap.26B, Longman, London.

Haemodialysis

Haemodialysis is that form of dialysis in which the blood is directly dialysed through a membrane (*see* 'Dialysis'). Whilst the process is very efficient, the dialysing coil must be primed with blood and this, in addition to imposing a load on any blood transfusion service, introduces the hazard of viral contamination which is common to all processes involving the use of human blood. The exclusion of such contamination is a major technical problem in renal treatment units.

See also: Dialysis; Hepatitis

Haemoglobinopathy

Haemoglobinopathies occur in two main types: those in which there is an alteration in the structure of the haemoglobin and those in which the synthesis of the globin part of the structure is defective. The first is exemplified by sickle cell disease; the latter are known as thalassaemias. Both are genetically determined on a monogenetic basis (see 'Genetic disease'). Both occur as major (homozygous) or minor (hetero-zygous) conditions, the latter often existing as no more than a symptomless carrier state. The thalassaemias are a major social problem in some areas of the world but have little medico-legal significance. Sickle cell disease, however, has a distinct association with hypoxia and may be of forensic significance.

See also: Erythrocytes; Genetic disease; Hypoxia; Sickle cell disease; Thalassaemia

Haemolytic Disease of the Newborn

The disease is due to immunisation of the mother by the red cells of the fetus through the medium of haemorrhages which cross the placenta — particularly during the birth process. The antibodies so formed may, if of the appropriate quality, pass back into the fetus and cause a second immune reaction with the fetal cells. The results in the fetus will range from mild jaundice, through severe brain damage to intrauterine death.

It is apparent that the fetal cells must contain a potent antigen which is absent from the mother and, in nature, this is almost always — over 95 per cent — the antigen D (see 'Rhesus system'). The genetic mechanism is therefore that a rhesus negative (dd) mother carries a child who is rhesus positive (D+), having received the D gene from its father. If the father's genotype is DD, all children will be Dd — i.e. rhesus-positive heterozygotes; if, however, the father is Dd, the statistical chance is that half the offspring will be dd and, therefore, not susceptible to the disease. The general pattern is that the mother is sensitised by her first D+ child and, thereafter, successive D+ children become increasingly severely affected. Other similarly stimulated antibodies have caused the disease, particularly anti-c, anti-E and anti-K (Kell, which is outside the rhesus system (see 'Blood groups').

Haemolytic disease of the newborn is diagnosable by amniocentesis and affected infants can be effectively treated by a combination of careful monitoring both of the fetus and of the mother, occasionally intrauterine transfusion, timing of delivery and replacement of the affected red cells of the infant by neonatal 'exchange' transfusion.

There are two major medico-legal aspects of haemolytic disease of the newborn. Firstly, a rhesus-incompatible transfusion is a potent sensitising process — the woman's first child may be grossly affected if such a transfusion has been given previously. Secondly, it is possible to protect the mother from immunisation by giving her suitable anti-D treatment immediately — or even soon — after delivery. Failure to do so would now undoubtedly be regarded as negligent and the disease should become very rare as a result of routine practice. Clearly, however, the anti-D needed to protect will also become rare and supplies may depend upon the use of male volunteers — a further potential inroad of commercialism into the provision of human biological materials.

A most interesting court case has been reported from the USA in which an action for preconception tort was allowed on the complaint of a neonate born with brain damage due to haemolytic disease. The allegation of negligence was based on the fact that a mother was not informed she was rhesus negative and was not protected after her first pregnancy; the second pregnancy was, consequently, managed inadequately[1].

See also: Amniocentesis; Blood groups; Blood transfusion; Causation; Negligence; Rhesus system

1. *Lazevnick v General Hospital of Monroe County, Inc.* Civ. Act. No. 78-1259 (MD Pa Aug 13, 1980).

Haemophilia

Haemophilia is a genetic disease which results in inadequate clotting of the blood. The sufferer may therefore bleed or bruise excessively easily and, apart from the obvious hazards of anaemia and shock due to haemorrhage, may die suddenly from intracranial haemorrhage which can result from relatively trivial injurious force.

Haemophilia may be of type A or type B (Christmas disease) depending upon whether Factor VIII or IX is deficient in the coagulation cascade (*see* 'Coagulation of the blood'). The deficiencies are X-linked; thus, whilst only males are affected, transmission is through the female line. Clearly, the haemophiliac of either type is at major risk during surgical operations even when these are of a relatively minor nature such as a dental extraction. Failure to screen for the disease before operation would be likely to attract an action in negligence.

Emergencies, such as surgery, can be covered by transfusion of Factor VIII or IX; maintenance doses are needed during normal activity. The haemophiliac is therefore at particular risk from conditions which are transmissible through blood or blood products — in particular, hepatitis or, now, the acquired immune defficiency syndrome.

See also: Acquired immune deficiency syndrome; Coagulation of the blood; Genetic disease; Hepatitis; X-linked disease

Haemorrhage

Haemorrhage is loss of blood from the intravascular circulation. It may be external to the body or internal — the blood then being extravasated into the tissues or into the natural body cavities. The pattern of a haemorrhage depends upon the vessel which is breached. Bleeding from an artery will be copious and forcible as the contained blood is under considerable pressure; haemorrhage from veins or capillaries will be relatively slow and more easily controlled because the pressure is low. The degree of a haemorrhage also depends upon other factors — the size of the defect, the size of the vessel and whether or not it can be contained naturally. The mode of vascular injury is also important. A lacerated injury, being due to crushing, will result in an irregular vascular defect and will be attended by effusion of tissue juices — the conditions for spontaneous coagulation of blood are, therefore, optimal; by contrast, it is a matter of common observation that a clean incision will cause persistent bleeding even when capillaries alone are involved.

The effects of external haemorrhage are surprisingly slight — we happily donate 500 ml of blood in return for a cup of tea. Any form of loss of blood of a litre or more may, however, result in collapse, due to a sudden loss of blood pressure, anaemia and hypovolaemic or surgical shock — the last being aggravated by the second. It is not always remembered that a litre of blood can be easily lost into the body cavities or even into the muscles.

The secondary effects of internal haemorrhage are physical rather than physiological. Arterial blood may plough into and disrupt soft tissues, of which the brain is by far the most important; intracranial haemorrhage may result in severe residual physical defect if it is survived. Alternatively, the blood may act as a space-occupying lesion causing pressure effects on nearby organs. The abdominal cavity is wide and expansile; the pleural or thoracic cavity is less so and collections of blood (haemothorax) may severely compromise breathing; but the cranial cavity is rigid and the brain highly sensitive, both anatomically and physiologically, to pressure changes — as a result, intracranial haemorrhages measured in millilitres may be fatal even though they do not involve the actual brain substance. Haemorrhage into the pericardial sac (haemopericardium) is of comparable danger as the pumping action of the heart is inhibited by pressure; this serious condition is known as cardiac tamponade.

Petechial haemorrhage is a form of capillary bleeding which is of particular medico-legal importance and is discussed separately.

See also: Anaemia; Arteries; Cardiac tamponade; Cardiovascular system; Coagulation of the blood; Hypovolaemia; Intracranial haemorrhage; Petechial haemorrhage; Surgical shock

Hallucinations

A hallucination is a sensory experience which occurs in the absence of a valid sensory stimulus. Hallcinations are characteristic of psychoses both of functional and of organic type. They may be transient when the underlying organic process is also impermanent — e.g. the classic hallucination of the presence of water when suffering from the cerebral effects of exposure to heat. A number of natural and synthetic chemicals are hallucinogenic.

See also: Hallucinogens; Psychoses

Hallucinogens

The term 'hallucinogen' is widely used to describe drugs which distort the senses or the appreciation of the environment. The use of the generic name is therefore a misnomer because a hallucination is defined as a sensory experience without a true sensory stimulus. Nevertheless, it is difficult to devise any acceptable alternative and hallucinogen is, at least occasionally, an apt description because the distortion of what is present may be so bizarre as to amount to a hallucination.

The group comprises a number of naturally occurring substances such as cannabis, derived from the leaves and flowers of *Cannabis sativa* and psilocin and psilocybin which are the active principles of, among others, the fungus *Psilocybe semilanceata* — the most important of a group of fungi popularly known as 'magic mushrooms'. In addition, there are an increasing number of synthetic drugs, including lysergic acid diethylamide (LSD) and phencyclidine (PCP), which have similar, though more potent, properties.

The effect of the drugs as a whole is to alter the senses of time, vision, hearing and interpretation. The nature of the distortion is, however, variable both as to extent and as to direction — the LSD user, for example, appears not to know if his 'trip' will be good or bad but generally the desire is for a further experience. Thus, whilst the hallucinogens are not addictive in the full sense, the user may acquire a psychological dependence. The use of Indian hemp under its derivative name 'cannabis' and of lysergic acid is discussed in greater detail under the appropriate headings.

The hallucinogens are controlled drugs as defined by the Misuse of Drugs Act 1971. They have, however, no known medical use and are further classified as Schedule 1 drugs under the Misuse of Drugs Regulations 1985[1]; although it does not appear to be stated to specifically in the Regulations, it is accepted that legal possession of hallucinogens is dependent upon the holding of a licence from the Secretary of State.

See also: Cannabis and its aliases; Drug addiction; Lysergic acid; Misuse of Drugs Act 1971

1. SI 1985/2066.

Hanging

Hanging is passive strangulation by ligature using the weight of the body to tighten the noose. Although this was once a method of execution, it must be distinguished from modern judicial hanging which causes death by distraction fracture of the cervical vertebrae with destruction of the brain stem[1].

Homicidal hanging must be so rare as to be ignored although occasional throttlings or other homicides are suspended after death in an effort to avoid detection[2]. Accidental death is most commonly associated with the sexual asphyxias although a number of emotionally deprived young people die in this way during what is intended to be a plea for attention; very occasionally, children may be accidentally hanged in the playground or in their restraining harnesses in prams and the like. Suicidal hanging is by far the commonest form of death by suspension and comes second only to ingestion as a method of self-destruction.

The pathological distinction between hanging and strangulation is to be made from the fact that, whereas the ligature abrasion will be horizontal in the latter, it rises in the former to the point of suspension — either at the back of the neck or beneath the angle of the jaw. Death may be due to venous occlusion, in which case there will be congestion and petechial haemorrhage above the ligature. In addition, however, the mechanics of hanging are likely to occlude the air passages and signs of hypoxia will be present throughout the body. Fracture of the laryngeal cartilages is far less common than in throttling, the noose usually passing between the hyoid and thyroid cartilage. *Post mortem* lividity will be very marked in dependent parts — arms, legs and even breasts — and congestion of these parts may be so severe as to cause widespread petechial haemorrhages.

On the other hand, suicidal hanging may be associated with severe emotional tension and death from vagal inhibition of the heart is by no means uncommon. In these circumstances, it is quite possible for a suicide to die with the feet still in contact with the ground. Signs of asphyxia will be correspondingly absent and the situation is one which the pathologist must consider with care.

Laceration of the intima of the carotid arteries is characteristic of a major jolt during suspension; it is very often seen in the unusual accidental hanging associated with parachuting — the rigging lines being entwined round the neck.

See also: Capital punishment; Changes after death; Parachuting injuries; Petechial haemorrhage; Sexual asphyxia; Strangulation; Suicide; Vagal inhibition of the heart

1. Abolished under the Murder (Abolition of Death Penalty) Act 1965 although it could still be used following conviction for treason, piracy or arson in HM dockyards.
2. A well-known instance being *R v Emmett-Dunne*, General Court Martial, Dusseldorf, 1954.

Hashish

See 'Cannabis and its aliases'

Head Injury

Head injury may be due to transmitted force — particularly through the spinal column, as occurs in falls from a height — or to direct violence, which is far commoner. Direct violence can be of crushing type, accelerative (as when the head is struck by an object) or decelerative which occurs when the moving head strikes an unyielding surface.

Very large numbers of lesions can be included under the title of head injuries. These include wounds of all sorts to the scalp, fractures of the facial bones or of the vault (or base) of the skull, concussion, brain swelling, intracranial and intracerebral haemorrhage and laceration of the brain substance. These are all described as separate entries.

For present purposes, only the general mechanism of severe head injury is considered, the most important point to be borne in mind being that a very high proportion of such injuries derive from differential movement of the brain within the skull. This is possible because the brain is suspended in the cranium within the cerebrospinal fluid which occupies the subarachnoid space. Forces acting on the intracranial structures may therefore be of compressive type where the head is struck;

this will occur in both accelerative and decelerative types of violence. In the latter type of injury, however, the tissues may also be subjected to suctional forces on the opposite — or contre-coup — surface where the brain is pulled from its attachments. In addition, more complicated movements may impose rotational or shearing forces on the brain and these will be exacerbated by contact with the relatively sharp edges of bone which fashion the cranial fossae.

The results of these complex forces may include rupture of the cerebral arterioles and veins, intracerebral bleeding, gross laceration of the brain and severe changes at cellular level within the brain tissue itself[1].

See also: Brain swelling; Cerebral injury; Concussion; Contre-coup injuries; Intracerebral haemorrhage; Intracranial haemorrhage; Skull fracture; Wounds

1. For a concise account of head injury, *see* Gordon A and Maloney AFJ 'Blunt head injury' in Mason JK (ed) *The Pathology of Violent Injury* (1978) Chap.12, Edward Arnold, London.

Health and Safety at Work etc. Act 1974

The safety of the work place is regulated under the terms of the Health and Safety at Work etc. Act 1974, which was designed to integrate the various pieces of legislation which had hitherto been applied to specific industries. The Act not only provides protection for the employee against harm to which he may be exposed in the work place but also controls exposure of the general public to industrial pollution. It provides for the promulgation of regulations concerning health and safety at work and for the development of codes of practice.

Part I of the Act established the Health and Safety Commission which consists of representatives of employers, employees and local authorities and is charged with effecting the purposes of the Act; it is also responsible for arranging research, training and provision of information relevant to safety at work. The Health and Safety Executive, established under s.11 of the Act, gives effect to the decisions of the Commission, enforcing these through inspectors, who replace the previous factory and other inspectorates and have wide powers of entry and discovery. Schedule 3 of the Act details the subject matter of health and safety regulations. This includes regulating safety precautions, the ensuring of regular medical examinations of employees and supervisory precautions relating to radiation, ventilation, noise, vibration, etc. A large number of regulations have been made and these now include areas of employment, such as hospitals and laboratories, which were not covered by the previous essentially 'industrial' legislation.

The 1974 Act lays down a number of general duties relating to health and safety. These, contained in ss.2–8, require, inter alia, that care be taken for the safety of those at work and those affected by working premises. Section 2 imposes a general duty on the employer 'to ensure, so far as is reasonably practicable, the health, safety and welfare at work of all his employees'. The phrase 'reasonably practicable' does not simply mean physically and financially possible; the degree of risk must be balanced against the effectiveness and onerousness of the available measures[1]. The inspectors may serve 'improvement' or 'prohibition' notices on employers; breach of the duties imposed in the Act does not give rise to civil liability (s.47) but may lead to criminal prosecution (s.33). The emphasis in health and safety at work is, however, on persuasion rather than on criminalisation.

The medical wing of the Health and Safety Executive is now provided by employment medical advisers, who have the same powers as inspectors appointed by the Executive. An accident is notifiable to the Executive if it involves the death of any person or injury to an employee resulting in more than three days absence from work; in the latter case, a consequent death occurring within one year must also be notified. Certain industrial diseases must also be notified (*see* 'Notifiable diseases'). The appropriate minister may direct that a full investigation be held into the causes and circumstances of any accident occurring or of any disease acquired in a factory. Deaths resulting from a notifiable disease or accident must be reported to the coroner or to the procurator fiscal. The former must then hold an inquest with a jury and the latter arrange for a fatal accident inquiry[2].

A major feature of the Act is the appointment of 'safety representatives' on the initiative of recognised trades unions[3]. Safety committees are to be established if two or more safety representatives so request.

See also: Fatal accident inquiry; Industrial injury; Inquest; Notifiable diseases; Occupational disease

1. *West Bromwich Bulding Society v Townsend* (1983) Times, 3rd January.
2. Criminal Law Act 1977, s.56(2); Fatal Accidents and Sudden Deaths Inquiry (Scotland) Act 1976, s.1(1)(a)(i).
3. Safety Representatives and Safety Committees Regulations 1977 (SI 1977/500).

Health Service Commissioner

A Health Service Commissioner, popularly known as the Ombudsman, is appointed for England, Wales and Scotland[1]. His function is to deal in a relatively informal way with alleged deficiencies in the service provided by the various bodies within the NHS and their officers and alleged failures to provide a service which it was their function to provide; the Commissioner may also investigate any other actions taken or not taken by the relevant body. The essence of a complaint is that the complainant must have sustained 'injustice or hardship in consequence of the failure or of maladministration'; a complaint may be made on behalf of a deceased person and may also be referred by the administrative body itself. There are strict time bars as to the laying of complaints but the Commissioner can override these if he thinks it reasonable. The powers of the Health Service Commissioner are, however, limited. In particular, he cannot consider a case where the complainant has a statutory avenue of appeal nor may he intervene if there is any remedy through the courts — allegations of frank negligence are therefore outside his province. Problems associated with pay and conditions of service are excluded. The Commissioner is also debarred from considering cases which arise from matters of clinical judgement; it is, however, often difficult to distinguish clinical care from administration, and the fact that the complaint involved an element of the former would not necessarily inhibit the Commissioner from investigating the administrative aspects. The Commissioner is not precluded from investigating a matter which is subject to inquiry under the Hospital Complaints Procedure Act 1985 (s.1(2)).

A combined report for the three countries is produced annually[2]. In the year 1983–84, 895 complaints were received and, of these, 584 were rejected; 119 reports were issued and the remainder were either referred back to the complainant or were still being considered. In view of the general informality of the Commissioner's inquiries, legal representation at the hearings is not usually regarded as appropriate. The Commissioner's procedures are governed generally by the Parliamentary Commissioner Act 1969.

See also: Complaints procedures in the NHS; Family practitioner committees

1. National Health Service Act 1977, s.106; National Health Service (Scotland) Act 1978, s.90. In fact, the same person holds all three appointments.
2. National Health Service Act 1977, s.119(4).

Hearsay Rule

The evidential rule against hearsay excludes accounts by witnesses of what was said on another occasion. Evidence of the fact that the statement was made is admissible but the statement cannot be adduced as proof of what was asserted[1]. The reason for the exclusion is that hearsay evidence is, by its very nature, less reliable than is direct evidence; the matter of the statement cannot be subjected to cross-examination and it could be that the witness is distorting, intentionally or otherwise, what was originally said[2].

Hearsay evidence is admissible in civil proceedings in certain circumstances provided for by statute[3] or where there is agreement by the parties. A party proposing to adduce hearsay evidence should serve notice to the others, who are entitled to require the presence of the maker of the original statement. The hearsay statement may be admitted in evidence if no such requirement is made or if the maker of the original statement is unobtainable for good reason.

Other exceptions to the inadmissibility of hearsay include the use of public documents and records and, importantly, certain admissions in civil cases and confessions in criminal proceedings. In the latter case, hearsay evidence may be adduced to indicate the state of mind of the person who made the statement or of the person to whom it was made; it will be allowed only if that is a clearly relevant issue[4].

See also: Best evidence rule; Confessions

1. *Subramaniam v Public Prosecutor* [1956] 1 WLR 465 at 470.
2. *Teper v The Queen* [1952] AC 480.
3. Civil Evidence Act 1968; Civil Evidence Act 1972.
4. *R v Blastland* (1985) Times, 30 July.

Heart Disease

Heart disease is the basis of the great majority of sudden deaths referred to the coroner or the procurator fiscal. The causes of such disease are therefore medico-legally important and most of the common types are discussed under separate headings.

Coronary heart disease is pre-eminent among these but other causes of sudden cardiac death include hypertensive disease, cor pulmonale, cardiomyopathy (or alterations in the structure of the heart muscle), myocarditis and valvular disease which is now relatively uncommon and is touched upon under 'Cardiomyopathy' and 'Embolism'.

Congenital disease is a major part of heart disease as a whole but, as a clinical condition, it has little medico-legal significance because the vast majority of cases are diagnosed at birth and are being treated with increasing skill and success. It is of aetiological importance on two counts. Firstly, it would appear to be a genetic disease of multifactorial type and the likelihood of its occurrence in a family cannot therefore be predicted with any statistical precision. It is, however, strongly associated with chromosomal defects and is a common manifestation of Down's syndrome. Secondly, the contribution made by drugs, radiation etc. to the environmental component of 'multiple factors' is often invoked but is virtually unassessable; proof of such causation is very rarely obtainable.

See also: Cardiomyopathy; Causation; Cor pulmonale; Coronary disease; Down's syndrome; Embolism; Genetic disease; Myocardial infarction; Myocarditis

Heat Effects

The human body is able to cool itself relatively effectively by the process of sweating and it is only when this mechanism becomes disordered that disability or death can be attributed to heat. Hyperthermia is therefore of rather less forensic significance than is hypothermia. There are two abnormal clinical responses to heat: heat exhaustion and heat stroke.

Heat exhaustion may be acute and results from inadequate evaporation of the sweat produced in response to a rising body temperature. This may be due to the wearing of unsuitable clothing or be associated with a simultaneous high ambient relative humidity and temperature. Some areas of the world (e.g. the Persian Gulf) are notorious for this combination; working areas may generate such a hostile atmosphere — a coal-burning boiler room is an example; or the humidity may build up when persons are confined in a closed environment — heat effects are then superimposed on hypoxia. An increase in body heat has a direct effect on the brain which may be lethal. Subacute heat exhaustion has a very different aetiology; in this condition, the loss of sweat and its contained salt is so profuse that the subject suffers from sodium depletion — it is important to take extra salt when such conditions are likely to be encountered, as a prophylaxis against what may be a severe metabolic upset. Chronic heat exhaustion is of little medico-legal significance; the sweat glands become blocked, often after prolonged periods of overproduction, and the ability to sweat is lost — the subject is then very susceptible to acute heat exhaustion and this may limit his domicile or employment.

Heat stroke is an acute and very serious condition in which the central temperature regulator in the brain is rendered defective by exposure of the head to intense heat — generally solar. The condition is seen in persons deliberately or accidentally exposed to the tropical sun without protection. The body temperature rises and there are severe cerebral and metabolic results. Death from heat stroke has been declared an industrial accident[1]. Heat stroke and heat exhaustion may co-exist; the prognosis is then exceptionally bad.

See also: Hyperthermia; Hypothermia; Hypoxia

1. *Ismay, Imrie and Co v Williamson* [1908] AC 437. But in *Pyper v Manchester Liners Ltd* [1916] 2 KB 691 death from what would now be called heat exhaustion was thought to be expected and, therefore, not an accident. The importance of semantics is emphasised in this case.

Helminthic Disease

Disease due to helminths (worms) is seldom of medico-legal significance.

Most helminths have a complicated life history and their effect in man depends on whether they exist within the bowel or within the tissues. The former generally results in little more than nuisance, although some bowel-situated helminths can cause significant disease; the hookworm, for example, feeds on blood and may cause a severe anaemia due to iron deficiency[1] whilst the fish tapeworm utilises the substances essential to the formation of erythrocytes, thus causing a vitamin deficiency anaemia. Involvement of the tissues, generally during the larval stage of development, may, however, be very serious[2]. Larvae of the pork tapeworm may cause intractable epilepsy if lodged in the brain whilst invasion by the larvae of the dog tapeworm, *Taenia granulosa*, results in the severe hydatid disease; hydatid disease is of forensic importance in that it is closely associated with the sheep farming industry although it is not a prescribed disease.

The complex life history of helminths means that very few are immediately transmissible from man to man (e.g. through the medium of food handlers); the pork tapeworm might be thus passed on but the least uncommon is the threadworm which is widespread and of little more than irritant significance. By contrast, many helminths are transmissible to man through the medium of undercooked flesh — pork and fish being the most important sources; routine inspections as authorised by the Food Act 1984 provide an essential preventive measure. Other helminths, including the dangerous *Schistosoma*, penetrate the skin of man while bathing in fresh water whilst those which mature in the soil are clearly liable to be transmitted from man to man if untreated human excrement is used as manure. From all of this it is apparent that helminthic disease is more likely to be contracted in tropical areas and particularly in those in which standards of hygiene and public health are poorly developed.

See also: Anaemia; Pathogenic organisms; Prescribed diseases and occupations

1. Ankylostomiasis is a prescribed disease for those occupied in mining.
2. The filarial worms, which are transmitted to man by insect bites, provide examples of tissue infestation by adult forms. Several varieties cause elephantiasis whilst one, *Onchocerca volvulus*, is a cause of intractable blindness in many parts of the tropical world.

Hepatitis

Hepatitis implies infection of the liver. For present purposes, discussion is limited to viral infection which is of three main varieties depending upon the precise infecting organism. Hepatitis A, commonly known as infective hepatitis, is spread by ingestion through faecal transmission. It is thus very common in institutions — particularly those in which the inhabitants are unable to maintain a high standard of hygiene. Sufferers may feel unwell and depressed — hence, 'looking on life with a jaundiced eye' but nearly all recover within a few months without sequelae. Hepatitis B, or serum hepatitis, spreads from blood or blood products to blood; it requires either to be injected or to be applied to open breaches in the skin. The disease has a definite mortality and may cause chronic liver damge, including a predisposition to cancerous growth; of major importance is that up to 10 per cent of persons affected become asymptomatic carriers of the virus. The carrier state may also follow from subclinical attacks. Patients who are subject to many injections are prone to the disease and to the carrier state — particularly if the conditions are less than ideal. Thus, drug addicts, haemophiliacs and the like are particularly at risk; increased susceptibility to hepatitis B is also part of the abnormality of Down's syndrome. The third variant of the disease is known as hepatitis non-A, non-B; it is diagnosed by exclusion of the other recognisable types and may have an origin and a clinical course similar to either.

Hepatitis B is by far the most important from the medico-legal aspect. Those in frequent contact with blood (e.g. pathologists, laboratory workers, postmortem room attendants, etc.) are at special risk and the disease is prescribed as an industrial disease for those in contact with human blood or blood products[1]. The disease is not uncommon — just under 1,000 cases were reported in 1979 in the UK[2]. The introduction of a carrier into a highly blood orientated organisation such as a haemodialysis unit could be catastrophic. Hepatitis B may be transmitted in a blood transfusion or infusion of blood products. It would almost certainly be negligent so to treat a patient without screening for or sterilising against the virus. Very many cases arose in the Second World War following the use of unscreened pooled blood plasma.

See also: Blood transfusion; Down's syndrome; Drug addiction; Haemophilia; Industrial injury; Prescribed diseases and occupations

1. Under the Social Security Act 1975, s.76(2). Hepatitis A and non-A, non-B are also prescribed by virtue of contact with a source of viral hepatitis.
2. Lowe CR (chairman) *Viral Hepatitis* Report of the Industrial Injuries Advisory Council (Cmnd 9147) (1984) HMSO, London.

Hermaphroditism

Hermaphroditism is a very rare condition in which a person possesses gonads of both sexes. Similarly, the chromosomal structure may be mixed. Either sex, but generally the female sex, may predominate as to the genitalia — and, hence, gender or awareness of sex — and this may be enhanced by surgical or endocrine suppression of the minor sex traits. Occasionally, the ambivalence is such that a conscious choice has to be made as to gender, and extensive surgery may then be necessary.

The assignation of sex for purposes such as marriage may then pose problems which are wellnigh insoluble on existing legal criteria. The only apposite decision was made on grounds of false identification rather than of false sex[1]; there are good grounds for suggesting, in the light of such evasion, that these cases should be decided by genital and social factors[2].

See also: Gender; Sex

1. In the marriage of C and D (falsely called C) (1979) 53 ALJ 659.
2. Finlay HA 'Sexual identity and the law of nullity' (1980) 54 ALJ 115.

Hijacking

Hijacking of aircraft is a criminal offence by virtue of the Aviation Security Act 1982, s.1. This ratifies the Convention for the Suppression of Unlawful Seizure of Aircraft[1]. The offence consists of unlawfully seizing or taking control of aircraft in flight; the nationality of the hijacker, the State in which the aircraft is registered and whether or not the aircraft is in the UK are generally immaterial. However, if the aircraft took off from and was intended to land in the State of registration, the perpetrator must be a British subject or the act must take place in the UK or involve a British registered aircraft for the crime to be constituted. 'In flight' includes taxiing to take-off and to the arrival ramp. Violence against the crew while in the process of hijacking constitutes the same offence as it would do if it were done in the UK. Special offences are retained of endangering the safety of an aircraft (s.2) and carrying dangerous articles (i.e. those designed or adapted to cause injury or incapacity) on an aircraft (s.4).

Heavy responsibility rests on the pathologist to demonstrate or eliminate hijacking as a cause of a fatal aircraft accident, and this may be a very difficult task owing to the various possibilities which may arise. One is that the hijackers may, in fact, have carried out a threat to destroy the aircraft in flight, in which case the findings will be those of an explosive decompression (see 'Decompression sickness'). Another is that the pilot may have been displaced; this would involve accurate identification and establishing an unusual pattern of injuries in the pilot. Thirdly, the possibility of the pilot or other crew having been shot must be considered and this, effectively, dictates X-ray examination of all suspicious bodies until the possibility has been ruled out on other grounds; it is to be noted that even X-rays may be difficult to interpret — a bullet is unlikely to lodge in the body and probably all that will remain is fragments of the bullet case — and these will be extremely difficult to differentiate from aircraft debris.

See also: Aircraft accidents; Bomb injuries; Decompression sickness; Patterns of injury

1. Cmnd 4577 (1971) HMSO, London.

Hippocratic Oath

A currently accepted translation of the Hippocratic Oath runs as follows[1]:

'I swear by Apollo the physician, and Aesculapius and Health, and All-heal, and all the gods and goddesses, that, according to my ability and judgement, I will keep this Oath and this stipulation:

'To reckon him who taught me this Art equally dear to me as my parents, to share my substance with him, and relieve his necessities if required; to look upon his offspring in the same footing as my own brothers, and to teach them this Art, if they shall wish to learn it, without fee or stipulation; and that by precept, lecture and every other mode of instruction, I will impart a knowledge of the Art to my own sons, and those of my teachers, and to disciples bound by a stipulation and oath according to the law of medicine, but to none other. I will follow that system of regimen which, according to my ability and judgement, I consider for the benefit of my patients, and abstain from whatever is deleterious and mischievous. I will give no deadly medicine to anyone if asked, nor suggest any such counsel; and in like manner I will not give to a woman a pessary to produce abortion. With purity and with holiness I will pass my life and practise my Art. I will not cut persons labouring under the stone, but will leave this to be done by men who are practitioners of this work. Into whatever houses I enter, I will go into them for the benefit of the sick, and will abstain from every voluntary act of mischief and corruption; and, further, from the seduction of females, or males, of freemen or slaves. Whatever, in connection with my professional practice, or not in connection with it, I see or hear, in the life of men, which ought not to be spoken of abroad, I will not divulge, as reckoning that all such should be kept secret. While I continue to keep this Oath unviolated, may it be granted to me to enjoy life and the practice of the Art, respected by all men, in all times. But should I trespass and violate this Oath, may the reverse be my lot.'

The Oath, while probably not truly attributable to Hippocrates, was certainly introduced at a time when medicine was being organised into a scholarly framework; for this reason, it contains a great deal of what can be described as medical etiquette — or intraprofession relationships. It had little influence on the practice of medicine until it was reintroduced into the early university medical schools where those elements referring to the ethical practice of medicine were given increasing prominence. Reiteration of the Oath at graduation is now rarely required but it has survived as a statement of ideals to be preserved in the doctor/patient relationship in those traditional universities in which a form of oath taking is maintained.

Most non-medical persons would suppose that the Hippocratic Oath remains the current expression of good medical ethics but its language is archaic and this was one reason for its partial replacement by the Declaration of Geneva, which was amended at Sydney in 1968.

It will also be seen that the Oath is a prime example of the need for modification of generalised declarations of intent to meet individual national requirements and the change of moral standards which arises with time. Thus, many would hold that the obligation to abstain from anything which is deleterious and mischievous has been eroded by the increasing use of humans for the purpose of medical experimentation (*see* 'Biomedical experimentation'). The specific prohibition of abortion is now of historical interest only and the extension in the Declaration of Geneva that the doctor 'will maintain the utmost respect for human life from the time of conception' has been vitiated not only by the Abortion Act 1967 and its successors around the world but also by the general acceptance of selective non-treatment of the newborn. The justifications for these departures are discussed under the appropriate headings, as is the general principle of the ordinary/extraordinary treatment test.

The somewhat obscure reference to cutting for stone has usually been taken as an undertaking not to dabble in a specialty for which one has no proper training but there is, in any event, no such reference in the Declaration of Geneva.

The two major obligations in the Hippocratic Oath which remain and which are strongly enforced by the disciplinary bodies controlling doctors around the world are to refrain from abusing one's privilege to enter the homes of patients and to maintain medical confidentiality. It is to be noted that even the latter is qualified in limiting the injunction to 'that which ought not to be spoken about'.

See also: Abortion Act 1967; Adultery; Biomedical experimentation; Confidentiality; Declarations; Euthanasia; General Medical Council; Neonaticide

1. This is the translation adopted in the British Medical Association *Handbook of Medical Ethics* (1984) p.69, BMA, London.

Homes

The requirement for, and the consequent increase of, homes for various types of disadvantaged persons has emphasised the need for their supervision. The relevant legislation is to be found in the Registered Homes Act 1984.

The Act considers three types of homes. The residential home is defined as one which provides residential accommodation for those in need of personal care by virtue of old age, disablement, past or present dependence of alcohol or drugs or past or present mental disorder (s.1). A nursing home is one which provides nursing care for those who are sick, injured or infirm (s.21). A mental nursing home provides treatment and accommodation for mentally disordered persons, these being defined as including persons with mental illness, psychopathy or arrested mental development (s.22) (*see* 'Mental Health Act 1983').

All such homes, whether or not they are run for profit, must be registered and the Secretary of State has wide powers to refuse a licence, to inspect the establishments and, if necessary, to revoke the licence. In particular, he may revoke the licence if it is found that the person in charge of a registered nursing home or registered mental nursing home is neither a registered medical practitioner nor a registered nurse (s.25(1)(f)).

It is to be noted that children's homes are not included in this legislation — the appropriate regulations are outlined in the Children's Homes Act 1982 which, at the time of writing, has not yet been enforced.

See also: Geriatric medicine; Mental Health Act 1983

Homicide

Homicide is the killing of another person. Only in exceptional circumstances will it be lawful, as in the case of a soldier carrying out a lawful order[1]. Since the life which is taken must be self-existent, homicide is distinct from abortion or child destruction. However, injury to the fetus *in utero* which results in the death of the child *after its birth* can amount to homicide[2].

There are four types of homicide. Of these, murder and manslaughter are prosecuted at common law; infanticide and causing death by reckless driving are statutory offences. Parenthetically, genocide — killing or harming with the intention to destroy, in whole or in part, a national, ethnical, racial or religious group[3] — includes a form of mass homicide which is, fortunately, unlikely to arise in everyday forensic practice. There is no offence of infanticide in Scotland, where child murder is a common law offence. Culpable homicide is the equivalent of manslaughter in Scots Law.

A positive act will normally be required for homicide, but there are narrowly defined circumstances in which homicide may result from an omission to act[4]; these arise where the law has imposed a positive duty to act on those who have responsibility for the welfare of others[5]. Such cases normally involve prosecutions for manslaughter but murder has occasionally been charged[6].

See also: Abortion; Child destruction; Culpable homicide; Infanticide; Manslaughter; Murder; Reckless driving

1. *HM Adv v Sheppard* 1941 JC 67. *See also* Nichols DB 'Untying the soldier by refurbishing the common law' [1976] Crim LR 181.
2. Coke Inst iii 50; *West* (1848) 2 Cox CC 500.
3. Genocide Act 1969.
4. For a full discussion, *see* Glazebrook P 'Criminal omissions: the duty requirement in offences against the person' (1960) 76 LQR 386.
5. *R v Instan* [1893] I QB 450; *R v Stone* [1977] QB 354.
6. *Gibbins and Proctor* (1918) 13 Crim App R 134.

Homosexual Offences

Homosexual acts between males which involve genital contact of any sort are criminal offences in the UK, being charged either as buggery or as gross indecency or, in Scotland, as shameless indecency. The criminal law does not extend, however, to acts of this nature which are committed in private and between consenting parties who are at least 21 years of age. This exception, which was introduced to English law by the Sexual Offences Act 1967 and into Scotland by the Criminal Justice (Scotland Act) 1980, s.80, goes some way to meeting the demands of the homosexual lobby but is still criticised as being discriminatory; it is, for example, illegal for a homosexual act to take place if it involves more than two participants. The definition of what constitutes a private place is narrow and specifically excludes a public lavatory, even if this is locked[1].

Other offences may be committed in a homosexual context. Attempts by homosexuals to make contact with other males for sexual purposes can lead to charges of soliciting under the Sexual Offences Act 1956, s.32, which provides that it is an offence 'for a man persistently to solicit or importune in a public place for immoral purposes'[2]. It was decided in *R v Ford*[3] that it can be left to the jury to decide what constitutes 'immoral purposes'; the court in that case indicated that, in its view, legal homosexual conduct (i.e. between consenting adults and in private) should be considered immoral. This approach was accepted in the later case of *R v Grey*[4]. The application of the law on homosexual soliciting has been criticised — often deservedly. It would seem that the entrapment of homosexuals by policemen in plain clothes has frequently gone beyond the bounds which might be thought necessary to protect the public against unwanted attentions.

It is not an offence to be a homosexual prostitute, although such persons may incur the risk of prosecution for soliciting. It is, however, an offence to procure the commission of homosexual acts, to live wholly or partly on the proceeds of male prostitution and to be involved in running a homosexual brothel[5].

Homosexual acts between women are not an offence unless there is no consent on the part of one participant or unless one of the participants is incapable of consenting.

See also: Buggery; Gross indecency; Indecent assault; Prostitution

1. Sexual Offences Act 1967, s.1(2)(b).
2. In Scotland, such conduct would also constitute the common law offence of shameless indecency.
3. [1978] 1 All ER 1129.
4. (1981) Times, 27 November.
5. Sexual Offences Act 1967, ss.4–6; Criminal Justice (Scotland) Act 1980, s.80 (12–13).
6. Sexual Offences Act 1956, s.14(2), (4); also, Indecency with Children Act 1960, s.1(1).

Homosexuality

Homosexuality is the state of being sexually attracted towards members of one's own sex. It is not an 'all or nothing' state; many authorities regard human sexuality as a spectrum with shades of emphasis varying between the purely heterosexual at one end and the exclusively homosexual at the other. In this entry, we are concerned with male homosexuality; female homosexuality (lesbianism) is dealt with under that heading.

There are no universally acceptable figures for the incidence of male homosexuality. The phenomenon, as with many aspects of sex, is difficult to measure and there are important cultural differences between societies. Kinsey's study, published in 1948, revealed that 37 per cent of American males had had some form of homosexual experience between adolescence and old age[1]. Later attempts to assess the incidence have come up with rather lower but widely varying estimates from 1 per cent of the population to a claim that one in ten persons is homosexual, even if not fully aware of the fact.

Homosexuality occurs in all social classes and in all societies. The homosexual may conceal the fact or he may 'come out' and make no pretence to be heterosexual. His sexual interests in other males may emerge during adolescence and may be translated at that time into sexual behaviour with other boys or, possibly, with other men[2]. Others may not become aware of their true interests until aged 20 or beyond; attraction is then frequently towards younger men, since physical appearance plays a very strong role in the homosexual psyche. The average homosexual, however, is not paedophilic and the suggestion that homosexuals as a group corrupt young boys is probably unfair. Nevertheless, there is a strong lobby within the homosexual movement for a reduction of the age of consent to homosexual practices to 16 years.

Homosexual activity takes many of the forms adopted by heterosexual lovemaking[3]. The public prejudice that homosexuals engage exclusively in anal intercourse is unfounded; the greater part of homosexual eroticism consists of fellatio or mutual masturbation[4].

From the medical point of view, certain homosexual practices are hazardous and can cause serious damage. The habit of inserting the fist into the rectum, which is not all that uncommon in certain, particularly American, homosexual quarters, hardly needs further medical comment. Sadistic homosexual practices are frequent and can result in serious injury or death. Homosexuals also tend to a form of morbid jealousy in relation to their partners. Certain communicable diseases (e.g. hepatitis and acquired immune deficiency syndrome) appear to be significantly associated with homosexual practices.

There are many theories which purport to explain the existence of homosexuality[5], ranging from the purely demographic to the more colourful psychoanalytical approach of the Freudian school[6]. The description of homosexuality as a disease has met with particular opposition. It is still described in some textbooks as a personality disorder and, indeed, appears as such in some official nosological systems; it has, however, been declassified as such in the USA[7].

Both church and state in the West have traditionally been hostile to homosexuality and, prior to 1861, buggery was a capital offence in England. The great majority of legal restrictions have now been removed so far as consenting adults are concerned. Public displays of homosexuality and the involvement of young persons are, however, still regarded seriously; offences connected with homosexuality are discussed in a separate entry. Even so, there is still a reservoir of public suspicion of and distaste for the homosexual, who may therefore find himself moving, as far as is possible, in exclusively homosexual circles[8].

The homosexual employee is theoretically afforded the same protection against unfair dismissal as is any other worker. In practice, however, the view is frequently taken that employers are entitled to take into account the susceptibilities of customers and of the public in general and that homosexuals may be disruptive or 'bad for business'[9]. Teachers and others who work with young people may be at a particular disadvantage. The fact that a schoolteacher had been convicted of gross indecency has been found sufficient grounds for his dismissal despite the absence of any evidence that he had had sexual relations with any pupils[10].

The breakdown of a marriage in which one party is homosexual may pose challenging problems for the courts. There is no evidence that the children of homosexual parents are psychologically disadvantaged, yet it is highly unlikely that courts will grant custody of a child to a homosexual parent[11].

Psychiatrists and clinical psychologists may be prepared to help the homosexual who is unhappy with his state or who is in difficulty with the criminal law. Such help may take the form of attempts to incorporate a heterosexual element in the patient's sexual fantasies and this may go hand in hand with efforts to establish heterosexual relationships[12]. Aversion therapy is sometimes used but there are ethical factors which must be taken into consideration[13].

See also: Acquired immune deficiency syndrome; Buggery; Fellatio; Hepatitis; Homosexual offences; Lesbianism; Paedophilia

1. Kinsey AC, Pomeroy WB and Martin CE *Sexual Behavior in the Human Male* (1948) WB Saunders, Philadelphia PA.
2. Humphreys L *Tearoom Trade* (1970) Aldine, Chicago.
3. Masters WH and Johnson VE *Homosexuality in Perspective* (1982) Little, Brown, Boston MA
4. Bell AP and Weinberg MS *Homosexualities* (1978) S & S, Greenville NC.
5. For a survey, *see* West DJ *Homosexuality Re-examined* (1977) University of Minnesota Press, Minneapolis MI.
6. Bieber I et al. *Homosexuality: A Psychoanalytic Study of Male Homosexuals* (1962).
7. Bayer R *Homosexuality and American Psychiatry* (1981) Basic, New York.
8. Tripp CA *The Homosexual Matrix* (1977) McGraw-Hill, New York.
9. *Saunders v Scottish National Camps Association Ltd.* [1980] IRLR 174; [1981] IRLR 277. But for a contrary decision, *see Bell v The Devon and Cornwall Police Authority* [1978] IRLR 283. For further cases, *see* Crane P *Gays and the Law* (1983) Pluto, London.
10. *Nottinghamshire CC v Bowly* [1978] IRLR 252.
11. For an indication of the attitude, *see Re D (an infant)* [1977] 2 WLR 79.
12. Bancroft J *Human Sexuality and Its Problems* (1983) p.159 et seq, Churchill Livingstone, Edinburgh.
13. Bloch S and Chodoff P *Psychiatric Ethics* (1981) p.174, Oxford University Press, Oxford.

Hormones

Hormones are secreted into the blood by the endocrine system. They act on specific target cells, the function of which is thereby stimulated; for example, the gonadotropic hormone stimulates the ovarian follicles to mature. Overproduction or absence of hormones results in disease or dysfunction of the target organs. The secretion of hormones is controlled, in turn, by the level of the target cell product in the blood; the whole system is subject to a type of feedback control which serves to maintain a biochemical equilibrium.

See also: Castration; Endocrine system

Hospices

The term 'hospice' is now reserved for institutions which cater particularly for the care of the dying. The movement has undoubtedly been accelerated by the inevitable concentration of fiscal aid on medical resources which favour those who have an economic potential if restored to health; the cynic might observe that the dying are even less valuable as voters than are geriatric patients. There have been many, however, who have independently appreciated the difficulties involved in a painful and long drawn-out death at home and have seen the need for their alleviation in some form of structured care which, if residential, is free, on the one hand, from the atmosphere of the 'workhouse' and, on the other, from the extortionist.

Nevertheless, very many families do care for their elderly relatives to whom withdrawal of family association may be the ultimate disappointment in their last weeks. Accordingly, it is a feature of the modern hospice movement to attempt to treat death as a family concern[1]; the emphasis is not based on the notion of long-stay capacity but rather on rehabilitation of the terminally ill so that they may return home for all but the final few days of life. The concept of hospice care may also be extendable to such groups as untreatable neonates[2].

It is central to such an achievement that the treatment of pain is refined and this, whilst being backed by occupational, religious and similar means of support, is, perhaps, the main focus of expertise in hospices. Essentially, the hospices offer an alternative approach to an easy terminal illness to that which is advocated by pro-euthanasia organisations. It has, indeed, been suggested that the need to invoke the doctrine of double effect in the treatment of terminal pain is virtually eliminated by the expert application of modern hospice care[3]. Hospice beds will not be, and probably should not be, available for every dying patient, and a major concern of hospice workers is to teach modern principles of terminal care to primary care physicians who will be in charge of such patients in their own homes; many undergraduate curricula in the UK do, now, include periods of hospice tuition.

The common factor among hospices rests in their clinical approach to terminal illness and death; their physical constitution is, however, very diverse and it is even possible for a 'hospice' to function on a home visiting basis. Separate buildings are probably ideal but it has been stressed in the UK that the intake should not be limited to cancer patients. A number of hospices in Britain are closely associated with the National Health Service but the majority are operated on a voluntary basis; it is a general feature, however, that hospice care is provided independently of payment.

See also: Double effect; Euthanasia; Terminal illness

1. *See* a resumé by the leader of the British hospice movement: Saunders C 'Hospices' in Duncan AS et al (eds) *Dictionary of Medical Ethics* (1981) p.218, Darton, Longman and Todd, London.
2. Silverman WA 'A hospice setting for human neonatal death' (1982) 69 Pediatrics 239.
3. Twycross RG 'Euthanasia — a physician's viewpoint' (1982) 8 J Med Ethics 86.

Hospital Orders

A criminal offender who is found to be mentally disordered and who is guilty of a crime other than one for which there is a fixed penalty (e.g. murder) may be regarded as being more suitable for treatment than for punishment. To this end, a court which could pass a custodial sentence may, instead, make a hospital order (Mental Health Act 1983, s.37)[1].

Two doctors, one approved for the purpose, must agree and must certify that the offender is suffering from mental illness, psychopathic disorder, severe mental impairment or mental impairment. The disorder must be one for which a period in hospital for treatment is appropriate and, in the case of psychopathic disorder or mental impairment, the treatment must be likely to alleviate or prevent a deterioration of the condition (s.37(2)(a)(i)). The diagnosis must therefore be specific, and the Act excludes sexual deviation as a reason for hospitalisation (s.1(3)).

The court's hands are, to an extent, tied. A hospital bed must be available within 28 days and the hospital may resist acceptance of the patient; whilst the court must be concerned for the public safety[2], the hospital may discharge the patient at any time on medical grounds. In any event, the patient, irrespective of the diagnosis, must still be treatable if he is to be detained in hospital for longer than six months and, if he escapes, he has only to remain at large for 28 days to achieve a statutory discharge; there is often something of a conflict between the medical profession and the courts in the operation of hospital orders which are, in fact, being made less frequently than was once the case. The patient who is the subject of a hospital order has most of the rights of a patient who is compulsorily detained for any reason but he may not apply to a tribunal within the first six months of the order taking effect.

The court also has powers, once a person is convicted, to make an interim hospital order when there is evidence from two doctors, one of whom is appointed for the purpose and one of whom is on the staff of the designated hospital, that the offender is suffering from a mental disorder for which a hospital order would be appropriate. The hospital has less autonomy in the case of an interim order; it must obey the terms of the order (s.40) and cannot discharge the patient without leave of the court. The order can be made for up to 12 weeks and is then renewable at 28-day intervals up to a maximum of six months (s.38). The court may then use any of its options — from making a hospital order, through making a probation order, to actually punishing the offender if the results of the interim order indicate that he was not suffering from a treatable condition.

See also: Compulsory medical treatment; Mental impairment; Mental patients' rights; Psychopathy

1. Magistrates may make a hospital order on a mentally ill or severely impaired defendant without a conviction, giving them an alternative to accepting a plea of insanity which they are not allowed to do. For full discussion, *see* Hoggett BM *Mental Health Law* (2nd ed, 1984) p.166 et seq, Sweet & Maxwell, London.
2. *R v Higginbotham* [1961] 1 WLR 1277.

Human Experimentation

Experimentation or research using humans can be justified on two main grounds. Human beings are not simply intelligent animals; they have a very specific physiology and the ultimate test of any treatment designed for humans is whether it is effective in humans. A more abstract justification rests on the need to conserve scarce resources; there is, nowadays, no justification for introducing new techniques or expensive drugs in the absence of proper evaluation[1].

Human experimentation covers the whole range of human existence from the embryo through the fetus and child to the adult. Each age carries its own practical and ethical dilemmas; the subject is, accordingly, discussed under the specific headings given in the cross-references.

See also: Biomedical experimentation; Child experimentation; Embryonic experimentation; Fetal experimentation

1. Hampton JR 'The end of clinical freedom' (1983) 287 Br Med J 1237.

Human Tissue Act 1961

The Human Tissue Act 1961 governs the use of parts of bodies of deceased persons; such use may be for therapeutic purposes (ie. transplantation of organs), educational (which includes the retention of specimens for museum purposes) or for research.

Section 1(1) of the Act allows the person lawfully in possession of the body after death to authorise removal of any part or any specified part of the body when the deceased has requested, either in writing at any time or orally in the presence of two or more witnesses during his last illness, that such parts of his body be used for these purposes after his death; the donor thus effectively 'contracts in' to the scheme. Under s.1(2), the person lawfully in possession of the body of a deceased person may authorise the removal of tissues if, having made such reasonable enquiry as may be practicable, he has no reason to believe that the deceased had expressed an objection to his body being so dealt with or that the surviving spouse or any surviving relative of the deceased objects; in these circumstances, the relatives of the deceased are empowered to 'contract out' of the scheme.

There has, in the past, been considerable debate as to who is the person lawfully in possession of the body[1]. Despite the absence of any specific case authority[2], it is now accepted that it is the hospital or institutional authority in whose care the body lies which is in lawful possession[3]. This can be inferred as a general rule from s.1(7) which allows for delegation of power by the person having control of the institution and by s.1(6) which specifically excludes funeral directors as being in possession for the purposes of the Act. The decision is of practical importance. If the relatives, who are undoubtedly entitled to possession, were, in fact, in lawful possession they could, if so minded, even obstruct the deceased's requests under s.1(1) as the power to act is permissive, not obligatory.

The coroner, or procurator fiscal, whilst not being in legal possession, has an absolute right to possession in cases which have been referred to him[4] and, in such circumstances, no authority can be given for removal of tissues except with the consent of the coroner or procurator fiscal (ss.1(5) and 1(9)). Many medico legal authorities will allow the removal of only such parts of the body as are specified by them; it is, however, important to remember that a coroner cannot authorise removal of tissue except in so far as is necessary for his investigations — he can only veto authorisations under s.1(1) or s.1(2).

Although it has been suggested that the restrictive provisions of the Act are a deliberate attempt to give protection to relatives, its main purpose is clearly to make therapeutic parts available and it follows that 'such reasonable enquiry as may be practicable' to disclose objections from relatives should be interpreted with regard to that end. It must be unreasonable to prolong enquiries until the organs are useless through anoxia and, in practice, it is customary to ask the opinion of those close relatives who, in modern conditions, are almost always available for interview during an unsuccessful period in intensive care. It must, on the other hand, be admitted that the availability of ventilator support lessens the urgency of the time factor; moreover, the nature of the request must be taken into consideration — there is no urgency in and there may well be very much wider objection to, say, removing tissue for preservation as a museum exhibit as compared with providing a life-saving organ.

There is further difficulty in deciding what, if any, offence is committed in disregarding the terms of the 1961 Act[5]. It is difficult to see what criminal offence could be committed apart from interfering with cases under investigation by the coroner or procurator fiscal; it does seem possible, however, that a civil action by relatives based on the infliction of nervous shock might succeed.

The Act lays down that removal of tissue can be done only by a fully registered medical practitioner who must have satisfied himself by personal examination of the body that life is extinct (s.1(4)). It also stipulates that a postmortem examination directed to establishing the cause of death or to investigating abnormal conditions must also be carried out by or in accordance with the instructions of a registered medical practitioner; the various subsections relating to consent or objection also apply to this academic type of investigation.

The Human Tissue Act 1961 has been criticised severely in that it is unduly restrictive and militates against the provision of badly needed organs; it has been noted also that it deters because of the onerous duties placed on doctors who will have no part in the later life-saving procedure of transplantation. As a result, a movement is very much alive to amend the law to a full 'contracting out' situation in which organs may be removed provided the deceased has not positively voiced objections during life. Similar legislation has been introduced, for example, in France[6]; at least five attempts to introduce such Bills in the UK Parliament have, however, failed.

An equally serious effect of the Act is on research, particularly on research into trauma and on the provision of controls for research into fatal disease — such controls being generally available only from persons killed accidentally. Nearly all such deaths will lie within the jurisdiction of the coroner or procurator fiscal, and the ambience of the medico-legal investigation makes it almost impossible to comply with the Act when cadaver tissues are needed for these purposes. There is, again, no evidence that the situation will be altered.

See also: Anatomy Act 1984; Autopsy; Coroner; Procurator fiscal; Transplantation of organs

1. See Skegg PDG 'The interpretation of the Human Tissue Act 1961' (1976) 16 Med Sci Law 193 for an exposition of the arguments.
2. R v Feist (1858) Dears & B 590 is often quoted but can hardly be applicable to modern conditions.
3. NHS Circular 1975 (Gen) 34, May 1975, DHSS, London.
4. R v Bristol Coroner, ex p Kerr [1974] QB 652.
5. For discussion, see Skegg PDG 'Liability for the unauthorized removal of cadaveric transplant material' (1974) 14 Med Sci Law 53, and Kennedy IM 'Further thoughts on liability for non-observance of the Human Tissue Act 1961' (1976) 16 Med Sci Law 49.
6. Farfor JA 'Organs for transplant; courageous legislation' [1977] 1 Br Med J 497.

Hunger Strike

The hunger strike is seldom other than a method of political protest. The medico-legal implications are discussed under 'Forced feeding'.

Hydrostatic Test

The hydrostatic test is used to distinguish stillbirth from death following a separate existence. It depends on the fact that aerated lungs will float in water but, in the difficult circumstances generally pertaining, the lungs will not be aerated uniformly. The test is therefore classically carried out by first placing the whole infant lung in water; if this sinks, individual lobes are tested for flotation and, if necessary, small pieces of lobes are then tested individually.

The test is of forensic antiquity and has been subject to severe criticism largely on the grounds that putrefied lungs will float due to the action of gas-forming organisms; this is certainly true and most observers would agree that evidence of a brief period of separate existence sufficient to satisfy the burden of proof required in cases of infanticide is impossible in the presence of significant *post mortem* changes. Other objections to the scientific accuracy of the test operate generally in favour of the mother, and we suggest that the test is of more value than is commonly stated provided that is it interpreted with reason. Inflation of the stillborn lung by artifical respiration is difficult to achieve but it has to be admitted that areas of aeration can be attained by mouth to mouth resuscitation; this is, perhaps, the most complex area of interpretation. Certainly, there can be no doubt that expert microscopy of the lungs is a far better test of a separate existence than is the hydrostatic test, although, even then, there are difficulties[1].

See also: Infanticide; Separate existence; Stillbirth

1. Osborn GR 'Pathology of the lung in stillbirth and in neonatal death' in Simpson K (ed) *Modern Trends in Forensic Medicine* (1953) Chap.2 (Butterworths, London) is a very valuable review. For an iconoclastic view *see* Knight B *The Coroner's Autopsy* (1983) p.127, Churchill Livingstone, Edinburgh.

Hymen

The hymen is a fibrous layer which separates the vulva from the vaginal cavity. Normally, it is perforated centrally with an opening sufficient to allow menstrual fluids and other secretions to escape. At the same time, it is generally inadequate to admit the erect male organ and is ruptured or lacerated on first coitus. Coital laceration is usually to be found posteriorly in the 4 or 8 o'clock position.

Much importance is attached to the hymen in descriptions of the findings in rape but bleeding lacerations are, in fact, the exception rather than the rule. Many women who are raped are married or are non-virginal, some hymens are naturally lax and others have been penetrated as a result of masturbation or the use of tampons. Defloration has always been considered the ultimate offence in rape and its comparative rarity as a result of the offence these days is an additional reason why the definition of rape deserves reconsideration.

See also: Rape; Sexual intercourse

Hyoid Bone

The hyoid bone is the uppermost of three major components of the skeleton of the larynx. It is attached by ligaments to the thyroid cartilage below and by ligaments and muscles to the floor of the mouth above. It is shaped in the form of a boomerang with the distal end (greater horns) being palpable below the angle of the jaw on each side.

As part of the process of ageing, the hyoid becomes calcified and the joints between the horns and the central body of the bone become fused. Thus, pressure on the horns, as may occur in manual strangulation, is likely to result in fracture — particularly in the aged subject. In fact, the importance attributed to the hyoid bone in the diagnosis of throttling is somewhat exaggerated, the most common injury to result from this trauma being to the upper cornua of the thyroid cartilage. But, since these are attached to the hyoid by strong ligaments, the latter is often injured at the same time as a result of distraction.

The hyoid bone can be damaged during a poorly performed autopsy and, in general, it is necessary to demonstrate *ante mortem* haemorrhage before attributing a hyoid fracture to throttling. Fracture of the hyoid is surprisingly uncommon in cases of strangulation by ligature; the ligature generally passes across the thyrohyoid ligament during this process.

See also: Larynx; Strangulation; Throttling

Hypertensive Disease

Hypertension is the medical term for high blood pressure. The disease is very prevalent in late middle age and is of medico-legal importance in that it is a potent underlying cause of sudden natural death; short of this, it can promote serious disability in the form of 'stroke'.

Hypertension may arise without obvious cause ('essential hypertension') or it may be secondary to kidney disease. The disease of the kidney which is responsible may be that known as glomerulonephritis; this is associated with streptococcal infection and is of no forensic importance. Alternatively, it may be due to chronic pyelonephritis; this is due to infection which often ascends from the urethra and bladder. Any injury which leads to urinary retention or to the need for repeated instrumentation (e.g. injury to the spinal cord or to the pelvis itself) predisposes to infection in the bladder and, possibly, ascending infection of the kidney. The result of such an injury may therefore become evident only years later when hypertension becomes apparent.

High blood pressure has two major effects of forensic importance. Firstly, the heart has to work harder to maintain the flow of blood and therefore hypertrophies (grows in bulk); the condition of hypertrophic cardiomyopathy is then established and such hearts are susceptible to sudden failure, presumably due to relative coronary insufficiency. Secondly, the arteriolar/capillary junction is placed under excessive strain and may give way, with consequent haemorrhage. Whilst this might cause morbidity at any site, it is most dangerous when it occurs in the brain; large areas of cerebral tissue may be disrupted and, by virtue of occupying space, the haemorrhage may be fatal in itself. Recovery will be accompanied by disability of varying degree and the elderly patient so affected constitutes a major socio-medical problem (*see* 'Geriatric medicine').

The correlation between hypertension and sudden death or disability is such that the disease ought to be eliminated from high risk occupations — particularly those which closely involve the public such as airline pilots. The conflict between public safety and unfair or unnecessary dismissal may then become acute.

See also: Cardiomyopathy; Coronary disease; Geriatric medicine; Intracerebral haemorrhage; Kidney failure

Hyperthermia

A rise above the normal body temperature is characteristic of endogenous overproduction of heat as occurs in many acute infections. The fact that the temperature does not also rise excessively during muscular exercise is attributable to the remarkable human compensatory mechanism of sweating, heat being conducted to the outside by evaporation; hyperthermia will therefore occur when there is failure of the sweat glands as may occur in chronic heat exhaustion (*see* 'Heat effects'). The same mechanism protects against the effects of environmental heat, and any condition which inhibits the evaporation of sweat may lead to hyperthermia — such conditions would include a high relative humidity, the absence of air currents or excess clothing; there is, indeed, some belief that a proportion of 'cot deaths' (*see* 'Sudden infant death syndrome') may be occult cases of hyperthermia.

It is difficult to dissociate the biochemical effects of sweating from those of heat itself but, in general, the adverse effect of a rise in body temperature *per se* is on the respiratory centre of the brain; such a pure effect is seen only in heat stroke (*see* 'Heat effects'). Conversely, hyperthermia may result from primary interference with the heat-regulating centre in the brain, a mechanism which probably accounts for the rise in body temperature in fat embolism and in some instances of cerebral hypoxia, including unusual conditions such as postdecompression shock.

Some brains are particularly sensitive to hypoxia which is induced by anaesthetics. The condition of malignant hyperpyrexia (an uncontrolled rise in body temperature which may be fatal) is an occasional complication of anaesthesia and appears to be genetically controlled. Failure to have sought a family history in such an event would be likely to be regarded as having been negligent.

See also: Asphyxia; Decompression sickness; Fat embolism; Genetic disease; Heat effects; Sudden infant death syndrome

Hypnosis

Hypnosis and the claims of its practitioners attract considerable controversy. Supporters of the procedure claim that the hypnotised subject enters a state of altered consciousness (the 'hypnotic trance') and that, while in this state, the subject is capable of performing in a way which is normally impossible. The hypnotised person may recall matters which were not recollected when awake; he may be 'regressed' in order to re-enact experiences of the past; he may even perform physical feats which would normally be beyond him[1].

The critics of hypnosis argue that there is nothing extraordinary in the hypnotised state[2]. No physiological evidence exists to differentiate the hypnotised from the waking state and EEG tracings from subjects under hypnosis have been found to be the same as from those who are awake[3]. Anecdotal evidence may exist of improved recall of events under hypnosis but it is argued that the phenomenon is consistent with other explanations and is not confined to hypnosis as a form of relaxant strategy.

Hypnotism is taken seriously by police forces and others concerned with criminal justice despite this atmosphere of caution[4]. It is most frequently used with a view to improving witnesses' recollection of events; the question then arises as to the admissibility of statements thus obtained.

No UK court has yet ruled on this point but it is likely that such statements would be considered inadmissible. If the witness can recall in court the events in question, then anything said under hypnosis would merely be a previously consistent statement and, accordingly, irrelevant[5]. In default of recollection in court, statements made under hypnosis and recounted to the court could be excluded by the hearsay rule.

The use of hypnosis in an attempt to establish the truthfulness of a witness (or of an accused) would be unlikely to be approved by courts in the UK. There has been an unwillingness to allow any expert evidence from psychiatrists as to the likely behaviour of accused persons on the grounds that this is an attempted usurpation of the function of the court as a trier of fact[6]. Both 'truth drug' and polygraph evidence have been rejected by Scottish and Canadian courts on similar grounds[7]. The evidence of a hypnotist as to the statements of an accused person or other witness made under hypnotism would probably also be considered inadmissible.

Although it raises no special legal issues, caution should be adopted in applying hypnosis to witnesses who are unlikely to be called to court. In the event of their evidence actually being required, the evident susceptibility and ready compliance of a hypnotic subject might well detract from the acceptibility of the evidence.

Hypnotism is also used as a theatrical spectacle and is controlled by the Hypnotism Act 1952, which, among other things, provides that a person below the age of 21 must not be used as a demonstration subject.

See also: Hearsay rule; Polygraph

1. Haward L and Ashworth A 'Some problems of evidence obtained by hypnosis' [1980] Crim LR 469. Compare Wagstaff G 'Hypnosis and the law: a critical review of some recent proposals' [1983] Crim LR 151.
2. Barber T *Hypnosis: A Scientific Approach* (1969) Van Nostrand Reinhold, New York and London; Wagstaff G 'Recall of witnesses under hypnosis' (1982) 22 J Forens Sci Soc 33.
3. Barber T, Spanos N and Chaves J *Hypnotism: Imagination and Potentialities* (1974) Pergamon, New York.

4. Kleinhauz M, Horowitz I and Tobin, T. 'The use of hypnosis in police investigation, a preliminary communication' (1977) 17 J Forens Sci Soc 77.

5. Cross R *Evidence* (6th ed, 1985) p.269, Butterworths, London; cf. Haward and Ashworth, n.1 above at p.478.

6. *R v Turner* [1975] QB 834. *See* Manning M and Mewett A 'Psychiatric evidence' [1976] Crim LQ 325.

7. *Meehan v HM Adv* 1970 JC 11 (truth drug); *Phillion v R* (1977) 74 DLR (3d) 136 (polygraph).

Hypoglycaemia

Hypoglycaemia is a deficiency of glucose in the circulating blood. Glucose being essential to the enzymatic cellular metabolism, the result will be an adverse effect at cellular level and this will present most prominently by virtue of the effect in the brain cells.

A mild degree of hypoglycaemia may result from inadequate intake of carbohydrate but, in normal circumstances, the stores of glycogen in the liver are able to make up for this with little delay. Transient nutritional hypoglycaemia is therefore unlikely to cause vehicular accidents *per se* but a synergistic effect of mental inertia combined with, say, fatigue, small amounts of alcohol, etc., may be a more important fact than is generally recognised. Acute hypoglycaemic attacks may, however, be precipitated in sensitive persons by ingestion of water and the condition may closely simulate acute alcoholism; this phenomenon was commonly suggested in the defence of drivers before the introduction of definitive laboratory tests in the Road Traffic Act 1972. Acute hypoglycaemia may also underlie those sudden deaths in which the only significant finding at autopsy is a severely fatty liver — a situation which occurs from unknown cause in infancy and which is commonly associated with a metabolic cause in adults; it is presumed that there are insufficient reserves of liver glycogen to respond to a crisis situation.

The most important cause of hypoglycaemia in legal medicine, however, is hyperinsulinism (*see* 'Insulin') which arises most often in the treatment of diabetes; it has particular significance in relation to the defence of automatism in criminal law.

Unfortunately, glucose in the blood is destroyed very rapidly after death and postmortem blood glucose estimations which disclose a low level are virtually useless in the investigation of unexplained natural or accidental deaths; better results are likely to be obtained from examining either the cerebrospinal fluid or the vitreous humour of the eye but, even then, the results must be interpreted with great caution[1].

See also: Alcohol; Automatism; Diabetes; Insulin; Liver disease and injury; Vitreous humour

1. But see the more useful results in the opposite condition — hyperglycaemia causing diabetic coma —.obtained by Gormsen H and Lund A 'The diagnostic value of postmortem blood glucose determinations in cases of diabetes mellitus' (1985) 28 Forens Sci Int 103.

Hypostasis

Hypostasis (*post mortem* lividity) is the result of sedimenting of the blood in a cadaver due to gravity. It commences as soon as the circulation ceases but a visible result — that is, the differentiation of the relatively bloodless, pale upper part of the body from the engorged lower portions — is seldom apparent before some 30–60 minutes after death; nevertheless, it is a comparatively early sign of death which is particularly useful if the conditions are such that the diagnosis of death is difficult (e.g. in hypothermia or drug-induced coma).

The visualisation of hypostasis is so capricious that it is relatively useless as a means of estimating the time after death. Its major importance is in indicating the position of the body after death. The appearances are enhanced by the fact that blood cannot gravitate into vessels which are closed due to pressure; the contrast between the pale pressure points and the engorged skin which, due, say, to body flexures, is not pressurised often provides a very accurate picture. The main practical difficulty occurs when the body is discovered face down; the problem then is to distinguish hypostasis from *ante mortem* pressure on the face in the presence of generalised congestion, as may occur in asphyxia due to suffocation. Hypostatic blood becomes increasingly difficult to move after a time and the tissues may become stained with haemoglobin; thus, a body which has been moved a few hours after death will almost always show some evidence of its original position, an observation which may be of considerable forensic significance. When the blood is concentrated by gravity into a relatively small volume of the body, as will occur in suspension by either extremity, the pressure may be so great as to burst the small blood vessels and lead to formation of petechial or even larger haemorrhages.

Hypostasis will reflect the colour of the blood at the time of death and will normally be of a dusky hue due to deoxygenation of the blood; this is part of the process of death and the colour of the blood can rarely indicate mechanical asphyxia as a specific cause. Cold inhibits oxygen dissociation, and the hypostasis in bodies lying in the cold (including those intentionally refrigerated) will be characteristically bright pink; cyanide, which inhibits enzymatic activity, gives a similar appearance. Some forms of industrial poisoning and poisoning by carbon monoxide are readily distinguishable from the appearance of the hypostasis.

See also: Asphyxia; Carbon monoxide poisoning; Changes after death; Coma; Cyanide; Industrial poisoning; Petechial haemorrhage; Timing of death

Hypothermia

In contrast to his resistance to environmental heat, man is able to adapt to the cold only poorly and does this mainly by increasing his protective clothing; specially ducted suits are essential in certain environments (e.g. in diving or in space operations). In the absence of such protection, death from hypothermia is probable in very cold conditions and is more rapid than is generally supposed.

There are two distinct types of hypothermic death which are of medico-legal significance — those occurring in elderly persons in conditions of deprivation and accidental deaths affecting the healthy adult or child exposed to a hostile environment, often the sea. Some rather inconstant pathology is to be expected in the former group; apart from the very general signs of malnutrition and, perhaps, personal neglgect, haemorrhages into the small bowel have been described, as has aseptic inflammation of the pancreas. These lesions may be associated with the formation of microthrombi (*see* 'Thrombosis') but it is not impossible that they are part of the pathology of hypothermia *and* subnutrition because they are found very infrequently in the second category in which death is essentially physiological.

Heat is generated, and lost, by exercise. A clothed man at rest is unlikely to be fully protected from the cold at temperatures below 0°C and will almost certainly die if left in an ambient temperature of −20°C[1]. Inadequate protection of the body against cold is provided by shivering but this mechanism fails when the body temperature falls to 33°C. All that is then left is a shift of the blood volume from the periphery to the deep core in order to limit heat loss through radiation; this causes profound physiological disturbance and the body may be unable to adapt — death is due to ventricular fibrillation which can be diagnosed at autopsy only by a process of exclusion. The shift of blood to the core may well cause a central sensation of heat as a surprising number of persons who have died from the cold are found to have removed their clothes. Mental disturbance is, however, a general prodromal symptom of hypothermic death — it is sad to think that Captain Oates' death in Antarctica may not have been a heroic sacrifice. The effect of alcohol is to accelerate death from hypothermia, possibly because its peripheral vasodilatory effect operates against the protective shift of blood volume.

The cooling body requires progressively less oxygen to maintain tissue integrity; the deeply hypothermic person may closely simulate one who is dead and this is particularly true if the condition is combined with drug overdose (*see also* 'Suspended animation'). It is to be noted that rewarming is the correct treatment of clinical hypothermia. This is of particular importance in the case of bodies removed from cold water; treatment by artifical repsiration following a mistaken diagnosis of near drowning may well provoke fibrillation in an already hypersensitive heart.

See also: Diving hazards; Drug overdose; Suspended animation; Thrombosis; Ventricular fibrillation

1. Hervey GR 'Physiological changes in hypothermia' (1973) 66 Proc R Soc Med 1053; Keatinge WR 'Hypothermia at sea' (1984) 24 Med Sci Law 160.

Hypovolaemia

Hypovolaemia means reduction of the circulating blood volume. This has profound physiological effects which can be summed up as being due to inadequate perfusion of the tissues with oxygen; hypovolaemia is therefore a potent cause of surgical shock.

The normal volume of the circulating blood is of the order of 5 litres; symptoms of hypovolaemia are likely to occur if more than 1.5 litres (30 per cent) of fluid are lost, although much depends upon the rate with which this occurs. Such a situation can arise from simple haemorrhage in which both plasma and red cells will be lost; fractures may result in severe haemorrhage which is often not evident on clinical examination. In many circumstances, however, the volume loss relates only to the fluid component of the blood; this classically follows burning but severe fluid loss may result from crushing of the tissues whilst severe diarrhoea and vomiting may provoke the same result — cholera presents as one of the most marked examples of hypovolaemia.

Treatment of hypovolaemia is urgent but is seldom simple as the various constituents of the blood may be lost unequally. Large quantities of blood, plasma substitutes and/or electrolyte solutions may be required, the nature of the need being established by careful monitoring.

See also: Burns; Crush injury; Haemorrhage; Surgical shock

Hypoxia

Hypoxia is the condition of the body when it is supplied with insufficient oxygen for its needs. Those conditions in which a normal atmosphere is prevented from oxygenating the tissues are described under 'Asphyxia'. In certain circumstances, however, the atmosphere itself may be deficient in oxygen.

The most obvious cause for exposure to such an environment is ascent to high altitude. Those living at high altitude compensate for the decrease in the partial pressure in oxygen in many ways, the most important of which is an increase in the number of oxygen-carrying red blood cells. Higher cerebral function begins to deteriorate in those who are unacclimatised and are rapidly or suddenly exposed to an atmospheric partial pressure of oxygen of less than 13 kPa (100 mmHg); this occurs at some 3,300 metres (11,000 ft) and supplemental oxygen is provided for pilots of unpressurised aircraft above this altitude (*see* 'Oxygen' for further details). The alternative to supplemental oxygen is, of course, to pressurise the environment and this is the measure taken in commercial aviation. The danger of pressurisation lies in the possibility of sudden decompression when the 'time of useful consciousness' (e.g. the time available to don an oxygen mask) becomes critical. In general, a sudden exposure to 12,000 m (40,000 ft) from a cabin altitude of 2,400 m (8,000 ft) will leave a time of useful consciousness of about 18 seconds[1].

Hypoxia may also occur in an airtight environment (*see* 'Environmental asphyxia'). Similarly, oxygen may be depleted when using a closed system such as in scuba diving[2] or during a poorly administered anaesthetic.

The cerebral effects of hypoxia are quite insidious to the subject but hypoxic convulsions are a common event and may result in some unusual artefacts — such as a simulated cry from a stillborn baby or terminal aspiration of stomach contents by children or adults.

Sustained hypoxia may cause irreversible damage to the body cells, the damage being related to the oxygen requirements of the particular cells. Brain cells are especially vulnerable — total absence of oxygen for even a short time may result in widespread brain damage and a persistent vegetative state; it is possible that even moderate hypoxia will cause minimal brain dysfunction in susceptible individuals. The effect of any diseased condition which is associated with local oxygen lack (e.g. myocardial ischaemia) will be exaggerated by environmental hypoxia.

See also: Aircraft accidents; Asphyxia; Carbon dioxide; Environmental asphyxia; Heat effects; Myocardial infarction; Oxygen; Persistent vegetative state

1. *See* Ernsting J 'Prevention of hypoxia — acceptable compromises' (1978) 49 Aviat Space Environ Med 495 for a review of hypoxia in aviation.
2. McAniff JJ and Schenck HV 'Investigation of scuba deaths' (1974) 2 J Sports Med 199.

Hysteria

Hysteria has many presentations, which may be of mental or physical character. These may include loss of sensation, paralysis, amnesia, deafness, blindness and the like. Hyperventilation is a common symptom and may lead to dangerous states of hypoxia in certain conditions — e.g. while piloting an aircraft.

Hysterical reactions are also known as dissociative states or conversion reactions and are essentially an escapist response to threatening or otherwise anxiety-producing situations. In essence, they represent a 'cry for help' — but this may be unappreciated because the severity of the triggering mechanism may not be apparent to the outside observer. The medical problem lies in distinguishing hysteria from, on the one hand, frank organic disease and, at the other end of the scale, from malingering (the deliberate production of symptoms with intent to benefit as a result). In the end, positive diagnosis may rest on a therapeutic test — do the symptoms improve with appropriate psychiatric treatment?

See also: Anxiety states; Compensation neurosis; Hypoxia

I

Iatrogenic Disease

Although of doubtful etymological accuracy, the term 'iatrogenic disease' implies disease which results from the attentions of the health caring professions themselves.

Theoretically, the list of potential iatrogenic diseases is almost endless and could include anything ranging from misdiagnosis to incompetent surgery. In practice, the great majority of iatrogenic disease, as opposed to physical injury, is associated with drug therapy, including overprescription and interaction of drugs prescribed in normal quantities.

Whilst certain unwanted side effects of drug therapy are inevitable (e.g. the depilation associated with chemotherapy for cancer) iatrogenic disease is of profound medico-legal significance as its very occurrence may provoke a suspicion of negligence.

See also: Drug interaction; Drug overdose; Negligence

Identification of the Dead

Identification of the dead is a straightforward matter of visual recognition in the vast majority of cases. There may, however, be considerable difficulty if the death is unnatural or if there has been extensive destruction of tissue due to the natural decomposition of the body. It is, in fact, convenient to discuss the subject in the worst possible context of the skeletonised body discovered in circumstances which give no clue to identity. This note is virtually confined to headings — most of the subjects are discussed in greater detail as indicated.

In the extreme case of fitting a name to an unknown skeletonised body, attention must be focused on the primary characteristics which will enable to the police to concentrate on a limited number of names in the list of missing persons. These will include:

(a) *Sex*. The distinction between the wide pelvic bone of the female and the relatively slim, funnel-shaped male pelvis provides by far the best sex differentiation in a skeleton. The associated contrasting appearances in the femur, in which the angle between neck and shaft is more acute in the female, provides evidence which is almost as good. In general, the bones of the female are less marked by muscular attachments and are more delicate; this applies in particular to the skull, which can

285

often be distinguished with certainty. The breast bone is rather more elongated in the male than in the female.

(b) *Age*. The methods for determining the age of the deceased from skeletal remains depend upon the broad age group concerned. It is a matter of observing centres of ossification, union of epiphyses and closure of skull sutures (*see* 'Age of a body at death'). The state of the dentition may, however, be the most accurate guide of all.

(c) *Stature*. Given the whole skeleton, a very reasonable assessment of stature can be given — certainly within the limits of most people's knowledge of the heights of their relatives. The determination of stature from individual bones is a matter for experts and is described under 'Stature'.

(d) *Hair colour*. Fragments of hair may persist when the greater part of the body has decomposed but it must be recognised that hair of any colour tends to fade to a nondescript dun hue with time.

The rather easier exercise of fitting a body to a probable name (i.e. when identification is suspected on general grounds) is a matter of comparing secondary characteristics in the body with those known to have been present in the missing person. These will include deformities and results of disease or surgical operation — which may be evident even in a skeleton; distinguishing marks, scars or tattoos may help if skin is still present. Personalised identification may be made from fingerprints but, for many reasons, including the effects of putrefaction, dental identification, which is possible even in the event of incineration, is likely to be more useful in the UK. Very good positive personal identification can often be made from a comparison of *ante* and *post mortem* X-rays of the frontal sinuses and pituitary fossa. Identification of the victim of homicide is, however, likely to be complicated by efforts to inhibit identification.

Circumstantial evidence of identification will be especially useful in the event of a major disaster. This can include clothing, documentation, jewellery and the like, the last being particularly valuable evidence following multiple deaths due to fire. Two aspects of identification in the disaster situation deserve emphasis. Firstly, circumstantial evidence must always be suspect and should always be corroborated. Secondly, the emotion surrounding a major disaster is such that visual identification should also be confirmed by other methods whenever possible — the tendency for distraught relatives to make mistakes cannot be overemphasised.

See also: Age of a body at death; Dentition; Fingerprints; Odontology; Ossification centres; Stature; Union of epiphyses

Ignorance of the Law

The maxim *ignorantia iuris neminem excusat* (ignorance of the law is no excuse) is one of the first apparent injustices which strikes the student of criminal law. The effect of this rule is to deny a defence to a defendant who has committed an offence without any knowledge that he was acting illegally[1]. The rule refers only to the criminal law; mistake as to the civil law may negative *mens rea*.

The justification of the rule lies in the fact that it would be impossible to administer a system of criminal justice without such a provision in the criminal code. This is particularly true as regards laws which are regulatory in nature; many defendants would undoubtedly be ignorant of the legislation under which they were charged and, consequently, the regulatory effect of the laws in question would be diluted[2].

An alternative approach to the issue would be to apply the rule in all cases other than those in which a defendant could not be expected to have a specialist knowledge of the law. This might allow justice to be done while, at the same time, preventing the more blatant injustices which the rule may bring about.

See also: *Mens rea*

1. *R v Esop* (1836) 7 C & P 456.
2. *See,* however, the qualification in *Lim Chin Aik v R* [1963] AC 160.

Illegitimacy

An illegitimate child is one who was born at a time when his parents were unmarried and who has not been legitimised by their subsequent marriage[1]. Children born of a voidable marriage are now considered legitimate; those born of a void marriage are legitimate provided that one or both of the parents were unaware of the defect in the marriage at the time of the child's conception[2]. An adopted child is treated for all purposes as the legitimate child of his parents but, whereas a person cannot marry his or her adopted child, sexual intercourse between the two does not, at present, constitute incest[3]. There is a legal presumption that a child is the legitimate offspring of its mother and her husband; this presumption is now rebuttable on the balance of probabilities which may include blood testing (*see* 'Parentage testing'). There is statutory support for this in England and Wales (Family Law Reform Act 1969) but not in Scotland.

The disadvantages of illegitimacy, which is increasing in the UK, are now a shadow of what once pertained. Some degree of social stigma probably persists but many of the adverse consequences in law have been abolished. The main disadvantages which the illegitimate child still experiences are in respect of financial support, which it may be technically more difficult for an illegitimate child to obtain from its parents, citizenship[4] and succession — an illegitimate child has less extensive rights of intestate succession than has his legitimate counterparts[5]. The only statutory disadvantage of legitimacy remaining is that such a child cannot succeed to titles of honour[6].

The father of an illegitimate child does not have the same parental rights as does the father of one who is legitimate; for example, his consent to adoption is unnecessary[7] unless he has obtained an order for custody — as he may do[8].

See also: Adoption; Incest; Nullity of marriage; Parentage testing

1. Legitimation through subsequent marriage was introduced into English law by the Legitimacy Act 1926.
2. Legitimacy Act 1959; Legitimacy Act 1976, s.1(1).
3. *HM Adv v RM* 1969 JC 52.
4. For a summary of citizenship implications, *see* Law Commission *Family Law: Illegitimacy* (Law Com No. 118) (1982) HMSO, London.
5. Mellows AR *The Law of Succession* (4th ed, 1983), p. 132 et seq, Butterworths, London.
6. Legitimacy Act 1976, Sch.1, para.4; Law Reform (Miscellaneous Provisions) (Scotland) Act 1968, s.5(5). *See also* Children Act 1975, Sch.1, para.10, for the position in adoption.

7. *Re Adoption Application 41/61* [1963] Ch 315.
8. Guardianship of Minors Act 1971, s.9.

Illusions

An illusion is a misinterpretation of a sensory stimulus which is real — as compared with a hallucination, for which there is no true sensory cause, or a delusion which is a belief having no foundation in fact. Illusions are certainly a feature of psychoses, particularly of the organic type, but they are by no means diagnostic of mental illness; we all experience optical and auditory illusions as a matter of daily routine. An illusion may give rise to an honest belief on the part of an individual; it may be legally important to distinguish this from a reasonable belief such as might be held by a reasonable man. The dilemma is exemplified in *DPP v Morgan*[1].

See also: Delusions; Hallucinations; Psychoses; Reasonable man

1. [1975] 2 All ER 347; [1976] AC 182. *See also R v Kimber* [1983] 1 WLR 1118.

Immersion

Immersion is a state of being in a liquid medium and one which may or may not be fatal. Common usage is to ascribe death in such circumstances to 'drowning' but, in fact, there are several modes of death to be considered. It is semantically more correct to ascribe death to immersion and then to define a more specific cause — of which inhalation of the medium, or true 'drowning', would only be one of many. Thus, homicidal or accidental deaths in the bath result most commonly from vagal inhibition of the heart following immersion rather than from drowning.

We feel, however, that it is simpler to bow to popular terminology and, for this reason, we describe the main types of immersion death under the heading 'Drowning'.

It is to be noted, however, that deaths due to immersion may be related only secondarily to the medium. They would thus include death from hypothermia in the sea or, in rather more bizarre circumstances, to scalding or to direct poisoning.

See also: Drowning; Hypothermia; Vagal inhibition of the heart

Immune Reaction

The immune reaction represents the defence of the body against invasion by foreign substances (e.g. bacteria or poisons). In its simplest form, the presence in the body of protein deriving from any 'non-self' origin acts as an antigen which stimulates an antibody which will, in turn, react specifically to neutralise that antigen. Being a matter of stimulus, the buildup of antibody is progressive so long as the antigen is present and active. The body is also capable of remembering an intruder; hence, a second attack is met by an antibody system which is already alerted — a minor antigenic invasion is then met with a major antibody response and is likely to be overwhelmed before it can establish itself. This is the basis of immunity to disease, which may be partial or absolute; this latter occurs in diseases such as chickenpox which are suffered not more than once.

Immunity is of two types. The humoral type is mediated through antibodies circulating in the plasma. The cellular type operates through the lymphocytic white cells of the blood and the rejection of the foreign substance is achieved by the concentration of such cells at the site — this is the typical reaction to a foreign implant.

The immune reaction can be abated by drugs — an essential, for example, in the transplantation of donor organs. Alternatively, the system may overreact, producing various forms of hypersensitivity, the most important of these from the medico-legal viewpoint being allergy in its many forms. Many of the adverse effects of the hypersensitivity reaction are due to the release of the substance histamine and can therefore be controlled to an extent by antihistaminic drugs or by the hormone adrenaline.

It will be seen that the immune reaction is basically a matter of appreciation of 'non-self'. A medically important aberration of the system occurs when the body, for any of a number of reasons, fails to recognise 'self' and reacts as if it were 'non-self'; this condition is known as autoimmune disease but it has negligible medico-legal significance.

Given the necessary antigens or antibodies, the alternates can be easily identified and, often, quantified in the laboratory. Many disease states can be diagnosed and previous exposure proved in this way; it also forms the basis of blood grouping.

See also: Acquired immune deficiency syndrome; Allergy; Antibody; Antigen; Blood transfusion; Transplantation of organs; Vaccination

Immunisation

Immunisation is the process whereby the normal immune reaction to invasion by a foreign substance is produced artificially. The most important types of invaders in this respect are the allergens (*see* 'Allergy') and pathogenic organisms.

Immunisation as to the latter can be of what is known as active or passive type. Active immunisation, which involves the use of dead or attenuated organisms, is described under 'Vaccination'. The use of passive immunisation is confined to circumstances in which an immediate effect is needed. Preformed antibody is injected and it is expected that this will react with and neutralise any organisms which are seeking to establish themselves in the body.

Such passive immunisation may be non-specific — highly purified human antibody is injected, some of which will react with a foreign protein; this is free from danger and can be very effective in special circumstances. Alternatively, specific antibodies may be deliberately produced in animals and the animal serum used to protect human subjects. Typical of such sources of immunity are those prepared against snake venoms and against the organism of tetanus. Such injections are not without danger as the animal protein contained in the injection may act as an allergen and provoke a severe, and sometimes fatal, reaction.

Any such injection should be covered by antiallergic drugs (such as adrenaline) but, even so, the potential dangers of passive immunisation must be weighed against the probability of the disease occurring — for example, the dangers of the bite of the only poisonous snake in Britain may be less than those of giving antivenin[1]. Nevertheless, failure to give antitetanus antiserum has been held to be negligent[2]; it would be hoped that most persons have been actively immunised against tetanus, in which case the prophylactic treatment of choice would be to give a 'booster' dose of actively immunising vaccine.

See also: Allergy; Immune reaction; Pathogenic organisms; Vaccination

1. Royal Society of Tropical Medicine and Hygiene 'Notes on the treatment of snake bite' (1962) 56 Trans R Soc Trop Med Hyg 93.
2. *Coles v Reading and District Hospital Management Committee and another* (1963) 107 SJ 115. There were, however, unusual features in the case.

Immunosuppression

'Immunosuppression' is a term generally reserved for the deliberate suppression of the immune reaction which is set up between the host and a transplanted (i.e. foreign) organ. The closer the antigenic similarity between host and graft, the more efficient is any applied immunosuppressive technique. It is to be noted that many forms of immunosuppression are non-specific and persons under the influence of such immunosuppressive drugs are susceptible to infection by pathogenic organisms and also to opportunistic infection. A new generation of immunosuppressives is now being developed from the drug cyclosporin which selectively depress the cellular type of immune reaction. Methods are thus steadily increasing in efficacy and graft rejection is no longer the very formidable hurdle it once was.

Natural immunosuppression is seen in several forms. The newborn infant has no immune system and acquires its immunity from its mother either as residual antibody or through the mother's milk; this is one reason why processes involving active immunisation are delayed for the first three months of life. Occasionally, the immune system fails to develop either completely or partially and a child is faced with many problems as to resistance to infection. Acquired immune deficiency disease is a new form of natural immunosuppression which appears to be due to a polyvalent virus and which is causing considerable concern.

See also: Acquired immune deficiency syndrome; Immune reaction; Pathogenic organisms; Transplantation of organs; Vaccination

Impotence

Impotence in the male may be caused by psychological or organic factors, the former being the more common. Many psychological explanations are possible: the patient may be anxious or inhibited sexually, he may feel himself to be incompatible with his partner or he may be fundamentally homosexual or trans-sexual. Organic causes of impotence include a low or non-existent level of secretion of sex hormones, neurological disorders and other conditions, including atherosclerotic disease which is possibly of major significance and is sometimes amenable to therapy. The ingestion of drugs, including alcohol, may lead to temporary impotence.

The principal medico-legal significance of impotence is that coitus is impossible and the condition is incompatible with consummation of marriage. Legal impotence, therefore, can be defined as an inability to achieve satisfactory sexual intercourse; neither orgasm nor ejaculation is essential to this concept[1]. For the purposes of avoiding a marriage, the impotence must be permanent and irremediable but it need relate only to the wife — a satisfactory physical relationship with other women is no bar to nullity.

A number of second marriages, in particular, are likely to be contracted with the partners being aware of, and prepared to live with, male impotence. The possibility of a later change of heart and of a petition for a decree of nullity is discouraged in such circumstances by the Matrimonial Causes Act 1973, s.13(1), which lays down that a decree of nullity shall not be granted if the respondent satisfies the court that the petitioner so conducted [her]self in relation to the respondent and to lead [him] reasonably to believe [she] would not do so and that it would be unjust to the respondent to grant the decree. This would not, however, simultaneously bar a petition for divorce.

See also: Consummation of marriage; Frigidity; Nullity of marriage; Trans-sexualism

1. *SY v SY* [1963] P 37.

In Vitro **Fertilisation**

In vitro fertilisation (IVF) implies the fertilisation of the human ovum by sperm in an artificial, extracorporeal medium[1]. As commonly practised, IVF is followed by transfer of the resultant embryo to the womb but the therapeutic process inevitably results in the production of surplus embryos — problems of embryocide and of embryonic experimentation are thus raised.

The process is primarily designed for the treatment of female infertility resulting from blockage of the fallopian tubes or other abnormalities consistent with adequate ovulation. Some 5 per cent of married women would probably benefit from the technique, which involves removal of the egg through the abdominal wall, fertilisation and implantation through the uterine cervix. The process is technically difficult but the results are steadily improving; at the time of writing, over 20 per cent of IVF implantations result in continuing pregnancy[2] although the miscarriage rate remains higher than normal. The occurrence of congenital abnormalities in fetuses which come to term appears to be no more frequent than in natural pregnancy.

Intramarital IVF using the ovum of the wife and the sperm of the husband can scarcely raise any any ethical issues *per se* — objections to this form of surgical treatment should, logically, include objection to attempted surgical correction of the underlying abnormality. Moral and legal issues may arise, however, if the process involves ovum donation, artificial insemination by donor or womb leasing. There are also incidental problems to be considered. Embryocide has been mentioned but, by contrast, the technique may also result in artificially induced multiple births; the production of quadruplets by this method in 1984 provoked considerable criticism[3].

Embryos for implantation may be preserved by freezing, and this raises specific problems related to succession and perpetuities. For these reasons, various recommendations have been made to limit the maximum storage time for such creations[4]; the problems of disposal of cryopreserved embryos are even more controversial than are those surrounding immediate destruction of the surplus embryo.

See also: Artificial insemination by donor; Embryonic experimentation; Ovum donation; Womb leasing

1. It is thus to be distinguished from the alternative method of transferring mixed ovum and sperm into the uterus and allowing natural fertilisation and implantation to occur; Craft I et al 'Human pregnancy following oocyte and sperm transfer to the uterus' [1982] 1 Lancet 1031.
2. Singer P and Wells D 'In vitro fertilisation: the major issues' (1983) 9 J Med Ethics 192.
3. *See* Phillips M 'A testing time' (1984) 10 BMA News Rev 6, 29. The importance of good faith in this area is well brought out by Craft I *'In vitro* fertilization — a fast changing technique: a discussion paper' (1982) 75 J Roy Soc Med 253.
4. The British Medical Association, for example, recommends disposal within 12 months ((1983) 286 Br Med J 1594). The Australian National Health and Medical Research Council in its 'Statement on human experimentation' (1982) (Supplementary note 4) suggests ten years but not beyond the time of conventional reproductive need or competence of the female donor. *See also* Brahams D 'In-vitro fertilisation and related research' [1983] 2 Lancet 726.

Inborn Errors of Metabolism

'Inborn errors of metabolism' includes a group of diseases which are determined by a genetic enzymatic defect (*see* 'Enzymes'). The severity of such diseases depends very much on the specific enzyme system which is defective but the most important are those which are accompanied by mental retardation — of which phenylketonuria and Tay–Sachs disease are the best known — or those which have a generalised effect — e.g. fibrocystic disease in which the enzyme deficiency is currently unknown.

Such diseases are untreatable but their effects can sometimes be minimised by following a dietary regimen which does not involve the missing enzyme (e.g. in phenylketonuria or galactosaemia). On the other hand, the defect can, in many cases, be identified *in utero* by amniocentesis. An inborn error of metabolism is very likely to be a legally acceptable reason for abortion under the Abortion Act 1967, s.1(1)(b), but the diagnosis may take up to six weeks to confirm. Abortion, if recommended, will therefore have to be undertaken with increasing risk to the mother and also with increasing proximity to legal viability of the fetus; this limitation is often used in argument against those who would wish to reduce the legal fetal age for abortion. In some cases — in particular, Tay–Sachs disease — the recognition of the carrier state in the parents is both possible and advantageous in restricted populations. Laboratory failure to report such cases accurately has led to some interesting decisions in the USA[1] (*see* 'Wrongful life').

Occasionally, as in phenylketonuria, the disease can be identified at birth by the detection of the abnormal metabolite in the urine; special dietary restrictions can then be instituted immediately. An element of resource allocation is introduced by routine screening for what is a rare condition, and it is only the simplicity of the test which makes it an acceptable economic/beneficial proposition.

See also: Abortion Act 1967; Amniocentesis; Enzymes; Genetic disease; Resource allocation; Wrongful life

1. For example, *Curlender v Bio-Science Laboratories* 165 Cal Rptr 447 (1980); *Noccash v Burger* 290 SE 2d 825 (Va, 1982).

Incest

Incest can be defined as sexual intercourse between near relatives; within this, however, the definition of near relative varies from one jurisdiction to another. Thus, the prohibited kinships in England and Wales, where incest has been an ordinary criminal offence only since 1908, are detailed in the Sexual Offences Act 1956, ss.10 and 11, which state that it is an offence for a man to have sexual intercourse with a woman whom he knows to be his grand-daughter, daughter, sister or mother; reverse relationships hold for women over the age of 16 — although, rather surprisingly, intercourse between a woman and her grandson is not prohibited; half-sibling relationships are included and the offence is committed notwithstanding the fact that the relationship is not traced through lawful wedlock. Incitement of a girl under the age of 16 to incest is proscribed under the Criminal Law Act 1977, s.54. The Incest Act 1567, which applies in Scotland, is based on biblical texts; the resulting prohibitions are, correspondingly, very much wider and include, *inter alia*, uncle/niece relationships and close relationships by affinity — this despite some erosion of the original law by the Marriage Enabling Act 1960. The maximum penalty for incest is seven years' imprisonment in England and life imprisonment in Scotland. Intercourse between parents and adopted children is not incest in the UK although such relationships are a bar to marriage — indeed, degrees of kinship prohibiting marriage are always wider than they are for incest.

The existence of an 'incest taboo' cannot be denied but its extent is variable — for example, incest, as such, is not a crime in France and Belgium — and the reason for its existence is uncertain. The propagation of genetic disease is often spoken of as a reason for prohibiting incest — and may well form a reason for, say, the strict control of donor semen banks — but it cannot have been the *reason* for an innate revulsion; moreover, it has to be emphasised that incest is a matter of sexual intercourse and not, primarily, of procreation. Most modern commentators now concentrate on the abuse of authority which is inherent in incest[1], the offence being philosophically allied to child abuse and to the impossibility of true consent in an atmosphere of domination by parents or by elder siblings. There are increasing attempts — notably made in Australia and Scandinavia — to revise the laws on incest along these lines[2]. At one end of the scale, it is considered that the offence should be abolished on the grounds that minors are already protected against sexual exploitation by age-related sex legislation and that consenting adults have a right to private activities. Such views are generally unacceptable to public opinion and the draft Incest and Related Offences (Scotland) Bill, proposed by the Scottish Law Commission, is an example of a compromise between strict logic and acceptability[3]. The draft provides that parent/child and sibling intercourse should still be categorised as incest and that adoptive relationships should be included; a separate offence is proposed to cover the step relationship and a new offence is to be created involving sexual intercourse between a person in a position of trust and authority and a child under the age of 16 who is subject to that trust and who is a member of the same household. The bill has been enacted as we go to press (Incest and Related Offences (Scotland) Act 1986).

The true incidence of incest is generally regarded as being higher than is apparent; this is a matter of under-reporting and, possibly, reluctance to act, there being no doubt that any criminal court proceedings place an enormous burden on young victims. Evidence of sexual intercourse must, of course, be corroborated and this may not be easy from the medical point of view. Incestuous intercourse must be *per vulvam* but, as in rape, neither penetration beyond the vulva nor emission is essential. Reporting and consequent examination are commonly delayed. Indeed, the first evidence of incest may be pregnancy, a fact which tends to exaggerate the importance of procreation in the offence and which may involve interesting laboratory testing for paternity not only of the resultant child but also of the child's mother.

See also: Adoption; Age of consent to sexual practices; Artificial insemination by donor; Genetic disease; Marriage; Parentage testing

1. Honoré T *Sex Law* (1978) pp.70–72, 79–81, Duckworth, London.
2. Bailey V and McCabe S 'Reforming the law of incest' [1979] Crim LR 749.
3. Mason JK '1567 and all that' 1981 SLT 301.

Incised Wounds

An incised wound is a break in the skin caused by a cutting edge. Its recognition is of importance because it almost certainly implies the use of a weapon, which, in a case of assault, will strongly influence what charges are brought. An incised wound is generally referred to as a stab wound if it is deeper than it is long on the surface.

Incised wounds will show little or no bruising, all the structures within the wound will be severed and bleeding will be severe from the ends of cleanly cut vessels.

Accidental incised wounds are extremely common (e.g. in the kitchen) but are not often dangerous. Homicidal or assaultive wounds may be distinguished from suicidal or self-inflicted wounds in that the former are usually deep and aimed at sensitive or obviously potentially lethal areas — suicides or exhibitionists very rarely make cuts in their faces or close to the eyes. Suicidal incisions, by contrast, are characteristically multiple and are of different depths — the most superficial of these 'tentative' cuts sometimes being little more than abrasions; such typical appearances are seen most commonly at the wrist. The distinction between homicidal and suicidal wounds may be difficult in the case of cut throat; one sign which will strongly indicate the former is the coincidental presence of 'defence injuries' on the palm of the hand or on the forearm.

Ritual incisions may be made by certain ethnic groups and may have to be distinguished from healed assaultive wounds. It is not uncommon in cases of homicide for incised wounds to be inflicted after death, in which case the genitals or breasts may be specifically attacked.

See also: Assault and battery; Cut throat; Defence injuries; Necrophilia; Stab wounds

Incompetence

A person suffering from a mental disorder or mental disability may be considered to be incompetent or incapable for certain legal purposes. The responsibility of such persons as to criminal matters is dealt with elsewhere (*see* 'Insanity and criminal responsibility' and 'Diminished responsibility') as is their inability to make a will (*see* 'Testamentary capacity'); there remain the questions of their ability to enter into legal transactions, such as contracts, and of their potential liability in tort.

The property affairs of an incompetent may be administered by the Court of Protection, the powers of which are derived from statute. This is not a court in the usual sense of the word, its function being performed by officers nominated by the Lord Chancellor and its procedures governed by the Mental Health Act 1983 and by the Court of Protection Rules 1984[1]. The court will intervene in the management of a person's affairs only if, after considering the medical evidence, it is satisfied that he is incapable of doing so himself. The court's actions may then include buying and selling property, transferring property to relatives and dealing with business commitments. The court has no power, however, over the incompetent's person and is not concerned with his medical treatment[2].

The contractual capacity of a mentally disordered or disabled person depends on the extent of the condition. It is possible that a person whose affairs are administered by the Court of Protection can have contractual capacity but this point is uncertain[3]. Any other mentally disordered person may enter into a contract but the contract may be set aside if it is shown that his mental incapacity prevented him from appreciating the significance of his actions and that the other party was aware of the mental incapacity[4]; this last proviso is not, however, essential[5]. Contracts for the necessaries of life may impose an obligation to pay for the services rendered on the mentally disordered person[6]. Mental disorder affects the ability to act as an agent and to execute deeds; an *inter vivos* deed may, however, be valid if it is executed during a lucid interval[7].

A person who cannot be considered incapable by virtue of mental disorder but who is, nevertheless, susceptible to pressure or influence as a result of age or weakness may be afforded legal protection against exploitation through the doctrine of undue influence under which unfair transactions may be set aside.

The liability for certain torts is independent of the state of mind of the tortfeasor and, consequently, a mentally disordered person may be successfully sued for civil damages[8]; although the issue is controversial, it is generally accepted in common law jurisdictions that liability should be imposed irrespective of the defendant's mental incapacity.

A mentally disordered person cannot engage in legal actions himself but must act through a next friend or guardian ad litem who is responsible for conducting litigation through the patient's solicitor.

Scots law on incompetence centres on the *curator bonis*.

A special meaning is attached to incompetence in the USA where an incompetent patient is one who cannot make an autonomous decision as to treatment. For further discussion, *see* 'Unconscious patient'.

See also: *Curator bonis*; Diminished responsibility; Guardian ad litem; Insanity and criminal responsibility; Mental Health Act 1983; Testamentary capacity; Torts; Unconscious patients

1. SI 1984/2035. *See* Heywood NA and Massey A *Court of Protection Practice* (11th ed, 1985) Stevens, London.
2. For criticism of the system, *see* Gostin L *The Court of Protection — a legal and policy analysis of the guardianship of the estate* (1983) MIND, London; Hoggett B *Mental Health Law* (2nd ed, 1984) p.337, Sweet & Maxwell, London.
3. *Re Walker* [1905] 1 Ch 160; *Re Marshall* [1920] 1 Ch 284. *See also* Guest AD (ed) *Anson's Law of Contract* (26th ed, 1984) p.207, Oxford University Press, Oxford.
4. *Imperial Loan Co v Stone* [1982] 1 QB 599 per Lord Esher MR at 601.
5. *Molton v Camroux* (1848) 2 Exch 487 at 503.
6. *Re J* [1909] 1 Ch 574.
7. For general treatment of agency, partnerships and power to make deeds, *see Halsbury's Laws of England* (4th ed, 1980) Vol.30, para.1010 et seq, Butterworths, London.
8. *Morriss v Marsden* [1952] 1 All ER 925; *see also* Fleming J *Law of Torts* (6th ed, 1983) p.21, Law Book Co, Sydney.

Indecency with Children

The Indecency with Children Act 1960 created the offence of gross indecency with or towards a child under the age of 14. The Act is designed to cover the situation whereby a person who, without the use of force, invites a child to handle him indecently, commits no offence because there is no assault. It is also concerned with those occasions on which a person acts indecently in the presence of a child without touching the child or causing the child to fear being touched. Thus, a man who masturbates in front of a child commits an offence under the Act, as does one who encourages a child to touch his sexual parts[1]. The offence is of strict liability, and a reasonable belief that the child was aged more than 14 would be no defence[2]. The Act does not extend to Scotland where the comparable offence is that of indulging in lewd, indecent or libidinous practices.

Children under the age of 16 are also protected against indecency through the Protection of Children Act 1978 which creates the offences, *inter alia*, of taking or permitting to be taken, distributing or showing indecent photographs of children; photographs include motion pictures or video recordings. The issue as to whether or not the photograph is indecent is a matter for the jury and evidence on the issue is not admissible[3]. Again, the Act does not extend to Scotland.

See also: Indecent assault; Lewd practices

1. *R v Speck* [1977] 2 All ER 859 in which inactivity, in failing to remove a child's hand from the genitalia, was deemed capable of amounting to an invitation to undertake the act.
2. *See Reginald Maughan* (1934) 24 Crim App R 130.
3. *R v Stamford* [1972] 2 All ER 427 would probably apply.

Indecent Assault

A common assault is rendered indecent by an added sexual connotation. It is stated that, for the offence to be committed, there must be a situation which would appear to the ordinary observer to be an affront to modesty[1]; a kiss, therefore, might or might not be an indecent assault depending upon the circumstances and the manner in which it was given[2]. Indecent assaults may be committed by both males and females against either sex. Persons under the age of 16 cannot consent to indecent assault whereas it is possible for a young person to consent to common assault (see 'Consent to injury'). There is, however, no age limit below which indecent assault cannot be committed; the common youngsters' 'petting party' thus tends to make a mockery of the law and, in practice, no action would be taken in such circumstances.

While it is theoretically possible for indecent assault to be charged when actual intercourse has occurred, the offence, as applied to women, is generally taken as meaning something less than vulval penetration. Thus, a man found not guilty of rape can be convicted of indecent assault; similarly, a boy aged less than 14 cannot be guilty of rape but can be convicted of indecent assault. It is somewhat anomalous that, whereas a man without previous similar charges against him and who is aged less than 24 years can defend himself against a charge of intercourse with a girl below the age of 16 on the grounds of a reasonable belief that she had attained the age of consent, no such defence is available in the case of indecent assault. However, a genuine mistake as to consent by an adult is now an acceptable defence[3]. A contrasting anomaly is that wholly revolting practices against women which do not involve vulval penetration — such as enforced fellatio — and which cannot therefore be rape, carry a maximum penalty of two years' imprisonment. Interestingly, indecent assault against a man results in a liability to ten years' imprisonment[4] but the distinction is seldom applied in practice. A woman who is mentally handicapped cannot consent to an indecent assault.

Indecent assault is not a specific crime in Scotland and it is not mentioned in the Sexual Offences (Scotland) Act 1976. It is simply an assault accompanied by circumstances of indecency. The assault is further aggravated when the victim is a child[5]. Intercourse with a voluntarily drunken woman would constitute a particular form of indecent assault[6]. The modern approach to indecent assault is exemplified in Canada where a three-tier approach has been in operation since 1983[7]; a sexual assault includes any assault made for the purposes of sexual gratification[8] — vulval penetration is regarded as specifically significant in so far as it results in bodily harm.

The most important aspect of indecent assault from the medical viewpoint lies in the possibility of charges being laid against doctors and dentists — the latter being particularly vulnerable during the modern practice of 'horizontal dentistry'. Whilst there must, in practice, be such a thing as 'implied consent' to medical examination, this is unlikely to apply to examination of the genitalia save in the context of the obviously gynaecological or obstetric consultation. Doctors would be well advised to obtain specific consent to examination of the sex organs, irrespective of the sexes involved, and this should be witnessed audibly by a third party whenever possible; the genitalia would include the female breasts in this context.

See also: Age and consent to sexual practices; Clandestine injury to a woman; Consent to injury; Consent to medical treatment; Fellatio; Rape

1. Williams G Textbook of Criminal Law (2nd ed, 1983), p.231, Stevens, London.
2. Maurice Leeson (1968) 52 Crim App R 185. For general discussion, see Mackesy AN 'The criminal law and the woman seducer' [1956] Crim LR 530.

3. *R v Kimber* [1983] 3 All ER 316, CA.
4. Sexual Offences Act 1956, ss.14, 15, Sch.2.
5. Gordon GH *The Criminal Law of Scotland* (2nd ed, 1978) p.823, Stevens, London.
6. *HM Adv v Logan* 1936 JC 100.
7. Criminal Code, ss.246.1, 246.2, 246.3.
8. *R v Alderton* (1985) 17 CCC (3d) 204, CA.

Indecent Exposure

Lewdly or obscenely exposing the genitalia is both a common law and a statutory offence. In the latter case, the offence is usually charged under the Vagrancy Act 1924, s.4 as amended by the Criminal Justice Act 1925, s.42. The Act speaks of 'exposing his person. . .with intent to insult any female' and it follows that only a man can be so charged. Theoretically, a woman could be charged under common law but it would be more likely to be regarded as a breach of the peace or, in Scotland, as shameless indecency. If the exposure takes place on private property, it will still be criminal if another person is present[1] but valid consent clearly renders the act non-criminal. The actual genitalia must be exposed to constitute the offence[2]. Indecent exposure is not a psychic indecent assault because the offended person does not anticipate any physical touching[3]. The action is often referred to as exhibitionism and this has been classified by the World Health Organization as a sexual deviation in which sexual gratification is the main purpose of exposure. It is this last qualification which defines the offence of indecent exposure; a 'streaker' is also an exhibitionist but is, nevertheless, not guilty of indecent exposure as he is not exposing himself to any particular person and obtains no sexual gratification. Eighty per cent of those brought before the courts for this offence do not offend again; psychiatric treatment of the persistent offender is labour intensive but some types of aversion therapy may be helpful if used with discrimination[4].

See also: Indecent assault

1. *Ford v Falcone* [1971] 2 All ER 1138.
2. *Evans v Ewels* [1972] 1 WLR 671.
3. *Fissington v Hutchinson* (1866) 15 LT 390.
4. Gayford JJ 'Indecent exposure: a review of the literature' (1981) 21 Med Sci Law 233.

Industrial Benefit

Three types of benefit can be obtained under the Social Security Act 1975 when industrial injury is sustained in an insurable occupation.

(a) Injury benefit is payable during the period in which the insured is unable to work through injury. It is paid for 156 days — which does not include Sundays and public holidays — and is then replaced by disablement benefit.
(b) Disablement benefit is payable according to the degree of disability (including disfigurement), which is expressed as a percentage of total disability. The degree of disablement is decided by medical boards which consist of two or more medical practitioners; appeal from the decision of the medical board is to the Medical

Appeals Tribunal which consists of a chairman and two consultant practitioners — the ultimate appeal is to the National Insurance Commissioner but this is available only on a point of law. Disablement benefit is paid weekly unless the disability is assessed at less than 20 per cent, in which case it is paid as a lump sum. There are means available (e.g. through unemployability supplement, special hardship or exceptional disablement payments[1]) to increase the disablement pension.

(c) Death benefit is payable to the widow in the event of fatal industrial injury. The rate of this depends, *inter alia*, on the number of dependents but it ceases upon remarriage — the happy event being celebrated with a final gratuity.

It is to be noted that special regulations apply in the case of prescribed diseases and, particularly, to compensation of the pneumoconioses. In this last instance, there is provision for both initial and periodic medical examinations, attendance at which is obligatory if benefit is to be continued.

See also: Industrial injury; Pneumoconioses; Prescribed diseases

1. Social Security Act 1975, s.36 substituted by Health and Social Security Act 1984, s.11.

Industrial Injury

The definition of and administrative arrangements for dealing with compensation for industrial injury are to be found in the Social Security Act 1975.

The nature of the great majority of industrial injuries is generally obvious and is due to frank trauma — a man catches his hand in moving machinery or a brick falls on a man's head. There is no way that all such injuries could be described in detail but they are clearly injuries which are entitled to compensation by way of industrial benefit. This note is concerned only with the more subtle medico-legal aspect of industrial injuries or accidents.

An industrial injury resulting from an accident need not be mutilating. An accident for this purpose is defined as an unlooked-for mishap or an untoward event which is not expected or designed; an injury includes any physiological injury or change for the worse. Thus, the term 'accident' includes any pathological or adverse physiological condition which is accidental merely by virtue of being unexpected. Moreover, the circumstances surrounding the unexpected event need not be exceptional; all that is required is that the event should be concerned with some engagement in work. The fact that the 'accident' is no more than an exacerbation of known pre-existing disease is immaterial[1], as is the fact that a worker's physical condition makes him more prone to a true traumatic accident[2]. Thus, the man who lifts a load and sustains a myocardial infarct is entitled to industrial benefit despite the fact that he was known to suffer from angina of effort. The 'Commissioners' Decisions' (*see* 'Industrial benefit') have progressively lengthened the list of circumstances which may be regarded as accidents, even going so far as to include nervous shock resulting from seeing a workman being killed. Any deaths associated with work must be the subject of a coroner's inquiry with a jury or of a fatal accident inquiry in Scotland.

Industrial injury does not necessarily have to occur while actually at work in order to qualify for industrial benefit. It is noted under that heading, for example, that accidents occurring as a result of another's skylarking will qualify (s.55). Some difficulty may be expected, however, in deciding what is a place of work. Transport provided by the employers is regarded as such (s.53) but the employee's own car is not. Elsewhere, the situation is not so clear cut — it has been held that the phrase 'in the course of his employment' is not capable of having a precise definition even though, in the actual case, the unsuccessful plaintiff had clocked on for work[3]. Both the examining physician and the pathologist should, however, anticipate that any condition arising during the working day is likely to attract action for compensation and their reports should be directed accordingly.

Diseases or conditions the origin of which cannot be pinpointed may be regarded as the result of an industrial process; such diseases are known as prescribed diseases and are discussed under that heading and under 'Occupational disease'.

See also: Coroner; Fatal accident inquiry; Industrial benefit; Occupational disease; Prescribed diseases and occupations

1. *Oates v Earl Fitzwilliam's Collieries Co* [1939] 2 All ER 498.
2. *Tankard v Stone-Platt Engineering Co Limited* (1946) 174 LT 277.
3. *Coult v Szuba* [1982] ICR 380 (QBD).

Industrial Poisoning

Industrial poisoning is another vast subject but one which is slowly changing in pattern. A number of conditions associated with poisoning are notifiable to the Health and Safety Executive[1] when they are contracted in a factory. The greatest danger from such poisons relates to their inhalation, although they may also be absorbed through the skin or be ingested. Industry is now so well aware of, and takes such precautions against, this type of industrial poisoning that the list of notifiable conditions is almost of historical interest only. Thus, poisoning by metals (e.g. by lead, cadmium or mercury) is now very rare. Inhalation of or skin contamination by the aromatic and aliphatic hydrocarbons is similarly decreasing, not only because of preventive measures but also because of the substitution of many of the more toxic solvents — toxic jaundice and toxic anaemia are now, correspondingly, uncommon.

At the same time, there is increasing interest in the more subtle effects of industrial poisoning and, in particular, in carcinogenesis (the induction of malignant disease). This is discussed in rather more detail under 'Occupational disease'.

Industrial poisoning in agriculture is particularly important. Pesticides are, by definition, toxic; the nature of their distribution prohibits the use of extraction techniques and the worker is, effectively, surrounded by a poisonous atmosphere of his own making. Many pesticides are acutely poisonous but their long-term effects are only now beginning to be questioned. The subject is discussed further under 'Pesticides'. Poisoning by radiation is also treated separately.

It is to be noted that positive efficiency in limiting industrial poisoning is provided by regular monitoring of the atmosphere and identification of a source of contamination before it has done any harm. The concept of threshold limit values is an essential basis for safety; all practicable measures must be taken to protect the workers once a limit is found to be exceeded. The notification of cases of poisoning, whilst being a valuable support, is really only a negative preventive method — the existence of a case is a clear indication that positive efficiency has broken down.

See also: Cancer; Notifiable diseases; Occupational disease; Pesticides; Radiation hazards; Threshold limit values

1. Reporting of Injuries, Diseases and Dangerous Occurrences Regulations 1985 (SI 1985/ 2023).

Infant Life (Preservation) Act 1929

This short Act has two main functions. Firstly, it introduces the offence of child destruction — causing the death of a child capable of being born alive — which is defined and discussed further under that heading. Secondly, it introduces a legal presumption to the effect that evidence that a woman had at any material time been pregnant for a period of 28 weeks or more shall be *prima facie* proof that she was at that time pregnant of a child capable of being born alive. The life of a fetus beyond the 28th week of gestation is thus protected save only when its destruction is necessary in good faith to preserve the life of the mother.

Section 5(1) of the Abortion Act 1967 lays down that nothing in that Act shall affect the provisions of the 1929 Act. The effect of the two Acts together is therefore to maintain the illegality of an abortion after the 28th week of pregnancy save in exceptional circumstances. The 1929 Act, however, does not presume that a woman of less than 28 weeks' gestation is *not* carrying a fetus capable of being born alive. An apparently legal abortion undertaken earlier than the 28th week may result in a living abortus or, indeed, one which is viable in modern circumstances[1]; strictly speaking, therefore, the Act may be being disregarded. There is, therefore, some pressure to amend the 1929 Act so as to lower the presumptive age of capability for a live birth to 24 or even 22 weeks[2]. On the other hand, antenatal diagnosis of fetal abnormality by amniocentesis takes some time and there are fears that such a change might result in some clearly indicated abortions being rendered illegal[3]. Whether or not this would be so, the arguments are finely balanced; in the near future, some modern techniques, such as chorionic sampling, may markedly lower the fetal age at which such diagnoses can be made.

The Infant Life (Preservation) Act does not run to Scotland[4]; the result is that any abortion performed within the terms of the Abortion Act 1967 is legal there irrespective of the gestational age of the fetus[5].

See also: Abortion Act 1967; Amniocentesis; Child destruction; Live birth; Living abortus

1. Infants of less than 28 weeks' gestation are now being successfully reared — *see* Dunn PM and Stirrat GM 'Capable of being born alive?' [1984] 1 Lancet 553.
2. *See*, for example, *The Times*, 1 June 1984, p.3. The probability is that a voluntary agreement to limit abortions to fetuses of less than 24 weeks' gestation will make an amendment of the 1929 Act unnecessary (*The Times*, 3 August 1985, p.2).
3. Alberman E et al 'Congenital abnormalities in legal abortions at 20 weeks' gestation or later' [1984] 1 Lancet 1226.

4. Where the offence of child destruction was already recognised as an innominate crime (*Jean M'Allum* (1858) 3 Irv 187; *HM Adv v Scott* (1892) 3 White 240).

5. Gordon GH *The Criminal Law of Scotland* (2nd ed, 1978) p.813, W Green, Edinburgh.

Infanticide

Although often taken to mean any killing of a young child, the term 'infanticide' should be reserved for the offence specifically defined in the Infanticide Act 1938. This provides that the offence is committed when a woman by any wilful act or omission causes the death of her child, being under the age of 12 months, but, at the time of the act or omission, the balance of her mind was disturbed by reason of her not having fully recovered from the effect of giving birth to the child or of lactation consequent upon the birth. The Act does not run to Scotland, where child murder is the comparable offence at common law.

When infanticide is charged, it is presumed that the child was born dead unless the prosecution can show proof to the contrary; any doubts that may exist must be resolved in favour of the mother. The onus on the pathologist is thus considerable and is complicated by several factors. Cases commonly present in one of two ways. The death may be very close to birth in which case any potentially fatal injuries — often associated with the head — may be difficult to distinguish from birth injuries, particularly in the circumstances of an unattended birth. Alternatively, the body of the newborn infant is likely to have been hidden and to have putrefied to a varying extent; incontrovertible proof of a live birth is then wellnigh impossible. Almost any means of killing a neonate can be, and have been, used but the pathologist will be aware, as examples, that babies *can* slip through the mother's hands to the floor, a young girl may genuinely mistake uterine contractions for the need to defaecate or a distraught mother may attempt to kill her infant that has never lived.

In practice, disturbance of the balance of the mind at the time of labour will be accepted in the vast majority of cases and, infanticide being punishable as manslaughter, the courts take an extremely lenient attitude in sentencing, the use of probation being the rule[1]. But it would be less easy today to attribute mental disturbance to lactation, and, in general, the older the infant, the more difficult will it be to bring convincing proof of the causal relationship of child birth to mental disturbance. Moreover, the older the child, the easier becomes the task of the forensic pathologist. It is, of course, open to any woman to set up a plea of diminished responsibility when charged with murder irrespective of the age of the child.

It goes without saying that only the mother can be afforded the sympathy of a charge of infanticide; a husband, say, who assisted his wife in the killing of their newborn child would be guilty of murder.

See also: Birth injuries; Concealment of birth; Diminished responsibility; Homicide; Live birth; Neonaticide; Separate existence

1. In 1973 it was found impossible to discern a level of sentencing in infanticide because instances were so rare (*R v Scott* [1973] Crim LR 708).

Infarction

An infarct is a segmental or conic zone of ischaemic necrosis in an organ or tissue and results from blockage of the end-artery supplying that tissue. Infarcts are therefore the result of obstruction of the arteriolar lumen by atheroma, thrombus or embolus; infarction is essentially a result of sudden deprivation of arterial blood — gradual occlusion commonly results in the establishment of a collateral circulation. Infarcts are usually pale in appearance but they may be haemorrhagic if the tissue concerned has a dual blood supply (e.g. in the lungs and liver). Occasionally, haemorrhagic infarcts are due to occlusion of a vein — the stagnant arterial blood is still rendered ineffective. Infarcts of the brain are unusual in presenting as areas of softening. An infarct is essentially a wound within an organ and characteristically heals by fibrosis; very often, however, the dead tissue becomes sealed off and a cystic cavity remains — this is particularly common in the brain.

Infarction occurs in many organs and is often symptomless or causes no more than acute pain. Incomparably the most important types are myocardial infarcts (*see* 'Coronary disease') and cerebral infarcts — the latter being the underlying cause of the often serious disability associated with 'stroke' in the elderly (*see* 'Geriatric medicine').

See also: Atheroma; Coronary disease; Embolism; Geriatric medicine; Thrombosis

Infectious Diseases

Strictly speaking, the term 'infectious diseases' should include all pathological conditions caused by infecting micro-organisms (*see* 'Pathogenic organisms'). Usage has, however, tended to equate infectious diseases with those diseases notifiable under the Public Health (Infectious Diseases) Regulations 1968 (SI 1968/1366); these would be better isolated as communicable diseases and are discussed under that heading.

See also: Communicable diseases; Notifiable diseases; Pathogenic organisms

Infertility

It is generally stated that some 10 per cent of married couples who desire a family are unable to have children but much depends on the geographical area. The reasons for infertility are rather more common in the female than in the male and abnormalities are present in both husband and wife in about 15 per cent of couples who seek advice.

The most frequent causes of infertility in women are to be found in disorders of ovulation which are generally susceptible to accurate diagnosis and treatment, albeit sometimes expensive. Abnormalities of the fallopian tubes account for about 20 per cent of female infertility problems. The majority of these are due to the results of infection; tuberculosis, which used to be a common source, is now rare but a number of causes are the result of sexually transmitted disease, in particular, gonorrhoea. Many other organisms cause tubal inflammation and a proportion of these result from pregnancy or abortion despite the fact that unqualified practitioners in the field are now virtually a matter of history; abdominal inflammation from any cause (e.g. appendicitis) may affect the fallopian tubes. Treatment of tubal blockage is primarily surgical but the chances of pregnancy following surgery are, at best, only about 50 per cent. Pregnancy then depends upon *in vitro* fertilisation and its allied techniques.

The infertile male presents a difficult problem as it is often little more than an opinion as to whether or not the ejaculate is abnormal. Some men can be shown definitely to have no or very few spermatozoa and these pose no problem in diagnosis; in a few others, a recognisable and treatable endocrine distrubance can be found. Some men appear to make antibodies to their own spermatozoa, and in others there is an immunological incompatibility between husband's sperm and wife's genital passage. But, in the great majority of cases of male infertility, no cause can be found other than a moderate reduction, of doubtful significance, in the number of spermatozoa and simple expedients such as multiple ejaculations are not successful. The available remedy is, then, artificial insemination by donor.

There is a persistent — about 5 per cent — group of infertile couples who are both apparently normal but who still fail to have children. Many treatments are attempted in such cases but their evaluation is difficult as the possibility of spontaneous pregnancy cannot be excluded. Occasionally, one is forced to wonder whether the cause may not lie in the mind — a successful pregnancy in an apparently infertile couple who have recently adopted a child is by no means infrequent.

See also: Abortion; Artificial insemination by donor; Immune reaction; *In vitro* fertilisation; Sexually transmitted diseases; Spermatozoa

Informed Consent

In recent years, informed consent has become more than simply a variation on consent to medical treatment and is now a philosophical concept: 'Because Anglo-American law starts with the premise of thorough going self determination. . .it follows that each man is considered to be master of his own body and he may, if he be of sound mind, expressly prohibit performance of life saving surgery or other medical treatment'[1]. Thus, in order to consent to medical treatment the patient must know to what he is consenting; he has a right to be informed and the doctrine of informed consent, runs the argument, is concerned not so much with the question of treatment without consent but rather with the breach of the patient's right to be given information on which to make the decision to consent[2]. It is now generally assumed that the provision of inadequate, as opposed to misleading, information does not completely vitiate consent and that actions for personal injury in battery (*see* 'Assault and battery') are not appropriate when related to the informed consent issue; such actions should, rather, be based in negligence (*see* 'Consent to medical treatment'). The patient then has two elements to prove: firstly, that the injury for which he seeks redress resulted from an undisclosed risk and, secondly, that he would not have consented to the treatment unless, or but for the fact that, there had been a failure in disclosure. The second limb, which is fundamental to the doctrine of informed consent, can be looked at in two ways — what is the proper extent of disclosure and how is 'proper' to be defined?

There is no doubt that the necessary extent of disclosure has been expanding in the USA. Of the many landmark decisions, one might quote *Williams v Menehan*[3] in which reasonable disclosure was demanded, the imposition of a fiduciary relationship[4] and the laying down of a full disclosure rule[5]; despite this rule, the professional, or therapeutic, privilege to withhold such information as is thought to be contrary to the patient's interest[6] has been retained.

The standard of disclosure can be regarded as being either patient orientated — i.e. what the patient regards as the required standard — or doctor orientated — the professional standard. The former, in turn, may be objective — i.e. what does the reasonable patient expect — or subjective — what did that particular patient require to know. The latter approach is closest to the philosophical concept of informed consent but, in allowing hindsight, it heavily weights the scales in favour of the patient[7]; it has also been pointed out[1] that the fully subjective standard cannot operate if the patient is dead. The general shift tends, therefore, towards an objective standard[5] — despite the fact that this offends against the patient's right to make an unreasonable decision. However, although there is a clear philosophical trend towards patient orientation, the majority of decisions in the USA still favour the professional standard[8] and several States have positively legislated to this end. The Canadian cases have also inclined towards a modified professional standard in that expert evidence may be taken as to reasonable medical practice but that the court's role is maintained in assessing what the patient wanted or needed to know[9].

The professional standard has been fully endorsed in the UK, whilst the right of the court to assess the expert medical evidence is retained. In the Appeal Court phase of *Sidaway v Board of Governors of the Bethlem Royal Hospital and the Maudsley Hospital and others*[10], the Master of the Rolls stated that the general duty of the doctor as to the provision of information was to give what was reasonable in the particular circumstances of the particular patient; 'the law', he said, 'could not stand by if the profession denied the patient a real choice'. The standard of such information was that of a practice 'rightly [as judged by the court] accepted by the profession'. The professionally orientated reliance on expert evidence was emphasised by Dunn LJ who said, in a concurring judgment, that 'informed consent formed no part of English law'. The interpretation must be that the Lord Justice meant by this that the subjective patient-orientated standard played no part in the law of England; nevertheless, only a short time later it was held that 'having regard to the decision in *Sidaway*, it was not open for it to be argued for the plantiff that "informed consent" was a consideration which could be entertained by the courts'[11]. The Appeal Court decision in *Sidaway* has been widely criticised[12] but, nevertheless, was upheld in the House of Lords[13]. Although the case was decided unanimously on its particular facts, the speech of Lord Scarman comes very close to acceptance of the transAtlantic interpretation. The general position now is that the test of negligence is as stated in *Bolam v Friern Hospital Management Committee*[14] — 'the standard [is that] of the ordinary skilled man exercising and professing to have that skill. . . [I]t is sufficient if he exercises the ordinary skill of an ordinary man exercising that particular art' — and the *Bolam* test applies also to providing the patient with information. It is, none the less, clear that the courts expect a doctor, and would impose a duty on him, to inform a patient of material or substantial risks involved in a medical or surgical procedure. Quite what constitutes the risk which is so regarded is still undefined but, as to incidence, it appears to lie somewhere between a 1 and 10 per cent chance of occurrence and, as to severity, something which no reasonably prudent medical man would fail to disclose.

It is apparent that the concept of informed consent, with its emphasis on rights and duties, introduces an element of confrontation; there is much to be said for Dunn LJ's concern[10] that it could be damaging to the relationship of trust and confidence between doctor and patient. It may well be preferable to regard 'informed consent' more in the light of improved communication and understanding and, by this means, to further what has been called a therapeutic alliance[15].

See also: Assault and battery; Causation; Consent to medical treatment; Negligence

1. *See* Koopersmith ERG 'Informed consent: the problem of causation' (1984) 3 Med Law 231.
2. Norrie K McK 'Standards of disclosure' 1984 SLT 237.
3. 379 P 2d 292 (Kan, 1963).
4. *Berkey v Anderson* 1 Cal App 3d 790 (1969).
5. *Canterbury v Spence* 464 F 2d 772 (DC Cir, 1972).
6. *Natanson v Kline* 350 P 2d 1093 (Kan 1960).
7. *Cobbs v Grant* 104 Cal Rptr 505 (1972).
8. For example, *Wooley v Henderson* 418 A 2d 1123 (Me 1980).
9. *See Reibl v Hughes* (1981) 114 DLR (3d) 1; *White v Turner* (1981) 120 DLR (3d) 269.
10. [1984] 2 WLR 778. The court confirmed the opinion in *Hills v Potter and another* [1984] 1 WLR 641.
11. *Freeman v Home Office* (No.2) [1984] 2 WLR 802.
12. *See*, for example, Kennedy I 'The patient on the Clapham omnibus' (1984) 47 MLR 454.
13. [1985] 2 WLR 480.
14. [1957] 1 WLR 582.
15. Teff H 'Consent to medical treatment: paternalism, self-determination or therapeutic alliance?' (1985) 101 LQR 432.

Inhalation of Gastric Contents

It is debated whether death can properly be attributed to inhalation of gastric contents. Whilst it must be virtually impossible for it to occur in the conscious adult, the great majority of authors concede that aspiration can and does result in death in subjects who are at special risk by reason of hypnotic drugs, alcohol or anaesthesia. The alternative view is that the majority of instances of inhalation are the result of, rather than the cause of, fatal hypoxia[1]. The problem is one of interpretation and corroboration, the best of the latter (although rarely possible) being clinical observation. The solution is generally clear if massive amounts of vomit are present in the air passages. It may be necessary to resort to microscopy if there are smaller quantities, the purpose being particularly to confirm the presence of vomit in the smaller air passages. It has been suggested that the finding of acid digestion of the respiratory mucosa is essential to the diagnosis of inhalation during life[2] but this sign, in the absence of an inflammatory reaction which must take some time to arise, is of doubtful value because physical digestion of tissues by acid can continue after death. Death may, moreover, be rapid because the acid content of the vomit has a bronchoconstrictive effect on the lungs[3]; death from vagal inhibition of the heart or from laryngeal spasm is a definite possibility even if the gastric material has been displaced no further than the nasopharynx. It is apparent that circumspection is needed in making such a *post mortem* diagnosis and this is particularly so when there are criminal connotations[4].

See also: Alcohol; Anaesthesia; Asphyxia; Hypoxia; Vagal inhibition of the heart

1. Knight BH 'The significance of the *post mortem* diagnosis of gastric contents in the air passages' (1975) 6 Forens Sci 229.
2. Gardner AMN 'Aspiration of food and vomit' (1958) 27 Quart J Med 227.
3. Lucas BGB 'Operational deaths and complications' in Camps FE and Lucas BGB (eds) *Gradwohl's Legal Medicine* (3rd ed, 1976), Chap.28, Wright, Bristol.
4. *See* the unreported case *R v Abrol* (1982) *The Times*, 14 July, p.3; (1983) *The Times*, 12 July, p.2; (1983) *The Times*, 27 October, p.3. A dentist was convicted of manslaughter but a judicial review set aside the sentence on the grounds that there was grave doubt as to the trial evidence that death was due to inhalation of vomit; a reopened inquest recorded a verdict of death by misadventure.

Inquest

The coroner's inquest is founded upon his duty to summon 'not less than 12 and not more than 23 good and lawful men. . .to inquire as jurors regarding the death [of a person who has died either a violent or an unnatural death or has died a sudden death for which the cause is unknown. . .][1]. Although the requirement to hold an inquiry in public remains, the composition of — particularly in relation to a jury — and indications for an inquest have been extensively revised and are now governed by the Coroner's Rules 1984 (SI 1984/552). The details are discussed under the heading 'Coroner'. There have been persistent criticisms of the inevitability of a public inquiry into unnatural deaths — particularly in cases of suicide. However, since the coroner is virtually unique among primary medico-legal authorities in being accountable only to himself, publicity is an essential safeguard.

It is possible to appeal to the Divisional Court if the findings of the coroner's inquest are contested but, curiously, the only course open to the court if they uphold the appeal is to order another coroner's inquest. The procedure generally results in less than satisfaction since the majority of complaints stem from a basic disillusionment with the role of the coroner and of the coroner's court[2].

See also: Coroner

1. Coroners Act 1887, s.3.
2. For a basis of criticism, *see* Mason JK 'Coroners from across the Border' (1983) 23 Med Sci Law 271.

Insanity and Criminal Responsibility

Although the majority of criminal offenders do not suffer from any mental disorder, a considerable proportion of persons in criminal institutions are found to be mentally disordered[1]; in many cases, the relationship between the offender's mental condition and his criminal conduct will be evident to all but the most sceptical.

Functional psychosis may provide the explanation for criminal conduct in some cases. Severe depression, for example, may lead to homicide[2]. A schizophrenic delusion may urge the sufferer to engage in courses of violent conduct which appear to him to be an appropriate or justified response to a deluded belief[3]. The presence of a less serious mental condition may also explain criminal conduct in a particular case; an out of character minor offence such as shoplifting may be attributable to minor depression.

Organic conditions may also cause criminal conduct of both a voluntary and involuntary nature. Senile or presenile dementia may lead to embarrassing antisocial behaviour which is out of character. Involuntary criminal conduct, such as that associated with hypoglycaemia or epilepsy, is discussed more fully in the context of automatism.

The question of the criminal responsibility of the mentally disordered offender goes to the heart of our notions of accountability[4]. There can be little argument over the offender's lack of responsibility in cases where the mental abnormality is such as to preclude consciousness. Otherwise, the issue is one of determining the extent to which the mental disorder relieves the offender of the requirement to observe the norms of society. The mere presence of mental disorder has never been accepted by the law as an excusing factor in itself; the disorder must affect the offender's attitude towards his conduct in such a way that he cannot be held responsible. The problem can be approached by considering the effect of mental disorder on *mens rea* (i.e. the offender might be considered to be acting without the necessary intent) or by the measuring of the offender's conduct against either cognitive or volitional criteria.

The test for criminal insanity which is currently applied in English law is formulated in the M'Naghten Rules. These provide for the special verdict of insanity if an accused person, suffering from a disease of the mind, did not know the 'nature and quality' of his act or, if he did know this, did not know that what he was doing was wrong. The Rules give rise to an array of problems. The definition of a 'disease of the mind' is controversial and what is meant by knowing the nature and quality of an act is problematic[5]. Knowledge of wrongfulness has also been interpreted in more than one way; although other views have been expressed[6], wrongfulness has been given a legal rather than moral meaning in England[7].

The most forceful criticisms of the M'Naghten test of insanity have, however, focused on the fact that it places undue emphasis on the cognitive aspect of mental disorder. It may well be that a mentally disordered person is quite aware of the wrongfulness of an act and yet cannot refrain from committing that act. Alternatively, objective appreciation of the wrongfulness of an action may not be accompanied by a similar subjective acceptance. A person suffering from a psychotic illness may know that society regards a particular form of behaviour as wrong and yet may not himself believe that it is.

Dissatisfaction with the application of the M'Naghten Rules in the USA has led to the formulation there of a series of alternatives. The *Durham* test[8], introduced in the District of Columbia in 1954, proposed that criminal responsibility would not be imposed if the unlawful act 'was the product of mental disease or mental defect'. This test had two drawbacks: firstly, the terms 'mental disease' or 'mental defect' tended to be interpreted as technical terms over which forensic psychiatrists argued at length; secondly, it was found difficult to determine when an unlawful act was a product of the disease or defect. The court adopted the American Law Institute's test, as laid down in the Model Penal Code, in the important decision in *United States v Brawner*[9]. This test holds that criminal responsibility will not be inferred when conduct is performed at a time when 'as a result of mental disease or defect he (the accused) lacks substantial capacity either to appreciate the criminality (wrongfulness) of his conduct or to conform his conduct to the requirements of the law'.

The Butler Committee, reporting in 1975, recommended 'not guilty on evidence of mental disorder' as a new formulation of the special verdict which could be reached either on the grounds that the offender was incapable of forming the requisite *mens rea* for an offence or that he was, at the time of the offence, suffering from severe mental illness or severe subnormality. 'Severe mental illness' was defined by the Committee not in terms of clinical labels, but in terms of characteristics of the condition — for example, delusional beliefs, highly disordered thinking and so on[10].

Scots law flirted with the M'Naghten Rules for a brief period during the nineteenth century but they are no longer applied in Scotland. The current Scots law, as laid down in the case of *HM Adv v Kidd*[11], has been described as being in broad agreement with the American Law Institute's approach, although the Scottish emphasis is on 'alienation of reason' and the accused's consequent inabiliity to use his reason to control his conduct[12].

See also: M'Naghten Rules; Manic–depressive psychosis; Psychoses; Schizophrenia

1. For discussion of the incidence of mental disorder amongst criminals, *see* Gunn J 'Criminal behaviour and mental disorder' (1977) 130 Br J Psychiat 317 and Guze SB *Criminality and Psychiatric Disorder* (1976) Oxford University Press, New York. *See also* Medicolegal 'Mentally ill offenders in prison' (1985) 290 Br Med J 447.
2. West DJ *Murder Followed by Suicide* (1965) Heinemann, London; Woddis GM 'Depression and crime' (1957) 8 Br J Delinq 85.
3. Prins H *Offenders, Deviants, or Patients?* (1980) p.64 et seq, Tavistock, London; Taylor P 'Schizophrenia and violence' in Gunn J and Farrington DP (eds) *Abnormal Offenders, Delinquency and the Criminal Justice System* (1982) Wiley, Chichester.
4. There is a voluminous literature on the philosophical basis of the insanity defence. Some important contributions to the debate include: Fingarette H and Hasse AF *Mental Disabilities and Criminal Responsibility* (1979) University of California Press, Berkeley CA; Flew A *Crime or Disease?* (1975) Macmillan, London; Gross H *A Theory of Criminal Justice* (1979) Oxford University Press, New York; Fletcher GP *Rethinking Criminal Law* (1978) Little, Brown, Boston MA.
5. Some writers take the view, however, that the wording of the Rules is helpfully simple. *See*, for example, Kuh RH 'The insanity defence — an effort to combine law and reason' (1962) 110 U Pa LR 771.
6. Schiffer ME *Mental Disorder and the Criminal Trial Process* (1978) p.132 et seq, Butterworths, Toronto.
7. *R v Windle* [1952] 2 QB 826.
8. *Durham v US* 214 F 2d 862 (1954)
9. 471 F 2d 969 (1972).
10. Butler Lord (chairman) *Report of the Committee on Mentally Abnormal Offenders* (Cmnd 6244)(1975) paras.18, 35, HMSO, London.
11. 1960 JC 61.
12. Gordon GH *The Criminal Law of Scotland* (2nd ed, 1978) p.376, W Green, Edinburgh.

Insects and Disease

The term 'insect-borne disease' is used here in its accepted colloquial form and includes diseases spread by organisms of the order *Arachnida* — ticks, mites, etc. It would be technically more correct to speak of arthropod-borne disease, which would cover all disease carried by organisms with multijointed legs. Disease thus spread is of forensic importance because its prevention is largely a matter of public health enforcement and, therefore, of legal control. Problems of medical negligence in diagnosis and treatment may also arise (*see* 'Protozoa').

Insect-borne injury can result from the direct injection of venom and this may, occasionally, be lethal of itself — deaths from wasp or bee stings occur even in the UK, and accidents may be precipitated by insect stings if they occur, say, while the subject is driving a motor vehicle.

Micro-organisms, however, can be transmitted by biting or by non-biting insects. In the former case, the pathogenic organisms usually pass an essential part of their life history within the insect carrier. They may then be injected when a blood feed is taken — as in malaria — or excreted into scratch marks — as in epidemic typhus. Whether or not such a disease becomes epidemic depends upon whether or not the infected insect takes multiple feeds from man. The spread of this type of insect-borne disease can be fought by attacking the breeding grounds of the carrier, by passive guarding against the biting insect and by immunisation. Classic infecting insects and the diseases caused include: lice — typhus and relapsing fever; fleas — plague; mosquitos — malaria and yellow fever; sandflies — leishmaniasis and sandfly fever; blood-sucking flies — sleeping sickness and types of filariasis; ticks — typhus and relapsing fever. Numerous viral diseases, many of which are of great severity, are also spread by insects.

Non-biting insects may carry pathogenic organisms on their bodies or in their excretions, these being picked up and transferred between man's excretions and his food. The best known of such diseases are typhoid and related fevers and poliomyelitis. Although houseflies have never achieved the same notoriety as, say, mosquitos, they have probably been responsible for as much, if not more, disease in man — the problems of epidemic disease associated with flies are very great as the insect vector is not an essential link in the man-to-man chain. The control of these conditions is essentially a matter of public health — sewage disposal and protection of food and water supplies, fly control, recognition and treatment of human carriers and immunisation.

See also: Pathogenic organisms; Protozoa; Public health; Vaccination

Insulin

Insulin is defined as a sterile solution of the specific antidiabetic principle of the mammalian pancreas and is used for the treatment of diabetes mellitus. It is ineffective when given by mouth and must be injected.

It is prepared in two forms — short acting (soluble or neutral insulin) and depot insulin — the latter having a prolonged action which reduces the need for multiple injections. It is normally prepared from pig or cattle organs but recombinant DNA techniques may rapidly lead to the availability of human material which will avoid the occurrence of occasional allergic reactions and the production of anti-insulin antibodies.

Insulin may need to be obtained or administered in an emergency. Since medicines can be given by injection only by practitioners or by persons acting on the instructions of a practitioner[1], and since all medicines needing to be so given are Prescription Only drugs, insulins have to be exempted from the general rules and are classified as Pharmacy medicines[2].

An excess of insulin, which may result, in the dabetic, from overdose or from an inadequate carbohydrate intake, carries with it the risk of hypoglycaemia which may cause mental confusion or coma. Insulin-induced hypoglycaemia may be mistaken for drunkenness but its main medico-legal significance is discussed under 'Automatism'.

See also: Automatism; Diabetes; Genetic engineering; Pharmacy medicines; Prescription Only medicines

1. Medicines Act 1968, s.58(2)(b). A patient may administer such drugs to himself.
2. Medicines (Products other than Veterinary Drugs) (Prescription Only) Order 1983 (SI 1983/1212).

Intent

The concept of basic intent has recently been particularly related to the effect of intoxication on *mens rea*. Crimes of basic intent are presumed not to require a high degree of mental awareness; an intoxicated person is thus thought to have enough mental capacity to commit an assault or a rape. By contrast, crimes of specific intent are considered to require rather more mental awareness or application. Consequently, intoxication may be a defence, *inter alia*, in a case of murder, forgery or theft[1]. Scots law is more strict in the case of murder, recklessness in being drunk eliding the specificity of intent[2].

The distinction between basic and specific intent is somewhat unsatisfactory. It would appear to be largely based on a policy which attempts to avoid the injustice of punishing those who could not have been aware of the implications of their actions whilst still making it possible to punish others who, for policy reasons, ought not to be acquitted[3]. Certain statutory offences (e.g. assault with intent to inflict grievous bodily harm) involve a specific intent and are subject to a defence of intoxication.

When directing a jury on the mental element in a crime of specific intent, judges are enjoined to avoid elaboration and to leave it to the jury's good sense to decide whether the accused acted with the necessary intent[4]. At the same time, the jury must be given an explanation that the greater the probability of a consequence, the more likely it was that the consequence was foreseen and that, if it was foreseen, the greater was the probability that it was also intended[5].

See also: Alcohol; Foreseeability; Mens rea

1. For judicial discussion, see the important case of DPP v Majewski [1977] AC 443. See also R v Garlick (1981) 72 Crim App R 291.
2. Brennan v HM Adv 1977 SLT 151.
3. For criticisms of the concept, see Williams G Textbook of Criminal Law (2nd ed, 1983)

p.471 et seq, Stevens, London. For the position in Scots law, *see* Gordon GH *The Criminal Law of Scotland* (2nd ed, 1978) p.733 et seq, W Green, Edinburgh.
4. *R v Moloney* [1985] 2 WLR 648.
5. *R v Hancock and Shankland* [1986] 1 All ER 641, HL (per Lord Scarman).

Intersex

The problems which surround the effects of chromosomal anomalies and endocrine imbalances in confusing the assignment of sex to an affected individual are discussed under the general headings of 'Sex' and 'Sex chromosomes'. Intersex related to deep psychological causes results in trans-sexualism, which is also treated separately.

See also: Sex; Sex chromosomes; Trans-sexualism

Intoxication and Criminal Responsibility

An association between the consumption of alcohol and crime, particularly crimes of violence, is extremely common.

It is possible to make out a case for the acquittal of an offender who has committed a criminal act while intoxicated. Responsibility for an offence normally requires *mens rea*; the intoxicated offender, however, may not know what he is doing (in the sense of not being able to appreciate the probable consequences of his action) and he may not have formed the requisite intention in relation to his physical act. Clearly, the extent to which this is the case will depend on the degree of intoxication; the man who is mildly drunk may be perfectly aware of his actions and of their moral or social implications[1].

The counter arguments are weighty. In the first place, the consequences of allowing intoxication as a defence would be serious, as it would be open to every offender to hide behind drunkenness when confronted with his criminal acts. The difficulties which the courts would then encounter in discriminating between the meritorious case — where an offence committed when drunk was one which the offender would never have contemplated nor wished to commit when sober — and the undeserving case would be overwhelming.

This pragmatic argument is supported on jurisprudential grounds. The man who becomes so intoxicated as to constitute a danger to the public is not morally blameless. Since the act of becoming drunk is socially irresponsible, it is not inappropriate that responsibility should be borne for the consequences[2]. A compromise is possible here — a new offence of becoming dangerously intoxicated might be created rather than charging any acts which took place under the influence of drink[3]. This has the attraction of avoiding conviction for serious crimes, such as murder, when intoxication has produced a lesser degree of moral guilt than is normally present in the convicted murderer.

English law on intoxication and criminal responsibility has a complex background. A convenient starting point is the decision in *DPP v Beard*[4] in which it was confirmed that intoxicaton would constitute a defence to a criminal charge if it was such as to render the defendant incapable of forming the *mens rea* necessary for the offence. A defendant who is intoxicated to a lesser extent may be convicted even if his drunkenness compromised his ability to distinguish between right and wrong.

The availability of intoxication as a defence is limited still further. In its decision in *DPP v Majewski*[5], the House of Lords elaborated on the suggestion in *Beard* that the defence will be available only in cases involving offences of specific intent and not in those of basic intent. The existence of a variety of confusing judicial dicta makes the distinction difficult to disentangle[6]; examples of each type of crime and further discussion are to be found under 'Intent'.

The status of involuntary intoxication is uncertain in English law[7]. There is a case for acquittal in some circumstances, even where the offence committed is one of basic intent, but it could be that it should be taken only as a mitigating factor. 'Dutch courage' intoxication, induced so as to build up the courage to commit an offence requiring specific intent, has been roundly rejected by the House of Lords[8]. Intoxication will be no defence in cases for which the *mens rea* requirement is satisfied by recklessness[9].

The Canadian courts have followed the *Majewski* approach to intoxication, not without criticism from academic writers[10]. The rule has, however, been abandoned in Australia, where it is now possible to claim a defence of intoxication for any offence following the decision in *R v O'Connor*[11]. Scots law has rejected the *Majewski* rule in relation to murder[12] but follows English law as to other offences of both specific and basic intent.

See also: Drunkenness; Intent; *Mens rea*

1. For discussion of 'degrees' of intoxication, *see* Lynch ACE 'The scope of intoxication' [1982] Crim LR 139.
2. The argument favoured in the Scots case *Brennan v HM Adv* 1977 SLT 151.
3. Recommended in Butler Lord (chairman) *Report of the Committee on Mentally Abnormal Offenders* (Cmnd 6244) (1975) HMSO, London. *See also* Colvin E 'Codification and reform of the intoxication defence' (1983–84) 26 Crim LJ 43.
4. [1920] AC 479.
5. [1976] 2 All ER 142.
6. Dashwood A 'Logic and the Lords in *Majewski*' [1977] Crim LR 532, 591; Beck SM and Parker GE 'The intoxicated offender — a problem of responsibility' (1966) 44 Can Bar Rev 563; Williams G 'Intoxication and specific intent' (1976) 126 NLJ 658; Colvin E 'A theory of the intoxication defence' (1981) 59 Can Bar Rev 850.
7. For a Canadian case on involuntary intoxication, *see R v King* 35 DLR (2d) 386 (1962).
8. *Attorney General for Northern Ireland v Gallagher* [1963] AC 349; [1961] 3 All ER 299.
9. *Commissioner of the Police of the Metropolis v Caldwell* [1982] AC 341. Allen MJ 'Recklessness and intoxication in the House of Lords' (1981) 32 NILQ 373.
10. *Leary v The Queen* [1978] ISCR 29.
11. (1980) 54 ALJR 349. *See also* Fairall P 'Majewski banished' (1980) 4 Crim LJ 264; Goode M 'Some thoughts on the present state of the "defence" of intoxication' (1984) 8 Crim LJ 104. For South African law, which rejected the *Majewski* approach in *S v Chretien* 1981 (1) SA 1097, *see* Burchell JM 'Intoxication and the criminal law' (1981) 98 SALJ 177.
12. *Brennan v HM Adv*, n.2 above. Gordon GH *The Criminal Law of Scotland* (2nd ed, 1978) p.407, W Green, Edinburgh; Gray JWR 'The expulsion of *Beard* from Scotland: murder north of the Border' [1979] Crim LR 369.

Intracerebral Haemorrhage

Haemorrhage within the brain substance may be due to natural disease or to trauma. The former occurs most commonly in the elderly whose arteries are damaged by atheroma and whose blood pressure is raised. Being arterial in nature, the extravasation of blood is under pressure and extensive destruction of brain tissue may result, with consequent loss of function in the event of survival — the classic 'stroke'. The vessels most frequently affected are those supplying the central nuclei of the brain and, occasionally, similar haemorrhage may result from direct violence to the head. The distinction as to whether the haemorrhage caused a fall and head injury or vice versa is often difficult to make at autopsy, but in the former case there may well be microscopic evidence of previous small bleeds.

Haemorrhage due to trauma may be petechial or confluent. Petechial haemorrhage results from generalised trauma which may be of forceful or hypoxic type. Confluent haemorrhage can be classified as being of primary or secondary type. Primary haemorrhage may be found at the site of injury (coup injury) or, when decelerative in origin, at the opposite sides of the brain; the possible reasons for this distribution are discussed under the heading of contre-coup injuries. Haemorrhage or contusions of this type can often be seen to result from confluence of localised petechial haemorrhages.

Primary haemorrhage may also occur in the brain stem as a result of injury to the base of the skull or as a type of contre-coup lesion following a fall onto the back of the head. The brain stem is, however, a classic area for secondary haemorrhage, which is a most dangerous complication of the presence of a space-occupying lesion elsewhere within the cranium. In the presence of such a lesion, or of generalised brain swelling, the brain stem becomes compressed and haemorrhagic due to a combination of direct pressure and impingement on the sharp edge of the dural flap which separates the cerebrum from the cerebellum (tentorium cerebelli); this process involves both the brain stem substance and its supplying blood vessels. Brain stem injuries are likely to be fatal; whilst little can be done about primary lesions in the area, secondary lesions are preventable in so far as the original space-occupying lesion may be reducible. Considerable onus may therefore lie upon the pathologist to distinguish the two types of injury; this in itself is no easy task but, in addition, secondary injury may be superimposed on and mask a primary injury[1]. The matter could be properly regarded as one which is best decided in the specialist neuropathology laboratory.

See also: Brain swelling; Contre-coup injuries; Head injury; Petechial haemorrhage

1. Crompton MR 'Brain stem lesions due to closed head injury' [1971] 1 Lancet 669.

Intracranial Haemorrhage

Intracranial haemorrhage may be classified in several ways. It may be arterial, venous or capillary in origin. It may result from violence or from natural disease (*see* 'Subarachnoid haemorrhage' and 'Intracerebral haemorrhage'). Most importantly, it can be classified on anatomical grounds as being extradural, subdural, subarachnoid or intracerebral. All these conditions are discussed under their appropriate headings.

The most important clinico-pathological features of intracranial haemorrhage are, firstly, that many cases are treatable without great difficulty and, secondly, that they may take some time to develop sufficiently so as to produce symptoms. Haemorrhages constitute space-occupying lesions within an inextensible cranium. A missed diagnosis may therefore result in severe damage at the cellular level, secondary obliteration of the cerebral circulation, irrecoverable brain damage including a persistent vegetative state or, even, brain stem death.

Unnatural intracranial haemorrhage is by no means always associated with fracture of the skull; whilst the presence of fracture is evidence of relatively severe applied force, serious haemorrhage can occur in the absence of any demonstrable external lesion. This will be especially so in the presence of a bleeding tendency such as haemophilia or even in association with the relatively poor haemostatic mechanisms of old age.

See also: Brain stem death; Extradural haemorrhage; Intracerebral haemorrhage; Persistent vegetative state; Subarachnoid haemorrhage; Subdural haemorrhage

Intramarital Rape

As many as 14 per cent of women may be the victims of sexual violence at the hands of their husbands at some time[1] but it is common law that intramarital rape is a contradiction in terms: 'The husband cannot be guilty of rape committed by himself upon his lawful wife, for by their mutual matrimonial consent and contract, the wife hath given herself in this kind unto her husband which she cannot retract'[2]. It was not until 1888 that an English court gave any proper consideration to this exemption[3]; although contradictory dicta were given, there was by no means unanimous support for Hale's proposition.

Several more recent decisions have identified circumstances in which a husband may be charged with the rape of his wife. In *R v Clarke*[4], a husband who raped his wife after she had obtained a separation order was convicted but a mere petition for divorce was held not to revoke consent to intercourse 'as given in marriage'[5]. It was stated in *R v O'Brien*[6] that a similar result could be obtained after a decree nisi of divorce had been granted. The Court of Appeal has also ruled that a husband who has non-consenting intercourse with his wife after he has given an undertaking to the court not to interfere with her can be charged with rape[7].

Reformers want the exemption removed but there are misgivings as to how this may be done[8]. A husband may genuinely believe that he has his wife's consent by virtue of their marriage and it might be difficult to establish *mens rea* in these circumstances. Some legal systems, however, recognise rape within marriage as an offence. There is a dictum indicating that Scots law is moving that way[9] even to the extent of regarding an amicable separation as voiding any 'surrender of the wife to the husband'. Legislation has been introduced in South Australia to allow conviction for marital rape in limited circumstances[10]. A number of the United States have passed laws giving women some protection from their husbands[11].

See also: Rape

1. Russell D *Rape in Marriage* (1982) p.2 Macmillan, New York; *see also* Walker L *The Battered Woman* (1979) p.107 et seq, Harper & Row, New York.
2. Hale in *Historia Placitorum Coronae* (1736) p.636.
3. *R v Clarence* [1888] 22 QBD 23. For discussion, *see* Freeman MDA '"But if you can't rape your wife who(m) can you rape?": the marital rape exemption re-examined' (1981) 15 Fam LQ 1, and Scutt J 'Consent in rape: the problem of the marriage contract' (1977) 3 Monash LR 255.
4. [1949] 2 All ER 448.
5. *R v Miller* [1954] 2 All ER 529.
6. [1974] 3 All ER 663.
7. *R v Steele* (1977) 65 Crim App R 22.
8. For a critical discussion of suggestions for reform, *see* Harman JD 'Consent, harm, and marital rape' (1983-84) 22 J Fam Law 423.
9. *HM Adv v Duffy* 1982 SCCR 182, 1983 SLT 7. See *HM Adv v Paxton* 1984 SCCR 311 for the extended proposition.
10. Criminal Law Consolidation Act 1935-1980, s.73(5) (South Australia).
11. *See* Schiff AF 'Rape: wife vs husband' (1982) 22 J Forens Sci Soc 235, who foresees some danger from the vindictive wife.

Ionising Radiation

Ionising radiation derives from the very high frequency fraction of the electromagnetic spectrum and includes X-rays, gamma rays and cosmic rays. This type of radiation is distinguished as 'ionising' in that it can change the chemical structure of cells. In so doing, it may alter the chromosomal makeup, may stimulate cell reproduction (i.e. cause cancer) or may kill the cell. All ionising radiations are therefore potentially dangerous (*see* 'Radiation hazards').

See also: Cancer; Chromosomal disease; Electromagnetic radiation; Radiation hazards

Irresistible Impulse

The test of insanity contained in the M'Naghten Rules focuses on the knowledge of the accused of the nature of his act and its wrongfulness, an emphasis which many commentators have regarded as unacceptable. It has been suggested that more attention should be paid to the inability of the mentally abnormal accused to control his behaviour; on this basis, the notion of irresistible impulse has been accepted as a feature of the insanity defence in a number of jurisdictions.

The debate on irresistible impulse goes back to the nineteenth century when the medical profession criticised the law's lack of attention to what psychiatrists of the time referred to as 'impulsive insanity'. Legal criticism was also voiced: Fitzjames Stephen, who had earlier taken a stern view of the idea of irresistible impulse as an excuse, later came round to an acceptance of the non-responsibility of a person acting under such influence[1]; the Atkin Committee, which reported on insanity and crime in 1924, recommended that 'it should be recognised that a person charged criminally with an offence is irresponsible for his act when the act is committed under an impulse which the prisoner was by mental disease in substance deprived of any power to resist'[2]. No changes were made in the law.

The theory of the irresistible impulse is that an accused may feel a compulsion to perform an act which he cannot resist in spite of intellectual appreciation of its wrongfulness[3]. This compulsion has been described by one judge as akin to the application of irresistible physical force leading to a situation where the accused 'could no more refrain from doing that which the impulse of the moment told him to do than if a strong man had taken hold of him and made him do it'[4]. Supporters of this concept argue that it is inappropriate to attribute responsibility for the effect of such an impulse to the person affected — one might as well hold a sneezer responsible for a sneeze.

Critics, however, point out that the ability to resist an impulse can be quite independent of mental illness. A person whose view of the world is distorted by psychotic illness may understand self-restraint as well as a person whose vision of reality is more normal. Failure to resist temptation may occur in either case and depends not on the mental abnormality or lack of it but on a deliberate decision to act as prompted[5].

The theory of irresistible impulse has been accepted in a number of countries. In the USA, the notion is embodied in the Model Penal Code, which speaks of a lack of 'substantial capacity either to appreciate the criminality of. . .conduct or to conform. . .conduct to the requirements of the law'. This provision has not been accepted in all American States. Canada has refused the idea of irresistible impulse as a defence[6] but there is a long line of cases in South Africa which embrace the notion with some enthusiasm[7]. English law rejected it in *R v Sodeman*[8] and *R v Rivett*[9] but it still has its supporters. Irresistible impulse may, of course, arise as an incidental factor supporting a plea of diminished responsibility under the Homicide Act 1957.

See also: Diminished responsibility; M'Naghten Rules

1. For a discussion of Stephen's views, *see* Walker N *Crime and Insanity in England* (1968) Vol.1, p.105 et seq, Edinburgh University Press, Edinburgh.
2. Report of the Committee on Insanity and Crime (Cmd 2005).
3. Gross H *A Theory of Criminal Justice* (1979) p.297, Oxford University Press, New York.
4. Per Innes CJ in *R v Smith* 1906 TS 783 at 787.
5. Williams G *Textbook of Criminal Law* (2nd ed, 1983) p.659, Stevens, London.
6. *R v Wolfson* [1965] 3 CCC 304; *R v Borg* [1969] SCR 551. *See also* Schiffer ME *Mental Disorder and the Criminal Trial Process* (1978) Butterworths, Toronto.
7. For South African Law, *see* Burchell EM, Milton JRL and Burchell JM *South African Criminal Law and Procedure* (2nd ed, 1983) p.259 et seq, Juta, Cape Town.
8. [1936] 2 All ER 1138 PC.
9. (1950) 34 Crim App R 87.

J

Jaundice

Jaundice is a yellow discoloration of the skin and tissues due to the presence of excess bile pigments. The bile pigments derive in the main from aged erythrocytes and are normally trapped by the liver cells and excreted in the bile. Primary disease affecting the function of the liver cells is therefore a potent cause of jaundice and is certainly the most important medico-legally. Liver cell death occurs following overdose of some anaesthetic agents and from exposure to some industrial hydrocarbons; liver failure is also caused by organisms of widely different types — e.g. the spirochaete of the industrial disease leptospirosis or the virus of hepatitis B which is transmitted in infected blood.

Jaundice may also be obstructive in type — bile is formed normally but cannot be excreted due, say, to the presence of stones or cancerous growth. The obstruction may occur within the liver due to the process of fibrosis.

Very occasionally, the liver is wholly normal but the breakdown of blood cells is so great that the organ is temporarily overwhelmed. This condition is known as haemolytic anaemia, the most important from the medico-legal aspect being that type which follows incompatible blood transfusion.

See also: Anaemia; Blood transfusion; Cirrhosis; Erythrocytes; Hepatitis; Industrial poisoning

Jehovah's Witnesses

Jehovah's Witnesses may conflict with good medical practice in their objection to blood transfusion. Their doctrine involves a rigid interpretation of the Bible[1] and, whilst there is no desire to avoid medical treatment, the doctor is restrained as to organ transplantation of any type, the commonest requirement being for blood; strict Witnesses may also refuse autotransfusion although cardiopulmonary pumps are regarded as appendages to the body[2]. There can be little doubt that the wishes of a

318

competent adult must be respected, and a surgeon would be justified in refusing to operate in such conditions save in an emergency.

Some American decisions are, however, interesting in demonstrating the interest of the State in protecting a patient against him or herself, particularly when the prognosis is good. Thus, in *Heston*[3], the court overruled the wishes of a mother and those previously expressed by her now incompetent daughter; in *Georgetown College*[4], the people were thought to have a compelling interest in preserving the life of the mother of a 7-month-old child; in *Powell*[5], the court ordered transfusions to be given so that time might be gained for a full hearing, Markowitz J assuming the role of 'my brother's keeper', saying 'this woman wants to live, I cannot let her die'. The dilemma has been well put in that this meant that the judge would go to heaven whilst the woman, having drunk blood, would be damned[6]!

The situation as regards minors is, however, different. In the UK, short of relying on the doctrine of necessity to elide a charge of battery, the doctor wishing to transfuse the child of a Jehovah's Witness in the absence of parental consent may initiate care proceedings[7]; Williams[8], however, thinks this is a doubtful process and advises application for court wardship. Absolute refusal for doctors to administer a life-saving transfusion has been regarded as manslaughter but there are no modern precedents[9]. The protection of children seems also to be a main consideration in the USA. An attempt to enjoin a Washington statute empowering judges to authorise transfusions for children in need despite their parents' objection failed in the US Supreme Court[10] and the principle has even extended to insisting on transfusion of the mother when the infant was still *in utero*[11]. Australian States have introduced legislation enabling a doctor to transfuse without parental consent when a child is in danger of dying and when blood transfusion is the best means of preventing the death[12].

See also: Assault and battery; Blood transfusion; Consent by minors; Consent to medical treatment; Necessity; Parental rights

1. Genesis ix: 3,4; Leviticus xvii: 14; Acts xv: 29; 1 Samuel xiv: 33.
2. Clarke JMF 'Surgery in Jehovah's Witnesses' (1982) 27 Br J Hosp Med 497.
3. *John F Kennedy Memorial Hospital v Heston* (1971) 279 A 2d 670.
4. *Application of President and District of Georgetown College Inc* (1964) 331 F 2d 1000.
5 *Powell v Columbian Presbyterian Medical Center* (1965) 267 NYS 2d 450.
6. Paris JJ 'Terminating treatment for newborns: a theological perspective' (1982) 10 Law Med Hlth Care 120.
7. Children and Young Persons Act 1969, s.23; Social Work (Scotland) Act 1968, s.16.
8. Williams G *Textbook of Criminal Law* (2nd ed, 1983) p.575, Stevens, London.
9. *R v Senior* [1899] 1 QB 283.
10. *Jehovah's Witnesses in Washington v King County Hospital Unit No. 1* (1968) 390 US 598, 88 S Ct 1260. For a survey of American cases, *see* Rampino KJ 'Power of court or other public agency to order medical treatment over parental religious objections for child whose life is not immediately endangered' 52 ALR 3d 1118.
11. *Raleigh Fitkin-Paul Morgan Memorial Hospital v Anderson* (1964) 201 A 2d 537. Contrast, however, with *Re Philip B* (1979) 92 Cal App 3d 796 where the parents' refusal to allow a cardiac operation on their 12-year-old child which would have improved his life expectancy was upheld — presumably, the test rested mainly on the risks of the procedure.
12. *See*, for example, Australian Law Reform Commission, Draft Bill concerning Human Tissue Transplants (1977) s.24(3).

Judges' Rules

The Judges' Rules deal with the procedure to be adopted by the police in questioning people, whether or not they are suspected of a crime. They lay down the requirement for a caution to be administered once the questioned person becomes suspected of a criminal offence; they restrict the questions which may be put to a suspect after he has been charged with an offence or informed of likely prosecution; and they specify the way in which written statements are to be taken from cautioned persons.

The aim of the Rules is to ensure fairness to the suspect and to create a framework in which statements may be said to have been given voluntarily. The Rules do not have the effect of law; it is for the presiding judge to determine whether any breach of the Rules will render the evidence in question inadmissible[1]. The Judges' Rules are now to be replaced and expanded in a Code of Practice introduced by the Police and Criminal Evidence Act 1984.

See also: Detention by the police

1. *R v May* (1952) 36 Crim App R 91 per Lord Goddard at 93.

Judicial Knowledge

Certain facts do not have to be proved in court but will be presumed to be within the knowledge of the judge or jury. These facts are matters of judicial notice which include things which the judge knows as general information rather than as any special, individual knowledge of particular topics or localities.

Judges may therefore be expected to know how many days there are in a particular month, that the streets of London are crowded and dangerous and that boys are mischievous[1]. Judicial notice is also taken of certain customs which have been accepted in the courts, but evidence will be required of practices which are accepted as routine in other disciplines — e.g. the usual way in which medical procedures are carried out.

1. These are examples of *notorious facts. See* Buzzard JH, May R and Howard MN *Phipson on Evidence* (13th ed, 1982) p.37, Stevens, London.

Juvenile Courts

The prosecution of juvenile offenders involves considerations and processes different from those which apply in the case of adults. When a child has admitted his guilt, the alternative of the police caution is used when possible; if prosecution goes ahead, the police are required to inform the local authority of their intention to take the child to court. The Children and Young Persons Act 1969 envisaged the ending of prosecutions of those under the age of 17, the intention being to replace criminal proceedings by care proceedings, but these provisions have not yet been put into effect. For the time being, therefore, children may still be prosecuted in the criminal courts[1].

Offenders under 17 years of age must be brought before a juvenile court except when: (a) the offence is one of homicide; (b) the juvenile is charged jointly with a defendant aged 17 years or over; (c) the magistrates' court only discovers during the trial that the defendant is a juvenile; or (d) in the case of a defendant aged between 14 and 17 years, the charge is a serious one which it is considered merits detention for a long fixed period.

Juvenile courts are magistrates' courts in another guise. The general aim is to keep them separate from the ordinary criminal courts — for example, juvenile courts cannot sit in the same room as has been occupied by an adult court within the previous hour. The magistrates are specially chosen for the role and at least one of the three justices sitting on a case must be a woman. An attempt is made to make the experience of a court appearance less daunting than occurs in an ordinary criminal case and, to this end, juvenile courts do not sit in public. Nevertheless, there are those who feel that the whole notion of court appearances for juveniles is inappropriate and that other, less formal, methods of disposal of juvenile offenders should be introduced. The Scottish system of children's hearings has attracted considerable attention in this respect. Children's hearings do not take the form of prosecutions adjudicated by a court but consist of hearings by a panel whose function is to determine the future of an errant child[2].

See also: Care proceedings; Juvenile crime

1. For a good account of juvenile courts, see Hoggett BM Parents and Children (2nd ed, 1981) Sweet & Maxwell, London.
2. In exceptional circumstances, the Lord Advocate may direct that a person under the age of 16 is prosecuted in terms of the Social Work (Scotland) Act 1968, s.31 (see Act of Adjournal (Summary Proceedings) (Children) 1971 (SI 1971/446)).

Juvenile Crime

Juvenile crime constitutes a discrete area of study in criminology. The young offender has become something of a political football in that juvenile crime is frequently seen as an indictment of society and its failures. The juvenile criminal is a reproach to his elders, yet he is viewed as potentially more salvageable than is the hardened adult criminal.

Juvenile crime is distinguished by a preference for theft and other offences against property, especially vandalism. There is a high incidence of violence between the ages of 17 and 21 which is greater than that amongst offenders over 21 years of age[1]. Drug-related offences are common amongst juveniles and this problem is increasing. The tendency for criminal offences to be committed when acting in groups is a particular feature of juvenile crime, and youth gangs have been the subject of extensive criminological study. In the USA, earlier works on gangs emphasised the institutionalisation within them of pointless, defiant violence[2]; later contributions, however, questioned this view and identified purposive features lying behind gang activity[3]. British studies have stressed the relatively unstructured nature of juvenile gangs, concluding that juvenile crime is often committed by informal groups or by one or two young people acting in concert[4]. National and regional differences within

Britain tend to affect the form of gang activity; it would be difficult to see the Glasgow youth gang operating in quite the same way in the south of England[5].

The cause of juvenile crime is highly problematic; the aphorism *quot homines tot sententiae* is particularly pertinent. Much attention has been paid to the significance of such factors as an extremely high incidence of parental divorce or separation in the homes of young offenders[6]; recently, more attention has been paid to broader issues such as family tension[7]. Economic factors, imitation of the violence seen daily on television programmes and the breakdown of parental and school discipline are also regarded as significant factors in the aetiology. The weight attached to such factors may depend to a large extent on the social and political standpoint of the commentator.

Psychological and psychiatric profiles of the juvenile offender have revealed some differences between offenders and non-offenders. Juvenile offenders would appear to have a higher incidence of health[8] and learning problems[9] and these, together with other environmental factors, may certainly contribute to the incidence of delinquency.

1. West DJ *The Young Offender* (1967) p.20, Duckworth, London. *See also* West DJ *Delinquency: Its Roots, Careers and Prospects* ('The Cambridge Study') (1985) Heinemann/ Gower, London.
2. Cohen AK *Delinquent Boys: The Culture of the Gang* (1971) Free Press, New York.
3. For discussion, *see* Hall Williams JE *Criminology and Criminal Justice* (1982) p.116 et seq, Butterworths, London.
4. Downes D *The Delinquent Solution* (1966) International Library of Sociology.
5. Patrick J *A Glasgow Gang Observed* (1973) Eyre Methuen, London.
6. Glueck S and Glueck E *Unravelling Juvenile Delinquency* (1950) Commonwealth Fund/ Harvard University Press, Cambridge MA; Burt C *The Young Delinquent* (1945) University of London Press, London.
7. Rutter M *Maternal Deprivation Reassessed* (1981) Penguin, New York.
8. Penner MJ 'The role of selected health problems in the causation of juvenile delinquency' (1982) 17 Adolescence 347.
9. *See*, for example, Satterfield JH et al 'A prospective study of delinquency in 110 adolescent boys with attention deficit disorder and 88 normal adolescent boys' (1982) 139 Amer J Psychiat 795; Wolff PH et al 'The neuropsychological states of adolescent delinquent boys' (1982) 23 J Child Psychol Psychiat 267.

K

Kicking Injuries

The human leg is a powerful weapon with a leverage system amplifying the action of the strongest muscles in the body and being assisted, often, by heavy boots. Moreover, the foot is a convenient instrument for the infliction of injury on an opponent who is already partially overcome. Kicking injuries are therefore not only common but also may be severe, the gravity of internal lesions often greatly surpassing what might have been expected from external inspection.

There is something of an atavistic impulse to embed the foot in the body — hence there is a predeliction for concavities such as the neck, beneath the ribs where the liver is at risk and in the lumbar region where the kidney may be severely traumatised. Head injuries are frequent and damage to the neck may result in traumatic subarachnoid haemorrhage[1].

Kicking is often accompanied by jumping or stamping, when the organs in the abdominal cavity may be extensively injured as the flaccid wall is compressed. Severe muscle damage beneath the point of contact is almost diagnostic of a kick. The heel of the shoe may be used as a screwdriver, producing particularly unpleasant injuries if inflicted by a female.

See also: Abdominal cavity; Subarachnoid haemorrhage

1. Watson AA 'Kicking, karate and kung-fu' in Mason JK (ed) *The Pathology of Violent Injury* (1978) Chap.16, Edward Arnold, London.

Kidney Failure

Kidney failure is basically of two types — due to damage to the glomeruli or to the tubules.

Glomerular damage is of major medical importance by virtue of the disease called glomerulonephritis — which results from a complex antigen/antibody reaction and is of no medico-legal significance. The glomeruli cannot recover once they are severely damaged and, if sufficient are destroyed to cause kidney failure, the available treatments are either lifetime dialysis or renal transplantation. Pyelonephritis is a different form of inflammation of the kidney which results from infection. Infection may be blood borne or ascend from the bladder; it follows that anything which predisposes to cystitis (inflammation of the bladder) — such as injury requiring repeated or prolonged catheterisation — may, after some time, also cause pyelonephritis. Pyelonephritis may also destroy the glomeruli and, thus, cause kidney failure. It is to be noted that any disease of the glomeruli may cause hypertension, with all the potential ills which that involves.

Acute renal failure is essentially a disease of the tubules and is of intense forensic importance in that the majority of cases spring from unnatural conditions. The common factor of all causes of acute renal failure is hypoxia of the organ; this is usually a matter of surgical shock although some cases may be due to poisoning. Among other causes, anything which reduces the blood volume — especially haemorrhage and burning — may give rise to the risk of acute renal failure. The condition is frequently associated with disseminated intravascular coagulation. The damaged renal tubules may well recover if reoxygenated; the treatment of acute renal failure is therefore a matter of treating shock and of dialysis until regeneration occurs[1].

See also: Antibody; Antigen; Dialysis; Disseminated intravascular coagulation; Hypertensive disease; Surgical shock; Transplantation of organs

1. Flynn CT 'Renal failure following injury and burning' in JK Mason (ed) *The Pathology of Violent Injury* (1978) Chap.19, Edward Arnold, London.

Knife Wounds

Serious wounds caused by knives may be of two main types — those due to the sharp edge of the weapon and those due to the use of the knife to cause penetrating injury.

The former depend upon a very sharp blade and are more realistically attributed to razors. Some knives will, however, be sharp enough to cause such injuries, which are described under 'Incised wounds'. They are particularly connected with cut throat and suicidal wounds of the wrist; defence injuries, described under that heading, also come into this category. The major distinction between suicidal and homicidal wounds lies in the presence of tentative cuts in the former; all cuts are likely to be clearly aggressive in the homicidal situation.

Penetrating knife wounds are described under 'stab wounds'.

The knife point abrasion is a minor, though important, knife wound. It is characterised by a thin linear abrasion which scabs readily. Such injuries may be evidence of overcoming the will through fear. These must, however, be distinguished from self-inflicted abrasions which are not uncommon as 'cris de coeur' or as attempts to fabricate evidence; the regularity of depth of the abrasions is often a clue to such an origin. Knife point abrasions are often inflicted after death particularly in killings with sexual overtones; these will show no vital reaction but the exuded tissue fluids will dry and give a spurious impression of infliction *in vivo*.

See also: Abrasions; Cut throat; Defence injuries; Incised wounds; Stab wounds; Vital reaction

L

Lacerations

Lacerations are, in general, of two types. In the first, the skin is torn by shearing and stretching forces; such injuries are the common result of road traffic or serious industrial accidents.

The second type is of greater medico-legal importance and results from compression and splitting of the skin between two hard objects. The injuries are therefore found characteristically over the skull and bony prominences. Lacerations will be irregular and ragged; they will show some degree of bruising because the causative object is blunt; not all structures within the wound will be equally damaged in the compression — thus, for example, strands of fibrous tissue may cross the wound, leaving the phenomenon known as 'bridging'; the small vessels will be crushed and bleeding will not therefore be a major feature; and superficial structures, such as hairs, may be found deep in the wound.

Lacerations of this second type will generally appear linear but this may be due to no more than the rounded shape of the underlying bone; those which result from assaults are commonly caused by bottles, pokers, wooden clubs and the like. The shape of the laceration thus gives little clue to its precise origin; the importance of recognising the injury for what it is lies in the fact that it clearly indicates attack with a blunt instrument. It may be noted that the boxer's so-called 'cut eye' is, in fact, a laceration of the skin overlying the supraorbital ridge.

Lacerations of the face and scalp may also arise as a result of falls onto hard surfaces. The bone underlying any laceration, whether inflicted or accidental, is liable to be fractured.

See also: Bruises; Fractures; Incised wounds

Lap Belts

Lap belts were at one time fitted in motor cars and were permitted in the front seats of light aircraft until 1980. There are both theoretical and practical reasons for supposing that these belts have their own specific dangers — mainly connected with forced flexion over a very efficient fulcrum. The main consequence is that, in the event of sudden deceleration, the head and upper torso strike objects in front such as the facia or windscreen with great force exaggerated by the 'dynamic overshoot' effect. Lap belts have also been responsible for the so-called 'lap belt injuries' which have been described in the abdominal cavity. All these dangers will be markedly limited by the wearing of an upper torso restraint which is now mandatory in the front seats of motor cars and aircraft (*see* 'Seat belts').

The use of lap belts in commercial aircraft is defensible on several grounds. From the negative aspect, it would be almost impossible to find adequate attachment points for torso harnesses and, if they were to be provided, the clutter of abandoned harnesses would probably cause more deaths during attempted egress following a crash than would be prevented. Positively, the lap belt is probably adequate for protection in accidents other than those which would be non-survivable with any form of restraint provided. This is because the fully flexed position can be assumed before impact and the seat in front is collapsed; the crash environment is thus converted into one which is relatively friendly.

See also: Abdominal cavity; Aircraft accidents; Seat belts

Larynx

The larynx, or voicebox, lies between the floor of the mouth and the trachea (windpipe). The voicebox itself is formed by the opposing vocal cords and is protected anteriorly by three structures labelled (from above downwards) the hyoid bone, the thyroid cartilage (or Adam's apple) and the cricoid cartilage which are interconnected by ligaments.

The medico-legal significance of the larynx is wide. The bone and cartilages are at risk of injury during strangulation — especially of manual type; the laryngeal opening is narrow and is liable to occlusion by foreign bodies as in choking; by the same token, swelling of the laryngeal mucosa, which is a common complication of allergy, may cause death through mechanical asphyxia. In such instances, or in severe infections, it may be necessary to make a hole in the trachea below the larynx (tracheostomy) in order to save life.

See also: Allergy; Choking; Hyoid bone; Strangulation; Throttling

Lead Poisoning

Lead is one of the most widely distributed metallic poisons. Its particular danger is that it accumulates in the body — especially in the bones — and minor exposure over long periods may therefore be of major importance. It is used widely in industry — and the scrap metal trade may be a potent source — but its use in the house (e.g. through paints, water pipes or, even, toys) has been greatly restricted by good practice, legislation[1] and expense. It may be absorbed by inhalation, which is the most dangerous portal of entry, by ingestion or through the skin.

Lead poisoning may be acute. This must now be very rare; its association with abdominal pain has led, in the past, to surgical operations for a supposed acute abdominal emergency. Far more general importance relates to chronic poisoning, the main features of which are muscle paralysis, anaemia and mental symptoms which may be misdiagnosed as psychoneurosis. Women and children are particularly affected by lead poisoning and their employment in lead manufacturing premises is strictly controlled[2]. Children, especially, may exhibit lead encephalopathy, the symptoms of which are not unlike those of intracerebral haemorrhage and which may be fatal. Severe chronic poisoning of this type can arise from emission of toxic vapours into the air — the prevention of which is specifically regulated[3].

Currently, greatest interest lies in insidious poisoning which may give rise to no more than lassitude and mental dullness. In this context, the motor vehicle provides probably the most significant source, tetraethyl lead being deliberately added to petrol. Pollution from this source is controlled by legislation[4] and the lead content of petrol now sold in the UK must not exceed 0.15 g/l; European Community legislation envisages the use of lead-free petrol, and discussions as to the form of motor engineering which is best suited to this aim is in progress at the time of writing. Inevitably, argument rages as to whether small increases in the body lead content do affect children materially but there is some evidence that insidious poisoning is responsible for mental retardation. The blood lead in children should be less than 0.4 mg/l; higher values demand investigation and, possibly, treatment. The comparable level in industrial workers is given as 0.8 mg/l; by contrast with many poisonous substances, the major proportion of the lead in blood is found in the erythrocytes.

Lead poisoning is a prescribed disease for social security purposes and is also a notifiable disease under the Factories Act 1961.

See also: Encephalopathy and encephalitis; Environmental poisoning; Erythocytes; Industrial poisoning; Intracranial haemorrhage; Notifiable diseases; Prescribed diseases and occupations

1. *See* Control of Lead at Work Regulations 1980 (SI 1980/1248), made under the Health and Safety at Work etc. Act 1974.
2. Factories Act 1961 ss.74, 128.
3. Health and Safety at Work etc. Act 1974, s.5; Health and Safety (Emission into the Atmosphere) Regulations 1983 (SI 1983/943).
4. Control of Pollution Act 1974, s.75.

Lesbianism

This form of homosexuality, involving sexual activities between women, has not attracted the same degree of legal attention as has male homosexual conduct. Lesbianism as such has never been outlawed in the UK, although it could constitute the offence of 'disgraceful conduct of an indecent kind' under military law. A Bill to criminalise lesbianism was introduced in 1921 but failed to attract the necessary support. One contributor to the debate in Parliament argued that it would be unwise to legislate in this way because it would only result in lesbianism being brought 'to the notice of women who have never heard of it, never thought of it, never dreamed of it'[1].

The only occasion then on which lesbian activity in private will attract criminal sanctions is when there is no consent on the part of one participant (indecent assault) or when one of the participants is under the age of 16 and therefore incapable of consenting[2]. Consent is likewise impossible in the case of a woman mental defective[3]. A woman who performs an act of gross indecency with a girl under the age of 14 or who incites the commission of such an act by a girl under 14, commits an offence under the Indecency with Children Act 1960, s.1(1). Similar behaviour in Scotland could be construed as lewd, indecent or libidinous practice[4].

See also: Homosexuality; Sexual offences

1. Quoted by Crane P *Gays and the Law* (1982) p.8, Pluto, London.
2. Sexual Offences Act 1956, s.14(2), (4).
3. Ibid, s.14(4).
4. Sexual Offences (Scotland) Act 1976, s.5.

Lewd Practices

Lewd and libidinous practices constitute the Scottish equivalent of indecency with children — i.e. sexual practices which fall short of indecent assault.

Lewd practices with children of either sex are an offence at common law when those affected are below the age of puberty. Similar conduct with girls between the ages of 12 and 16 years is a statutory offence[1]; consent is no defence nor is error as to age, but it is to be noted that there is no such offence in relation to boys over 14 years old.

See also: Indecency with children

1. Sexual Offences (Scotland) Act 1976, s.5.

Libel and Slander

Libel is a form of defamation, being distinguished from slander in that the former is recorded in permanent form, usually in writing[1]. Words which are broadcast on radio or television are considered to have been published in permanent form and may therefore be libellous[2]. A libel action can be taken both in tort and as a criminal offence although there is some opposition to the latter form[3]. Libel is actionable *per se*, unlike slander which, in most circumstances, requires proof of special damage — or damage which is quantifiable in monetary terms. The requirement of publication of a statement is satisfied provided that it has been made to a person other than to the plaintiff.

Liability will be imposed in respect of a defamatory statement if that statement can lower the plaintiff's reputation in the eyes of ordinary, right thinking people. Examples of the type of statement which may be considered defamatory include allegations of dishonesty, of sexual deviance or of incompetence in the exercise of a profession. An imputation that a person suffers from a contagious disease may also be defamatory; there may be many who will give a wide berth to those thought to be suffering from socially unpopular conditions, particularly venereal diseases[4]. The use of innuendo may transform apparently innocent words into a defamatory statement.

The most important defences in defamation are those of truth, fair comment and privilege. Truth justifies a defamatory comment even if this is made maliciously; the defence of fair comment will protect statements which are made on the basis of correct facts and which are matters of public interest; privilege is either absolute or qualified, and protects a person who makes potentially defamatory statements in the discharge of his duties or in any other similar context.

See also: Confidentiality; Privilege

1. Dias RW and Markesinis BS *Tort Law* (1984) p.322, Oxford University Press, Oxford; Dias RWM (ed) *Clerk and Lindsell on Torts* (15th ed, 1982) p.895 et seq, Sweet & Maxwell, London.
2. Defamation Act 1952, s.1.
3. *Goldsmith v Pressdram Ltd* [1977] QB 83 is a recent instance of criminal libel.
4. Dias RWM (ed) *Clerk and Lindsell on Torts* (15th ed, 1982) p.909, Sweet & Maxwell, London.

Lightning

The effects of a strike by lightning can be very variable. The flash incorporates the application of an electric current of very high intensity, the primary effects of 'flash' burning, secondary thermal burning due to ignition of clothing or surroundings and the pressure effects of a severe blast wave.

Lightning strike may well occur while the victim is alone, and the discovery of a body with severe injuries — including fractures — may lead to a suspicion of assault. The diagnostic sign, when present, is of superficial arborescent skin burns but careful search may also disclose clothing burns; ferrous material in the pockets may become magnetised and, due to the heat generated, may imprint the skin where it is in contact.

Beyond these aspects of differential diagnosis, deaths due to lightning are of little forensic significance. It is, however, remarkable that the passage of the electric current may be so rapid that injury is recoverable with prompt treatment. More than half those struck by lightning can, in fact, be salvaged.

See also: Blast injuries; Burning; Electricity

Limitation of Liability

The Limitation Act 1980 imposes a limit of time in which an action in tort involving personal injuries can be brought. In general, this limit is three years, which dates either from the time at which the cause of action occurred or from the time the person injured had knowledge of his injury (s.11). In the event of death, the limiting period is, again, three years dating either from the time of death or from the time the personal representatives of the deceased would have had knowledge of the cause for action. Moreover, an action under the Fatal Accidents Act 1976, as amended by the Administration of Justice Act 1982, s.3, cannot be brought if the death of the person occurred at a time when an injured person could not, himself, do so[1]; a limitation of three years imposed in the Fatal Accidents Act 1976 applies either to the date of death or from the date on which the person for whose benefit the action is being taken had knowledge of the cause of death — this applies separately to each dependant if there is more than one such person (s.13).

In all cases, the date of knowledge means the date on which the person concerned first had knowledge that the injury was significant, that it was attributable wholly or in part to alleged negligence, nuisance or breach of duty and of the identity of the defendant (s.14). Section 14(3) also defines a person's knowledge as including that which he might have been expected to acquire from facts obtainable or ascertainable by him or which could be obtained with the help of such medical or other expert advice which it might have been reasonable for him to seek.

Knowledge, it has been held[2], is a word which has a clear meaning and to which full effect must be given — reasonable belief or supposition is not enough to trigger the time-bar clock.

Under s.33 of the 1980 Act, the court has strictly delineated powers to allow an action to proceed, despite its being apparently time disbarred, if it is thought to be equitable to both parties.

See also: Personal injuries

1. Limitation Act 1980, s.12.
2. *Davis v Ministry of Defence* (1985) Times, 7 August.

Live Birth

Live birth is best defined as the contrast to stillbirth — that is, it is the status of a fetus which has achieved a separate existence from its mother and has breathed or shown other signs of life.

The condition is essentially legal in concept and is to be distinguished from viability, which is a medical term implying a capacity to survive apart from the mother. There seems no reason why failure to attempt to maintain a live birth in the living state should not be regarded as homicide or as an offence against the Children and Young Persons Act 1933, s.1. Doctors in the USA have been accused of homicide on at least two occasions, having failed to maintain abortuses which lived[1], and several States have adopted provisions making it a crime to fail to sustain the life and health of a living aborted infant.

See also: Abortion; Amniocentesis; Homicide; Separate existence; Stillbirth; Viability

1. *Commonwealth v Edelin* 359 NE·2d 4 (Mass, 1976) — acquitted as a matter of law on appeal; *see also* Towers B 'The trials of Dr Waddill' (1979) 5 J Med Ethics 205 — no further action after two 'hung juries'.

Liver Disease and Injury

The liver is a massive, solid organ weighing approximately 1.5 kg and lying behind the right lower ribs. It has a wide range of functions, including the storage of carbohydrates, the metabolism of fat and protein, the formation of bile and detoxification; the last includes manipulation of the normal waste products of the body's metabolism and also of many drugs and extraneous poisonous substances including alcohol. It is therefore clear that all the blood must pass through the liver; moreover, since it has a secondary portal supply bringing digested food products from the gut, toxic substances or pathogenic organisms in the bowel may well be passed to the liver and be lodged there. This is the basis of the almost invariable involvement of the liver in metastatic malignant growth which is primary in the gut; however, other tumours metastasise readily to the liver by virtue of its blood-clearing function.

The liver may be overcome in its attempts to detoxify, and many poisonous substances damage the organ in this way. Alcohol has such an action although its precise mode is uncertain but there are, in addition, many substances of medico-legal importance, including, particularly, the halogenated hydrocarbons used in industry and as anaesthetics which are hepatotoxic — the effect of the latter is potentiated by any concurrent hypoxia. Some drugs have an action not on the liver cells themselves but rather on the bile-forming mechanism — the tranquilliser chlorpromazine was a good example of this type of toxic action. There are many organisms which specifically attack the liver. The virus of hepatitis is an obvious example but bacteria of the genus *Leptospira* are important in industry and leptospirosis is a prescribed disease; many helminths lodge in the liver and one, *Taenia echinococcus*, is closely associated with dogs and sheep farming. The liver which has sustained toxic or microbiological necrosis is capable of regeneration but its organised structure is often lost and the organ is less able to withstand further insults; recovery from liver damage is almost always accompanied by some degree of cirrhosis. Death of the liver means death of the person, and courageous efforts are being made in the field of liver transplantation; the technique is considerably harder than that involved in renal transplantation but rejection of the organ is less marked[1].

A major function of the liver is to excrete in the bile the bile pigments which are derived from the breakdown of effete erythrocytes. Liver failure is associated with the accumulation of bile pigments in the plasma; jaundice, or yellowness, is therefore a common sign of liver disease — toxic jaundice, or jaundice arising from industrial poisoning, is listed as a prescribed disease although the jaundice itself is no more than a marker of underlying liver disease.

The sheer size of the liver and its relative immobility render it liable to crushing injuries and, for the same reason, it is likely to be injured in gunshot or knife attacks or in assaults involving kicking; laceration of the liver is common in vehicular accidents. The anatomy of the organ makes surgical repair a very difficult procedure, and death from haemorrhage is common following such injuries. The structure of the liver renders it very sensitive to vibration. Widespread destruction of liver tissue is therefore a common finding in severe deceleration injuries such as those resulting from falls from great heights; such injuries are, however, of little more than academic interest as they are always associated with other untreatable traumatic lesions.

See also: Anaesthesia; Cancer; Cirrhosis; Deceleration injuries; Hepatitis; Industrial poisoning; Malignant disease; Prescribed diseases and occupations; Transplantation of organs

1. Calne RY et al 'Improved survival after orthoptic liver grafting' (1981) 283 Br Med J 115.

Living Abortus

In 1984, 2,032 abortions were carried out on residents of England and Wales late in pregnancy (20th week or over). Sixteen per cent of these were performed on the ground of a substantial risk of handicap to the child. This ground comprised only 1.6 per cent of all English and Welsh abortions and it is reasonable to attribute the great discrepancy to the delay imposed by current methods of antenatal diagnosis[1]. Thus, with improved medical care, a number of fetuses aborted late may well be delivered alive and a high proportion are likely to be physically or mentally handicapped.

The obstetrician is thus in a clinical, legal and moral dilemma. It has been authoritatively stated that it is: 'Unlawful for termination of pregnancy to be carried out by a method which destroys a foetus capable of being born alive, even if its chances of survival are slight or non existent, unless this is done in order to preserve the life of the mother. . .If a live and apparently viable foetus emerges from the termination, there is a statutory duty to try and (sic) keep it alive, however unwanted or abnormal it may be, and for the mother and child to be cared for by a midwife for 10 days. Further, if after delivery a foetus shows signs of life, an offence is committed if its birth and death are not registered or if it is incinerated other than in a crematorium'[2].

Attitudes have changed since 1974 and it would now be possible to consider the position in the light of the fetus being either normal or abnormal. In the former case, it is difficult to see how a doctor who deliberately contrives the death of a living abortus is not guilty of some form of homicide; in the absence of an offence of feticide, this would probably be most appropriately child destruction as the lethal sequence began with the victim *in utero* but it could be manslaughter or murder depending upon the circumstances[3]. The obstetrician might attempt to justify his failure to sustain the infant on the grounds that the primary object of the procedure was to relieve the woman of her fetus. He could also deny that he has a duty of care to the abortus; this has been suggested as being a genuine option[4] but it seems a far cry from the Hippocratic ideal. The courts seem anxious to avoid public examination of the real issues; what appears to be the only relevant British case resulted in an unprecedented rejection of a prosecution instigated by the DPP[5]. Perhaps the only way of satisfying the doctor's conscience, observing the law and, at the same time, achieving the purpose of an abortion is for it to be recognised that a mature abortus has the same rights as a prematurely born infant and that any resulting viable fetuses should be regarded as parentless infants and offered for adoption.

The treatment of the living but defective abortus should logically follow the pattern adopted for the defective neonate (*see* 'Neonaticide') with the exception that, in the abortion case, the views of the parents should be considered only if they have a change of mind and agree to support the child. The principles of ordinary/

extraordinary treatment would then apply, the overriding feature being the best interests of the infant — the likelihood of a successful adoption would weigh heavily in the balance of treatment decisions.

See also: Abortion; Abortion Act 1967; Adoption; Amniocentesis; Child destruction; Feticide; Homicide; Negligence; Neonaticide; Ordinary/Extraordinary treatment

1. Although this is clearly not always the reason. For example, more than half (53 per cent) of the total abortions carried out in England and Wales in 1984 on women who were 20 or more weeks pregnant were classified as being performed on non-residents.
2. Lane Justice (chairman) *Report of the Committee on the Working of the Abortion Act* (Cmnd 5579) (1974) para.278, HMSO, London.
3. Based on *R v West* (1848) 2 C & K 784, 175 ER 329.
4. Paul EF and Paul J 'Self ownership, abortion and infanticide' (1979) 5 J Med Ethics 133.
5. *R v Hamilton* (1983) *The Times*, 16 September, p.1.

Local Anaesthesia

Local anaesthesia can be achieved by injection of anaesthetic into a sensory nerve, which will free the whole of the receptor area from pain, or by injection of the terminal endings of the nerve by local infiltration, which will be adequate for a very circumscribed operation. The needs for the latter can, in fact, be sometimes met by local freezing but we are here concerned with the anaesthetic properties of the group of drugs which are derived from cocaine.

Whilst local anaesthetics are generally very safe, that safety depends upon recognition of the fact that a proportion of the drug is inevitably absorbed into the circulation and on how well that amount is detoxified. The latter is a matter of general fitness but the former is subject to some well-known hazards. Absorption from certain areas — especially the nasopharynx — is notoriously fast whilst widely dilated vessels will absorb relatively rapidly. The local anaesthetic is therefore often combined with a vasoconstrictor substance and this, in itself, may have a profound effect on heart function if it is absorbed in too great a quantity. There is also a general hazard that the whole dose may be injected into the lumen of a blood vessel.

The hazards of local anaesthesia therefore include overdosage of either the anaesthetic or of the vasoconstrictor agent — which is a matter of correlation with the age, stature and physical condition of the patient — or of rapid absorption from whatever cause. Severe reactions in the form of central nervous system involvement or of direct cardiac effect are, however, very rare — albeit sufficient to indicate caution in, say, the elderly and infirm. Of perhaps greater importance is the possibility of permanent damage if an excess of anaesthetic is injected directly into a nerve.

Spinal anaesthesia is a form of local anaesthesia which is discussed as a separate entry.

See also: Spinal anaesthesia

Lumbar Puncture

Lumbar puncture is an invasive method of examining the cerebrospinal fluid and, by derivation, the central nervous system. It involves inserting a needle of fairly wide bore through the spinal processes and dura mater into the subarachnoid space. The fluid withdrawn can be examined in the laboratory.

The alteration in volume induced can lead to some disability. Headache occurs in about a quarter of those so investigated and is probably made worse by a continuing leak of fluid from the puncture hole. In addition, the patient may complain of dizziness and abnormal hearing and there may be vomiting. These conditions are normally transient but may last for weeks. In some disease states — especially when there is cerebral tumour or subdural haemorrhage — the procedure may precipitate a dangerous shift of the brain and there is always a remote risk of introducing infection.

Modern non-invasive techniques have now eliminated much of the need for lumbar puncture but it is still essential for the diagnosis of meningitis (*see* 'Nervous system') and it will be indicated as part of the investigation of many neurological diseases; it is needed for the induction of spinal anaesthesia and for the introduction of radio-opaque material; and it may sometimes be necessary to introduce drugs directly to the subarachnoid space. Otherwise, the test should probably not now be undertaken as a primary means of diagnosis[1].

See also: Central nervous system; Nervous system; Spinal anaesthesia

1. Pearce JMS 'Hazards of lumbar puncture' (1982) 285 Br Med J 1521.

Lung Disease and Injury

The lungs occupy the greater part of the thoracic cavity. Each is divided into lobes — upper and lower on the left, and upper, middle and lower on the right. The structure consists essentially of a mass of alveoli (air sacs) which are surrounded by a network of capillaries. It is here that the atmospheric oxygen is transferred to the blood and the excess carbon dioxide is removed from the plasma. The alveoli are the end-points of the bronchioles, which derive from the bronchi; the left and right main bronchi form the terminal division of the trachea (windpipe).

The lungs are surrounded by two layers of serous membrane known as the pleura and are maintained in an expanded formation by a negative pressure which exists between the pleural layers; any penetration of the pleura which breaks this pressure differential will lead to collapse of the lung, and a collapsed lung is a potent nidus for infection. Partial collapse of a lung occurs when air is excluded by blockage of a bronchus or bronchiole; any foreign body — including a tooth inhaled during dentistry — can do this, as may plugs of mucus or of pus.

Bacteria and dust from the air are prevented from reaching the alveoli and are removed from the bronchial tree by the action of cilia (brushes) on the bronchiolar epithelium. Chronic inflammation of the bronchi — chronic bronchitis — destroys the cilia and pus accumulates; the process is thus self-perpetuating and is aggravated by many irritants such as excess dust or cigarette smoke. The alveoli may also become affected and break down into far larger, inefficient spaces — emphysema. Chronic bronchitis and emphysema almost invariably complicate the pneumoconioses, or dust diseases.

Acute inflammation within the alveoli is known as pneumonia. This may be primary and involve whole lobes — lobar pneumonia — or spread secondarily from the bronchioles — bronchopneumonia. The distinction is described under 'Pneumonia'. Tuberculosis is — or was — the most important chronic bacterially mediated inflammation of the lung tissue. Chronic irritation of the lung by mineral dust results in fibrosis which may be progressive (*see* 'Pneumoconioses').

Carcinoma (cancer) of the bronchus is the commonest malignant tumour occurring in British men. There is a very marked association with cigarette smoking and this is exaggerated if there is simultaneous exposure to asbestos. Asbestosis is also associated with the rare malignant tumour of the pleura — mesothelioma.

The delicate structure of the lungs is very sensitive to the mechanical stresses of deceleration or blast — widespread pulmonary haemorrhage is a feature of both. Expansion of air in the alveoli may also result in rupture (*see* 'Diving hazards'). Wounds of the lungs by bullets or by knives are usually unilateral and, unless a major vessel is involved, may well be survivable given timely treatment — the associated collapse actually protects against serious capillary haemorrhage.

Pulmonary oedema — 'water on the lungs' — may be primary or secondary and is discussed under that heading.

See also: Asbestosis; Cancer; Emphysema; Pneumoconioses; Pneumonia; Pulmonary oedema; Smoking; Stab wounds; Tuberculosis

Lysergic Acid

Lysergic acid diethylamide (LSD) is a major example of a group of synthetic drugs which alter the senses — known popularly as either hallucinogens or psychedelics, neither of which is semanticaly accurate but both of which are descriptively acceptable.

The main features of LSD are, firstly, the very small amount which needs to be taken for an effect; the corollary is that equally small variations in dose may lead to major alterations in response. Secondly, the effect is dramatic, the distortions of sensation being vivid and transcendental. Thirdly, the precise effect is unpredictable and depends to an extent on the environment in which the drug is taken — the use of LSD in solitude is probably uncommon because the distorted perceptions are then likely to exaggerate the intrinsic anxieties of isolation.

In general, however, the effects are gratifying and the desire for a repetition is likely to progress to a psychological dependence. True addiction does not seem to occur and there is no evidence that the use of LSD is detrimental *per se* — any apparent social deterioration is probably an expression of the life style of the drug taker rather than the result of its use. There is, however, no doubt that users of LSD can be dangerous to themselves and to others when under the influence of the drug — many reported instances of affected persons 'flying out of the window' are undoubtedly true[1]. The detection of LSD in the tissues, particularly at autopsy, is technically difficult but is, nevertheless, possible in a good laboratory.

Lysergic acid is a Class A controlled drug under the Misuse of Drugs Act 1971; its possession is always illegal unless it is licenced by the Secretary of State[2].

See also: Drug addiction; Hallucinogens; Misuse of Drugs Act 1971

1. *R v Lipman* [1969] 3 All ER 410.
2. Misuse of Drugs Regulations 1985 (SI 1985/2066), Sch.1.

M

M'Naghten Rules

The M'Naghten Rules form the basis of the defence of insanity in English law and have greatly influenced the development of criminal law in the USA and in the Commonwealth[1].

Daniel M'Naghten was a paranoid schizophrenic who suffered from delusions of political persecution. In 1843, he shot the Prime Minister's secretary, believing him to be the Prime Minister himself. A great deal was made at his trial of modern psychiatric studies which discredited the then popular notion that insanity was either total and starkly evident or was absent. M'Naghten was eventually found to be insane and a special verdict was brought in which committed him to hospital. The resultant public outcry led to the summoning of the judges before the House of Lords, an unusual step, and the posing to them of five questions as to the basis and operation of the legal rules relating to insanity. The judges' answers lay down the grounds of responsibility when an accused person is thought to be insane. Some of the answers ceased, in due course, to be of legal significance in that they embodied early nineteenth century notions of 'partial insanity', a concept which envisaged the person who harboured delusions on a particular subject or subjects as being otherwise sane. It is the answers which were provided to the second and third questions which have survived as the core of the defence of insanity.

In brief, this section of the M'Naghten Rules provide that an accused person is to be held to be insane if, acting under the influence of a disease of the mind, he either does not know the nature and quality of his act or he does not know that it is wrong. The objections to this view of insanity and criminal responsibility are discussed under that heading.

See also: Insanity and criminal responsibility

1. There is a full account of M'Naghten's trial in Walker N *Crime and Insanity in England* (1968) Vol.1, p.84 et seq, Edinburgh University Press, Edinburgh.

Maceration

Maceration is aseptic necrosis of tissues. The effect is similar to putrefaction but the latter is due to bacterial action. In either case, the tissues are irrevocably dead at cellular level.

The most important manifestation in medico-legal terms is the macerated fetus. The appearance of maceration clearly indicates that the fetus has died *in utero* and its recognition is one of the few ways in which a doctor who was not present at a birth can certify a stillbirth with certainty.

See also: Putrefaction; Stillbirth

Maim

Maim, or mayhem, is a common law offence involving an act which permanently disables a man and consequently reduces his military usefulness[1]. The offence is an archaic one but it would still be technically possible to secure a conviction[2]. The essence of the offence is that the act deprives the victim of a limb or of an important organ; consequently, cases have tended to relate to the cutting off of legs or feet but have also included damage to eyes, ears and nose[3].

No crime is committed if there is sound reason for the damage, as in the case of amputation of a limb for medical reasons. Consent to the harm is no defence in the absence of such justification. Castration provides a modern example of a potential maim in the absence of therapeutic indications.

See also: Castration; Consent to injury; Sterilisation

1. There is a full discussion of maim in Skegg PDG *Law, Medicine and Ethics* (1985) p.43 et seq, Oxford University Press, Oxford. *See also* Meyers DW *The Human Body and the Law* (1970) pp.15, 18, Aldine, Chicago.
2. Ormrod R 'Medical ethics' [1968] 2 Br Med J 7.
3. Turner JWC (ed) *Russell on Crime* (12th ed, 1964) Vol.1, p.625, Stevens, London.

Malice Aforethought

A confusing term, 'malice aforethought' describes the *mens rea* of murder. It is clearly present when the defendant intended to kill his victim; it may also be present when he committed an act without such intention but, nevertheless, knew there was a high degree of probability that it would cause the death of another. Malice aforethought would also be present if he acted with an intention to cause grievous bodily harm to another or if he knew there was a high degree of probability that such harm would arise[1]. This rule is riddled with anomalies and it has been suggested that it should be confined to cases where the act was known to the defendant to involve a risk of causing death. The doctrine of constructive malice, whereby a death occurring in the course of unlawful conduct could be treated as murder irrespective of the mental attitude of the perpetrator, was abolished by the Homicide Act 1957, s.1.

See also: Homicide; *Mens rea*; Murder

1. *R v Cunningham* [1981] 2 All ER 863.

Malignant Disease

Malignant disease is the excessive overgrowth of body tissues which, for reasons which are only partially understood, break free of the restraints which nature puts upon normal growth and replacement (*see* 'Cancer'). Benign tumours or overgrowths also occur but the malignant tumour is distinguished as being of the nature of a parasite; death occurs either as a result of destruction of vital organs (eg the liver) or from cachexia — the energy designed to support the body is drained away to satisfy the needs of the tumour.

A massive amount of research is applied to the causes and treatment of malignant disease, the nature of which imposes very great ethical dilemmas for the researchers[1] (*see* 'Biomedical experimentation'). Treatment designed to destroy malignant cells by the use of cytotoxic drugs must also affect normal tissues which are rapidly dividing for the purpose of replacement; such effects are often unpleasant and, again, raise both ethical and practical problems in the management of terminal illness. The use of ionising radiation in the treatment of malignant disease is discussed briefly under 'X-rays'.

See also: Biomedical experimentation; Cancer; Euthanasia; X-rays

1. A very good exposition is to be found in Bliss BP and Johnson AG *Aims and Methods in Clinical Medicine* (1975) Chap.8, Beekman, New York.

Malpractice

'Malpractice' is a term which is increasingly widely used as a synonym for 'medical negligence'. It tends to have a somewhat broader meaning in the USA, where it is also used to cover a doctor's behaviour which would constitute serious professional misconduct in the UK and which would lie within the disciplinary ambit of the General Medical Council.

See also: General Medical Council; Negligence

Manic-Depressive Psychosis

Manic–depressive psychosis is the functional psychosis which is affective in type and is, thus, associated with disorders of mood. The distinction between the normal response to environment — which runs from great happiness to despair — and psychosis is often blurred but the precipitating factors are generally inadequate to justify the response which occurs in the psychotic; in the extreme case there is little or no relation to reality. Reactive depression, or the occurrence of a true depressive illness in a stable personality, is a response to severe stress which bridges the gap.

The severe manic–depressive has a cyclothymic personality with sudden swings from elation to depression. Delusions are frequent and these are often self-critical to an extent which may precipitate suicide; since the depressive is likely to be under treatment, the ready availability of potent drugs greatly increases that risk. The very serious extension of this aspect of the illness is that the depressive may also murder his family. The manic–depressive in a manic phase is likely to commit various offences associated with intolerance of others — including road traffic offences. Shoplifting is frequently committed by depressives. The underlying condition need not be the classic psychosis but may be of reactive type; this is particularly common in middle-aged women, in whom commission of the offence may be an indication of an urgent need for treatment.

Treatment of the depressive is not without danger. The increased possibilities of suicide have been mentioned. The monoamine oxidase inhibitor group of drugs inhibit the breakdown of the amino acid tyrosine; tyrosine is present in excess in many foods — of which cheese is the most important — and actions for negligence have been successful when doctors have failed to warn their patients of the likelihood of interaction. Many psychiatrists regard electroconvulsive therapy as a treatment of choice, and this has its own hazards. The place of brain surgery in the treatment of depression is discussed separately (*see* 'Psychosurgery').

Chronic reactive depression may so much impair a person's mental responsibility as to justify reducing a charge of murder to one of manslaughter[1].

See also: Diminished responsibility; Drug interaction; Electroconvulsive therapy; Psychoses; Psychosurgery

1. *R v Seers* (1984) 79 Crim App R 261.

Manslaughter

Manslaughter is a variety of homicide, less serious than the crime of murder, which does not attract a fixed penalty on conviction. There are two varieties — voluntary and involuntary. Voluntary manslaughter occurs when the defendant has the *mens rea* of murder, malice aforethought, but when, at the same time, there is a mitigating factor. Provocation was the only such factor acknowledged under common law but two additional factors — diminished responsibility and killing within a suicide pact — have been introduced by statute[1].

Involuntary manslaughter is a somewhat vague legal concept. Many cases of homicide, although falling short of murder, will, nevertheless, include some element of unlawfulness which distinguishes them from accidental killings and it is this 'elusive factor' which identifies them as manslaughter[2]. Unlawfulness may exist in relation to deaths resulting from neglect, negligence or recklessness or to deaths resulting from frankly unlawful conduct.

Failure to perform duties which would be expected by virtue of a relationship with another person may result in criminal liability if that person dies from neglect. Well-known instances of this proposition are *R v Senior*[3], in which the defendant was charged with the manslaughter of his child for whom he had failed to secure necessary medical aid, and *R v Instan*[4], which concerned the neglect of an elderly relative. It has been affirmed in a number of other cases that there may be a conviction for manslaughter when death is due to a failure to provide food, shelter or medical treatment in circumstances where the deceased was dependent on the defendant for such assistance[5].

Negligence resulting in death should lead to a charge of manslaughter only if its degree amounts to *gross* negligence. The courts have been reluctant to impose liability for manslaughter in lesser degrees of negligence, which have been considered as 'misadventure'[6]. In *R v Bateman*[7], a doctor was charged with the manslaughter of a woman patient whom he had allegedly treated negligently. The court's ruling, which has since been widely accepted, was that criminal liability should not be imposed when the negligence was such as would normally attract only civil liability — liability for manslaughter was appropriate when there was such negligence as to be deserving of criminal punishment. The distinction is between making a 'mere mistake, an error of judgement, and doing something which is grossly and palpably wrong'[8].

Prosecutions of doctors for manslaughter following upon negligent treatment are, in fact, rare and most of the reported cases come from the nineteenth century[9]. Simpson drew attention to the importance of alcohol as a cause of improper treatment[10]. In a recent example from South Africa a doctor serving his internship was convicted of culpable homicide following the death of a patient to whom he had administered a drug in excessive quantities. His ignorance of the dosage could have been easily rectified by consultation or reading[11]. A very recent and interesting case concerned a dentist whose patient died while undergoing single-handed dentistry and anaesthesia; although the conviction for manslaughter was later quashed on judicial review, the dentist's name was still erased from the dental register[12].

Reckless action may also lead to conviction for manslaughter. The act may be lawful in itself but the *mens rea* of manslaughter may be present if it is performed in a way which demonstrates reckless disregard for the possibility of injury to others.

A death resulting from an unlawful act may be prosecuted as manslaughter — so-called 'constructive manslaughter'. The essence of the offence is that there must be an unlawful act directed at another and that the unlawful act must be one which all sober and reasonable people would realise was likely to cause some, albeit not serious, harm[13]; whether or not psychiatric damage can be regarded as actual bodily harm is a complex issue[14] (*see* 'Special sensitivity'). An act is directed at another if it is done with some sort of animosity towards that person. The supply of a controlled drug from which the recipient later died has been held not to be manslaughter as there had been no act directed at the victim which was likely to cause injury[15].

See also: Culpable homicide; Malice aforethought; Provocation; Recklessness; Special sensitivity

1. Homicide Act 1957, s.4.
2. Per Lord Atkin in *Andrews v DPP* [1937] AC 576 at 581; 2 All ER 552 at 554; Smith JC and Hogan B *Criminal Law* (5th ed, 1983) p.311, Butterworths, London.
3. [1899] 1 QB 283; *R v Bonnyman* (1942) 28 Crim App R 131.
4. [1893] 1 QB 450.
5. *R v Gibbins and Proctor* (1918) 13 Crim App R 134; *R v Jones* (1901) 19 Cox CC 678; *R v Curtis* (1885) 15 Cox CC 746.

6. *R v Finney* (1847) 12 Cox CC 625; *Andrews v DPP* [1937] AC 576, [1937] 2 All ER 552.

7. (1925) 19 Crim App R 8.

8. At p.13. For criticism of the 'circularity' of the *Bateman* test, *see* Smith and Hogan (n.2 above), p.322.

9. *See*, for example, *R v Macleod* (1874) 12 Cox CC 534 and cases cited in Mitchell S and Richardson PJ (eds) *Archbold: Pleading, Evidence and Practice in Criminal Cases* (42nd ed, 1985) pp.1639–1640, Sweet & Maxwell, London.

10. Simpson K *Forensic Medicine* (8th ed, 1979) p.53, Edward Arnold, London (9th ed, 1985, Simpson K and Knight B).

11. *S v Mkwetshana* 1965 2 SA 493.

12. *Abrol v GDC* (1984) 156 Br Dent J 369.

13. *Brian Dawson, Stephen Thomas Nolan, Ian Walmsley* (1985) 81 Crim App R 150 per Watkins LJ.

14. Stallworthy M 'Can death by shock be manslaughter?' (1986) 136 NLJ 51.

15. *R v Dalby* [1982] 1 All ER 916; cf. *R v Cato* [1976] 1 All ER 260.

Marihuana

See 'Cannabis and its aliases'.

Marriage

Marriage, as defined by the registrar at civil ceremonies, is the union of one man with one woman voluntarily entered into, for life, to the exclusion of all others. The widespread use of divorce has clearly eroded this ideal but the principle remains. Marriage by 'cohabitation with habit and repute' is still possible in Scotland[1] but, in general, certain well-defined preliminaries and ceremonials are required before a legal marriage; not all of these invalidate a marriage if they are infringed and, then, they do so only if the disregard was 'knowing and wilful'[2]. Only those requirements which are of potentially medico-legal interest are mentioned here.

The legal age for marriage is 16 years, and a marriage is void if either party is below that age[3]; a genuine belief that one's 'wife' was over 16 years old is a defence to charges under the Sexual Offences Act 1956, s.6. Parental or custodial consent is needed if a party is aged less than 18 years but the lack of consent does not invalidate the marriage[4]. The conditions under which a marriage is void or voidable are discussed under 'Nullity of marriage'. It is to be noted that a decree of nullity entitles a wife to the same consideration as when the marriage has been dissolved.

The prohibited degrees of marriage are to be found in the Marriage Act 1949, Sch.1, and the Marriage (Scotland) Act 1977, Sch.1. The list in the latter is rather longer as the possibility of a relationship more distant than that of grandparent is accepted. The prohibited degrees include half blood and illegitimate relationships. Marriage between a man and his adoptive mother or adopted daughter is forbidden but first cousins may marry and marriage is permissible between a man and his former wife's sister, aunt or niece[5]. There has been a general move towards eliminating prohibitions due to affinity and this has been achieved in Australia. The prohibited relationships for marriage are wider than those for incest in England and now in Scotland (Incest and Related Offences (Scotland) Act 1986).

See also: Age of consent to sexual practices; Age of majority; Incest; Nullity of marriage

1. *Shaw v Henderson* 1982 SLT 211.
2. Marriage Act 1949, ss.25, 49.
3. Marriage Act 1949, s.2.
4. Marriage Act 1949, s.48.
5. Marriage (Enabling) Act 1960, s.1.

Matricide

Matricide — the killing of one's mother — is a rare crime which is very markedly related to sons. The crime is some twice as common as patricide but, even then, results in only 4–12 cases per year in England and Wales. It is strongly associated with schizophrenia and the homicides are characterised by extreme violence[1]. Other relatively common features include the absence of a father in the home and sexual immaturity in the son. Chiswick[2] has, however, pointed out that thousands of schizophrenics live at peace with their mothers and that family murder, which accounts for almost half of all homicides in Britain, is a complex interaction of individual characteristics of both victim and murderer. A significant proportion of the crimes are due to no more than sudden rage. Attempts to conceal the crime are very rare.

See also: Homicide; Schizophrenia

1. Green CM 'Matricide by sons' (1981) 21 Med Sci Law 207.
2. Chiswick D 'Matricide' [1981] 2 Br Med J 1279.

Medical Examiner

The medical examiner is the primary medico-legal authority in many of the United States and in some parts of Canada. The office of medical examiner, rather than of the legal authority, is responsible for the investigation of sudden and suspicious deaths. Under this system, a single medical man visits the locus of death and decides upon the need for autopsy examination. He may, indeed, perform the autopsy himself but it is usual for two pathologists to testify as to the postmortem findings.

On the conclusion of his inquiries, the medical examiner, who has been in close liaison with the police, may drop the case and certify death or he may refer the matter to the district attorney.

The precise arrangements differ from State to State but it is apparent that the system is streamlined and potentially most efficient; nevertheless, it depends to a very great extent on the confidence of the public in the holder of the office.

The medical examiner system has very largely displaced the office of coroner in the USA. There, however, the coroner may well be unqualified in either medicine or law and he is generally elected, sometimes on a political basis; the position is scarcely comparable with that of the coroner in England and Wales.

See also: Coroner

Medical Referee

The medical referee is appointed by the appropriate Secretary of State on the nomination of the cremation authority; his main function is to provide written authority for the cremation of individual bodies. He must be a registered medical practitioner of at least five years' standing[1]. A deputy medical referee must also be appointed and, in an emergency, the medical referee of one cremation authority may act for another authority.

The medical referee has wide powers. In addition to authorising a cremation, having, *inter alia*, satisfied himself that the death has been registered, or that a coroner's or procurator fiscal's certificate has been issued, and that the inquiries into the death have been adequate, he may in any case decline to allow cremation and need not give his reasons for so doing[2]. He may, if he so wishes, investigate the death himself — including the performance or authorisation of a postmortem examination — or he may report the case to the coroner or procurator fiscal.

There is no reason why a medically qualified coroner should not be a medical referee, in which case he may give his own coroner's certificate (Form E).

See also: Coroner; Cremation; Procurator fiscal; Registered medical practitioner

1. Cremation Regulations 1930 (SR&O 1930/1016), r.10.
2. Ibid, r.12(7).

Medicines Act 1968

This is a massive Act, the main concern of which is to regulate the pharmaceutical industry so that medicinal substances are supplied safely to the public. Medicinal products are defined (s.130) as any substances (not being instruments, apparatus or appliances) that are manufactured, sold, supplied, imported or exported for use by being administered to human beings or animals for medicinal purposes or that are ingredients of a substance or article used for medicinal purposes. A medicinal purpose includes treatment or prevention of disease, diagnosis, contraception, induction of anaesthesia or interference with a normal physiological function in either a negative or positive way.

The Act introduces licensing and certification relating to the manufacture and sale of medicinal products (Part II), regulates how they may be sold (Part III), defines and registers pharmacies (Part IV), lays down rules for labelling, packaging and identification of medicinal products (Part V) and circumscribes the advertising of such products (Part VI). Thus, a large number of potential offences are introduced, many of which are beyond the scope of a relatively short note. Those aspects of the Act which most closely concern the doctor (or dentist or veterinarian) relate to the supply of medicines to the public and to the promotion of drugs to the medical profession.

Section 52 of the Act makes it illegal for any person other than a pharmacist working in a registered pharmacy to sell or offer for sale any medicine which is not specified as being in the General Sale List (s.51)[1]. Section 58 introduces a class of medicinal product which may be sold only in accordance with a prescription given by an appropriate practitioner. The list of these is long, covering the great majority of drugs likely to be used in modern treatment, and is to be found in the Medicines (Products other than Veterinary Drugs)(Prescription Only) Order 1983[2]. One effect of ss.52 and 58 is to leave a group of drugs which may be sold without a prescription but only from a pharmacy — these are known as Pharmacy medicines. Regulations concerning the various types of medicinal products are described under the appropriate headings[3].

The most important aspect of Part VI, medico-legally speaking, is s.96 which institutes 'data sheets' for all medicinal products. These must contain all reasonable information, both favourable and prejudicial, which will enable the practitioner to assess the value of the particular product[4]. A *Data Sheet Compendium* is issued annually by the Association of the British Pharmaceutical Industry. Data sheets have two main effects — they ensure that advertising is not biased but, at the same time, their existence provokes a strong presumption of negligence should any precautions advised in them be ignored.

Part I of the Act is of great importance to the medical profession in establishing a Medicines Commission[5] which has the power to recommend the setting up of committees. Of those extant, the Committee on the Safety of Medicines is the most significant.

See also: General Sale List medicines; Medicines Commission; Pharmacy medicines; Prescription Only medicines

1. Medicines (Products other than Veterinary Drugs) (General Sale List) Order 1984 (SI 1984/769).
2. SI 1983/1212.
3. For an effective overview of the supply situation, *see* Hay CE and Pearce ME *Medicines and Poisons Guide* (2nd ed, 1980) Pharmaceutical Press, London.
4. Medicines (Data Sheet) Regulations 1972, SI 1972/2076.
5. The Medicines Commission and Committees Regulations 1970, SI 1970/746.

Medicines Commission

The Medicines Commission[1], which consists of a Chairman and 13 members, is appointed to advise the lisensing authorities as to the regulation of the supply of medicinal substances under the Medicines Act 1968. The Commission has power to appoint committees whose function is to oversee the safety, quality or efficiency of medicines and to promote the collection and investigation of information relating to adverse reactions to drugs on which such advice is based.

The most significant of these is the Committee on the Safety of Medicines[2], which receives notification of adverse reactions from practitioners. The practitioner need have no proof of a causal relationship between a drug and a reaction — a suspicion is sufficient — nor need the Committee have evidence which would satisfy a statistician before they take action. Once a sufficient volume of suggestive evidence has been collected, however, the Committee can move rapidly on its own authority and can circulate warning notices drawing the attention of practitioners to areas of danger. A drug may also be withdrawn from circulation or the Commission may advise that it be further regulated. At the time of writing, an action in negligence against the Medicines Commission has been raised by sufferers from the ill-effects of an antirheumatic drug.

See also: Medicines Act 1968

1. Medicines Commission and Committees Regulations 1970 (SI 1970/746).
2. Medicines (Committee on Safety of Medicines) Order 1970 (SI 1970/1257).

Mens Rea

Mens rea is the guilty state of mind required for a conviction in the majority of criminal offences[1]. The main exception to this rule is that there is no such requirement in statutory offences of strict liability. The *mens rea* requirement will vary from offence to offence. That of murder, for example, is malice aforethought — an intention to kill; the *mens rea* of rape is intention to have sexual intercourse without the woman's consent or a recklessness as to whether or not she consented.

Mens rea may exist if there was intention to do the illegal act at the time of its commission, if there was recklessness in relation to the act or if there was negligence. Intention is the most important concept and one which has given rise to considerable confusion in the courts and in legal writing. Many crimes require an intention not only to act wrongfully but also to achieve certain consequences; this is the case with murder. In *Hyam v DPP*[2] the House of Lords affirmed that foresight of the high probability of a consequence could constitute an intention to bring that consequence about. The concept of recklessness has also been the subject of much legal debate which is considered under that heading. Negligence may amount to *mens rea*, as when the defendant has engaged in risky conduct and has failed to take reasonable steps to ensure that his actions do not result in harm to others. The degree of negligence required for attracting criminal liability is relatively high; the concept is one which has mainly civil implications.

Certain criminal law defences operate to negative *mens rea*. These include mistake and also a failure to foresee the consequences of an action.

See also: Foreseeability; Negligence; Recklessness

1. For general discussion, *see* Smith JC and Hogan B *Criminal Law* (5th ed, 1983) p.47 et seq, Butterworths, London. The issue is extensively reviewed in the Law Commission *Criminal Law: Report on the Mental Element in Crime* (Law Com No.89) HMSO, London.
2. [1974] 2 All ER 41, HL.

Menstrual Extraction

A form of birth control, menstrual extraction involves aspirating the uterine cavity between one and three weeks after a missed menstrual period, using a thin suction curette.

The term would seem to be a euphemism for early abortion but neither semantically nor legally can it be properly so regarded, because the fact of pregnancy is uncertain. The present state of the law in this area is unclear[1] but it is difficult to see how the precise conditions of the Abortion Act 1967 can be satisfied by the procedure. All in all, it seems wise to take a pragmatic view. Whilst it is possible that an offence in terms of the Offences Against the Person Act 1861, s.58 is committed in any event[2], it is equally certain that menstrual extraction is one of the least traumatic forms of abortion available — in particular, there can be no question of maternal bonding; the criminal law would surely lose respect were it to insist on such delay as necessarily entailed the destruction of a more mature fetus. At the same time, it has to be admitted that a difficult situation would arise in the unlikely event of perforation of the uterus and death following the procedure. It is hard to see why the recommendations of the Lane Committee[3], designed to close this anomalous gap, were not put into force.

See also: Abortion; Abortion Act 1967; Offences Against the Person Act 1861

1. Tunkel V 'Abortion: how early, how late and how legal?' [1979] 2 Br Med J 258.
2. There could be no offence in Scotland unless the fact of pregnancy were proved — a near impossibility.
3. Lane Justice (chairman) *Report of the Committee on the Working of the Abortion Act* (Cmnd 5579) (1974) HMSO, London.

Mental Health Act 1983

The three major legislative landmarks in the English law of mental disorder are the Mental Treatment Act 1930, the Mental Health Act 1959 and, finally, the Mental Health Act 1983. The philosophy underlying these Acts has become progressively more liberal and has moved away from the former 'asylum' view of mental illness to one which emphasises voluntary admission to hospital and the avoidance of coercive treatment as far as is possible. The 1983 Act consolidates most of the law relating to mentally disordered persons, including the mentally ill, those who are mentally impaired and those who are suffering from psychopathic disorder.

The Act provides for the compulsory admission to hospital of those who have a degree of mental disorder which warrants detention for assessment or treatment; the criteria for such detention are that the patient needs to be detained either in the interests of his own health or safety or with a view to the protection of others (*see* 'Detention in mental hospitals'). Provisions are made for the appointment of a guardian to a mentally disordered person under the age of 16 (ss.7–15). The rights of the patient in a mental hospital are principally protected by Part IV of the Act, which deals with consent to treatment, Part V, which deals with mental health review tribunals, and Part VII, which deals with the management of patients' property and affairs. It is specifically provided in the Act that it is an offence to ill-treat or neglect patients in hospitals or mental nursing homes (s.127).

Part III of the Act considers mentally disordered persons who are the subject of criminal proceedings. In certain circumstances, the Crown Court or Magistrates' Court may remand an accused person to hospital for a report on his mental condition (s.35). Such removal cannot be for more than 28 days at a time nor for more than 12 weeks in all. The Crown Court may also remand an accused person to hospital for treatment, for similar periods, if it has evidence from two medical practitioners that treatment is required for mental illness or for severe mental impairment.

It is also open to the courts, on the evidence of two medical practitioners, to impose hospital and guardianship orders on those who are convicted of offences punishable by imprisonment (s.37); the details are discussed under 'Hospital orders'. A restriction order may be imposed on a patient admitted to hospital by the Crown Court under Part III of the Act (s.41). These orders, which have been the subject of controversy[1], are detailed under that heading.

The Scottish legislation on mental health, the Mental Health (Scotland) Act 1984, embodies much the same therapeutic philosophy as does the English Act although there are major differences in structure and in some of the provisions. Particular features of the Scottish Act include the Mental Welfare Commission, which has a broader brief than does the English Mental Health Act Commission, and the functions of the sheriff in respect of reception into guardianship and detention in hospital (*see* 'Detention in mental hospitals').

See also: Consent to medical treatment; Criminal responsibility; Detention in mental hospitals; Hospital orders; Mental Health Act Commission; Mental Welfare Commission for Scotland; Restriction orders

1. *X v United Kingdom* (1982) 4 EHRR 118; *Kynaston v Secretary of State for Home Affairs* (1981) 73 Crim App R 281; *see*, now, s.41(6) of the 1983 Act.

Mental Health Act Commission

The concept of an independent body charged with the task of protecting the interests of mental patients is one which is not new to Scotland[1] but one which was introduced in England only in 1983[2]. The Commission includes both medical and lay membership drawn from varying walks of life. It has a number of duties, the most important of which are:

(a) The appointment of doctors and others who will issue certificates relating to certain forms of trust.
(b) Receiving reports on treatment carried out on certain categories of patient and of non-consensual treatment given under the Mental Health Act 1983, s.58.
(c) Exercising general protection over detained patients (this does not include power to order the release of patients).
(d) Advising the Secretary of State on the code of practice to be drawn up to guide doctors, social workers and others on the problems of dealing with mentally ill patients.
(e) Scrutinising censorship of patients' mail.

Legally, the Commission is a special health authority under the National Health Service Act 1977, s.109(d).

See also: Mental Health Act 1983

1. The Mental Welfare Commission was introduced in Scotland by the Mental Health (Scotland) Act 1960, s.2.
2. Mental Health Act Commission Regulations 1983 (SI 1983/894).

Mental Impairment

The Mental Health Act 1983 provides for the compulsory admission to hospital, both for assessment and for treatment, of those suffering from mental impairment and severe mental impairment — these terms being substituted for those of 'subnormality' and 'severe subnormality' which appeared in earlier legislation. Mental impairment is defined as: 'A state of arrested or incomplete development of mind (not amounting to severe impairment) which includes significant impairment of intelligence and social functioning and is associated with abnormally aggressive or seriously irresponsible conduct on the part of a person concerned' (Mental Health Act 1983, s.1(2)).

The significance of this definition lies in the fact that the non-offending mentally impaired person may now be compulsorily detained in hospital only when his behaviour is socially dangerous; there was no such qualification in the previous legislation. Furthermore, he may be detained compulsorily only if detention is likely to prevent or alleviate a deterioration of the condition; on the other hand, the severely mentally impaired non-offender does not have to be considered treatable in order to be eligible for long-term admission.

A guardian may be appointed to the mentally impaired person. The 1983 Act requires that such an appointment should be necessary for the welfare of the patient or for the protection of others (s.7(2)(b)). It follows that a guardian may be appointed to a mentally impaired patient only if that person is behaving in an abnormally aggressive or irresponsible way; the grounds for intervention in the lives of mentally impaired people are, thus, strictly limited.

A mentally impaired person who commits a criminal offence may be considered unfit to plead, in which case he is detained in hospital until he is discharged by the authority of the Home Secretary or is sent back for trial; this situation is rare. Alternatively, mental impairment may lead to a plea of not guilty by reason of insanity or, in the case of homicide, to one of diminished responsibility. If a conviction results, or could result, in cases (other than murder) in which the sentence might be custodial, the court may make a hospital order. Such an order can be made only if the court is satisfied that a hospital bed will be available within 28 days (s.37(4)). The practical effect is that the hospital authorities can block the admission to hospital of unwelcome offenders. This has been the subject of both academic criticism and judicial disapproval[1] in so far as the likelihood of mentally impaired persons ending up in prison is, thereby, increased.

It has been pointed out that a useful alternative method of dealing with the mentally impaired offender would be the imposition of a guardianship order[2]. Such an order gives a guardian considerable discretion over the life style of the offender.

See also: Diminished responsibility; Hospital orders; Insanity and criminal responsibility; Mental Health Act 1983; Unfitness to plead

1. *R v Harding* (1983) Times, 15 June. *See also* 'Mental disorder and prison' (1984) 289 Br Med J 1387.
2. Hoggett B *Mental Health Law* (1984) p.182, Sweet & Maxwell, London.

Mental Patients' Rights

A mentally disordered person who is a voluntary patient in a psychiatric hospital enjoys the same rights as to his personal freedom as does a patient in an ordinary hospital. He may leave whenever he wishes and may be subject only to such restrictions as are necessary for the effective and smooth running of the institution. He may, of course, be restrained in order to protect either himself or others, such restraint being limited to what is strictly and immediately necessary in the circumstances[1].

The patient detained involuntarily is in a different position. He may be prevented from leaving the hospital until he is discharged on expiry of his period of detention or until he is discharged following upon appeal to a mental health tribunal. The hospital has other powers over his person additional to this restriction of his liberty.

It is now clear that there is statutory power to treat the patient for his mental illness without his consent provided that the requirements for non-consensual treatment are observed. One effect of these requirements is to limit substantially the application of the more serious treatments in the case of patients who do not consent.

The powers of the hospital in relation to the day-to-day life of detained patients are nowhere specifically stated but there can be no doubt that courts would uphold the right of hospital authorities to take steps needed to run the hospital efficiently and to ensure that the patients harm neither themselves nor others. A reasonable restriction of visiting hours and restrictions on the property brought by patients into hospital would be acceptable. A patient could not be compelled to work unless the work was part of a programme of occupational therapy. Placing a patient in solitary confinement may be necessary in some circumstances and, therefore, legally acceptable but such steps must not infringe the statutory provision which makes it a criminal offence for the staff of a hospital to ill-treat a patient (Mental Health Act 1983, s.127). The Royal College of Psychiatrists considers the use of isolation to punish patients as unacceptable unless it is part of the process of treatment[2].

A patient detained under the Mental Health Act 1983 is entitled to receive an explanation of his legal position from the hospital managers (s.132(1)). This explanation must be given as soon as is practicable and must be provided both orally and in writing. Hospital managers are required to include in this information, *inter alia*, an explanation of rights to apply for a hearing by a mental health tribunal, of the statutory provisions relating to treatment and of the relevant powers vested in the Mental Health Act Commission. Other pieces of information which must be conveyed to the patient include any reclassification of his disorder and any renewal of a period of detention (ss.16(4) and 20(3)).

The mail of detained patients may be censored and this includes the interception of mail unwanted by the addressee (s.134(1)(a)) and, in the case of special hospitals, of mail likely to cause distress to persons outside the hospital. Incoming mail for the latter category of patient may be withheld in the interest of safety of the patient or others (s.134(2)). Censorship must be recorded and both the sender and the intended recipient informed of the action taken. The hospital managers cannot interfere with mail from correspondents such as Members of Parliament, officers of the Court of Protection or mental health tribunals.

The restrictions placed on the right of the detained patient to litigate over acts done in connection with mental health legislation have been the subject of controversy. Liability of the authorities to civil or criminal proceedings will be imposed only if the act in question was done in bad faith or without reasonable care (s.139(1)); the section does not, however, exclude the possibility of judicial review nor of a writ of habeas corpus[3]. Criminal proceedings may be brought only by the Director of Public Prosecutions or with his consent (except in cases of ill-treatment or neglect arising from s.127 of the Act) and civil proceedings require the leave of the High Court. This latter provision has now been clarified[4]. The Court of Appeal has held that a detained patient wishing to bring civil proceedings against a doctor does not have to establish a prima facie case before High Court leave is given; the question to be determined is whether the applicant's complaint deserves such fuller investigation as would be possible if an action were allowed to proceed. This interpretation certainly makes it easier for a patient to assert his rights.

The legal rights and the general legal position of the mentally disorderd are affected by the fact of mental disorder whether or not they are detained patients. The contractual and testamentary capacities of the mentally disordered are dealt with under the latter heading. The 'family rights' of the mentally disordered are also subject to restrictions. The marriage of a mentally disordered person may be annulled on the grounds of absence of valid consent[5] or on the grounds that one of the parties was suffering from mental disorder of such a nature as to make him unfitted for marriage[6]. Mental disorder may, of course, provide grounds for divorce if it leads the respondent to behave in such a way that the petitioner cannot reasonably be expected to live with him.

A mentally disordered parent involved in a custody dispute may be denied custody if the court considers that it would not be in the best interests of the child to live with such a parent. The child of a mentally ill parent might be taken into care by a local authority on the grounds of the parent's inability to look after him[7].

The property needs of a mentally disordered person may be dealt with in a variety of ways. Although private arrangements are possible, these will not apply in every case and a power of attorney granted before the onset of the illness is rendered invalid by the later incapacity; consequently, the most common method of dealing with property will be through the Court of Protection.

See also: Care proceedings; Court of Protection; Divorce; Habeas corpus; Mental Health Act 1983; Mental Health Act Commission; Nullity of marriage; Testamentary capacity

1. *Pountney v Griffiths* [1976] AC 314; Hoggett B *Mental Health Law* (2nd ed, 1984) p.205, Sweet & Maxwell, London.
2. Royal College of Psychiatrists *Isolation of Patients in Protected Rooms during Psychiatric Treatment* (1980).
3. *In re Waldron* (1985) Times, 8 October.
4. *Winch v Jones and Others*; *Same v Hayward and Others* (1985) Times, 16 July.
5. Matrimonial Causes Act 1973, s.12(c).
6. Ibid, s.12(d). *Bennett v Bennett* [1969] 1 WLR 430.

7. Child Care Act 1980, s.3.

Mental Welfare Commission for Scotland

The Mental Welfare Commission for Scotland was established by the Mental Health (Scotland) Act 1960 but is now governed by the terms of the Mental Health (Scotland) Act 1984, Part II. The purposes of this body are, essentially, to prevent ill-treatment of patients, to remedy deficiencies in their care or treatment, to ensure that they are not improperly detained and to protect the property interests of patients. The Commission operates on a relatively informal basis but may hold formal inquiries under the National Health Service (Scotland) Act 1978, s.76. The most commonly received complaints of ill-treatment relate to physical assault; the Commission's investigations are then designed to prevent a recurrence. The police and procurator fiscal may be informed and criminal prosecution may follow, as will internal disciplinary measures. The Commission also investigates accidents involving patients, allegations of financial irregularities in conducting the affairs of patients and may, as a last resort, exercise a power to discharge a patient.

See also: Mental Health Act Commission

Further reading
The work of the Mental Welfare Commission for Scotland is outlined in the Commission's publication *Does the patient come first?* (1981) HMSO, Edinburgh.

Mercy Killing

Mercy killing is euthanasia by another name. The motive in mercy killing is one of relieving the victim of intolerable pain or suffering and it is therefore morally different from killing a victim with malice aforethought.

Nevertheless, the act is *prima facie* murder in that the person performs it with the intention of ending life. The fact that the motive might be viewed as benevolent is of no signficance as far as the theoretical criminal law is concerned but, in practice, mercy killings will most probably be prosecuted as manslaughter rather than as murder. Such cases tend to attract much sympathy from both judge and jury, as the killing is frequently carried out by a person who has nursed the victim with great devotion. The removal of a fixed penalty for murder and its substitution by a flexible and responsive scale of sentencing would remove the need for the legal pretence that such killings are not premedidated homicide and would, at the same time, protect the concept of diminished responsibility against undue extension. The Law Commission did, in fact, at one time recommend the introduction of an offence of mercy killing but retracted this on further consideration[1].

See also: Euthanasia; Manslaughter; Murder

1. For suggestions for reform, *see* Criminal Law Revision Committee, Report 14, *Offences Against the Person* (Cmnd 7844) (1980) HMSO, London. *See also* Leng R 'Mercy killing

and the CLRC' (1982) 132 NLJ 76; and Smith KJM 'Assisting in suicide; the Attorney General and the Voluntary Euthanasia Society' [1983] Crim LR 579.

Methanol

Methanol (or methyl alcohol) is far more toxic than is ethyl alcohol (ethanol). It is deliberately added to ethanol (ethyl alcohol) which is intended for industrial and household use. Industrial methylated spirits consists of ethanol with 5 per cent added methanol; it can be issued only from pharmacies on the written order of medical or laboratory practitioners and not more than 1 pint can be dispensed at any one time; the container must be marked 'for external use only'. The ordinary household equivalent, known as mineralised methylated spirits, is ethanol containing 9 per cent methanol with added colouring matter and disgustants. The sale of methylated spirits is limited in Scotland to the terms of sale of Part II Poisons (*see* 'Poisons Act 1972')[1]. Pure methanol is used as an antifreeze.

The toxicity of methanol depends to some extent on its very slow metabolism, the greater part of that which is ingested being excreted in the breath. The symptoms of poisoning — drunkenness, blindness, coma and death — are likely to be delayed, sometimes by as much as a day. Death due to respiratory depression is likely if more than 100 ml methanol is consumed.

Occasional cases of poisoning have been reported from absorption through the skin but the great majority are due to accidental drinking — including deliberate 'spiking' by others — with a few being due to deliberate drinking. This last is a not uncommon practice — the 'meths' being used to supplement relatively palatable forms of alcoholic drink — and, although it is possible that ethanol acts to inhibit the toxic effects of methanol, some form of habituation to methanol must occur. Recovery from methanol poisoning generally leaves some residual blindness and, sometimes, severe kidney damage.

See also: Alcohol; Drunkenness; Poisons Act 1972

1. Methylated Spirits (Sale by Retail) (Scotland) Act 1937.

Minors

Minors are persons aged under 18 years, which is the legal age of majority. Scots law embodies a further classification of this group — that of pupils, who are girls under the age of 12 and boys under the age of 14.

The legal capacity of the minor differs from that of the adult; in general, the law protects the minor from any adverse consequences of his actions, as, for example, in the area of contract. The most important issue from the medico-legal point of view relates to the minor's ability to consent to medical treatment (see 'Consent by minors').

Minors are protected against sexual activity of varying types at varying ages, being shielded from sexual exploitation by the laws relating to unlawful sexual intercourse and indecency. A minor can, however, contract a legal marriage at the age of 16. The consent of a male minor to homosexual practices is invalid, legal protection in this case existing to the age of 21 years. By contrast, homosexual practices between women are not illegal provided both are aged over 16 years.

See also: Age of majority; Consent by minors; Homosexual offences; Indecency with children; Lesbianism; Marriage; Sexual offences

Miscarriage

Etymologically, miscarriage is a failure to carry a fetus to term; the word has, however, come to be applied to the loss of a fetus in the early stages of gestation and certainly before viability. It is synonymous with spontaneous abortion.

Some women have no difficulty in conceiving but persistently miscarry; the reason for this is obscure but possibly is related to an immune rejection — this is one type of condition which may be greatly benefited by researches associated with modern reproductive technology. Several natural diseases are known to predispose to miscarriage (e.g. renal disease or diabetes). It is also probable that many chromosomally abnormal fetuses are rejected as miscarriages. As pregnancy advances, disease or abnormality of the placenta becomes of major importance and this is particularly so in the context of injury as a cause of miscarriage. It is surprisingly hard to dislodge a fetus by violence to the abdominal wall — any success probably depends upon the production of surgical shock in the mother rather than on fetal death. Dislodgement of a placenta lying anteriorly is, however, not uncommon and follows upon retroplacental haemorrhage.

The semantic association between miscarriage and abortion is interesting in that the Offences Against the Person Act 1861, which proscribes abortion at ss.58 and 59, mentions the word only in the marginal note; the text of the Act refers to procuring the miscarriage of a woman. The Abortion Act 1967, however, relates to termination of a pregnancy. Taking the two Acts together, it would seem that abortion implies a positive act to separate the fetus from its mother. 'Spontaneous abortion' is thus a useful medical description but is something of a contradiction in legal terms. It is to be noted that neither Act refers to feticide either directly or by necessary implication.

The term 'miscarriage' also has relevance to the question of whether postcoital contraception or the use of an intrauterine device contravene the Abortion Act[1]; we would agree with the view which holds that there can be no miscarriage without carriage of the embryo.

See also: Abortion; Abortion Act 1967; Contraception; Feticide; Menstrual extraction; Offences Against the Person Act 1861; Placenta; Reproductive technology

1. *See* Keown IJ '"Miscarriage": a medico-legal analysis' [1984] Crim LR 604.

Misuse of Drugs Act 1971

Until 1971, legislation on drug addiction had been very markedly related to the international control of narcotic drugs. It had, however, become clear that the drug problem was wider than was covered by the existing regulations; the scene was constantly shifting whereas the law was rigid. Moreover, there was an obvious need to introduce a constructive rather than a purely prohibitive approach to the problem. The Misuse of Drugs Act 1971 represents an attempt to address drug addiction in a comprehensive way.

Arguably, the most important part of the Act lies in s.1 which establishes an Advisory Council on the Misuse of Drugs. The Council, which consists of not less than 20 persons with wide and recent experience involving the misuse of drugs, has a very wide remit in monitoring the national situation and advising on measures to be taken in the light of changing circumstances. Apart from this available rapid response to practical misuse, the Council is directed to promote co-operation between all the social services involved in the eradication of drug abuse and to further the education of the public as to its dangers.

A basic requirement to achieving these goals is to identify drugs of a special danger and, to this end, the Act introduces a category of drugs known as 'controlled drugs'. These are subdivided into Classes A, B and C[1], the basic distinction being made on the penalty for their unlawful supply and possession (see below). In practice, it follows that the most dangerous drugs are placed in Class A which does, indeed, include all the narcotics which were previously controlled under the now repealed Dangerous Drugs Acts. In addition to drugs of addiction, Class A includes a number of the important hallucinogens, including LSD and pure cannabinol; these, having no medicinal use, are further controlled in that a special licence is required for their lawful possession (1985 Regulations (SI 1985/2066), Sch.1).

The most common offences are those of possession; the concept of possession has consequently spawned a number of intricately argued court decisions. The Act makes it an offence for any person, without lawful excuse, to have in his possession a controlled drug and it is also an offence to be in possession of a controlled drug with the intention of supplying it to others (ss.4 and 5). The significance of this distinction lies in the more severe penalties which the latter attracts. A doctor, or other authorised person, may possess a controlled drug for professional purposes, as may a person to whom the drug has been prescribed; no offence is committed if a person possesses a controlled drug under the impression that the substance was something other than what it really was. This is the mistake of fact defence allowed under s.28 of the Act.

The simplest concept of possession is that described by Lord Wilberforce in *Warner v Metropolitan Police Commissioner*[2]: 'ideally a possessor of a thing has complete physical control over it, he has knowledge of its existence, its situation and its qualities — he has received it from a person who intends to confer possession of it and he has, himself, the intention to possess it exclusively of others'.

Knowledge of the existence of the object is essential but its precise nature need not be known[3]. The courts have dealt with he problem of defendants who have been found in possession of sealed packages or containers in a series of cases known as the 'Container Cases'. The rules laid down in *Warner* apply in such cases and, in certain circumstances, lay on the accused an evidential burden to show that he had no authority or chance to open the container, that he had no reason to suspect that its contents were unlawful and that he honestly believed the contents to be of a different kind from those actually present[4].

The consumption of a drug probably means that it is no longer possessed by the consumer[5]. Minute quantities were formerly considered to be incapable of possession if they were not usable; this test has now been replaced by that which holds that a drug can be possessed if its amount can be weighed and measured[6].

It is an offence under the Criminal Law Act 1977, s.52, to possess any plant of the genus *Cannabis* with the exception of the mature stalk and seed. It is not an offence, however, to possess mushrooms containing the Class A drug psilocin unless there has been some human involvement in their preparation for consumption; 'preparation', however, is open to interpretation[7].

Section 4 of the Act outlaws the production of controlled drugs and any involvement in such production by another. Production is defined as producing the drug 'by manufacture, cultivation or any other method. . .' (s.37(1)). The supply of drugs consists of handing over possession of a drug to another; distribution is included within the meaning of the word 'supply' and consists of a number of separate acts of supply[8]. The production, supply and possession with intent to supply of Class A controlled drugs is now punishable by imprisonment for life (Controlled Drugs (Penalties) Act 1985).

Other offences under the Act include that of unlawful importation or exportation of controlled drugs (s.3(1)), permitting drug-related offences on the premises (including smoking opium) (s.8) and cultivating any plant of the genus *Cannabis*. The question of what constitutes cultivation has been construed so as to include any act designed to facilitate the growth of the plant[9].

The lawful possession of controlled drugs by doctors, dentists, veterinary surgeons and pharmacists is subject to their use being restricted to their professional capacity. Strict regulations, particularly related to Class A drugs, are enforced to ensure safe custody[10]; a locked car is not a locked receptacle for this purpose[11] but a locked glove compartment in a locked car would probably qualify. The form to be followed in prescription of controlled drugs is standardised and is detailed in the 1973 Regulations (r.15); it is to be noted, in particular, that 'repeat prescriptions' are not allowed. The Act makes a fairly major inroad into the principle of medical confidentiality in that regulations made under the Act require the medical practitioner to notify the Home Office (including notification in Scotland) of any person he attends whom he suspects is a drug addict[12]. A further innovative restriction on the power of the doctor to prescribe drugs is also introduced; a doctor is prohibited from prescribing cocaine or heroin to an addict (other than for treatment of organic disease or injury) unless he is specially licenced to do so.

Serious penalties may be imposed on doctors for committing offences under the Act and certain allied offences under the Customs and Excise Act 1952. The Secretary of State may prohibit an offending doctor from possessing or prescribing controlled drugs (s.12); such a prohibition is immediately operative once notified but it may be suspended or cancelled at any time. The Secretary of State can also prohibit a doctor from possessing or prescribing controlled drugs if the doctor prescribes drugs to an addict without notification of the case, if he supplies heroin or cocaine in non-organic conditions without the necessary licence or if it is believed that the practitioner has been prescribing controlled drugs in an irresponsible manner (s.13). The rather complex arrangements for hearings in such cases by tribunals and advisory bodies is described in s.14. It is to be noted that actions under s.14 and proceedings before the General Medical (or Dental) Council can reach independent conclusions[13].

The sentencing of offenders under the Act is controversial. The principles to be observed by the courts were laid down in the recent case of *Aramah*[14] in which the

Court of Appeal stressed that importers should be treated more severely than suppliers and users. There is, however, a strong body of opinion to the effect that punishment by the criminal law of those convicted only of possession for personal use is inappropriate and that more serious efforts should be made to help addicts to conquer their problem. At the time of writing, the Government appears to be redoubling its efforts.

In addition to regulating the possession and consumption of controlled drugs, the Act gives special powers to the police and to customs officers, the most significant from the day-to-day point of view being the power given to the police to stop and search people, vehicles or vessels, reasonably suspected of harbouring controlled drugs (s.23(2)). For further discussion, see 'Detention by the police'.

See also: Detention by the police; Drug addiction

1. Controlled drugs are listed in Sch.2 of the Act and Schs.2, 3 and 4 of the Misuse of Drugs Regulations 1985 (SI 1985/2066). Scheduling of drugs is also used in the USA under the Drug Abuse Prevention and Control Act 1970.
2. [1969] 2 AC 256.
3. *Fernandez* 1970 Crim LR 277.
4. For further discussion, *see* Lord R *Controlled Drugs, Law and Practice* (1984) p.141 et seq, Butterworths, London.
5. *Hambleton v Callinan* [1968] 2 All ER 943.
6. *Bocking v Roberts* [1974] QB 307; *R v Boyesen* [1982] AC 768.
7. *R v Stevens* [1981] Crim LR 568; extended in *R v Cunliffe (Kenneth John)* (1986) Times, 2 May. An alternative view appears in *Murray v MacNaughton* 1984 SCCR 361.
8. *See also* Customs and Excise Management Act 1979, s.170(2).
9. *Tudhope v Robertson* 1980 SLT 60.
10. Misuse of Drugs (Safe Custody) Regulations 1973 (SI 1973/798).
11. *Rao v Wyles* [1949] 2 All ER 685.
12. Misuse of Drugs (Notification of and Supply to Addicts) Regulations 1973 (SI 1973/799).
13. *Dasrath Rai v General Medical Council* [1984] 1 Lancet 1420.
14. (1983) 76 Crim App R 190. *See also Virgin* (1983) 5 Crim App R 148 (S); *McCullough* (1982) 4 Crim App R 98 (S).

Mongolism

'Mongolism' is the term which was at one time used to describe the syndrome due to trisomy-21 (*see* 'Chromosomal disease'). It tended to be dropped as giving offence to those of Asian origin and to be replaced by Down's syndrome, the eponym being derived from the physician who coined the original term. This, in turn, has been criticised in so far as Down did not discover the condition and his original paper contained what might be regarded as racist overtones. Some geneticists would prefer the retention of the terms 'mongol child' and 'mongolism'[1].

See also: Chromosomal disease; Down's syndrome

1. Edwards JH 'Mongolism' in Duncan AS et al (eds) *Dictionary of Medical Ethics* (1981) p.297, Darton, Longman and Todd, London.

Morbid Jealousy
See 'Othello syndrome'.

Mummification

A body may dry out, or mummify, if it is left in an arid environment and particularly if it is exposed to drying draughts. If the process is sufficiently fast, putrefaction is prevented, the skin becomes hard and parchmented and the human form is relatively well preserved.

The bodies of infants are comparatively sterile and putrefaction is commonly delayed; mummification is therefore a frequent finding in cases of infanticide and/or of concealment of birth. Similarly, elderly persons have relatively little tissue to putrefy and mummification is not uncommon. One medico-legally important aspect of mummification is that features indicating an unnatural cause of death may be retained far longer than would be the case in the face of normal putrefaction.

See also: Changes after death; Concealment of birth; Infanticide; Putrefaction

Murder

Murder is the most serious form of homicide, attracting a mandatory life sentence. Capital punishment has not been imposed in the UK for murder since the Murder (Abolition of Death Penalty) Act 1965, although there remains a vocal body of opinion in favour of its restoration.

The classic definition of the crime is given in Coke's Institutes:

> 'Murder is when a man of sound memory, and of the age of discretion, unlawfully killeth within any county of the realm any reasonable creature *in rerum natura* under the King's peace, with malice aforethought, either expressed by the party or implied by law, so as the party wounded, or hurt etc. die of the wound or hurt etc. within a year and a day after the same'[1].

The requirement that the victim be a 'reasonable creature *in rerum natura*' restricts the crime to the killing of self-existent human beings[2]. The year and a day rule was intended to provide an arbitrary solution to problems of causation in an age when reliable medical evidence as to the cause of death was not available. The rule still applies, although its modern justification rests on the desire to avoid an indefinite threat of serious criminal charges.

No physical injury to the victim is necessary for murder. The offence is committed, for example, if the accused has literally frightened his victim to death[3]. Similarly, frightening the victim into causing his own death may amount to murder in certain circumstances[4].

The term 'malice aforethought' is singularly unhelpful in describing the *mens rea* of murder, as neither malice nor a high degree of forethought is required. The decision in *R v Cunningham*[5] has established that the *mens rea* is present if:

(a) There was an intention to kill the victim; or

(b) There was an intention to perform an act with the knowledge that death would probably ensue; or

(c) There was an intention to cause grievous bodily harm; or

(d) There was an intention to perform an act with the knowledge that grievous bodily harm would probably result.

Specific intent is a requirement for the crime of murder; acute alcoholism could negate such intent in England but not in Scotland[6]. Murder by neglect could be charged but, in practice, a charge of manslaughter is far more likely following a death in such circumstances.

Particular difficulties arise in the context of medical practice in relation to the cessation or denial of treatment and to therapies which have the effect of shortening life. Cessation of treatment is dealt with under 'Euthanasia'. Treatment which shortens life may amount to murder if it is directed towards that specific goal. It is irrelevant that a patient may have only hours or minutes to live; to terminate that life deliberately still amounts to murder[7]. No criminal offence need be committed, however, if the treatment administered is intended to alleviate pain or suffering but has the additional effect of shortening life. Thus, in the charge to the jury in *R v Adams*, it was stated: 'If the first purpose of medicine, the restoration of health, can no longer be achieved, there is still much for a doctor to do and he is entitled to do all that is proper and necessary to relieve pain and suffering, even if the measures he takes may incidentally shorten life'[7]. Clearly, no exact rule can be stated but it is reasonable to conclude that murder will be committed only when the predominant aim is that of killing the patient rather than alleviating his discomfort. It is unlikely that the *mens rea* of murder will be inferred unless this test can be satisfied[8].

See also: Capital punishment; Causation; Double effect; Euthanasia; Homicide; Intent; Manslaughter; *Mens rea*; Neonaticide

1. 3 Coke Inst 47.
2. As to what constitutes a self-existent being, *see* 'Homicide'.
3. *R v Hayward* (1908) 21 Cox CC 692.
4. *R v Lewis* [1970] Crim LR 647.
5. [1981] 2 All ER 863.
6. *DPP v Majewski* [1976] 2 WLR 623; *Brennan v HM Adv* 1977 SLT 151.
7. Per Devlin J. Quoted in Palmer H 'Dr Adams' trial for murder' [1957] Crim LR 365.
8. *See* Beynon H 'Doctors as murderers' [1982] Crim LR 17. The importance of the doctor's intention was stressed in the judge's instruction to the jury in *R v Arthur* (unreported, 1981); *see* Medicolegal 'Dr Leonard Arthur: his trial and its implications' (1981) 283 Br Med J 1340.

Mutation

Very occasionally, a genetically determined disease appears in a family with no recognisable history. The probability is that this arises as a result of mutation or a spontaneous change in a gene. The mutation rate is not easy to evaluate because many variables are introduced except when the new gene is dominant and is always recognisable (fully penetrating). Such would certainly be the case in a mutant blood group, and the Family Law Reform Act 1969, s.25. speaks of exclusion of paternity subject to mutation. In fact, the expectation of blood group gene mutation is rarer than 1 in 1 million gene generations[1]; it is nevertheless interesting that a very early, but exhaustive, review of paternity testing experience discovered two cases in which mutation was thought to have occurred[2].

Ionising radiation exerts the most important influence on mutation and an increase in the mutation rate is proportional to the radiation dose. It is now generally agreed there is no dose of radiation which can be regarded as certainly non-mutagenic — i.e. there is no threshhold of safety (see 'Threshold limit values') — and the effect is cumulative. The majority of mutations are harmful and therefore tend to die out naturally.

See also: Parentage testing; Radiation hazards; Threshhold limit values

1. Dodd BE and Lincoln PJ Blood Group Topics (1975) p.129, Edward Arnold, London.
2. Brownlie AR 'Blood and the blood groups — a developing field for expert evidence (1964) 5 J Forens Sci Soc 124.

Myocardial Infarction

Myocardial infarction, or ischaemic death of portions of heart muscle, is the common result of acute blockage of a coronary artery, this being superimposed on coronary atheroma. The immediate effect of this is likely to be acute ischaemic pain — or angina pectoris; both patients and, occasionally, doctors may confuse this stage with acute indigestion. The heart muscle may recover completely if the limitation of blood flow is transient; at the other end of the scale, very rapid death may ensue if the part rendered ischaemic is of major importance in the nervous control of the heart beat. Otherwise, the process of infarction may be relatively slow and death depends upon the amount of muscle infarcted and the degree of shock induced in the patient. Both the presence of and the extent of infarction can be predicted from an assay of various enzymes in the blood; the persistence of enzymatic activity indicates a poor prognosis. It is possible at autopsy to assess the time interval between the original ischaemic insult and death by considering the stage of vital reaction within the infarct. The microscopic changes take some six hours to become appreciable but special histochemical methods may demonstrate the presence of an infarct before it is otherwise visible[1].

The pathologist investigating a sudden cardiac death may be in considerable difficulty. No infarct may be established and no recent thrombus will be discovered in some two-thirds of cases which will be the subject of a coroner's inquiry. The great majority of such cases will show severe coronary atheroma but it is often difficult to see why this should have caused the death at any precise moment. The probability is that hypoxia of the muscle causes ventricular fibrillation; indeed, it is likely that death results from ventricular fibrillation even when an infarct is associated with obviously occlusive arterial disease.

A full-thickness infarct may so weaken the heart wall that it ruptures, this being the mechanism of death in the majority of those who survive an infarct only to die a few days later. In very many instances, however, the damaged muscle will be repaired, leaving a fibrous scar. This scar itself may be weak and may dilate, forming an aneurysm which may, again, rupture some considerable time after the event. Thrombus may form within the aneurysmal sac, and emboli may detach from this giving rise to secondary infarcts in the brain and other tissues.

It is to be noted that, whilst coronary atheroma is widespread, the incidence of myocardial infarction varies very greatly in different populations. Scotland, for example, has a relatively high incidence of death from ischaemic heart disease even as compared with England whilst such deaths are rare amongst the Japanese[2]. Of the major factors involved, exercise is important (presumably as a way of promoting a collateral circulation), whilst smoking, with the added vasoconstrictor effect of nicotine, is undoubtedly predisposing. The role of diet is obscure; a high carbohydrate diet may be as big a risk factor as is the more widely known heavy consumption of animal fats — and both may predispose to atheroma rather than to myocardial infarction.

Modern sophisticated imaging techniques are being introduced to increase the efficiency of diagnosis and assessment of myocardial infarction. In general, however, the investigations depend upon electrocardiography. The electrocardiograph will closely define an acute infarct but is rather less efficient in the demonstration of fibrous areas — a matter of some importance as a person who has had an infarct is at greater risk of having another than is a similar person of sustaining a primary attack.

It is debatable whether or not trauma can precipitate myocardial infarction. It is possible that direct injury to a coronary vessel could institute reparative and constrictive fibrosis but the circumstances would be unusual and each case would have to be judged on the facts. Direct trauma to the heart muscle could, however, produce conditions comparable to an infarct; it might then be difficult to distinguish with certainty the underlying aetiology of a subsequent cardiac rupture. It is, however, clear that if the circulation is already compromised, a fall in blood pressure will further worsen the situation. Infarction may thus occur as an indirect result of shock due to trauma which may, occasionally, be due to operative surgery. Coronary heart disease is a not uncommon cause of death on the operating table, and this is one reason for the thorough investigation of the cardiovascular system prior to operation[3].

By and large, women are less susceptible to myocardial infarction than are men; there is, however, some evidence that women taking high oestrogen contraceptive pills are at increased risk[4].

See also: Aneurysm; Atheroma; Coronary disease; Electrocardiogram; Embolism; Shock; Thrombosis

1. *See* Knight B *The Coroner's Autopsy* (1983) App. 2, Churchill Livingstone, Edinburgh.
2. *World Health Statistics Annual,*WHO, Geneva.
3. Leading Article 'Anaesthesia for patients with coronary disease' [1980] 281 Br Med J 341.
4. *See*, for example, Mann JI and Inman WHW 'Oral contraceptives and death from myocardial infarction' [1975] 2 Br Med J 245.

Myocarditis

Myocarditis is inflammatory disease of the heart muscle and can therefore be protozoal, bacterial or, more commonly, viral in origin. As such, it is part of a generalised condition which is recognisable; it is reasonable to attribute death to involvement of the heart when it occurs during such a disease.

Medico-legal interest in myocarditis is far more concentrated on deaths occurring in apparently healthy persons for which there is no obvious cause. So-called 'isolated myocarditis' has been described as a sensitivity reaction, sometimes to drugs, and may, occasionally, be evident to the naked eye. Most commonly, however, there is no relevant medical history and evidence of inflammation has to be sought with a microscope. In the absence of symptoms, the diagnosis rests on the finding of inflammatory cells within the heart muscle; the secondary problem, however, is to interpret such a finding.

There can be no doubt that one of the forensic pathologist's frequent problems is to establish a certifiable cause of manifestly natural death in which autopsy demonstrates none of the usual pathological patterns. The temptation to 'use' the finding of small foci of cardiac inflammation to fill the gap is considerable but the validity of such an inference has been challenged by studies which indicate that such pathology is present as a chance finding in some 5 per cent of autopsies[1].

The correct interpretation may be of very great practical importance in the allocation of blame for, say, a major transportation accident[2]. The feeling of most observers is now that the finding of inflammatory cells in the heart muscle should not, of itself, be accepted as an explanation of death; it is necessary to discover evidence of associated necrosis of muscle before 'myocarditis' can be an acceptable diagnosis. The condition does, however, emphasise the importance of microscopy in the elucidation of obscure deaths and of accidents for which there is no obvious cause.

See also: Heart disease; Sudden natural death

1. Plueckhahn VD and Cameron JM 'Traumatic "myocarditis" or "myocarditis" in trauma' (1968) 8 Med Sci Law 177; Stevens PJ and Underwood Ground KE 'Occurrence and significance of myocarditis in trauma' (1970) 41 Aerospace Med 776.
2. Stevens PJ *Fatal Civil Aircraft Accidents* (1970) Acc No. 152, p.19 et seq (Wright, Bristol) is a classic example.

N

Narcotic Drugs

The control of narcotic drugs has been a matter of international co-operation since shortly after the First World War and has been the subject of several conventions and agreements[1]. A narcotic drug is, etymologically, one which causes drowsiness and relief of pain; since drugs having such effects are nearly all addictive (see 'Drug addiction'), narcotic drugs became synonymous with drugs of addiction and the original international regulations dealt with only seven drugs. The list, however, increased with the production of synthetic narcotics, and the scope of international proscription extended to include drugs which were neither clearly addictive nor somniferous — in particular the hallucinogens. The list of regulated drugs now extends to approximately 100 substances[2]. The term 'controlled drugs' now used in the Misuse of Drugs Act 1971 is greatly preferable but the concept of narcotics persists in the limited list given in the Schedule to the Misuse of Drugs (Notification of and Supply to Addicts) Regulations 1973. By far the most important of these are morphine, diamorphine (or heroin) and cocaine, although methadone and pethidine have their own problems.

Morphine is a naturally occurring alkaloid derived from *Papaver somniferum* and heroin is a synthetic variant on the natural substance. Heroin is some five times as effective, as is, therefore, the major problem in drug abuse; addiction to heroin is the reason for inclusion of some 95 per cent of those on the narcotic register of New York City. The drug can be 'snuffed', smoked or injected either subcutaneously or intravenously; absorption by the last route is absolute and immediate and its effect is therefore generally sought by the addict and particularly by the habituated addict whose requirements are more urgent. Thus, the autopsy in a heroin addict frequently shows the signs of injection which, as likely as not, will include evidence of sepsis and of thrombosis of vessels. Findings in the UK and the USA are not, however, strictly comparable as therapeutic supply to the addict is available in the former; as a consequence, deaths from hepatitis, acquired immune deficiency syndrome (AIDS), septicaemia and pulmonary disease due to lodging of particles of foreign impurities in the lungs (see 'Embolism') are rather more common in the USA. Recovery of heroin at postmortem dissection is a major difficulty as it readily breaks down in the tissues to morphine, and even morphine is, for some obscure reason, very difficult to

364 National Health Service

quantify at autopsy — the bile is probably the best material to search. Even then, the precise significance of the discovered drug is difficult to assess; a fatal dose in a novice may be no more than a coincidental finding in a confirmed addict. It should not be forgotten that morphine and heroin are, still, ideal drugs for the legitimate medical treatment of severe pain.

Cocaine is extracted from the shrub *Erythroxylum coca* and has been used in its natural form for a long time past as a stimulant. Cocaine has a minor medical use as a local anaesthetic but it has been wholly replaced by synthetic substitutes. It is therefore now almost entirely a drug of abuse and would seem to be increasing in popularity, especially among the higher economic social strata. It is generally 'snuffed' — and may cause perforation of the nasal septum — but can be inhaled or injected. The euphoric effect is said to be relatively brief and may be followed by depression; since the cocaine addict was probably depressed originally, the combination of personality and drug effect may lead to a recognisable affective psychosis. It is apparent that the use of cocaine causes neither sleep nor analgesia; its continued association with the narcotic drugs has been attacked both in the United States courts and by academics[3].

Pethidine and methadone are active when taken by mouth. The former is a valuable drug in the practice of midwifery and may be possessed and administered under supervision by a registered midwife. Methadone is of considerable importance as it is used to treat heroin addiction — the rationale being that the number of injections of heroin can, thereby, be diminished; unfortunately, therapeutic methadone addiction is, as a result, not uncommon.

See also: Drug addiction; Embolism; Hallucinogens; Misuse of Drugs Act 1971; Psychoses

1. For example, Convention for limiting the manufacture and regulating the distribution of narcotic drugs, Geneva (1931); Single Convention on Narcotic Drugs, New York (1961).
2. A list of narcotic drugs under international control (series no. E.CN.7/513) (1968).
3. *People v McCarty* 418 NE 2d 26 (Ill, 1981); Schultz CB 'Statutory classification of cocaine as a narcotic: an illogical anachronism' (1983) 9 Am J Law Med 225.

National Health Service

The British National Health Service came into being by virtue of the National Health Service Act 1947 and the National Health Service (Scotland) Act 1947. There has been much subsequent legislation, the bulk of which is now consolidated in the National Health Service Act 1977[1].

Under s.1, it is the Secretary of State's duty to continue the provision of a comprehensive health service designed to secure improvement in the physical and mental health of the people and in the prevention, diagnosis and treatment of illness. The service so provided shall be free of charge unless expressly provided for otherwise. The Secretary of State has power to provide such services as he considers appropriate for the purpose of discharging his duty (s.2).

It is the Secretary of State's duty to provide to such extent as he considers necessary to meet all reasonable requirements under s.3(1)(a) hospital accommodation, (c) medical, dental, nursing and ambulance services, (d) other facilities for the care of nursing mothers and young children, (e) facilities for prevention of illness, the care of persons suffering from illness and their aftercare, and (f) such other services as are required for diagnosis and treatment. The provision of special hospitals for the treatment of those whose illness makes them a potential danger to the public, is obligated under s.4.

The Secretary of State has other duties (s.5), including providing school dental services and contraceptive advice and services. He may also provide invalid carriages, overseas treatment for tuberculosis and a public microbiological service — and he may assist research.

The Secretary of State depends for advice on the discharge of his duties from the Central Health Council; this consists of 15 persons nominated by the Royal Medical Colleges and allied professional organisations, 27 professional persons selected and appointed by the Secretary of State and a further number, up to a total membership of 46, appointed by the Secretary of State as he thinks fit. The Central Health Council may appoint such committees as are thought necessary.

The distribution of practices is arranged by medical practices committees; family practitioner committees (FPCs), whose function is to provide primary care, are established under s.10 with their duties described under s.15. The constitution and duties of FPCs have recently been amended[2].

The administrative arrangements for provision of general medical, dental, ophthalmic and pharmaceutical services are detailed in Part II of the Act. As a result of the deliberations of a Royal Commission[3], the administration of the NHS has been simplified, the day-to-day responsibility now resting upon District Health Authorities (DHAs)[4].

A practitioner can be disqualified if it is represented, after due inquiry, by the DHA that his continued inclusion in the list of practitioners would be prejudicial to the efficiency of the service (s.46). In these circumstances, the case is heard by a tribunal consisting of a chairman appointed by the Lord Chancellor, one representative of the FPC and one practitioner member drawn from a panel of six persons designated for the purpose; legal representation is allowed for those appearing before the tribunal.

Part III deals, *inter alia*, with the treatment of private patients within the NHS and Part V established the Health Service Commissioner.

The NHS is now a vast operation and is a major employer of labour in the UK. Inevitably, an important part of the work force can be expected to have relatively little professional concern with patient care and situations accordingly arise which are more appropriate to industry; the Service is also a fairly simple target for politicians. A far more responsible attitude than was apparent, say, a decade ago has now developed in this sphere but, nevertheless, there are other areas of legitimate criticism including, particularly, the length of waiting lists for elective surgery. A reasonably good symbiotic relationship appears to be growing between the free NHS and the private practice of medicine which is, itself, certainly increasing; there are also movements towards 'privatising' some of the non-professional components of the Service. The misuse of the public service on behalf of private practice is, however, a persistent source of proper resentment.

The clear difficulty facing the health authorities is that of allocating scarce, or certainly finite, economic resources when attempting to discharge the various duties of the Secretary of State. So far as can be discovered, there has been only one challenge on this score[5], when it was alleged that the Minister was in breach of his duty to provide hospital facilities for what was, in the particular case, orthopaedic surgery. The judge of first instance remarked: 'If the money is not there then the services cannot be met in a particular place'. It was held that the formula employed in s.3 of the 1977 Act gives the Secretary of State a clear discretion as to how financial resources are to be used and the law could interfere only if he had acted so as to frustrate the policy of the Act. In the Court of Appeal, Lord Denning MR held that the Minister could be considered to have failed in his statutory duty only if his exercise of discretion was so thoroughly unreasonable that no reasonable Minister could have reached it. Bridge LJ pointed to the economics of the bottomless pit which would be exacerbated the further medical and technological advances go in the direction of comprehensive patient care. Nevertheless, he felt extremely sorry for the applicants who had to wait a long time for necessary surgery. 'They shared that misfortune', he said, 'with thousands up and down the country'. Even so, it would be difficult to find anyone who would wish to abandon the NHS in favour of an alternative in which, effectively, a person's health was balanced against his ability to pay for the necessary treatment. There seems little other than political ideology to prevent the best of a NHS working in harmony with the best of insurance-based private health care to the benefit of both.

See also: Complaints procedures in the NHS; Family practitioner committees; Health Service Commissioner; Resource allocation; Special hospitals

1. With comparable legislation in National Health Service (Scotland) Act 1978.
2. Health and Social Security Act 1984, s.5 and Sch.3.
3. Merrison AW (chairman) *Report of the Royal Commission on the National Health Service* (Cmnd 7615) (1979) HMSO, London.
4. Health Services Act 1980, s.1.
5. *R v Secretary of State for Social Services, ex parte Hincks* (1979) 123 SJ 436. The case, together with the unreported appeal phase, is discussed in detail in Finch JD *Health Services Law* (1981) pp.37–39, 202, Sweet & Maxwell, London.

Natural Death

With all the discussion of traumatic and sudden unexpected death which is associated with legal or forensic medicine, it is sometimes forgotten that the great majority of deaths are natural and anticipated. Theoretically, the moment of death should be scarcely perceptible but, in point of fact, it is almost always obvious and abrupt when the death is witnessed — it is easy to understand the concept of the soul leaving the body. In such circumstances, attempts at resuscitation would not only be fruitless but also quite unethical; it would, however, be proper to allow a period of observation to ensure the permanence of the cessation of cardiorespiratory function.

Occasionally, however, the moment of death is less easy to define. This is particularly so when it is essentially due to no more than senility or when it occurs during persistent and deep coma. It is because of such difficulties that some jurisdictions require the establishment of *post mortem* lividity, or hypostasis, before death can be certified. No diagnostic rules are laid down in the UK, the declaration of natural death being regarded as a matter of good clinical practice. Deaths which are unobserved and which are associated with hypothermia and/or drug taking are not natural and are discussed under 'Hypothermia'.

See also: Death; Hypostasis; Hypothermia

Necessity

The doctrine of necessity applies in both civil and criminal law and serves to legitimise acts which would otherwise be illegal. The basis of the doctrine is that it is better to avoid the occurrence of a major evil even if one commits a lesser criminal or tortious act in so doing. One example of such a circumstance would be the destruction of property in order to effect a life-saving rescue.

The legal status of the defence of necessity is not clearly defined[1]. Its availability is, however, now beyond doubt and there are a number of medical contexts in which it may be invoked. For example, the treatment of a patient without that patient's consent may be justified by necessity if the patient is unconscious and if treatment is required immediately. On a more contentious note, the administration of a blood transfusion to a child which is resisted by the parents might be supported on the grounds of necessity if it were considered life saving, although many doctors would feel happier if the minor were first made a ward of court.

It is less certain that the law would accept a plea of necessity if it involved the taking of life. The *locus classicus* of this dilemma is the case of *R v Dudley and Stephens*[2], where the principle was not accepted; this case echoed one which occurred in the USA some years previously[3].

See also: Consent to medical treatment; Hunger strike; Wardship proceedings

1. For full discussion, *see* Law Commission *Codification of the Criminal Law*, Working Paper No.55 (1974) HMSO, London.
2. (1884) 14 QBD 273.
3. *US v Holmes* (1842) 26 Fed Cas 360, No.15383.

Necrophilia

Necrophilia can be defined as sexual love for a dead body. The term should cover more than normal sexual intercourse as the act may be homosexual in nature[1]; *post mortem* mutilation of the body may also be a manifestation of necrophilia which is probably rooted in a suppressed desire for power, the dead body being wholly defenceless.

Such cases as are reported generally come to light only because the necrophilic act follows upon murder; one extraordinary incident is reported in which the act of necrophilia was perpetrated on a body which was, unknown to the offender, the victim of murder by another man[2]. The prevalence of pure necrophilia is unknown because it must be a strictly private matter; it must also be virtually confined to those who have ready access to dead bodies.

In point of fact, it is difficult to see what criminal offence is perpetrated in such circumstances. It could, conceivably, be an instance of the Scottish common law offence of violation of a sepulchre but this would seem to involve interference with a corpse only after it has been buried or entombed[3]. There is no similar offence in English law; a Parliamentary move towards legislation following *R v Ward*[4] has not been followed up.

1. Bartholomew AA et al 'Homosexual necrophilia' (1978) 18 Med Sci Law 29.
2. *R v Ward* discussed in Price DE 'Necrophilia complicating a case of homicide' (1963) 3 Med Sci Law 121. The DPP considered there was no criminal offence in the necrophilic activity.
3. Gordon GH *The Criminal Law of Scotland* (2nd ed, 1978), p.999, W. Green, Edinburgh. Whether a mortuary would constitute a place of safe keeping is uncertain (*see Dewar v HM Adv* 1945 JC 5).
4. 631 HC Official Report (5th series) col.90. *See also* Brownlie AR 'Necrophilia: need Parliament trouble?' (1963) 3 Med Sci Law 313, who tends the view that necrophilia could be charged in both England and Wales and in Scotland as an 'outrage to decency'.

Neglect

Neglect of a child or of a helpless person may attract criminal liability if it is sufficiently serious. It is not a criminal offence in England and Wales to neglect an adult[1] but a charge of manslaughter could arise in the event of death from neglect of a person for whom the defendant had a responsibility. Scots law, however, incorporates the crime of cruel and unnatural treatment, which includes neglect of children by their parents, of an invalid in the defendant's charge and of wives by their husbands; the cruel treatment must, however, be specific[2].

Children are protected by the Children and Young Persons Act 1933 and by the Children and Young Persons (Scotland) Act 1937 under which a parent or other person having custody of a child who wilfully neglects it in a manner likely to cause it unnecessary suffering or injury to health may be convicted of an offence. This can include failure to provide proper medical or dental treatment. In *R v Sheppard and another*[3] it was held that parents who failed to obtain medical attention for their 16-month-old son, who was found to be suffering from hypothermia and malnutrition, were required to have known of the need of medical help. The case establishes that the offence of wilfully neglecting a child is not one of strict liability but that conviction is appropriate only if the defendant had realised the risk of harm and had decided not to act or if he did not obtain help because he was uncaring as to the child's welfare.

See also: Manslaugher; Recklessness

1. With the exception of the statutory offence committed in certain circumstances by a person who fails to maintain his or her spouse (National Assistance Act 1948, ss.42, 51(1)).
2. Gordon GH *The Criminal Law of Scotland* (2nd ed, 1978) p.833, W Green, Edinburgh.
3. [1980] 3 All ER 899.

Negligence

Medical negligence is one of the issues most frequently discussed in contemporary tort law and one which warranted separate treatment in the Pearson Report[1]. The level of litigation involving doctors in alleged negligence is certainly rising although the situation in the UK is not as intense as is that in the USA[2]. The practice of so-called defensive medicine is a direct response to what is seen as the imposition of an unduly onerous burden on the medical profession and, to avoid this, various alternatives have been suggested to fault-based systems of liability[3]. However, the existing system, with all its flaws, must currently provide for the victims of medical misadventure.

A fundamental principle of the law of torts is that injury caused by negligence gives rise to an obligation to compensate, provided that the defendant owed the plaintiff a duty of care[4]. In the practical context, the problems are, firstly, those of determining what conduct fails to meet the standard of care expected in the circumstances and, secondly, of determining that there was a causal link between the defendant's negligent act and the injury. The latter can be a complex matter. It is not always easy to determine the cause of a medical problem — pre-existing conditions may complicate the picture, as may subsequent injuries or illnesses which have nothing to do with the original insult and which might have developed in any circumstances. The problem of causation is particularly acute in the area of consent, and is discussed under 'Informed consent'.

As to the former, there is a considerable body of dicta which indicate that the British courts accept a professional standard of care in relation to medical negligence. This implies an acceptance that the determinant of proper treatment is that standard which is defined by the medical profession itself. In practice, expert witnesses inform the court of what is regarded as appropriate conduct by doctors and it is that standard which is then applied by the court — but see below[10] for potential restrictions on this simplification.

The definitive case adopting the professional standard is *Bolam v Friern Hospital Management Committee*[5] in which it was stated that medical negligence consists of a 'failure to act in accordance with the standards of reasonably competent medical men at the time'. It was stressed: 'a doctor is not guilty of negligence if he has acted in accordance with a practice accepted as proper by a responsible body of medical men skilled in that art'. The judgment in the Scottish case of *Hunter v Hanley*[6] has been interpreted as making a similar point[7] and there are a considerable number of Canadian cases in which the professional standard (or custom test) has been adopted[8]. In *White v Turner*[9], for example, the court took the view that 'if the work of a plastic surgeon falls below the accepted practices of his colleagues, he will be held civilly liable for any damage resulting. But, if his work complies with the custom of his confreres, he will normally escape civil liability for his conduct, even where the result of the surgery is less than satisfactory'.

It has, however, been confirmed recently that the court is the final arbiter of a professional standard — this being defined as acting in accordance with a practice *rightly* accepted as proper by a body of skilled and experienced medical men[10].

There is thus a reversion to earlier decisions which included putting to the jury the question of what was an appropriate standard of care[11]. This tendency was foreshadowed by Lord Denning, normally a strong defender of the professional standard, who said that, in some circumstances, he would be prepared to consider as negligent a practice generally adopted by the medical profession;[12] a commonly accepted practice in relation to the removal of surgical swabs was held to be negligent in *Urry and Urry v Bierer and others*[13].

A doctor is not bound in all circumstances to follow the standard practice of his profession. The classic dictum on this point is that of Lord Clyde in *Hunter v Hanley*[6] who said: 'to establish liability by a doctor where deviation from normal practice is alleged, three facts require to be established. First of all it must be proved that there is a usual and normal practice; secondly, it must be shown that the defender has not adopted that practice; and, thirdly,...it must be established that the course the doctor adopted is one which no professional man of ordinary skill would have taken if he had been acting with ordinary care'. The effect of this is to increase the burden on the doctor to justify unconventional treatment. It does not exclude experimental treatment — at least not of the sort which would be endorsed by acceptable expert witnesses — but it does exclude that which is totally idiosyncratic and which is not based on scientific premises[14].

Failure by a doctor to reach a correct diagnosis may constitute negligence. He is expected to make such investigations as would be made by a competent doctor but he need not explore remote possibilities nor need he conduct exhaustive tests which would be regarded as excessive by his peers. Rare diseases may be misdiagnosed without attracting negligence[15] but this would not apply if the condition could be detected by routine investigations which were appropriate to the case[16].

Misdiagnosis is one aspect of errors of judgement. Controversy in this area was raised by Lord Denning in *Whitehouse v Jordan*[17] when he stated in the Court of Appeal that an error of judgement did not amount to negligence. This view was expressly rejected when the same case came to the House of Lords: 'To say that a surgeon committed an error of clinical judgement is wholly ambiguous for, while some such errors may be completely consistent with the due exercise of professional skill, other acts or omissions in the course of exercising "clinical judgement" may be so glaringly below proper standards as to make a finding of negligence inevitable[18].

Inexperience is, in general, no defence to negligence. The subject is discussed in greater detail under 'Novice doctors'.

There can be no denying the difficulties involved in the bringing of an action for medical negligence although this appearance is, to an extent, exaggerated by the fact that only the more difficult cases will come to court and be reported — the more obvious instances will almost always be settled. Even so, there are problems inherent in obtaining medical records (*see* 'Disclosure of medical records') and obstacles often arise to obtaining expert medical evidence for the plaintiff. As stated, it may be difficult to establish causation although the recent case of *Clark v MacLennan*[19] has made matters very much easier for the plaintiff by reversing the burden of proof. This tactic may be pursued when there is failure by the defendant to take precautions designed to prevent the damage which has actually occurred; this has a different effect to that of the doctrine of *res ipsa loquitur* which may occasionally be invoked on behalf of the plaintiff.

See also: Causation; Compensation; Defensive medicine; Disclosure of medical records; Informed consent; No-fault compensation; Novice doctors; *Res ipsa loquitur*

1. Pearson CH (chairman) *Report of the Royal Commission on Civil Liability and Compensation for Personal Injury* (Cmnd 7054) (1980) HMSO, London.
2. Harland WA and Jandoo RS 'The medical negligence crisis' (1984) 24 Med Sci Law 123; Taylor JL *Medical Malpractice* (1980) p.31, Wright, Bristol; 'The influence of litigation on medical practice' (1977) 70 Proc R Soc Med 579.
3. For discussion, *see* Smith R: 'The world's best system of compensating injury?' (1982) 284 Br Med J 1243; 'Problems with a no-fault system of accident compensation' (1982) 284 Br Med J 1323; 'Compensation for medical misadventure' (1982) 284 Br Med J 1457.
4. Most medical negligence issues arise in tort rather than in contract although, in the context of private medical treatment, contractual remedies are available — e.g. *Scuriaga v Powell* (1979) 123 SJ 406. For general discussion on medical negligence, *see* Dugdale AM and Stanton KM *Professional Negligence* (1982) Butterworths, London.
5. [1957] 2 All ER 118.
6. 1955 SC 200.
7. See, however, the misgivings of Howie, n. 13 below.
8. *See McFadyen v Harvie* [1941] 2 DLR 663, affd [1942] SCR 390; *Chubey v Ahsan* (1975) 56 DLR (3d) 231; *Florence v Les Soeurs de Misericorde* (1962) 33 DLR (2d) 587. For discussion, *see* Linden AM *Canadian Tort Law* (3rd ed, 1982) Butterworths, Toronto.
9. (1981) 120 DLR (3d) 269.
10. Donaldson MR in *Sidaway v Bethlem Royal Hospital and others* [1984] 2 WLR 778 at 792; also Hirst J in *Hills v Potter* [1983] 3 All ER 716 at 728. The test is discussed in Norrie K McK 'Standards of disclosure' 1984 SLT 237.
11. *Lanphier v Phipos* (1838) 8 Car & P 475; *Rich v Pierpont* (1862) 3 F & F 35.
12. *Roe v Ministry of Health* [1954] 2 All ER 131. For discussion of Lord Denning's attitudes, *see* Maclean SAM 'Negligence — a dagger at the doctor's back?' in Watchman P and Robson P (eds) *Justice, Lord Denning and the Constitution* (1981) Gower, Aldershot, Hants.
13. (1955) Times, 16 March; on appeal, (1955) Times, 15 July. For discussion of this case, *see* Howie RBM 'The standard of care in medical negligence' 1983 Jur Rev 193. *See also* the important case of *Hucks v Cole* (1968) Times, 9 May.
14. *See* Giesen D *Medical Malpractice Law* (1981) p.164 (Gieseking Verlag, Bielefeld) and cases cited at n.88.
15. *Bell v R* (1973) 44 DLR (3d) 549; *Ostash v Sonnenberg* (1968) 67 DLR (2d) 311.
16. *Cusson v Robidoux* [1977] SCR 650; *Dale v Munthali* (1977) 16 OR (2d) 532; *McCormack v Redpath Brown* (1961) Times, 24 March.
17. [1980] 1 All ER 650 at 658.
18. [1981] 1 WLR 246 at 257. For comment, *see* Robertson G 'Whitehous v Jordan — medical negligence retired' (1981) 44 MLR 457.
19. [1983] 1 All ER 416. For comment, *see* Jones MA 'Medical negligence — the burden of proof' (1984) 134 NLJ 7.

Neonatal Death

The neonatal period is defined as the first 28 days of extrauterine life.

The most dangerous time within this period is the first 24 hours during which some 30–40 per cent of neonatal deaths occur, the precise proportion depending upon the quality of the services available; a further 15 per cent of deaths occur within 48 hours of birth.

The high incidence of early neonatal death is closely associated with prematurity — at least half such deaths will occur in premature infants and the smaller the baby, the less are its chances of survival. Nevertheless, given good modern medical attention, some three-quarters of infants weighing between 1.5 and 2.5. kg ($3\frac{1}{3}$–$5\frac{1}{2}$ lb) should survive.

Death is due to hypoxia, resulting from injury to either the cord or the placenta, in about 10 per cent of cases and is due to birth trauma in a further 5 per cent. Both these causes of death will be prominent among cases of infanticide; infanticide is, however, now very rare following the Abortion Act 1967. Congenital defects account for at least 15 per cent of neonatal deaths; a very small number of these will be of such severity that treatment will be deliberately withheld — this very important aspect of modern legal medicine is discussed under 'Neonaticide'.

Other conditions which were once potent causes of neonatal death — including infections and haemolytic disease of the newborn — are being steadily eliminated by either preventive or curative methods. The neonatal death rate is, in some ways, a measure of the sophistication and effectiveness of a health service and it is encouraging that the rate has fallen in England and Wales from 28.3 per 1,000 live births in 1939 to 8.2 per 1,000 live births in 1979; the comparable rates for death in the first 24 hours of life were 10.3 and 3.7. It is less satisfactory to note that the improvement is far less obvious in Social Classes IV and V[1] — a finding which indicates the need for a general raising of social standards.

See also: Birth injuries; Congenital disease; Haemolytic disease of the newborn; Infanticide; Neonaticide; Prematurity

1. Black D (Chairman) *Inequalities in Health*: Report of a research working group (1980) DHSS/University of Birmingham.

Neonaticide

'Neonaticide' is a derived word which here means allowing or encouraging an infant to die in a medical setting. The term is neutral as to implication and is used in preference to the more common 'selective non-treatment of the newborn' because it includes failure to feed a mentally affected but otherwise physically healthy neonate and failure to provide routine surgery to the newborn on grounds other than those of non-feasibility.

There can be no doubt that, despite the increasing use of amniocentesis and other antepartum diagnostic techniques, some infants are born with disabilities which are so disabling, and so likely to remain disabling after treatment, that they should be allowed to die without medical or surgical intervention; infants with severe neural tube defects offer the commonest example[1]. The rearing of a disabled child is also likely to affect the health of the mother or of the existing children of the family. There are therefore grounds for regarding neonaticide as merely an extension of the Abortion Act 1967, and legislation to this end has been proposed[2]. The major difference is, however, that, whilst the fetus has very limited rights in law, the neonate should be entitled to full legal protection. Thus, there is a potential conflict in this area between good medical practice and strict legality — a conflict which has been presaged in articles bearing such titles as 'The legal threat to medicine'[3] and, on the other hand, 'Doctors as murderers'[4].

To a large extent, this conflict of ideals stems from a failure to distinguish between, at one end of the scale, the neonate who is physically ill and likely to die without treatment — exemplified by the severe spina bifida child — and, at the other extreme, the child who is physically anxious to live but is mentally abnormal — the uncomplicated sufferer from Down's syndrome; the downsian infant suffering from an additional remediable physical defect occupies an intermediate position and, at the same time, offers some solutions to the problems of management.

The concept of patient autonomy includes the right to accept or refuse treatment. The neonate cannot, however, make a decision for himself and some form of substituted judgement[5] — that is, an assessment of what a competent patient would choose for himself — must be provided; since the judgement of the 'productivity' of treatment must be a medical matter, it is the doctor who must be primarily responsible for making the decision, a right to good medical practice which was clarified in the *Baby Quinn* affair[6]. The parents clearly have a right to express their views but, in the end, they and their medical advisers will not be permitted to act otherwise than in the best interests of the child. But does this include a parental right to reject their child if it has, so far as can be judged at the time, no defect other than a probable degree of mental subnormality?

This was a major issue in *R v Arthur*[7] where a doctor was tried, and acquitted, of attempted murder, having noted 'Parents do not wish it to survive. Nursing care only' and having prescribed a drug to inhibit appetite — the patient being a downsian infant who was only later shown to have been also physically disabled. The *Arthur* decision turned on the particular medical facts and is probably valueless as a precedent[8]; the case in *Re B*[9], taken through the civil courts, is far more important. In *Re B* the parents refused permission for a relatively simple life-saving operation on their downsian infant. After considerable legal activity, the Court of Appeal ordered the operation as being in the best interests of the child, stating, *inter alia*, that 'the child should be put in the same position as any other mongol child and must be given the chance to live an existence' — thus giving a clear indication that they would not expect an uncomplicated case of Down's syndrome to be abandoned without food. At the same time, the judgment inferred that, had it been probable that the child's life would have been intolerable, they would *not* have ordered the operation — thus confirming the 'productive treatment' test adopted by the DPP in *Quinn*.

Thus, the tenuous rights of the parents to reject a child because it is imperfect are now even less certain and, after some hesitation, the British Medical Association have now conceded that, irrespective of parental wishes, the physically fit downsian infant should be fed[10]. The situation seems, therefore, to be now stabilised on the basis of the *infant's* best interests and it is important to avoid extending the principle of selective non-treatment of the physically defective neonate similarly to the way in which the interpretation of the Abortion Act 1967 has expanded.

The American scene appears confused but is, nevertheless, instructive. It is notable that failure to feed an uncomplicated case of Down's syndrome would not be an option in the USA where a severely defective newborn is defined as one not likely to survive without surgical and medical intervention[11]; but the parents' authority carries very great weight once treatment is required[12]. In a crisis of controversy, the Federal Administration issued a directive virtually dictating maximum treatment of all defective neonates; but these regulations were challenged immediately in the

Federal District Court which decided against the Administration[13]. This incident exemplifies the dangers of lay interference in what are essentially medical decisions.

See also: Abortion Act 1967; Amniocentesis; Down's syndrome; Euthanasia; Neural tube defects; Parental rights; Paternalism

1. *See* Lorber J and Salfield SAW 'Results of selective treatment of spina bifida cystica' (1981) 56 Arch Dis Childh 822 for a full discussion.
2. Limitation of Treatment Bill proposed by Brahams D and Brahams M '*R v Arthur* — is legislation appropriate?' (1981) 78 Law Soc Gaz 1342.
3. Havard JDJ (1982) 284 Br Med J 612.
4. Beynon H [1982] Crim LR 17.
5. A useful concept elaborated in the American case *Superintendent of Belchertown State School v Saikewicz* 370 NE 2d 417 (Mass, 1978).
6. The DPP refused to prosecute a surgeon who had been reported for his failure to operate on a severe case of spina bifida (1981) *The Times*, 6 October, p.1.
7.(1981) *The Times*, 6 November, pp.1, 12.
8. Although Kennedy I ('Reflections on the Arthur Trial' (1982) 59 New Society, No.999, 7 January, p.13) believes that it establishes new law relating both to medical practice and to the rights of parents.
9. [1981] 1 WLR 1421, CA.
10. (1983) 286 Br Med J 1593.
11. Sherlock R 'Selective non-treatment of newborns' (1979) 5 J Med Ethics 139.
12. *Re Phillip B* App 156 Cal Rptr 48 (1979) where the court refused to authorise a cardiac operation on a 12-year-old Down's syndrome boy.
13. Paris JJ and Fletcher AB 'Infant Doe regulations and the absolute requirement to use nourishment and fluids for the dying infant' (1983) 11 Law Med Hlth Care 210.

Further reading
There is a mass of literature on this subject. For a defence of the in *Re B* decision, *see* Freeman MDA 'Using wardship to save a baby from its parents' (1982) 12 Fam Law 73. Trans-Atlantic views are well put in MacMillan ES 'Birth defective infants: a standard for non treatment decisions' (1978) 30 Stan LR 599, and Ellis TS 'Letting defective babies die: who decides?' (1982) 7 Am J Law Med 393. Attention is also directed to two articles by Glanville Williams 'Down's syndrome and the duty to preserve life' and 'Down's syndrome and the doctor's responsibility' (1981) 131 NLJ 1020, 1040.

Nervous Shock

The law of torts permits damages to be recovered for nervous shock (or emotional shock). This was not always the case; in the nineteenth century, the courts were suspicious of claims for apparently non-physical personal injury and refused them on the grounds, *inter alia*, that symptoms could easily be simulated.

Damages will not be awarded for those transient emotional responses which may follow upon being involved in or witnessing a distressing event. Such emotional responses include grief, sorrow or fear and the courts have stressed that these are normal responses to harrowing or alarming experiences and are, as such, noncompensable[1]. In a recent case[2], however, 'worry, strain and distress' were regarded as the consquences of 'ordinary shock' — which the court considered to be a concept which everyone understood and which was to be preferred to 'nervous shock'; damages were recovered in respect of that shock despite the fact that it was not 'psychiatric' in type. The effect of shock may be the development of long-lasting secondary responses. These may manifest themselves as recognised psychiatric illnesses such as depression or schizophrenia. Physical reactions, such as miscarriage, may also be precipitated. These are medical and psychiatric effects for which damages are clearly recoverable. In addition, a claim for damages in respect of nervous shock will be readily accepted as parasitic upon physical injury when the plaintiff has, himself, been injured in the incident.

Judges have consistently expressed concern as to the limitations which are to be placed on nervous shock claims made by witnesses of accidents. In the past, the 'impact rule'[3] and the 'zone of danger rule'[4] have required that the plaintiff either suffers some impact in the incident or, at least, be placed in personal danger. These rules have now been abandoned in English law. Nevertheless, the courts will require that the plaintiff be in close proximity to the incident and that there be a reasonably near personal relationship between the plaintiff and the principal victim of the negligent act. Proximity to the incident has been interpreted increasingly liberally. It is now clear that the plaintiff need not have witnessed the actual incident; in a series of cases, referred to as the 'aftermath cases', the courts have allowed claims where the plaintiff has come to the scene of the accident, or has seen the victims, shortly after its occurrence[5]. In *McLoughlin v O'Brian*[6] damages were awarded to a woman who saw her injured family shortly after their arrival in hospital. The House of Lords in that case also laid down broad guidelines upon which nervous shock cases will be judged, eschewing hard and fast rules of the sort proposed in the influential American decision *Dillon v Legg*[7].

The basic test in English law is now one of foreseeability, qualified by considerations of proximity and relationship. The courts are likely to be particularly sympathetic to those who have engaged in rescue operations[8].

See also: Foreseeability

1. *Mount Isa Mines Limited v Pusey* (1971) 45 ALJR 88 at 92, (1970) 125 CLR 383; *Hinz v Berry* [1970] 1 All ER 1074.
2. *Whitmore and another v Euroways Express Coaches Ltd and others* (1984) Times, 4 May.
3. *Victorian Railway Commissioners v Coultas* (1888) 13 AC 222
4. *Dulieu v White and Sons* [1901] 2 KB 669
5. *Boardman v Sanderson* [1964] 1 WLR 1317; *Benson v Lee* [1972] VR 879
6. [1982] 2 WLR 982
7. 441 P 2d 912, 69 Cal Rptr 72 (1968)
8. *Chadwick v British Railways Board* [1967] 1 WLR 912. For a recent application of the principles, *see Wigg v British Railways Board* (1986) Times, 4 February.

Further reading
Teff H 'Liability for negligently inflicted nervous shock' (1983) 99 LQR 100; Havard J 'Reasonable foresight of nervous shock' (1956) 19 MLR 478.

Nervous System

The nervous system controls muscular movement, sensation and the special senses. It consists essentially of three elements — the central, peripheral and autonomic nervous systems.

The central nervous system comprises the brain and spinal cord. The brain is described separately. The spinal cord carries sensory messages to the brain and passes motor messages to the tissues. The fibres through which this is done are collected in tracts or bundles which are very specifically located in the cord — in general, the motor pathways lie anterior and the sensory tracks posterior. Sensation is further divided into pathways for pain, thermal appreciation and the like. Injuries to or diseases of the spinal cord may therefore produce very selective results; the fibres cross over at the level of the lower brain — thus, injuries to the spinal cord will produce results on the same side of the body.

The central nervous system is covered closely by a thin membrane called the pia mater and, outside this, by the arachnoid mater. The intervening subarachnoid space contains cerebrospinal fluid, which cushions the brain and allows some margin for changes in size. Inflammation of the membranes is known as meningitis. A diagnosis of meningitis may be made from examination of the cerebrospinal fluid, which is collected by means of lumbar puncture — a procedure which is not without hazard. Drugs and anaesthetics may be introduced in this way and will act directly on the central nervous tissue.

The peripheral nerves divide into two main groups. The cranial nerves emanate from the brain itself and control the eyes — both movement and vision — hearing, facial movement and sensation, and the tongue and pharynx; the important vagus nerve is a cranial nerve. The spinal nerves either leave the spinal cord anteriorly or enter posteriorly; the motor and sensory routes join within the spine so that the peripheral nerve bundles contain both sensory and motor elements. Peripheral nerves are capable of regeneration if their sheaths are rejoined after they have been cut.

The autonomic nervous system is essentially that which controls involuntary function. It is intimately connected with the peripheral nervous system through junctions in the spinal cord; thus, even if the spinal cord is severed, some action of the organs supplied by nerves arising below the lesion may be maintained through spinal reflexes.

The special senses of hearing and eyesight are transmitted through the cranial nerves but are interpreted in special sensory areas in the brain, under which entry they are described in greater detail.

See also: Autonomic nervous system; Brain; Central nervous system; Lumbar puncture; Spinal anaesthesia; Spinal cord injuries

Neural Tube Defects

Neural tube defects include a range of congenital malformations in which the bony skeleton fails to close over parts of the central nervous system. The abnormalities range from anencephaly, in which the skull bones do not close, to spina bifida occulta, where a defect in the lower spine is fully compensated by the skin; the former is likely to be incompatible with life beyond a short period, the latter may be symptomless.

Whatever the causes predisposing to the abnormalities may be, they appear to apply to the whole range of neural tube defects. The fact that there are clear geographical differences in rates of occurrence suggests that environmental factors may be at work — the incidence in various parts of the UK ranges from 1:100 to 1:500 births whilst the general incidence in North America is said to be in the region of 1:1000 births. A widespread investigation into the effect of vitamin supplements in pregnancy is in operation at the time of writing. Certainly, there appears to be a genetic effect. If one child of a marriage is affected, the likelihood of a second abnormal infant is between 7 and 15 times that of the random population — a recurrence risk of 3–5 per cent; the recurrence risk rises to 10 per cent if two children are affected, whilst the risk of an affected parent having such offspring is, again, in the region of 3–5 per cent. The conclusion must be that neural tube defect is a genetic disease of multifactorial type.

Two major issues then arise — those of genetic counselling and of intrauterine diagnosis. The simplest aid to prenatal diagnosis is the level of alpha-fetoprotein in the serum of the pregnant woman. The degree of elevation of the normal level depends upon the 'openness' of the fetal lesion — thus, about 90 per cent of cases of anencephaly are so diagnosable but only 50 per cent of the various forms of spina bifida. Moreover, several conditions — including multiple pregnancy, intrauterine fetal death and rhesus immunisation (see 'Haemolytic disease of the newborn') — may give rise to false positive results. A further check can therefore be made using ultrasound visualisation or, alternatively, the invasive techniques of amniocentesis or fetoscopy can be employed.

In the event of a positive finding, and following counselling, abortion is clearly available under the terms of the Abortion Act 1967, s.1(1)(b). However, in the event of a neural tube defective infant being born unexpectedly, very serious problems as to the propriety of treatment or of selective non-treatment arise. Whether these are approached from the practical angle[1] or from general ethical principles[2], the decisions are bound to be controversial; modern medical opinion would be in favour of assessing the results of treatment in terms of the quality of life offered.

See also: Abortion Act 1967; Amniocentesis; Fetoscopy; Genetic counselling; Genetic disease; Haemolytic disease of the newborn; Neonaticide; Quality of life; Spina bifida; Ultrasound

1. Lorber J and Salfield SAW 'Result of selective treatment of spina bifida cystica' (1981) 56 Arch Dis Childh 822.
2. For general discussion, *see* Mason JK and McCall Smith RA *Law and Medical Ethics* (1983) Chap.7, Butterworths, London.

No-fault Compensation

The common law remedy for negligent medical treatment has well-known disadvantages — in practice, the burden of proof is weighted against the plaintiff, the process is long and often harrowing, and the final results have been described as a forensic lottery. The problems of drug-related injury include such special factors as proof of causation and identification of the wrongdoer; these make such negligence a distinct case which is discussed separately under 'Pharmaceutical liability'. The common law approach suffers from the general criticism that it is concerned to punish the wrongdoer rather than to compensate the injured. The most widely advocated alternative is the no-fault system of compensation.

New Zealand introduced, in 1972, legislation to provide a comprehensive no-fault compensation scheme for all accidents, including those occurring in the home and at sport[1]. In Sweden, compensation for injuries sustained in road traffic accidents and at work is paid without proof of fault and the Patient Insurance Scheme, introduced in 1975, provides that a patient has only to prove that injury resulted from 'medical misadventure' for compensation to be paid. The scheme involves private insurance paid for by taxes and is administered by county councils; any rights the patient may have in tort are transferred to the council once compensation has been paid[2].

The New Zealand scheme, which has been widely praised[3], is administered by an Accident Compensation Corporation. Under it, a person or his dependants may receive either a lump sum or up to 80 per cent of his earnings in the event of accidental injury. All actions for tort in respect of injury are abolished although doctors may still be sued for negligence which is not associated with accidental injury — e.g. consent based actions may be allowable[4] — and not all claimants are admitted to the scheme. Nevertheless, any such scheme has difficulties — these are mainly associated with causation and include the definition of accident in relation to disease, problems of self-infliction and the like. The Accident Compensation Act 1982 now attempts to define what precisely is included or excluded from the scheme.

As a result, the Pearson Commission[5] declined to recommend a no-fault system of compensation following medical negligence. Apart from the difficulties involved in financing and limiting the scope of such a scheme, the Commission could not find that there was a special case for exempting the medical profession alone from legal liability. The Commission did recommend no-fault compensation for road traffic injuries but it seems unlikely that legislation will result[6].

See also: Causation; Informed consent; Pharmaceutical liability

1. Accident Compensation Act 1972.
2. *See* Harland WA and Jandoo RS 'The medical negligence crisis' (1984) 24 Med Sci Law 123.
3. Smith R 'The world's best system of compensating injury?' (1982) 284 Br Med J 1243, 1323, 1457. For a full discussion, *see* Palmer G *Compensation for Incapacity: A study of law and social change in New Zealand and Australia* (1979) Oxford University Press, Melbourne, or, more recently, McLean SAM 'Liability without fault — the New Zealand experience' [1985] J Soc Welf Law 125.
4. Osborne PH 'Informed consent to medical treatment and the Accident Compensation Act, 1972' [1979] NZLJ 198.
5. Pearson CH (chairman) *Report of the Royal Commission on Civil Liability and Compensation for Personal Injury* (Cmnd 7054) (1978) HMSO, London.
6. *See* Smith R 'Malpractice: a New Zealand solution to an American crisis?' (1985) 291 Br Med J 812.

Noise Pollution

Noise is now one of the major environmental pollutants and is responsible for much anxiety and for both threatened and actual litigation. It may take the form of a minor irritation — the neighbour's radio — or of a major onslaught on the sense of hearing. The medical implications in the latter case are considerable.

Noise affects not only the hearing but also the psychological and physical health. There is now a body of evidence which indicates that noise can lead to the development of psychiatric symptoms ranging from irritability or excessive sensitivity to neurotic states[1]. A number of studies focus on the rate of admission to psychiatric hospitals in areas affected by a high level of airport noise[2] but the significance of the result is questionable.

There are similar doubts as to the precise connection between exposure to high noise levels and physical illness[3]. Suggestions that exposure to noise has a teratogenic effect on the fetus[4] are particularly alarming but it has been pointed out that any such effect may result from related exposure to chemical pollutants (e.g. aircraft fuel) emanating from the noise source.

The impact of noise on human hearing, at least, is established beyond doubt. High intensity impulse noise, such as that caused by an explosion, can result in immediate acoustic trauma including damage to the eardrum and the ossicles; this may or may not recover. Long-term exposure to continuous high intensity noise, such as that encountered in machine shops, can cause severe hearing loss[5].

Various legal restrictions on the environmental noise level are available. The private citizen can bring an action under the law of private nuisance, seeking an injunction against further noise or claiming damages for that which has already been suffered. Alternatively, an action may be taken either by an individual or by a local authority seeking a noise abatement order under the Noise Pollution Act 1974. Byelaws passed by local authorities may also contain noise control regulations[6]. The noise levels permitted from various types of ground vehicle are stipulated from time to time[7]. Air traffic noise is controlled in the design of aircraft[8]; moreover, there are strict flying regulations as to the use of noise abatement procedures or limited approach pathways related to individual airports[9].

General control of noise at work rests in the Health and Safety at Work etc. Act 1974. The Health and Safety Executive has published a Code of Practice for reducing the exposure of employed persons to noise. A simple measure of decibels (dB) is inadequate for assessing the effect of noise on the human ear; high frequency noise is more damaging than is that at low pitch given the same noise intensity. Industrial noise levels are therefore 'weighted' to take account of this phenomenon and are expressed in dBA. Permissible exposure to noise is expressed on a dBA/time scale. Thus, the threshold limit value for an eight-hour working day is 90 dBA; only one hour would be permissible at a level of 99 dBA[10]. Occupational deafness is a prescribed disease in certain occupations although the conditions laid down are somewhat stringent. An ordinary civil claim may be successful against an employer if negligence can be shown in respect of a failure to take proper precautions against hearing damage[11]. Personal protection includes the use of ear muffs, of acoustic glass wall or of ear plugs; periodic audiometric testing may also be advisable.

See also: Health and Safety at Work etc. Act 1974; Prescribed diseases and occupations; Safety equipment; Threshold limit values

1. For a discussion of the literature, *see* Clark CR 'The effects of noise on health' in Jones DM and Chapman AJ (eds) *Noise and Society* (1984) p.116, Wiley, Chichester.
2. Tarnopolsky A et al 'Aircraft noise and mental health' (1980) 10 Psycholog Med 638.
3. For example, Knipschild P and Ondshoorn N 'Medical effects of aircraft noise: a drug study' (1977) 40 Int Arch Occupat Environ Hlth 197.
4. Jones FN and Tausher J 'Residence under an airport landing pattern as a factor in teratism' (1978) 33 Arch Environ Hlth 10.
5. Ward WD 'Noise induced hearing loss' in *Noise and Society* (n.1 above) p.77.
6. For a full discussion of the law relating to noise, *see* Penn CN *Noise Control* (1979) Shaw, London.
7. Motor Vehicles (Construction and Use) Regulations 1978 (SI 1978/1017).
8. Air Navigation (Noise Certification) Order 1984 (SI 1984/368).
9. Nevertheless, the Department of Trade and Industry *Report of the Public Inquiry into the causes and circumstances of the accident near Staines on 18 June 1972* (Civil Aviation Aircraft Reports 4/73, 1973) (HMSO, London) concluded that any procedure which demands that an aircraft should fly at less than its optimum power is undesirable; it was, however, agreed that aeronautical and social considerations have to be blended as best as possible.
10. The decibel scale is logarithmic. Normal speech is at the level of 50 dB; the jet engine produces something of the order of 130 dB, which is a pressure wave 100 million times more intense.
11. *Berry v Stone Manganese Marine Ltd* (1971) 12 KIR 13.

Non-accidental Injury in Children

Probably most parents become exasperated with their children and strike them at one time or another. Such outbursts will, however, be regretted and the child will be taken to the doctor immediately if any harm has resulted. The 'non-accidental injury (NAI) syndrome' is, however, different, the characteristics being the appearance of obscure injuries or illness of repetitive type which result from the actions of a caring agency — a parent, step-parent, babysitter or the like; typically, there is delay in reporting the injuries and, when this is done, the history of causation is deceptive and inconsistent with the clinical findings.

The deception is such that the syndrome, when first observed, was wrongly attributed to natural disease[1]. Thus, the classic findings are of fractures associated with evidence of subdural haemorrhage. Much more common, however, are bruises which, by their different ages, may provide the crucial evidence of repetitive injury. The bruises are commonly of 'fingertip' type and, indeed, much of the pathology of NAI is due to shaking the child rather than to direct violence. Black eyes, swollen ears and scalp bruises are, nevertheless, frequent. Lacerations, other than the almost diagnostic tearing of the frenum of the lip, are relatively uncommon; instruments are seldom used. Fractures are often of twisting type and the epiphyses of the long bones are torn off; radiological evidence of failure to treat or of infliction at different times is often discovered. Fractures of the ribs are found posteriorly and are due to forcible gripping of the torso. Severe intra-abdominal injuries are found in a proportion of fatal cases although death is probably seldom intended; the syndrome is to be distinguished from infanticide or child murder which more commonly result from a single 'mental explosion'.

Whilst no social class is immune from NAI, it remains true that it is commonest in those families which are under greatest stress and this, inevitably, focuses on the lower socio-economic groups. Many 'child batterers' were, themselves, subject to similar abuse. There appear to be two types of child abusers — those who are stretched to the limit by extraneous conditions and those who inflict bizarre sadistic injuries on their children such as seating them on hot stoves or immersing them in hot water. Bites are common — surprisingly, in both groups.

Some 300–400 deaths may result from NAI each year in the UK[2], about 50 per cent occurring in the first year of life, and there is a far greater morbidity, particularly in the form of brain damage. The solution of the problem depends upon early recognition. Suspected subjects can be admitted to hospital where it is now customary to convene a 'case conference' of interested parties, including social workers who can advise on subsequent policy. The modern trend is towards maintaining the family unity through parental help rather than punishing the parents. Occasional disasters occur[3] and some children have to be removed from parental care — a process described under 'Care proceedings'. Nevertheless, a disturbing proportion of such children are 'rebattered' on return to their parents.

Most local authorities therefore maintain an 'at risk register' to which recourse may be had should any health agency suspect they have a case in their care. The ethics of medical confidentiality are not thereby infringed as it is the child, not the parents, who is the patient. The register is not, however, an unmixed blessing as there is the possibility that parents whose children have been truly accidentally injured are deterred from seeking treatment for fear of suspicion[4]. Such matters are most commonly overseen by local 'review committees' which may, at the same time, issue guidelines for health care practitioners.

Some authorities regard incest as a form of non-accidental injury but, whilst both the NAI syndrome and incest involve child abuse, the conditions can be differentiated on very many counts (*see also* 'Child abuse').

See also: Bite marks; Bruises; Care proceedings; Child abuse; Confidentiality; Fractures; Incest; Infanticide; Subdural haemorrhage

1. Caffey J 'Multiple fractures in the long bones of infants suffering from chronic subdural haematoma' (1946) 56 Am J Roentgenol 163.
2. Court SDM (chairman) *Fit for the Future: Report of the Committee on Child Health Services* (Cmnd 6684) (1976) HMSO, London. Recent appraisal suggests this figure is put too high (Jackson ADM 'Wednesday's children: a review of child abuse' (1982) 75 J Roy Soc Med 83).
3. Field-Fisher TG (chairman) *Report of the Committee of Inquiry into the care and supervision provided in relation to Maria Colwell* (1974) HMSO, London.
4. Leading Article 'Child abuse: the swing of the pendulum' (1981) 283 Br Med J 170.

Non-accidental Injury of Adults in the Home

Violence in the home involving adults is very largely a matter of physical abuse by spouses or cohabitors upon each other, generally under the influence of alcohol. The subject is discussed in greater detail under 'Domestic violence'. Physical injury occasionally becomes lethal, particularly if there is a convenient weapon at hand. Husbands who stab their wives seldom attract much sympathy from the courts but wives who kill their husbands are frequently regarded as acting under extreme provocation — including the comparatively recent concept of cumulative provocation — in which case, a conviction for manslaughter is often punished with a minimum sentence; the courts will also often accept the possibility of self-defence which results in an absolute discharge. Killing may also be accidental — it is not uncommon for one spouse to be temporarily concussed in a drunken brawl and to die from inhalation of vomitus while the other is also semi-comatose from alcohol.

Injuries to the aged — sometimes colloquially known as 'granny-bashing' — is also fairly frequent although psychiatric abuse, comparable to that seen in the case of children, is very much more widespread and is equally damaging. The correct medico-social disposal of the abused elderly often presents as an acute problem. The inclination must be to remove the old person from a hostile environment and such an option is open under the National Assistance Act 1948, s.21. Residential care can, however, be soul destroying and it is by no means certain in every case that minor abuse is not preferable to emotional solitude; close co-operation between the physician and the social work department is very necessary in such circumstances (*see also* 'Geriatric medicine').

See also: Domestic Violence; Geriatric medicine; Provocation

Non-consummation of Marriage

Non-consummation of marriage may result from the incapacity of one or both of the parties to have sexual intercourse (as defined in 'Consummation of marriage') or from the refusal of the respondent to do so. Incapacity may be physical or psychological in origin. In legal theory, the incapacity should be incurable to constitute grounds for nullity but the real test is whether intercourse is practicable in the circumstances. The courts will not expect an affected party to undergo risky or possibly unsuccessful surgery in order to correct the defect. Non-physical incapacity includes frigidity and other psychological states which militate against intercourse[1]; the revulsion may be so strong as to establish vaginismus — uncontrollable spasm of the vaginal muscles.

Wilful refusal by the respondent to consummate the marriage will afford grounds for nullity in England and Wales but not in Scotland (where such behaviour would be grounds for divorce). In such cases the court will look at the whole circumstances of the parties' relationship in order to assess whether there was in fact a refusal to consummate and not merely a misunderstanding. The refusal need not be expressed but may be inferred from the conduct of the respondent[2]. The English courts may order an examination of the parties by their medical expert; such a direction would be extremely unlikely in Scotland[3].

See also: Consummation of marriage; Nullity of marriage

1. *G v G* [1924] AC 349.

2. *Ponticelli v Ponticelli* [1958] P 204, [1958] 1 All ER 357.
3. *G v G* 1961 SLT 324.

Non-ionising Radiation

Non-ionising radiation can be regarded as that part of the electromagnetic spectrum which lies below and including the frequency of ultraviolet light — that is, below a frequency of 10^7 GHz. It thus includes radio, radar, microwave, infrared heat, visual light and ultraviolet light. Although electromagnetic frequencies of this order do not change the chemical structure of the cells, they are not without danger to humans.

Very low frequencies may, in fact, strike a resonance with the body rhythms and may be harmful; this may also occur at the range 10–100 MHz at which the body can act as an aerial and develop hot spots of high energy deposition. Currently, major interest centres upon the frequencies of 1–100 GHz, which is the range for radar and domestic microwave ovens. The effect here can be divided into that which is thermal and that which is non-thermal and depends upon the power density achieved at the target point — this being measured in W/m^2 (watts per square metre). Non-thermal effects in radar workers have been reported, particularly from the Warsaw Pact countries. These include non-specific mental changes together with some minor cardiovascular aberrations; the effects are, in any event, reversible. Thermal changes are more important: exposure to 'microwave oven' frequencies can lead to burns — which may include long-lasting sensitivity to radiation energy of all types — cataract of the eyes and, in some cases, neurological injury to both the peripheral and sympathetic nerve fibres. Leaks from microwave ovens can also affect cardiac pacemakers which have been fitted. Microwave ovens, even when properly serviced, can still leak at the rate of 50 W/m^2. This is within the currently accepted limits of exposure standard in the UK of 100 W/m^2 — a limit value which is rather in excess of the majority of national standards.

Electromagnetic frequencies in excess of 10^3 GHz produce heat as is evidenced in infrared heaters and toasters; the danger to humans is not great as the heat is perceived and avoided. Ultraviolet light (10^5–10^9 GHz) is not perceived and can lead to severe 'sunburning'. Moreover, high intensity ultraviolet light is approaching the range of ionising radiation and there is firm evidence that it predisposes to cancer of the skin — most commonly this is of the non-metastasising type known as basal cell carcinoma or rodent ulcer.

At the same time, non-ionising radiation has very positive medical advantages — apart from the social assets of radio, television and the like. Infrared heat is widely used for improving the local circulation and, hence, the relief of ischaemic pain. Infrared thermography is used particularly for the detection of breast cancer and, although it is by no means ideal, may well be preferred to X-ray mammography which carries with it a very slight hazard of actually inducing cancer. The use of ultrasound in obstetrics is described under that heading; ultrasound may also be used at high power to deposit heat — and relieve pain — and to destroy tissue, currently superficial structures but now being also adapted to certain destructive operations on the brain. A particularly interesting developing technique is that of nuclear magnetic resonance imaging. This non-invasive process introduces no radiation hazards and depends upon imaging the radiofrequency fields which the atomic nuclei in the body release when they are excited at a frequency of 1–10 MHz. It is possible by this means to image natural body matter with, so far as can be seen at present, no ill-effects. There may, however, be some as yet undetected effects of tissue heating and, as with the use of ultrasound, the situation must be kept under review.

The whole field of the beneficial use of non-ionising radiation is developing rapidly and surveillance is through the National Radiological Protection Board.

See also: Electromagnetic radiation; Ionising radiation; Radiation hazards; Ultrasound

Notifiable Diseases

The Public Health (Control of Disease) Act 1984 defines only five conditions which are notifiable to the proper officer — i.e. the community health physician (or community medicine specialist) — of a local authority; the local authority will then inform the district health authority of the existence of the case. These diseases are cholera, plague, relapsing fever, smallpox and typhus fever, all of which can be regarded as 'exotic diseases' — i.e. conditions which occur only by virtue of importation from abroad; they are presumably isolated because of the emphasis of the Act on the control of ports and aerodromes.

Nevertheless, cases of food poisoning are added through s.11 and, by virtue of the secondary legislation which survives the repeal of a statute[1], there are a further 22 conditions which are notifiable under s.13(1) of the 1984 Act[2]; the Secretary of State may add to or subtract from the list of infectious diseases as he thinks fit. A registered medical practitioner must notify such cases unless he has good reason to believe that that has already been done. The local authority also has powers to add to the list when conditions so warrant[3]. German measles for example, is a very common addition now that its association with congenital disease has been established.

A number of occupational diseases are reportable to the Health and Safety Executive but this is the responsibility of the employer rather than of the individual doctor; employers can, however, act only on receipt of a written diagnosis from a doctor. There are currently 28 such conditions[2], which include poisonings, skin diseases, pulmonary disease, certain infections and cancers which are known to be associated with occupation; decompression sickness is also included (*see* 'Diving hazards'). It is to be noted that all notifiable diseases of this type are also prescribed diseases but the reason for notification is different — the main purpose of notification of industrial diseases is to identify inefficient preventive measures at the place of work.

See also: Communicable diseases; Diving hazards; German measles; Infectious diseases; Prescribed diseases and occupations; Toxic jaundice

1. Public Health (Infectious Diseases) Regulations 1968 (SI 1968/1366); Public Health (Infectious diseases) (Scotland) Regulations 1975 (SI 1975/308), both as amended by later additions and deletions.
2. Up-to-date lists are unlikely to be found in current textbooks. Information for doctors is available in Health and Safety Executive *Occupational Disease Reporting*, HSE 18, HMSO, London.

3. Public Health (Control of Disease) Act 1984, s.16(1); National Health Service (Scotland) Act 1972, s.53.
4. Reporting of Injuries, Diseases and Dangerous Occurrences Regulations 1985 (SI 1985/2023), Sch.2.

Nova Causa Interveniens

An apparent causal link between an act and a subsequent event may be severed by the occurrence of an intervening event. This breaking of the 'chain of causation' is sometimes referred to as a *nova causa* (or *novus actus*) *interveniens*.

The intervening event may be an act of God, an act of a third party or an act of the plaintiff or of the victim himself. Whether or not it becomes a *nova causa interveniens* will depend on the extent to which it comes to be regarded as causally significant in itself. The intervening event 'eclipses' the original act if it becomes so potent and unanticipated a cause that it would strike one as being inappropriate to investigate any prior events; or, in the classic opinion, 'it is something ultraneous, something unwarrantable. . .a new cause which disturbs the sequence of events'[1].

The normal hazards of medical treatment will not break the chain of causation[2] but extreme forms of medical negligence or quite extraordinary developments in the patient's condition might do so. The principle in criminal law is usually illustrated through homicide cases. In an Australian case[3] the victim had been discharged from hospital after an apparently successful operation to deal with stabbing injuries but died 11 months later as a result of bowel obstruction caused by a fibrous tissue ring about the site of the operation; a conviction for manslaughter was upheld on appeal. The British Court Martial Appeal case, *R v Smith*, provides a well-known and succinct statement of the rule to be applied:

'If at the time of death the original wound is still an operating cause and a substantial cause, then the death can properly be said to be the result of the wound, albeit that some other cause of death is also operating. Only if it can be said that the original wounding is merely the setting in which another cause operates can it be said that the death does not result from the wound. Putting it another way, only if the second cause is so overwhelming as to make the original wound merely part of the history can it be said that the death does not flow from the wound.[4]'

Exceptions to this rule in criminal law are very rare. *Jordan*[5], in which the cause of death was given as bronchopneumonia, which might have resulted from overtransfusion, is commonly quoted but the circumstances of the appeal were unusual and Hallett J (at p.157) emphasised that the treatment given was not normal; Lawton LJ believed the case should not be regarded as an authority relaxing the common law approach to causation[6]. The unreported case of *R v Vickers*[7] provides a classic example of *nova causa*. A man was kicked in the face and bled severely from the nose. He died on the operating table because the anaesthetic tube was placed in the oesophagus and not in the trachea — the accused was found not guilty of manslaughter but guilty of inflicting grievous bodily harm.

The problem has been highlighted in two cases involving removal of ventilator support from victims of assaults whose hearts were still beating at the time[8]. Appeals against conviction by reason of *nova causa* were rejected in both cases on the grounds that the action constituted good medical practice; the courts did not address themselves to the problem of the precise cause of death. The apparently contradictory decision in *Re Potter*[9], in which a charge of manslaughter was reduced to one of common assault when the victim was used as a transplant donor, was dealt with before the implications of brain stem death had been properly evaluated.

The subsequent conduct of a plaintiff may also give rise to causal problems in tort actions. The plaintiff was successful in *Wieland v Cyril Lord Carpets*[10] when, as a result of having to wear a surgical collar following injury, she was unable to see properly through her spectacles and consequently fell. In *McKew v Holland et al*[11], however, the House of Lords stressed that the plaintiff could not expect to be compensated if he took unreasonable risks and a fall ensued.

The suicide of a victim of a criminal assault would not result in criminal liability for the death, but the rule in tort may be different. The leading English case is *Pigney v Pointers Transport Services Ltd*[12] in which damages were awarded when the victim of an accident hanged himself while suffering from a neurosis caused by an accident. A similar result has been achieved in Canada in *Cotic v Gray*[13], a suicide case in which the 'thin skull principle' was invoked. It must be borne in mind, however, that *Pigney* was decided prior to the decision in *The Wagon Mound*[14], which introduced a foreseeability test into causation; a quite different result might ensue if a foreseeability test were to be applied by a court now faced with such a situation.

See also: Brain stem death; Fluid replacement therapy; Negligence; Refusal of medical treatment; Special sensitivity; Torts; Ventilator support

1. Lord Wright in *The Oropesa* [1943] P 32 at 39.
2. *Robertson v Post Office* [1974] 1 WLR 1176 CA. See also *James Clinton Jordan* (1956) 40 Crim App R 152 per Hallett J at 157.
3. *R v Evans and Gardiner* (No.1) [1976] VR 517; (No.2) [1976] VR 523.
4. [1959] 2 QB 35 per Lord Parker CJ at 42.
5. *Jordan* n.2 above. For clinical comment, *see* Camps FE and Havard JD 'Causation in homicide: a medical view' [1957] Crim LR 576. For general discussion of causation in the law of homicide, *see* Gerber P 'Impeaching medical evidence — causation in the law of homicide' (1983) 57 ALJ 407.
6. In *R v Blaue* [1975] 1 WLR 1411 at pp.14–15.
7. (1981) *Daily Telegraph*, 9 October, p.3.
8. *Finlayson v HMAdv* 1978 SLT (Notes) 60; *R v Malcherek, R v Steel* [1981] 2 All ER 422, [1981] 1 WLR 690 CA.
9. (1963) 31 Med-Leg J 195.
10. [1969] 3 All ER 1006. See also *Block v Martin* (1951) 4 DLR 121; *Boss v Robert Simpson (Eastern) Ltd* (1968) 2 DLR (3d) 114.
11. [1969] 3 All ER 1621 HL.
12. [1957] 2 All ER 807.
13. (1981) 124 DLR (3d) 641.
14. *The Wagon Mound* [1961] AC 388.

Novice Doctors

In general, it can be said that inexperience is no defence to an allegation of negligence[1]. The standard of skill expected of a doctor is essentially the standard expected of practitioners with whom he claims to have similar skills; thus, all that will required of the junior doctor is the proper level of competence to be expected of juniors[2]. There are, however, a number of limitations to this generality. Firstly, all persons practising medicine must measure up to the minimum standards of the ordinary practising doctor. Secondly, it may be negligent for an inexperienced doctor not to seek the advice of a senior or specialist when the prudent junior would have done so. Thirdly, if the novice undertakes procedures, other than in an emergency, in which he is not experienced, he is, in effect, claiming the skills of a suitably trained practitioner and will be judged on that standard. The situation is then similar to the man who has or claims to have special skills and from whom greater care is to be expected[3]. Fourthly, the junior doctor must, in general, carry out the instructions of his senior unless they are manifestly wrong[4] — an invidious position is thus created in that the courts will judge what is clearly wrong objectively whereas the decision as to what seemed wrong at the time must have been taken subjectively. Nevertheless, the principle is fair in that both the consultant who gave the instructions and the hospital authority would be resposible for the actions of the junior[5]. A young doctor working under powers which are only generally delegated is, however, doing so on his own initiative.

See also: Negligence; Vicarious liability

1. *Nettleship v Weston* [1971] 2 QB 691.
2. *Vancouver General Hospital v Fraser* [1952] 2 SCR 36.
3. *Ashcroft v Mersey Regional Health Authority* [1983] 2 All ER 245; *Wimpey Construction UK Ltd v Poole* (1984) Times, 3 May.
4. *Junor v Inverness Hospitals Board of Management and McNicol* (1959) Times, 26 March.
5. *See* discussion in Speller SR *Law of Doctor and Patient* (1973), p.78, HK Lewis, London. *Also*, Dyer C 'Is inexperience a defence against negligence' (1986) 293 Br Med J 497.

Noxious Substances

The Offences Against the Person Act 1861 defines the offences of administering or causing to be taken by any person any poison or other noxious thing so as thereby to endanger the life of such person or to inflict upon him grievous bodily harm (s.23) or with intent to injure, aggrieve or annoy such a person (s.24). It is also an offence to administer a noxious thing intending to procure the miscarriage of a woman (s.58).

Poison is therefore a noxious thing although it would seem that it must be given in sufficient quantity to have an ill-effect if offence is to be committed[1]. Otherwise, the law is inexplicit. Whether or not a substance is a noxious thing must depend not only on the quantity given but also upon the intention with which it was administered. Preparations of ergot are medicinal substances when given for the treatment of migraine; they become noxious substances if the intention is to procure a miscarriage. A further distinction lies in what might be called the 'pharmacological wrapping'.

Thus antimony is a powerful poison and a noxious thing but, when injected as sodium antimony tartrate, it becomes a medicinal substance; sodium antimony tartrate given deliberately in excess of the therapeutic margin would, however, revert to being noxious. The subject is also discussed under 'Drugs'

See also: Abortion; Drugs; Offences Against the Person Act 1861

1. *R v Cato* [1976] 1 WLR 110.

Nuclear Medicine

Nuclear medicine can be defined as the application of radioactive trace substances to medical diagnosis and treatment. The principle of use depends on the fact that radionuclides — unstable variants of atoms (which are prepared in the laboratory and are sometimes known as radiopharmaceuticals) — will emit radiation which can be quantified by simple counters or be imaged by scintigraphy. A modification of nuclear medicine is the use of isotopes for quantifying drugs and biological substances in laboratory specimens. This process is known as radioimmunoassay and is a highly sensitive technique — it has revolutionised the quantification of substances such as insulin or digoxin in the body fluids. Unfortunately, whilst the technique is invaluable in clinical medicine, it has slightly limited evidential value as it is not entirely specific; for example, it may not be possible to identify a particular member of the group of benzodiazepines.

The choice of diagnostic radionuclide to be used depends upon the organ under investigation. A necessary prerequisite is that it will concentrate in the target organ whether that be the brain, heart, kidney or an endocrine gland. In this way, radionuclide imaging, whilst giving a far less clear anatomical picture than do either X-rays or ultrasound, is unique in effectively imaging function. It is essential that the radionuclide used has a short half-life so that the dose of radiation given to the body is strictly limited (*see* 'Radiation hazards').

Nuclear medicine has no special medico-legal significance *per se* — the normal standards of medical negligence apply. Nevertheless, the introduction of radioactivity into the body has its hazards; we can shield ourselves or remove ourselves from external radiation but there are no such escapes from an internal source. These facts are well known and suitable precautions are always taken; even so, the use of internal radiopharmaceuticals is now confined to practitioners who are licensed for the purpose[1].

See also: Endocrine system; Radiation hazards; Toxicological analyses; Ultrasound; X-rays

1. Medicines (Administration of Radioactive Substances) Regulations 1978 (SI 1978/1006).

Nullity of Marriage

A decree of nullity may be obtained in respect of a marriage which is void or voidable. Void marriages are those which are void *ab initio*; voidable marriages are valid marriages until a decree to annul them is obtained. The grounds upon which marriages contracted after 31 July 1971 may be void or voidable are set out in the Matrimonial Causes Act 1973, ss.11 and 12.

A marriage is void if there is lack of capacity to contract a marriage or if certain formalities have not been observed. Incapacity will have been present if the parties are within the prohibited degrees of relationship; if one of the parties is under the age of 16; if either of them is already married; if they are of the same sex; if one of them is party to a polygamous marriage celebrated abroad but while he is domiciled in England.

A marriage is voidable if it is unconsummated; if there is lack of consent to marriage (e.g. through fraud or mental unsoundness); if there is mental disorder; if the respondent suffered at the time of the marriage from a communicable venereal disease; or if the respondent was, at the time of the marriage, pregnant *per alium*.

There is a time bar, which is circumventable in the event of mental disorder or of injustice, of three years beyond which a decree of nullity may not be granted on grounds other than non-consummation[1]. Moreover, as regards venereal disease and pregnancy by another man, the petitioner must have been unaware of the facts at the time of the marriage; the same does not apply in the case of mental disorder. The most common bar to avoidance of a marriage is, however, approbation — a marriage cannot be annulled if the petitioner, although knowing that a petition was open to him, so behaved as to make it apparent to the respondent that he would not seek an annulment and that there would be injustice to the respondent if the decree were granted; both conditions must be fulfilled for the bar to operate[2].

In Scots law, a marriage may be declared void if one of the following conditions is satisfied: (a) legal incapacity to marry; (b) unsoundness of mind; (c) relationships within the forbidden degrees; (d) one of the parties being already married; (e) absence of consent; (f) non-compliance with certain formalities. Non-consummation provides the single and only ground for voidability[3]. Approbation is also a bar to a declarator of nullity in Scotland[4].

See also: Marriage; Non-consummation of marriage

1. Matrimonial Causes Act 1973, s.13 as amended by the Matrimonial and Family Proceedings Act 1984, s.2.
2. *D v D (Nullity: Statutory Bar)* [1979] Fam 70.
3. Clive E *The Law of Husband and Wife in Scotland* (2nd ed, 1982) p.85 et seq, W Green, Edinburgh.
4. *G v G* 1961 SLT (Reps) 324 *sub nom AB v CB* 1961 SC 347.

Nurses, Midwives and Health Visitors

The profession of nursing, along with those of midwifery and health visiting, is now controlled under the Nurses, Midwives and Health Visitors Act 1979. The statutory bodies concerned with the training and governance of the professions are a UK Central Council for Nursing, Midwifery and Health Visiting (s.1) and National Boards for England, Wales, Scotland and Northern Ireland (s.5). Each board nominates at least five of their members to be members of the Central Council — these five being two nurses, one midwife, one health visitor and one tutor; the Secretary of State may nominate additional members. The functions of the Council include preparing and maintaining a register of qualified nurses, midwives and health visitors (s.10), and establishing and improving the standards of training and professional conduct of the professions; to this end, it may appoint committees of which one must be a midwifery committee (s.3(1)).

The members of the national boards are both appointed and elected — the latter being in a majority. The functions of the boards are to arrange courses of training so as to satisfy the standards of the Central Council, to arrange suitable examinations and to carry out investigations of cases of alleged misconduct with a view to proceedings before the Central Council or its committees for a person to be removed from the register. In addition to each board having a Midwifery Committee, there is also a Health Visiting Joint Committee consisting of members of both the Council and the boards.

The register consists of persons who have passed the necessary qualifying examinations — which includes recognised qualifications in the EEC countries or elsewhere, subject to a language proficiency condition. The register has 11 parts related to the profession and degree of qualification of those registered[1].

A person may be removed from the register, whether or not for a specified period, for misconduct or otherwise (s.12) and may also be restored. Committees are constituted to hear and determine proceedings which are relevant; both the Council and its committees may have an assessor to advise on points of law. An appeal against removal from the register can be made to the High Court, or the Court of Session in Scotland, within three months of the decision being made. There are no stated restrictions on this in the Act and it would seem that, contrary to the rules governing the professional conduct committees of the General Medical and General Dental Councils, a nurse can question the validity of a conviction in a court of law when appearing before the Central Council for Nursing, Midwifery and Health Care[2].

It is an offence to represent falsely that one has qualifications in nursing, midwifery or health visiting (s.14).

Midwives are subject to special regulations and, in particular, come under the supervision of the appropriate health authority or board who may report any case of misconduct to the national board (s.16). It is to be noted that a person other than a registered midwife or a registered medical practitioner shall not attend a woman in childbirth other than in the case of sudden or urgent necessity (s.17); it is not clear whether this prevents a husband being present at his wife's delivery — one's feeling is that the word 'attend' in the Act implies some active participation.

See also: General Dental Council; General Medical Council

1. Nurses, Midwives and Health Visitors (Parts of the Register) Order 1983 (SI 1983/667).
2. (1985) *The Times*, 16 July, p.3.

Occupational Disease

There are virtually no occupations which do not carry some medical hazard — even writer's cramp is a prescribed disease. As a result, a comprehensive medical specialty of occupational medicine has grown up and is of very great importance not only in therapy but also, more importantly, in the prevention of disease; it should not be forgotten that the study of the effect of health on work is another most significant dimension of the specialty. One difficulty is that occupations differ so much in type and in danger that it is almost impossible for one man to be competent in all aspects — there is a wealth of difference between coal mining and flying a commercial aircraft; the tendency is therefore for each occupation to attract its own medical officers. In any branch of employment, the specialist in occupational medicine will need not only clinical and environmental medical expertise but also an appreciation of managerial and employees' problems and of the maintenance of good industrial relations. Both occupational physicians and those in employment or training will receive advice on request from the Employment Medical Advisory Service in matters related to occupational health and disease[1].

If an occupation causes a disease, then those employed in that occupation should be compensated if they contract that disease; this is the basis of the definition of prescribed diseases and occupations which are discussed under that heading. Not all occupational diseases are prescribed because it takes some time to establish that work and disability are undoubtedly associated. Equally, many conditions which are claimed as being occupational may well not be so associated; the natural desire to establish a claim for strict compensation often results in a conflict between political urgency and scientific caution.

Particular interest currently centres on the causative link between occupation and cancerous growths. Localised malignancies, clearly associated with contact, have been known for many years — the classic mule-spinner's cancer of the scrotum due to persistent contact with mineral oil has given way to some newer specific tumours such as carcinoma of the nasal membranes following exposure to nickel fumes or to wood dust. Indeed, the nature of cancer, its ubiquity in the general population and its long incubation period, make proof of causation extremely difficult unless the tumour is of unusual type. Angiosarcoma of the liver is just such a tumour and the comparatively rapid acceptance of its association with vinyl chloride, an essential in the modern plastic manufacturing industry, can be attributed largely to that fact. Mesothelioma, which is now firmly associated with asbestosis, is a further example. It is, however, far more difficult to attribute common cancers, such as carcinoma of the prostate, to occupational factors. Exposure to pesticides is a particularly sensitive area and is discussed further under that heading.

Occupational disease covers all aspects of health and employment but would also cover conditions associated with leisure occupations and with self-employment. For all practical purposes, however, it can be regarded as synonymous with industrial disease.

See also: Cancer; Employment medical advisers; Industrial poisoning; Pesticides; Prescribed diseases and occupations

1. Health and Safety at Work etc. Act 1974, s.55.

Odontology

Odontology (the study of the teeth) is synonymous with the practice of dentistry. Forensic odontology is the application of this science to assist the legal system.

The two main areas in which forensic odontology is of legal importance are in identification, particularly in the context of major disasters, and in the investigation of bite marks. Both these applications are discussed under the appropriate headings.

Traditional dentistry is fast expanding in such fields as maxillo-facial surgery and the dental surgeon can be of very great assistance in the investigation of accidents and, consequently, in advising on aspects of protection of the face and head; this is particularly true in vehicular accidents.

See also: Bite marks; Identification of the dead; Road traffic accidents

Offences Against the Person Act 1861

The Offences Against the Person Act 1861 covers a wide spectrum of offences against human beings. Many of the original clauses have been extensively amended or replaced by later legislation (especially the Criminal Law Acts 1967 and 1977). The significant offences are discussed under the appropriate titles but some sections are mentioned briefly here.

Section 18 deals with unlawfully and maliciously wounding or causing any grievous bodily harm, with intent to do some grievous bodily harm to any person. It therefore defines an offence of specific intent — a matter of importance in the adjudication of an accused's state of mind[1].

Grievous bodily harm means 'really serious harm'[2]. A wound might or might not be grievous bodily harm but is distinguished in that it must, by definition, involve a breach of the skin or adjacent mucous membrane (e.g. the inside of the lip)[3].

Section 20 covers unlawfully and maliciously wounding or inflicting grievous bodily harm — unlawful wounding — which must, therefore, be intentional or the result of recklessness[4]. Section 47 refers to an assault occasioning actual bodily harm, which would seem to encompass any injury — including a bruise — but the severity of the injury is likely to be considered in sentencing[5].

Offences associated with poisoning are dealt with under s.23 — 'unlawfully and maliciously administering. . .any poison or other destructive or noxious thing as thereby to endanger life or inflict grievous bodily harm' — and s.24 — '. . .with intent to injure, aggrieve or annoy'. It is to be noted that the intention, the dose and the effect[6] are taken into consideration in defining what is noxious.

Sections 58, 59 and 60 are discussed under the headings 'Abortion' and 'Concealment of birth'.

The Offences Against the Person Act 1861 does not extend to Scotland, where the majority of relevant offences are dealt with at common law[7].

See also: Abortion; Bruises; Concealment of birth; Homicide; Intent; Murder; Poisoning; Wounds

1. *DPP v Majewski* [1977] AC 443; *Garlick* (1981) 72 Crim App R 291.
2. *DPP v Smith* [1961] AC 290.
3. *JJC (a minor) v Eisenhower* [1983] 3 All ER 230.
4. *R v Cunningham* [1957] 2 QB 396.
5. *Christopher Jones* [1981] Crim LR 119.
6. *R v Marcus* [1981] 1 WLR 774.
7. The Criminal Law (Scotland) Act 1829 has been repealed.

Offensive Weapons

The Prevention of Crime Act 1953 makes it a criminal offence to have with one in a public place an offensive weapon without lawful authority or reasonable excuse. Offensive weapons are divided into three categories:

(a) Articles made for the purpose of causing an injury (offensive weapons *per se*). These include such weapons as bayonets, coshes and flick knives and also defensive weapons such as ammonia guns which are not covered by the Firearms Act 1968.
(b) Articles adapted for causing injury to others — these include sharpened combs, socks filled with sand, etc.
(c) Articles which have an innocent everyday purpose and which have not been manufactured with the intention of causing injury. An example of a weapon in this category would be a knife which has a domestic purpose, such as a penknife.

The implications of this categorisation are evidential. As far as the first two are concerned, the prosecution has only to prove that the defendant had the weapon in his possession in a public place; it is then for the defendant to show lawful authority or reasonable excuse. In the case of possession of a weapon in the third class, the prosecution must also prove that the defendant had the weapon with the intention of causing injury — which can be interpreted so as to include causing fright or shock[1].

The question of what constitutes a reasonable excuse in terms of the Act has been considered in a number of cases. Claims that the weapon was carried in self-defence are closely scrutinised and will be justified only if there is an immediate and obvious threat[2]. The test in each case is whether the reasonable man would have considered it appropriate to carry the weapon[3].

See also: Flick knives

1. *Woodward v Koessler* [1958] 3 All ER 557.
2. *Bradley v Moss* [1974] Crim LR 430; *Greive v Macleod* 1967 JC 32.
3. *Bryan v Mott* (1975) 62 Crim App R 71.

Further reading
Supperstone M *Brownlie's Law of Public Order and National Security* (2nd ed, 1981) p.148 et seq, Butterworths, London.

Omission

An omission to act may have consequences in both civil and criminal law. In the civil context, an omission to perform an action may be considered negligent, and give rise to legal liability, so long as the court is prepared to take the view that there was a duty to act on the part of the defendant. This duty will not be inferred readily; English law is reluctant, for example, to impose a duty to rescue, although such a duty may arise where there is a close relationship between the parties or where the defendant has created a dangerous situation. To illustrate the principle in a medico-legal context: a doctor who is responsible for a patient, and who omits to warn him of a possible dangerous side effect of a drug he prescribes, commits an omission which could amount to negligence. This is a simple case in that the doctor undoubtedly had a duty of care for the patient in question; by contrast, a doctor who comes across an injured person is under no legal obligation to assist him and an omission to help would not give rise to a legal claim[1]. The position of hospitals which decline to treat in an emergency is different. Liability may be imposed on a hospital which has a statutory obligation to provide medical assistance but a private hospital or clinic will incur no similar liability[2].

Criminal liability for omissions may be imposed on persons who have failed to perform a required duty and who have consequently caused death or injury. The circumstances in which such liability will be imposed are, however, limited and, in general, it is only in the most serious cases that an omission to act will be treated as criminal negligence. The subject is discussed in greater detail under 'Manslaughter'.

See also: Manslaughter

1. This would not be so in some countries — e.g. France (Decree 79-506 of 28 June 1979, art.4).
2. Fleming J *Law of Torts* (6th ed, 1983) p.138, Law Book Co, Sydney.

Ordinary/Extraordinary Treatment

The moral justification for doctors adopting a quality of life approach to treatment rather than the classic Hippocratic sanctity of life ethos is contained in the ordinary/ extraordinary treatment test. As enunciated by Pope Pius XII, this reads:

> 'Man has a right and a duty in case of severe illness to take the necessary steps to preserve life and health.That duty. . .devolves from charity as ordained by the Creator, from social justice and even from strict law. But he is obliged at all times to employ only ordinary means. . ., that is to say those means which do not impose an extraordinary burden on himself or others'[1].

This statement of the moral position has been approved by Protestant leaders[2] although it is less certainly acceptable in the Jewish tradition[3].

The important aspect of the test is that it is personalised to the individual patient. There is no implication that a generalised therapy (e.g. cytotoxic drug treatment) is or is not 'ordinary'; such a definition would depend upon the era and upon the medical sophistication of the health service. Rather, the test is to be made in the context of the patient's condition and prognosis, and it is acceptable to take into account his non-medical status and that of his family — or, indeed, of others in the competition for scarce resources. It follows, for example, that minimal treatment may be 'extraordinary' for the brain-damaged patient maintained by a ventilator; considerable therapeutic effort might, by contrast, be regarded as 'ordinary' for the fully conscious patient suffering from paralysis of the respiratory muscles. Similarly, what might be justifiable invasive therapy in a young person could be 'extraordinary' when applied to a patient already suffering from the infirmities of old age. It is therefore rather more appropriate to refer to a productive/non-productive treatment test, thereby firmly focusing on the individual case. Whilst the wishes of the relatives may properly be taken into account when reaching a decision, the determining factor must be the best interests of the patient.

The policy of the courts in the UK has been very much to rely on the twin pillars of good faith and good medical practice. The few precedents available apply more properly to the associated legal doctrine of necessity and the moral principle of 'double effect'. United States judges have tended to interpret the principle more in terms of a feasible/non-feasible treatment test[4] which implies a philosophy orientated to the doctor rather than to the patient.

See also: Double effect; Euthanasia; Necessity; Resource allocation; Terminal illness

1. (1957) 49 Acta Apostolicae Sedis 1027.
2. Coggan D 'On dying and dying well' (1977) 70 Proc R Soc Med 75.
3. Jakobovits I 'Jewish medical ethics — a brief overview' (1983) 9 J Med Ethics 109.
4. MacMillan ES 'Birth defective infants. A standard for non-treatment decisions' (1978) 30 Stan LR 599. *See also Maine Medical Center v Houle* No.74-145 (Sup Ct, Me) (1974)

Further reading
The following two articles have been found particularly useful:
   Kuhse H 'Extraordinary means and the sanctity of life' (1981) 7 J Med Ethics 74.

Campbell AGM 'The right to be allowed to die' (1983) 9 J Med Ethics 136.

Ossification Centres

The shafts of the long bones calcify early in fetal life. Calcification of the ends (epiphyses) takes rather longer and is established through the formation of centres of ossification within the fetal cartilage. These appear in a relatively regular order; the assessment of the presence of centres thus provides a fairly good indication of the age of the fetus or infant. The order and time of appearance are to be found in many standard works[1]. Perhaps the most important centres from the medical aspect are those in the talus bone of the foot and in the first segment of the sternum (breast bone); these form at about the 28th week of gestation and are valuable indications of whether or not the fetus can be presumed in law to be viable[2] and also assist in the distinction between a dead fetus and a stillbirth. The centres in the lower end of the femur and in the cuboid bone of the foot appear at full term and are useful observations in the interpretation of suspected infanticide.

Centres of ossification are clearly visible if cut through at postmortem dissection; they are, however, most satisfactorily demonstrated by X-ray.

The centres also fuse with the main bone in regular chronological order and this process can be used in the same way to estimate the age of a child or adolescent (*see* 'Union of epiphyses').

See also: Age of a body at death; Identification of the dead; Infant Life (Preservation) Act 1929; Stillbirth; Union of epiphyses; Viability

1. For example, Mason JK *Forensic Medicine for Lawyers* (2nd ed, 1983) App.F, Butterworths, London.
2. Infant Life (Preservation) Act 1929.

Othello Syndrome

This condition, more accurately described as morbid jealousy, is said occasionally to play a role in crimes of violence. The essential feature of the syndrome is the delusion that the sufferer's spouse is being unfaithful; it can occur either in 'pure' form or as part of a psychosis with other features[1]. Morbid jealousy is also sometimes associated with psychopathy and with certain organic illnesses, particularly alcoholism.

The subject of the Othello syndrome spends much time searching for evidence of the suspected infidelity. Traps may be laid and the spouse may be followed and interrogated at length. Violence and even homicide may result[2].

The syndrome may include feelings of inadequacy which some psychiatrists interpret as being connected with homosexuality — jealousy of this sort is regarded as a projection onto the spouse of suppressed homosexual inclinations. Psychiatric treatment may assist in some cases but requires much time. The sufferer may need to be hospitalised for the protection of the spouse.

There are few reported decisions in which the Othello syndrome, or morbid jealousy, is discussed. It may provide grounds for a plea of diminished responsibility in cases of homicide. There is at least one recent decision in which the court found that morbid jealousy was not the sort of medical condition which would justify the success of such a plea[2] but the unreported case of *R v Asher*[3] indicates that there is some room for sympathy.

See also: Delusions; Diminished responsibility; Homosexuality; Psychopath; Psychoses

1. There is a useful summary of the syndrome and its features in Enoch MD and Trethowan WH *Uncommon Psychiatric Syndromes* (2nd ed, 1979) p.36 et seq, Wright, Bristol.
2. *R v Vinagre* (1979) 69 Crim App R 104.
3. (1981) *The Times*, 9 June, p.4.

Overlaying

Overlaying is the process of asphyxiation of an infant due to the physical presence of its mother or other bed fellow while she is asleep or otherwise unaware. Although it was at one time diagnosed frequently as a cause of infant death, it is probable that this reflects, firstly, the once prevalent combination of overcrowding and alcoholism[1] and, secondly, a medical inability to recognise the natural occurrence of sudden death in infancy. Occasional cases are still seen although they are almost always associated with some accident such as entanglement of bed clothes.

See also: Asphyxia; Sudden infant death syndrome

1. An association which is still recognised in the Children and Young Persons Act 1933, s.1(2)(b).

Ovum Donation

Ovum donation involves the provision of human eggs by any means for the use of other parties. Such ova are usually either surplus following *in vitro* fertilisation or are recovered from the ovaries of women undergoing sterilisation operations; the consent of the woman is required for removal and for the subsequent use to which the eggs are put.

In the present state of the law, such ova may form the basis of embryonic experimentation although this may not be so at the time of publication[1]. Less controversially, they may be used as the material for *in vitro* fertilisation of sterile women who are unable to provide their own ova.

Used in this way, ovum donation is the female equivalent of artificial insemination by donor. Although, strictly speaking, the same difficulties as to registration and legitimacy apply, they are even less likely to arise in practice. Disputed maternity is extremely unlikely; moreover, it seems inevitable that a rule along the lines of *mater est quam gestatio demonstrat* will be applied in the future[2].

See also: Artificial insemination by donor; Embryonic experimentation; *In vitro* fertilisation

1. Unborn Children (Protection) Bill 1985 may yet reach the Statute Book.
2. In conformity with Warnock M (chairman) *Report of the Committee of Inquiry into*

Human Fertilisation and Embryology (Cmnd 9314) (1984) para.6.8, HMSO, London. There is statute law to this effect in Victoria (Status of Children (Amendment) Act 1984).

Oxygen

Oxygen, which contributes approximately one-fifth of the earth's atmosphere, is literally the breath of life. The cells of the body will die without oxygen and will do so with a speed proportional to their oxygen requirements in life.

The partial pressure of oxygen in the alveoli at ground level is approximately 13.7 kPa (103 mmHg). Oxygenation of the erythrocytes becomes clinically inadequate when this falls to about 6.7 kPa (50 mmHg). Chronic environmental exposure to a reduced partial pressure of oxygen is compensated for, *inter alia*, by the production of more erythrocytes (polycythaemia). Acute oxygen loss must be countered by increasing the supply — and, hence, the partial pressure — artificially. However, even pure oxygen is inadequate when the total atmospheric pressure is reduced to 20 kPa (150 mmHg); this occurs at an altitude of some 12,000 m (40,000 ft), beyond which oxygen must be provided under pressure.

The supply of oxygen to the tissues is compromised by heart failure, by anaemia and by abnormalities of the haemoglobin; excess oxygen may therefore be required in many chronic disease states. The use of oxygen in high concentration, and particularly its use at excess pressure (hyperbaric), is not without complication — oxygen poisoning is a well-established entity. Poisoning results in fibrosis of the lung and is therefore self-perpetuating; it is possible that this is the mechanism by which paraquat produces its lethal effects.

See also: Anoxia; Asphyxia; Aspiration; Hypoxia; Paraquat poisoning

P

Paedophilia

Paedophiles are persons who are sexually attracted to children. There is a strong case for restricting the use of the term to those whose activity is with children who are pubescent or younger. Many adults who are relatively 'normal' sexually find themselves, on occasion, attracted to teenagers who are three or four years past puberty[1].

Paedophiles are overwhelmingly male and may be heterosexual or homosexual in disposition. They may range from adolescent boys to elderly men. Many are married and most have been married. A relatively high proportion have personality disorders[2]. Their sexual approaches to children are seldom initiated through violence and are frequently met with compliance on the part of the child; it would seem that danger to the child's life arises only when the paedophile appreciates the possibility of discovery and punishment. Sexual contact is often restricted to fondling the sexual parts. In many cases, the offender will be known to the child and may, indeed, be a member of the victim's family. The aetiology of the condition is as disputed as is that of any other sexual deviation but there is general agreement that paedophiles are recruited from those who find it difficult to make social contact with women.

Treatment of paedophilia is difficult and often disappointing. Counselling may help the patient to deal with his sexual impulses and to avoid the occasions of temptation; it may also assist in making his sexual approaches to adults more confident. Aversion therapy and other attempts at behaviour modification have also been used on a small scale.

The law's response to the adult who engages in sexual conduct with children is usually unambiguously punitive. The criminal law penalises most forms of sexual activity involving girls under the age of 16 and boys below 21 years of age. Prison sentences are common and may be lengthy in the case of a repeated offender; a particularly distasteful aspect is that such offenders often have to be isolated from other prisoners for their own safety.

See also: Indecency with children; Sexual offences

1. Taylor B (ed) *Perspectives on Paedophilia* (1981) Batsford, London.
2. Swanson DW 'Adult sexual abuse of children: the man and the circumstances' (1968) 29 Dis Nerv Syst 677.

Paper Chromatography

Paper chromatography is a relatively old and coarse form of chromatography in which drugs in solution are carried by suitable solvents which are allowed to travel by capillary action on filter paper. The distance travelled by the drug related to the distance travelled by the solvent is known as the R_f value of the drug.

An unknown drug can be identified by comparing its R_f value in several solvents with the R_f values of known drugs. The method is therefore limited to the identification of those drugs for which R_f values have been established.

See also: Chromatography

Parachuting Injuries

The nature of parachuting injuries depends to a large extent on the purpose of the exercise — whether it was an emergency escape from military aircraft, whether it was a military operation or whether it was performed as part of a spectacle or recreational sport.

The first is of little forensic interest although of absorbing interest to the forensic pathologist. Injuries can result from striking the aircraft, from premature parachute opening — which, paradoxically, becomes increasingly dangerous with high altitude — from entanglement with equipment and from ground impact injury which may be enforced through the need to make an emergency escape at low altitude; the so called 'chin–sternum–heart syndrome', in which the body is severely flexed so as to compress the heart beneath the fractured sternum, is an interesting and common result of this last hazard[1]. The majority of such injuries have been eliminated by the almost universal use of powered ejection from high performance aircraft[2]. Military parachuting is scarcely significant in the present context but sports parachuting — and hang-gliding — are becoming increasingly popular. Fatalities from the former are uncommon as the sport is well supervised, the aircraft used are generally specialised and reserve parachutes are carried for use in the event of primary failure. Injuries which are sustained are generally those of poor ground impact technique and are concentrated on the lower limbs and shoulder girdles. Fatal injuries due to virtual free fall to the ground include rupture of the heart and aorta and rupture of the liver; an interesting ring fracture of the base of the skull, surrounding the foramen magnum, occurs following partial parachute development when the force of a heavy feet-first impact is transmitted through the spine. Injuries due to dragging on the ground, which are not uncommon in emergency and military parachuting, are unlikely to be seen as drops will not be undertaken in adverse wind conditions.

The legality of display and sports parachuting is fully ensured by the decision in *Attorney General's Reference (No.6 of 1980)*[3].

See also: Deceleration injuries; Falls; Sports injuries

1. Simson LR 'Chin–sternum–heart syndrome: cardiac injury associated with parachuting mishaps' (1971) 42 Aerospace Med 1214.
2. For review, *see* Mason JK 'Transportation accidents' in Camps FE and Lucas BGB (eds) *Gradwohl's Legal Medicine* (3rd ed, 1976) Chap.21, Wright, Bristol.
3. [1981] QB 715.

Paralysis

Paralysis of a muscle implies loss of motor power in that muscle.

Medically speaking, paralysis may be of spastic or flaccid type; the muscle in the former appears to be in a state of contraction whilst it is limp in the latter. Spastic paralysis results from an injury in the brain or spinal cord; flaccid paralysis is due to injury of the peripheral motor nerves. The common result is that spastic paralysis is widespread and involves whole segments of the body whilst flaccid paralysis affects groups of or even single muscles. Both may, however, result in considerable deformity as contractures will result either from spasticity of the major muscle groups or from the unimpeded action of normal muscles which are unopposed by flaccid paralysed antagonists.

Since regeneration of the central nervous system is impossible, spastic paralysis is permanent whilst some recovery of function of flaccid paralysed muscles may be possible if the nervous connection is reinstated.

See also: Central nervous system; Nervous system

Paranoia

Paranoid reactions are present in a number of serious mental illnesses and are characterised by delusions which are typically those of persecution or of aggrandisement.

They occur in schizophrenics (*see* 'M'Naghten Rules') and in depressive psychotics. Persons with organic psychoses may also develop paranoid symptoms — including those of suspicion of all around them. The individual with the so-called paranoid personality — that is, one who is naturally suspicious or self-satisfied — may be precipitated into a fully fledged paranoid state when under stress. An extreme example of the paranoid state is that of morbid jealousy (the Othello syndrome). Many psychiatrists believe that paranoia is particularly a part of the homosexual personality.

See also: Delusions; Homosexuality; Othello syndrome; Psychoses; Schizophrenia

Paraplegia

Paraplegia is the loss of motor function, or paralysis, of both legs. From the medico-legal aspect, the most common cause is an injury to the spinal cord in the lower thoracic or upper lumbar region which, in turn, results from fracture of the spine.

The spine in this area is very sensitive to forced flexion; paraplegia therefore often results from vehicular or industrial — in particular, mining — accidents.

Paraplegia will be accompanied by loss of voluntary control of the organs supplied by nerves originating from the lumbar spinal cord — e.g. the bladder, the rectum and the penis. Involuntary function, including some sexual capacity, may, however, be restored through a spinal reflex mechanism; the spinal cord below the injured region is still supplied with oxygenated blood and is therefore viable.

See also: Paralysis; Spinal cord injuries

Paraquat Poisoning

Poisoning by paraquat was at one time common and involved suicide, accident and an occasional homicide. It is now comparatively rare — probably because the extremely unpleasant nature of death has been widely publicised and also because the availability of the herbicide in its concentrated form is now controlled under the Poisons Rules 1978 (SI 1978/1), Sch.4.

Paraquat causes localised chemical burning and is a generalised poison. The lethal effect in the latter context is on the lungs where the action appears to be to sensitise the alveoli to atmospheric oxygen — the result being progressive fibrosis of the lung tissue. The high mortality of paraquat poisoning stems from the fact that, whilst the patient is dying from hypoxia, treatment with oxygen merely accelerates the disease process[1]. The indications are that the total effect is immediate and the pathology progressive once a threshhold concentration has built up in the tissues; a fatal outcome has been initiated by very small doses. Although over 500 deaths have been reported world wide as being due to paraquat, the substance can be used with safety if reasonable industrial precautions are employed. The dangers of paraquat must be viewed in the light of the very great agricultural benefits it confers.

See also: Pesticides; Poisons Act 1972

1. Rebello G and Mason JK 'Pulmonary histological appearances in fatal paraquat poisoning' (1978) 2 Histopathology 53.

Parasuicide

The term 'parasuicide' is used as a preferred alternative to attempted suicide which presupposes motivation; indeed, parasuicide itself implies a resemblance to suicide and it has been suggested that 'deliberate self-harm' is a still better and less definitive term[1]. There must, however, be an association between the two conditions in that nearly half those committing suicide have a history of parasuicide at some time in the past[2].

Drug ingestion is by far the commonest form of parasuicide although incised wounds of the wrist are occasionally seen. Whereas barbiturates are the commonest ingested drugs resulting in suicide, the benzodiazepines are implicated more often in parasuicide[3]. By contrast with suicide, parasuicide is commonest in young females, in whom it is some 40 times more frequent than is suicide. There is a marked association of parasuicide with the lower social groups and overcrowded housing areas. It has been suggested that, whereas probably a third of those who actually kill themselves do so on account of overt mental disorder, an even higher proportion of those who make unsuccessful attempts do so primarily for social reasons[4]. Some concept of the scale of the problem is to be obtained from the fact that as many persons are admitted to intensive care units in a major city by reason of drug overdose as are admitted from vehicular accidents[5].

See also: Drug overdose; Incised wounds; Road traffic accidents; Suicide

1. Morgan HG et al 'The urban distribution of non-fatal deliberate self-harm' (1975) 126 Br J Psychiat 319.
2. Kennedy P et al 'The prevalence of suicide and parasuicide ('attempted suicide') in Edinburgh' (1974) 124 Br J Psychiat 36.
3. Proudfoot AT and Park J 'Changing patterns of drugs used for self-poisoning' [1978] 1 Br Med J 90.
4. Trethowan WH 'Suicide and attempted suicide' [1979] 2 Br Med J 319.
5. Murray JC et al 'Severe self-poisoning — a ten year experience in the Glasgow area' (1974) 19 Scott Med J 279.

Parentage Testing

The transmission of genes is described under 'Genetic disease'. For the purposes of paternity testing, a gene should express itself as an antigen which can be identified through its specific antibody. There are alternative immunological methods available, such as electrophoresis, and these are used for the identification of genetically controlled enzyme systems or of other protein molecules. Substances which are to be used for parentage testing must be passed on 'true', they must be unaffected by extraneous conditions such as disease and they must be readily available. For practical purposes, the process is limited to the examination of the blood; the antigens and other determinations available are described under 'Blood groups'.

Save in very exceptional circumstances (e.g. error in the hospital nursery or kidnapping) maternity is not in question. The vast majority of tests for parentage involve questions of disputed paternity which arise in the context of affiliation orders, divorce proceedings and questioned legitimacy; evidence of a relationship might also be required in incest cases. The intricacies of modern reproductive techniques may confuse matters in the future (*see*, for example, 'Artificial insemination by donor' and 'Ovum donation').

The 'rules' of parentage testing are:

(a) One antigen-producing gene of an allelic pair is derived from each parent. Each parent has one of two genes to donate at random.
(b) A blood group antigen cannot be present in a child unless it is present in at least one parent.
(c) If one parent is homozygous for a given antigen then that antigen *must* appear in all his or her offspring.

These principles can be applied to each blood group system independently; the more systems tested, the more conclusive will be the result. The 'value' of each system depends on several factors — the number of antigens in the system, the power of expression of those antigens, the availability of antibodies with which to demonstrate them and their distribution in the population. The ABO system suffers from the fact that the antigen O cannot be demonstrated — thus a phenotypical group A man who was in fact of genotype AO could father either a group A or a group O child; similarly, the potential rhesus antigen d is silent. The Kell blood group system is of very little value because 90 per cent of persons are 'Kell negative' — that is, they have the genotype kk. In all, the MNS system is the most useful single diagnostic tool.

Serum proteins (especially of the haptoglobin and Gc systems) are effective in excluding parentage, as are several of the red cell enzyme systems — the erythrocyte acid phosphatase and the glutamate–pyruvate transaminase reactions are particularly useful. The inheritance of abnormal haemoglobins (e.g. HbS which is responsible for sickle cell disease) is also mendelian in principle; the use of such characteristics depends very much on the ethnic group being considered.

Parentage testing — or, in practical terms, paternity testing — can only exclude a wrongly accused father, and the certainty with which this can be done depends on the number of systems tested. Thus, 17 per cent of falsely suspected fathers will be excluded if only the ABO system is studied; this rises to 60 per cent if the rhesus and MNS systems are added whilst a full battery of tests involving red cell antigens, red cell enzyme systems and serum proteins can exclude 89 per cent of such men. The figure is effectively 100 per cent if the laboratory is able to interpret the HLA antigen system. It is therefore one of the failings in equity of paternity testing that, whereas the woman and her baby have little to gain from the procedure, the man has little to lose. It is, however, possible to give some idea of the likelihood of a given man being the father. This is generally done by calculating the proportion of men in a similar general population who would not be excluded from paternity by the tests done; the lower the figure, the greater is the pointer to fatherhood — but it will remain no more than a pointer to which the court will have due regard. As Lord Reid put it: 'If 50 per cent of men could supply the necessary antigens, the test would be valueless in proof of paternity; if only one in 1,000 could do so, the result would go a long way to proving that the man was the father; but if the figure was 1 per cent or 10 per cent, the test might go some way to making paternity probable'[1]. With the increased specificity made possible by the discovery of more test systems, it is doubtful if figures as high as 10 per cent would be regarded as significant today. Evidence of transmission of a very rare antigen would add to the statistical probability but would also be persuasive in its own right.

Parentage testing is statutorily constrained in England and Wales under the Family Law Reform Act 1969, Part III. The court may direct the use of blood tests to see whether or not a person is excluded from paternity on application from any party to the proceedings (s.20(1)). Consent is needed but the court may draw inferences from the fact that a person has failed to accept a direction (s.23(1)). There is, of course, nothing to stop the parties coming to an agreement in the absence of a court direction. Specimens must be obtained as a minimum from the mother, the child and any putative fathers. The specimens must be identified by the parties and by their legal advisers. Declarations of consent and of validation of specimens must be signed, together with declarations that no blood transfusions have been received in the last three months. Ideally, an infant should be at least 6 months old at the

time of testing. The majority of specimens will be taken by general practitioners —
who are specifically assured of non-attendance at court — and, since the parties may
well not be known to the sampler, corroboration of identification from passport
photographs is advisable lest the putative father send a friend to donate blood in his
place[2]. The actual testing may be undertaken only by a specialist appointed and
authorised for the purpose by the Home Office (s.22).

'Excluded from paternity' means excluded subject to the occurrence of mutation
(s.25); in fact, no proven case of a blood group mutating between two generations
has ever been recorded. There is, however, some evidence that the secretor status
may change under the influence of alcoholism, and a notorious complication is the
spurious appearance of the B antigen as a result of bacterial interaction[3]; the use of
fresh blood is essential. Rare blood groups are discovered only in the course of
time — it is just possible that the presence of a group unknown at the time was
responsible for the unusual result in the Scottish case of *Imre v Mitchell*[4] when a
1:1,000 chance of error was regarded as sufficient to discredit a blood test result; it
seems highly improbable that such an eventuality could occur today, although testers
will be aware of the possibility.

The Family Law Reform Act 1969 does not run to Scotland, where blood grouping
for paternity purposes has not been widely used. This is because of an innate
reluctance to do something which may be to the disadvantage of a child[5]. This
approach shows slight evidence of change and the Inner House has recently ordered
blood testing on the grounds that 'the best interests of the child would be secured if
the truth relating to her parents were ascertained'[6].

At the time of writing, there are some interesting developments in the field of
genetic engineering; it is possible that the new techniques will be able to show
parentage positively and that they may come to supplant the conventional methods
described above[7].

See also: Artifical insemination by donor; Blood groups; Genetic disease; Genetic
engineering; Ovum donation

1. *S v S; W v Official Solicitor* [1970] 3 All ER 107, HL, at 110. The corroborative value of
blood tests in paternity disputes has been confirmed recently (*T v B* (1985) Times, 30
November).
2. The Scottish case of *Sproat v McGibney* 1968 SLT 33 may have been confused in this
way.
3. Dodd BE and Lincoln PJ *Blood Group Topics* (1975) Chap. 11, Edward Arnold, London.
4. 1958 SC 439.
5. Ibid, per Lord Clyde.
6. *Docherty v McGlynn* 1983 SLT (Reports) 645.
7. *See* Jeffreys AJ et al 'Individual-specific "fingerprints" of human DNA' (1985) 316 Nature
76; and a practical application 'Positive identification of an immigration test-case using human
DNA fingerprinting' (1985) 317 Nature 818.

Parental Rights

Parental rights are basically rights in common law which have the statutory backing
of the Children Act 1975. In so far as they are not defined, they must be assumed

to include the right to physical possession of a child — a right which has been, admittedly, eroded in that, when it is in doubt, the court will now decide on the basis of the child's best interests irrespective of any assumed parental rights. A parent has rights[1] to legal custody which include the right to control the manner and place in which a child spends his time[2].

A number of other rights exist — e.g. to impose discipline, to dictate the child's religion and to control his education[3] — but the outstandingly important right in the medico-legal field is the parents' right to consent to medical, surgical or dental treatment on behalf of their children. This right has been transferred to the minor aged between 16 and 18 years through the Family Law Reform Act 1969, s.8(1), but s.8(3), which states that nothing in the section is to be construed as making ineffective any consent which would have been effective if the section had not been enacted, introduces an element of confusion. Speller[4] has pointed out that the section could mean that parental consent could still overrule refusal of treatment by the minor; on the other hand, the subsection may preserve the right of the minor below the age of 16 to give valid consent to treatment provided he has sufficient understanding of the circumstances.

The problem is discussed further under 'Consent by minors' but, here, it is noted that, whilst the Court of Appeal in *Gillick v West Norfolk and Wisbech Area Health Authority and another*[5], relying largely on the concept of legal custody as defined in the Children Act 1975 and on the rules of wardship procedure, decided in favour of parental rights over the under-16, the House of Lords considered that the right to control a child existed for the benefit of the child and that it would be unrealistic for the courts to fail to recognise, *inter alia*, that most wise parents relax their control gradually as the child develops and encourage him to become increasingly independent[6]. An equally important aspect of parental rights in this connection lies in the parents' problematic right to refuse treatment on behalf of a child. There is a strong medical bias towards this right — 'in the absence of a clear cut code to which society adheres, there is no justification for the court usurping the parents' rights'[7]. The courts, however, have consistently demonstrated their general inclination to give preference to the best interests of the child. In the important case of *Re B (a minor)*[8], the court overruled the refusal by the parents of a life-saving operation for a downsian infant. 'The child', said Dunn LJ, 'should be put in the same position as any other mongol child and must be given the chance to have an existence'. Kennedy[9] has suggested that the parallel case of *R v Arthur*[10] in which a downsian infant was annotated as 'Parents do not wish it to survive. Nursing care only', makes new law in that it is now possible to withhold treatment for an infant if it has a medical condition which is both disadvantageous and incurable and the infant is rejected by its parents. It would, however, seem that *Re B* is a far more persuasive authority, particularly as a decision in that case might have been different had the child been likely to be forced into a life of pain. Indeed, this interpretation of the two cases must be correct; were it not, the way would be open for parents to reject their children at any time of minority, a concept which is directly opposed to the duty imposed in the Children Act 1975, s.85.

If the situation in the UK in this particular respect appears complex, it is as nothing when compared with the trans-Atlantic scene where contradictory decisions are frequent[11]. Nevertheless, the opinion in the USA appears to be hardening in favour of parental rights to refuse treatment. There is a change from the attitude:

'Children are not property whose disposition is left to parental discretion without hindrance'[12] to one of regarding refusal of care as a treatment elected by the parents which was within accepted medical standards[13]. A recent Canadian decision[14] has, however, gone the other way, holding that a shunting operation on a hydrocephalic child was a necessary procedure to which the parents could not object.

See also: Consent by minors; Down's syndrome; Jehovah's Witnesses; Neonaticide; Wardship proceedings

1. Both parents of a legitimate child have an equal right over him: Guardianship Act 1973, s.1(1).
2. Children Act 1975, s.86.
3. Education Act 1980; Education (Scotland) Act 1981.
4. Speller SR *Law of Doctor and Patient* (1973) p.29, HK Lewis, London.
5. [1985] 2 WLR 413.
6. [1985] 3 WLR 380 per Lord Fraser.
7. Leading Article 'The right to live and the right to die' (1981) 283 Br Med J 569.
8. [1981] 1 WLR 1421.
9. Kennedy I 'Reflections on the Arthur trial' (1982) 59 New Society, no.999, p.13.
10. (1981) *The Times*, 6 November.
11. For discussion, *see* Mason JK and Meyers DW 'Parental choice and selective non-treatment of deformed newborns: a view from mid-Atlantic' (1986) 12 J Med Ethics 67.
12. *Matter of Cicero* 101 Misc 2d 699, 421 NYS 2d 965 (1979).
13. *Weber v Stony Brook Hospital* No.83-672 slip op (NY, 1983).
14. *Re Superintendent of Family and Child Service and Dawson et al* (1983) 145 DLR (3d) 610.

Parole

Parole is a scheme whereby a prisoner may be released into the community before the end of his sentence. The release takes place on licence which lasts for the duration of the original sentence or for the rest of life in the case of a person sentenced to life imprisonment. The parolee may be recalled and the licence revoked if he fails to observe its conditions. These may include such obligations as complying with the terms of supervision set out and remaining within the country. The conditions of eligibility for parole are satisfied after one-third of a determinate sentence has been served or after one year, whichever is longer; thus, a prisoner must have been sentenced for a term of over 18 months in order to qualify for parole. Decisions as to the granting of parole are made by the Parole Board which is composed of lay and professional members, including psychiatrists. The Board estimates the risk of granting a licence, taking into account the nature of the offence, the response to prison training and the likelihood of further offences being committed.

Further reading
West DJ *The Future of Parole* (1972) Duckworth, London.

Partnerships in Medicine

Medical partnerships, like others, are subject to an extensive range of rules regulating the rights and duties of the partners[1]. Unlike many other partnerships in the UK, however, they are also subject to specific statutory rules related to the NHS. These rules do not affect private medical partnerships, which will operate in much the same way as, say, those involving lawyers or architects.

The National Health Service Act 1977 (s.54 and Sch.10) makes it an offence for any medical practitioner offering to provide services under the Act to sell the goodwill in his partnership. Any person purchasing such goodwill also commits an offence. The effect is to exclude any 'buying-in' to a NHS medical partnership for any consideration other than the future provision of services. Any disguised sale of goodwill will be covered by the prohibition; providing services for a payment which is substantially less than that which might reasonably have been expected is considered to be a sale of goodwill, as would be requiring an excessive payment for surgery premises. The prohibition against the sale of goodwill can cause problems if the partnership is dissolved; an agreement to divide the patients between partners will be void, and the only acceptable way of proceeding will be through the family practitioner committee[2].

Restrictive covenants in a partnership agreement which purported to prevent a doctor from carrying out his obligations to his patients were at one time considered to be void[3]. However, the relevant case has been overruled and it has been held recently that there can be no objection on the ground of public policy or interest to a doctor resigning from a partnership thereafter being under a reasonable restriction as between himself and his former partners; the *ratio* for this decision depends very much on the principle that goodwill, although not saleable, is one of the most valuable assets on which the livelihood of partners depends[4]. The normal rules governing restrictive covenants will be applied to private medical partnerships. These rules stipulate that restrictions will be enforced by the courts only if they go no further than is reasonably required in order to protect the goodwill of the practice.

Misconduct on the part of a partner may lead to the dissolution of the partnership; the misconduct would, of course, have to be of a nature which compromised the partners in their practice of medicine. Members of a partnership are liable for the torts of their partners provided that these are committed during the course of partnership business. This liability is both joint and several — i.e. the partnership can be sued for the torts of one partner whilst proceedings can also be taken against a partner in respect of a tort committed by another. The importance of insisting that each member of a partnership carries appropriate insurance cover scarcely needs to be stressed. The vicarious liability of a partnership for the torts of employees is a further potential source of concern.

See also: Family practitioner committees; National Health Service; Vicarious liability

1. Partnership Act 1890.
2. Scamell EH and Banks RCI *Lindley on the Law of Partnership* (15th ed, 1984) p.677, Sweet & Maxwell, London.
3. *Hensman v Traill* (1980) Times, 22 October.
4. *Kerr and others v Morris* (1986) Times, 22 May. *See also* the similar decision in the earlier Scottish case *Anthony v Rennie* 1981 SLT (Notes) 11.

Passengers in Vehicles

Injuries to passengers in motor vehicles are likely to be severe in the absence of adequate restraint. Those in the front seat are unprotected by a steering wheel and, having been precipitated forwards following a crash, will meet their first obstacle at greater velocity than will the driver. The head will impact with windscreen with great force and the facia will damage the heart and aorta as much as, if not more so, than will the steering wheel in the case of the driver. One injury which is almost specific to passengers is fracture of the base of the skull resulting from a blow to the chin as the head strikes the facia; this injury was particularly common in the unfortunate period when lap belts were fitted to front seats of cars. 'Dynamic overload' will also apply to passengers in rear seats and this will be particularly so if they are standing at the time and the body's centre of gravity is high — this situation is particularly likely to apply in the case of children; the Transport Act 1981, s.28, introduces the offence of allowing a child to stand unrestrained in the front seat of a car but the danger still exists for those standing in the rear compartment. It is possible to develop an argument — which we believe to be spurious — that the provision of seat belt restraint for drivers increases accidents and, hence, pedestrian deaths; no such reasoning can apply to passengers whose protection by adequate restraint is an essential feature of road traffic safety[1].

Drivers of cars must have insurance in respect of their passengers. Nevertheless, passengers injured in vehicular accidents can scarcely be responsible and are likely to sue their driver in negligence. The concept of contributory negligence has assumed considerable importance in this context in recent years.

Any damages accruing from negligent driving fall to be reduced by up to 25 per cent if the plaintiff was not wearing a seat belt[2]. For this restriction to apply, however, it must be shown that the injuries sustained would have been lessened or prevented in the individual case[3]. It is not open to the court to consider what other injuries might have resulted from the use of restraint[4]. Similar considerations may apply in fatal cases and the pathologist conducting the postmortem has, therefore, responsibilities additional to determining the cause of death.

The same principles now apply to the passenger who rides knowing that his driver is drunk[3]. It is also perhaps worth noting that the blood alcohol of a passenger may have other consequences in so far as exclusion clauses as to intoxication which form part of personal accident insurance policies are applied on a temporal rather than a causative basis[5].

See also: Contributory negligence; Deceleration injuries; Road traffic accidents; Seat belts

1. See The medical effects of seat belt legislation in the United Kingdom: DHSS Research Report No.13 (1985) HMSO, London.
2. Froom and others v Butcher [1976] QB 286; Salmon v Newland and others (1983) Times, 16 May; Patience v Andrews [1983] RTR 447.
3. Owens v Brimmell [1976] 3 All ER 765. The question of the applicability of the violenti rule here is uncertain: see Road Traffic Act 1972, s.148(3); Ashton v Turner [1981] QB 137.
4. Patience, n.2 above.
5. Louden v British Merchants Insurance Co [1961] 1 All ER 705.

Paternalism

Inevitably, the doctor knows more about medicine and medical treatment than does his patient. Paternalism can be defined as an abuse of that knowledge so as to distort the doctor/patient relationship in such a way that the patient is deprived of his autonomy — or of his ability to make a rational choice.

The balancing of paternalism and autonomy is most clearly seen in the context of disclosure to the patient. Some form of professional privilege — that is, the considered decision of the doctor to withhold such information from his patient as he considers to be in the patient's best interests — must be available as part of clinical judgement. Equally, the patient, should he so demand, has a claim to be treated as a thinking adult. It seems important that some middle ground should be established before the Hippocratic aim of the doctor 'to follow that system of regimen which, according to my ability and judgement, I consider for the benefit of my patient' is usurped by an equally sincere reaction in favour of 'patients' rights'. An analysis of the opinions given in the various stages of *Sidaway*[1] indicates that this is no easy task.

See also: Autonomy; Informed consent

1. *Sidaway v Bethlem Royal Hospital and Maudsley Hospital HA and others* (1982) 19 February, unreported (QBD); [1984] 1 All ER 1018 (CA); [1985] 1 All ER 643 (HL).

Further reading
For a philosophical approach, *see* Buchanan A 'Medical paternalism' (1978) J Philosophy Pub Aff 370, and Basford HA 'The justification of medical paternalism' (1982) 16 Soc Sci Med 731.

Pathogenic Organisms

Pathogenic organisms are those which cause disease — which, for present purposes, can be confined to human disease. The term should be reserved for organisms which are parasitic on the internal tissues. These can be simply divided into the helminths (worms), fungi, bacteria and viruses, all of which are described in rather greater detail under appropriate headings.

Organisms may be invariably pathogenic in that, in the absence of natural or induced immunity, they are always likely to cause disease on gaining access to man; the *Mycobacterium* which causes tuberculosis is an example. Other organisms may be harmless to man in ordinary conditions but may become pathogenic if circumstances change. Thus, the widely distributed bacterium *Escherichia coli* is a normal constituent of the bowel; it will, however, cause serious disease if it is introduced to the urinary tract. Pathogenic infection of this type is known as opportunistic infection. Clearly, the overall condition of the host will be significant. Many organisms can be coped with easily so long as the body's defences are adequate; but, given debility or physical alteration in the body structure, the growth of many organisms may become difficult to control; the common yeast, *Candida albicans*, is a good example of such potential pathogenicity.

The strict control of pathogenic organisms is an essential prerequisite to the control of disease and, in general, this is the function of the various Public Health Acts. Laboratories where organisms are diagnosed and studied are a potential source of particular hazard both to the staff and to the public. Specially 'dangerous pathogens' are therefore listed and their handling is subject to particular restrictions[1]. Work with Category A pathogens requires the endorsement of the dangerous pathogens advisory group of the Department of Health and Social Security; this category includes a number of rare viruses of which the organisms responsible for smallpox, rabies and Lassa fever are perhaps the best known. Category A pathogens are rarely encountered in clinical practice but Category B1 organisms comprise those which offer special hazards to ordinary laboratory workers and include the organisms responsible for tuberculosis, glanders, typhoid and allied fevers, plague, amoebiasis and a number of other diseases. All material suspected of containing B1 pathogens must be clearly labelled 'Danger of Infection' and be processed in special accommodation. Category B2 pathogens and materials are those which require special conditions for containment but do not need special accommodation. They include all specimens known to contain the virus of hepatitis B (hepatitis virus is treated as a Category B1 organism when it is deliberately introduced into the laboratory) and specimens from 'at risk' groups such as sufferers from leukaemia, Down's syndrome or drug addicts; central nervous system tissue from cases of a number of nervous diseases are also subject to restrictions. Category C organisms are those which offer no special hazard to laboratory workers provided high standards of technique are observed.

The accommodation used for Category B1 materials must be locked when not in use and must be clearly labelled 'Danger of Infection' within the international 'biohazard' symbol.

Similar precautions, with suitable adaptation, must be taken in postmortem rooms (see 'Autopsy'). The need for a 'high risk' postmortem involving Category B1 pathogens must be carefully evaluated and postmortem examinations must never be made in cases suspected of involving Category A pathogens other than with special approval. Bodies of those who have died from Category A infection must be cremated and the community medicine specialist is empowered to certify the cause of death and authorise cremation without the usual medical certificates.

See also: Autopsy; Bacteria; Cremation; Fungi; Helminthic disease; Hepatitis; Viruses

1. Health and Safety (Dangerous Pathogens) Regulations 1981 (SI 1981/1011). For general classification and precautions, see Howie J (chairman) Report of the Working Party to Formulate a Code of Practice for the Prevention of Infection in Clinical Laboratories (1978) HMSO, London.

Pathology

Pathology is the study of disease. Since death is the ultimate in disease, pathologists — and particularly forensic pathologists — tend to be associated with the study of disease through the autopsy. The art of the postmortem dissection is sometimes referred to as morbid anatomy but the anatomical pathologist also studies structural disease in the living; since much of the technique of diagnosis depends upon microscopic study, he is also often referred to as a histopathologist.

Pathology as defined above covers much more than anatomical changes. Thus, a pathologist may be, among other specialties, a microbiologist, a biochemist, a haematologist or an immunologist. The field is, in fact, now so vast that the 'general' pathologist is virtually a thing of the past; the examination for Membership of the Royal College of Pathologists can be taken in a subspecialty.

Patterns of Injury

The rapid recognition of repetitive patterns of injury is the hallmark of the experienced forensic pathologist. This facility is one of the main justifications for the insistence on the attendance of the forensic medical expert at the scene of a crime or accident. A great deal of police time and public money can be saved by an early answer to the mode of death — was it homicidal, suicidal, accidental or natural? Recognisable patterns of injury in the individual can also be related to any weapon or instrument used. But perhaps the least appreciated, but very useful diagnostic patterns, evolve from the distribution of injuries in a number of casualties stemming from a major disaster.

It is impossible to describe all patterns of injury — many are dealt with as separate injuries (e.g. 'Fingernail marks'), but a few examples will suffice. As regards the mode of death, one might particularly mention the typical tentative incisions of the suicidal razor death, the savagery of homosexual homicide and the whole range of diagnostic points in the pattern of deaths due to firearm injuries — not the least being the almost invariable site of election in suicidal shooting.

As to the pattern of injury related to the responsible instrument, mention may be made of the characteristic minimal external and the maximal internal injury due to kicking attacks, of the typical depressed circular fracture of the skull produced by a hammer blow, of the parallel abrasions caused by the sides of a baton and of the fingertip bruising due to gripping. Features such as the uniformity of self-inflicted knife point injuries also provide a readily recognisable diagnostic pattern.

The pattern of injuries in a major disaster is well exemplified in the commercial aircraft accident. The pattern is generally uniform, the precise details depending on the form of the accident; for example, fracture of the lower legs due to seat displacement is typical of the landing time accident whilst fracture of the femora, associated with internal injuries due to vertical deceleration, indicate a deep stall type of incident. Patterns often correspond from accident to accident — including the proportions of casualties dying from, on the one hand, burning and, on the other, from injury; the repetition of similarities may enable the pathologist to give a relatively firm opinion as to the type of the disaster[1]. Equally important is the recognition of a discordant pattern — either involving the immediate casualties or as compared with what was thought to be a similar accident which had occurred previously[2]. Similar principles can be applied in, say, the investigation of mining accidents.

See also: Aircraft accidents; Blast injuries; Bomb injuries; Fingernail marks; Kicking injuries; Knife wounds; Suicide

1. Mason JK 'Passenger tie-down failure: injuries and accident reconstruction' (1970) 41 Aerospace Med 781.

2. Mason JK 'The importance of autopsy examination in major disasters' (1984) 13 Ann Acad Med Singapore 12.

Pedestrian Casualties

Pedestrians contribute between one-third and one-half of all road traffic fatalities, the incidence depending very much on the locality — obviously, there will be a higher proportion of pedestrian casualties in urban areas than in the country[1]. Rather more male pedestrians are killed than are females, although the sex difference is far less than, say, in the case of drivers. There is a bias towards the very young and the very old among pedestrian fatalities and, in general, the proportion of pedestrians among road users who are killed is higher than the proportion among those injured — an illustration of their vulnerability. Whilst the general record of the UK in relation to road traffic deaths is reasonably good[2], the ratio of pedestrians to other road users killed is among the highest in the industrialised world, probably reflecting the almost total absence of sanctions against errant pedestrians in Britain.

The disadvantages from which the pedestrian suffers in a vehicular accident are fairly clear. He is unprotected, he is exposed to primary impact injuries occurring below the pelvis and, as likely as not, secondary impact injuries on striking the windscreen structures of the car. He will then sustain tertiary injuries of an unpredictable character as he impacts the roadway or surrounding structures. It is therefore not surprising that the head is the most frequent site of injury when the general index of injury is severe but the legs become the most commonly injured parts when minor injuries are included. Head injuries are the most frequent cause of death but are closely followed by neck and chest injuries in this respect. Laceration of the aorta is a particular feature of the latter and, as might be expected, the liver is especially at risk in the abdomen[3].

Disease is, of course, likely to promote pedestrian accidents but such disease will, in general, merely serve to emphasise the frequent involvement of the aged (see 'Trauma and disease'). It is to be noted that as many, if not more, pedestrians as drivers will be found at autopsy to have been intoxicated at the time of death; equity and the principles of contributory negligence would suggest that pedestrians injured in road traffic accidents should be subjected to breath analysis as are drivers but there is, of course, no law on the subject.

See also: Road traffic accidents; Trauma and disease

1. For a very typical analysis of a major city, *see* Tonge JI et al 'Traffic-crash fatalities (1968–73): injury patterns and other factors' (1977) 17 Med Sci Law 9.
2. Mason JK 'Road traffic accidents' in Anthony PP and MacSween RNM (eds) *Recent Advances in Histopathology — 11* (1981) Chap.15, Churchill Livingstone, Edinburgh.
3. For a full review of pedestrian injuries, *see* Ashton SJ and Mackay GM 'Pedestrian injuries and death' in Mason JK (ed) *The Pathology of Violent Injury* (1978) Chap.3, Edward Arnold, London.

Penetrating Wounds

Penetrating wounds include all those in which the linear depth of injury exceeds that on the surface. The injuries most often semantically associated with penetrating wounds in forensic pathology are stab wounds but a bullet wound, injuries due to explosive fragments and the like clearly come within the definition of penetrating injury. In addition to the effects of the penetration of a knife or particle, a major danger of the penetrating injury is that the inexperienced surgeon will mistake it for a superficial injury and treat it by suture — complications such as haemorrhage and sepsis are then particularly liable to arise in the deeper areas.

See also: Firearm injuries; Stab wounds

Persistent Vegetative State

This condition was first fully explored in 1972[1], and its understanding is central to addressing the questions of the quality of life, of selective non-treatment and, indeed, of death. The essential concept is that the brain is differentially susceptible to hypoxic damage. The cortex, which dictates our intellectual life, is the most sensitive whilst the brain stem, which controls the simple vegetative functions of respiration and reflex existence, is the least. Hypoxic damage which has already affected neurones is irreversible but progressive involvement of brain structures can be stopped by reoxygenation. The end-result of a treated hypoxic insult can therefore be anything from a minor intellectual deficit to a body which exists only in the vegetative sense; it is decerebrate, non-volitional and is in the persistent vegetative state.

The patient in this condition responds to stimuli of varying severity according to the degree of brain damage but can no longer be regarded as a sapient human being. The body breathes and, accordingly, the heart beats; the eyes may react and a reflex swallow may be maintained in occasional cases but, certainly, the bowel can absorb material presented through a nasogastric tube. The liver and kidneys are oxygenated and will therefore function; and this state will continue for periods depending upon the quality of nursing care — the best known example being Karen Quinlan[2] who survived in this condition for nearly nine years, this being by no means an extreme example.

In the wake of the movement to measure existence in terms of personality, there is a tendency to regard such persons as being 'for all practical purposes dead' a concept which is not without informed non-medical support[3]. Nevertheless, it seems essential to retain an absolutist view of death — either the body is alive or it is dead, and the persistent vegetative state is to be clearly distinguished from brain stem death. To destroy such a body either by commission or by omission — which would include non-feeding — is to invoke all the complexities of euthanasia. If death is apparently preferable, the only ethical and legal route lies through the application of the ordinary/extraordinary treatment test which, in practice, resolves itself into the selective non-treatment of intercurrent infection. The appalling quandary is well studied through the intricacies of the Californian case *Barber v Superior Court*[4] in which two doctors were charged with murder having removed an intravenous feeding line from a patient in the persistent vegetative state in accordance with the ethical guidelines issued by their Medical Association.

The application of the ordinary/extraordinary treatment test depends upon an accurate prognosis and this may be particularly difficult to reach in children; in this case, it has been suggested that a minimum of three months' observation should be given before a child is deemed to be permanently unconscious[5]. Even so, there would seem to be a requirement that death is imminent (e.g. likely within a maximum of one year) before such a basic facility as feeding could be withdrawn with majority acceptance[6].

See also: Brain stem death; Euthanasia; Hypoxia; Ordinary/Extraordinary treatment

1. Jennett B and Plum F 'Persistent vegetative state after brain damage: a syndrome in search of a name' [1972] 1 Lancet 734.
2. *Re Quinlan* 355 A 2d 647 (NJ, 1976).
3. *See*, for example, Lord Scarman 'Legal liability and medicine' (1981) 74 J Roy Soc Med 11.
4. 147 CA 3d 1006 (Calif, 1983), discussed in its early stages by Towers B 'Irreversible coma and withdrawal of life support: is it murder if the IV line is disconnected?' (1982) 8 J Med Ethics 203. *See* Meyers DW 'Legal aspects of withdrawing nourishment from an incurably ill patient' (1985) 145 Arch Intern Med 125 for a fuller review of that and related cases.
5. A sympathetic approach is to be found in Campbell AGM 'Children in a persistent vegetative state' (1984) 289 Br Med J 1022.
6. Mason JK and Meyers DW 'Parental choice and selective non-treatment of deformed newborns: a view from mid-Atlantic' (1986) J Med Ethics 67.

Personal Injuries

Causing injury to the person may lead to the award of damages either in tort or in contract, the former being the more common. The aim of such damages is to try to make good to the sufferer the loss which he has been caused[1] or, alternatively expressed, to put the plaintiff back into the position in which he would have been had the injury not occurred. The difficulty with this approach, however, is that of calculating the 'value' of an injury; unlike material loss, many injuries can be quantified only arbitrarily. Pain and suffering, for example, can hardly be assessed in cash terms — and yet the courts are required to do so.

The technique by which non-pecuniary damages are assessed in personal injury cases involves an examination by the courts of the awards made in the past. In this way, a 'tariff' has been developed which provides consistency and a reasonable degree of predictability. The level of awards is known as the quantum of damages.

Any personal injury — other than the slightest, to which the *de minimis* rule might be applied — may be recognised by the court. At one end of the scale there are devastating injuries involving consequences such as permanent unconsciousness, paralysis or severe brain damage; these injuries will attract a very high level of compensation. An example of such an award is to be found in *Rialas v Mitchell*[2], the appeal stage of which was decided in 1984: a boy aged 6½ at the time of the accident was awarded, amongst other heads, £50,000 for pain and suffering and loss of amenity, £42,000 for future loss of earnings and £143,552 for future nursing care and attention. Minor injuries from which the plaintiff makes a complete recovery lie at the other end of the spectrum; the sums awarded here are small and are essentially those for pain and suffering with, possibly, a certain loss of amenity. A plaintiff in this category may expect under £1,000 damages. The value of an undisplaced nasal fracture was assessed by the Criminal Injuries Compensation Board in 1984 at £450[3].

Damages to the senses are compensated in the same way as are other forms of personal injury. The loss of sight is an understandably serious matter and will attract extremely high damages, a major element of which will be for loss of amenities. The loss of taste and smell are treated seriously by the courts, it being accepted that these senses are important to a full appreciation of life.

It is a feature of personal injury that the full extent of the injury may only become apparent at a late stage. For this reason, the medical reports may need to state the expected development in the plaintiff's condition, drawing attention to likely deterioration and to loss of expectation of life. A common example of this is to be encountered in head injury cases, when the likelihood of the development of epilepsy must be a factor in the award of damages[4].

Until recently, the basic rule in this regard has been that damages are assessed as at the time of judgement although changes in the plaintiff's condition between the time of starting litigation and the time at which the court has given judgement have been taken into account. Deterioration is not considered when it is caused by some factor unassociated with the defendant but the causing of further injury to the plaintiff by another party does not relieve the first tortfeasor of liability[5].

A worsening in the plaintiff's condition or the emergence of some new fact about the injury between the date of the judgment in the court of first instance and any decision in a court of appeal may be taken into account; the courts have, however, been reluctant to allow this[6]. The inevitable limitation placed on compensating for any changes in the plaintiff's state once all possible appeal stages have been exhausted has led to a number of calls for the reform of the rules in favour of a system which allows for periodical payments rather than single lump sum awards, an approach endorsed by the Pearson Committee[7]. A compromise has now been reached whereby the court can either proceed on the old basis or can award provisional damages for injury already sustained, leaving open the possibility of a further award in the event of a consequent deterioration in the plaintiff's condition[8]. Which form of compensation is adopted is at the option of the plaintiff; whilst the new system has obvious advantages in that the damages awarded will be more equitable and, perhaps, greater, the plaintiff takes a calculated risk on the defendant remaining solvent — something which is by no means certain in these days of increasingly high awards to multiple parties to a single action[9]. It is to be noted, in passing, that the court cannot take the existence of the NHS into consideration when awarding damages for personal injury[10].

The British Law Societies regard it as unethical for their members to undertake personal injury litigation on a contingency basis — that is, being remunerated through a proportion of the damages obtained. This practice is common in the USA and probably accounts for at least part of the escalation in personal injury cases of all types. Nevertheless, it is arguable that such practice allows deserving plaintiffs access to the courts which they would, otherwise, be denied; there can be no doubt that many persons in the UK who are ineligible for legal aid are inhibited in bringing an apparently justifiable action for fear of the financial consequences of failure.

See also: Damages; De minimis; Epilepsy; Limitation of liability; Quantum of damages

1. *Admiralty Commissioners v S.S. Valera* [1922] 2 AC 242 at 248 per Lord Dundedin.
2. (1984) Times, 17 July.

3. Kemp DA *The Quantum of Damages* (4th ed, 1975) Supp. p.12003, Sweet & Maxwell, London.
4. *Kaiser (an infant) v Carlswood Glassworks Ltd* (1965) 109 SJ 537 (CA).
5. *Baker v Willoughby* [1970] AC 467.
6. *Jenkins v Richard Thomas and Baldwins* [1966] 1 WLR 476 (CA); *Lim Poh Choo v Camden and Islington Area Health Authority* [1979] 3 WLR 44 (HL).
7. Pearson CH (chairman) *Report of the Royal Commission on Civil Liability and Compensation for Personal Injury* (Cmnd 7054-1) (1978) para.57.4, HMSO, London.
8. Supreme Court Act 1981, s.32A inserted by the Administration of Justice Act 1982, s.6. (s.12 achieves the same end for Scotland).
9. Medicolegal 'Can't pay, won't pay' (1985) 291 Br Med J 1195.
10. *Lim Poh Choo* (*see* n.6 above).

Personality Disorders

'Personality disorder' is a difficult term to define. None of us is perfect — we may be excessively selfish, extroverted or dependent on others — but it would be wrong to describe the majority as disordered. This can apply only when the divergence of personality from the norm is sufficient to have serious effects on private or public relationships such as may lead to frank wrongdoing. The origin of such abnormalities is a complex matter possibly including hereditary factors but more likely directed by parental attitudes, experiences at school and more general socio-environmental influences. At least half of all crime is committed by persons under the age of 21 years and much of this can be said to be associated with 'personality disorder'. But its prevention is in the realm of social politics; the underlying conditions are to be clearly distinguished from mental illness (*see* 'Psychoses').

The extreme of personality disorder is expressed in psychopathy. Such egocentrics present as a major problem both to criminologists and to psychiatrists yet they are generally regarded as untreatable because there is no underlying illness; the term 'psychopathy' has been dropped from the International Classification of Diseases and has been replaced by 'personality disorder'.

See also: Psychopathy; Psychoses

Pesticides

A pest is defined as any organism harmful to plants or to wood or other plant products, any undesired plant and any harmful creature. A pesticide means any substance, preparation or organism prepared or used for destroying any pest[1]; the word thus includes herbicides, of which paraquat is a commonly available example.

The control of pesticides is of particular importance because they are, by definition, toxic substances and because of their wide distribution. The latter may put workers at special risk (*see* 'Industrial poisoning'); the pesticide may upset the ecology by destroying desirable animals, insects or plants; and, of particular importance, it may be distributed widely in the air and be integrated in foodstuffs with consequent ill-effects on the population as a whole. It is this last hazard, coupled with an understandable antipathy of many to wholesale tampering with nature, that produces so much emotion on the subject.

Until recently, the control of the wider problems of pesticide toxicity has been the function of the Notification of Pesticides Scheme of 1955 under which expert advisory committees were set up to regulate the introduction of new agricultural chemicals. The scheme involved licensing for trials, limited licensing and full commercial licensing subject to such restrictions as to use as were thought necessary. This somewhat loose arrangement has now been given statutory effect with the establishment of an Advisory Committee on Pesticides[2] which, in general, will advise the Ministers on methods of protecting the health of human beings, creatures and plants, and safeguarding the environment while, at the same time, securing safe, humane and efficient methods of controlling pests; the Committee will also advise on making information about pesticides available to the public. A very specific part of the advice on which the Ministers may act relates to how much residue may be left in any crop or food; the Committee must also work in co-operation with the Health and Safety Commission. In addition to this general control, there are many existing specific regulations made under previous legislation[3]. Inevitably, a number of pesticides, of which the organophosphorus compounds, or 'nerve poisons', are the most notorious, can be absorbed through the skin and there is much regulation of the protective clothing which must be worn when handling these.

Pesticides offend many who are concerned for the environment — as, indeed, they might well be when they are used as weapons of war; they can affect many persons who have no control over their use; as a result, it is often extremely difficult to distinguish the adverse results of pesticides from diseases which affect the population as a whole and this problem is accentuated by the fact that many of the supposed ill-effects of pesticides take a considerable time to develop. Causation is thus difficult to prove but is eagerly sought and scientific fact becomes tangled with 'witch-hunting'. This was well brought out in a major Canadian case[4] in which an injunction was sought to prevent the spraying of 2-4-5T; in rejecting the claim, Nunn J said, *inter alia*: ' [the prohibition of the pesticide in Sweden] seems to have been a political decision. . .The totality of evidence does not come close to establishing any probability of a risk to health. . .Some [of the plaintiffs' expert witnesses] seemed at many times to be protagonists defending a cause and, thereby, losing objectivity'.

Even greater heat has been engendered by the action of some 15,000 veterans of the Vietnam war who claim to have been harmed in various ways by the dioxin-containing defoliant known as 'Agent Orange'. Despite the fact that no study has provided any proof of an increased mortality in those exposed to the agent, and despite an out of court settlement by several manufacturers in favour of a trust fund of $180 million to treat disabled veterans and their families, the suits continue. One reporter records the suggestion that publicity has so prejudiced the case that no jury would ever rule against disabled veterans and comments on the merits of 'publicity campaigns masquerading as legal proceedings'[5]. The cause of scientific proof is scarcely assisted in such circumstances.

Many of the immediately poisonous pesticides used against larger animals are, by their very nature, likely to be toxic to man. Indeed, a large proportion of the famous poisoning cases of the past related to rodenticides. All such substances are now rigidly controlled — strychnine, fluoroacetic acid and thallium are typical examples[6]; at the same time, pests themselves are protected against some of the more inhumane means of extermination such as by the use of yellow phosphorus, red squill and strychnine[7].

See also: Causation; Health and Safety at Work etc. Act 1974; Industrial poisoning; Paraquat poisoning; Poisoning

1. Food and Environment Protection Act 1985, s.16(15).
2. Ibid, s.16(7).
3. For example, Farm and Garden Chemicals Act 1967. *See*, now, Poisonous Substances in Agriculture Regulations 1984 (SI 1984/1114).
4. *Palmer and Others v Nova Scotia Forest Industries* (1984) 2 DLR (4th) 397, per Nunn J at 500, 505.
5. Dunea G 'Sense and senselessness' (1985) 290 Br Med J 776.
6. Poisons Rules 1978 (SI 1978/1), r.13 and Sch.12.
7. Animals (Cruel Poisons) Regulations 1963 (SI 1963/1278).

Petechial Haemorrhage

Petechial haemorrhages are characteristically of pinpoint size and, whilst they may be present anywhere, are most easily seen beneath the serous surfaces (e.g. pericardium, pleura or conjunctivae). They were originally described in infant asphyxial deaths and there is no doubt that hypoxia plays a part in their origin — hence, petechial haemorrhages may be found, particularly on the pleural surfaces, in cases of natural death in which the agonal period is hypoxic as, for example, in myocardial infarction. Petechial haemorrhages may be a very prominent feature in the natural sudden infant death syndrome (cot death)[1].

There is, however, no doubt that petechiae are most characteristic of local hypoxia and of venous congestion. Thus they appear very commonly in the facial tissues during strangulation or hanging and are always most prominent in the lax tissues (e.g. of the eyelids). It is probable, then, that petechiae form as a result of either hypoxia or increased intracapillary pressure and that a combination of these conditions may be a self-perpetuating mechanism. It follows that petechiae are likely to occur in association with cyanotic congestion and may, indeed, not be obvious until the area is drained of blood during postmortem dissection. Technically, it may be difficult to distinguish petechiae from the ends of congested vessels cut at autopsy (e.g. during the examination of the brain tissue); confirmation, if necessary, must be by means of microscopy.

See also: Asphyxia; Hypoxia; Myocardial infarction; Sudden infant death syndrome

1. For the classic iconoclastic view of this sign of asphyxia, *see* Gordon I and Shapiro HA *Forensic Medicine* (2nd ed, 1982) pp.89–90, Churchill Livingstone, Edinburgh.

Pharmaceutical Liability

The compensation of those who suffer injury as a result of the medical use of drugs is a most controversial issue. Several factors serve to single out drug-involved from other forms of product-caused injuries. The first is the scale of the damage; drug injuries tend to be serious and to affect the lives of a large number of people. The thalidomide disaster is an instance of the scale which can be achieved and one which also demonstrates some of the political issues which are at stake[1]. Secondly, there is the problem of causation. By the very nature of a drug injury, it may be difficult to attribute responsibility to the use of a particular product. Many conditions are multifactorial in their aetiology and it is difficult to say with certainty that damage was caused by a particular agent. Birth defects, for example, can be caused by a wide range of genetic, organic or environmental factors as well as by the use of drugs during pregnancy; consequently, the rigorous standards of causation demanded by the law of torts may be difficult to satisfy in such cases. Other problems which dog the potential plaintiff in a drugs injury case include that of identifying the manufacture of the offending drug. This is particularly acute in the case of substances which are made by a number of manufacturers on a world-wide basis[2].

To all intents, it is impossible for a plaintiff to base such a claim on breach of contract. The law of contract can be invoked against the seller if a person buys a drug from a chemist and is injured, but such instances must be extremely rare. There is no contract between the patient and either the chemist or the manufacturer when a prescription is dispensed and, effectively, a patient so injured can obtain redress only through tort law.

The existing law of torts requires the plaintiff in a drug injury case to establish that he has suffered injury from the use of a defective drug and that the defect in the drug resulted from the defendant's negligence. The defendant may be the doctor who prescribed the drug, the chemist, or other, who supplied it, or the manufacturer — this last will be the natural party to proceed against in practice.

Awesome difficulties now face the plaintiff. Even if the criteria of causation are satisfied, the hurdle of negligence remains. As the law stands in the UK at present, a drug manufacturer will not be liable for damages if a plaintiff is unable to establish that there was a failure on his part to discharge the duty of care he owed to the eventual consumer of his produce — e.g. in development, testing, production and marketing of the product. The complexities of drug production are such that it is beyond the means of most litigants to establish the presence of negligence without assistance from the doctrine of *res ipsa loquitur*[3].

One method of providing compensation, short of introducing a system of state-funded compensation along the lines applied in New Zealand, is to continue to use the law of torts but to introduce the principle of strict liability. Such an approach still requires proof of causation and, in most cases, the identification of a particular defendant, but it imposes liability even on the non-negligent drug manufacturer. The need to establish negligence is therefore removed and this eliminates prolonged litigation. For obvious reasons, it is a prospect which appeals neither to the pharmaceutical industry nor to insurers.

Over the last few decades, courts in the USA have increasingly leant towards the strict liability approach in the case of injuries caused by purchased products. The philosophy behind this move has essentially been one of 'profit liability' mixed with elements of the 'created risk' theory: the manufacturer makes a profit from the product and is best placed to bear the risk that he creates by marketing an item which causes damage. The American Restatement of the Law of Torts embodies this approach in providing that the seller of a product in 'a defective condition and unreasonably dangerous to the user or consumer' may be held strictly liable for any resulting damage[4]; this rule has been reflected in several decisions in favour of the injured consumer. However, certain dangers are inherent in the ingestion of drugs and, consequently, pharmaceutical products have not been seen as being unreasonably dangerous; proof of negligence in manufacture has, therefore, still been required.

Even so, a change in American attitudes is to be noted in the cases arising out of the marketing of diethylstilboestrol (DES), a drug which has been shown to be linked, *inter alia*, with the development of vaginal and cervical cancer in the daughters of women for whom it was prescribed. Successful actions against manufacturers of the drug have been maintained by such daughters, some courts taking the view that the drug companies should have known of, and should have warned against, the possible dangers[5]. Other tort-based approaches to the problem are possible. The German courts, whilst adhering to the requirement that fault must be demonstrated by the plaintiff, have so adjusted the burden of proof as to make it progressively more difficult for any manufacturer, including a manufacturer of drugs, to avoid liability.

Pressure for the introduction in the UK of strict liability in products liability cases has been intense. The Law Commission recommended a scheme in its report on liability for defective products, as did the Scottish Law Commission in the same report. Similar recommendations emerge from the Pearson Commission in its extensive survey of the whole question of compensation for personal injuries[7], and the weight of opinion in favour of this solution grew following the approach adopted by both the Council of Europe[8] and the EEC Commission[9].

The original EEC Draft Directive on Products Liability was additionally potentially threatening to the financial interests of the pharmaceutical industry in that it dispensed with the state of the art defence. This defence enables the manufacturer of a defective product to escape liability for damage caused by that product if he can prove that he took all possible care given the state of knowledge and manufacturing ability at the time of marketing. To remove such a defence means that the manufacturer of a drug may still be liable despite the fact that there was no possible way in which he could have known at the relevant time that the drug could have deleterious effects. The final EEC Directive represents something of a political compromise[10]. The UK Government was particularly committed to a state of the art defence[11] which is retained (art.7(e)) but member States may derogate from this directive which is, at any rate, to be reviewed in ten years (art.15(3)).

There is still no certainty that a strict liability system would solve satisfactorily the problem of drug injuries; the twin difficulties of initiating litigation and proving causation still remain. Developments of doctrines such as the innovative American notion of market share liability may ease the causation difficulty but do not remove it altogether. In these circumstances, attention focuses on even more radical solutions including the establishment of compensation funds, financed by the State or by pharmaceutical companies, like those which have been introduced in Sweden and Japan[12]. Such schemes are open to criticism in that they single out one group of injured persons for particularly favourable attention but, in a climate where an all-embracing system such as the New Zealand scheme lacks political backing, one which concentrates on drug injuries may be a useful trail blazer.

As something of a postscript, we note that the United States courts have allowed yet a further extension of liability on the part of drug companies; damages have recently been awarded to a physician who prescribed a defective drug to a patient.

It was held that manufacturers have a duty to physicians to inform them accurately of the potential adverse effects of a drug — compensation was awarded to the doctor on the grounds of resulting damage to his reputation[13].

See also: Causation; Compensation; Negligence; No-fault compensation; Strict liability

1. Teff H and Munro CR *Thalidomide: the legal aftermath* (1976) Saxon House, Farnborough, Hants; Sunday Times *Suffer the Children* (1979) Deutsch, London.
2. *See* Teff H 'Products liability in the pharmaceutical industry' (1974) 24 McGill LJ 102.
3. For a general critique of the existing system of tort law, *see* Atiyah PS *Accidents, Compensation and the Law* (3rd ed, 1980), Weidenfeld & Nicolson, London.
4. Section 402A. For discussion of the American position, *see* Smith R 'Product liability all dressed up American style' (1981) 282 Br Med J 1535.
5. For a useful review of DES cases, *see* Norris JA et al 'Product quality and safety' (1981) 7 Am J Law Med 213.
6. Law Commission and Scottish Law Commission *Liability for Defective Products* (Cmnd 6831) (1977) HMSO, London.
7. Pearson CH (chairman) *Report of the Royal Commission on Civil Liability and Compensation for Personal Injury* (Cmnd 7054) (1978) HMSO, London.
8. Council of Europe Convention on Products Liability in regard to personal injury and death (1977).
9. Commission of the European Community, 3rd Draft Directive on Products Liability (OJ No. C 127, 21.5.1979, p.62). For discussion, *see* Teff H 'Proposals for compensating the victims of drug injury' (1984) 24 Med Sci Law 208.
10. OJ No. L 210, 7.8.1985, p.29.
11. Smith R 'Two solutions to an insoluble problem' (1981) 282 Br Med J 1610.
12. For details of the approach adopted in these jurisdictions, *see* Fleming JG 'Drug injury compensation plans' (1982) 30 Am J Comp Law 297.
13. *Oksenholt v Lederle Laboratories* 656 P 2d 293 (Or, 1982).

Pharmacy Medicines

Medicines for human use may be sold only from a registered pharmacy unless they are specified in the General Sale List. Not all other medicines are constrained by the Medicines (Products other than Veterinary Drugs)(Prescription Only) Order 1983[1] and it follows that there is a group of drugs which are available to the public without prescription but only through a pharmacy — there is no list of such 'pharmacy medicines' which are, effectively, defined by exclusion. Containers for Pharmacy medicines must be clearly marked 'P'.

There are some significant types of drug within this group, notably many antihistamines, used for the treatment of hay fever and other allergies, some antinauseants, used, for example, in the prophylaxis of sea-sickness and some drugs for the treatment of angina. The insulins are also included because they must be available for injection by non-professionals. Some Pharmacy medicines are therefore not without danger. In particular, the antihistamines must carry a warning that they may cause drowsiness and should not be combined with alcohol nor used by persons in charge of a vehicle or machinery.

See also: General Sale List medicines; Insulin; Medicines Act 1968; Prescription Only medicines; Road traffic accidents

1. SI 1983/1212.

Phenotype

The clinical geneticist defines a phenotype as the appearances resulting from the interaction between the individual's genotype and his environment[1]. Thus, a person's genotype for fatness might be expressed Ff, indicating the genetic constitution of a fat person; if, however, he is starved, he will not put on weight and will be phenotypically thin.

From the medico-legal aspect, however, it is more usual to regard a phenotype as an incomplete genotype, the deficiency resulting either from an inability to demonstrate both the genetic factors in the allele or because a number of closely associated allelic pairs cannot be placed with certainty. Thus, taking an example from the rhesus blood group system, we can say that a person has the phenotype CcDe but it is only on the basis of probability that we can assume he has the common genotype CDe/cde rather than the exceptionally rare Cde/cDe.

See also: Blood groups; Genes; Genotypes; Rhesus system

1. Emery AEH *Elements of Medical Genetics* (6th ed, 1983) p.8, Churchill Livingstone, Edinburgh.

Phosphatase, Acid

The prostatic secretions and, hence, the semen contain large amounts of the enzyme acid phosphatase. This enzyme is readily detectable by comparatively simple laboratory tests and its occurrence is particularly helpful in indicating that part of a sheet or specimen of clothing which should be examined for definitive spermatozoa. The acid phosphatase test will be positive in the event of azoospermia whether the condition be due to natural causes or results from vasectomy; the test, in general, has very high evidentiary value in the USA where it is considered to be the most conclusive test for the presence of semen[1].

This specificity is not, perhaps, so well accepted in the UK because of the occurrence of acid phosphatase in some plant extracts and in other tissues, of which the most important is the vaginal fluid. There are, however, acceptable methods to distinguish the two — seminal phosphatase gives a far more rapid result than does vaginal and the two forms can be distinguished by electrophoresis. The identification of human semen in a vaginal swab is perfectly feasible and is done repeatedly but the occasional occurrence of a strongly reactive vaginal enzyme cannot be wholly excluded[2].

The strength of the reaction falls off as the semen is lost from the vagina and is, at the same time, diluted by the vaginal secretions; as a result, attempts have been made to estimate in this way the length of time since intercourse. Despite sophistication of the method[3], the inherent variables between persons — and between samplers — make it extremely difficult to generalise in this field; however, in many cases, an informed opinion can be given as to whether the semen is fresh or 'old' (e.g. over 24 hours old). Similarly, a distinction can be made between 'old' in terms of days and fresh seminal stains in fabric, but it would be very doubtfully valid to attempt to put a precise age on a stain purely on the basis of its phosphatase content — storage conditions, including refrigeration, have a profound effect on the persistence of the enzyme.

See also: Rape; Seminal stains; Spermatozoa

1. Schiff AF 'Rape' in Tedeschi CD et al (eds) *Forensic Medicine* (1977) Chap.37 at p.954, WB Saunders, Philadelphia PA.
2. Davies A 'Evaluation of results from tests performed on vaginal, anal and oral swabs received in casework' (1977) 17 J Forens Sci Soc 127.
3. Rutter ER et al 'Estimation of time since intercourse from acid phosphatase/UV_{270} absorbance ratios' (1980) 20 J Forens Sci Soc 271.

Placebo

A placebo may be defined as inert substance having no known pharmacological action. The use of placebos is indicated in certain clinical trials in order to control the subjective effect of 'having treatment'; equally, their use may be the optimal way of distinguishing any specific ill-effects of the substance under trial.

There are some who would condemn their use on the grounds that it offends against the fundamental virtue of honesty[1]. That view might well hold in the event of a placebo being used as a treatment[2]; but, in the context of a trial, it can be said that an experiment which is known to be bad is, in itself, unethical — a minor deception is acceptable if it is needed to validate a useful research project.

A more substantial criticism of the placebo is that it may deprive patients of recognised treatment and a major deception then becomes of very doubtful morality. A placebo could not, for example, be used as a control in the experimental treatment of known organic disease nor could it be employed when pain was a prominent feature of the condition — the reference substance would then have to be the standard analgesic. Given the fact that there is a standard treatment, it would, however, be proper to add a new supplement and a placebo at random, always subject to the overriding need to design such an experiment so that it was completed as soon as possible. The introduction of a placebo into a trial is, of course, dependent upon the consent of the patients enrolled.

The use of placebos in preventive trials raises more difficult issues. Such researches must, by their very nature, take a long time to mature whilst the mere fact that a preventive method is being tried strongly suggests that there is an underlying belief that it will be effective — in which case, it could be argued that the control subjects should not be deprived of prophylaxis for, perhaps, years. In such circumstances, every effort should be made to obtain a statistically valid result by, say, comparing the results of protecting everyone with the situation which obtained before the start of the trial. This approach has obvious drawbacks and a trial in parallel may be the only acceptable design; once again, the onus is then on the researchers to complete the experiment as fast as possible.

The fact that 'placebo ethics' is a viable subject for discussion tends to show how far modern medicine has advanced. Physicians who are old enough to remember prescribing various floral tinctures now realise that they were probably using placebo medicine for much of their early practice.

See also: Biomedical experimentation

1. Simmons B 'Problems in deceptive medical procedures: an ethical and legal analysis of the administration of placebos' (1978) 4 J Med Ethics 172.
2. For an American view, *see* Kapp MB 'Placebo therapy and the law: prescribe with care' (1983) 8 Am J Law Med 371.

Placenta

The placenta can be considered as a highly complicated membrane which divides the fetal blood from the maternal circulation; its primary function is to act as the 'lungs' of the fetus, the gases of respiration being transferred across the placental membrane.

The placenta forms from both sides. On the one hand, the fertilised ovum attaches itself to the uterine wall, normally posteriorly, and some of its dividing cells develop into invading trophoblasts. These develop into what are known as chorionic villi; since the villi are developed from the ovum, their cells will have the characteristics of those of the embryo, a feature which allows for the modern technique of chorionic villus sampling as an early (8–11 weeks) aid to the diagnosis of fetal abnormality (*see* 'Prenatal diagnosis'). At the same time, the maternal capillaries are forming lakes of blood into which the villi grow.

As development continues, the placenta separates and at about the tenth week of gestation is present as a pancake-shaped mass of vessels which ultimately grow to a diameter of some 25 cm. The fetus is joined to the placenta by the umbilical cord, which carries fetal blood in umbilical arteries and veins.

The placenta is the life support system of the fetus, and disease or injury may result in fetal hypoxia and death. An abnormally placed anterior placenta is at risk in circumstances such as vehicular accidents. When making invasive investigations of the fetus, including amniocentesis, care must be taken not to injure the placenta; preliminary location is essential and this is best achieved by the use of ultrasound.

It is to be noted that substances which can pass through a biological membrane will pass the placental barrier. The important substances which pass from maternal to fetal circulation include drugs, viruses and antibodies. The first may be so severe as to lead to genuine fetal dependence; the last is responsible for haemolytic disease of the newborn. Fetal products will also pass to the mother, one of importance being alpha-fetoprotein — a fact which allows for a simple but coarse screening test for neural tube defect in the fetus.

See also: Amniocentesis; Haemolytic disease of the newborn; Neural tube defects; Prenatal diagnosis; Road traffic accidents; Ultrasound; Umbilical cord

Plasma

The plasma is the fluid component of the circulating blood and comprises some 55 per cent of the adult blood volume. Anything which is described as 'dissolved in the blood' (e.g. ethanol) is really dissolved in the plasma; when reading reports, it is therefore important to know whether the result relates to a concentration in blood or in plasma, the latter being likely to be about twice the value of the former.

The functions of the plasma are legion. A main component consists of the plasma proteins which are largely responsible for maintaining the osmotic pressure which, in turn, regulates the balance between intra- and extravascular fluid; thus, for example, starvation, which depletes the proteins, results in 'famine oedema'. The globulin fraction of the plasma proteins contains the essential immunoglobulins which are responsible for antibody response to infection. The plasma carries the electrolytes, blood clotting factors and the hormones secreted by the endocrine glands. It also distributes the waste products, including urea, which are to be excreted by the kidney and the carbon dioxide which is excreted through the lungs.

Plasma can be lost without simultaneous loss of erythrocytes. The prime example of this occurs in burning but it is also a feature of other forms of trauma such as the crush injury syndrome. Replacement of plasma is complicated by the fact that the plasma for transfusion may contain pathogenic organisms of which the most important is the virus of hepatitis; it is thus generally preferable to use synthetic plasma expanders — such as dextran — in which colloids of varying molecular weight are used to restore and maintain normal plasma osmotic pressure.

See also: Burning; Coagulation of the blood; Crush injury; Electrolytes; Endocrine system; Fluid replacement therapy; Hepatitis

Pneumoconioses

The pneumoconioses are otherwise known as dust diseases of the lungs and are defined as fibrosis of the lungs due to silica dust, asbestos dust or other dust and include the condition of the lungs known as 'dust reticulation'. The various occupations associated with pneumoconiosis are known as prescribed occupations[1]. Other than in the condition of asbestosis, which has particular importance and is discussed separately, and in some less important conditions (*see* 'Dust diseases'), the underlying fibrogenic dust is that containing the silica particle and it has been officially stated that simple coal miners' pneumoconiosis, which occurs independently of silica, is not, itself, a cause of disability. Coal miners' pneumoconiosis is undoubtedly associated with chronic bronchitis and emphysema, and disability due to these is added to the assessment of the dust disease for the purposes of benefit provided that the disability would, otherwise, have been assessed as being more than 50 per cent (*see* 'Industrial benefit').

This association with other diseases, which include tuberculosis, renders the assessment of coal miners' pneumoconiosis somewhat complicated. It is divided into simple and complicated types, the former being graded on the size of fibrous nodules seen radiologically (Group p nodules are up to 1.5 mm in diameter, Group m 1.5–3.0 mm and Group n 3.0–10.0 mm). The severity of the disease is also assessed on the extent of pulmonary involvement — Category 3 disease implies involvement of all of both lungs. Complicated pneumoconiosis is also known as progressive massive fibrosis — large nodules aggregate and there is extensive destruction of lung tissue with severe resulting respiratory symptoms; the relationship between simple and complicated pneumoconiosis seems to be more complex than that of a mere progression in severity.

The assessment of disability due to coal miners' pneumoconiosis is made by the Pneumoconiosis Panel which bases its findings on the radiological distribution of disease, the vital capacity of the lungs and the forced expiratory volume of the breath which effectively measures the elasticity, or functional reserve, of the lungs. Respiratory symptoms need not necessarily be due to pneumoconiosis and this somewhat pragmatic approach, which is essential to the cause of objectivity, sometimes leads to apparent anomalies — a man with symptoms may be denied benefit whilst another who is apparently healthy may be a certified sufferer because of his X-ray picture.

Further confusion arises as to death certification. A doctor certifying a death has no obligation to include pneumoconiosis in his certificate as to cause of death if he does not believe it had any association with the proximate cause. Although he must now state that an industrial disease was present even if only as an incidental[2], this may not always be done and some cases may be missed. If, however, pneumoconiosis is mentioned in the certificate, the death must be reported to the coroner, who must notify the Pneumoconiosis Panel of the arrangements for autopsy and the panel may be represented there[3]. The coroner may not, however, employ a member of the Pneumoconiosis Panel to carry out the postmortem dissection[4] — although the thoracic organs may be sent to the Panel afterwards. Thus, the coroner's certificate may include pneumoconiosis as relevant to the cause of death whilst the Panel may deny this — and the opposite may occur. Whilst this may cause great confusion when entitlement to death benefit is under consideration, it is the opinion of the Pneumoconiosis Panel which exerts the main influence on the insurance officer.

Silicosis, which is a disease of mining in general — including driving the tunnels in coal mines — is a more severe disease, as is asbestosis. Both are described under separate headings.

Although industrial benefit is payable in respect of the pneumoconioses, there is nothing to prevent an affected workman suing his employer in negligence; the Secretary of State is empowered to make a lump sum payment in respect of pneumoconiosis, byssinosis or diffuse mesothelioma if no employer remains to be sued[5].

See also: Asbestosis; Death certification; Dust diseases; Emphysema; Industrial benefit; Industrial injury; Lung disease and injury; Prescribed diseases and occupations; X-ray

1. Social Security (Industrial Benefit) (Prescribed Diseases) Regulations 1985 (SI 1985/967), Sch.1, Part II.
2. Industrial Diseases (Notification) Act 1981.
3. There is no such requirement on the procurator fiscal in Scotland.
4. Coroners Rules 1984 (SI 1984/552), r.6(d).
5. Pneumoconiosis etc. (Workers' Compensation) Act 1979.

Pneumonia

Pneumonia is acute inflammation of the lung tissue, leading to an inflammatory exudate in the alveoli. It is essentially of two types.

Primary or lobar pneumonia involves whole lobes of the lung and is generally attributable to a single specific infecting organism (e.g. the pneumococcus). Whilst the attack may be so widespread and virulent as to cause death irrespective of treatment — the historic example of pneumonic plague, or pneumonia due to the plague bacillus, illustrates how catastrophic such infection can be — the great majority of such organisms are sensitive to antibiotics and, as a result, bacterial lobar pneumonia is now comparatively rare. The relatively new 'Legionnaire's disease' may prove to be an exception until it is thoroughly understood. Virus pneumonia, as, for instance, that associated with measles, may be devastating in susceptible populations such as those of central Africa.

Secondary or bronchopneumonia is rather different and results from an extension of inflammation of the bronchi and bronchioles. The infecting organisms are therefore comparatively non-specific, of several types and relatively resistant to antibiotics. Bronchopneumonia arises most commonly when the lungs are inflating poorly — the classic situation being during bed rest after surgical operation or immobilisation during prolonged unconsciousness. The condition is also typical of a general break-down in the defences of the body to the presence of organisms which are usually of little more than potential pathogenicity (*see* 'Pathogenic organisms'). Thus, bronchopneumonia is a classic fatal termination of debilitating disease or of simple senility. The treatment of pneumonia occurring in such circumstances presents one of the commoner ethical problems arising in medical practice and is referred to further under the heading 'Ordinary/Extraordinary treatment'.

See also: Lung disease and injury; Ordinary/Extraordinary treatment; Pathogenic organisms

Poisoning

Poisoning in man is a vast subject which is far removed from its usual connotation with a Victorian melodrama. In fact, homicidal poisoning is now very rare; this is due to two main factors. Firstly, the operation of statutes such as the Poisons Act 1972 or the Medicines Act 1968 severely inhibits the poisoner and, secondly, the availability of the NHS not only simplifies the admission to hospital of cases unresponsive to treatment but, at the same time, also separates the poisoner from his victim; a third, not entirely irrelevant, reason is that there are easier ways today than death for parting from one's spouse. Many homicidal poisonings stem nowadays from the 'mercy killing' situation and some are therefore concerned with members of the health caring professions. As a consequence, the poisonous substance used may be unusual and, if of a physiological nature (e.g. insulin), may be very difficult to detect.

The doctor who is unfortunate enough to be confronted with a case which he believes to be of attempted homicidal poisoning is in a difficult position. The target is his patient and therefore commands all possible care; it is certainly not impossible that a victim or his family could bring a successful action in negligence for failure to warn of a continuing risk. Yet the consequences of a false accusation could be catastrophic. The most sensible, pragmatic approach would seem to be to investigate the case as would be done in an obvious natural disease state but to involve university departments of forensic medicine or public analysts rather than clinical laboratories which are less likely to have the particular expertise — or, indeed, desire — to be involved in criminal litigation. In view of this possibility, particular care must be taken in noting times etc. and accurately labelling and sealing specimen containers. In modern circumstances, admission to hospital can, and should, be arranged as an emergency and there would be no objection to a confidential exchange of views with the admitting consultant. What to do in the event that poisoning is proved, is less easily solved. If the victim has to return to the same environment after discharge, it would seem to be a matter of patient care that action be taken; it would be good sense to restrict reporting to a senior police officer and, at the same time, to involve a medical defence society. The doctor's duty in the event of death is clear — any case in which there is a suspicion of poisoning must be reported to the medico-legal authority; no reason need be given to other interested parties beyond an inability to complete the death certificate with adequate certainty.

Poisoning other than of homicidal type may be environmental, industrial, accidental, suicidal or iatrogenic. The first of these, which is generally man made or, at least, man provoked, undoubtedly results in the greatest morbidity due to poisoning; its control, which will include the control of radiation, is, however, a major public health problem and is referred to only briefly under 'Environmental poisoning'. Industrial poisoning is also considered separately — it includes both poisoning of workers, which is now relatively rare, and poisoning of the general public by industrial waste; despite stringent legislation, this may occur accidentally but deliberate circumvention of the regulations cannot be excluded as a cause.

Accidental poisoning may occur on a disaster scale — as when there is a major industrial polution; it may affect several people as, say, when a container lorry is involved in an accident; or it may be limited to the individual. The majority of individual accidental poisonings are due to errors of identification — whether of naturally occurring substances such as fungi or berries or of drugs or poisons in use in the household. It follows that children are common casualties. Accidental poisoning due to bacteria and their toxins is discussed under 'Food poisoning' and poisoning by drugs under 'Iatrogenic disease'. Accidental poisoning by carbon monoxide consitututes a real and somewhat unique hazard to the adult family and is described separately.

Poisoning is the commonest method of suicide and also the one form of suicide which is more frequent in women than in men (see 'Suicide').

The study of poisons is known as toxicology but, strictly speaking, this refers only to the investigation of poisonous substances and their effects. Poisoning by living organisms such as bacteria and fungi is more a matter for the microbiologists who are often involved in medico-legal work as public analysts (see 'Food and drug leglislation'); there is, however, some confusing nomenclature in the discipline which often results from historical associations — the title of government chemist, for example, scarcely describes the wide range of his responsibilities.

See also: Carbon monoxide poisoning; Environmental poisoning; Food and drug leglislation; Food poisoning; Iatrogenic disease; Industrial poisoning; Radiation hazards; Suicide; Toxicological analyses

Poisons Act 1972

The Poisons Act 1972 now has surprisingly little relationship to the medical profession but, being concerned with the supply of non-medicinal poisons to the public, is still a major safeguard against homicidal as well as accidental and suicidal poisoning.

The Act provides for the maintenance of a Poisons Board which advises on the classification of poisons and on limitations as to their supply; to these ends, the Board draws up a Poisons List and Poisons Rules[1]. It is probable that the functions of the Poisons Board will be taken over by the Health and Safety Executive.

The Poisons List is divided into two parts. Part I poisons may be sold only by a pharmacist from registered premises. Part II poisons may be sold only by pharmacists or, from specific premises, by persons who are approved by the local authority as sellers of Part II poisons. In general, Part II poisons are substances which, although poisonous, are needed for normal household chores.

All listed poisons must be sold in impervious containers which show the name of the poison and the proportion of the poison in any mixture. The container must show the word 'Poison' and must display specified warnings[2]. The name and address of the seller must also be shown.

The Poisons Rules contain a number of schedules, many of which are of very specific application and all of which relate to safety in supply and possession of poisons. Schedule 1 lists a number of poisons for which special conditions apply. Schedule 1 poisons may be supplied only to a person known to the retailer or to a person providing a certificate of need signed by a householder known to the pharmacist or by a police officer in charge of a station. The sale must be detailed in a book kept for the purpose and the purchaser must sign the entry. Since Schedule 1 now contains no medicinal substances, doctors, dentists and veterinarians are as restricted to supply as is the man in the street.

Schedule 4 must be distinguished from Schedule 4 of the obsolete 1972 Rules which applied to the group of barbiturate drugs. The present Sch. 4 restricts the sale of certain Part II poisons either to pharmacists or to listed sellers of Part II poisons but then only to persons engaged in horticulture, agriculture or forestry for the purposes of their trade or business; many potent herbicides or pesticides are thus additionally controlled. It is now important to distinguish such Sch. 4 poisons from those substances listed under Sch. 4 of the Misuse of Drugs Regulations 1973 (SI 1973/797); these are substances which, having no medicinal use, can be possessed only by virtue of a licence from the Home Secretary.

See also: Health and Safety at Work etc. Act 1974; Medicines Act 1968; Misuse of Drugs Act 1971

1. Poisons List Order 1978 (SI 1978/2); Poisons Rules 1978 (SI 1978/1).
2. Poisons Rules 1978 (SI 1978/1), Sch.6.

Polygraph

The polygraph, or lie detector, is an instrument designed to enable to investigator to test a person's truthfulness. The instrument measures physiological changes which are considered to be responses to fear; these include alterations in blood pressure, respiration, pulse rate and galvanic skin response. The peak graphic change in these functions will, it is hoped, indicate the degree of fear triggered by a particular question.

The reliability of the polygraph has been indicated in a number of studies[1]. The average subject is unlikely to be able to mask his anxiety over a revealing or crucial question and an indication of deception is, then, likely to be accurate. It may, however, be difficult to use the instrument satisfactorily with some subjects. Psychotics may be prevented by their inner confusion from understanding the significance of questions; some psychopaths, whose emotional experience and receptiveness may be abnormal, may also be inappropriate test subjects.

The general technique involves asking a number of both relevant and control questions and comparing the responses. A 'peak of tension' test, whereby a question is asked as to a detail of a crime which will not be publicly known, is included at some point.

Whilst polygraphic evidence is used in some United States jurisdictions, it is not at present admissible in UK courts. Its use by employers to screen employees is not illegal but may be objected to on the grounds that it represents an intrusive and alarming form of prying; in certain circumstances, however, the State may claim an overriding security requirement.

1. Reid JE and Inbal FE *Truth and Deception* (1966) Williams & Wilkins, Baltimore MD; Abrams S 'Polygraph validity and reliability: a review' (1973) 18 J Forens Sci 313.

Post Mortem Changes in the Body

See 'Changes after death'

Precognition

Precognition is an aspect of evidence in criminal justice which is peculiar to Scotland. It consists of a relatively informal provision of evidence to the procurator fiscal or to the defence; its main purpose is to provide the fiscal with the grounds on which to decide whether or not to proceed to or advise upon the laying of criminal charges. Precognition is taken on oath before a fiscal only exceptionally and in the face of a recalcitrant witness. Normally, there is no oath, the fiscal takes his own notes of evidence and the witness is not bound in court by his precognition which cannot be quoted against him (cf. the English deposition). Precognition is essentially a private affair.

Each side in criminal proceedings has a right to precognosce the witnesses of the other but they may have to call upon the witness to take the statement which he is under a duty to give them. The defence can cite an unwilling witness to attend court even though he has failed to provide a precognition.

The procedure in England and Wales has gradually been approaching that operating in Scotland. The Criminal Justice Act 1967 did away with the publicity associated with preliminary hearings in the magistrates' courts whilst the Police and

Criminal Evidence Act 1984, s.81, now allows for Crown Court rules to be so framed as to ensure the exchange of expert evidence between the parties before a criminal trial.

See also: Procurator fiscal

Preconception Torts

An action is afforded in English law under the Congenital Disability (Civil Liability) Act 1976 to a child who is born defective as a result of a tortious occurrence which affected either parent 'in his or her ability to have a normal, healthy child' (s.1(2)(a)). Such an action will not apply if, at the time of conception, either or both of the parents knew of the particular risk of their child being born disabled as a result of the occurrence in question. An action will, however, be possible against the father of the child if he knew of the risk but the mother did not know.

There are no reported UK cases in which an action for a preconception tort has been raised but such actions have been successful in a number of United States jurisdictions[1]. Damages have been allowed in respect of injuries suffered by a child whose mother's blood group had been wrongly recorded[2]; had this error not been made, steps could have been taken prior to the child's conception to ensure that rhesus sensitization did not occur.

An obvious difficulty in such cases is that the time between the tortious act and the emergence of the defect can be considerable. An infant plaintiff would not be time-barred were he to be born disabled after a preconception tort which occurred, say, ten years previously, as time will not begin to run until the parties are in existence[3]. Exposure to radiation which leads to chromosomal aberration might, however, have consequences for the injured person's offspring only decades later. A limitation period of 30 years then applies under the Nuclear Installations Act 1965 (s.14(1)).

See also: Wrongful life

1. *Jorgensen v Meade Johnson Laboratories Inc* 483 F 2d 237 (1973); *Bergstresser v Mitchell* 577 F 2d 22 (1978); cf. the refusal of the New York Supreme Court to allow such a claim in *Abala v City of New York* 434 NYS 2d 401 (1981); *see* B.A.R. 'Preconception tort as a basis of recovery' (1982) 60 Wash ULR 275.
2. *Lazevnick v General Hospital of Monroe County Inc*, Civ. Act No 78-1259 (MD, Pa Aug 13, 1980).
3. Percy RA *Charlesworth and Percy on Negligence* (7th ed, 1983) p.205, Sweet & Maxwell, London; *Thomson v Lord Clanmorris* [1900] 1 Ch 718.

Pregnancy

There is a strong presumption in law that a child born to a married woman is the child of the woman's husband: *pater est quem nuptiae demonstrant*. This presumption applies to children born after the death of the husband[1], after a divorce[2], and in cases where the man has married a woman knowing her to be pregnant[3]. The presumption is rebuttable on the balance of probabilities[4] that the husband could not be the father. Medical evidence in rebuttal will generally be on the basis of blood tests but the courts may consider the duration of pregnancy when genetic evidence is either not available or, for some reason, is not adduced.

The normal average duration of pregnancy is 280 days but this may easily vary by 10 days or so on purely physiological grounds. The courts have gone to some length to support the *pater est* presumption. In *Preston-Jones v Preston-Jones*[5] the House of Lords ruled that the fact that a husband had not had access to his wife for 360 days before the birth of a child was not, in itself, sufficient to establish adultery although, taking into account the fact that such a long gestation period was extremely unlikely, the case, as a whole, went against the defendant. Divorce has been refused when petitions have been based on the fact that children were born 346 and 349[6] days after the last intramarital coitus. Grossly extended periods of gestation may be medically explicable as resulting from impregnation which immediately follows a missed abortion but such an explanation would be of no value in rebuttal of adultery.

The minimum gestation time for the production of a living infant is imponderable and depends very largely on the medical facilities available (*see* 'Viability'); even in times of relative obstetric inexperience, it has been held that the fact that a child lived when the history of marital relations indicated that it could only have been of less than 28 weeks' gestation was not proof of illegitimacy[7].

The age range in which pregnancy is possible is difficult to establish with certainty. Some remarkable reports of youthful pregnancy, often as a result of incest, are available but, in the general climate of Western civilisation, it is reasonable to accept that conception before the 12th year is extremely unlikely. A woman is regarded in England and Wales as being incapable of pregnancy after her 56th year[8].

At one time it was a working rule that a sudden unexpected death in a young woman was likely to be associated with pregnancy until it was disproved. The picture has been completely changed by the Abortion Act 1967; however, a ruptured ectopic pregnancy still remains as a potential cause of such deaths.

See also: Abortion Act 1967; Adultery; Divorce; Ectopic pregnancy; Parentage testing; Viability

1. *Re Heath* [1945] Ch 417.
2. *Knowles v Knowles* [1962] P 161.
3. *Gardner v Gardner* (1877) 2 AC 723 HL.
4. Family Law Reform Act 1969, s.26.
5. [1951] AC 391.
6. *Wood v Wood* [1947] P 103; *Hadlum v Hadlum* [1949] P 197.
7. *Clark v Clark* [1939] P 228.
8. Perpetuities and Accumulations Act 1964.

Prematurity

A premature baby is defined as one which weighs less than 2.5 kg (5½ lb) at birth. Over 50 per cent of all stillbirths and neonatal deaths occur in premature babies and, in general, the smaller the baby, the less are the chances of survival. Not more than 5 per cent of infants weighing less than 1.25 kg (2¾ lb) will survive for 28 days but it needs only a slight increase in weight to increase the survivability markedly; thus, nearly 75 per cent of babies born in the bracket 1.5–2.0 kg (3⅓–4½ lb) should survive given modern medical treatment.

Premature babies are susceptible to birth trauma. The sudden infant death syndrome also appears to be associated with a low birth weight; it is, however, to be emphasised that this is only a statistical association — most premature babies who are successfully brought through the neonatal period (the first 28 days of extrauterine life) survive to be healthy children and adults.

See also: Birth injuries; Sudden infant death syndrome

Premenstrual Syndrome

Premenstrual syndrome, sometimes known as premenstrual tension syndrome, is a condition occurring during the eight-day paramenstruum (the last four days of the premenstruation period and the first four days of menstruation). A variety of symptoms are experienced, including physical fatigue, irritability and depression[1]. Estimates of the proportion of the female population thus affected range from 20 to 40 per cent[2].

Medical interest in the syndrome has been most marked since the late 1970s. The particularly important legal aspect has been that a number of studies have pointed to an association between the syndrome and delinquent behaviour[3]. This has been used to support the argument that the syndrome should be taken into consideration in the criminal justice process, as the basis of a complete defence, as grounds for a plea of diminished responsibility or in mitigation of sentence[4].

The difficulty in attempting to base any form of defence on this condition is that of determining where it should be accommodated within existing legal categories. Premenstrual tension would clearly not satisfy the M'Naghten test of insanity, although it might be included within an insanity defence based on volitional rather than cognitive factors. It must also be distinguished from automatism in that the essential feature of that defence — lack of consciousness of action — is unlikely to be present[5]. There has been a generally cool response by the courts to pleas of psychogenic automatism.

The premenstrual syndrome is more likely to succeed as the basis of a plea of diminished responsibility in a charge of manslaughter and there have already been indications that courts will be sympathetic to it in this context[6]. Its future in this role, as, indeed, its future as a mitigating factor generally, will ultimately depend on the legal response to the syndrome's wider acceptance in medical circles as well as on the degree to which individual cases attract the sympathy of courts and juries.

See also: Automatism; Diminished responsibility; M'Naghten Rules

1. Endicott J et al 'Premenstrual changes and affective disorders' (1981) 43 Psychosom Med 519.
2. Reid R and Yen S 'Premenstrual syndrome' (1981) 139 Am J Obstet Gynec 851.
3. D'Orban P and Dalton K 'Violent crime and the menstrual cycle' (1980) 10 Psychiat Med 353; Dalton K 'Cyclical criminal acts in premenstrual syndrome' [1980] 2 Lancet 1070. For

a note of caution, *see* Press M 'Premenstrual stress syndrome as a defense in criminal cases' (1983) Duke LJ 176 at p.192.
4. Taylor L and Dalton K 'Premenstrual syndrome: a new criminal defense' (1983) 19 Cal West LR 269.
5. *R v Smith* [1982] Crim LR 531: the Court of Appeal held that automatism is not applicable where premenstrual syndrome is involved.
6. Dalton, n. 3 above.

Prenatal Diagnosis

The importance of prenatal diagnosis of fetal abnormality has been accentuated by the passing of the Abortion Act 1967 under which the substantial risk that the neonate will suffer from significant physical or mental abnormality is a permissible reason for legal abortion (s.1(1)(b)). Whilst the purpose of the Act is to prevent a life of suffering or undue hardship to the family, it is equally important that normal fetuses should not be aborted unnecessarily.

Methods for the detection of abnormalities while in the womb are discussed under separate headings but can be summarised here as being of invasive or non-invasive type. The latter include X-rays, which are strongly discouraged owing to the possibility of genetic damage to the fetus — something which is particularly possible in the first trimester of pregnancy; the modern imaging method of ultrasound is, so far as can be judged, without danger.

Of the invasive techniques, amniocentesis is now well established and is the major source of fetal cells and excretions for study. The procedure is, however, extravagant in time and often involves comparatively late abortions. The technique of chorionic villus sampling has been developed to overcome this difficulty. In this test, cells are taken from the developing placenta; they — and cells obtained by amniocentesis — can be examined by methods involving recombinant DNA[1] (*see* 'Genetic engineering'). An early diagnosis of the majority of important genetic diseases can thus be made. The technique is said to cause spontaneous abortion in 2–5 per cent of cases and must be regarded as being currently in the research stage.

The fetus can be directly visualised through fetoscopy and fetal blood samples can be taken; the need for the later will, however, be greatly reduced as recombinant DNA techniques are perfected.

See also: Abortion Act 1967; Amniocentesis; Fetoscopy; Genetic engineering; Ultrasound; X-rays

1. Emery AEH *An Introduction to Recombinant DNA* (1984) Wiley, Chichester.

Prescribed Diseases and Occupations

The basis of industrial benefit is the occurrence of an accident — that is, an unlooked-for mishap or an untoward event which is not expected or designed — and this implies the identification of a moment at which an injury occurred. In certain circumstances, however, a disease or other pathological condition arises as a consequence of continued exposure to a work hazard — the development of such a condition is the result of a process rather than of an accident; clearly, industrial benefit should be paid in such cases. At the same time, not every disease contracted by an employee is due to his working conditions and, to qualify for industrial benefit, a disease must be one which can be attributed with reasonable certainty to the occupation and one which does not constitute a risk to the whole population. Such a disease is prescribed by regulation[1], and a worker who is poisoned or who contracts a disease in a designated occupation is treated for purposes of industrial benefit as if he had sustained an accident. At the time of writing, there are 54 prescribed diseases[2].

All poisonings which are notifiable to the Health and Safety Executive are also prescribed diseases, but the reasons for their being so classified are different — notification is a matter of preventive medicine, prescription is entirely related to industrial benefit. The dust diseases, or pneumoconioses, are not, however, detailed in the list of prescribed diseases; instead, occupations which result in pneumoconiosis are listed as prescribed occupations[3]. Special arrangements are made for dealing with diseases associated with prescribed occupations.

See also: Industrial benefit; Industrial injury; Notifiable diseases; Occupational disease; Pneumoconioses

1. Social Security Act 1975, s.76.
2. Social Security (Industrial Benefit) (Prescribed Diseases) Regulations 1985 (SI 1985/967), Sch.1. The difficulties associated with identifying a new 'prescribed disease' are discussed further under 'Occupational disease'.
3. SI 1985/967, Sch.1, Part II.

Prescription Only Medicines

The great majority of effective medicinal drugs now require the prescription of a relevant practitioner — doctor, dentist or veterinarian[1]. Officially, the list of such drugs includes: all drugs specified as such in the Medicines (Products other than Veterinary Drugs)(Prescription Only) Order 1983[2]; all drugs included in Sch.2 of the Misuse of Drugs Act 1971 — with certain exceptions when the drug is in low concentration; all drugs for use by parenteral administration — excluding, in particular, the insulins[3]; and drugs with a limited product licence. Containers for Prescription Only medicines must be clearly marked 'POM'. A record must be kept of all sales or supplies of Prescription Only medicines unless they are prescribed through the NHS — and this includes medicines supplied in an emergency (*see* below); records and prescriptions must be preserved for two years.

Rules are laid down as to how a valid prescription must be completed; the most important of these relate to repeat prescriptions. A prescription directing a repeat but not specifying the number of times it may be repeated may not be dispensed on more than two occasions. Moreover, unless it is a repeat prescription, the medicine may not be dispensed later than six months following the date of the prescription.

If a doctor (or other practitioner) is unable to provide a prescription, the pharmacist may supply a medicine subject to the doctor undertaking to provide the prescription within 72 hours — this exemption does not apply if the drug is listed in the Misuse of Drugs Act 1971, Sch.2. The pharmacist may also supply a drug to a patient without a prescription in an emergency provided he knows that it has been prescribed previously. The total supply must not be greater than that needed for three days (excluding public holidays) and the supply must not include a drug listed in the Misuse of Drugs Act 1971, Sch. 2, other than one used for the treatment of epilepsy[4].

See also: Barbiturates; Epilepsy; Insulin; Misuse of Drugs Act 1971

1. A closely defined number of drugs may be supplied by a midwife in the course of her profession.
2. SI 1983/1212.
3. Certain other drugs for the treatment of acute cardiorespiratory incidents may be given by injection by anyone in an emergency for the saving of life.
4. Medicines (Products other than Veterinary Drugs) (Prescription Only) Order 1983 (SI 1983/1212), Sch.2.

Prisoners

The medico-legal implications associated with prisons and prisoners are very wide. The population from which prisoners are drawn is, itself, selected; the conditions in which prisoners are kept are, in general, appalling; and the conflict between punishment and the preservation of human rights — of which medical rights form a large part — raises serious ethical issues.

Suicides are some three times as common in the prison population as they are in the outside world[1]; there is a high rate among prisoners of mental abnormality which does not fall within the terms of the Mental Health Acts; and the sickness rate is very much higher among prisoners than in the general NHS population even when allowing for the low social class of most prisoners[2]. Such figures cannot, however, be accepted without considerable reserve as there are obvious advantages in the present prison environment of reporting sick and even of being sick.

The medical treatment of prisoners thus becomes a matter of fine judgement; the distinction between malingering and a suicidal potential would tax many doctors working in far better conditions and under far less pressure than is the prison medical service. The treatment given is a particularly sensitive area and is subject to public scrutiny. The probability is that most prison doctors do not overprescribe and several actions for libel against prison medical officers in this respect have been successful[3]. On the other hand, occasional disclosures in responsible newspapers give cause for concern[4]. The prison medical officer's dilemma is compounded by the fact that, unlike patients admitted involuntarily to mental hospitals, the disturbed prisoner can be treated compulsorily only if there is a threat to life or of grievous harm to the individual, staff or other inmates or there is a likelihood of irreversible deterioration of the patient's condition — clearly, there is room for interpretation. Indeed, it is arguable whether a prisoner is ever capable of giving true consent to medical treatment and the only relevant British case was decided on the facts of the individual case rather than on the principle, although this was part of the plaintiff's case[5]; the tenor of the judgment was such as to suggest, however, that the courts would not regard the somewhat complex relationship between the prisoner, the prison medical officer and the prison authorities as invalidating consent of itself.

The problem of consent becomes more acute when related to experimentation, particularly if the prisoners are used as a useful homogeneous population to provide evidence which bears no relation to their own predicament. Although the regulations have been very markedly tightened up, including the withdrawal of government funding, there was a period in the USA when prisoners were extensively used as experimental subjects on behalf of the pharmaceutical and cosmetic industries. It is almost self-evident that a prisoner cannot give a true consent when inducements go so far as to include a note of approbation for having taken part in such experiments in his parole board documents[6]. On the other hand, it might be proposed that the mere fact of partaking in an altruistic research programme could form part of the rehabilitation of the criminal into normal society and, on this basis, limited consensual research could be permitted. We would suggest, however, that research involving pain or debility should never be permitted on prisoners even with apparent consent — the advantages of admission to the prison hospital would represent an unacceptable inducement.

The problem of experimental treatment of prisoners still remains — in fact, since no treatment is known to prevent recidivism, any treatment given with this aim must be experimental. Non-invasive treatment such as that offered for psychopathic personalities at Grendon Underwood must be acceptable so long as there is no inducement of premature release and the option of return to normal prison life is retained. Other, increasingly invasive, techniques must, however, be suspect. Many have had periods of enthusiastic approbation, particularly in relation to the treatment of sex offenders, but few have been shown to have any unequivocal therapeutic value. Castration is such a mutilating operation that it is discussed as a separate issue under that heading. Psychosurgery is also treated as a spearate entry but, since the great majority of sex offenders are not mentally abnormal within the context of the Mental Health Act 1983, it is difficult to see how it could be justified in modern conditions. The use of antiandrogenic implants is, at least, reversible but can scarcely be regarded as ethical if it is combined with inducements of early release[7]. Clearly, some research is essential to improve any 'curative' element of imprisonment but, even so, the boundary between treatment and psychiatric research becomes blurred[8].

The ultimate frontier between prisoners and medicine is reached in the context of cruel and inhuman treatment or torture; clarification of this was the object of the Declaration of Tokyo (see 'Punishment and torture'). Arguments can be adduced to justify the use of torture in certain circumstances, but this must be a political decision. One thing seems certain — the only ethical association with torture open to the doctor is to treat and care for the injuries of the subject.

See also: Biomedical experimentation; Castration; Compulsory medical treatment; Consent to medical treatment; Punishment and torture; Psychosurgery

1. Smith R 'Deaths in prison' (1984) 288 Br Med J 208.
2. Smith R 'The physical health of prisoners' (1984) 288 Br Med J 129. This and n.1 are part of a weekly series by Dr Smith appearing under the general heading 'The state of the prisons'.
3. For example, 'The "liquid cosh" libel' (1983) 286 Br Med J 153.
4. See 'Home Office confirms forcible drugging of prisoners' (1982) The Guardian, 24 August, p.3.
5. Freeman v Home Office (No 2) [1984] 2 WLR 802.
6. Herch F and Flower R 'Medical and psychological experimentation on California prisoners' (1974) 7 U Cal Davis LR 351.

7. Halleck SW 'Ethics of antiandrogen therapy' (1981) 138 Am J Psychiat 642.
8. Sissons PL 'The place of medicine in the American prison: ethical issues in the treatment of offenders' (1976) 2 J Med Ethics 173.

Privilege

The relationship between a legal adviser and his client is governed by the rule of so-called 'legal professional privilege' under which what passes between them must remain confidential unless the client waives the privilege. The rule applies to documents related to legal advice whether these are prepared in the process of an action or whether disclosure is sought before the action is raised[1]. Similarly, the lawyer cannot be questioned in court as to what transpired between him and his client. The doctor in Britain enjoys no such privilege in relation to disclosures made to him by a patient in the course of treatment. He must produce any notes when required to do so by statute[2] although he might be well advised to decline to do so in the absence of an order of the court (*see* 'Disclosure of medical documents'). Moreover, he must answer if questioned in court as to what passed between him and the patient. The *locus classicus* of this proposition is the dictum of Lord Mansfield in the *Duchess of Kingston's Case* where the Lord Chancellor said: 'a surgeon has no privilege, when it is a material question, in a civil or criminal cause, to know whether parties were married, or whether a child was born, to say that his introduction to the parties was in the course of his profession, and in that way he came to the knowledge of it. . .if a surgeon was voluntarily to reveal these secrets, to be sure, he would be guilty of a breach of honour and of great indiscretion; but to give that information in a court of justice, which by the law of the land he is bound to do, will never be imputed as any discretion whatever'[3].

A judge may, however, exercise his discretion in the doctor's favour if the doctor declines to answer. This may be because the question is judged to be irrelevant, or only marginally relevant, and that there is inadequate reason for justifying the breaking of confidence. Relevance is the only consideration in Scots law; in England and Wales it would also have to be a proper and necessary question to be put in the course of justice[4]. A written answer may be provided if allowed but this may complicate further examination. The consent of the patient, of course, relieves the doctor of his ethical obligation in this respect.

There have been some demands for the introduction of evidentiary privilege for doctors in the UK but these have not met with approval[5]. Other jurisdictions, however, have recognised the need. Civil law countries have traditionally recognised the right of the doctor to remain silent and, indeed, a serious view is taken of any professional person who does not respect a client's confidences even in the witness box; in fact, pressures from members of the EEC may induce some change in British practice. New Zealand introduced a statutory medical privilege in the Evidence Further Amendment Act 1885 (s.7)[6] covering both civil and criminal proceedings but this was rapidly changed to exclude the criminal element (Evidence Act 1908, s.8); the Australian State of Victoria had legislated as early as 1857 for privilege in civil proceedings. The majority of jurisdictions in the USA recognise medical privilege in evidentiary matters, psychiatrists and other psychotherapists enjoying particular sympathy in this respect.

See also: Confidentiality; Disclosure of medical records

1. *Lee v South West Thames RHA* (1985) *The Times*, 23 April, p.3.
2. Administration of Justice Act 1970, ss.31, 32.
3. (1776) 20 St Tr 355 at 357.
4. *Att Gen v Mulholland and Att Gen v Foster* [1963] 2 QB 477; *HM Adv v Airs* 1975 SLT 177.
5. Law Reform Committee *Privilege in Civil Proceedings*, 16th Report (Cmnd 3472) (1967) HMSO, London; Davies E (chairman) *Report of the Criminal Law Revision Committee, Evidence (General)* (Cmnd 4991) (1972) para.272, HMSO, London.
6. For discussion of medical privilege in New Zealand, *see* Report of the Torts and General Law Reform Committee *Professional Privilege in the Law of Evidence* (1977) TGLRC, Wellington.

Procurator Fiscal

To describe the procurator fiscal as the Scottish equivalent of the coroner is an oversimplication. To all intents, the coroner has no duties other than to inquire into deaths which either are or are potentially unnatural or of which the cause is uncertain. The primary function of the procurator fiscal, who is a salaried member of the Fiscal Service administered through the Crown Office, is to act as a public prosecutor and, in this role, he not only prepares but also presents cases for the prosecution in the criminal courts. Nevertheless, an integral part of this function is to inquire into uncertain or suspicious deaths and, in this respect, he does assume the function of the English coroner.

The strict rule, similar to that in England and Wales, is that the registrar must report to the procurator fiscal any of 19 types of death which are indicated by the certificate of cause of death[1]; these are essentially the same as for the coroner with the addition of some rather anachronistic references to public health. Again, however, it is customary for the doctor to report cases directly. The fiscal then institutes an inquiry through his deaths officer and this will include investigation into the medical history of the deceased. This will be reported to the fiscal's medical adviser — the police surgeon[2] — who will have examined the body externally. As a result of his information from both police and medical sources, the fiscal may decide that no further action is called for and will invite the police surgeon to sign a certificate of cause of death. It should be noted that the function of the procurator fiscal is essentially legal, being to exclude criminality or negligence associated with the death; the accuracy of the mortality statistics is of minor significance. Alternatively, the fiscal may petition the sheriff for a warrant to obtain a postmortem dissection of the body; this will be performed by two doctors in any case likely to come to court[3]. Whilst it is highly unlikely that the sheriff would ever refuse to authorise such an examination, it is apparent that the system as a whole tends to reduce the number of medico-legal autopsies; rather fewer deaths are reported to the fiscal than to the coroner and only about a quarter of the former are dissected — the precise proportion depends very much on the locality. The pathologist who performs the autopsy will sign the certificate of cause of death. There is no other equivalent to the coroner's certificate of death or certificate after inquest but the registrar cannot issue a certificate of registration until the fiscal certifies that he has completed his necessary inquiries.

In the event of his following up the case, the fiscal obtains further evidence by way of precognition. This is a private discussion between the fiscal and a witness in which evidence, save in very exceptional circumstances, is not given on oath. As a result of his precognitions, the fiscal may decide to take no further action or may refer the matter to Crown counsel. There are, however, certain types of death which the procurator fiscal *must* report to the Crown Office. These include those in which the circumstances were suspicious, those arising from vehicular accidents, possible suicides, industrial deaths, those occurring in police or prison custody, unusual anaesthetic deaths and gas poisoning. Deaths which would be reportable to any other government department, deaths which occurred in conditions likely to be prejudicial to the public, those associated with the activities of a third party and those in which a desire for a public inquiry has been expressed must also be notified.

The investigation is private unless and until the case reaches the civil or criminal courts or is the subject of a public fatal accident inquiry held under the Fatal Accidents and Sudden Deaths Inquiry (Scotland) Act 1976. A major criticism of the unnecessary publicity of many coroners' inquests is, thereby, eliminated; on the other hand, the system dictates the maintenance of a high degree of public confidence in the officials.

See also: Coroner; Death certification; Fatal accident inquiry; Precognition; Registrar of births, deaths and marriages

1. Registration of Births, Deaths and Marriages (Scotland) Act 1965, s.28.
2. The *Report of the Working Party on Forensic Pathology Services in Scotland* (1976) (Crown Office, Edinburgh) recommended that this function be taken over by university departments of forensic medicine and this policy is being gradually implemented.
3. But only one need give evidence (Criminal Justice (Scotland) Act 1980, s.26(7)).

Professions Allied to Medicine

The Professions Supplementary to Medicine Act 1960 constituted a Council of Professions Supplementary to Medicine which was given the functions of co-ordinating and supervising the various Boards established under the Act (s.1). A Board was appointed for each of the following professions: chiropodists, dieticians, medical laboratory technicians, occupational therapists, orthoptists, physiotherapists, radiographers and remedial gymnasts (s.1(2)).

The Council consists of 23 members — four appointed by the Privy Council and one by the Governor of Northern Ireland, four appointed by the Secretary of State (with a limitation of two medical practitioners), eight appointed by the Boards represented, three medical practitioners from England and Wales, two from Scotland and one appointed by the General Medical Council; the number of medical practitioners must equal the number of representative members.

The composition of the Boards varies from 11 to 17; they include 'representative members' — who must be in a majority of one — medical practitioners appointed by various medical establishments and an expert in professional education.

The Boards keep a register of all appropriate professionals, who must be properly trained and qualifed (s.3). The Board itself approves courses, qualifications and institutions providing them; in the event of a wish to withdraw approval, the proposal is passed to the Council and the decision, after due inquiry and consultation, then rests with the Privy Council (s.4). Registration entitles the professional to use the title 'State Registered. . .' and it is an offence for anyone who is not registered to use such a title (s.6).

Each Board has an Investigating and a Disciplinary Committee, and the latter may remove from the register the name of a person who is convicted in any criminal court or who has been found guilty by the Committee of infamous conduct in any professional respect. An appeal is available to Her Majesty in Council and the name may be restored to the register on application to the Committee.

The number of professions supplementary to medicine may be extended or decreased, or be amalgamated, on the recommendation of the Council to the Privy Council but, as the Act stands, there must not be more than 12 Boards.

The profession of optician is covered under the Opticians Act 1958. The General Optical Council may erase the name of an optician from the Opticians Register, suspend his registration or penalise him (up to £1000 at present) if he has been convicted in a criminal court or is found guilty of serious professional misconduct[1].

Pharmaceutical chemists are controlled under the Pharmacy Act 1954 by which the administrative and disciplinary functions in the profession are taken over by the Pharmaceutical Society of Great Britain. A pharmacist must be one who is conducting a lawful retail pharmacy business in a registered pharmacy and it is an offence to use any title which would cause people to suppose a person to be a pharmacist unless he is a pharmacist as defined[2].

See also: Nurses, Midwives and Health Visitors

1. Opticians Act 1958, ss.10–11 inserted by the Health and Social Security Act 1984, s.4 and Sch.2.
2. Medicines Act 1968, s.78.

Prostitution

There is no law to prevent a woman receiving money for providing a sexual service; such legal regulation of prostitution as exists has two major aims — to protect women against exploitation and to preserve public decency.

The latter objective is covered, firstly, in the Street Offences Act 1959 which makes it an offence for a common prostitute to loiter or solicit in a street or public place for the purposes of prostitution. The Act does not extend to Scotland, where the same offence is chargeable under the Civic Government (Scotland) Act 1982. The second defence of the public relates to the keeping of brothels — an offence under the Sexual Offences Act 1956, s.33[1]. A brothel is defined as premises kept for the purposes of people having illicit sexual intercourse; it need not be obviously so to persons outside[2] and payment for services is not necessary — the essential requirement would seem to be that a number of women use the same premises[3]. Sections 34 and 35 of the 1956 Act also prohibit leasing or permitting premises to be used as a brothel.

Much of the legislation in relation to the above and to the protection of women refers to a common prostitute. 'Common' is regarded as an important additon implying a woman who is 'prepared for reward to engage in acts of lewdness with all and sundry or with anyone who might hire her for that purpose'[4]. Ordinary sexual intercourse is not essential to common prostitution[5] but repetition is. It was thought to be necessary to prove the profession when statute speaks of a prostitute[6] but this is not so — at least in Scotland — when the wording of a new Act repeals that of another[7].

The definition is of importance in the context of procurement of women. Thus, to procure a woman to become a common prostitute (1956 Act, s.22) does not include procurement for a single act of indecency[4]; it is significant that those offences in which procurement refers to women under the age of 16 years or to those suffering from mental impairment, and offences relating to detention against the woman's will, relate to single acts of unlawful sexual intercourse rather than to common prostitution. Simple persuasion may constitute procurement[8]. Male prostitution exists but only a woman can be a common prostitute. A man commits a specific offence if he persistently solicits or importunes in a public place for immoral purposes (1956 Act, s.32).

See also: Sexual offences

1. Similar legislation is found in the Sexual Offences (Scotland) Act 1976, s.13.
2. *R v Rice* (1866) LR 1 CCR 21.
3. *Singleton v Ellison* [1895] 1 QB 607.
4. *Smith v Sellers* 1978 SLT Notes 44; *R v Morris-Lowe* [1985] 1 All ER 400 per Lord Lane LCJ at 402.
5. *R v De Munck* [1918] 1 KB 635.
6. Civic Government (Scotland) Act 1982, s.46.
7. *White v Allan* 1985 SLT (Reps) 396.
8. *R v Broadfoot* [1976] 3 All ER 753.

Protective Helmets

The very high incidence of head injury as a cause of accidental death has led to an increase in the use of protective helmets in a wide variety of sports and occupations. The design adopted depends largely on the type of accident to be anticipated. Thus, whilst all effective helmets incorporate the design factors of an inner suspension harness separating the skull from a hard outer shell, coverage of the vault of the skull is generally considered adequate when protection from missiles is the main consideration — as in construction engineering or, come to that, in warfare.

Skull injury in the temporal region is, however, very common when the body itself becomes a missile and the head is subjected to deceleration impact forces. The provision of ear flaps is therefore a prerequisite of helmets used in aircraft, racing cars and on motor cycles[1]. This increases the cost and, to an extent, the discomfort but it is still doubtful if the relatively small helmets used by many pedal cyclists would be of major value in a serious accident.

The use of helmets in industry is governed by safety regulations made under the Health and Safety at Work etc. Act 1974. The fact that injury was sustained while authorised equipment was not being worn would not prevent the payment of industrial benefit[2]; it would, however, be recognisable as contributory negligence in the event of an action in negligence being taken against an employer and, indeed, the employer can prohibit a worker who refuses to use equipment from taking employment in which the use of such equipment is justified[3].

The use of protective helmets in vehicles is compulsory only in relation to motor cycles and motor scooters[4], when both drivers and passengers must wear equipment satisfying the British Standards Institute[5]; only the person not wearing a helmet is guilty of an offence unless that person is a child under the age of 16[6]. Although the compulsory use of protective helmets has provoked less resistance than has the introduction of compulsory wearing of car seat belts — possibly because of a smaller lobby or because the helmet can appear as something of a status symbol — there are still protests[7]; their value has, however, been strongly indicated by the results of differential repeal of similar legislation in various of the United States on libertarian grounds[8]. The British courts have adopted a similar attitude towards contributory negligence in failing to wear a protective helmet when motor cycling as they have to the failure to use seat belts in cars[9]. It is in many ways surprising that legislation in respect of protective helmets has not been extended. There are, for example, no regulations covering the use of helmets in light aircraft or gliders where they would be expected to be of major benefit in the event of an accident.

See also: Contributory negligence; Industrial benefit; Safety equipment; Seat belts

1. The professional cricketer's helmet provides an exception to such a 'missile' rule but, in that case, the temporal region is that part of the skull which is most likely to be struck.
2. Social Services Act 1975, s.52.
3. *Singh v British Rail Engineering Ltd* (1985) Times, 6 August.
4. Motor Cycles (Protective Helmets) Regulations 1980 (SI 1980/1279).
5. Road Traffic Act 1972, s.33.
6. Motor-cycle Crash-helmets (Restriction of Liability) Act 1985.
7. The special position of the Sikhs has been recognised in the Road Traffic Act 1972, s.32A added by Motor Cycle Crash Helmets (Religious Exemption) Act 1976, s.1. This, however, is a particular case (*see* n.4 above).
8. *See* Leading Article 'A grim experiment' (1980) 281 Br Med J 406.
9. *O'Connell v Jackson* [1971] 3 WLR 463.

Protozoa

Protozoa are unicellular organisms distinguished by the presence of a nucleus.

Taken on a world-wide scale, protozoal disease is responsible for a vast morbidity and mortality. Such diseases include malaria, trypanosomiasis (sleeping sickness), leishmaniasis and amoebiasis, to name but a few. It is apparent that the majority of serious protozoal diseases are tropical or subtropical in distribution; when introduced into temperate climates, as is particularly likely in these days of extensive and rapid travel, they are known as exotic diseases. The medico-legal significance of exotic disease is that it is likely to be misdiagnosed by the unwary physician despite the fact that the recognition of most protozoa is relatively easy in the laboratory. It would certainly be regarded as negligent to fail to diagnose, say, malaria in a person returned from an endemic area, and there have been a number of court decisions to that effect[1]. A very large proportion of the UK population are likely to have been abroad during the last year and most hospitals now insist on a specific question as to overseas travel to be recorded in their patients' clinical notes.

See also: Infectious diseases; Negligence

1. For example, *Langley v Campbell* (1975) Times, 6th November (malaria); *Tuffil v East Surrey AHA* (1978) *The Times*, 15 March, p.4 (amoebiasis). *See*, in general, Medicolegal 'Malaria: A medico legal hazard' [1975] 4 Br Med J 474.

Provocation

The criminal law recognises that acts may be committed under the influence of extreme anger and that culpability may be accordingly diminished in some cases. The plea of provocation, which serves to reduce murder to manslaughter, is based on the notion that a defendant may have been sufficiently provoked to have temporarily lost control of himself. The defence applies only in homicide cases although it may be used to plead mitigation of sentence in other contexts. Fairly strict limits have been placed on the doctrine in English law. Firstly, the provocation must have been such as would have affected a reasonable man; peculiar circumstances will not be taken into account in this calculation although the age of the defendant may now be considered a relevant factor[1]. New Zealand law has been more liberal in this respect, allowing the courts to take into account the physical characteristics of the individual defendant.

The time lapse between the provocation and the response of the defendant must not be too great — the killing must take place in the 'heat of the moment' and before the defendant has had time to recover his self-control. The physiological basis of such a rule has been criticised on the grounds that a provoked person is more likely to be angry after the insult has had time to 'sink in'[2].

Cumulative provocation is a new development in the law. This has arisen in a number of cases when the defendant has been subjected to long periods of abusive treatment and has eventually taken his tormentor's life. This doctrine has been applied particularly when women have eventually killed their violent husbands but have not done so in response to an identifiable act of provocation which would satisfy the traditional test.

See also: Diminished responsibility

1. *DPP v Camplin* [1978] AC 705. For discussion of recent developments in Commonwealth law, *see* Sharma KM 'Provocation in New South Wales: from Parker to Johnson' (1980) 54 ALJ 330.
2. Brett P 'The physiology of provocation' [1970] Crim LR 634.

Psychedelic Drugs

The term 'psychedelic drug' is often used to describe drugs which distort the senses. The term is unsatisfactory because the sensual aberrations derived from the use of such drugs are by no means always visual. An alternative term is 'hallucinogens', under which they are further described.

Psychiatric Evidence

The psychiatrist may be called upon to assist a court of law in a number of contexts. In civil matters, psychiatric evidence as to competency may be of importance in relation to contractual or testamentary capacity, and the psychiatrist might also be involved in a range of cases involving matrimonial and personal injury problems. More controversially, he may also be deeply concerned in the process of criminal justice, pronouncing on issues of responsibility or assisting the court in the determination of an appropriate sentence. This is an area of forensic work which troubles the psychiatric profession[1].

A fundamental ethical problem overshadows psychiatric involvement in legal work. The psychiatrist's relationship with his patient in other aspects of his expertise is a therapeutic one and it is implicit in this relationship that nothing will be done to harm the patient's interests. Conditions in the forensic context are, however, different and, certainly, considerations other than the immediate welfare of the patient may apply.

Many objections have also been voiced as to the way in which the courts sometimes cast the psychiatrist as an expert in responsibility who is, in effect, asked to rule on the defendant's accountability[2]. It is felt that this is not the role of an expert witness but involves a decision which the court should make for itself. Whilst the psychiatrist may be prepared to reveal the existence of mental disorder which might affect responsibility, the actual determination of guilt is another matter.

Psychiatric examinations can play an important part in the sentencing process, affording courts the opportunity of a medical rather than a penal disposal. A recent study of postconviction psychiatric reports in Scotland has shown that the courts, by and large, pay considerable heed to the recommendations made[3]. The psychiatric report can, of course, make no comment as to further medical treatment but, by identifying problems such as alcoholism or a history of psychiatric illness, it may reveal mitigating factors which will lead the court to take a more sympathetic view of the offender.

The psychiatrist may also be called upon to assess the competence and credibility of witnesses. The witness' competence to testify may be compromised by mental unsoundness; if the matter is raised, it is for those alleging incompetence to show that the witness is unable, by virtue of mental unsoundness, to recall or to describe accurately the subject matter of his evidence[4]. This determination is made by the judge after a *voir dire* examination in the presence of the jury. The issue of credibility is somewhat different. Here, psychiatric evidence may be addressed as to whether, by reason of his mental condition, a witness *is* telling the truth as opposed to being *capable* of telling the truth.

Psychiatric evidence of the defendant's character is usually inadmissible on the grounds of irrelevance but there will be some cases where, by nature of the offence, it becomes acceptable[5]. Essentially, what a defendant may be attempting in these circumstances is to show that he is unlikely to have committed a crime of such a

Psychoneuroses   447

nature because it is alien to his character. If there is a co-accused, there may be an attempt by one to show that the other, rather than he, himself, has the necessary character disposition. The courts are generally wary, however, of psychiatric evidence brought for this purpose; in *R v Turner*[6] a warning was sounded against attempts to displace the function of judge and jury by relying on expert psychiatric testimony.

See also: Diminished responsibility

1. For general discussion, from an American viewpoint, of the ethical issues posed in forensic psychiatry, *see* Rappeport J 'Ethics and forensic psychiatry' in Bloch S and Chodoff P (eds) *Psychiatric Ethics* (1981) p.255, Oxford University Press, Oxford.
2. Chiswick D 'Use and abuse of psychiatric testimony' (1985) 290 Br Med J 975.
3. Schaffer E 'A study of post-conviction psychiatric reports in Glasgow Sheriff Court' (1983) 23 Med Sci Law 283. *See also* Gibbens TCN et al *Medical Remands in the Criminal Court* (1977) Oxford University Press, Oxford.
4. *R v Hill* (1851) 169 ER 495.
5. *Toohey v Metropolitan Police Commissioner* [1965] AC 595 (HL).
6. [1975] 1 All ER 70 (CA). For discussion, particularly of Canadian cases, *see* Manning M and Mewett AW 'Psychiatric evidence' (1975-6) 18 Crim LQ 325.

Psychiatric Illness

Psychiatric or mental illness is a vast subject but one which is of great importance in legal matters — particularly those pertaining to the criminal law.

The various conditions range from the mild anxiety state, to which we are all prone, to the full-blown picture of insanity in its many forms. Compartmentalising of psychiatric illness is difficult and is subject to some criticism by psychiatrists. We have, however, attempted to explain the various conditions under the following headings:

(a) Anxiety states.
(b) Psychoneuroses.
(c) Psychoses, these being divided into the functional — including the affective disorder of manic-depression and schizophrenia — and organic types.

In addition to frank psychiatric illness, one must consider personality disorders including, particularly, psychopathy whilst some sexual disorders, such as trans-sexualism, qualify for inclusion in psychiatric illness. The mental problems of ageing are discussed under 'Dementia'.

See also: In addition to the above, see Disease of the mind; Insanity and criminal responsibility; Mental impairment; Testamentary capacity

Psychoneuroses

The psychoneuroses, or neuroses, are a group of mental disorders which present most often in the form of anxiety, depression or hysteria. The syndromes may give rise to mild effects or they may cause considerable distress to the patient but they are not associated with severe affective change nor with disturbances of thought. In this way, they can be separated from the psychoses but the distinction is often blurred — indeed, some authorities hold that a neurosis is but a lesser form of psychosis.

Anxiety is perhaps the commonest of the reactions which characterise neurosis and is discussed briefly under 'Anxiety states'. Neurotic depression is sometimes very difficult to distinguish from depressive psychosis but the former is more often episodic, the episodes being precipitated by recognisable stress (reactive depression). Hypochondriasis, or an obsession with ill-health, is common to both but tends to be generalised in neurosis rather than 'organ-fixed' as it may be in psychosis. It is also said that the neurotic becomes more depressed as the day wears on. Either form of depression can lead to withdrawal into isolation but, as can be imagined, suicide by positive effort is likely to be a feature of the more serious form.

Hysteria, sometimes referred to as a dissociative state, is discussed separately, as is the medico-legally important variation of compensation neurosis.

Psychoneuroses are recognisable mental illnesses which can be precipitated by external events. Neurosis is to be distinguished from what might be called 'normal' distress or worry and is clearly a compensatable injury when negligence and causation can be shown (*see* 'Nervous shock').

See also: Anxiety states; Compensation neurosis; Hysteria; Manic–depressive psychosis; Nervous shock; Psychoses

Psychopathy

The term 'psychopath' (alternatively 'sociopath') is sometimes used to describe those who, as a result of abnormal personality, persistently behave in an antisocial or disruptive manner and who appear unable to appreciate the moral implications of their actions[1]. The precise nature of the condition, its scope and aetiology — and, indeed, nomenclature — are the subject of considerable controversy in modern psychiatry. There is broad agreement, however, that psychiatry can offer little useful therapy for the psychopath and, as a result, psychiatric institutions are unwilling to accept such patient for treatment. Nevertheless, mental health legislation both in England and Wales and in Scotland allows for the admission of psychopaths to hospital for treatment provided that the patient in question is considered treatable. It is therefore possible for a court to make an order on these lines. Psychopathy will not provide grounds for an insanity defence, as the condition is unlikely to satisfy the requirements of the M'Naghten Rules or of most other modern tests of insanity in criminal law. The condition may, however, provide the basis for a plea of diminished responsibility and may thus lead to the reduction of a charge of murder to one of manslaughter or culpable homicide. Most psychopaths who commit offences tend, in fact, to be dealt with by the criminal courts in the same way as normal offenders and are disposed of accordingly[2]. The Butler Committee, reporting in 1975, recommended that training units be established for psychopathic offenders committed to prison but there does not appear to have been any resulting official commitment to this proposal[3].

See also: Insanity and criminal responsibilty; M'Naghten Rules

1. Blair D 'The medicolegal implications of the terms "psychopath", "psychopathic person-ality" and "psychopathic disorder"' (1975) 15 Med Sci Law 51, 110; Prins HA 'Who is the psychopath? A rejoinder and a comment' (1977) 17 Med Sci Law 241.
2. Ashworth A and Shapland J 'Psychopaths in the criminal process' [1980] Crim LR 628.
3. Butler Lord (chairman) *Report of the Committee on Mentally Abnormal Offenders* (Cmnd 6244) (1975) HMSO, London.

Psychoses

Psychoses are those forms of mental illness which supervene upon a normally developed mental faculty. The conditions are characterised by deterioration in the personality and by a progressive loss of contact with reality. It is customary to divide the psychoses into organic types in which there is a clearly defined structural or biochemical change in the brain and functional types where, although a specific defect is suspected, it has not yet been shown.

The causes of organic psychoses are many. The lesion may be localised yet still lead to marked personality changes which are sometimes of an aggressive type. Head injury has a major part to play here — at one end of the spectrum, epilepsy and frankly dangerous personality alterations may be precipitated whilst, at the other, the somewhat controversial state of post-traumatic or compensation neurosis may result. Far more commonly, however, the organic lesions are of diffuse, generalised type and are related to degenerative changes, infection, biochemical alterations or toxic insults.

In general, the symptoms of generalised degenerative brain damage include amnesia — particularly for recent events — disturbances of consciousness and of attention, lack of spontaneity and, occasionally, bizarre forms of disinhibition such as may be expressed in indecent exposure. Whilst such psychosis may be a natural result of ageing, it is accelerated by atherosclerosis of the cerebral vessels. Idiopathic presenile dementia may also occur — this is premature atrophy of the brain, one type of which is known as Alzheimer's disease, a condition of additional medico-legal interest as somewhat similar lesions appear in the brains of boxers who sustain chronic trauma to the head.

Infection of the brain tissue itself is known as encephalitis, of which there are many types; the specific psychosis due to neurosyphilis (once known as general paralysis of the insane) is now very rare. Organic changes due to non-infective external agents are known as encephalopathies; lead poisoning is a classic example. A number of psychotic states are associated with vitamin deficiencies.

Functional psychoses can be broadly divided into the affective and the schizophrenic psychoses. The former — manic–depressive psychosis — is exemplified by a disorder of mood, and the latter by a disorder in thought processes. Both manic–depressive psychosis and schizophrenia are of considerable medico-legal importance and are described under their separate headings.

See also: Atheroma; Boxing; Compensation neurosis; Encephalopathy and encephal-itis; Indecent exposure; Lead poisoning; Manic–depressive psychosis; Schizophrenia

Psychosurgery

Psychosurgery is a most controversial form of surgical treatment. It is distinct from reparative forms of brain surgery in that it involves the destruction of normal organic brain tissue with the express purpose of alleviating psychiatric illness. Psychosurgery is aimed at altering the behaviour of the patient and it is for this reason that it causes such disquiet amongst its critics[1]. The prospect of a society in which surgery to the brains of antisocial elements is used to ensure political compliance, although currrently a fanciful one, should not be completely discounted if one is to judge by reports of the abuse of psychiatry in some totalitarian countries.

There is nothing new in the idea that physical interference with the brain can relieve psychiatric symptoms. The early notion of allowing 'humours' to escape from the cranial cavity by boring holes in the skull represents an attachment to crude psychosurgery; the scientific application of surgery to the brain for the relief of mental illness is, however, a product of the twentieth century. A large number of operations for prefrontal lobotomy[2] were performed between the 1930s and 1950s and there is currently growing international interest in the more sophisticated techniques that are becoming available. Psychosurgery is therefore not a thing of the past; the ethical and legal issues it raises remain relevant.

Modern psychosurgical techniques[3] use stereotaxic instruments which give access to virtually any part of the brain. Brain tissue may be destroyed by section or by suction, by the implantation of electrodes or by a variety of other methods, including ultrasound. Earlier psychosurgery concentrated upon the frontal lobes; the modern approach involves the destruction of tissue in a number of other areas of the brain, one operation often being directed towards several targets.

The choice of patients for psychosurgery is contentious. Even psychosurgeons would agree that surgery should be offered only after less radical treatments have been tried and have failed to relieve symptoms. The majority of patients receiving psychosurgery are suffering from severe depression, anxiety and obsessional compulsive disorders. Despite occasional reports of success within the group, schizophrenics are generally held to be unsuitable subjects for psychosurgical treatment.

The ethical issues involved in the use of psychosurgery to control violent behaviour are self-evident and hotly debated. Some would welcome the possibility of surgically 'neutralising' violent and aggressive persons but the consequences of allowing the attempt in the absence of a clearly identified mental illness are disturbing. The success rate following upon psychosurgery in abnormally aggressive patients with symptoms of brain disease is better than in those who have been operated on purely on account of aggressive behaviour[4].

When it is successful, psychosurgery achieves a degree of improvement in the symptoms of many acutely troubled patients and consequently alleviates significant suffering; such success is, however, often attended by adverse reactions which may include considerable lethargy and disinhibition — at least in the short term. Such postoperative complications are far fewer using modern sophisticated techniques which result in a far safer operation than was possible 20–30 years ago[5].

Psychosurgery is performed in the majority of, if not all, western European countries (the Soviet Union purports to outlaw it); it is not, however, common. It is estimated that only 200 such operations were performed in the UK in 1975[6]. This figure is much higher, on a proportional basis, than that for the USA where there are both legislative and case law hurdles for the prospective psychosurgeon to overcome[7].

There are no British common law objections to psychosurgery performed in good faith for the relief of psychiatric symptoms. A proper consent must be obtained and, in the case of a patient who is either detained under the Mental Health Act 1983 or is an informal patient, no form of psychosurgery, including hormonal implantations aimed at reducing the male sex drive, can be undertaken unless: (a) an independent doctor and two non-doctors have certified that the patient is capable of understanding the implications of the treatment and has given his consent, and (b) the independent doctor, having consulted two persons concerned with the patient's treatment (one a nurse and one neither a nurse nor a doctor), certifies that the treatment should be given as being likely to alleviate the patient's condition or to prevent its deterioration[8].

This legislation would appear to exclude the use of psychosurgery for patients who are incapable of understanding the procedure. Whilst this may satisfy the opponents of surgical intervention, the denial of the possibility of such help to those to whom it may offer the sole remaining hope of relief seems questionable.

See also: Mental Health Act 1983

1. For a summary of the arguments, *see* Carnahan WA and Mark VH 'Legal and ethical reflections on neurosurgical intervention' in Valenstein ES (ed) *The Psychosurgery Debate* (1980) p.456, WH Freeman, Oxford; also, Neville RC 'Pots and black kettles: a philosopher's perspective on psychosurgery' (1974) 54 Boston ULR 340.
2. For a historical survey, *see* Dax EC 'The history of pre-frontal leucotomy' in Smith JS and Kiloh LG (eds) *Psychosurgery and Society* (1977) Pergamon, Oxford.
3. Sweet WH 'Treatment of medically intractable mental disease by limited frontal leucotomy — justifiable?' (1973) 289 New Engl J Med 1117.
4. Small IF et al 'Follow-up of stereotaxic amygdalotomy for seizure and behavior disorders' (1977) 12 Biol Psychiat 401.
5. Valenstein ES 'Review of the literature on post-operative evaulation' in Valenstein ES (ed) *The Psychosurgery Debate*, n.1 above.
6. Robin A and Macdonald D *Lessons of Leucotomy* (1975), Kimpton, London.
7. For the arguments in favour of this approach, *see* Gostin LO 'Psychosurgery: a hazardous and unestablished treatment? A case for the importation of American legal safeguards to Great Britain' [1982] J Soc Welf Law 83.
8. Mental Health Act 1983, s.58.

Public Health

The prevention of disease by major public health measures has undoubtedly done more for the general health of industrialised nations than have the curative efforts of the medical profession; it is arguable that the most effective single health measure in recent times has been the organisation of an efficient sewage system. The great majority of public health measures — including sanitation and buildings, sewage and sewage disposal, the supply of pure water, etc. — are beyond the control of the individual and are of little relevance in the context of a short note such as this; the basic statutory control lies in the Public Health Act 1936[1]. We are here concerned only with public health as it affects the individual, the current legislation being consolidated in the Public Health (Control of Disease) Act 1984.

This Act contains many provisions which affect the independence of both the doctor and the patient and which provide good examples of the principle that individual rights must, on occasion, be sacrificed to the good of the community. Foremost among these provisions is that which places a duty on the doctor to notify cases of certain epidemic, endemic or infectious diseases (s.11) (*see* 'Notifiable diseases'). The notification must be to the proper officer of the local authority, who will be the community medicine specialist; the statutory breach of professional confidence is, thus, still constrained by the 'need to know' principle (*see* 'Confidentiality').

The Secretary of State is given wide powers under s.13 to make regulations with a view to the treatment of such persons or to prevent the spread of disease; amongst these, he has the specific power to detain persons arriving or leaving the country by ship or by aircraft. The control of imported disease is, in fact, a major aspect of public health.

Many specific controls are authorised in relation to individuals suffering from infectious disease. A person commits an offence by exposing himself to the public when infected, or by exposing a person under his care who is infected or by distributing infected bedding and the like (s.17) and the occupier must answer all reasonable questions put to him by the proper officer when there has been a case of a notifiable disease or of food poisoning in the house (s.18). The local authority can insist upon disinfection of premises which may have been contaminated (s.31).

The officer may prevent a person who is infected from going to work (s.20) and he may, similarly, stop an infected child going to school (s.21); children may be prohibited from places of entertainment, swimming pools, sports grounds and the like if there is danger of their becoming infected or of spreading disease (s.23).

Persons who are at risk of infection may be moved from an infected house with their consent and an infected person can be removed, if necessary without consent, to a temporary shelter or home (s.32). Furthermore, a justice of the peace can order the removal of an infected person to hospital with the consent of the district health authority (s.37) and, if there is a likelihood that the patient would receive inadequate care if discharged, the justices can order detention in that hospital (s.38).

The carrier state (i.e. the state in which a person is clinically normal yet is capable of passing the carried disease to others) is a link of immense importance in the spread of infectious disease. Under s.35 of the Act, the justices can order such a person, or a person who is an overt sufferer, to undergo a medical examination and, for this purpose, a medical practitioner can enter premises by warrant — being constituted, in effect, as an officer of the local authority.

The Act also controls the disposal of bodies dead from infectious disease. Such bodies must be transferred direct to a mortuary or/and then directly to burial or cremation (s.43). Among other precautions, wakes may not be held over the bodies of persons who have died from notifiable diseases (s.45).

Although there are many severe limitations of liberty inherent in the Act, the need is apparent and there has not been, nor is there ever likely to be, any objection to the reasonable implementation of the provisions.

See also: Communicable diseases; Confidentiality; Notifiable diseases

1. As amended by the Public Health Act 1961; also Public Health (Scotland) Acts 1879–1945.

Public Inquiries

Public inquiries provide a way by which Parliament or Ministers may obtain an independent investigation into matters of public concern. The general *modus operandi* is that the inquirers, having taken such evidence as they think appropriate, make findings and recommendations but the decision as to what should be done as a result still rests with the responsible Minister. A distinction is, thus, to be drawn between a public inquiry and a tribunal — of which latter there are very many; a tribunal can, to a large extent, be regarded as a specialised and, accordingly, more efficient form of judicial court[1]. The number and mode of operation of tribunals is kept under review by the Council of Tribunals which is continued in being by the Tribunals and Inquiries Act 1971.

Public inquiries are, generally speaking, authorised by statute and they may then be obligatory or discretionary. As an example of the former, the Minister who wishes to site a new airport must hold a public inquiry if his decision is protested. Discretionary public inquiries have two main origins. Firstly, Parliament may itself call for a tribunal of inquiry into subjects of urgent public importance[2]; such inquiries are rare and often concern allegations of corruption in high places. An important feature is that the 1921 Act confers the powers of the High Court on the tribunal, which can therefore compel persons to give evidence under oath.

Secondly, there are many statutes which allow a Minister to call for a public inquiry and, from the medico-legal aspect, the most important of these relate to the investigation of accidents or other disasters involving the public at large; the powers given by the Civil Aviation Act 1982, f.75 s.10[3], are a good example. The arrangements as to evidence, compellability and the like are derived from the 1921 Act and the judicial atmosphere is thus maintained.

Many would question whether the inquisitorial atmosphere, with personal legal representatives of any interested parties having authority to cross-examine, is the ideal way to establish the cause of an accident resulting from a highly technical operation such as, say, running an airport. Nevertheless, technical experts normally constitute part of the tribunal of inquiry, natural justice is served by publicity and, notwithstanding what action is subsequently taken by the responsible Minister, the proceedings lay the foundations for any further litigation.

In addition to statutory inquiries, Government and Ministers may set up inquiries of various composition and powers as they see fit in the public interest.

1. For a full discussion, *see* Wade ECS and Bradley AW *Constitutional and Administrative Law* (10th ed, 1985) Chap.37, Longman, Harlow, Essex.
2. Tribunals of Inquiry (Evidence) Act 1921.
3. Civil Aviation (Investigation of Accidents) Regulations 1983 (SI 1983/551), part iii.

Pulmonary Embolism

The precursors of thrombosis — changes in the composition of the blood, alterations in the inner walls of vessels and stasis of the blood — are particularly well met in the veins of the legs and pelvis of persons who are confined to bed. The process of thrombosis may continue until a large clot is formed which is attached only lightly to the vessel wall. When such a thrombus breaks off, it will travel to the right side of the heart and, depending on its size, will block the pulmonary trunk, a major pulmonary artery or a lesser pulmonary vessel. This process is generally known as pulmonary embolism although, strictly, it should be more closely defined as pulmonary thrombotic embolism.

The effect is directly related to the size of the vessel occluded. Blockage of a major vessel may cause sudden death; blockage of lesser arteries will result in anything from pain and impaired respiratory function to being symptomless. As might be expected, the effects are more severe in the elderly and it is not uncommon for such persons to die suddenly a few days after surgical operation. It is possible to reduce the risk of pulmonary embolism but not to exclude it entirely; death from this cause and medical negligence are seldom, if ever, causally associated.

See also: Embolism; Sudden natural death; Thrombosis

Pulmonary Oedema

Pulmonary oedema is the presence of tissue fluid in the alveolar air sacs. The effusion of fluid is a standard response to injury, and any injury to the broncheolar or alveolar epithelium is likely to result in pulmonary oedema. Such injury may be physical — e.g. exposure to fire or to any irritant gas — or toxicological — paraquat poisoning being a specific example; any cerebral depressant drugs such as the barbiturates may have a similar, but non-specific, effect. The condition may develop as part of generalised processes including severe allergy or surgical shock. Hypoxia also leads to capillary permeability; pulmonary oedema is a relatively constant feature of any asphyxial type of death.

— Pulmonary oedema may also result from mechanical difficulties in the cardiovascular system. Thus, the failing left ventricle will cause secondary pressure on the pulmonary veins and capillaries which are, consequently, stretched and porous. Acute left ventricular failure, as in an attack of coronary insufficiency, is generally accompanied by acute pulmonary oedema; such oedema is also a feature of chronic heart failure whether this be due to disease or simply to old age. Hypervolaemia (too much circulating fluid in the cardiovascular space) may occasionally result from the overtransfusion of blood or fluids during treatment (*see* 'Fluid replacement therapy'); the excess fluid is then liable to transude into the lungs. A similar effect will result from kidney failure when an inadequte amount of fluid is excreted in the urine.

The major ill-effect of pulmonary oedema is mechanical. The air sacs are filled with fluid and gaseous interchange is compromised; in lay terms, the patient 'drowns in his own body fluids'. Bacteria will flourish in oedema fluid and this explains, at least in part, the frequency with which bronchopneumonia terminates old age.

See also: Allergy; Asphyxia; Burning; Fluid replacement therapy; Heart disease; Hypoxia; Pneumonia; Surgical shock

Punch Drunkenness

Punch drunkenness was originally described in 1928[1] and is now a well-established syndrome occurring in those who have been exposed to repetitive head injury. It is primarily a feature of boxing and has been the focus of the campaign to outlaw professional boxing as a spectacle. Those who do not support this lobby point out that there are other sporting activities such as parachuting and hang-gliding which are inherently traumatic to the brain; the emotional difference would seem to be that the primary intention to cause brain damage exists only in boxing.

The punch drunk syndrome — or traumatic encephalopathy — is characterised by dysarthria, ataxia and progressive dementia; in addition, there are changes of mood. Well-recognised pathological changes occur in the brain and are, in general, explicable on the grounds of repetitive minor haemorrhages, shearing forces to the brain and consequent death of neurones; there is widespread loss of nervous tissue and, whilst similar changes are found in natural senility, those in boxers are readily distinguishable by reason of their extent and distribution.

Professional boxing has done much to improve its medical image in the last quarter of a century and punch drunkenness has declined correspondingly. The classic syndrome appeared to be mainly a condition of the poor quality boxer who had to fight frequently, and often at a gross disadvantage, in order to earn a living. Many top professionals survive to carry on a simple business with success; even so, the deterioration in personality of even the most successful is sometimes very apparent.

See also: Boxing; Encephalopathy and encephalitis; Intracranial haemorrhage

1. Martland HS 'Punch drunk' (1928) 91 JAMA 1103.

Punishment and Torture

The problems of punishment and torture are addressed at the international level in the Declaration of Tokyo, which was drawn up by the World Medical Association in 1975 and which is especially concerned with the position of the doctor in relation to the prisoner.

The question of torture is unlikely to have much relevance to general medico-legal practice. It is defined as the deliberate, systematic or wanton infliction of physical or mental suffering...to force another person to yield information, to make a confession, or for any other reason; it is further laid down that the doctor will not render assistance of any sort to facilitate torture nor ought he to be present during any such procedure.

The trend of the Declaration suggests that it was motivated to express strong, and manifestly correct, disapproval of the use of pathophysiological and psychological methods of this type for party political ends. It is less certain whether the Declaration can be applied in all other circumstances without restriction. The ban on the presence of a doctor at torture must, for example, be, at times, inconsistent with a later statement that 'the doctor shall be bound to alleviate the distress of his fellow men and no motive — whether personal, collective or political — shall prevail against this higher purpose'. And it is reasonable to ask: 'Is there never a time when torture of the type envisaged is admissible?'. The use of cruel means to discover the name of a collaborator is of a different nature from that designed to establish the whereabouts of a bomb placed in a shopping centre. There is a case to be made for regarding homicide by wanton terrorism as the ultimate in crime, the prevention of which is justified by any means on the basis of necessity; nevertheless, the legality of 'in-depth investigation' for any purpose, is very doubtful[1]. Fortunately, only very few are required to test their conscience in this way.

There is, however, a steady move towards applying the concepts of, and attitudes to, torture to punishment for crimes committed and even to such exercises as body searches. Thus, an 'intimate search' for narcotic drugs is likely to be regarded as 'degrading treatment' under the European Convention on Human Rights, but is the supply of narcotics to young people any less degrading in total human terms? Degrading procedures in relation to punishment seem to be increasingly equated with corporal punishment. A reasonable degree of corporal punishment is clearly legal within the home in the UK[2] — although it is not, for example, in Sweden. There is strong pressure from the European Commission to ban such punishment in schools and only the Isle of Man within the British Isles maintains the right to use a beating as a method of punishing criminality; that corporal punishment, even if only of a symbolic nature, is, however, a feature of Moslem justice. Again, it is a little difficult to see why a sharp and painful lesson should be regarded as degrading when locking four men up for years in a cell designed for one is acceptable practice — there can be little which is more inhuman than is the latter course.

In practice, it is extremely difficult for the prison doctor to be seen to be wholly dissociated from punishment even if it is only of a custodial nature; merely keeping people fit for imprisonment is assisting in punishment in so far as there can now be little credibility left in the concept of imprisonment providing remedial therapy[3]. The position of prison medical officers, who must have considerable allegiance to the State, is, at best, difficult. They must pronounce on fitness for solitary confinement or for dietary restriction, and the fact that a medical opinion is required implies the possibility of a danger to health; their duties are seen at their most complex in relation to practices such as forced feeding. It has even been suggested that a two-tier system of prison medicine might be employed[4]. Meantime, it is remarkable what a good job is done by the prison medical service in such conditions; it is noteworthy that allegations against prison doctors are most likely to result in their receiving substantial damages[5].

See also: Detention by the police; Forced feeding

1. Parker Lord (chairman) *Report of the Committee of Privy Counsellors Appointed to Consider Authorised Procedures for the Interrogation of Persons Suspected of Terrorism* (Cmnd 4901) (1972) HMSO, London. *See also* Jones GE 'On the permissibility of torture' (1980) 6 J Med Ethics 11.
2. *Attorney General's Reference (No.6 of 1980)* [1981] QB 715.
3. Despite the good intentions of the Prison Rules 1964 (SI 1964/388).
4. Bowden P 'Medical practice; defendants and prisoners' (1976) 2 J Med Ethics 163.
5. Medicolegal 'Prison medical officers and the Guardian' [1979] 2 Br Med J 448.

Putrefaction

Putrefaction of the body proceeds along two main channels. Autolysis is the general disintegration of structure which results from dissolution of the ground substance of the tissues in an anoxic state and from residual enzymatic activity in the cells; this occurs particularly in those tissues which have minimal fibrous supporting structure such as the brain and spleen. Bacterial destruction is the direct result of the proliferation of micro-organisms in the body tissues which are used as substrate; the widespread formation of gases during the process accounts in large measure for the odour of putrefaction. Bacterial growth in the cadaver is unbridled by the defence mechanisms of the living body.

Putrefaction will begin where endogenous bacteria are most common — in the large bowel. This will manifest itself in two to three days by discoloration of the abdominal wall. Blood being an ideal medium for growth, bacteria will proliferate in the vessels which become discoloured and prominent in some four days, the phenomenon being known as 'marbling'; this will appear more rapidly if organisms were present in the blood before death (septicaemia). At the same time, the skin begins to lose coherence and the superficial layers rub off easily; blisters will form and the hair and nails will detach about three weeks after death.

Gas formation leads to ballooning of the tissues, especially those of loose texture, at the end of the first week and there is gross disfiguration in about three weeks. The body is likely to be partially liquefied in a month and may burst open. Putrefaction in water is generally rather slower unless the water is severely contaminated by bacteria. An immersed body will tend to float at the end of a week but may never do so in deep, cold water.

The process of putrefaction is assisted by carnivorous animals and crustacea and by the action of maggots. A skilled entomologist may be able to give a good estimate of the length of time since death by an examination of larval phases, pupal cases and the like.

Skeletonisation probably means that the body has been dead for over a year but this period may be greatly shortened in temperate summer conditions. Indeed, it is apparent that so many variables, both intrinsic and extrinsic, affect the process of putrefaction that an estimate of the time of death at this stage can be given only in terms of weeks or even months. Bodies in coffins putrefy slowly and may, rather, turn to adipocere.

The most important artefact at the stage of putrefaction is the formation of serosanguinous fluid which may exude into the body cavities or through the body orifices; care is called for in distinguishing this from *ante mortem* haemorrhage.

See also: Adipocere; Timing of death

Quadriplegia

Quadriplegia (or tetraplegia) is paralysis of all four limbs including the intervening torso and results from damage to the cervical spinal cord. If this occurs below the third vertebra, the diaphragm will continue respiration; a higher lesion is likely to be fatal although the respiration can be maintained electronically or by means of a respirator. The ventilation of such patients provides classic examples not only of decisions related to the quality of life but also to the utilisation of scarce resources[1].

The overwhelmingly commonest cause of quadriplegia is a crush fracture of the cervical spine and this is most likely to be sustained in a vehicular accident; sporting injuries are the second most common cause and most of these are due to diving into shallow water; industrial accidents also contribute significantly. In the event of survival, the cord below the lesion is viable and reflex nervous activity is still possible.

See also: Quality of life; Resource allocation; Spinal cord injuries

1. *See* Gardner BP et al 'Ventilation or dignified death for patients with high tetraplegia' (1985) 291 Br Med J 1620.

Qualified Privilege

The communication to a third person of an untrue and defamatory statement about another may form the basis of an action for slander or for libel. It will be a defence to such an action if the person who made the statement acted in circumstances of privilege, which may be absolute or qualified. Absolute privilege attaches to statements made in Parliament or in judicial proceedings; qualified privilege is relevant to statements made in more everyday circumstances.

A classic definition of the doctrine of qualified privilege in defamation is: 'A privileged occasion is, in reference to qualified privilege, an occasion when the person who makes the communication has an interest or a duty, legal, social or moral, to make it to the person to whom it is made, and the person to whom it is made has a corresponding interest or duty to receive it. This reciprocity is essential'[1].

There are many occasions in the medical context in which statements will be made in circumstances of qualified privilege. Obvious instances include a letter from a general practitioner to a specialist to whom a patient is referred or an assessment of a patient by his social worker or psychologist which is passed on to a third person professionally involved in the subject's welfare. The essence of such examples is their reasonableness. Unnecessary disclosure of information will not be protected; the revelation of a medical history in response to an inquiry from an employer, for example, would not be covered by qualified privilege in the absence of consent by the subject.

In some circumstances, a doctor or other person involved in treatment of a patient may feel that he has a duty to disclose information about the patient; an example might be a belief that the patient is a child molester[2]. In such circumstances, the doctor might claim qualified privilege even if the information turned out to be false. If the plaintiff in an action for defamation is to overcome such a defence, he must establish that there was malice on the part of the defendant. Malice does not exist when there is mere negligence or mistake; there must be an attitude of mind which is malignantly disposed towards the plaintiff.

See also: Confidentiality; Libel and slander

1. *Adam v Ward* [1917] AC 309 per Lord Atkinson at 334.
2. *Jenoure v Delmege* [1891] AC 72, 77.

Quality Control

'Quality control' is a phrase used as shorthand for the maintenance of the quality of results in clinical or laboratory medical practice. The term is used most often in the latter sense because the repetitive performance of laboratory tests — often by means of automated machines — is a process particularly at risk from imperceptibly lowering standards. It is therefore important that periodic checks are made in addition to the normal control runs which will be used in conjunction with any battery of tests. There is an increasing use of quality control specimens which are distributed from a central laboratory to those in the less technically endowed periphery.

Similarly, there is a movement towards systematic periodic quality control of physicians' clinical expertise and this is becoming accepted practice in the USA. Currently, there is no great pressure in that direction in the UK where, to some extent, the same result is achieved by a rather complex system of higher qualifications aided by facilities for continuous training which can be made available within a national health service. It may well be, however, that some system such as the American 'recertification' will come to be expected, particularly in the area of primary care.

See also: Royal Medical Colleges

Quality of Life

The concept of the value of life being measured by its quality as opposed to the absolutist view of the sanctity of human life is currently receiving much support both from the public and from the medical and legal professions.

The movement does not rest entirely on a change of moral attitudes — although it cannot be denied that such a change is in progress — but it is also greatly influenced by increasing medical abilities to maintain life in circumstances which would have been impossible a quarter of a century or less ago. The simplest example is that of the elderly dement who would have died from any current infection before the introduction of antibiotics. The medical profession has, thus, been almost forced away from the ethos of preserving life as an end in itself; instead, it has increasingly interpreted the adjuration that 'the health of my patient will be my first consideration' in terms of the quality of the existence provided.

The morality of such an approach to medical treatment is now unequivocal and is contained in the ordinary/extraordinary treatment doctrine. The principle is applied particularly at each end of life's spectrum in the form of selective non-treatment of the newborn (*see* 'Neonaticide') and 'passive euthanasia'.

British courts appear happy with the concept in general but are unwilling to allow doctors an open-ended remit in the field. Thus, Stevenson LJ was of the opinion that:

'It was better to be born maimed than not to be born at all except, possibly, in the most extreme cases of mental and physical disability'[1].

In the important case of *Re B*[2], the question was posed: 'Was the child's life going to be so demonstrably awful that it should be condemned to die or was the kind of life so imponderable that it would be wrong to condemn her to die?'. Clearly, the law expects a substantial reduction in the quality of life before it will condone abandonment of an infant.

The legal difficulties at the end of life are somewhat less because a relatively subjective view can be formed of the patient's quality of life. The importance of an expression of opinion by the patient in this respect has been a feature of decisions in the USA[3]. The US courts have not, however, had an easy passage in the sea of neonaticide. In *Re McNulty*[4], for example, it was held that: 'If there is any life saving treatment available, it must be undertaken regardless of the quality of life that will result' and, again, 'it is our function to secure the child's opportunity for "life, liberty and the pursuit of happiness"'[5]. More recent decisions have, however, concentrated on the range of potential qualities of life available[6].

See also: Euthanasia; Neonaticide; Ordinary/Extraordinary treatment; Sanctity of human life

1. *McKay and another v The Essex Area Health Authority and another* [1982] 2 WLR 890.
2. [1981] 1 WLR 1421.
3. *See*, for example, *In the matter of Mary Hier* 464 NE 2d 959 (Mass. App, 1984).
4. No.1960 (Probate Ct) (Mass, 1978).
5. *Matter of Cicero* 421 NYS 2d 965 (1979).
6. *In Re Infant Doe* 52 USLW 3369 (US Nov 8, 1983) — an important case which was only partially approved for reporting.

Quantum of Damages

The quantum of damages is the amount of damages which a court will award a plaintiff. Assessing quantum may involve the calculation of actual pecuniary loss (as in damage to property) or it may entail an estimate of what sum may reasonably compensate the plaintiff for non-pecuniary loss — such as pain and suffering. It is the latter issues of quantum which pose problems and for which 'tariff' systems are observed. Quantum is affected by issues of remoteness and by the conduct of the plaintiff himself. Failure to mitigate damage (*see* 'Refusal of medical treatment') may reduce the amount of damages, as will contributory negligence.

See also: Contributory negligence; Damages; Refusal of medical treatment

R

Radiation Hazards

Becquerel, who discovered natural radioactivity in 1896, is said to have sustained a burn from his demonstration specimen, and the whole history of early radiation work is strewn with examples of serious injuries resulting from the use of radioactive materials while unprotected. Nowadays, however, such gross attributable damage is virtually unknown, the nearest approach being the occasional 'sunburn' lesions sustained by patients undergoing radiotherapy of deep-seated tumours. Far greater importance attaches to the more diffuse and insidious effects of generalised ionising irradiation and it is these dangers to which this note is directed.

The absorption of ionising radiation results in changes in the chemical state of the atoms of the absorbing tissue. Such 'charged' atoms are more active than are the normal and it is, presumably, that greater activity which results in abnormal and harmful changes in cellular structure. Certainly, the effects of radiation are most likely to manifest themselves in cells with a high turnover — especially the blood-producing cells and those of active epithelium; this applies to all rapidly proliferating tissues and, therefore, particularly to those of the fetus or child. In addition to this general effect, radiation has a specific effect on the sex cells. The dose of radiation is measured in grays — 1 Gy corresponding to the energy absorbed when 100 roentgens of electromagnetic radiation are received by 1 gram of tissue. The effective absorption of radioactivity in human soft tissue is now measured in sieverts (Sv); in general, a sievert is equal to a gray but for alpha particles and neutron absorption, 1 Gy is equivalent to 10 Sv (see 'Electromagnetic radiation').

The hazards of exposure to radiation can best be appreciated in relation to the dose delivered to the tissues. Very large doses of the order of 5–10 Sv and above are unlikely to be received by other than those in the direct zone of a nuclear explosion; such a dose will kill within weeks due to infection consequent upon death of the bone marrow and massive damage to the epithelium of the gastrointestinal tract.

Far more concern is merited by moderate dosage and it is here that difficulties arise as to both understanding and interpretation. It is to be noted that the effect of the total dose is time dependent — i.e. 1 Sv applied for ten minutes will have the same effect as 10 Sv applied for one minute. Secondly, the effects of repeated exposure are probably cumulative; and, thirdly, it is still uncertain whether or not there is a threshold dose below which radiation is harmless — the probability is that there is no such threshold effect. Whatever the interpretation of such variables may be, it is an observed fact that cancer or malignant disease — particularly, but by no means exclusively, of the blood, lung and thyroid gland — is the most important general disease caused by radiation; such malignant disease is unlikely to show itself until several years after the relevant exposure. The final result of these imponderables is that a causative association between disease and a given exposure is extraordinarily difficult to prove — many persons are exposed to radiation and have no ill-effects whilst many who have never been exposed will die of cancer. Malignant disease of the skin or subcutaneous tissues or of the bones, or blood dyscrasia, is a prescribed disease when associated with exposure to ionising radiation, and, in general, a sympathetic view of cancer is taken by the Insurance Officer and National Insurance Tribunals. Presumably, however, even the State must defend itself against liability at some stage and, at the time of writing, a major inquiry, closely bound with litigation, is proceeding as to the effects of what would now be seen as quite unusual exposure of military personnel to the Antipodean nuclear weapon tests undertaken in the 1950s. Uncertainty as to causation is not confined to Europe — a similar controversy rages in the USA as to the likely long-term effects of a disastrous leak of radioactivity from a nuclear power station[1].

Low dosage radiation is particularly important in its gonadal effect — higher doses will kill such cells whereas, for a genetic effect to appear, the cells must not only survive but must also retain the power to multiply; moreover, any resultant damage to the embryo must be less than that which will cause a spontaneous abortion (see 'Genetic disease' and 'Chromosomal disease'). The gonadal effect of radiation is probably to alter the chromosomal structure and to increase the mutation rate in genes. The former is likely to be lethal; the latter mutants will become fixed in the population and, being probably of multifactorial significance, may be difficult to detect until generations later.

There have only been two exposures to the maximum effects of a nuclear explosion and the results of follow-up of survivors are equivocal. It may well be, however, that, despite the dose/time response rule, the effects of a single massive radiation dose may display themselves differently from those of chronic exposure. Scientists are therefore still working in something of a vacuum and the only reasonable policy is to do everything possible to limit any increase of environmental radioactivity.

Greatest effectiveness in this respect is to be gained from regulating medical radiology (see 'Radiology') but, in addition, there are a very large number of regulations controlling the use of radioactivity which are currently being consolidated under the Health and Safety at Work etc Act 1974[2]. The whole operation is overseen by the National Radiological Protection Board whose inspectors have wide ranging powers of entry, search and prohibition[3]; standards are further set by the International Commission on Radiological Protection. The current rule is to limit the exposure of those who are occupationally exposed to radiation to 50 mSv per year and of the general population to 5 mSv per year; the difference represents an enforced compromise between desirable safety and operational efficiency. All who work with or near radioactive material are strictly monitored by the use of radiation-sensitive film badges and by periodic blood analyses.

This is not the place to discuss in detail the relative morbidity and mortality of the various sources of domestic energy; whilst it is apparently true that far fewer people are killed or injured in producing nuclear power than are in the production of coal-fired electricity, this does not take into account the morbidity among, say, uranium miners — a matter which is extremely difficult to establish. Nor is it appropriate to discuss the extremely important environmental problem of the disposal of nuclear waste; the basic difficulty with this and many associated concerns is to disentangle science, politics and emotion[4].

See also: Chromosomal disease; Electromagnetic radiation; Genetic disease; Mutation; Prescribed diseases and occupations; Radioactivity; Radiology; X-rays

1. Culliton BJ and Waterfall WK 'Low-dose radiation' [1979] 1 Br Med J 1545.
2. Made under the Radioactive Substances Act 1960.
3. Radiological Protection Act 1970.
4. Mole RH 'Radioactive waste and its disposal' (1984) 288 Br Med J 91.

Radioactivity

Radioactivity is the energy which results from the fragmentation of large atoms, with the production of others which are smaller and stable. Fractions, often minute, of all the earth's elements exist in natural radioactive form — the so-called unstable isotopes; these can also be produced artifically in nuclear reactors and are, in fact, widely used in medical diagnosis and therapy.

Radioactivity is of two main types — particulate or in the form of very high frequency sinous waves (*see* 'Electromagnetic radiation'). The former appear as alpha particles which are the same as helium nuclei and which penetrate tissue very poorly, beta particles which are equivalent to electrons and have moderate tissue penetrance, and neutrons which are unsplit and which differ very much in their effect on tissue. Electromagnetic radiations contributing to radioactivity include X-rays and gamma rays; such radiations penetrate tissue deeply, which accounts for the diagnostic value of the former.

Since radioactivity is the result of breakdown of atoms, it must have a recognisable limit. This is measured as the half-life of an isotope — that is, the time taken for half the available atoms of an isotope to disintegrate. The longer the half-life, the more persistent will be the radioactivity. Half-lives vary enormously and this can often be put to good use. Thus, carbon-14, which is a product of cosmic radiation, has a half-life of 5,640 years; it can thus be used for estimating the age of archaeological human remains. On the other hand, it is essential that isotopes deliberately introduced into the body have a very short half-life — iodine-131, which is used in the investigation of thyroid dysfunction, satisfies this criterion. Although a degree of radioactivity is a feature of all elements, the activity of some — such as uranium and radium — is such that they are known as radioactive elements; they retain this property because their half-lives are about the same as the age of the earth.

It follows that there is a persistent background of radiation, and the density of this depends mainly upon the nature of the terrain — granite rock is far more radioactive than is, say, limestone. Some electromagnetic radiation comes from space in the form of cosmic rays — the extent of this dose depends upon altitude and geographical latitude. But, in addition, the tissues of the body are themselves radioactive, largely due to the presence of potassium-40 which comprises about 1/10,000th of the total body potassium. In additon, industrialised man produces excess radiation, the most notorious of which derives from the testing of nuclear weapons but by far the most significant of which is the product of medical diagnosis (*see* 'X-rays'); industry also makes a measurable contribution and there is an occasional addition as a result of a mishap in the provision of nuclear power.

Radioactivity was originally measured in curies. The curie was, however, so large a unit as to be unusable and has been replaced by the becquerel (1 Bq = 1 disintegration per second = approximately 0.25×10^{-9} curie). The unit of electromagnetic radiation is the roentgen but the amount absorbed (measured in grays (Gy)) or the biological effect on man (measured in sieverts (Sv)) are of far greater importance in medicine.

See also: Electromagnetic radiation; Radiation hazards; X-rays

Radiology

Radiology is the specialty which studies images of the body. Such images may not only define and diagnose disease but, so long as a permanent record is kept, successive images can also be used to plot the course of disease over the years.

The medical use of radiology began with X-irradiation and this still constitutes its main arm. The simple plain X-ray has now been developed to a sophisticated state and is increasingly combined with techniques of varying invasiveness by which it is possible to measure the function and anatomy of the organs. Thus, the simple barium meal which is used to study the intestinal canal can scarcely be considered invasive but, at the other extreme, we have the complexities of the angiogram. Other contrast X-rays depend upon the activity of the organ under review — thus, different substances may be used which are concentrated in the kidney, by the gall bladder, etc. None of these methods is entirely without risk — in particular, allegy to the contrast medium may occasionally occur[1]. Moreover, X-rays as such present their hazards to the patient and to the population as a whole; as a result, radiologists have increasingly turned to the use of non-ionising forms of electromagnetic radiation to produce useful images. All such methods have their individual advantages and disadvantages but those which appear to have the greatest potential at present are the use of ultrasound and of nuclear magnetic resonance imaging.

Additionally, the radiologist is involved in the practice of nuclear medicine and may be the preferred practitioner to be licensed to inject radioactive substances.

Diagnostic radiology is generally distinguished from therapeutic radiology, the latter being very largely a matter of the treatment of malignant disease. There is, in fact, a movement towards treating such patients in departments of clinical oncology in which the expertise of the physician, the surgeon, the radiologist and the pathologist are combined.

Radiology has a most important role to play in forensic pathology. The permanence, and acceptability, of radiographs make them particularly useful in demonstrating an internal injury (e.g. a fractured laryngeal bone) to a judge or a jury. Similarly, comparative radiographs may provide evidence of identification which will satisfy the most sceptical; the use of radiology in assessing the age of a skeleton or decomposed body is also very considerable. Radiology is a near essential to the investigation of deaths due to firearm injuries or to bomb explosions; aside from providing a record, they assist the pathologist in locating fragments which may be of fundamental importance to the investigation of crime[2].

Radiology also has its place in the investigation of violence in the living. It is an essential adjunct to the investigation of non-accidental injury in children and, of course, it has a major role in the clinical management of accidental injuries. Failure to diagnose a fracture by virtue of failure to X-ray an injured part is a common source of actions in negligence. At the same time, the general hazards of X-irradiation must be recognised and it is right that efforts be made to limit exposure to unnecessary radiation[3]. It has also been stated legally that negligence is not proved simply by failure to take an X-ray — the question of negligence depends upon the circumstances of each case[4].

Finally, the fundamental place of radiology in the management of the pneumoconioses requires special mention.

See also: Allergy; Angiography; Identification of the dead; Negligence; Non-accidental injury in children; Non-ionising radiation; Nuclear medicine; Pneumoconioses; X-rays

1. For an authoritative description, *see* Ansell G (ed) *Complications in Diagnostic Radiology* (1976) Blackwell Scientific, Oxford.
2. *See* Evans KT and Knight B *Forensic Radiology* (1981) Blackwell Scientific, Oxford.
3. Jennett B 'Some medico-legal aspects of the management of acute head injury' [1976] 1 Br Med J 1383
4. Lord Denning MR in *Braisher v Harefield and Northwood Hospital Group Management Committee* [1966] 2 Lancet 235

Randomised Trials

The randomised trial is designed to test the relative efficiency of two or more treatments, the principle being that patients suffering from the relevent condition are treated by one of the trial methods at random; the purpose is to eliminate subjective inferences on the part of the treating clinicians. There are several difficulties associated with randomised trial which are broadly practical and ethical in nature. The practical design and statistical complications of a research protocol are beyond an entry such as this save for the fact that the methods of obtaining an adequate accrual rate are clearly allied to the ethical issues. The latter relate to the researchers themselves, to the caring physicians and to the patients concerned.

As to the researchers, a randomised trial can be ethically justified only if the answer which the trial will produce is unknown. A problem arises as to the standard of proof required — is the research to continue until a statistically valid result is obtained or should it be discontinued when it appears to the researchers that one group of patients is being victimised? The answer must depend, *inter alia*, upon the importance of the result and the severity of the condition but it is perfectly possible for the research team to hold a morally acceptable view which is different from that of the caring physicians.

The physicians responsible include both the primary care physician, on whom falls the burden of allowing his patient to enter the trial, and the doctors responsible for care while he is undergoing treatment. The former, who probably has an instinctive feeling as to which of the randomised treatments is preferable, is often ill-considered in the conduct of trials. The latter, who must be distinct from the researchers if randomisation is to succeed, are in particular difficulty in the context of the double blind trial — in which neither the researcher nor the physician is aware of the patient's allocation. It is doubtful if the double blind trial is ethically acceptable if the condition under treatment is severe — the physician ought then to know what treatment is being administered; at the other end of the scale, it is open to question whether a trial which is of no concern to the physician is, in fact, worth undertaking. The acceptability of a placebo as one of the test substances is of sufficient importance to be discussed separately.

The general philosophy of the randomised trial is dominated by the question of consent which, one would have thought, should be subject to greater information than might be made available in a simple therapeutic situation[1]. It can be questioned whether the ordinary patient can make a rational decision when even the medical profession is in doubt[2] but, despite this, truly responsible medical opinion is that a genuine attempt should be made to obtain real consent to a randomised trial[3]. It is somewhat disconcerting to find that serious therapeutic experiments are being undertaken without the knowledge of the subjects[4]. Consent by or on behalf of children is discussed under 'Consent by minors'.

There have been several attempts to evade the issue of informed consent for the benefit of both the patients and the researchers — these include what is known as prerandomisation of patients before entry into the trial, which means that the patient need not be informed of the choices open to him[5]. One aim of such devices is to improve the accrual rate to the trial; it is more than doubtful if a stratagem which achieves a consent which would not be forthcoming in its absence is ethically acceptable.

Any randomised trial must now be subject to approval by the appropriate ethical committee. The structure and function of such committees is discussed separately.

See also: Biomedical experimentation; Consent to medical treatment; Consent by minors; Ethical committees; Informed consent; Placebos

1. *Halushka v The University of Saskatchewan* 53 DLR (2d) 436 (1966).
2. Taub S 'Cancer and the law of informed consent' (1982) 10 Law Med Hlth Care 61.
3. Cancer Research Campaign Working Party in Breast Conservation 'Informed consent: ethical, legal, and medical implications for doctors and patients who participate in randomised clinical trials' (1983) 286 Br Med J 1117.
4. Editorial 'Secret randomised clinical trials' [1982] 2 Lancet 78.
5. Ellenberg SS 'Randomization design in comparative clinical trials' (1984) 310 New Engl J Med 1404.

Rape

The offence of rape is committed when a man has unlawful sexual intercourse with a woman without her consent. This definition is modified in Scotland to involve sexual intercourse with a woman against her will — a distinction not without practical significance. The common law was refined in England by a statutory formula introduced in the wake of *DPP v Morgan*[1]. This reads 'A man commits rape if (a) he has unlawful sexual intercourse with a woman who at the time of the intercourse does not consent to it; and (b) at the time he knows she does not consent to the intercourse or he is reckless as to whether she consents to it'[2].

Any degree of penetration of the vulva is sufficient to constitute the offence and emission of semen is not required[3]. But, whilst penetration completes the act of rape, sexual intercourse is a process which continues until withdrawal of the male organ[4]. A boy under the age of 14 is presumed to be incapable of rape; this unreal, though irrebutable, presumption does not run to Scotland. A boy — or, indeed, a woman — could be guilty of rape as a principal in the second degree (art and part in Scotland).

Unlawful sexual intercourse is defined as intercourse outside the bonds of marriage; it follows that, in general, a husband cannot rape his lawful wife. This inevitable conclusion is now under fierce attack and the problem is discussed under 'Intramarital rape'.

The decision in *Morgan*[1] clearly indicated that a genuine mistake as to consent negated the *mens rea* of rape even though the mistake was, objectively, unreasonable. Far more difficulty has been met in interpretation of the concept of reckless rape[5]. Possible approaches include, firstly, to follow the reasoning in *R v Caldwell*[6] and to conclude that a man is reckless if he is indifferent and gives no thought to the possibility that the woman might not be consenting in circumstances when, if any thought had been given to the matter, it would have been obvious that there was a risk that she was not. Alternatively, he might be considered reckless if he is aware of the possibility that she might not be consenting but, nevertheless, persists regardless of whether or not this is so[7]. Another approach is to adopt the 'couldn't care less' test — that, even if a man appears to have a mistaken belief, the jury can still find him guilty of reckless rape if 'they come to the conclusion that he could not have cared less whether she wanted to or not but pressed on regardless', the rationale being that he would not only have been reckless but also could not have believed that she wanted to[8]. Whichever theory of recklessness is preferred, there is now a strong case for applying a subjective test to the question[9]. It is a characteristic of recklessness in rape that it is recklessness in relation to the circumstances of the act (the presence or absence of consent) rather than as to its consequences (as was the case in *Caldwell*).

Some modern writers interpret rape in a purely sexist framework: '[it] is nothing more or less than a conscious process of intimidation by which *all* men keep *all women* in a state of fear'[10]. Others regard it as being, in large part, a crime of aggression directed against a woman and as an extreme form of personal violence[11]. The continued isolation of rape as a separate and definable offence may be a reaction to the very severe trauma which a victim can suffer or it might be connected historically with the property implications of virginity[12]. It is argued that 'to take the emotion out of rape trials is to ignore the very nature of the crime'[13] but, equally, it may be that present attitudes are self-defeating in that the offence is one which is difficult to prove.

Considering this last proposition from the medical viewpoint, rape under the influence of threats will leave no trace of violence with which to convince a jury; evidence of penetration will not be found if this was vulval only or if, as is likely, the victim was married or otherwise non-virginal; in the absence of emission, no spermatozoa will be found and, in practice, spermatozoa are often undetectable even though there has been emission; injuries are improbable in the rapist in the event of a disparity in size and, especially, if there have been several assailants. From the criminological aspect, the victim, who has gone through a harrowing experience, may well be unable to convince the police at the time or a jury later of the truth of her story. Evidence as to the complainant's sexual life apart from that with the accused, may no longer be adduced without leave of the court and anonymity of the victim is preserved[14]; nevertheless, the court appearance is likely to be distressing and the reluctance of juries to convict of so serious an offence as rape is notorious[15].

For these, and other, reasons, there is a movement towards simplifying criminological attitudes to rape; for example, the crime of rape by that name has been abolished in Canada[16] and in New South Wales[17] where the three alternative offences are designed to assimilate rape into a category of aggravated sexual assault[18]. Many jurisdictions have also come to appreciate the absurdity of concentrating on vulval intercourse when other forms of sexual assault, which currently come under the general heading of indecent assault, may be equally or more revolting. Thus, in Victoria and South Australia, rape can be committed homosexually as well as heterosexually and involves the introduction of the penis into any orifice or of an object into the vagina or anus; many of the United States have responded by substituting the word 'person' for 'female' in describing the victim and the concept of rape other than *per vulvam* is firmly established. The Heilbron Committee[19] found they had insufficient time to consider the law of all offences of violence which such changes would have entailed; the inference is that they would have found it useful to do so given the opportunity.

See also: Clandestine injury to a woman; Indecent assault; Intramarital rape; *Mens rea*; Recklessness; Sexual intercourse; Unlawful sexual intercourse

1. [1976] AC 182.
2. Sexual Offences (Amendment) Act 1976, s.1(1).
3. Sexual Offences Act 1956, s.44.
4. *Kaitamaki v The Queen* [1984] 3 WLR 137.
5. Temkin J 'The limits of reckless rape' [1983] Crim LR 5.
6. [1981] 1 All ER 961.
7. As in *R v Pigg* [1982] 1 WLR 762; commentary by Smith JC [1982] Crim LR 446.
8. *R v S* (1983) Times, 6 December; sub nom *R v Satnam and Kewal* (1984) 78 Crim App R 149 (per Bristow J).
9. *R v Mohammed Bashir* [1982] Crim LR 687.
10. Brownmiller S *Against our Will* (1974) p.15, Bantam, New York.
11. For a profile of the rapist, *see* Groth A and Birnbaum H *Men who Rape* (1979) Plenum, New York; Hall Williams JE 'Serious heterosexual attack' (1977) 17 Med Sci Law 140.
12. Schwendinger JR and Schwendinger H. 'Rape, the law and private property' (1982) 28 Crim Delinq 271.
13. National Council for Civil Liberties *Sexual Offences*, Report No.13 (1976) NCCL, London.
14. Sexual Offences (Amendment) Act 1976, ss.2 and 4.

15. McCall Smith A 'The complainant's condition in rape cases' (1979) 19 Med Sci Law 25.
16. Criminal Code, ss.246.1, 246.2, 246.3. A sexual assault includes the unlawful touching of a woman's breasts (*R v Ramos* (1984) 42 CR (3d) 370).
17. Crimes (Sexual Assaults) Amendment Act 1981.
18. The modern Australian law on sexual offences is well précised in Plueckhahn VD *Ethics, Legal Medicine and Forensic Pathology* (1983) Chap.16, Melbourne University Press, Melbourne.
19. Heilbron Justice (chairman) *Report of the Advisory Group on the Law of Rape* (Cmnd 6352) (1975) para.80, HMSO, London.

Reactive Depression

'Reactive depression' is a term sometimes used to distinguish a depressive state for which there is an apparent extraneous cause from an endogenous, or constitutional, condition. Any dividing line must, however, often be unclear and it is probably better to speak of depressive illness as a whole — the role of precipitating factors can well be taken into account during diagnosis and therapy.

See also: Manic–depressive psychosis; Psychoneuroses

Reasonable Force

Although the use of force against the person is, in general, not legally permissible and will normally constitute an assault, it is possible to use reasonable force in certain narrowly defined circumstances without incurring civil or criminal liablity. The question of what constitutes reasonable force is decided by way of the surrounding circumstances.

The use of corporal punishment in the course of lawful correction is legal provided only reasonable force is used[1]; resonable force is an objective concept in such circumstances and amounts to that degree of force which is considered acceptable by the reasonable man. A parent has the right to administer corporal punishment of this sort to his child and the same power is extended to those *in loco parentis*. Teachers may currently use reasonable force in disciplining their charges but the availability of this deterrent is increasingly subject to restriction following upon decisions of the European Court of Human Rights[2].

Reasonable force may be used in defending persons or property — the requirements for this are discussed under 'Self-defence'. It may also be used in making an arrest and when searching a detained person. The latter is regulated by the Police and Criminal Evidence Act 1984, s.54; the use of reasonable force by a policeman for the purpose of searching for objects on the person is specifically permitted (s.117). Intimate body searches may be made for objects capable of causing harm or for the presence of Class A controlled drugs provided they are authorised by a police officer of at least the rank of superintendent (s.55). An intimate body search for the presence of Class A drugs must normally be carried out by a registered medical practitioner or by a nurse. A doctor or a nurse would not be legally entitled to use force to effect the search in the event of the detained person refusing consent; whether this apparent omission from the Act is deliberate or fortuitous, it is, in practice, unlikely that a doctor or a nurse would be prepared to carry out an intimate body search on an unwilling person.

See also: Assault and battery; Controlled drugs; Detention by the police; Punishment and torture; Reasonable man; Self-defence

1. *Attorney General's Reference (No.6 of 1980)* [1981] QB 715; R v Mackie [1973] Crim LR 54.
2. *Campbell and Cosans v United Kingdom* (1982) 4 EHRR 293; *Mr and Mrs X and their Son v United Kingdom* (1983) 5 EHRR 265.

Reasonable Man

The concept of the reasonable man is one which is widely used throughout the law when behaviour has to be judged against an objective standard of conduct. The reasonable man is the man of average caution and ability who is neither excessively foresighted nor particularly unable to judge the likelihood of future occurrences. He is neither timorous nor lion hearted, showing just the right degree of wariness when it comes to assessing risks and taking them.

The reasonable man is readily translated into specific contexts. He becomes the reasonable doctor — who embodies the professional wisdom of the averagely talented member of the profession — the reasonable nurse or, even, the reasonable patient. The court is thus able to apply a professional or objective standard to issues of negligence.

See also: Negligence

Reckless Driving

The Road Traffic Act 1972 includes the offences of causing death by reckless driving (s.1)[1] and of driving recklessly (s.2).

The concept of recklessness causes difficulty but Williams has said there is no word in the language more suitable than recklessness either to bridge the gap between negligence and intention or to express the position of one who consciously runs an unjustified risk[2]. The seminal driving case is *R v Lawrence* where it was held that, for a charge of reckless driving to be sustained, the jury must be satisfied of two things — that the defendant was in fact driving the vehicle in such a manner as to create an obvious and serious risk of causing physical injury to some other persons who might happen to be using the road or of doing substantial damage to property and, second, that in driving in that manner, the defendant did so without having given any thought to the possibility of there being any such risk or, having recognised that there was some risk involved, had nevertheless gone on to take it[3]. The intention of the Act, although perhaps not expressed in the judicial interpretation, was to distinguish the very serious offence of reckless driving from gross negligence. The offence of killing by reckless driving may have been introduced as a sop to juries who were unwilling to convict of manslaughter; the common law offence of manslaughter by driving may, however, still be charged when the negligence is of higher degree than that needed for a charge of causing death by reckless driving and when the risk of death is very high[4]. In the event of a charge of killing by reckless driving being laid, the coroner must accede to a request from the Director of Public Prosecutions to adjourn his inquest and, in the unnecessary event of this being reopened, the findings of the inquest must not be inconsistent with those of the criminal court[5].

It is to be noted that recklessness as applied to driving is not only a matter of handling or control of the vehicle; driving with a load known to be unsafe can, for example, also be regarded as reckless[6].

See also: Homicide; Manslaughter; Recklessness; Road Traffic Act 1972

1. As amended by the Criminal Law Act 1977, s.50.
2. Williams G *Textbook of Criminal Law* (2nd ed, 1983) p.100, Stevens, London.
3. [1982] AC 510 per Lord Diplock at 526. This is severely criticised by Williams (n.2) p.314 et seq.
4. *R v Seymour* [1983] 2 All ER 1058.
5. Criminal Law Act 1977, s.56 and Sch.10.
6. *R v Crossman* [1986] RTR 49.

Recklessness

The person or property of others may be damaged intentionally, negligently or recklessly. Reckless conduct may result in criminal prosecution either at common law (such as for manslaughter) or for a statutory offence (such as reckless damage under the Criminal Damage Act 1971).

The nature of recklessness has been the subject of intense legal controversy since the House of Lords' judgments in *R v Caldwell*[1] and *R v Lawrence*[2]. Prior to these cases, the law was that a person was reckless who carried out a deliberate act knowing that there was a risk of damage and that this risk was one that it was unreasonable to take. It was stressed in *R v Stephenson*[3] that the risk of damage must have 'entered the mind' of the defendant before he could be held to have been reckless.

But the decision in *Caldwell* indicated that a person is reckless if he does an act in which there is an obvious risk of damage and either (a) he gives no thought to the possibility of risk or (b) having recognised the existence of a risk, he has, nevertheless, proceeded in his act. A similar approach was taken in *Lawrence* and has recently been reaffirmed by the Privy Council[4]. The effect of the decisions on the law has been disputed[5]. They would seem to penalise the thoughtless defendant — that is, the man who just does not address his mind to a risk which would be obvious if the situation were considered. The defendant who thinks about the possibility of a risk, but who forms the impression that there is none, is not reckless; one who considers the possibility, decides, correctly, that a risk exists and who, nevertheless, thinks it a reasonable risk, would be considered reckless if the risk was not one which a reasonable person would have taken.

Much of the medico-legal interest in recklessness must lie in the application of the concept to the offence of rape. The decision in *DPP v Morgan*[6] and legislation in the form of the Sexual Offences (Amendment) Act 1976 confirm that recklessness is part of the *mens rea* of rape. The introduction of an objective approach to the concept of recklessness, as set out in *Caldwell*, means, however, that it is now possible to convict of rape a man who did not, in fact, think that there was any risk of the woman in question not being a consenting party. In *R v Pigg*[7] the Court of Appeal took the view that a man is reckless in this context if he did not consider the possibility of non-consent in circumstances where, had he thought of this, it would have been obvious to him that such a risk existed. This would suggest that, in certain situations — namely, those in which a reasonable man would feel that there was a risk that the woman was not consenting — the failure of the defendant to apply his mind to the risk question may be culpable. The decision in *Pigg* has been welcomed by those who favour an extension of the *mens rea* of rape[8] but not by those who believe that only subjective guilt — in this case, *actual knowledge* of the risk — should be sufficient to secure a conviction.

The rather distinct offence of reckless driving is considered separately.

See also: Rape; Reckless driving

1. [1981] 1 All ER 961.
2. [1981] 1 All ER 974.
3. [1979] QB 695.
4. *Kong Cheuk Kwan v The Queen* (1985) Times, 12 July.
5. *See* the debate in Griew E 'Reckless damage and reckless driving: living with Caldwell and Lawrence' [1981] Crim LR 743; Syrota G 'A radical change in the law of recklessness?' [1982] Crim LR 97; Williams G 'Recklessness redefined' [1981] CLJ 252.
6. [1976] AC 182.
7. [1982] 1 WLR 762. *See also* the approach adopted in *R v S* (1983) Times, 6 December.
8. *See* Temkin J 'The limits of reckless rape' [1983] Crim LR 5.

Reflex Cardiac Arrest

'Reflex cardiac arrest' is an alternative name for vagal inhibition of the heart. Many would regard it as a preferable expression as it does not imply, as does the latter, that the precise mechanism of sudden physiological cardiac arrest is fully understood.

See also: Cardiac arrest; Vagal inhibition of the heart

Refusal of Medical Treatment

The general rule in regard to the law of tort is that an injured party is under a legally imposed duty to mitigate his loss. This requires him to take steps to ensure that the damage he has suffered is minimised by proper palliative action. Failure to secure medical treatment in a case involving personal injury may mean that the defendant is held not liable for those complications or consequences of the original injury which would have been avoided had medical attention been obtained. The standard will be that of reasonable treatment — the plaintiff may be denied damages in respect of the avoidable part of his injury if he declines treatment which a reasonable man would have accepted[1]. He would not be expected to accept unusual or exceptionally risky treatment although the justification for his judgement would, itself, have to be reasonable.

In contradistinction to the civil law position, there are a number of decisions in the criminal law which confirm the liability of the accused for the death of a victim who refuses medical treatment. Such liability will be imposed despite the fact that the refusal is in the face of strong medical warnings as to the possible medical consequences. In *R v Holland*[2] the victim refused the amputation of a finger and died from tetanus two weeks later; the accused was held responsible for the death. In a case more appropriate to modern conditions[3], the victim of a stabbing refused to accept a blood transfusion on the grounds that she was a Jehovah's Witness; the Court of Appeal approved the direction of the trial judge that the stab was still, at the time of her death, the operative cause — or a substantial cause — of death and, consequently, upheld the accused's conviction for manslaughter.

Lawton LJ's opinion in this case[4] explains the differences between the civil and criminal law as regards mitigation of loss. He said:

'...Those who use violence on other people must take their victims as they find them. This means the whole man, not just the physical man. It does not lie in the mouth of the assailant to say that his victim's religious beliefs...were unreasonable.

'If the victim's personal representatives claim compensation for his death, the concept of foreseeability can operate in favour of the wrongdoer in the assessment of such compensation; the wrongdoer is entitled to expect his victim to mitigate his damage by accepting treatment of a normal kind...A policy of the common law applicable to the settlement of tortious liability may not be, and in our judgement is not, appropriate for the criminal law.'

See also: Contributory negligence; Foreseeability; Jehovah's Witnesses; *Nova causa interveniens*; Torts

1. *Steele v Robert George and Co (1937) Ltd* [1942] AC 497; *Marcroft v Scruttons Ltd* [1954] 1 Lloyds Rep 394. *See*, generally, Hudson AH 'Refusal of medical treatment' (1983) 3 LS 50.
2. (1841) 2 M & R 351, 174 ER 313. Such treatment would not be advised a century and a half later.
3. *R v Blaue* [1975] 3 All ER 446, 1 WLR 1411.
4. Ibid, 1 WLR at pp.1415–1416.

Registered Medical Practitioner

A registered medical practitioner is one registered with the General Medical Council under the terms of the Medical Act 1983, Parts II and III. Doctors may be fully registered by virtue of holding one of the qualifications obtained in the UK which are currently detailed in s.4 of the Act, by holding a primary qualification of a country in the EEC (Sch.2) or by holding a qualification in a Commonwealth or foreign country which is recognised by the GMC — currently, there are 22 universities recognised in seven such countries. Limited registration is offered to those from other countries who wish to practise in the UK. Such registration is limited to employment in hospitals or institutions which are approved by a post-graduate governing body and which is supervised by a fully registered doctor. It is contingent, when first granted, upon having passed, or having been exempted from, a test of professional competence and of proficiency in English — in 1985, 418 out of 1,984 candidates passed both these tests. Limited registration cannot be granted for more than five years in aggregate. Full registration may be granted after satisfying the GMC as to professional competence; there is a right of appeal to a review board in the event of refusal of full registration (ss.28 and 29). Provisional registration is granted to doctors during their first year after qualification, during which time their practice is limited to specific appointments; full registration is given subject to certification of satisfactory compliance with their compulsory postgraduate training.

A number of postgraduate degrees, Royal College memberships or fellowships and diplomas are registrable with the GMC but these are currently ancillary only; EEC legislation, which seeks to register specialists, may alter their significance.

Certain functions of the medical doctor are specifically barred to those who are not registered. The non-registered doctor cannot practise in the Armed Forces, nor in prisons, nor in any hospital or institution other than one which is wholly supported by voluntary contributions. He cannot prescribe drugs which are designated as 'Prescription Only medicines' and cannot sign the many certificates for which being a registered medical practitioner is, among others, a qualification. He may not attend a woman in childbirth[1] nor may he treat venereal disease[2].

It is no offence to practise a 'healing art'; any offence relates to pretending to be registered (s.49). No offence occurs, however, if the person honestly believes he is in the right as describing himself as he does[3].

See also: General Medical Council; Prescription Only medicines

1. Nurses, Midwives and Health Visitors Act 1979, s.17 (replacing Midwives Act 1951, s.9).
2. Venereal Disease Act 1917, s.1.
3. *Younghusband v Luftig* [1949] 2 KB 354, [1949] 2 All ER 72; *Wilson v Inyang* [1951] 2 All ER 237, [1951] 2 KB 799.

Registration of Births and Deaths

The registration of births and deaths is regulated in England and Wales by the Births and Deaths Registration Act 1953 and in Scotland by the Births, Deaths and Marriages (Scotland) Act 1965[1].

The law requires the registration of all births and stillbirths. Information on births may be given within 42 days of the event by any qualified informant — usually the father or mother, although information may be given by, amongst others, any person present at the birth. The particulars which must be provided are the date and place of the birth, the names of the parents (if known) and the name of the informant. The name of the father of an illegitimate child must not be included in the register other than at the joint request of both parents or when a declaration as to fatherhood is made by either the mother or the father[2]. An illegitimate person's birth may be re-registered when that person is legitimised (s.14) and the Registrar General may require re-registration in the event of legitimation on the marriage of a person's parents.

In the event of a child being 'found exposed', the person finding the child or the person into whose care it is given must inform the registrar within 42 days of the discovery[3].

The registrar can demand attendance of the informant if a birth has not been registered within 42 days and he may then register the birth within three months of the event; if registration is delayed for up to a year, it can be effected only following a declaration to the superintendent registrar; the authority of the Registrar General is needed before a birth can be registered more than 12 months after the birth (s.21).

In the case of stillbirths, the registrar requires from the informant a certificate of stillbirth. This certificate states that the child was not born alive and should give the cause of death[4] — in the absence of which, the case will be referred to the coroner (*see* below).

It is the duty of a qualified informant notifying the registrar of a death to deliver a certificate of the cause of death to him within five days of the death. Qualified informants include relatives of the deceased and, in the case of a death which occurs other than in a house (which includes a hospital and other premises), persons finding the body or causing its disposal. The contents of the death certificate are discussed under that heading.

Following notification, the registrar will either register the death and issue a certificate for disposal or he will report the death to the coroner (*see* below). It is an offence for any person to dispose of a body unless the registrar has given such a certificate or the coroner has given either an order for burial or a certificate for cremation[5]. The person effecting the disposal — normally the person who keeps the burial register or the registrar of the crematorium — is required to notify the registrar of the details within 96 hours of disposal of the body; this is not, however, necessary in the case of a stillbirth. Deaths which are notified more than a year after the occurrence are registrable only on the authority of the Registrar General.

The registrar must inform the coroner of a death notified to him if the certificate of the cause of death indicates it to be a case in which the cause of death is unknown, that the body was neither seen by the certifying doctor after death nor seen in life within 14 days of death or that the death occurred in suspicious or unnatural circumstances; these last are detailed in regulations made under the Act[6].

Any error of fact or substance can be corrected in the margin of the register of births or deaths on a declaration by two qualified informants or, in the case of death, on a certificate given by the coroner (s.29). Registers of births and deaths are public documents and may be searched by members of the public on payment of a fee (s.32). A short copy of a birth certificate can also be obtained but this must not include any details referring to parentage or adoption.

Special provisions as to registration of births, marriages and deaths apply to the armed forces and their associated organisations when they are serving overseas[7].

The Scottish provisions as to registration of births and deaths are broadly similar to those discussed above save that a birth must be registered within 21 days and a death within 8 days. There are no coroners in Scotland, their roles being performed by sheriffs and procurators fiscal. The circumstances in which a registrar must inform the procurator fiscal of a death and vice-versa are stated in s.28 of the 1965 Act.

See also: Coroner; Death certification; Disposal of the dead; Illegitimacy; Procurator fiscal; Stillbirth

1. For a full description of the position as regards death in England and Wales, *see* Davies MRR *The Law of Burial, Cremation and Exhumation* (5th ed, 1982) Shaw, London.
2. Family Law Reform Act 1969, s.27.
3. *See* Registration of Births (Abandoned Children) Regulations 1976 (SI 1976/2080).
4. Registration of Births, Deaths and Marriages Regulations 1968, (SI 1968/2049) rr. 48–56.
5. Births and Deaths Registration Act 1926, s.1.
6. Note 4, above, r.51.
7. Registration of Births, Deaths and Marriages (Special Provisions) Act 1957.

Remoteness of Damage

The topic of remoteness of damage overlaps to a considerable extent with the related concepts of causation and foreseeability in the law of tort. Remoteness is essentially a limiting convention which is used by the courts to exclude from the ambit of the defendant's liability those consequences which are too remote or distant from the original wrongful act[1]. Without this exclusion, the law of tort would be involved in attributing responsibility for events which, although caused by the defendant's act, were not consequences for which he could realistically be expected to bear blame. An example of a remote possibility would be when the plaintiff, as a result of a leg injury caused by the defendant some months previously, loses his balance and injures his head. Damage which is foreseeable is unlikely to be excluded as being too remote if it is damage 'of a kind' foreseen by the defendant. Intended consequences are certainly not to be considered as being too remote for liability to be attributed[2].

See also: Causation; Foreseeability; Torts

1. For a classic statement of the principle, *see* Lord Wright's judgment in *Liesbosch Dredger v S.S. Edison* [1933] AC 449 at 460.
2. *Quinn v Leathem* [1901] AC 495, per Lord Lindley at 537.

Reproductive Technology

This is something of a neologism and refers, in general, to modern aids to reproduction for the infertile. It is believed that about 10 per cent of married couples are seeking some sort of aid to creating a family.

Some techniques require minimal expertise — these include artificial insemination by husband or by donor and surrogate motherhood; the last may, of course, be accomplished by purely natural means. Other techniques require considerable skill, are both time consuming and labour intensive and have a success rate which is often disappointing but which is related to the competence of the professionals involved. Such techniques derive from *in vitro* fertilisation, which can include ovum donation and may be extended to embryo donation and womb leasing.

All the techniques involved are discussed under the appropriate headings. They have recently been the subject of in-depth study[1] and many recommendations as to their legal control have been made. It is of interest that such techniques when applied to animals may already be controlled by regulation[2].

See also: Artificial insemination by donor; Artificial insemination by husband;

Embryo donation; Embryo transfer; *In vitro* fertilisation; Ovum donation; Surrogate motherhood; Womb leasing

1. Warnock M (chairman) *Report of the Committee of Inquiry into Human Fertilisation and Embryology* (Cmnd 9314) (1984) HMSO, London.
2. Animal Health and Welfare Act 1984, s.10.

Res Ipsa Loquitur

The maxim *res ipsa loquitur* (the matter speaks for itself) finds its classic expression in the judgment of Erle CJ:

> 'There must be reasonable evidence of negligence. But where a thing is shown to be under the management of the defendant or his servants, and the accident is such as in the ordinary course of things does not happen if those who have the management use proper care, it affords reasonable evidence, in the absence of explanation by the defendant, that the accident arose from want of care'[1].

The principle of *res ipsa loquitur* may therefore be invoked by a plaintiff who has suffered an injury in circumstances where the incident is explicable only as an occurrence in which there was negligence on the defendant's part. The cause of the occurrence must be unknown and it is a further requirement that the defendant should have been in control of the situation at the time when the damage was sustained.

The effect of the doctrine has been the subject of considerable legal debate and differing positions are adopted in various Commonwealth countries. The prevailing view in the UK is that, if *res ipsa loquitur* is applied, the plaintiff is entitled to succeed unless the defendant brings evidence to rebut the possibility of negligence[2]. The position is different in Canada. The application of the principle merely creates an inference of negligence but does not transfer the onus of proof onto the defendant[3].

A defendant who is able to provide an explanation of the accident which is as consistent with the absence of negligence as it is with its presence succeeds, thereby, in reimposing the evidential burden on the plaintiff. The plaintiff then has to establish negligence on the defendant's part in the usual way.

In general, the courts are fairly reluctant to use the doctrine of *res ipsa loquitur*[4] although there are a number of examples of its application in medical negligence cases. Lord Denning made his colourful pronouncement on the subject in one of these: 'If the plaintiff had to prove that some particular doctor or nurse was negligent, he would not be able to do it. But he was not put to that impossible task; he says, "I went into the hospital to be cured of two stiff fingers. I have come out with four stiff fingers, and my hand is useless. That should not have happened if due care had been used. Explain it if you can"'[5]. A further good example is to be found more recently in *Clark v MacLennan and another*[6] where it was held that, in the face of universal opinion that an operation should have been delayed, the onus lay on the defendant to show that he was not in any breach of duty in operating soon after childbirth.

There have been indications in other cases that the courts are hesitant to allow the imposition of too heavy a burden on the doctor. In the important Canadian case of *Wilcox v Cavan*[7] the court urged caution in the application of the *res ipsa loquitur* doctrine to medical cases where 'differences of expert opinion are not unusual and the sequence of events often appears to have brought about a result which has never occurred in exactly the same way before'.

See also: Burden of proof; Negligence; Swab cases

1. *Scott v London and St Katherine Docks* (1865) 3 H & C 596 at 601.
2. Dias RWM (ed) *Clerk and Lindsell on Torts* (15th ed, 1982) p.485 et seq, Sweet & Maxwell, London. *See also* Shiff S 'A res ipsa loquitur nutshell' (1976) 26 U Toronto LJ 451; Atiyah PS 'Res ipsa loquitur in England and Australia' (1972) 35 MLR 337. A good general survey is to be found in Giesen D *Medical Malpractice Law* (1981) p.259 et seq Gieseking Verlag, Bielefeld.
3. Linden AM *Canadian Tort Law* (3rd ed, 1982) p.253 et seq, Butterworths, Toronto.
4. For an example of judicial reluctance, *see Mahon v Osborne* [1939] 2 KB 14.
5. *Cassidy v Ministry of Health* [1951] 2 KB 343 at 365.
6. [1983] 1 All ER 416.
7. (1975) 50 DLR (3d) 687. Other Canadian cases on the subject include *Cardin v La Cite de Montreal* (1961) 29 DLR (2d) 492; *Finlay et al v Auld* (1974) 43 DLR (3d) 216 and *Ferguson v Hamilton Civic Hospitals* (1983) 144 DLR (3d) 214.

Resource Allocation

Resources can never be infinite and a positive limitation is imposed when a health service is funded from a central source. To allocate such limited resources on the basis of consumer demand alone is to invite chaos and it becomes necessary to ration health care according to medically defined needs[1]. To reach that definition requires a solution to a virtually insoluble dilemma[2].

It is possible to consider health resource allocation on a global scale, at national level and in relation to the individual. The former is a matter of international policy and is irrelevant to this entry. The distribution of health care in the UK has been reviewed recently by national working parties and attempts have been made to correlate the financial help given with the actual needs of the various health authorities. Such studies raise considerable doubts as to the basis of calculation — should it, for example, be orientated towards hospital-based treatment or to primary care? Is it correct to equate the actual financial burden imposed by various patterns of illness with justification for their continued support? And, inevitably, is it possible to keep the more distasteful aspects of politics out of such decisions? Politics in the broad sense must apply because, essentially, the allocation of any scarce resource, including health care, is a matter of maximising societal benefit. Some form of 'cost–benefit' analysis is essential and this involves placing a value on human life which, again, cannot be infinite. It is neither politically nor morally wrong to impose such controls; rather, it must be accepted that there is likely to be an unethical maldistribution of resources in the absence of regulation[3].

Legally, the Secretary of State has a statutory duty to provide health services to such extent as he thinks necessary to meet all reasonable requirements of the health service[4]. There seems to be only one case in which the adequacy of such provision has been challenged[5]. The case failed, predictably, on the grounds that there would be a failure of duty only if the Minister's action was thoroughly unreasonable; as a matter of policy, it was noted that we should be faced with the economics of a bottomless pit if no limits in respect of long-term planning were to be read into public statutory duties.

Nevertheless, no matter how fairly is the national budget distributed, the ultimate decision as to resource allocation at the individual patient level must be a clinical matter — the parameter of objectivity is replaced by actual need and this, in turn, involves value judgements for which an ethical guideline must be sought. There is no legal precedent to direct the doctor who is faced with decisions which may involve life or death, although the general legal principle of necessity would apply; a possibly apposite British case, concerning survival in a life boat, decided that inactivity is the correct policy in such circumstances[6]. No legal liability arises if a doctor refuses to accept further patients when there is no further capacity for treatment available but there is still a moral choice to be made. Some idea of the difficulty is expressed in the deliberately extreme suggestion that some economic logic might emerge whereby those who would receive heavy damages if not treated would be given treatment and those whose damages would be small would be left to their remedy in damages. 'Those who find such a method revolting', says the author, 'should put forward better methods to make the inevitable selection'[7].

There are a variety of more valid alternatives. There is a growing tendency to discuss the choices in terms of triage but it is more than doubtful if an essentially military expedient can be applied in the civilian situation. Comparisons which attempt to distinguish the relative gain to society of saving one life rather than another involve judgements which are wholly beyond the remit of the clinician who should, ethically, be concerned only with the needs of his individual patient. For similar reasons, the allocation of resources on the basis of the general merits or social worth of the recipient is unacceptable save in the negative sense that a person who might destroy the system (e.g. a carrier of hepatitis in a renal dialysis unit) might be properly excluded. Other suggestions have included consideration of the capacity of the patient to enjoy or profit from treatment — but who is to judge other people's standards of satisfaction? The most widely acceptable criterion of selection would seem to be medical benefit; but prognosis is uncertain, whilst medical and social benefit are difficult to dissociate. It is clearly wrong, using the productive/non-productive treatment test, to provide a scarce resource for a patient who is receiving no benefit but it would be equally wrong to withdraw such a resource from a patient simply because a better medical proposition was a later contender. In the end, one is almost forced to accept the principle of randomisation of allocation based on the needs of the individual patient — although such a conclusion arises from little more than the inadequacy of the remaining alternatives, it has the merits of fairness in eliminating comparative judgements. There might, however, be a good case for combining the potentials of private medicine with the merits of the national service when the scarcity is simply one of 'hardware' for which central financing is not available.

Arguments as to the allocation of resources — particularly to groups of patients — are likely to escalate as more exotic forms of diagnosis and treatment evolve and as the nature of the population changes[8]. Scarcity is not, however, necessarily a wholly bad thing; abundance carries with it the hazard that investigation and treatment may be forced upon unwilling recipients — or that activity will become an end in itself irrespective of the outcome for the patient[1]. One thing is certain — the success of a group of patients in achieving an allocation of resources can, in existing circumstances, only be at the expense of other groups. Decisions should be made in an atmosphere of scientific evaluation; emotional and partisan appeals to the news media or from the political hustings are not good ways by which to establish a balanced health service.

See also: National Health Service; Necessity; Ordinary/Extraordinary treatment; Triage

1. Klein R 'Rationing health care' (1984) 289 Br Med J 143.
2. We have discussed the problem at length in Mason JK and McCall Smith RA *Law and Medical Ethics* (1983) Chap.11, Butterworths, London. *See also* Leenen HJJ 'The selection of patients in the event of a scarcity of medical facilities — an unavoidable dilemma' (1979) 1 Int J Med Law 161.
3. *See* a series of articles by Mooney GH and Drummond MF under the general heading 'Essentials of health economics' (1982) 285 Br Med J 949 to (1983) 286 Br Med J 40; also Mooney GH 'Cost-benefit analysis and medical ethics' (1980) 6 J Med Ethics 177.
4. National Health Service Act 1977, s.3.
5. *R v Secretary of State for Social Services, ex parte Hincks* (1979) 123 SJ 436. For the appeal stage, *see* Mason and McCall Smith, n.2 above at 147, or Finch JD *Health Services Law* (1981) pp.38–39, Sweet & Maxwell, London.
6. *R v Dudley and Stephens* (1884) 14 QBD 273.
7. Medicolegal 'Rationing of resources' (1985) 290 Br Med J 374.
8. *See* Gardner BP et al 'Ventilation or dignified death for patients with high tetraplegia' (1985) 291 Br Med J 1620.

Respirator Support

Respirator support is virtually a matter of historical interest only following the almost total elimination of acute anterior poliomyelitis (infantile paralysis). It is essentially a treatment for those diseases which cause peripheral respiratory failure and is to be contrasted with ventilator support which is used to overcome central failure due to brain damage. The two processes differ mechanically in that the respirator operates by creating a vacuum around the chest which effects inspiration whereas air is forced into the lungs during ventilation.

The difference from the practical management aspect is that the patient in the respirator is conscious and fully competent whilst the ventilated patient is comatose and incompetent. Problems of treatment of intercurrent disease or of removal of support are therefore of quite different dimensions[1]. 'Switching off' the respirator before death would, inevitably, constitute some form of assisted suicide — a potential offence against the Suicide Act 1961, s.2. The defence of good medical practice would not be easy to sustain; such a situation might well be one in which it would be proper to follow US precedent and to obtain a judicial opinion — and it is unlikely that authority to remove support would be granted[2].

See also: Euthanasia; Ordinary/Extraordinary treatment; Suicide; Ventilator support

1. See Mason JK and McCall Smith RA *Law and Medical Ethics* (1983) p.183 (Butterworths, London) for discussion.

2. The US case of *In the matter of Claire C Conroy*, Sup Ct NJ App Div A 2483-82 T1 (1983) provides something of a parallel.

Respiratory System

The function of the respiratory system is to trap the atmospheric oxygen and to make it available for transfer to the tissues by the cardiovascular system; in addition, it excretes the gaseous products of the combustion which takes place at cellular level.

Air intake is achieved by the positive action of expanding the thoracic cavity using the intercostal muscles and diaphragm; the movement of expiration is a passive one. Respiration is under the control of the respiratory centre in the brain stem and is normally activated through the autonomic nervous system. It is, however, possible to alter one's breathing volitionally through the peripheral motor nervous system; ultimately, however, the autonomic system will prevail and it is impossible to hold one's breath indefinitely in a hostile gaseous or fluid atmosphere. The major stimulus to respiration is the level of blood carbon dioxide as perceived by the respiratory centre; overbreathing, such as occurs subconsciously when frightened or deliberately prior to breath holding, flushes out the carbon dioxide and inhibits the respiratory reflex — dangerous states of hypoxia may result.

Air inspired passes through either the nose or the mouth, through the larynx and into the trachea, or windpipe; since the oesophagus, or gullet, lies behind the trachea, the laryngeal opening must be closed during swallowing and this is done reflexly by the epiglottis — this reflex is lost in states of diminished consciousness. The trachea splits into two main bronchi to supply the left and right lungs and these divide into smaller bronchi and even smaller air tubes known as bronchioles. These ultimately lead to air sacs or alveoli which are microscopic chambers surrounded by capillaries; gaseous interchange takes place between the alveolar spaces and the erythrocytes across the avleolar wall — the alveolar walls being kept apart by the action of an important substance known as surfactant. Grossly, the lungs are divided into lobes, three in the right lung and two on the left, the third left lobe being substituted by the heart which occupies the left thorax; the right lung is therefore always heavier than is the left. Friction during the necesssary movement between the lung and the chest wall is minimised by a lining consisting of two layers of fibrous tissue called the pleura. The space between the two layers is under negative pressure and it is this which serves to maintain the lungs in an expanded state. The lungs have a separate pulmonary blood supply, the pulmonary artery arising from the right ventricle of the heart and the pulmonary veins entering the left atrium — blockage of the former may cause rapid hypoxia and sudden death (*see* 'Pulmonary embolism'). The fetal lungs are, of course, inoperative, oxygenation of the fetus being accomplished through the placenta; pulmonary intake of air is therefore an important sign of live birth.

The delicate alveoli must be protected against the dust and bacteria which are present in the air. To achieve this, the cells lining the air passages are equipped with hairs (cilia) which waft particulate matter towards the glottis — hence the phlegm which is occasionally coughed up. Any substances poisonous to the cells, such as cigarette smoke, inflammation of the bronchial tree (bronchitis) or simple overpowering of the cilia by excess dust lay the alveoli open to foreign matter. The results of invasion by bacteria or dust are discussed under 'Lung disease and injury' and 'Pneumoconioses'.

Any process which inhibits the free transfer of oxygen from the air to the erythrocytes gives rise to asphyxia; this intensely important aspect of forensic pathology is discussed in detail under that heading (*see also* the various mechanical forms of asphyxia such as 'choking', 'strangulation', 'drowning', etc.). Any penetrating injury of the chest will involve the pleura and the lungs (*see* 'Lung disease and injury'); fortunately, the body can survive on one lung with only partial decrement and repair of damaged lungs is very feasible.

See also: Asphyxia; Autonomic nervous system; Carbon dioxide; Hypoxia; Live birth; Lung disease and injury; Placenta; Pneumoconioses; Pulmonary embolism

Restriction Orders

Restriction orders were intended to be, in effect, hospital orders without limit of time. The Mental Health Act 1959 permitted the Home Secretary to recall a convicted person who had been detained in and released from a special hospital; shortly before the passing of the Mental Health (Amendment) Act 1982 these powers were appealed to the European Court of Human Rights which found in favour of the plaintiff[1]. As a result, persons subject to a restriction order must now be medically examined and a report sent to the Home Secretary at least yearly, and they cannot be detained once they are found to be no longer suffering from a mental disorder which makes compulsory hospital detention appropriate. The restriction order has thus lost some of its 'life sentence' implications but, nevertheless, is to be used only with reserve.

The restriction order can be made only by the Crown Court (s.41) although the magistrates can commit an offender to the Crown Court with the intention that an order be made. A bed must be available, and the evidence of two doctors, one approved for the purpose, must be available from at least one of them attending the court in person. An order can, however, be made only to protect the public from serious harm and, in view of this serious basis for the direction, any appeals which are available can be difficult to sustain.

Although restriction orders can be made for a finite period, they are generally made without time limit. The restricted patient cannot be discharged without the permission of the Home Secretary, he may be recalled (in which case he may appeal to a tribunal after six months) and he cannot gain his freedom by escaping successfully for 28 days. The Home Secretary can lift the restriction or he can discharge the patient either absolutely or conditionally (s.42). If a restriction order is lifted when the patient is still in hospital, he reverts to the position of one who is subject to a hospital order.

It is to be noted that the Home Secretary has the power, subject to the medical criteria applicable to a hospital order, to transfer a prisoner to hospital (s.47). The transfer has the same effect as a restriction order if restrictions are imposed; the patient may appeal to a mental health tribunal six months after transfer but, should he be regarded as fit for discharge, the Home Secretary may either do so or return him to prison. If a hospitalised prisoner no longer requires treatment, or if treatment is no longer effective, the Home Secretary can leave the patient in hospital or he can release him on licence or discharge him under supervision. The hope is that the powers of transfer to hospital will release those who are mentally ill from the prison environment but, ultimately, the whole scheme depends upon the availability of secure beds.

See also: Hospital orders; Mental Health Act 1983

1. *X v United Kingdom* (1982) 4 EHRR 118. This and other cases are discussed in detail in Hoggett BM *Mental Health Law* (2nd ed, 1984) p.174 et seq, Sweet & Maxwell, London.

Resuscitation

The problem of attempting resuscitation in the event of cardiorespiratory collapse sometimes presents as an acute dilemma both of practice and of ethics. Reclamation is not difficult, particularly when the cardiac failure results from ventricular fibrillation — so-called cardioversion can be achieved either by electrical stimulation or by physical means following natural acute myocardial ischaemia, electric shock and the like.

Whilst every instinct calls for resuscitation, the possibility of hypoxic brain damage having been already caused has to be considered. This is, perhaps, even more so when the primary cause for cardiorespiratory collapse is in the respiratory system, as may occur after a drug overdose or, more acutely, following a mishap during anaesthesia. In this case, the result of resuscitation — which is as likely as not to need no more than reoxygenation — may well be no more than a persistent vegetative state. The words of Lord Denning MR, in deciding such a case, are particularly chilling: 'Many would say', he said, '"'twere better she had died"'[1]. The practical problem rests on the fact that it is almost impossible to reach a prognosis until after the event.

The ethical concerns are compounded if the original hypoxic insult was iatrogenic in origin. In practice, there seems no way that the very great majority of such dilemmas can be resolved other than in favour of being hopeful to salvage a useful life.

Resuscitation in the chronic sick and old has also caused some crises of conscience. The hospital notes of many such patients have been marked 'Not to be resuscitated in the event of collapse' and such instructions may well be a good and humane practice of medicine. The situation is not, however, so clear cut to the layman and public reaction has probably stopped 'blanket' directives of this type although it is still perfectly proper to decide each case on its merits as it appears. The issue is discussed further under 'Euthanasia'.

See also: Euthanasia; Persistent vegetative state; Ventricular fibrillation

1. *Lim Poh Choo v Camden and Islington AHA* [1979] 1 All ER 332.

Rhesus System

The rhesus (Rh) blood group system derives its name from the fact that blood cells of the monkey *Macaca rhesus* provoked antibodies in rabbits which showed the same reactions in human beings as did the serum of certain persons who had exhibited transfusion reactions. There has been much academic debate as to the nature of the Rh genes and antigens, and it is intended here to describe the system only in terms of the British or Fisher notation[1].

The system consists basically of three allelic pairs of genes and resultant antigens — Cc, Dd, Ee. Since one gene of each pair is derived from each parent, eight possible complexes can be derived. The genes in each complex are 'linked' — that is, the whole complex is passed on true to the offspring. Thus, the eight complexes can be combined to give 36 genotypes. Some complexes are, however, very rare and 94 per cent of linked gene groupings consist of CDe, cDE or cde.

The 'strongest' antigen is D and, in common parlance, the terms 'rhesus positive' and 'rhesus negative' refer to the presence or absence of D in the genotype. A rhesus positive person may be homozygous (DD) or heterozygous (Dd); the diagnostic limitation of the rhesus system lies in the fact that d is 'silent' and provokes no antibody by which it can be identified. Antibodies to the remaining five antigens are, however, available; phenotypes can be built up through their use and, by a process of positive identification and elimination, potential genotypes can be derived. Thus, cells reacting with anti-C, anti-D and anti-c but not with anti-E, the most common finding, could be of the genotypes CDe/cde, CDe/cDe or Cde/cDe but nearly 94 per cent showing such a reaction would, in proven fact, be of the first type and 6 per cent will be of the second.

The failure to demonstrate d obviously limits the system in regard to parentage testing but the inability to identify the precise groupings with certainty is immaterial, save in a few instances, because the individual antigens are each inherited on mendelian principles and the probablity of the particular genotype being derived from a given phenotype drops below 90 per cent in only one numerically important instance. It may be important to decide whether the father is homozygous or heterozygous for a given gene/antigen when investigating haemolytic disease of the newborn but, again, the probabilities, aided by family studies, will generally give a satisfactory answer.

The antigen D, with its capacity to produce anti-D, is outstandingly important in provoking both transfusion reactions and haemolytic disease of the newborn but antibodies to all the remaining members of the group, other than d, have been provoked either alone or in combination. The rhesus system is complicated by the fact that rare variants of the basic antigens occur. Thus, the antigen C^w replaces C in some 2 per cent of British persons. The demonstration of transmission of such a variant goes a considerable way to positive identification of a putative father.

See also: Antibody; Antigen; Blood groups; Blood transfusion; Haemolytic disease of the newborn; Parentage testing

1. A very adequate discussion of the rhesus group is contained in Dodd BE and Lincoln PJ *Blood Group Topics* (1975) Chap.6, Edward Arnold, London.

Rifled Weapon Injuries

Rifled weapons are those in which the barrel is grooved spirally. They include handguns — pistols, which may well be automatic, and revolvers — and the typical long-barrelled rifle (*see* 'Firearms'). The rifled weapon fires bullets, and injuries inflicted by them can be described alternatively as bullet wounds. The discharge of a rifled weapon results in a shockwave as the air in the barrel is forced outwards followed by the products of explosion — flame, soot, rapidly expanding gas and unburnt powder. The bullet lies at the head of this mass as it leaves the barrel. The muzzle velocity of bullets fired from rifles is very much greater than that of those discharged from handguns. Hence, injuries sustained at relatively close range will be more severe from rifles than from handguns, and the rifle will be lethal at far greater distances.

Bullet injuries are characterised by showing both entry and exit wounds. The shape of the entry wound depends upon the distance from which the shot was fired. A contact wound may show bruising and burning but its shape will be irregular since it has been caused in the main by the expansion of air and explosive gases within the tissues; these gases may contain carbon monoxide, and carboxyhaemoglobin can often be seen or demonstrated in the extravasated blood within the wound. A short range shot will show no bruising but, depending upon the distance, burning of the tissues or clothing may still be evident. Beyond this, and up to about one metre (one yard), the characteristic finding is of tattooing — the embedding of particles of unburnt powder in the skin or clothing. As the effect of the explosion decreases with distance, so will the bullet entry wound become more regularly circular and, despite the elasticity of the skin, this often reflects the calibre of the firearm; soiling, or peripheral deposition of the oil collected from the barrel of a rifled weapon, is a diagnostic feature of bullet entry wounds.

By contrast, the exit wound will be caused by a bullet which has perhaps been deformed or is, at any rate, no longer gyroscopically orientated and which may be carrying with it fragments of tissue or bone. The wound will therefore be everted and irregular and will show neither burning nor soiling. An exit wound caused by a very high velocity missile may be the same size as the entry wound but, in ordinary circumstances, it will be appreciably larger than is that due to entry. It will be seen that a very good estimate can be made of the direction of a firearm injury but, beyond one metre (one yard), the wounds are likely to appear the same irrespective of distance until the end-stage of flight is reached; at that point, the entry wound may be irregular and the bullet may remain lodged in the tissues.

Tissue damage is due to two main factors other than the actual penetration of the bullet. Firstly, there is major damage due to cavitation behind the bullet in its track but, more importantly, there is a dissipation of energy in its path; since energy is proportional to the square of the velocity, a high velocity missile is very destructive even though its mass may be deliberately reduced.

A major function of the autopsy following death from rifled weapon injuries is to distinguish between homicide, suicide and accident. Suicidal wounds are generally of contact type and are almost invariably in a 'site of election' — the entry wound is in the mouth, the centre of the forehead or the temple; a shot below the left ribs is also characteristic of election. Multiplicity of shots is suggestive of homicide but does not certainly exclude suicide as the first shot may not be fatal. The diagnostic feature of homicide is a contact or very close range injury in a site inaccessible to the victim — the executioner's shot in the nape of the neck is a classic example. Otherwise, the distinction between homicide and accident is likely to be made only on the basis of circumstantial evidence. Death from bullet injuries is either due to destruction in a vital centre (e.g. the brain or heart) or results from haemorrhage from an organ or a major vessel. Damage to the spinal cord is a common and particularly tragic effect of a bullet wound; the survivor of such an injury is likely to be paraplegic.

X-ray cover is a near essential of any gunshot injury autopsy. The bullet may be fragmented or, in the case of small calibre weapons, may still be present in the body and be difficult to find having been deflected by contact with bone. The recovery of such evidence is an important contribution to the discovery of the offending weapon and, hence, of the culprit.

See also: Bullets; Carboxyhaemoglobin; Firearms; Homicide; Paraplegia; Suicide; X-rays

Rigor Mortis

Rigor mortis is the process of stiffening of the muscles which occurs after death. It is due to the accumulation of waste products of metabolism and to the failure of the anoxic tissues to replenish chemicals essential for the elasticity and plasticity of the muscle fibres — in particular, adenosine triphosphate. As a result, the muscles become rigid and the joints fixed; breaking down the rigor through manipulating the joints results in tearing of the muscle fibres which will not, therefore, recover their rigor.

Whilst the process of rigor formation proceeds in all muscle groups from the time of death, it is most likely to be demonstrable in the smaller muscle masses. Thus, it commonly appears first in the muscles of the face and last in the major muscle groups of the legs. As a result, whilst rigor is rarely demonstrable before some three hours after death, there is a tendency for apparent progression, the whole body being affected after about 12 hours. Rigor will persist until secondary flaccidity sets in due to commencing putrefaction. When this occurs will depend upon many factors but, as a rule of thumb, it can be expected to become manifest some 24 hours after death, rigor passing off in the ensuing 12–24 hours in much the same order as it appeared. In favourable conditions, however, rigor may persist for several days.

Rigor develops poorly in infants and in the elderly. Its passage is accelerated by a warm ambient temperature. It will appear more rapidly in muscles which have been exercised shortly before death and, since putrefaction is unaffected, it will remain established for a longer period in the bodies of those who were active at the time of death. Rigor also occurs in the involuntary muscles and may account for *post mortem* defaecation or expression of semen.

Rigor must be distinguished from freezing of the body fluids or cold stiffening of the body fat. Its distinction from heat contracture, which occurs in burnt bodies, is important[1]; shortening of the muscles is not a feature of rigor mortis. The possibility of the rare condition of cadaveric spasm occurring must also be considered.

See also: Burning; Cadaveric spasm; Putrefaction; Timing of death

1. At least one celebrated murder trial revolved on this differentiation: *see* Blom-Cooper, L 'A miscarriage of justice — English style' (1981) 49 Med-Leg J 98.

Risk

Most human activities entail a risk of causing damage, a matter which is generally accepted as an inevitable part of day-to-day life. The level of risk is taken into account when assessing the wisdom of a particular course of action and will be considered to be excessive in some cases. To ignore a considerable risk and to hazard its occurrence may amount to negligence or to recklessness which may, in turn, lead to civil or criminal legal consequences.

A risk of some sort is inherent in most medical procedures. The risk may be described as negligible in procedures or treatments which are known to be extremely safe and need not cause concern to either the doctor or the patient. A pin prick made to obtain a specimen of capillary blood exemplifies such a negligible risk.

Other procedures may carry considerable hazard and the doctor may then have to pay careful attention to the risk/benefit ratio involved in investigation or treatment. The calculation of this ratio, which can be expressed with some precision in certain cases, is essential if the doctor and his patient are to reach a decision as to whether to proceed with the treatment in question. It may, for example, be appropriate to compare mortality and morbidity rates in the absence of treatment with those arising from complications of therapy.

The difficulty is acute when deciding to proceed to an extremely risky treatment of cases in which less radical therapy has failed. The question may be reduced essentially to one of deciding whether the patient's life can be hazarded against an uncertain, or possibly remote, prospect of a cure. It is submitted that the consent of the patient to the taking of the risk justifies proceeding with the treatment in such circumstances provided that, viewed objectively, the prospect of improvement by virtue of the treatment is better than negligible.

The disclosure to the patient of inherent risks is necessary if such risks can be considered material and if they are such as the reasonable doctor would consider necessary for the patient to know[1]. The issue is essentially that of 'informed consent', which is discussed at length under that heading.

The concept of risk is also applicable to the criminal law. The ambulance driver hurrying to the scene of an accident takes a risk if he crosses an adverse traffic light or exceeds the speed limit, and he has a statutory right so to do[2]. The essential feature justifying this lies in its being a calculated risk — was it an action which a reasonable man would have taken? The legal principle of necessity applies and, in concord with this, the permissive regulations specifically do not limit the criminal or civil liability of emergency driving. Acceptable risk taking can be distinguished from recklessness by the question — did the person foresee that his action might produce an adverse result and, if so, was it unreasonable for him to take the risk of producing it[3]? The social need to do so must also be considered in assessing the reasonableness of taking a risk. The courts do, however, appear to take a somewhat unsympathetic view of the overzealous rescuer[4].

See also: Informed consent; Necessity; Recklessness

1. *Sidaway v Bethlem Royal Hospital and Others* [1985] 2 **WLR** 480 HL.
2. Road Traffic Act 1972, s.22 qualified by Traffic Signs Regulations and General Directions 1981, r.34(1)(b) (SI 1981/859); Road Traffic Regulation Act 1984, s.87.
3. Law Commission *Criminal Law: Report on the Mental Element in Crime* (Law Com No.89) (1978) HMSO, London.
4. *Ward v London County Council* [1938] 2 All ER 341; *Wardell-Yerburgh v Surrey County Council* [1973] RTR 462; *Wood v Richards* [1977] RTR 201.

Road Traffic Accidents

There is a vast literature on the epidemiology and morbidity of road traffic accidents and only an outline will be attempted here.

It is a matter of observation that road travel is more dangerous in some countries than in others. So far as Europe is concerned, however, there does appear to be something of a log linear relationship between traffic density and deaths — the lower the density of vehicles related to the population, the higher is the death rate provoked by those vehicles[1]. If that is so, the UK has a rather better than average fatality rate on the roads, the number killed in Britain remaining remarkably constant at some 6,000–7,000 persons annually — or 12–14/100,000 population. At the same time, there has been a dramatic fall in the fatality rate as related to the vehicle density — the rate has dropped from 25 deaths/10,000 vehicles licensed 50 years ago to less than 4 deaths/10,000 vehicles today.

There is, however, little uniformity as to the pattern of road traffic accidents which can be looked at, *inter alia*, on a geographic basis — as anticipated, for example, pedestrian fatalities are the most serious problem in urban areas — or through a classification by users, or as related to the type of vehicle.

It is convenient to divide users into drivers, passengers and pedestrians; all have their separate problems. The driver's chest and upper abdomen are at particular risk from the steering wheel but, against this, he has the protective use of his hands and arms against same wheel. Steering wheels of collapsible type are being installed more often but, in general, injuries to the heart, aorta and liver are as commonly fatal in drivers as are head and neck injuries. The problems of passengers are discussed as a separate entry. The mechanism of fatal injury to those using front seats in cars is obvious but the campaign against the compulsory use of upper torso restraint still continues[2]. This is now concentrated on an apparent associated increase in the number of pedestrians killed and injured on the roads. Pedestrians, who form a wholly distinct class of road user, are considered in a separate entry; for the present, we would suggest that the depressing casualty rate amongst them is more likely to be due to the now almost universal disregard of speed limitations than to an improbable tendency to risk taking by seat belt users[3].

The type of vehicle and of the resultant accident is, again, a subject which includes a large number of variables. For example, the total number of kilometre-hours for the vehicle type must be taken into consideration; then, a somewhat surprising result is that a bus is 12 times more likely to injure a pedestrian than is a car[4]. Even so, it can be pointed out that a bus is more likely to come into contact with a bus queue and so the epidemiological arguments continue. The motor cycle, however, constitutes a unique type of vehicle in which the driver is exposed to high speed accidents with minimum protection. Motor cycle deaths are not decreasing and, despite the compulsory use of protective helmets, head injury constitutes the commonest cause of death amongst such road users; multiple injuries, particularly of the abdominal organs, are, however, very frequent. The peak of motor cycling injuries is very narrowly concentrated in the age group 17–20 years and, for obvious reasons, practical tuition in driving a motor cycle is difficult; several voluntary schemes for ensuring minimum instruction to first time purchasers have been introduced but none has been shown to be clearly successful. The Transport Act 1981, s.23, introduces far more stringent regulations as to the issue of provisional licences to drive motor cycles and, in particular, now defines a learner motor cycle, the most important item of the complex definition being that its engine capacity must not exceed 125 cc. The full effect of such regulations has yet to be assessed.

The association of alcohol with road traffic accidents is discussed under 'Alcohol' and 'Road Traffic Act 1972'; disease as a cause of accidents is considered under 'Trauma and disease'. Of other types of medical or toxicological causes of accident, carbon monoxide poisoning has to be considered but, with modern standards of vehicle maintenance, this should be significant very rarely and, then, probably only in a synergistic role. The contribution of medication to road traffic accidents is unclear; it is probably true to say that the use of any drug which induces behaviour change is to be deprecated in drivers but solid evidence as to widespread ill-effect is conflicting[5]. Certainly, the combination of alcohol, drugs and driving is one to be scrupulously avoided.

Although great publicity is given to road traffic fatalities, they should be looked at in proportion. As many people die from accidents in the home as die on the roads; nearly half as many children are killed as a result of child abuse; and certainly more than half as many children die from the sudden infant death syndrome. The major significance of road traffic deaths lies in the age and sex group most commonly affected; not only is the man aged 20–35 at maximum economic value to the community, he also belongs to the group most likely to have relatively helpless dependants.

It is to be noted that a proportion of the cost of medical treatment resulting from road traffic accidents is borne by the insurers rather than wholly by the NHS[6].

See also: Alcohol; Passengers in vehicles; Pedestrian casualties; Protective helmets; Road Traffic Act 1972; Seat belts; Trauma and disease

1. Mason JK 'Accidents and travel' in Royal Society of Edinburgh *Travel: Disease and other hazards* (1982) p.63, RSE, Edinburgh.
2. *See*, for example, Wardroper J 'How seat belts are killers' (1985) *Sunday Times*, 12 May.
3. Mackay M 'Seat belts and risk compensation' (1985) 291 Br Med J 757.
4. Ashton SJ and Mackay GM 'Pedestrian injuries and deaths' in Mason JK (ed) *The Pathology of Violent Injury* (1978) Chap.3, Edward Arnold, London.
5. For example, Betts TH et al 'Effects of four commonly-used tranquillizers on low speed driving performance tests' [1972] 4 Br Med J 580; Special Correspondent 'Road accidents: are drugs other than alcohol a hazard?' [1978] 2 Br Med J 1415; Skegg DCG et al 'Minor tranquillisers and road accidents' [1979] 1 Br Med J 917.
6. Road Traffic Act 1972, ss.154, 155.

Road Traffic Act 1972

Only Part I of this large Act is relevant in the medico-legal context and this note can deal only with certain sections which are of particular significance.

Section 1 defines the offence of causing death by reckless driving[1] and s.2 deals with the general offence of driving recklessly. The concept of reckless driving is sufficiently important to be considered separately (*see* 'Reckless driving').

Sections 5–12[2] are of wide significance in the medico-legal field. Section 5 defines the offence of driving or attempting to drive a motor vehicle on a road or other public place while unfit to drive through drink or drugs. Unfitness to drive can be assessed only through a medical examination, which is a notoriously capricious measure of fitness; in practice, therefore, charges are laid under s.5 only very rarely other than in respect of drugs. Offences concerned with drink are normally charged under s.6(1) which defines the offence of driving or attempting to drive after consuming so much alcohol that the proportion of it in the breath, blood or urine exceeds the prescribed limits. The current prescribed limits are 35 μg alcohol/100 ml breath; 80 mg alcohol/100 ml blood; and 107 mg alcohol/100 ml urine (s.12(2)). The offence relates to the body substance tested — extrapolation from one to the other is not allowed[3].

The provisions of s.8 are to the effect that analysis of the breath is the definitive test, when two specimens will be required and only the lower reading used. A requirement to provide a specimen of blood or urine can be made only at a police station or a hospital and then only if the constable has reasonable cause to believe that, for medical reasons, a specimen of breath cannot be provided or should not be required, or no suitable breathalyser is available, or it is suspected that the condition of the driver is due to some drug. Somewhat surprisingly, in the absence of a clear medical reason, it is left to the constable to decide between a specimen of blood or of urine. In the event that the breath specimen gives a result showing an alcohol content of no more than 50 μg/100 ml, the driver may claim that it be replaced by a specimen of blood or urine. Failure without reasonable excuse to provide a specimen carries the same penalty as having an excess of alcohol and, in general, the courts have been extremely reluctant to accept excuses as reasonable[4].

The original arrest under s.6(1) is made on the basis of a screening breath test which may be required if a constable in uniform has reasonable cause to suspect that a person is or has been driving or attempting to drive with alcohol in his body or if he has committed a moving traffic offence; a requirement may also be made if an accident has occurred. The constable may arrest without warrant if the test indicates that the breath alcohol is above the prescribed limit or if the driver refuses to provide a specimen. A constable may enter, if need be by force, any place where the driver is or is expected to be in order to require such a specimen when an accident has resulted in injury (s.7(6))[5]; this power specifically does not extend to Scotland[6]. Specimens may only be taken in a hospital if the medical officer in immediate charge of the case has been notified of the proposal; the medical officer may then object on the grounds that the requirement or the provision of the specimen, or the warning associated with a refusal to provide a specimen, would be prejudicial to the proper care and treatment of the patient (s.9).

Section 10 provides a specific defence to the effect that the assumption that the proportion of alcohol in the accused's breath, blood or urine at the time of the alleged offence was not less than that in the specimen provided shall not be made if the accused proves that he consumed alcohol after he had ceased to drive and before he provided the specimen and that, had he not done so, the proportion of alcohol in the specimen would not have exceeded the prescribed limit[7]. This closes a loophole in the law whereby, as a result of *Rowlands v Hamilton*[8], the consumption of *any* alcohol after the accident was sufficient to invalidate the certificate. In face of the many variables inherent in a biological situation, the provision of accurate evidence on which to discharge the second limb of the s.10 defence is difficult. Nevertheless, the fact that it is so stated in the statute must mean that Parliament intended such a defence to be possible; a reasonable approach is to use the theoretical tables provided by the British Medical Association in 1960[9] while allowing for, and admitting, the possible pitfalls.

Conviction under s.5(1) and s.6(1) of the Act carries with it mandatory disqualification from driving. This may be draconian in its effect and it is not surprising that a large number of technical defences have been set up and, in many cases, accepted. The great majority of these are made irrelevant by the Transport Act 1981 but there is no doubt that a similar situation will evolve in respect of breathalysers. Drivers may, in the process of pleading guilty, put forward special reasons why they should not be disqualified — very often the reasons involve unexpected 'lacing' of drinks. In these circumstances, the onus is on the defendant to produce admissible and relevant evidence; scientific evidence on the lines of the s.10 defence need not always be called but will be needed if the cause and effect position is not obvious to the layman[10]. The courts are increasingly inclined to regard the 'lacer' of drinks as procuring an offence under s.6(1)[11].

See also: Alcohol; Breathalysers; Reckless driving; Recklessness; Road traffic accidents

1. As amended by the Criminal Law Act 1977, s.50.
2. As amended by the Transport Act 1981, s.25 and Sch.8.
3. *McGarry v Chief Constable of Bedfordshire* [1983] RTR 172.
4. Although juries are entitled to conclude that a man has an invincible repugnance to the use of the needle (*Alcock v Read* [1980] RTR 71). *See also* the unusual case of 'emotional shock': *Spalding v Laskaraina Paine* (1985) Times, 21 May.
5. But *only* if injury has occurred (*Fox v Gwent Chief Constable* [1985] 1 WLR 33, DC; (1985) Times, 18 October, HL).
6. Where the right to privacy presumably still exists by virtue of *Morris v Beardmore* [1980] 2 All ER 753 confirmed in *Finnigan v Sandiford, Clowser v Chaplin* [1981] 2 All ER 267.
7. This has always been the law in Scotland (*Wood v Brown* 1969 SLT 297 strengthened in *Campbell v Mackenzie* 1981 SCCR 341).
8. [1971] 1 WLR 647.
9. *See* Mason JK 'The Section 10 defence to charges of driving with excess alcohol' (1984) 128 SJ 539. The use of the tables has been given judicial approval (*R v Somers* [1963] 3 All ER 808).
10. *Pugsley v Hunter* [1973] RTR 284.
11. For a review, *see* Medicolegal 'Impaired driving: responsibility from a distance' (1984) 289 Br Med J 1606.

Royal Medical Colleges

The Royal Medical Colleges are corporations which are, in the main, designed to secure the standards of competence of those holding themselves to have a particular expertise in the various branches of medical practice. By and large, this is achieved through a strict system of qualifying examinations[1] although the Colleges also undertake a vigorous programme of continuing education.

With the exception of the Royal Colleges of Surgeons, the Colleges offer membership to those candidates who have satisfied the examiners; fellowship is then granted following a successful period of specialist practice — the exception being that the Colleges of Surgeons offer fellowship by examination without the need for intervening membership. There is nothing to prevent a university graduate (or a licentiate of the Royal Colleges or of the Society of Apothecaries) practising any branch of medicine or surgery he wishes — the standards set legally will be those of the ordinary competent person professing to have a particular skill. Membership of a Royal College shows, however, that the practitioner has a special interest and, therefore, a special knowledge in a more limited field; it places him in a peer category within the profession and, at the same time, provides the courts with a measure of the expertise of a witness. It needs to be stressed, however, that the courts can take equal notice of experience, publications and the like when assessing the competence of a witness.

The Royal Colleges have no disciplinary powers over their members and fellows but they contribute a substantial number of members appointed to the General Medical Council.

At the time of writing, there are Royal Colleges of Physicians (of London and of Edinburgh), Surgeons (of England and of Edinburgh), Obstetricians and Gynaecologists, Pathologists, Psychiatrists, Radiologists and General Practitioners. There is a Royal College of Physicians and Surgeons of Glasgow and the Colleges incorporate Faculties of Occupational and Community Medicine and of Anaesthetics. In appropriate cases (e.g. surgery and pathology) membership and/or fellowship is extended to dental practitioners.

As part of the continuing process of education, the Royal Colleges, either individually or in collaboration, offer diplomas in a large number of subspecialties (e.g. child health or tropical medicine); in many cases, these are 'stepping stones' to membership, the examination for which may have a special orientation.

See also: Discipline in the medical profession; General Medical Council

1. In certain circumstances, the Colleges will confer membership or fellowship without examination on practitioners of outstanding academic merit.

S

Sadomasochism

The sadist obtains psychological and sexual gratification from the infliction of pain upon others. Sadistic conduct is, of course, possible in the non-sexual sphere[1] but it is sexually motivated sadistic violence which is likely to be of medico-legal interest.

The application of minor violence in a sexual context may fall well within the bounds of what is considered normal; moderate spanking (known in North America as 'paddling') may raise no eyebrows. The sadist, however, goes further and gains pleasure from causing considerable pain in his partner. The use of whips and other instruments is common and these may cause significant injury to the victim.

Sadistic activity may involve a willing partner and, in such cases, the only legal consideration will be the extent to which consent can be given to self-injury[2]; there must be limits beyond which the defence of consent will not be available (see 'Consent to injury').

Sadistic attacks on non-consenting victims are relatively common and may be performed in the context of another crime such as burglary. Sadistic homicides are particularly distressing as the victim may be subjected to torture or to mutilation either before or after death. Such crimes are most frequently performed by men against women and the sexual element may be particularly underlined by the mode of killing which may involve violence to the genitalia. Child murder may be sadistic, a notorious instance being the so-called Moors Murders.

Masochism is the mirror-image of sadism, sexual pleasure being derived from submission to violence or general domination[3]. Some women crave such domination from men and may, as a consequence, be at some risk from the overenthusiasm of the sadist; the majority of serious end-results, and of death in particular, of heterosexual masochism derive from mistake rather than intention. Perhaps the most common masochist is the middle-aged man who is forced to seek a professional female partner; death in such circumstances is intrinsically unlikely to be homicidal although a strong possibility of sudden natural death is often present. Serious sadomasochism is, however, a frequent concomitant of male homosexual activity; the brutal pattern of a homicide is often an indication of such a basis.

See also: Child murder; Homosexuality; Patterns of injury

1. For a discussion of the sadistic personality, *see* Fromm E *The Fear of Freedom* (1960) p.121 et seq, Ark, London.
2. Leith LH 'Sado-masochism, consent and the reform of the criminal law' (1976) 39 MLR 130; *R v Donovan* [1934] 2 KB 498.
3. TE Lawrence ('Lawrence of Arabia') was a well-known sufferer from masochistic perversions. For an analysis, *see* Meyers J *The Wounded Spirit* (1973) p.114 et seq, Martin Brian & O'Keeffe, London.

Safety Equipment

Accidents account for some 5 per cent of all deaths in the UK and for a serious morbidity and strain on the health care provisions; nearly four times as many industrial working days are lost each year as a result of accidents as derive from industrial disputes. The provison of safety equipment in an attempt to stem the tide is an integral part of industrial, transportation and sports medicine. Some specific aspects of safety equipment are described elsewhere (*see*, for example, 'Protective helmets' and 'Seat belts'); this note attempts no more than generalisations.

It is sometimes not appreciated that the provision of safety equipment always involves some form of compromise. For example, the provision of head rests in cars undoubtedly protects against whiplash injury but, at the same time, general visibility is reduced; or, the use of ear muffs may be considered essential for those working in aviation to protect the ears but this is done at the expense of a loss of sensitivity to other warning signals. Safety design essentially consists of identifying the major hazard, deciding how to protect against it and then balancing the likely advantage gained against potential disadvantages introduced. The safety picture must always be seen as a whole; advocacy and acceptance of the introduction or modification of individual items of equipment in isolation are likely to have unhappy results. It is also important to emphasise that safety equipment does not stop accidents; its function is to transform fatal accidents into those which are non-fatal — e.g. the trapeze artist's safety net — or to eliminate injury in non-fatal conditions — the rationale of, say, the industrial eye-shield.

The pathologist has much more to do than establish the cause of death if safety equipment fails with a fatal result — he has a major role to play in preventive medicine. Thus, if a preventable injury is discovered at postmortem and safety equipment was not provided, he must attempt to assess whether such provision would affect the outcome in future similar cases or if it would have done so in the instant case — indeed, this latter is now a legal need[1]. If the equipment was provided and used and has failed in its purpose, he should seek to assess whether it was properly used, whether it was quite inadequate or whether it required modification; he must also consider whether the equipment positively contributed to the death. Such an exercise can be most rewarding professionally in addition to providing important information for employers, insurers and the estates of the deceased.

The use of safety equipment in industry is a matter for discussion at the safety committees established under the Health and Safety at Work etc. Act 1974[2]; codes of conduct or practice are provided for many industrial undertakings. Occasionally, there is a statutory duty on workers to take or use precautions[3] but the general rule is that an insured worker will not be deprived of industrial benefit because of failure to use the equipment provided. An employer is, however, entitled to protect himself against actions in negligence and can properly refuse to employ a person who would not conform to the standards of practice[4]; the courts may, in certain circumstances, decide that no distinction can be made between the doctrine of *volenti non fit injuria* and 100 per cent negligence[5].

See also: Health and Safety at Work etc. Act 1974; Industrial injury; Protective helmets; Road traffic accidents; Seat belts; *Volenti non fit injuria*

1. *Patience v Andrews* (1982) Times, 22 November.
2. Safety Representatives and Safety Committees Regulations 1977 (SI 1977/500).
3. *See*, for example, *McMullen v National Coal Board* [1982] ICR 148.
4. *Singh v British Rail Engineering* (1985) Times, 6 August.
5. *Imperial Chemical Industries v Shatwell* [1965] AC 656.

Safety of Sports Grounds

Sports grounds become more dangerous for spectators as the size of crowds enlarges and the increasingly competitive atmosphere melds with the general aggressiveness of modern society. There are, thus, two outstanding dangers — those of overcrowding in general and of mob violence.

Overcrowding is unlikely to be a serious hazard in open air conditions (*see* 'Environmental asphyxia') unless there is some superadded event causing panic. Then, should the overcrowding suddenly become insufferable, as when concentrated in the exits, crushing will occur and death may result either from crush asphyxia or from trampling. A serious example of this phenomenon in the UK occurred at Ibrox Park in 1971 when the problem was not so much to get out of the stadium as to return to it when the game appeared to be improving in quality; heavy damages were awarded to the families of those killed. The horror of the situation will escalate if the mass exodus is impelled by a further lethal hazard of which fire is the most likely example; 56 persons died from this cause at Bradford in 1985.

These dangers have, to some extent, been met by the Safety of Sports Grounds Act 1975 which requires safety certificates for stadia capable of accommodating more than 10,000 persons. The granting of such certificates depends upon regulated admission and the provision of adequate entrances, exits and crush barriers, these being established through consultation between the local authority and the police, fire and community health officers. Improved standards, however, take time and money to effect; regulations had not extended to stadia such as that of Bradford at the time of the disaster.

Mob violence depends upon many factors including the quality of the crowd itself — there is surprisingly little violence at rugby union stadia such as Twickenham despite the fact that alcohol is freely available. Nevertheless, alcohol and the carrying of offensive weapons are probably the most significant determinants of sports hooliganism. The situation was first addressed in Scotland[1] where the prohibition of alcohol at specified sports grounds and increased powers of police search and confiscation have gone some way to ameliorating conditions. Injuries discovered are likely to be those due to kicking, bottles and knives, but, occasionally, bizarre conditions may lead to panic and to crushing effects as described above. Prevention is largely a matter of good policing, the ultimate responsibility for which may be at high level; it is extraordinary to record the collapse of the Belgian Government purely as a result of a disaster due to mob violence at an international football match in Brussels in 1985. The British Government, possibly stimulated by a reluctance to be deposed in similar unusual circumstances, has accelerated legislation to control the sale or possession of alcohol at designated sports grounds and sporting events[2]; designation will be by order made by the Secretary of State, which suggests that many sporting authorities may take voluntary steps to avoid being so branded.

Apart from these special conditions related to major episodes, the owner of a sports stadium is liable to the spectators in tort and is statutorily responsible for their safety under the Occupier's Liability Act 1957, s.2 and 1984, s.1. The occupier must take care to protect spectators from foreseeable risks which good practice suggests should be provided for[3] but the spectator goes to the event aware of some risk — the principle of *volenti non fit injuria* applies[4].

See also: Alcohol; Crush injury; Environmental asphyxia; *Volenti non fit injuria*

1. Criminal Justice (Scotland) Act 1980, Part V.
2. Sporting Events (Control of Alcohol etc.) Act 1985.
3. *Latchworth v Spedeworth International* (1983) Times, 11 October; *Wilks v Cheltenham Home Guard Motor Cycle Club* [1971] 1 WLR 668.
4. *Wooldridge v Sumner* [1963] 2 QB 43.

Saliva Testing

Saliva testing is of particular medico-legal importance in the examination of bite marks but may also be needed in the investigation of sexual assaults in general. Saliva may also be identified on stamps, envelopes, cigarette ends and the like although these are applications more in the field of forensic science than forensic medicine.

A stain or fluid may be identified as being salival from its amylase content. Personalised identification depends on the fact that A, B and H substances are secreted in high concentration in the saliva. The capacity to secrete depends upon the possession of the secretor gene (Se) which is a property of some 75 per cent of the population. It is of some interest that no persons of the Lewis blood group Le a+b− possess the Se gene; the presence of the Lewis antigen, which is also secreted in the body fluids, may therefore be a useful check on the absence of ABH substances. All secretors secrete H substance but this is in maximal concentration in persons of blood group O. Those of blood group A secrete mainly A substance and those of group B secrete B substance. A, B and H substances can normally be demonstrated by relatively simple techniques; the practical aspects are discussed under 'Bite marks'. Spurious findings do, however, occur, especially as regards saliva, and these must not be ignored[1].

The specific group substances are destroyed by enzymes present in the saliva. Thus, all specimens of saliva must be boiled before being transmitted to the laboratory; false negative results for secretion may be obtained if this precaution is omitted.

See also: Bite marks; Blood groups

1. Pereira M and Martin PD 'Problems involved in the grouping of saliva, semen and other body fluids' (1976) 16 J Forens Sci Soc 151.

Sanctity of Human Life

On an extreme view, human life is sacrosanct and must on no account be destroyed; the even more rigid interpretation is that every effort must be made to preserve it. The general principle of the sanctity of human life is widely and properly held — murder is the only crime for which life imprisonment is mandatory — but there are exceptions on every hand. The State has no qualms in demitting the principle in time of war and acknowledges the right to self-destruction in the Suicide Act 1961. Both legislators and the medical profession combine to condone 170,000 abortions annually in Great Britain, an attitude which contrasts curiously with the insistent pressure of the former for recognition of the sanctity of the *in vitro* human embryo[1]. The courts have shown themselves particularly sympathetic to relaxing the rule in a medical context — the jury in *R v Arthur* were advised to 'think long and hard before concluding that eminent doctors have evolved standards that amount to committing a crime'[2].

It is, indeed, in medical practice that the doctrine is of greatest general significance, particularly in relation to the preservation of life, and few would now regard a rigid imposition of a sanctity of life ethos as being tenable in that area. The move is strongly towards an appreciation of the quality of life and the current position is discussed more fully under that heading.

It might be supposed that the Roman Catholic Church would be the bastion of the sanctity of human life, yet the medical need for dispensation was clearly set out by Pope Pius XII in his exposition of the ordinary/extraordinary treatment test; the validity of the pronouncement has been confirmed recently by the Catholic hierarchy[3]. It is to be noted, however, that whilst this path would be followed by the Church of England[4], the attitude of the orthodox Jewish faith is far more inclined to an absolute view of the sanctity of human life[5].

See also: Abortion; Embryonic experimentation; Neonaticide; Ordinary/ Extraordinary treatment; Quality of life

1. The Unborn Children (Protection) Bill 1984 was defeated only by way of a procedural ruse.
2. *See* Palmer H 'Dr Adams' trial for murder' [1957] Crim LR 369; *R v Arthur* (1981) *The Times*, 6 November, pp.1, 12.
3. Sacred Congregation for the Doctrine of the Faith *Declaration on Euthanasia* (1980).
4. Coggan D 'On dying and dying well' (1977) 70 Proc R Soc Med 75.
5. Jakobovits I 'Jewish medical ethics — a brief overview' (1983) 9 J Med Ethics 109.

Scalds

A scald is a burn due to hot fluid. It has precisely the same effects as a burn although scalds involving deep tissues are extremely unlikely.

Scalding is almost invariably accidental and is not uncommon in industry, particularly as a result of exposure to the vapour of boiling fluids. It is most often seen in everyday practice in children, largely due to curiosity in the kitchen; scalds from fat may be especially severe as the liquid is very hot and clings to the skin.

Perhaps the main, although still uncommon, exception to accidental causation lies in the field of child abuse; dipping a child in hot water is a well known variant of this offence.

See also: Burns; Child abuse

Scars

The natural process of wound healing involves the formation of vascular granulation tissue, the invasion of this by collagen and its ultimate transformation into fibrous tissue or a scar (cicatrix). In general, the cleaner the wound and the less haemorrhage present, the less will be the scarring — a principle which is particularly observed in the practice of plastic surgery.

Early scars are pink due to contained blood vessels but are later quite avascular and white. They do not grow with the body and therefore tend to disappear with age. Scar tissue contracts in its terminal development; thus, disability due to contracture around joints may be added to the basic disfigurement of a skin scar. Internal scarring and contraction may result in restriction of a hollow viscus (e.g. the bowel) whilst the formation of fibrous bands may have much the same effect due to compression of the viscus. Excessive or hypertrophic scarring may occur, particularly following burns; keloid is a particular form of scar which, although uncommon, occurs in susceptible individuals and which is progressive and extremely resistant to treatment. Scar tissue which forms in muscle is likely to be weaker than the original structure; thus, for example, rupture of a scarred area is a frequent complication of a healed myocardial infarction. Malignant tumours may form in scar tissue and a causative link is generally acceptable[1].

Scars are widely used in identification procedures but allowance must be made for changes in appearance if description and inspection are separated by a long time interval. Occasionally, skin folds may appear to be scars but the pathologist can distinguish the two at postmortem by the absence of elastic tissue in the cicatrix.

See also: Burns; Identification of the dead; Infarction; Wounds

1. *Barty-King and another v Ministry of Defence* [1979] 2 All ER 80.

Schizophrenia

Schizophrenia is a form of affective psyhosis which is characterised by a disorder of thinking manifested by distorted perception; the mind of the schizophrenic is dominated by hallucinations, illusions and delusions.

The disease usually begins to show itself around the age of 20 years and its cause is unknown. There is some evidence of an underlying biochemical disorder in cerebral metabolism but, at the same time, a genetic association cannot be excluded; it is probably safest to regard schizophrenia as an example of multifactorial genetic disease. Indeed, it may well be that there are a number of conditions which have the same presenting signs of mental illness.

These signs are referable to abnormal thinking — the schizophrenic may have great difficulty in self-expression, he may suddenly attack another person for no reason and this may stem from an immutable sense of grievance, the so-called paranoid schizophrenic. He may therefore be a dangerous person who can be impelled to violent acts by hallucinatory instructions; on the other hand, the paranoid schizophrenic may be capable of leading an apparently normal life and of deep meditation in planning retaliation on those who are his supposed enemies[1]. Somewhat contrary to previous findings, recent work has indicated a very definite excess of schizophrenics who have been violent towards others; although much of the violence was of minor type, schizophrenics made up 11 per cent of a group of men convicted of homicide[2]. The classic, and somewhat unique, homicidal crimes associated with schizophrenia are those of matricide and uxoricide (*see* 'Othello syndrome').

Otherwise, the schizophrenic is likely to commit petty crimes with some persistency; the propensity results largely from his unemployability and the need to exist[3].

See also: Delusions; Genetic disease; Hallucinations; Illusions; Matricide; Othello syndrome; Paranoia; Psychoses

1. For all the result of the trial in *R v Sutcliffe*, it would seem that the accused showed considerable evidence of schizophrenia. *See* an interesting appraisal in Prins HA 'diminished responsibility and the Sutcliffe case: legal, psychiatric and social aspects (a "layman's" view)' (1983) 23 Med Sci Law 17.
2. Taylor PJ and Gunn J 'Violence and psychosis. I — Risk of violence among psychotic men' (1984) 288 Br Med J 1945.
3. Mackay RD and Wight RE 'Schizophrenia and anti-social (criminal) behaviour — some responses from sufferers and relatives' (1984) 24 Med Sci Law 192.

Seat Belts

The wearing of restraining belts — either in the form of lap belts alone or including upper torso restraint — in the front seats of motor vehicles has been compulsory in many countries for some time; it is now also required in the UK[1]. The regulations[2] state that the belts must include torso restraint but they do not apply to children under the age of 14 years. The latter may not now be carried in the front of a vehicle unless wearing a seat belt in conformity with special regulations[3]. The regulations are also inapplicable to any person holding a valid certificate signed by a medical practitioner to the effect that it is undesirable on medical grounds for that person to wear a seat belt (s.33A(2)(b)(iii)).

The importance of seat belts was recognised before the statute in *Froom v Butcher*[4] which finally established that failure to wear a seat belt amounted to contributory negligence in personal injury cases. The importance of the medical evidence in each particular case was emphasised in *Owens v Brimmell*[5]. The reduction in compensation under this heading has increased to 25 per cent and it is not open to the court to reduce that percentage by speculating upon what other injuries the plaintiff might have suffered if he had been wearing a seat belt[6].

Lord Denning MR indicated in *Froom* that a pregnant woman might provide an exception to the rule but there is no country in which pregnancy is an automatic ground for exemption from the seat belt laws[7]. Most medical opinion would agree that the chances of death of a mother who is not wearing a belt are greater than those of death or injury to the fetus by virtue of being restrained; the problem is of considerable interest in relation to the Congenital Disabilities (Civil Liability) Act 1976, s.2, which specifies driving a motor vehicle as the only circumstance from which a child injured *in utero* can sue its mother; but the matter has not, to date, been decided in the courts. There are, in fact, very few proven indications for exemption from the regulations on medical grounds, the general opinion being that any indications which could be cited would simultaneously indicate unfitness to drive; a passenger genuinely unable to wear a belt should be restricted to the rear seat of a vehicle.

Prior to the UK regulations, which became law in 1983, there was abundant evidence from elsewhere that the compulsory use of seat belts significantly reduced both morbidity and mortality in vehicular accidents[8], and a similar pattern is already evident in the UK[9]. Occasional criticisms based on the occurrence of 'seat belt injuries' fail to take account of the fact that the alternative to such surgically treatable injuries is death; death from burning of an entrapped person is very rare on the roads where immediate assistance is almost always available. Opposition is also based on the premise that drivers who are belted-in take more risks and that this is at the expense of pedestrians; there is little informed medical support for this view[10]. The regulations under the 1981 Act are due to be reviewed in 1986, when the medical evidence in their favour is almost certain to overcome the contrary libertarian arguments; the further likelihood is that the regulations will be extended to include rear seat passengers.

Full harness restraint has been compulsorily fitted to the seats of pilots of commercial aircraft for many years. Torso restraint is now obligatory for pilots and front seat passengers in light aircraft[11]. Failure to supply torso restraint for passengers in commercial transport aircraft derives, primarily, from the virtual impossibility of fitment. The alternative use of lap belt restraint is justified by the fact that torso flailing during deceleration will be accompanied by collapse of the seat back in front of the passenger; the combination of high decelerative loads and simple lap belt restraint is, however, likely to produce treatable seat belt injuries.

See also: Aircraft accidents; Fetal rights; Road traffic accidents

1. Road Traffic Act 1972, s.33A as amended by Transport Act 1981, s.27. The regulations extend to Northern Ireland by virtue of s.41(3) of the 1981 Act.
2. Motor Vehicles (Construction and Use) (Amendment) (No.3) Regulations 1979, SI 1979/1062; Motor Vehicles (Wearing of Seat Belts) Regulations 1982, SI 1982/1203.
3. Road Traffic Act 1972, s.33B as amended; Motor Vehicles (Wearing of Seat Belts by Children) Regulations 1982, SI 1982/1342.
4. [1976] QB 286.
5. [1976] 3 All ER 765.
6. *Patience v Andrews* (1982) Times, 22 November per Croom-Johnson J; *See also Salmon v Newland and others* (1983) Times, 16 May.

7. Christian MS 'Exemption from compulsory wearing of seat belts — medical implications' [1979] 1 Br Med J 1411.

8. *See*, for example, McDermott FT and Hough DE 'Reduction in road fatalities and injuries after legislation for compulsory wearing of seat belts: experience in Victoria and the rest of Australia' (1979) 66 Br J Surg 518.

9. Pye G and Waters EA 'Effect of seat belt legislation on injuries in road traffic accidents in Nottingham' (1984) 288 Br Med J 756.

10. Mackay M 'Seat belts and risk compensation' (1985) 291 Br Med J 757.

11. Air Navigation Order 1980, SI 1980/1965, art.32 and Sch.5.

Self-defence

Self-defence, or private defence, which includes the protection of others, is a full defence in criminal law, conceptually related to that of necessity. The basis is that a person is entitled to use force to protect his person against unjustified force. The wrongful act of striking an attacker is justified by the necessity of self-preservation.

This proposition is subject to important limits. The use of force must be the only acceptable course open to the defendant; the option of disengagement is to be preferred, although the law will not always require the attacked party to take to his heels in flight[1]. It is also essential that the defendant should have reacted in a way which is proportional to the threat; it is inappropriate to resort to a lethal weapon in the face of a threat of mild physical violence. The test in each case is one of reasonableness: was the response a reasonable one in the circumstances[2]? It might be difficult for a court to regard the response as reasonable when the result is the death of an unarmed attacker. To deal with this sort of situation, the Australian courts have developed a doctrine of excessive self-defence, the operation of which has served to reduce to manslaughter what would otherwise be murder[3].

Pre-emptive action may come within the scope of the defence but it is not enough for a defendant to have felt that there was some possibility of an attack in the future; the attack must be imminent and unavoidable before a man will be entitled to defend himself in this way[4].

See also: Necessity; Reasonable force; Reasonable man

1. *R v Julien* [1969] 2 All ER 856; *R v McInnes* [1971] 3 All ER 295.

2. *See*, however, *James Russell Shannon* (1980) 71 Crim App R 192.

3. *R v Howe* (1958) 100 CLR 448.

4. A liberal view of pre-emptive action was taken in *Attorney General for Northern Ireland's Reference* [1977] AC 105.

Seminal Stains

Seminal stains fluoresce in ultraviolet light but this method of identification is non-specific and is vitiated by the widespread use of modern detergents which also fluoresce. Currently, the most sensitive and specific general test for semen is that for the presence of acid phosphatase which is very concentrated in the prostatic fluid[1]. The test sometimes give false positive results; its specificity and sensitivity are discussed in greater detail under 'Phosphatase, acid'.

Demonstrable spermatozoa, which constitute the ultimate finding for positive identification of semen, may be found in the fabric several months after deposition, particularly if the stain has dried rapidly. They may be visible directly under the microscope, especially when using polarised light. Alternatively, they may be soaked from the material or dislodged by ultrasound treatment and subsequently stained. Old stains are unlikely to yield complete forms, the general finding being of heads shorn of their tails. The normal human spermatozoal head measures some 4 μm in diameter; in the absence of tails, it is essential to demonstrate typical bipolar staining in order to distinguish the spermatazoon from a degenerating pus cell (*see* 'Spermatozoa').

Human semen contains large amounts of A, B or H substances in those who are secretors (*see* 'Saliva testing') and this property can be used towards personal identification of the donor. However, since only the ABO blood group system can be tested, it is likely that a given specimen will be identified no more accurately than to the extent that it could have been donated by approximately 40 per cent of the male population — as a consequence, the findings have greatest usefulness in excluding a suspect. Vaginal secretions also contain group-specific substances and it must be appreciated that stains resulting from sexual intercourse, particularly those on the garments of women, are likely to contain a mixture of both semen and vaginal fluid. It will be possible to distinguish serologically between the two only in exceptional circumstances. Failure to make this clear has been regarded as a reason for discrediting scientific evidence in a criminal trial[2].

See also: Blood groups; Parentage testing; Phosphatase, acid; Saliva testing; Spermatozoa

1. For a full appraisal, *see* Kind SS 'The acid phosphatase test' in Curry AS (ed) *Methods of Forensic Science* (1964) Vol.3, p.267, Interscience, New York and London.
2. *Preece v HM Adv* [1981] Crim LR 783.

Senility

The capacity of the tissues of the body to replace themselves and to resist the secondary effects of degenerative change is not unlimited and varies from tissue to tissue; for example, no regeneration of brain cells is possible whilst the capacity of, say, the cartilage of the joints to repair the effects of constant use depends very much on the loads to which the individual joints are subjected. At the same time, the enzymatic systems which constitute the body's 'engine' wear out with time.

Senility can be regarded as the state reached when the ageing process becomes detrimental and clinically obvious. As might be expected, it is commonly most evident in the brain and presents as dementia, but enzymatic exhaustion manifests itself more subtly and the resultant state of hypothermia often goes unnoticed. Ultimately, the heart will succumb to 'fair wear and tear' and the old person passes quietly from stupor, to coma, to death — indeed, the distinction may often be a difficult clinical decision.

In such circumstances, it is perfectly proper to ascribe death to senility and this is often a far more honest form of certification than is the invention of a hypothetical pulmonary infection or myocardial ischaemia. Nevertheless, it will be seen that neglect is often little other than accelerated senility and, for this reason, many registrars tend to set an age limit below which they will not accept senility as a cause of death. A number of geriatric deaths are referred to the medico-legal authority in this way and, often, postmortem examination serves to improve the accuracy of the mortality statistics.

See also: Death certification; Dementia; Hypothermia

Separate Existence

Separate existence is a legal concept which is designed to establish the point at which a fetus, whose legal rights are extremely limited, becomes a human being and, therefore, entitled to the full protection of the law. Two criteria must be met before a separate existence is established. Firstly, the fetus must have completely proceeded in a living state from the body of the mother and, secondly, it must have breathed or shown some other sign of life — in the absence of which it is either a miscarriage or, if it has achieved a gestational age of 28 weeks, a stillbirth. It is to be noted that severance of the umbilical cord is not a prerequisite of a separate existence.

Glanville Williams holds that the test of whether a fetus is born alive lies in the functioning of the heart[1]. This conclusion is difficult to accept in view of the specific reference to breathing in the definition of stillbirth. Moreover, reliance on the heart beat would pose an almost insoluble problem for the pathologist in attempting to distinguish between a stillbirth and an early death. Every fetus of some 18 weeks' gestation or more will demonstrate some form of life so long as the placental connection — and, hence, oxygenation of the tissues — is maintained[2]; a confident distinction could, in fact, be made only if the fetus was macerated and, in practice, it is necessary to concentrate on the respiratory system. Fetal lungs which have not respired are relatively solid, dark red in colour and do not fill the chest; normal infant lungs are pink, expanded and crepitant to the touch. Theoretically, lungs containing air should float whilst those which have not been filled will sink; this is the basis of the widely criticised hydrostatic test. The appearances at each end of the spectrum can generally be interpreted with assurance but intermediate cases may be very difficult to decide — the infant can, for example, breathe in the genital tract of the mother, anoxic convulsions may direct air into the respiratory passages and, in any case, the aeration of the lungs can be patchy. Microscopic examination is essential in cases of uncertainty and particularly serves to distinguish putrefactive gas formation from aeration[3]. Air discovered in the stomach may, again, be the result of convulsive movements and is of no diagnostic significance. Other oft-quoted signs of a separate existence include inflammatory changes in the umbilical cord and the presence of food in the stomach but these are signs of long-term survival and are useful only when putrefaction inhibits the use of more sophisticated methods.

It is for the prosecution to prove the fact of a separate existence in relation to the offence of infanticide.

See also: Child destruction; Hydrostatic test; Infanticide; Live birth; Maceration; Stillbirth; Viability

1. Williams G *Textbook of Criminal Law* (2nd ed, 1983) p.290, Stevens, London.

2. A point noted by the Brodrick Committee — *Report of the Committee on Death Certification and Coroners* (Cmnd 4810) (1971), para.8.10, HMSO, London.
3. Osborn GR 'Pathology of the lung in stillbirth and neonatal death', in Simpson K (ed) *Modern Trends in Forensic Medicine* (1953) (Butterworths, London) is an old but still classic exposition of the subject.

Sex

The law is largely indifferent to sex[1]. There are, however, certain situations in which it may be important — these include matrimony, some aspects of sexual offences and the quasi-legal situation of competitive sport. There are four criteria to be considered in cases of doubt — the chromosomal makeup of the individual, the gonadal complement, the genital appearances and the social role accepted.

The infant's sex is registered at birth and this cannot be altered unless a mistake has been made[2]; a mistake does not include later anatomical changes even if these are natural[3]. There is abundant case law to support the inference that the chromosomal configuration is fundamental to the legal definition of sex as it applies to marriage[4] or to sexual offences which are grounded in the sex of the perpetrator[5]. Whilst it is true that the presence of the Y chromosome indicates maleness, it is equally true that abnormalities of chromosomal differentiation may cause considerable difficulties and these are discussed under 'Sex chromosomes'. Moreover, endocrine disturbances, distinct from the genetic bases, may cause very great problems of intersex.

In such instances, the diagnosis at birth will have been made on the apparent genital sex — e.g. an extreme case of failure to form the male organs (hypospadias) being mistaken for a girl or one of overgrowth of the female genitalia (adrenogenital syndrome) appearing to be a boy — and the error is recognised only at or about puberty. Since much psychiatric damage may be done by effecting a change of habit, it may be good medical practice to take a conscious decision to adhere to the adopted social sex. Marriage may well be debarred but, even in the alternative, the marriage of a hypospadiac in a male role will probably be voidable on the grounds of non-consummation.

Certain cases of intersex will clearly be justifiably assignable to the 'wrong' social sex and, among these, examples of the testicular feminisation syndrome are prominent. In this condition, the external appearances are those of femininity but the sex chromosomes are of XY pattern and the presence of intra-abdominal testes inhibits the development of female genitalia. The resultant vaginal atresia is correctable by surgery and the cases vividly illustrate the difficulties into which the law may be forced. Thus, in the well-known nullity case of *SY v SY (otherwise W)* it was held: 'If a woman with an artificial vagina is incapable of true sexual intercourse, she cannot be raped or commit adultery. I would regard such a result as bordering on the fantastic'[6] and a petition for nullity was rejected. Yet, in default of natural justice, a testically feminised 'woman' with an artificial vagina would be in the same ultimate position as obtained in *Corbett*[4] where the marriage was declared void. Ormrod[1] has forecast that the genital sex would probably be decisive were the testicular feminisation syndrome to be tested in court but it is difficult to follow this in strict logic.

A similar paradox arises in sport where many competition organisers insist on examination of buccal smears from female contestants in order to demonstrate the presence of nuclear 'Barr bodies' which indicate femininity — a heavily masculinised subject of the adrenogenital syndrome will survive the test whilst the obviously feminine testicular feminisation case will fail.

The arguments in favour of generally accepting a genital and social standard rather than a chromosomal definition of sex rise to a maximum in cases of trans-sexualism, which is discussed separately. It has been suggested that a social standard should apply in the application of the Equal Pay Act 1970 and of the Sex Discrimination Act 1975[7] and, in theory, there is nothing to stop a person being registered for social security purposes in the sex of his or her choice. It was, however, held in *White v British Sugar Corporation* that *Corbett* should apply in relation to the 1975 Act[8]; but this rather unsatisfactory case was decided on the basis of dishonesty rather than of sex discrimination.

True hermaphrodites, who possess both functioning male and female gonads, are very rare and are discussed under that heading. Gonadal sex will, in fact, be used only rarely to distinguish true sex as, in the vast majority of apposite cases, positive proof would rest on an abdominal operation which would probably be unacceptable.

See also: Gender; Hermaphroditism; Intersex; Marriage; Non-consummation of marriage; Sex chromosomes; Trans-sexualism

1. Ormrod R 'The medico-legal aspects of sex determination' (1972) 40 Med-Leg J 78.
2. Births and Deaths Registration Act 1953, s.29; Registration of Births, Deaths and Marriages (Scotland) Act 1965, s.42(5).
3. *X Petitioner* 1957 SLT (Sh Ct) 61.
4. *Corbett v Corbett* [1971] P 83.
5. *R v Tan and others* [1983] 3 WLR 361.
6. [1963] P 37 per Wilmer LJ at 60.
7. Thomson JM 'Transsexualism: a legal perspective' (1980) 6 J Med Ethics 92.
8. [1977] IRLR 121.

Sex Chromosomes

The sex chromosomes are designated X and Y. The possession of a Y chromosome indicates maleness. It is apparent that the genotype YY cannot exist, the normal sex genotypes being XX in the case of a female and XY in the case of a male.

The existence of the XX configuration may be deduced from examination of the nuclei of cells — either of tissue type or of those found in the blood. The diagnostic feature in tissue cells is known as the Barr body which stains and can be seen microscopically as an aggregate of chromatin on the inner surface of the nuclear membrane. This can be seen in several types of cell in tissue sections obtained surgically or at postmortem but epithelial cells rubbed from the mucosa of the mouth offer the most readily available source in the living subject. At least 2 per cent of cells must show Barr bodies before a diagnosis of femininity can be made; in good hands, the proportion of 'chromatin positive' cells discovered is usually very much higher. The diagnostic feature in the blood is the so-called 'Davidson body' in the polymorphonuclear leucocyte — the cell primarily responsible for the acute reaction to infection. The Davidson body appears as a drumstick-like excrescence on the multilobed nucleus. Discovery of six drumsticks in fewer than 300 consecutive cells examined indicates feminism. The Y chromosome is far more difficult to demonstrate but can be seen to fluoresce with the dye quinacrine; some 20–80 per cent of cells in a male are 'Y positive'.

Abnormal sex chromosome genotypes occur due to trisomy or deletion. Thus, the formation XXY results in Klinefelter's syndrome — a rather feminine type of male, a proportion of whom show a degree of mental retardation; an XO genotype results in Turner's syndrome with decreased sexual development and associated mental problems. The XYY constitution has caused much debate because a number of such men show antisocial behavioural characteristics and the genotype is said to be over-represented in prison populations. Many XYY men are, however, perfectly normal and it seems unlikely that the demonstration of the abnormality will be accepted, *per se*, as evidence of diminished responsibility or as sufficient to elide the *mens rea* of an offence[1]. The chance finding of an XYY formation at amniocentesis raises complex problems in genetic counselling.

See also: Amniocentesis; Genetic counselling

1. Fox RG 'XYY Chromosomes and crime' [1969] Aust & NZ J Crim 5; Price W 'XYY male and criminal behaviour' (1967) 213 Nature 815.

Sexual Asphyxia

Sexual asphyxia is part of a syndrome of sexual aberration which, although it is reported occasionaly in women, is almost always exhibited by young men who are frustrated in heterosexual attachments. The syndrome is masochistic in nature and typically involves transvestism, autoerotic stimulation enhanced by a pornographic environment and, particularly, by bondage; bondage is augmented by suspension by the neck and/or the wearing of a hood, either of which mechanism may lead to death from asphyxia. Occasionally, other bizarre hypoxic arrangements are made such as self-sealing in a plastic bag[1]. The use of an asphyxial mechanism may be associated with the widepsread belief that a degree of hypoxia enhances sexual pleasure.

The typical surroundings of a sexual asphyxial death will indicate it was accidental rather than a suicidal hanging. In both, however, the subject is likely to have gone to some trouble to ensure privacy. This particular form of sexual deviation is so uncommon in women that what appears to be a case might be suspected of being one of sadistic love play which has 'gone wrong'; on the other hand, the simple use of plastic bags appears to be a common form of suicide in women[2].

See also: Asphyxia; Hanging; Hypoxia; Sadomasochism; Transvestism

1. Chapman AJ and Matthews RE 'Accidental death during unusual sexual perversion' (1970) 17 J Forens Med 65.
2. Crompton MR 'Alcohol and violent accidental and suicidal death' (1985) 25 Med Sci Law 59.

Sexual Intercourse

Sexual intercourse is the penetration of the female genitalia by the male organ but the precise interpretation of this definition differs as to whether criminal law or family law is being considered. In neither case is emission of semen required[1] but the possibility of some satisfaction must be present when sexual intercourse is considered as a measure of consummation. Thus, it was held in the very old case of *D-e v A-g (otherwise D-e)*[2] that it could not be regarded as intercourse if that intercourse were so imperfect by reason of inadequate penetration as to be scarcely natural. This judgment has been upheld more recently[3]. It is clear that the intention to procreate children is unnecessary as a part of normal intramarital sexual intercourse[4] and family law as to sexual intercourse is essentially related to the deterrence of adultery.

Criminal law, on the other hand, is concerned with the protection of women and, accordingly, the slightest degree of penetration of the vulva constitutes sexual intercourse[5]. It also constitutes 'complete' sexual intercourse, complete in this instance being used in the sense of having come into existence[6].

Despite the very rigid interpretation of sexual intercourse as being heterosexual and of 'normal' character, there are indications of a general trend to extend the definition in so far as the criminal law is concerned. Thus, the Sexual Offences Act 1956, s.44, itself speaks of sexual intercourse 'natural or unnatural'. The situation elsewhere is changing rapidly; for example, sexual intercourse is now defined in the criminal law of New South Wales as including both anal and oral penetration[7]; many States of the USA have introduced similar statutes[8].

Intercourse within marriage is lawful; the problems of unlawful sexual intercourse are discussed under that heading.

See also: Adultery; Consummation of marriage; Rape; Unlawful sexual intercourse

1. Sexual Offences Act 1956, s.44; *R v R* [1952] 1 All ER 1194.
2. 1845 1 Rob Eccl 279.
3. *W (otherwise K) v W* [1967] 1 WLR 1554.
4. *Baxter v Baxter* [1948] AC 274; White v White [1948] P 330.
5. *R v Hughes* (1841) 9 C & P 752. Williams G *Textbook of Criminal Law* (2nd ed, 1983) (Stevens, London) describes it as a common law definition (p.236).
6. *Kaitamaki v The Queen* [1984] 2 All ER 435, PC, interpreting Crimes Act 1961, s.127 (NZ).
7. Crimes (Sexual Assault) Amendment Act 1981, s.61A. The same result is achieved in Victoria in the definition of rape and sexual penetration (Crimes (Sexual Offences) Act 1980, s.2A).
8. *See* Schiff AF 'Rape: wife vs husband' (1982) 22 J Forens Sci Soc 235.

Sexual Offences

The term 'sexual offences' includes acts in which the predominant aim is sexual aggression against the victim, acts where aggression may be absent and both parties consent to the act in question but which are considered to be against public policy and acts which are not directed against a particular person but which, none the less, offend public decency. A further classification can be made into those acts perpetrated against adults and those which involve children. Many such offences may be committed in a heterosexual or homosexual context.

The primary aim of the criminal law in this area is to protect the individual against non-consensual sexual activity. The law, however, goes further, protecting those who are incapable of giving a proper consent and, in certain circumstances, paternalistically preventing adults from performing acts which are deemed to be offensive in themselves. The prevailing view in legal philosophy, at least since the Wolfenden Report[1], has been that, provided the young and the vulnerable are protected, consenting adults should be allowed to engage in such sexual activity as they choose provided that this does not involve excessive physical violence.

Rape is generally considered to be the most serious sexual offence that can be committed against a woman although, in practice, there are other acts of sexual aggression which may be viewed as equally, if not more, traumatic and offensive. Further sexual offences against women include sodomy and indecent assault whilst there are a number of statutory provisions which proscribe unlawful sexual inter-course, many of which relate to age[2]. Statute also protects women by a variety of provisions relating to procurement and by the law concerning incest. The great majority of the offences covered are discussed in greater detail under their specific headings.

In addition to specific offences related to acts by men against young girls, the law provides further protection for children of both sexes against exploitation by both males and females. A child under 16 cannot consent to an indecent assault and this effectively prohibits the legal involvement of any child under that age in any form of sexual encounter with an adult; children under the age of 14 are specifically protected against sexual activities which do not involve physical touching[3]. Neither boys nor girls can give valid consent to homosexual practices; for this purpose, a girl is defined as being below the age of 16 but, in the case of boys, the prohibition extends to the age of 21[4]. There is pressure in some quarters to reform the law so as to narrow the age gap between the sexes but this is unlikely to meet with broad approval at present.

The principal unnatural offences against males are sodomy and gross indecency. Both of these are now permissible provided they are committed by consenting adults over the age of 21 in private[4]. Most prosecutions brought for homosexual offences relate to acts committed with youths or acts of sexual solicitation committed against *agents provocateurs*. Gross indecency or simple indecency do not require physical contact between the participants although the most usual form of such behaviour involves sexual contact short of anal penetration.

The major Sexual Offences Acts also contain provisions restricting prostitution and brothel-keeping.

As is the case with most forms of antisocial behaviour, there is much speculation and varied interpretation of the basic causes of sexual offences. The treatment of sexual offenders is a particularly vexed subject. Whilst some authors claim successful hormonal or even surgical treatment, others deny that this is either ethical or useful. Psychiatric treatment of the sexual offender is unlikely to be effective unless there is strong motivation on both sides[5].

See also: Age of consent to sexual practices; Incest; Indecent assault; Indecency with children; Lewd practices; Prostitution; Rape; Sodomy; Unlawful sexual intercourse

1. Wolfenden J (chairman) *Report of the Committee on Homosexual Offences and Prostitution* (Cmnd 247) (1957) HMSO, London.
2. Sexual Offences Act 1956, ss.5, 6; Sexual Offences (Scotland) Act 1976, ss.3, 4.
3. Indecency with Children Act 1960.
4. Sexual Offences Act 1967, s.1; Criminal Justice (Scotland) Act 1980, s.80.
5. Chiswick D 'Sex crimes' (1983) 143 Br J Psychiat 236.

Sexually Transmitted Diseases

Sexually transmitted diseases (STD) used to be known as venereal diseases; as a further part of the attempt to remove the stigma of, and disincentive to seek, treatment, departments of venereology are now known as departments of genitourinary disease. The change in emphasis is justified to an extent by the changing content of the subject, many more conditions now being known to be transmitted sexually[1]. Partly as a consequence, the number of cases of STD is growing, although the control of the most serious disease, syphilis, has been most successful.

The increase in sexual disease is probably due to several factors, including the decreasing use of sheaths *pari passu* with the widespread availability of oral contraceptives. The increasing importance of viral disease suggests that multiplicity of partners may have some effect. Non-specific genital infection and gonorrhoea remain the commonest forms of STD, and the latter is of particular concern in that the organism is fast becoming resistant to antibiotic therapy. The viral disease herpes is, however, the most rapidly increasing sexually transmitted disease although the organism is the same as that which affects the rest of the body and which is not sexually associated. There are a few diseases which are clearly related to male homosexuality — in particular, genital warts and the acquired immune deficiency syndrome — and the recent slight increase in the occurrence of syphilis is very largely accounted for by homosexuality. Adler has pointed out, however, that nearly a quarter of those attending departments of genitourinary medicine are there for reassurance only.

The existence of sexually transmitted disease has some importance in relation to a declarator of nullity of marriage and its contraction will, of course, have a significant bearing on divorce. Other aspects of STD which are of marginal medico-legal importance are the transmission of disease to the fetus and neonate and the relationship of cancer of the female cervix to sexual activity.

The transmission of syphilis to the fetus *in utero* is virtually inevitable if the mother is suffering from the acute disease during pregnancy; congenital syphilis is now very rare thanks to routine screening of pregnant women, the main difficulty being that the disease may become apparent to laboratory tests only after the original screening has been completed. Several diseases may be passed to the fetus during the act of birth. Genital herpes, which may also infect and kill the fetus *in utero*, is the most important of these; the condition when it affects the infant has a 60 per cent mortality and it may give rise to permanent brain damage — there are good reasons for ruling that a baby carried by a mother with genital herpes should be delivered by caesarian section. Maternal infections with the organism *Chlamydia trachomatis* may result in inflammation of the eye in up to half the offspring and to pneumonia in many of these. Gonococcal conjunctivitis is a better known complication but is very much less common than is chlamydial infection; ophthalmia neonatorum is a notifiable infectious disease[2].

Carcinoma of the cervix appears to be related to early sexual intercourse followed by intercourse with multiple partners — the only type of cancer of the cervix which has been reported in nuns is of a wholly different nature to that commonly acquired. The condition is, however, also related to the husband's sexual habits and there is growing evidence that the disease is at least potentiated by a virus; the virus need not, however, be typical of sexually transmitted disease.

Very strict rules are laid down as to the preservation of confidentiality in the treatment of sexually transmitted disease[3]. As a result, considerable care is needed in the very desirable tracing of contacts and this can be done only through recognised health care providers. The importance of confidentiality may be one reason why there has been reluctance to declare the acquired immune deficiency syndrome a notifiable disease.

See also: Acquired immune deficiency syndrome; Confidentiality; Divorce; Nullity of marriage

1. The reader interested in the clinical aspects of STD is referred to a series of articles mainly by Adler NW collected as *ABC of Sexually Transmitted Diseases* (1984) British Medical Association, London.
2. Public Health (Infectious Diseases) Regulations 1968 (SI 1968/1366); Public Health (Infectious Diseases) (Scotland) Regulations 1975 (SI 1975/308).
3. National Health Service (Venereal Diseases) Regulations 1974 (SI 1974/29), r.2. Strangely, there are no similar regulations applicable to Scotland.

Shock

Great care must be taken in distinguishing the physical and mental meanings of the word 'shock'.

Medically speaking, shock is a condition usually resulting from loss of circulating blood volume which may well be fatal if left untreated; it is described under 'Surgical shock'. In the popular sense, and often as used in legal discussion[1], 'shock' is the mental state resulting from an unpleasant experience whether this be physical or psychic (*see* 'Nervous shock'). Persons who are described as 'suffering from shock' following an accident, and who are discharged from medical care the same day, fall into the latter category.

Even so, the courts are not unsympathetic towards the concept of emotional shock as being mitigating in the criminal law; emotional shock after an accident may be sufficient to make a person unaware of the surroundings and of current legal obligations[2].

See also: Nervous shock; Surgical shock

1. 'Ordinary shock': *Whitmore and another v Euroway Express Coaches Ltd and others* (1984) Times, 4 May per Comyn J.
2. *Spalding v Laskaraina Paine* (1985) Times, 21 May.

Shoplifting

Shoplifting — the theft of merchandise from stores during their trading hours — is a widespread crime which has considerable economic implications for the retail trade; it is said that as much as a 10 per cent loss can be anticipated from this cause. The crime is frequently undetected and prosecution does not always result even when a shoplifter is apprehended.

Shoplifting is committed by a broad range of offenders, from young children to the elderly, and these are drawn from all social backgrounds[1]. The proportion of shoplifters who are professionals is relatively low. Some are ordinary thieves in the sense that they steal the goods in order to satisfy material needs — there is no doubt that many employees fall into this category; others, who are of greater medico-legal interest, commit the offence for no apparent motive. The latter constitute a particularly remarkable group of offenders in that the offence will often be quite out of character and may blight an otherwise blameless life. The tragedy of a respectable person being arrested for shoplifting and later committing suicide is not unknown[2].

There may be evidence of neurosis or of depression in many cases of apparently motiveless shoplifting and this may provide a medical explanation for the offence. Middle-aged women are particularly likely to fall into this category and, in some instances, the offence may be interpreted as a 'cry for help' — apprehension will at least lead to attention. Confusion may be a feature in some elderly shoplifters; recollection of the incident may be absent and an attempt to explain the theft is unlikely. Resentment, originating in social maladjustment or emotional disappointment, may be a motivating factor in some offenders.

Shoplifting will usually be charged as theft under the Theft Act 1968, s.1, although some forms of shoplifting, such as the switching of labels on products, may fall under a different section of the Act — e.g. s.15. The *actus reus* of the offence may take place before the defendant leaves the premises, as was the case in *R v McPherson*[3] in which it was held that the theft took place when the goods it was intended to steal were placed in the defendant's basket[4].

See also: Dementia; Manic–depressive psychosis

1. For a study of the offence and the characteristics of a group of offenders, *see* Gibbens TCN and Prince J *Shoplifting* (1962) Helmond, London; also, Won G and Yamomoto G 'Social structure and deviant behavior: a study of shoplifters' (1968) 53 Sociol Soc Res 44.
2. Low NC 'Neither guilty nor insane' (1983) 23 Med Sci Law 275.
3. [1973] Crim LR 191.
4. For discussion, *see* Smith ATH 'Shoplifting and the Theft Acts' [1981] Crim LR 586.

Shotgun Injuries

Shotguns are designed for killing small animals, and certificates for their use are comparatively easy to obtain; it follows that injuries due to shotguns are the most likely to be seen of those due to gunshot in the UK — this would not necessarily apply in the USA, where firearms are far more readily available.

Shotguns are either single or double barrelled, one barrel being usually 'choked' or tapered so as to retain the 'shot' in a solid mass for a longer time. Their calibration is remarkable. If the bore is less than 0.5 inch in diameter, the gun is calibrated in that diameter. If it is greater, the bore is related to the number of lead balls, exactly corresponding to the bore of the barrel, the total weight of which would be 1 lb; thus, an 8-bore gun is larger and more effective than is one of 12-bore.

As with any gunshot injury, those due to shotguns at close range are due to emergent air, smoke and flame, unburnt powder and the actual missile which, in this case, consists of a large number of metal pellets and the wads, made of paper or plastic, which hold the 'shot' in place within a paper or plastic cartridge case.

A contact wound will therefore show bruising and burning, and the whole of the shot will penetrate the skin through a large round hole. In these circumstances, an exit wound is possible and, if it occurs it will be irregular; the whole head may be blown off if the contact is in the mouth. Shot penetrates very badly, however, and exit wounds are exceptional in injuries due to shotguns. At close range there may still be evidence of burning, tattooing (impregnation of the skin or clothing with unburnt powder) will be present and it can be said that the distance of the shooting was less than two metres (two yards) if wads are found within the wound.

The function of the shotgun is to provide a cone of pellets through which the target will pass. The diameter of the cone increases with distance and, although the precise measurement depends to a large extent on the 'choking' of the gun, a usable rule of thumb is that the diameter of the spread of shot in inches equals the distance in yards from which it was discharged (diameter in centimetres divided by 2.5 equals the distance in metres); this diameter can be measured in injury cases by the spread of pellet injuries on the skin. The spread may not be exactly circular if the shot was from an angle but, in general, it is possible to give a very fair estimate of the distance from which a shotgun injury was inflicted. This is of very great value in attempting to answer the standard question of whether it was the result of suicide, homicide or accident. But it is clear that a murderer may use a close-range shot and the distinction between homicide and accident or, indeed, between suicide and accident, is generally only possible on the basis of the circumstantial evidence.

At close range, the mass of shot is deadly and can scarcely fail to penetrate a major organ or vessel. Otherwise, the danger of a shotgun injury depends upon the penetration of the individual pellets and their location; their removal may pose a formidable surgical problem. Shotgun injuries are unlikely to be dangerous to man above some 25 metres unless a pellet penetrates a delicate organ such as the eye.

See also: Firearms

SI Units

Laboratory and other scientific data should now be recorded in SI units (*Systeme Internationale d'Unites*); reports will be increasingly so framed as younger doctors come into the medico-legal arena.

The independent base units of SI are (physical quantity, name of unit and symbol):

length	metre	m
mass	kilogram	kg
time	second	s
electric current ampere A		

thermodynamic temperature	kelvin	K
luminous intensity	candela	cd
amount of substance	mole	mol

Decimal multiples and fractions of the units are formed by prefixes, with appropriate symbols:

10^{12}	tera	T	10^{-1}	deci	d
10^{9}	giga	G	10^{-2}	centi	c
10^{6}	mega	M	10^{-3}	milli	m
10^{3}	kilo	k	10^{-6}	micro	μ
10^{2}	hecto	h	10^{-9}	nano	n
10^{1}	deca	da	10^{-12}	pico	p
			10^{-15}	femto	f
			10^{-18}	atto	a

Other units are easily derived and designated by powers. Thus, the unit of area is the square metre (m^2) and the unit of volume is the cubic metre (m^3) although the litre (l) will continue in use.

The divider ('per') is shown by the use of negative powers. Thus, speed = metres per second = $m \cdot s^{-1}$; acceleration = metres per second per second = $m \cdot s^{-2}$.

A number of new names have been introduced for example the unit of force is the newton = $N = kg \cdot m \cdot s^{-2}$ (mass $\times$ acceleration) and the unit of pressure (including the measurement of blood pressure) is the pascal = $Pa = N \cdot m^{-2}$ (force per square metre).

The most difficult SI unit for the non-scientist to appreciate is the mole, which relates to the molecular weight of a substance in solution rather than to its weight in grams. It is therefore possible that, say, the breath alcohol will, in future, be reported as 7.6 $\mu mol \cdot l^{-1}$ rather than the customary 35 $\mu g/100$ ml.

Sickle Cell Disease

Sickle cell disease is specifically entered only because it provides an example of a genetic disease which has wide medico-legal and medico-social implications. The disease depends upon the presence of an abnormal genetically determined variant of haemoglobin known as HbS[1]. Red cells containing HbS are sensitive to hypoxia, which causes the cells to take on abnormal shapes, to become more easily broken down and to clump together causing multiple thromboses. The very severe disease, the signs and symptoms of which are dependent upon these abnormalities, occurs only in the homozygous state; heterozygotes are said to have the sickle cell trait and are clinically normal unless the red cells are subjected to hypoxia when symptoms may be precipitated.

The sickle cell gene is very ethnic dependent and is maximal in areas where malaria due to *Plasmodium falciparum* is endemic; the probability is therefore that the heterozygous state protects against malaria and this accounts for its extreme frequency in central Africa — the gene is dying out in the negro population of the USA because malaria does not occur there.

The medico-legal significance of sickle cell disease — aside from considerations of genetic counselling and antenatal diagnosis — are twofold. Firstly, a person with sickle cell trait is likely to be at risk under anaesthesia; failure to seek the gene in a patient of a relevant ethnic group would certainly be negligent. Secondly, the association with hypoxia raises problems of employment in certain occupations — particularly those associated with aviation; questions of a political nature and of relevance to industrial relations may, thereby, be raised[2] but cannot be regarded as being within the ambit of the ordinary practising doctor or lawyer.

See also: Anaesthesia; Genetic counselling; Genetic disease; Haemoglobinopathy; Hypoxia; Protozoa; Thalassaemia; Thrombosis

1. This is not the only variant — HbC, for example, occurs but is less dangerous than is HbS.
2. Diggs LW 'The sickle cell trait in relation to the training and assignment of duties in the Armed Forces: IV. Considerations and recommendations' (1984) 55 Aviat Space Environ Med 487.

Silicosis

Silicosis is a form of nodular fibrosis of the lungs which results from the inhalation of particles of silica which are of smalll size — large particles merely act as inert foreign bodies.

Small particles can, however, dissolve to form silicic acid and it is this which is believed to be the fibrogenic factor. The process of fibrosis in silicosis is progressive, the destruction of the lung tissue being out of proportion to the amount of silica contained in the tissue. Fibrotic nodules may collect to form massive conglomerate nodular silicosis. The whole process is severely destructive of lung tissue and death ultimately results from cardiorespiratory failure of the cor pulmonale type.

Silica will be dissipated whenever rock is drilled or sand is particularised and this will occur in the cleaning of blast furnaces, grinding, building in sandstone or working in slate or sandstone quarries. Silicosis is rarely associated with simple coal miners' pneumoconiosis but is found in anthracite miners and in miners of any type who are engaged in driving the tunnels to reach the face. The disease is at a maximum incidence in deep gold mines.

Silicosis is very clearly associated with tuberculosis and potentiates the virulence of the causative organism. Somewhat surprisingly, silicosis is not related to an increased incidence of cancer of the lung and, thus, contrasts markedly with asbestosis.

Silicosis is a prescribed disease and all processes involving the production of silica particles are prescribed occupations.

See also: Cor pulmonale; Pneumoconioses; Prescribed diseases and occupations; Tuberculosis

Simultaneous Death

The subject of simultaneous death is discussed more fully under 'Commorientes'.

The English courts appear to take the view that it is impossible to prove pathologically that deaths occurred simultaneously[1]. The test when disposing of the estates of two persons who have died in circumstances which make the order of death uncertain is therefore not whether there *was* a simultaneous death but whether there was uncertainty as to which person survived the other. However, when the words 'simultaneous death' are used in a will, it is likely that the courts will decide the matter on common sense principles[2].

See also: Commorientes

1. *Hickman v Peacey* [1945] AC 304.
2. *Pringle, in re Baker v Matheson* [1946] Ch 124.

Skull Fracture

The skull is composed of vault and base. The vault is formed by two tables of bone between which is a space filled with connective tissue. The base of the skull is irregular, showing alternating buttresses and weaker floors which form so-called fossae — anterior, middle and posterior — in which the brain lies. The floors of the fossae are further weakened by the presence of foramina through which the cranial nerves and blood vessels pass; the posterior fossa contains the large foramen magnum through which passes the medulla and its extension — the spinal cord.

The basic feature of fractures of the vault of the skull is their capacity to radiate — the effect of the head striking a flat surface is that the skull fractures rather like a pane of glass. A blow from, say, a hammer may, however, cause a depressed fracture of 'pond' type, when the lesion in the outer table may closely simulate the shape of the striking object. Other types of force may produce a comminuted, or fragmented, fracture with deep depression of the individual pieces of bone.

Fracture of the vault of the skull is not a cause of death in itself but secondary effects may be very dangerous. The most important of these is haemorrhage — classically extradural but often subdural; the haemorrhage is a space-occupying lesion which will affect the whole brain. Localised brain damage due to depressed fracture may, by contrast, result in surprisingly mild sequelae.

Fracture of the base of the skull is generally due to transmitted force. A blow to the side of the head may cause a radiating fracture of the base which will follow the lines of weakness. The classic fracture of the base is seen typically in front seat passengers in motor vehicle accidents when a blow to the chin is transmitted through the jaw to the base of the skull on each side; the result is a fracture running from side to side in the middle fossa and involving the pituitary gland. Such an injury is rarely survivable. An unusual fracture of the base of the anterior fossa occasionally results from a blow to the eyeball which acts as a hydraulic ram and 'blows out' the thin frontal plate. Fracture in the posterior fossa is most often seen as radiating from the point of contact in a fall on the back of the head. The ring fracture surrounding the foramen magnum is a specific type of fracture due to force transmitted through the spinal column — particularly following a fall landing on the buttocks; in extreme cases, the hydraulic pressure 'blows out' the whole vault of the skull. Fractures of the base of the skull are generally more serious than are those of the vault. They are very difficult to treat, they involve important structures passing through the bone and, since the air sinuses are likely to be involved, infection in the form of meningitis is likely even if the immediate injury is survived.

See also: Brain; Fractures; Intracranial haemorrhage; Parachuting injuries

Smoking

Tobacco has been smoked in Europe for centuries. The habit of smoking first became extensive in Britain during the First World War and grew rapidly in the following decades; consumption of cigarettes had increased by nearly 300 per cent over the 1920 figures by the end of the Second World War. Deaths from lung cancer also increased greatly during the same period[1].

Evidence that tobacco smoking is closely linked with a number of serious diseases was first widely publicised in the early 1960s. Two reports made significant impacts — the first report of the Royal College of Physicians, published in 1962[2], and the First Report of the American Surgeon-General, which appeared in 1964[3]. These reports reached an apparently inescapable conclusion that there was a strong link between smoking and the development of carcinoma of the lung. In addition, a link between smoking and chronic bronchitis, emphysema and heart disease was established[4]. It is, in fact, arguable that the major adverse effect of smoking is that which it has on the heart and on the predisposition to coronary insufficiency; although this association is clear, its mechanism is still uncertain — whether the causative factor is carbon monoxide or nicotine and whether the fatal mechanism is narrowing of the arteries due to the production of atheroma or spasm induced by nicotine are questions which have yet to be answered[5]. Another worrying conclusion of medical research is that the smoking of cigarettes by pregnant women can damage the fetus[6]. Pregnant women who smoked were found to be more likely to miscarry, and the children of such mothers tended to be below the expected birth weight. It was also found that children exposed to tobacco smoke in the house ran a higher risk of respiratory disease than their counterparts from non-smoking households[7]. The response of governments to these warnings was lukewarm; little more was done than to inform the public of the risks and to ban certain forms of advertising.

There is strong pressure in many countries for the further legal regulation of the promotion and use of tobacco[8]. There have been a number of product liability cases brought in the USA against tobacco manufacturers by persons who believe they have suffered injury as a result of the use of cigarettes but none of these has, as yet, been successful. Some jurisdictions in the USA have also introduced relatively stringent regulations governing the conditions in which employees may smoke at work. The aim of this legislation is to protect non-smokers from the harmful effects of 'passive or second-hand smoking'; this form of exposure to tobacco smoke may constitute a major risk to the health of the non-smoking population[9].

The sale of tobacco products to children under the age of 16 is an offence in Britain[10]. Despite this, the amount of money spent by children on cigarettes each year in Britain has been estimated to be in the region of £60 million. Undoubtedly, this is an area in which strict control should be applied and the ban on 'seductive' advertising on the television may be having an effect. Ultimately, however, the control of smoking is a matter of conditioning — children are unlikely to resist a peer temptation to smoke when their parents are seldom to be seen without a lighted cigarette.

See also: Atheroma; Cancer; Carbon monoxide poisoning; Heart disease

1. Taylor P *Smoke Ring* (1984) p.3, Bodley Head, London.
2. Royal College of Physicians *Smoking and Health* (1962) Pitman, London.
3. US Surgeon-General's Advisory Committee on Smoking and Health *Smoking and Health* (1964) Van Nostrand, Princeton NJ.
4. For general discussion of the health issues, *see* Ashton H and Stepney R *Smoking: Psychology and Pharmacology* (1982) Tavistock, London.
5. *See*, for example, Heliovaara M et al 'Smoking, carbon monoxide, and atherosclerotic disease' (1980) 280 Br Med J 268; Ramsdale DR et al 'Smoking and coronary artery disease assessed by routine coronary arteriography' (1985) 290 Br Med J 197.
6. Donavan JW et al 'Routine advice against smoking in pregnancy' (1975) 25 J Roy Coll Gen Pract 264.
7. Leading Article 'Warning: smoking may damage your children's health' [1977] 1 Br Med J 1179.
8 Leading Article 'The avoidable holocaust' (1980) 280 Br Med J 959.
9. Trichopoulos D et al 'Lung cancer and passive smoking' (1982) 27 Int J Cancer 1; Hirayama T 'Non-smoking wives of heavy smokers have a higher risk of lung cancer: a study from Japan' (1981) 282 Br Med J 183.
10. Children and Young Persons Act 1933, s.7; Children and Young Persons (Scotland) Act 1937, s.18 (as amended by Protection of Children (Tobacco) Act 1986).

Snake Bite

Snake bite is of only marginal forensic interest in the UK but is of great importance in many parts of the world — particularly in India, Central America and Australia; it has been said that, in some areas, snake bite is not uncommonly used as a cover for homicidal deaths.

The majority of snakes are non-poisonous; those which are dangerous are divided into the *Colubridae* — which group includes many non-poisonous varieties — and the *Viperidae*, all of which are poisonous. As a wide generalisation it can be said that the venom of the *Colubridae* (cobras, etc.) is neurotoxic whilst that of the vipers affects the blood-clotting mechanism. Venom is reflexly injected into the body when the snake bites or strikes. Few snakes are aggressive and most bites result from their accidental disturbance. A given amount of venom will be injected for every bite and the prognosis of snake bite is therefore worst in children. Prognosis in general depends greatly on the species of snake responsible and is also affected by the efficiency of the bite.

The treatment of snake bite is both general and specific. The latter consists of passive immunisation with antivenin (*see* 'Immunisation'). The antivenin will be most effective if it is prepared from and available against the actual species of snake involved[1] but, in practice, it must often be used as a polyvalent preparation. The antivenin will be prepared in animals and the injection of animal protein may produce a severe sensitivity reaction. The danger of such a reaction must be balanced against the expected toxicity of the venom; failure to appreciate this may give rise to problems in negligence. Thus, the toxicity of the venom of the only poisonous

British species, *Vipera berus*, is so slight that it could be good medical practice to withhold antivenin from an adult; but this might well not be so in the case of a small child[2].

See also: Immunisation; Sensitivity reaction

1. Diagnostic kits may be available in heavily snake ridden areas. *See* Plueckhahn VD *Ethics, Legal Medicine and Forensic Pathology* (1983) p.213, Melbourne University Press, Melbourne.
2. Royal Society of Tropical Medicine and Hygene 'Notes on the treatment of snake bite' (1962) 56 Trans R Soc Trop Med Hyg 93.

Sodomy

Sodomy in England and Wales consists of anal intercourse with another person and is part of the more general offence of buggery. The definition is more circumscribed in Scotland, where sodomy consists of penetration of the anus of one man by the penis of another.

It is an offence under the criminal law for a man to commit sodomy with another man[1] unless the act is committed in private between consenting persons who are aged over 21 years[2]. Outside these circumstances, consent to the agent's act is irrelevant although whether or not there was consent will bear upon the sentence imposed[3]. Penetration of some degree is essential to the offence but emission is not needed[4]; short of penetration, the agent can be charged with assault with intent to commit buggery. A boy under the age of 14 years is deemed incapable of sexual intercourse generally and, furthermore, cannot be an accomplice to buggery.

The medical investigation of sodomy is often unrewarding. The finding of a fissured, or of a classically expanded inelastic anus, may be evidence of habituation but not necessarily of recent buggery. Spermatozoa may be recovered from the rectum but failure to discover does not exclude the offence. Faecal material may be recovered from the penis of the active partner and evidence of lubricant from either party but it is rare for the parties not to have washed by the time an examination takes place. A charge of gross indecency can be sustained in the event of lack of proof of sodomy.

There are no circumstances in which it is legal to commit buggery with a woman in England and Wales; although, strictly speaking, the offence does not depend upon consent, a wife who submits but does not consent to acts of sodomy is not an accomplice[5]. By contrast, it appears that anal intercourse with a consenting adult woman is not a crime as such in Scotland. It is to be noted that, whether in a heterosexual or a homosexual partnership, sodomy or buggery is strictly confined to anal penetration.

See also: Buggery; Fellatio; Homosexual offences; Homosexuality; Indecent assault

1. Sexual Offences Act 1956, s.12.
2. Sexual Offences Act 1967, s.1; Criminal Justice (Scotland) Act 1980, s.80. It is still an offence to commit sodomy while serving in the armed forces or in the merchant navy irrespective of age or consent (Sexual Offences Act 1967, s.1(5), s.2(1)).
3. Sexual Offences Act 1967, s.3(1). *R v Courtie* [1984] 1 AC 463.
4. *R v Reekspear* (1832) 1 Mood CC 342.

5. *Lawson v Lawson* [1955] 1 **WLR** 200.

Solvent Abuse

Although sporadic cases were known many years ago, inhalation of solvents for their psychotropic and even hallucinogenic properties is comparatively new as a major feature in forensic medicine; an appreciable number of deaths have been reported only since the early 1960s. It is interesting that the habit appeared simultaneously in many places and does not seem to have spread from a single main source[1].

The precise extent of the problem cannot be assessed but the number of deaths associated with solvent abuse has increased in the UK year by year; 80 cases were reported in 1983[2]. Many hydrocarbons are used, the most popular being cleaning agents and glues; gas fuels and aerosol sprays[3] are also widely abused. The solvent may be placed on a rag or in a plastic bag but actual placing of the bag over the head occurs mainly in those rare cases associated with autoeroticism. Males are overwhelmingly the most frequent abusers and deaths in all series peak at the ages 13-20 years. There appears to be an association between solvent abuse and social or emotional deprivation. Anderson et al[2] have shown, surprisingly, that 71 per cent of deaths resulted from inhaling while alone but it may simply be that sniffing in company is of less intense degree and deaths do not occur because of the circumstances. Nineteen non-fatal cases of toluene encephalopathy were found to be of a generally younger age group than fatal cases[4], again suggesting a rather different epidemiology. The repetitive solvent abuser can often be identified by the presence of erythematous spots around the nose and mouth.

Death from solvent abuse is probably due to direct cardiac toxicity but many deaths result from plastic bag asphyxia or from inhalation of gastric contents. Deaths are commoner in Scotland than elsewhere in the UK and it was there that the first attempts to legislate against the practice were made[5]. A conviction at common law for culpable and reckless conduct in selling solvent abuse 'kits' to children has been successful[6] and it was said 'we wish to make it perfectly clear to persons who may be convicted of this wicked crime in the future that more serious sentences may be expected at the hands of the High Court'[7]. English prosecutions of the practice were first taken under the heading of nuisance[8] but legislation making it an offence to supply inhalants to persons under the age of 18, having reason to believe that they will be used for the purpose of causing intoxication, has now been introduced[9]. It is to be noted that toluene in glue is regarded as a drug — at least for the purposes of the Road Traffic Act 1972 (s.5)[10].

See also: Encephalopathy and encephalitis; Inhalation of gastric contents; Sexual asphyxia

1. One hundred and ten deaths were reported from the USA in 1970: Bass M 'Sudden sniffing death' (1970) 212 JAMA 2075. Twelve occurred in Finland between 1968 and 1971: Alha A, Korte T and Tenhu M 'Solvent sniffing death' (1973) 72 Z Rechtsmed 299.
2. The fullest report available is that of Anderson HR, Macnair RS and Ramsey JD 'Death from abuse of volatile substances: a national epidemiological study' (1985) 290 Br Med J 304.

3. Reinhardt CF et al 'Cardiac arrythmias and aerosol sniffing' (1971) 22 Arch Environ Hlth 265.
4. King MD et al 'Solvent encephalopathy' (1981) 283 Br Med J 663.
5. Solvent Abuse (Scotland) Act 1983. The Act does no more than establish 'glue sniffing' as a reason for ordering compulsory care of a child under the Social Work (Scotland) Act 1968, s.32(2).
6. See Sourindrhin I 'Solvent misuse' (1985) 290 Br Med J 94; *Khaliq v HM Adv* 1983 SCCR 483, 1984 SLT 137.
7. *Khaliq and Ahmed v HM Adv* 1984 SCCR 212 per Lord Justice General Emslie at 215.
8. *Sykes v Holmes and another* (1985) Times, 16 July.
9. Intoxicating Substances (Supply) Act 1985.
10. *Bradford v Wilson* [1984] RTR 116.

Somnambulism

The sleeping state is usually characterised by very slight physical activity. In some cases, however, the sleeping subject may perform complex actions, a phenomenon known as somnambulism (or 'sleep walking'). Somnambulism may be preceded by night terrors which may result in the subject's rising and reacting violently — this condition was once thought to be associated with epilepsy but this has been shown not to be the case[1].

Somnambulism is significant from the legal point of view in that it may entail behaviour resulting in death or injury to others. There are several accounts of such occurrences although the issue of somnambulistic violence has received comparatively little attention in modern legal and psychiatric literature. A very early instance was the case of Colonel Culpepper who was tried, in 1686, for shooting 'in his sleep' a soldier and his horse. Several witnesses came forward to testify to the bizarre sleep walking of the Colonel and the result was an eventual pardon[2]. There were several cases reported in the nineteenth century, including the well-known Scottish example of *Simon Fraser* who battered his infant son to death while allegedly dreaming that he was dealing with a wild beast in his bed. Fraser was not acquitted but the Crown deserted the diet on receipt of an undertaking from him that he would in future sleep alone[3].

Less ambiguous results were achieved in the twentieth century. In the case of *Boshears*[4], the accused went to sleep in front of the fire and awoke to find the girl beside him strangled. His plea of somnambulism was put to the jury and was accepted. Similar acquittals have been noted, even if inadequately recorded, in the law reports[5]. It appears to be a feature of offences committed in a state of somnambulism that they are out of character and incxplicable. The subject may have been prey to anxiety-producing events during the day which provoke later somnambulistic violence. In one case involving a 14-year-old boy, the day preceding the somnambulistic episode had been characterised by depression and feelings of anger. The conclusion of the psychiatric witnesses was that his senseless stabbing during the night of his 5-year-old cousin, with whom he enjoyed a good relationship, could be explained only in terms of somnambulism[6].

There is no distinct legal defence of somnambulism. Such behaviour may, however, be treated as automatism, in which case it should be considered to be of the non-insane type. The alternative is to approach the question from the point of view of *mens rea*[7]. The difficulty with the automatism solution is that the courts may be unwilling to allow an acquittal when there is a possibility of recurrent violence. Perhaps the only sensible and just conclusion in these rare cases is to accept a plea of not guilty provided satisfactory practical arrangements can be made to prevent further damage to others. Short-term pharmacological assistance can be given in the form of sleeping tablets but the effect of these is likely to diminish with time.

See also: Automatism; Insanity and criminal responsibility

1. Soldatos CR et al 'Sleep walking and night terrors in adulthood: clinical EEG findings' (1980) 11 Clin Electroenceph 136.
2. Walker N *Crime and Insanity in England* (1968) Vol.1, p.167, Edinburgh University Press, Edinburgh.
3. (1878) 4 Cowp 70.
4. (1961) *The Times*, February, p.5.
5. Walker, n.2 above, p.170 et seq.
6. Oswald I and Evans J 'On serious violence during sleepwalking' (1985) 147 Br J Psychiat 688.
7. Medicolegal 'Sleep walking and guilt' [1970] 2 Br Med J 186.

Special Hospitals

Special hospitals are managed by the Department of Health and Social Security, rather than by district health authorities, and are designated for the care of those patients who are compulsorily detained and who 'require treatment under conditions of special security on account of their dangerous, violent or criminal propensities'[1]. The majority of patients in special hospitals are the subject of a restriction order; others may have been transferred from an ordinary hospital which has found them too difficult to manage. Special hospital patients are not necessarily serious offenders; those who have offended may have committed only minor crimes but have, nevertheless, been judged to be dangerous. Concern for conditions in special hospitals has been expressed in more than one official report[2].

The placing of a patient in a special hospital may be challenged in the courts on the grounds that no reasonable Secretary of State would have reached such an administrative decision; the courts will, however, always be aware of the difficulties involved in finding alternative arrangements for certain patients[3]. The publication in 1980 of the Boynton Report on conditions in Rampton Hospital has resulted in an effort to clear the special hospital system of many patients who are inappropriately so detained but this is a slow and complicated process, particularly when undertaken in a climate of financial restraint[4].

See also: Restriction order

1. National Health Service Act 1977, s.4.
2. For example, in the Butler Reports: *Interim Report of the Committee on Mentally Abnormal Offenders* (Cmnd 5698) (1974); *Report of the Committee on Mentally Abnormal Offenders* (Cmnd 6244) (1975) HMSO, London.
3. *R v McFarlane* (1975) 60 Crim App R 320. For comment, *see* Hoggett B *Mental Health Law* (2nd ed, 1984) p.31 et seq, Sweet & Maxwell, London.

4. Boynton J (chairman) *Report of the Review of Rampton Hospital* (Cmnd 8073) (1980) HMSO, London.

Special Sensitivity

This is the problem well known as the 'thin skull' rule which was first described as such in *Dulieu v White and Sons*:

> 'If a man is negligently run over or otherwise negligently injured in his body, it is no answer to the sufferer's claim for damage that he would have suffered less injury, or no injury at all, if he had not had an unusually thin skull or an unusually weak heart'[1].

The essence of the rule (which applies equally in both civil and criminal cases) is that one takes one's victim as one finds him; the accused or the defendant is still liable for the unusually severe consequences of his act if his victim has a pre-existing condition or an unusual anatomical feature which dictates that physical injury has more serious consequences for him than it would have for others. This rule has survived the introduction of the foreseeability test for causation in tort[2].

There is a wealth of cases illustrating the application of the thin skull rule although, ironically, few of them actually involve head injury. In *Wilson v Birt Ltd*[3], however, the plaintiff actually had a weakness in his skull and, as a consequence, sustained a subarachnoid haemorrhage when subjected to no more injury than that resulting from a pole falling on his head; in *Warren v Scruttons Ltd*[4], the plaintiff, who already had an ulcer on his eye, developed further ulcers after contracting an infected finger wound; in *Smith v Leech Brain and Co Ltd*[5], the presence of premalignant tissues at the site of a lip burn resulted in liability being imposed for the subsequent development of a cancerous condition; and, in *Watts v Rake*[6], the awakening of quiescent spondylitis was laid at the defendant's door even though the plaintiff would have, in any case, developed the condition an estimated 13 years later.

The 'thin skull' rule also applies if the defendant's act renders the plaintiff more susceptible to further illness or injury[7]. The subsequent development of a psychiatric condition following injury may be compensated but this is regarded as an injury of a kind different from the original injury and must therefore be found to be foreseeable before liability will be imposed[8].

The rule's application in criminal cases can have major implications for an accused. An assault on a person who is particularly at risk from physical violence may, theoretically, result in a charge of murder even if the death of the victim could not possibly have been contemplated by the assailant. In practice, courts in England will prefer charges of manslaughter in such cases and sentencing will reflect more closely the degree of moral guilt shown[9]. Scottish courts have, however, been more rigorous in adhering to the rule. In *HM Adv v Rutherford*, the Lord Justice Clerk stated: 'It is no answer for an assailant who causes death by violence to say that his victim had a weak heart or was excitable or emotional. . .He must take his victim as he finds her. It is just as criminal to kill an invalid as it is to kill a hale and hearty man in the prime of life'[10].

The death of the victim through fright or shock poses particular problems for the thin skull rule. Frightening a person to death is certainly possible, albeit rare, and, in principle, there is no reason why a person who causes another to die as a result of putting him in fear of his life should not be guilty of homicide. In the Scottish case of *Bird v HM Adv*[11], the opinion of Lord Jamieson that this would also include putting the victim in reasonable fear of his safety or in reasonable fear of further violence was approved on appeal. In a recent English case involving a heart attack, the court assumed, albeit without deciding the point, that harm in the context of manslaughter included injury to the person through the operation of shock emanating from fright; they were not, however, prepared to regard 'emotional disturbance' as coming within that definition[12]. Specific problems arise when such action is associated with the suicide of the victim[13].

See also: Causation; Culpable homicide; Foreseeability; Manslaughter; Murder; Tort

1. [1901] 2 KB 669 per Kennedy J at 679.
2. *See* Fleming J 'The passing of *Polemis*' (1961) 39 Can Bar Rev 489. The decision in *Re Polemis and Furness, Withy & Co Ltd* [1921] 3 KB 560 implied a strict liability for the consequences of an action irrespective of their likelihood.
3. (1963) 2 SA 508 (South Africa).
4. [1962] 1 Lloyds Rep 497.
5. [1962] 2 QB 405
6. (1960) 108 Crim LR 158.
7. *Oman v MacIntyre* 1962 SLT 168.
8. *Malcolm v Broadhurst* [1970] 3 All ER 508.
9. As was observed by the Chief Justice of Gibraltar in the unusual case of *R v Cooper* discussed by Knight B 'Trauma and ruptured cerebral aneurysm' [1979] 1 Br Med J 1430.
10. 1947 JC 1 at 3.
11. 1952 JC 23. *See also* the unreported case of *John Mason Taylor* Criminal Appeal Court (Edinburgh) June, 1975 (death due to general harassment). In general, Williams G *Textbook of Criminal Law* (2nd ed, 1983) p.395, Stevens, London; Gordon GH *The Criminal Law of Scotland* (2nd ed, 1st supp, 1984) para.23–08, W Green, Edinburgh.
12. *Brian Dawson, Stephen Thomas Nolan, Ian Walmsley* (1985) 81 Crim App R 150. There is a useful discussion of the whole problem in Stallworthy M 'Can death by shock be manslaughter?' (1986) 136 NLJ 51.
13. Lanham DJ 'Murder by instigating suicide' [1980] Crim LR 215. *See also* Watson AA 'Death by cursing — a problem for forensic psychiatry' (1973) 13 Med Sci Law 192.

Spectrometry

Spectrometry (the use of optical measurement) is one of the most widely used principles in forensic science. There are, however, many variations on the theme.

Emission spectrometry depends upon the fact that elements will produce characteristic electromagnetic vibrations when vaporised. All the elements are identifiable and the pattern produced by a specimen of, say, paint, can be compared with paint from the suspected origin. The sample is, of course, destroyed in the process but the modern laser-beam technique can be applied to very small quantities.

The most useful variant is known as absorption spectrometry. This can be applied to identifying elements in the process known as atomic absorption spectrometry which measures the energy absorbed when the vaporised substance is exposed to radiations of varying wavelength. Absorption spectrometry is, however, more commonly applied in the simple and relatively cheap methods of passing radiations of the wavelength between 200 and 50,000 nm (10^3–10^7 GHz frequency) through the substance and observing how much radiation is absorbed in various wavelength bands. Thus, one can speak of ultraviolet spectrometry, visible light spectrometry, or colorimetry, and infrared spectrometry, the last having its most well-known use in breath analysis for alcohol. Usually, a tracing is made of the absorbance over the chosen range and this can be compared with known tracings from known substances. The methods are used widely for the identification of drugs after isolation and purification, ultraviolet spectrometry being the standard method for identification of barbiturates; in general, the infrared absorption spectrum is rather more characteristic than is that of ultraviolet radiation. All absorption spectrometry methods can be used quantitatively.

Emission and absorption spectrometry can be combined in fluorimetry, the principle being that ultraviolet radiation is absorbed by certain substances and simultaneously emitted as visible light. The method is very sensitive and is used for the detection of substances present in minute amounts such as lysergic acid; even so, far more sensitive methods, including radioimmunoassay (*see* 'Nuclear medicine') are needed for the identification of LSD in biological samples.

Mass spectrometry is the most modern spectrometric technique but operates on a completely different principle, producing a print-out of the breakdown pattern of a drug when it is bombarded by electrons; whilst the mass spectrometer is undoutbedly one of the most efficient tools available, the apparatus is very costly and can only be installed at a central establishment.

See also: Electromagnetic radiation; Nuclear medicine; Toxicological analyses

Spermatozoa

Spermatozoa are the male gametes found in the testes and ejaculated along with secretions from the prostate, seminal vesicles and epididymis as semen during the male orgasm. Normal semen contains up to 200 million spermatozoa per millilitre and the ejaculate may be of any quantity up to about 6 ml. Ejaculation is not an essential element of legal sexual intercourse nor, therefore, of rape, incest or buggery but the finding of spermatozoa in the female genital tract or in the rectum is very good evidence when such circumstances are suspected.

A spermatozoon consists of a head, a small neck and a body which is slightly wider than the long filamentous tail (50 μm). The head measures 4–5 μm in length and is ovoid in shape. Motile sperm can be recognised easily but staining provides the clearest and most objective evidence of their presence in a swab. The head then appears as an acorn with a pale-staining tip and a darker base; the recognition of this bipolar staining is important as, once the sperm has lost its tail, the degenerate head may be confused with other cellular debris from the vagina or rectum.

The length of time for which spermatozoa retain their normal morphology is a matter of some debate. Some observers believe that spermatozoa with tails can be recovered from the female genital tract up to 26 hours following intercourse[1]; others have found considerable difficulty in demonstrating normal forms as recently as three to four hours after the event[2]. In general, it appears that some of the difference may depend on whether the results of normal intercourse or of rape are under study[3]. Spermatozoa retain their integrity on cloth for a long time and are readily recognisable even after some weeks.

Both spermatozoa and semen in secretors contain blood group substances. The blood group of an ejaculate is therefore demonstrable generally by the method known as haemagglutination inhibition. The delicate technique of mixed agglutination will demonstrate contamination of individual fibres by semen. The origin of non-human spermatozoa can be ascertained serologically, and the spermatozoa of various animal species have differing shapes which may be recognised by an expert.

See also: Bestiality; Blood stains; Rape; Saliva testing; Sexual intercourse

1. Willott GM and Allard JE 'Spermatozoa — their persistence after sexual intercourse' (1982) 19 Forens Sci Int 135.
2. Sharpe N 'The significance of spermatozoa in victims of sexual offences' (1963) 89 Can Med Ass J 513.
3. For discussion, *see* Mason JK *Forensic Medicine for Lawyers* (2nd ed, 1983) p.222, Butterworths, London.

Spina Bifida

The condition spina bifida results from failure of fusion of the spinal column and, as a result, there is herniation of the spinal cord; the resultant state is properly called meningomyelocele. The congenital defect occurs anywhere in the spine and the higher the lesion, the more severe are the consequences. The detection, elimination and treatment of meningomyelocele constitute one of the burning issues in current medical practice; this is largely because the advances in neonatal care and surgery have been so rapid that what would, only a decade or so ago, have been fatal or grossly disabling conditions are now treatable but with varying results. The therapy of spina bifida affects the infant, its parents and the resources of the State in general and of its medical services in particular. The subject is discussed in some detail under 'Neural tube defects', of which spina bifida is but one part.

See also: Neonaticide; Neural tube defects

Spinal Anaesthesia

If a local anaesthetic agent is applied to a nerve root, a whole segment of the body can be anaesthetised. Further, if the cerebrospinal fluid (*see* 'Brain') is replaced by anaesthetic which is injected at the lower end, the whole of the body can be anaesthetised in ascending fashion, the level of anaesthesia depending upon the level to which the anaesthetic is allowed to rise. This is the principle of spinal anaesthesia. However, the higher the anaesthetic rises, the closer it comes to the nerves which supply the life system functions; there is, then, a very definite limit to the level to which spinal anaesthesia can be administered and, since some upward diffusion is inevitable, the technique has a built-in risk which is probably higher than that of general inhalation anaesthesia. These risks are compounded by the fact that the anaesthetic agent will also affect the autonomic nervous system, which may have serious effects on the blood pressure and on the circulation as a whole. In addition, the injection site through the dura mater must leak for a time and the resultant pressure changes cause a headache and other subjective nervous disturbances which may last for weeks.

For these reasons, the injection of anaesthetic into the subarachnoid space has been very largely replaced by epidural anaesthesia in which the anaesthetic is introduced into the extradural space. The technique is rather more difficult but anaesthetists include a number of tests to ensure that the injection site is correct. Occasional misplacements do, however, occur. The danger is, then, that, since more anaesthetic is required in epidural than in spinal anaesthesia, a gross excess may be introduced into the subarachnoid space with consequent severe injury and even death due to direct brain stem damage. The *post mortem* diagnosis of such a disaster may not be easy as death is likely to be delayed in the presence of ventilator support and something in the region of 50 per cent of the holes made inadvertently in the dura will have healed in ten days; microscopic evidence of healing may, however, still be present.

Epidural anaesthesia is, however, extremely safe when confined to the lower nerve roots which supply the perineum, and the technique is widely used in modern obstetrics.

See also: Autonomic nervous system; Brain; Brain stem death; Dura mater

Spinal Cord Injuries

Injuries to the spinal cord may be unilateral in unusual conditions such as when the cord is damaged in the process of surgical operation. Far more commonly, injury will amount to complete transection which will involve sensory loss of a segmental distribution below the lesion and motor loss to an extent pending upon which spinal nerves below the point of injury supply the muscles; partial loss of motor function may occur at the upper limit of the injury as most motor nerves have an origin from two or more spinal segments.

Regeneration of the spinal cord is impossible. The result of transection is therefore permanent loss of voluntary motor and sensory function below the injury. Both the arms and legs will be affected if the injury is in the neck region — the condition is known as quadriplegia; an injury in the thoracic area will result in the loss of use of the legs — paraplegia. Voluntary control of other muscles will also be lost. Thus, high cervical lesions are usually fatal because the ability to use the muscles of respiration is lost. Similarly, the paraplegic will lose the voluntary use of his bowel and bladder function. Limited involuntary movement may, however, persist through spinal reflex action — the cord is well supplied with blood and is thus viable although cut off from its nervous connection with the brain (*see* 'Paraplegia' and 'Quadriplegia'). Voluntary function may improve after injury as the swelling due to haemorrhage and oedema subsides.

The commonest source of injury to the spinal cord is fracture of the spine sustained in vehicular accidents or during risk sports. Bullet wounds tend to involve the spine and such injury is a very typical war wound. It is something of a tragic paradox that improved methods of emergency care and casualty transportation result in the survival of persons who are severely and irretrievably handicapped; special treatment units can, however, have a remarkable effect on the acceptance of disability. Injury to the upper cervical spine leads not only to spinal cord damage but also to involvement of the medulla of the brain stem which contains the vital centres; this was the rationale of judicial hanging as a method of execution.

See also: Capital punishment; Firearm injuries; Paraplegia; Quadriplegia; Road traffic accidents; Sports injuries

Splenic Injury

The spleen lies superficially beneath the left lateral ribs. Its major function is to dispose of effete erythrocytes and it is therefore distended with blood and its capsule is generally under tension. Injury to the spleen is thus likely to produce serious intra-abdominal haemorrhage. It is probably the commonest severe abdominal visceral injury sustained in generalised trauma such as occurs in vehicular accidents or in serious assaults; rupture of the spleen should be anticipated in such circumstances and should be diagnosed readily in any accident department. The organ is not essential to life and its removal is a relatively simple surgical operation.

The spleen will be hyperactive, and therefore larger and more susceptible to rupture, when it is dealing with an increased load of broken down erythrocytes. This occurs, *inter alia*, in malaria and sickle cell disease. It has been said, though probably apocryphally, that a blow to the spleen is a recognised method of homicide in malarious areas; whether or not this is so, an enlarged spleen is certainly more susceptible to accidental injury than is a normal organ. This is of importance also in temperate climates as the spleen is enlarged in many infectious diseases — rupture during the course of the very common condition of infectious mononucleosis (or glandular fever) is by no means unusual.

The spleen is grossly enlarged in the various malignant diseases involving the blood cells (e.g. leukaemia). The medico-legal significance is not great as such sufferers will already be very ill and are unlikely to be involved in violence.

See also: Erythrocytes; Protozoa; Road traffic accidents; Sickle cell disease

Sports Injuries

Virtually every sport has its potential for injury and this is increasing as all sport becomes more competitive. The incidence of death and injury depends, however, on the definitions involved. Looking merely at death, it would seem that golf is the most dangerous sport but few would regard the coronary attack of the middle-aged long handicapper as a true injury — clearly, the term 'sports injury' must be reserved for traumatic conditions. It would be impossible in an entry of this type to detail all such injuries which are possible; only generalisations will be attempted and, in truth, most are self-evident.

Some sports are intrinsically dangerous by virtue of the environment in which they take place — e.g. parachuting and hang gliding[1]; likely injuries in the event of catastrophe will be those of falls from a height. At the other end of the atmospheric spectrum, one could cite underwater diving, the hazards of which are discussed separately; similarly, mountaineering and pot-holing could be contrasted. All have it in common that part of their attraction is a 'calculated flirtation with death'[2].

Such risk sports are of solitary type. A further group can be isolated as being solitary in nature but undertaken in a group configuration — motor racing and steeple chasing are examples. Here, the injuries likely to be sustained are those of exaggerated road traffic accidents and falls.

More general danger arises from those which are loosely described as contact sports and which range in hazard from, say, American football to field hockey — although modern cricket probably qualifies for such classification. Contact sports can be defined as those in which injury may be sustained but is regrettable when it occurs. They can be distinguished from those sports which are essentially legalised assaults, prominent among which are boxing and wrestling.

The distinction between legal and illegal assault is not easy to make but is founded in the UK on the ruling in *Attorney General's Reference No.6 of 1980*[3]. It is important to note that the doctrine of *volenti non fit injuria* is one which applies in civil law; we are here concerned with a criminal law, the gist of which is that a consensual fight with fists is unlawful no matter how it is undertaken, the salient factor being an intention to cause actual bodily harm or to be reckless as to its causation. This decision was based on public policy but Lord Lane CJ went on to say: 'Nothing which we have said is intended to cast doubt upon the accepted legality of properly conducted games and sport, lawful chastisement or correction, reasonable surgical interference, dangerous exhibitions, etc. These apparent exceptions can be justified. . .as needed in the public interest'. Clearly, the public interest may change and the subject is reverted to under 'Boxing'.

The practical result of the ruling would seem to be that, to be properly conducted, a sport must have rules and, preferably, a governing body, that an official should be present to impose the rules and that, to keep within the law of the land, the players must keep within the rules of the game. Even then, the use of weapons which are intended to cause harm might be illegal; 'chain wrestling' provides an example[4].

The importance of a governing body for contact sports is perhaps best exemplified in rugby union football (boxing is a special case and is discussed separately). The nature of what was designed as a purely amateur game is changing rapidly with the concept of the need to win and it is, consequently, becoming more dangerous. Spinal injuries are increasing and rugby may be a significant cause of quadriplegia; the governing body has, therefore, a duty to amend the rules urgently and, in fact, does so[5]. A person deliberately flouting the rules and causing injury lays himself open to criminal charges.

Cricket provides an example of the importance of the official. It is often a moot point as to whether a short fast ball is designed to strike the batsman or to induce a rash stroke; causing injury after a warning from the umpire would, however, certainly expose the bowler to criminal prosecution.

As to the players themselves, it has been reported, for example, that between 12 and 31 per cent of injuries sustained in rugby are caused deliberately[6]. Successful prosecutions for manslaughter following death resulting from a foul are believed to have occurred but do not seem to have been reported; a case of prosecution for assault has, however, been considered[7].

As to solitary dangerous sports, the importance of organisations such as the British Sub-Aqua Club in the promotion of safety cannot be overemphasised. Yet their role can only be advisory and, if they have any legal responsibility, which is doubtful, it can only be in the civil field. There is no such criminal offence as self-manslaughter; the organisers of a hang-gliding exhibition, for example, cannot be convicted of being accessories to manslaughter if there is a fatality[2].

As a final word, it may be mentioned that, in several sports, a substitute cannot be played unless a doctor certifies an injury as being such as to prohibit a player continuing. The issue is, perhaps, most applicable to boxing, but any doctor involved remains liable both in civil and in criminal negligence in the event of a player being wrongly certified fit to continue.

See also: Bodily harm; Boxing; Diving hazards; Falls; Parachuting injuries; Quadriplegia; Recklessness; *Volenti non fit injuria*

1. Balfour AJ 'Icarus anatomised' (1982) 50 Med-Leg J 43.
2. *See* Williams G *Textbook of Criminal Law* (2nd ed, 1983) p.592, Stevens, London.
3. [1981] QB 715.
4. Parliamentary Report (1985) *The Times*, 12 July, p.4.
5. Silver JR 'Injuries of the spine sustained in rugby' (1984) 288 Br Med J 37.
6. Davies JE and Gibson T 'Injuries in rugby union football' [1978] 2 Br Med J 1759.
7. *R v Billinghurst* [1978] Crim LR 553.

Stab Wounds

Stab wounds are incised wounds which are deeper than they are long on the surface. Only very rarely will they be accidental. On the other hand, suicide by stabbing is not uncommon in some communities whilst killing by stabbing is presently the commonest form of murder in the UK[1]. The carrying of knives by youths — and even by young girls — and their use under the influence of alcohol is widespread. It would be extremely difficult to prohibit the carrying of all knives save in specific conditions — e.g. within sports grounds; flick knives, however, may not be sold or dealt in[2] and constitute offensive weapons *per se*[3].

Due to the elasticity of the tissues, a stab wound always looks elliptical in the skin. A wound which is cleanly angular at each end is probably made by a double-edged weapon; fraying (so-called fish-tailing) at one end indicates a single cutting edge but this is not a constant finding. Bruising at any point suggests that the weapon has penetrated to the hilt — an observation which, taken in conjunction with the depth of the wound, may be of great help in identification. The width of the incision — which should be measured with the edges apposed — cannot be less than the width of the knife at a particular depth of penetration; it may, however, be greater because the knife may be 'rocked' in the wound or the victim may move. Measurement of the depth of a stab wound — particularly at postmortem dissection — must take into account the flexibility of the skin (e.g. over the abdominal wall) and also the displacement of organs due to gravity. The depth of the wound is of surprisingly little value in assessing the force of the blow; once the point of a knife has penetrated the skin, the remaining blade slips in very easily[4].

The main danger of a stab wound is haemorrhage from which the victim is unlikely to die immediately; consequently, homicidal stab wounds are often multiple. Suicidal wounds may also be multiple, particularly in the case of a mentally deranged victim. Often, however, the suicidal wound is single, electively placed below the left ribs and aimed towards the heart. The presence of 'defence injuries' clearly distinguishes assault from self-infliction.

Although this note has concentrated on knifing, stab wounds may be inflicted by any pointed instrument — e.g. needles, screwdrivers, scissors — and the appearances will be correspondingly modified.

See also: Defence injuries; Homicide; Incised wounds; Suicide

1. It certainly is so in Scotland (Scottish Home and Health Department *Criminal Statistics, Scotland* 1979 (Cmnd 8215) (1981) HMSO, Edinburgh).
2. Restriction of Offensive Weapons Act 1959 and 1961.
3. *R v Simpson (Calvin)* [1983] 3 All ER 789, CA.
4. Knight B 'The dynamics of stab wounds' (1975) 6 Forens Sci 249.

Further reading
Johnson HRM 'Stabbing and other knife wounds' in Mason JK (ed) *The Pathology of Violent Injury* (1978) Edward Arnold, London.

Starvation

Starvation may be accidental as when a person is trapped or marooned, it may very rarely be associated with deliberate neglect, or it may be voluntary — the result either of conscious determination, as in the hunger striker, or from psychiatric disorder — the well-known state of anorexia nervosa. Cases associated with occlusive disease of the gullet (e.g. carcinoma of the oesophagus) are now virtually unknown.

The ability to withstand starvation appears to depend very much on whether or not fluid is available. Water loss is acute, and, in the absence of replacement, death is likely to occur in some ten days; life may be prolonged for several weeks if water is drunk. The typical appearances of starvation are due principally to loss of fat, body protein being consumed as a last resort. The postmortem picture will, however, differ markedly from case to case; the grossly emaciated body is generally that of a person who has been obtaining minimal nutriment whereas the case of total starvation may well succumb from metabolic disorder before the full-blown appearances have developed. The typical signs of chronic starvation are those of widespread loss of fat and reduction in the size of the organs, particulary of the heart; a translucent appearance of the bowel wall is said to be very characteristic.

A person who is starved will be additionally deprived of essential elements, vitamins, etc. and will be prey to intercurrent infection. But many infections — particularly tuberculosis — will lead to wasting, and the pathologist's problem often becomes that of deciding between cause and effect. This is particularly likely to be so in the case of children; deprivation and starvation in childhood is said to be as common a cause of death as is battering of the child[1].

See also: Forced feeding; Neglect; Non-accidental injury in children

1. Emery JL 'The deprived and starved child' (1978) 18 Med Sci Law 138.

Stature

Occasionally it may be necessary to establish the stature of a deceased person from the evidence available from one or a few bones. This can be attempted through the use of anthropological tables which have been drawn up following painstaking research[1].

There are several important provisos to be made when using any such tables. Firstly, the results depend very much upon the ethnic origin of the skeletal remains. Secondly, the greater the number of observations available — i.e. the more bones which can be measured — the finer will be the bracket of probability as to the actual height. Thirdly, the accuracy claimed is seldom greater than a total height of $\pm$ 2.5 cm (1 in). Finally, and perhaps of greatest practical importance, very few people are likely to know the height of a missing person with any greater accuracy than obtains scientifically. It should be remembered that height is also a matter of deportment; it is not only that the cartilages of old persons shrink, the aged also fail to hold themselves upright.

All in all, it is doubtful if there is very much practical advantage in attempting to improve on simple rules of thumb — for example, the length of the humerus (upper arm bone) is about 20 per cent of the total height; that of the femur (thigh bone) 27 per cent; and that of the tibia (lower leg) 22 per cent.

See also: Identification of the dead

1. *See* Krogman WM *The Human Skeleton in Forensic Medicine* (1962) CC Thomas, Springfield IL.

Sterilisation

Surgical sterilisation is a procedure directed at ending the ability to reproduce. In males this is most commonly achieved by vasectomy, in which the vas deferens is cut or tied; in females, the most frequently used methods involve the dividing or clipping of the fallopian tubes, thus preventing the passage of the ova between the ovary and the womb. Sterilisation is usually permanent although, in a few cases, it is possible to reverse the procedure and restore reproductive capability. Sterilisation is highly effective as a method of contraception although the success of the procedure cannot be guaranteed in every case. Failure may occur even without negligence on the part of the doctor performing the operation. An operation undertaken with a view to reversibility is less likely to be successful and many surgeons will not operate if so constrained by the patient. The concept of irreversibility has caused some confusion and has led to some finely balanced litigation. To describe an operation as irreversible means that it cannot be successfully rectified surgically — it does not imply a guarantee of sterility in the face of natural repair; the decided cases have turned mainly on the twin concerns of explanation and understanding[1].

Because of the improbability of successful reversal, sterilisation should not be undertaken lightly. There is nothing illegal in the operation in the UK (in spite of some earlier doubts[2]) but it is important that a full and informed consent be obtained from the patient. It might be considered ethically desirable to obtain the consent of the patient's spouse but failure to do so would be unlikely to have legal repercussions for the doctor; sterilisation without the consent of the spouse might, however, be regarded as intolerable behaviour from the point of view of divorce.

The sterilisation of minors and of the mentally handicapped raises complex legal issues. As far as minors are concerned, it is unlikely that the consent either of the patient or of his parents would be adequate to justify the operation save in exceptional circumstances. Any decision in relation to the procedure is best left until full legal capacity has been attained.

Mentally subnormal minors might be considered as constituting a different category in which strong reasons could be adduced for sterilisation. There is a case for ensuring that a female child should never become pregnant if her condition is such that she is unlikely ever to be able to give a proper consent to intercourse or to understand the implications of child birth or child rearing. The difficulties of supervising compliance with chemical or mechanical forms of contraception in these circumstances make surgical sterilisation an attractive option.

The permissibility of sterilising a mentally subnormal 15-year-old girl was considered in the case of *In Re D (a minor)*[3]. D suffered from Sotos' syndrome, a condition which led to her having an intelligence quotient of 80. A move to have her sterilised was prevented by the court because it was likely that she would be able to make her own choice in later years. D clearly fell into the category of those mentally subnormal people whose condition is not sufficiently serious to justify sterilisation but the case does provide a general indication of the caution with which the courts will approach the matter. By contrast, the later Canadian case of *Re Eve*[4] provides an example of circumstances in which a court will allow the parents of a mentally handicapped person to consent to the sterilisation of their offspring. Although there should, in theory, be no distinction between a subnormal child and a subnormal adult, it is likely that the court will exercise greater caution when it is a minor who is the proposed subject. One reason for this might be the possibility of improvement in the condition.

Enthusiasm for eugenic sterilisation in the USA led to the enactment earlier this century of a number of statutes providing for the compulsory sterilisation of certain types of person[5]. In some cases the categories of persons involved were extremely broad; in others, only the mentally retarded have been affected. The American courts have recently tended to interpret sterilisation statutes narrowly, requiring strict procedural safeguards in order to prevent abuse.

See 'Wrongful pregnancy' for further discussion of claims for negligence in respect of failed sterilisation.

See also: Consent by minors; Eugenics; Genetic disease; Informed consent; Mental impairment; Wrongful pregnancy

1. *Thake and another v Maurice* [1984] 2 All ER 513, QBD; [1986] 1 All ER 497, CA (vasectomy). *Eyre v Measday* [1986] 1 All ER 488, CA (laparoscopy).

2. Dicta of Lord Denning in *Bravery v Bravery* [1954] 3 All ER 59, CA.
3. [1976] 1 All ER 326.
4. (1981) 115 DLR (3d) 283.
5. Soskin RM 'Sterilization and the mentally retarded' (1983) 2 Med Law 267.

Further reading
For further discussion, *see* Meyers DW *The Human Body and the Law* (1970) Chap.1, Aldine, Chicago; McLean SAM and Campbell TD 'Sterilization' in McLean SAM (ed) *Legal Issues in Medicine* (1981) Gower, Aldershot, Hants.

Sterility

Sterility can be regarded as absolute infertility — women are sterile after the menopause. There are, however, conditions occurring or appearing during child-bearing life which are so untreatable that they can be said to render a person sterile rather than infertile. In women, these will include premature menopause, failure of the ovaries to develop — often associated with abnormalities of the sex chromo-somes — and several rare developmental abnormalities of the ovaries; some tubal conditions (e.g. bilateral tuberculous infection) might be regarded as being so untreatable as to render the women sterile. A man with genetically determined failure of testicular development or with undescended testes will be sterile and there a few cases in which male sterility is due to congenital absence of the vas deferens on each side. Ionising irradiation of the gonads can cause sterility in both sexes; the operations of tubal ligation and vasectomy are usually intended to sterilise — *see* 'Sterilisation' for discussion of the problems of reversal of the operation.

It should, perhaps, be noted — despite its obviousness — that reproductive sterility has a completely different meaning from microbiological sterility. The latter implies that no viable micro-organisms are present in a given medium. Microbiological sterility is not without medico-legal importance as the introduction to the body of pathogenic micro-organisms may lead to accusations of medical negligence.

See also: Infertility; Pathogenic organisms; Sterilisation

Steroids

The steroid hormones are elaborated by both the cortex of the adrenal glands and by the sex organs. The hormonal secretions of the latter are of medico-legal importance in that abnormalities in development of the testes or ovaries may lead to alterations in the genitalia and secondary sex characteristics and, accordingly, to the misinterpretation of the chromosomal sex. Thus, testicular failure will result in female appearances and social acceptance as such. Alternatively, complex interactions between the androgenic and oestrogenic steroids which are provoked in persons who have both male and female gonads may lead to unusual states such as the testicular feminisation syndrome (*see* 'Sex'). Sex hormones are, however, also secreted by the adrenal cortex and, whilst not as powerful as those from the gonads, may exert a profound effect particularly when present in excess and when present congenitally. Such excess production may be due to overgrowth (hyperplasia) or to tumour. In this way, the adrenogenital syndrome results in sexual precocity in boys and virilism in girls.

The main steroids produced by the adrenal cortex, however, are concerned with the biochemistry of the body, including electrolyte balance; from the medico-legal aspect, the most important relationships are those related to 'stress' and to the control of the inflammatory response and sensitivity reactions of the body. Thus the adrenocortical hormones have an important part to play in the successful outcome of surgical operations and of the response to trauma in general. Steroids of the glucocorticoid type may be used to suppress both inflammation and the immune response, and they are currently a major component of immunosuppressive methods which are needed to sustain organ transplantation therapy.

The use of steroids involves two major difficulties. Firstly, despite continual refinement, their use as, say, immunosuppressants is likely to produce signs of hyperadrenalism. Secondly, withdrawal of the hormones may be accompanied by serious biochemical upset. Steroid therapy is also a not infrequent cause of drug interactions. All these complications are, however, well documented and known.

The use of steroids in sport is something of a bizarre development, the most usual concept being that the use of anabolic — or tissue constructive — steroids will improve the physical ability of women. Whether this is so is still debated but there is no doubt that the athletic performance of women improved very greatly from 1968 onwards — which is about the time when steroids were first seriously considered in this light. The control of such 'drugs', which are essentially part of the human body, is obviously not easy although complicated laboratory tests are available. The use of steroids in sport is condemned by the International Federation of Sports Medicine but the onus of discovery and elimination rests on the governing bodies of the sports concerned.

See also: Drug interaction; Gender; Genitalia; Immune reaction; Immunosuppression; Sex; Transplantation of organs

Stillbirth

A stillborn child or stillbirth is defined as one which has issued forth from its mother after the 28th week of pregnancy and which did not at any time after being completely expelled from its mother breathe or show any other sign of life[1]. The Brodrick Committee[2] considered this definition in detail and concluded there were no sufficient grounds to recommend a change either as to gestational age or as to the reference point in time which distinguishes a live birth from a stillbirth.

The pathologist, in making the distinction, has therefore to seek evidence as to the precise age of the fetus and also as to whether there were any signs of life. The former depends to a large extent on the size of the fetus (classically, 35 cm (14 in) from crown to heel at the 28th week) and on the presence of centres of ossification which are discussed under 'Age of a body at death'; in the present context, the most important are those in the talus bone in the heel and in the first segment of the breast bone. The determination of a live birth is discussed under 'Separate existence'; many stillbirths are premature[3] or show obvious deformity which is incompatible with life.

Stillbirths must be registered, a prerequisite being the provision of a medical certificate of stillbirth; this indicates the presumed cause of stillbirth which may be either maternal or fetal. The certifier, who may be a registered medical practitioner or a certified midwife, may either have been present at the birth or have examined the body after being informed of its birth. In all parts of the UK there is provision for a declaration by the informant that there was no professional person able to certify and that the infant was born dead[4]. A stillbirth is a birth rather than a death and, accordingly, the informant has 42 days in England and Wales or 21 days in Scotland to register the event. It will be seen that not only may the determination of stillbirth be technically difficult, but also the current process of disposal is open to abuse; for these reasons, among others, the Brodrick Committee[2] recommended the introduction of a certificate of perinatal death to include both stillbirths and early infant deaths — a recommendation which shows no signs of implementation.

If the registrar, or the certifier, is in any doubt as to whether the infant lived, the matter must be referred to the coroner or procurator fiscal, who will then take responsibility for certification and disposal. Although it is unlikely that the mother's right to dispose of the stillbirth's organs would be challenged, the Human Tissue Act 1961 takes no account of stillborn infants, who must therefore be either buried or cremated. Both are contingent upon the certificate for disposal or of registration but, unless this has, for some reason, not been provided before burial, there is no requirement on the superintendent of the place of disposal to notify the registrar that disposal has been effected.

See also: Age of a body at death; Disposal of the dead; Homicide; Human Tissue Act 1961; Infanticide; Live birth; Separate existence

1. Births and Deaths Registration Act 1953, s.41; Registration of Births, Deaths and Marriages (Scotland) Act 1965, s.56.
2. Broderick N JL (chairman) *Report of the Committee on Death Certification and Coroners* (Cmnd 4810) (1971) Chap.8, HMSO, London.
3. A premature infant is defined as one with a birth weight of less than 2.5 kg (5½ lb).
4. 1953 Act, s.11(1)(b); 1965 (Scotland) Act, s.21(2)(b).

Stomach

The stomach lies covered by the left lower ribs and consists of two parts — the fundus into which the oesophagus opens and the pylorus from which the duodenum arises.

A main function of the stomach is to macerate and partially digest the food. To do this, the muscular action of the stomach wall is supported by the action of the gastric juice. This is strongly acid due to its content of hydrochloric acid and contains enzymes which start the digestion of protein food. The ingested food is thus turned into semi-fluid mass which is also rendered sterile by the acidity of the medium. An additional function of the stomach is to elaborate the anti-anaemic factor — vitamin B_{12}.

The stomach is anchored at both ends but is otherwise mobile and is surprisingly seldom injured in vehicular accidents. It is, however, vulnerable to knife wounds and is particularly injured when knife attacks are aimed at the heart from below. A leak of acid gastric juice into the peritoneal cavity causes intense irritation — or peritonism — but not infection. For a variety of reasons, including undue stress and vagal activity, the stomach may digest its own lining, leading to the disease of gastric ulceration. The ulcerative process may extend through the wall, resulting in perforation of the stomach, or it may involve relatively large vessels with consequent haemorrhage; either event may result in sudden natural death. Refractory gastric ulcers may have to be treated by partial gastrectomy, in which case the whole regularity of stomach emptying may be distorted. The major effect from the medico-legal aspect is on the absorption of the alcohol which, being passed rapidly into the small intestine, may produce symptoms of acute alcoholism despite the ingestion of quantities which would normally have no major effect. Similarly, the blood or breath alcohol level is likely to peak faster and higher in such persons as compared with the norm.

See also: Alcohol; Road Traffic Act 1972

Strangulation

Strangulation, or death resulting from compression of the neck, may be manual (throttling) or due to a ligature which, in turn, may be applied actively (classic strangulation or garotting) or passively (hanging). In any case, there are several potential modes of death.

Obstruction of the windpipe by direct pressure is unlikely because of the relatively incompressible nature of the laryngeal cartilages but it may occur if the constriction is on or below the cricoid cartilage[1]. Compression of the arterial blood supply to the brain would result in death but this, again, is mechanically difficult to achieve and is unlikely on anatomical grounds because the brain has a dual blood supply through the anterior carotid arteries and the posterior vertebral arteries — the latter being protected by the bony cervical vertebrae. Venous occlusion is easy to achieve and will also cause cerebral hypoxia; it occurs frequently and is indicated by the presence of petechial haemorrhages above the obstruction. Such signs are, however, absent in many cases of strangulation, when the probable cause of death is vagal inhibition of the heart — a mechanism involving an afferent stimulus of the sympathetic nervous system and an efferent reflex in the vagus nerve leading to slowing or stopping of the heart beat. The carotid sinus in the neck is a particularly sensitive sympathetic stimulus receptor and several lethal techniques of unarmed combat make use of this fact; strangled victims of the Indian thugs of the last century would die rapidly and noiselessly.

Thus, the signs of strangulation by ligature will vary. An abrasion associated with the ligature may be present and will be characteristically horizontal and of uniform appearance — allowing for the interposition of hair or clothing; soft materials such as nylon tights are, however, often used and may leave surprisingly little evidence. If the agonal period has been prolonged, petechial or frank confluent haemorrhages will be seen above the ligature; the rest of the body is, however, adequately oxygenated and they are seldom seen in the general tissues. Diagnostic importance rests on the presence of fingermark abrasions indicating an attempt to relieve the constriction, an interpretation which can sometimes be confirmed by an examination of fingernail scrapings. Damage to the laryngeal cartilages is less common in strangulation by ligature than it is in throttling. None of these signs is likely to be seen if death was due to vagal inhibition of the heart which results in very rapid death. Death due to venous congestion takes a variable time which is very difficult to estimate. Theoretically, a period of some two or more minutes is necessary for death to result but it is difficult to sustain pressure for this length of time in homicide; it is likely that death occurs in 30–60 seconds in most cases. This relatively short time is probably due to the increased physical and physiological activity in the victim; this is borne out by the contrasting marked asphyxial changes which are common in suicidal strangulations.

Classic strangulations are most commonly due to homicide but may be suicidal, in which case there is often evidence of a method — including knotting — to maintain the ligature. Accidental self-strangulation is sometimes seen during an act of bravado or in abnormal sexual activity. Sexual activity may also result in accidental death or manslaughter of the partner due to the occurrence of vagal inhibition of the heart; this is often compounded by a moderate degree of alcoholic or drug intoxication. Garotting is still occasionally used in some countries as a method of judicial execution.

Unusual forms of strangulation have to be considered in the very young. Children in cots may strangle themselves in their harness or bed clothes or even in assocation with the side rails, particularly if these are defective[2]. Homicidal strangulation of the newborn by the umbilical cord must be extremely uncommon but wrapping of the cord around the neck is a valid cause of stillbirth.

See also: Agonal period; Autonomic nervous system; Fingernail marks; Garotting; Hanging; Larynx; Petechial haemorrhage; Throttling; Vagal inhibition of the heart

1. *See* Gresham GA 'Violent forms of asphyxial death' in Mason JK (ed) *The Pathology of Violent Injury* (1978) Ch.11 (Edward Arnold, London) for a review of the subject.
2. Variend S and Usher A 'Broken cots and infant fatality' (1984) 24 Med Sci Law 111.

Strict Liability

Strict liability is a concept applied in both civil and criminal law. In civil law, it constitutes a liability which is independent of negligence of the defendant and is based on proof that he caused the injury for which compensation is claimed. The plaintiff still, however, must seek his redress against a named defendant and he still requires to prove causation; it therefore differs from no-fault compensation schemes under which compensation may be payable in the absence of a specific defendant. For further discussion of strict liability and civil law, *see* the entry on 'Torts'.

The doctrine of strict liability in the criminal law allows conviction of an accused person in the absence of *mens rea*; a defendant can thus be convicted even if he was unaware what constituted the *actus reus* of the offence[1]. In one well-known example of the application of strict liability, the owners of a factory discharging pollutants into a river were convicted of the offence of polluting water although they were unaware of the failure of their equipment[2].

The doctrine of strict liability became entrenched during the nineteenth century when Parliament commonly legislated on offences without referring in the statute to the need of *mens rea* on the part of the defendant. The early strict liability offences were all regulatory, being concerned with such matters as the handling and selling of food[3]. But sexual offences, traffic violations and, subsequently, industrial control offences became increasingly absorbed into the strict liability framework of the criminal law.

The injustice of convicting the morally innocent offender has struck both the courts and academic commentators on the law, with the result that a distinction has now developed in English law between purely regulatory offences and those which involve an element of moral opprobrium. In the former, the doctrine of strict liability is still imposed but, in the latter, a presumption is generally made to the effect that Parliament intended a *mens rea* requirement[4]. This compromise goes some way towards removing potential injustices.

See also: Causation; Negligence; No-fault compensation; Torts

1. For a general discussion, *see* Leigh LH *Strict and Vicarious Liability* (1982) Sweet & Maxwell, London.
2. *Alphacell v Woodward* [1972] AC 824.
3. Paulus I 'Strict liability: its place in public welfare offences' (1978) 20 Crim LQ 445.
4. *Lim Chin Aik v R* [1963] AC 160; *Sweet v Parsley* [1970] AC 132.

Subarachnoid Haemorrhage

Some degree of subarachnoid haemorrhage is common in any severe head injury but generally represents no more than an extension of cerebral contusion; only occasionally is such a haemorrhage significant in itself. This note is concerned with subarachnoid haemorrhage which is fatal *per se* and this differs from other intracranial but extracerebral haemorrhages in being more commonly natural than traumatic in origin.

Severe subarachnoid haemorrhage stems most often from the arteries of the circle of Willis which ring the brain stem. The result is a bleed which is maximal in a vital area and which passes almost unopposed into the cerebrospinal fluid. The fluid cannot drain itself so as to accommodate the effused blood and the combined result is rather rapid death if the condition is untreated; this may well be so — the primary symptom usually being severe headache for relief of which the average person looks to the aspirin bottle rather than to the neurosurgeon.

The common source of bleeding is rupture of a congenital ('berry') aneurysm of the circle of Willis. The propensity to aneurysm lies in a deficiency of the muscular coat of the arteries, particularly at the rather angular junctions of the various vessels involved. There may be small bleeds as the aneurysmal sac increases in size before a potentially fatal burst. The underlying aetiology is congenital and the catastrophe can therefore occur at any age. Subarachnoid haemorrhage constitutes a potent cause of sudden unexpected death in young adult life although recent work has shown that berry aneurysms may persist into late middle age and rupture long after the age of 50 years[1]. A weak vessel is clearly more likely to rupture when the blood pressure and pulse volume are increased. Ruptured aneurysms are thus not uncommonly found following unexpected death during an altercation; the significance of such a finding is discussed under 'Special sensitivity'. At autopsy, it may sometimes be impossible to demonstrate an aneurysmal sac, in which case the underlying lesion may be atheroma in an elderly person[2]; alternatively, the pathologist should then think of the possibility of traumatic subarachnoid haemorrhage.

Fatal traumatic subarachnoid haemorrhage commonly results not from head injury but from injury to the neck and, in particular, to the region of the first cervical vertebra (atlas bone). The subject is of special importance and is discussed separately (*see* 'Traumatic subarachnoid haemorrhage').

See also: Aneurysm; Atheroma; Congenital disease; Inhalation of gastric contents; Special sensitivity; Traumatic subarachnoid haemorrhage

1. Bowen DAL 'Ruptured berry aneurysm: a clinical, pathological and forensic review' (1984) 26 Forens Sci Int 227.
2. Crompton MR 'The coroner's cerebral aneurysm: a changing animal' (1975) 15 J Forens Sci Soc 57.

Subdural Haemorrhage

Subdural haemorrhage has it in common with extradural haemorrhage that it is virtually always traumatic in origin. The degree of trauma needed may, however, be relatively slight and is age dependent. Primary subdural haemorrhage may be acute, subacute or chronic in type.

Acute subdural haemorrhage is, as often as not, unassociated with fracture of the skull or cerebral injury. A specific type relates to birth trauma and accounts for some 5 per cent of deaths which follow rapidly upon live birth. The lesion results from rupture of a venous sinus within the dural membranes and is a characteristic feature of death in premature and precipitate births; babies with unusually large heads are also at risk. Otherwise, acute subdural haemorrhage results from rupture of one or several of the many venules which 'bridge the gap' between the brain substance and the dural sinuses. Anything which predisposes to differential movement between the brain and the skull or which extends the gap to be bridged is therefore likely to increase the liability to subdural haemorrhage. Thus, it is a characteristic lesion in child abuse, in which the main assault is generally in the form of shaking[1], and it may be provoked by comparatively minor trauma in the aged whose brains are, to a degree, shrunken. The extent of any subdural haemorrhage is less well defined than is that of extradural haemorrhage as the subdural space is comparatively unrestricted.

Subacute subdural haemorrhage gives rise to a situation comparable to extradural haemorrhage in that, following head injury, there is a deterioration in the condition following apparent recovery; the distinction from the acute condition is generally a matter of the speed with which the haematoma develops. It is, however, apparent that it may be essential to assess the age of a subdural haemorrhage in cases of suspected homicide as there may, in fact, be no causal connection; such ageing can often be done by microscopic examination of the clot which begins to become organised in two to three days.

Chronic subdural haemorrhage often appears to be unassociated with head injury but this appearance is probably spurious. Bleeding, which is often bilateral, leads to progressive compression of the brain and the subtle changes in function or behaviour which are provoked may be missed until they are severe or they may be misdiagnosed as senile dementia; as in the acute condition, the pliable brains of infants and the atrophic brains of the aged are more likely to be affected. The lesion is easily identifiable pathologically as the blood clot organises from the outside, often leaving a cystic centre, whilst there is simultaneous evidence of repetitive fresh bleeding.

Secondary subdural haemorrhage can result from an extension of a subarachnoid or intracerebral haemorrhage.

See also: Child abuse; Extradural haemorrhage; Intracranial haemorrhage; Subarachnoid haemorrage

1. Caffey J 'On the theory and practice of shaking infants' (1972) 124 Am J Dis Child 161.

Sudden Infant Death Syndrome

The term 'sudden infant death syndrome' (SIDS) has been accepted by the Registrars General since 1970 to describe the sudden death of infants who were apparently previously healthy and in whom no cause for death can be demonstrated at autopsy[1]. This definition has been criticised in so far as it depends to a large extent on the depth of postmortem investigation and on the acceptance or rejection by the pathologist of minor autopsy findings as being causative of death; such critics would regard the cause of death as being less fundamental than its mode — the sudden death of an apparently healthy infant while asleep or seeming to be asleep.

The precise incidence of the SIDS depends upon the definition accepted but may rise as high as 3 deaths per 1,000 live births; it is the commonest cause of death in children between the ages of 1 week and 1 year and presents a major medico-social problem. The deaths peak at 12–16 weeks of age, they are commonest in the winter months and there is an excess of cases in the low socio-economic groups — although, paradoxically, social class I is also overrepresented. The second child appears to be at greatest risk[2].

Many theories have been adduced to explain SIDS but none suffices to explain all cases. 'Cot deaths' seem to result from sustained sleep apnoea — bouts of cessation of breathing which occur normally in infants; the reasons for the failure to restart breathing are unknown and may be many, but a high proportion of SIDS deaths are preceded by mild upper respiratory tract infections and many of the infants have been seen by the doctor in the last few weeks of life. Thus, whilst some parents may be subject to a severe guilt reaction, others will transfer this to the practitioner. It is to be emphasised that these deaths are sudden, unexpected and unpredictable and neither guilt nor negligence can be attributed to any party; nevertheless, the deaths must, by definition, be reported to the medico-legal authority.

The findings at autopsy may be completely negative. Alternatively, non-specific signs which are commonly attributed to hypoxia — including severe petechial haemorrhages in the thoracic organs — may be found. It is very probable that the many infant deaths which used to be attributed to overlaying were, in fact, instances of SIDS.

The postmortem distinction between SIDS and suffocation by a soft object, such as a pillow, may be impossible to make; it is, however, generally agreed that, whilst cases of child murder or infanticide may be misdiagnosed, their number is extremely small in relation to those deaths which are due to natural causes.

See also: Asphyxia; Hypoxia; Overlaying; Suffocation

1. *See* Bergman AB, Beckwith JB and Ray GC (eds) *Proceedings of the Second International Conference on Causes of Sudden Death in Infants* (1970) University of Washington Press, Seattle.
2. Mason JK et al 'Cot deaths in Edinburgh: infant feeding and socioeconomiic factors' (1980) 34 J Epidem Comm Hlth 35. The incidence of the condition is exceptionally high in Tasmania, where it is a notifiable disease.

Further reading
There is a mass of literature world wide on this subject. Knight B *Sudden Death in Infancy: cot death syndrome* (1983) (Faber, London) gives an up-to-date review. *See also* Kendeel SRM and Ferris JAJ 'Sudden infant death syndrome: a review of literature' (1977) 17 J Forens Sci Soc 223.

Sudden Natural Death

Some 80 per cent of deaths reported to the English coroner are natural deaths — and are expected to be so — and over 98 per cent of these will be examined by postmortem dissection. The logic is, of course, that criminality cannot be excluded as a cause of sudden unexplained death other than by autopsy. Yet, other than in infant deaths which form a separate category, the number of homicides that are discovered at a coroner's autopsy is minuscule and, most probably, it is the external examination which has alerted the pathologist in those cases which are uncovered. Moreover, the sheer volume of the work militates against an exhaustive examination and, in particular, a toxicological examination, which is most likely to disclose an occult homicide, is logistically impossible in the vast majority of cases[1]. It seems more realistic to accept the conclusion of the Brodrick Report[2] that the main function of coroners' service in modern times is to improve the accuracy of the mortality statistics. Whether this is the best way of achieving that end is still open to discussion (*see* 'Autopsy').

The causes of sudden natural death depend very much on the age group under consideration; it can, however, be said that, in general, the great majority of deaths which are unexplained, and which occur so rapidly after the onset of symptoms that they cannot be certified with certainty by a doctor unfamiliar with the patient, are associated with abnormalities of the cardiovascular system. The major exception to this rule is in infancy when, although sudden deaths *may* be associated with congenital heart disease, the great majority are examples of the sudden infant death syndrome.

Sudden cardiovascular death in young adults may be diagnosed, perhaps tenuously, as having resulted from myocarditis; cardiomyopathy, when it is present, is a far less controversial finding. Subarachnoid haemorrhage from a congenital abnormality of the cerebral vessels is not uncommon; bleeding into a metastatic tumour is the only other reasonably frequent cerebral cause of sudden death in this age group. There is, however, a steady trickle of cases for which no cause can be found at autopsy — a young adult dies, very often after exercise, and no abnormality is discovered other than, frequently, an enlarged spleen for which no explanation is forthcoming. In many ways, it is unfortunate that pathologists are effectively required to certify a cause of death for which the grounds are less than certain; an acceptance of the situation and, following the precedent in infancy, of certification in terms of 'sudden unexplained death in young adulthood' would be more honest and would serve to stimulate research in the area.

Haemorrhage associated with the reproductive organs must be considered as a real possibility in young women. Ectopic pregnancy remains the most likely example now that the sequelae of criminal abortion have been all but eliminated.

Sudden natural death in middle age is almost entirely a matter of coronary insufficiency which may be a product of coronary atheroma or of hypertrophic cardiomyopathy (see 'Cardiomyopathy'). Coronary insufficiency extends into old age as a cause of sudden death but disease of the cerebral vascular system then assumes an equal importance and may take the form of haemorrhage, thrombosis or embolism. Haemorrhage from a ruptured aortic aneurysm must also be suspected.

Epilepsy takes precedence in the non-vascular causes of sudden death; status epilepticus may occur but that particular clinical condition is not essential as epileptics can die suddenly without obvious cause. Often, the epileptic drowns or suffocates during a simple attack. Respiratory diseases may cause sudden death but it is rarely unexpected or unexplained. So-called status asthmaticus is the best known example but must now be very rare. It is important to consider the possibility of the therapy being at fault whenever death is attributable to a condition which has been under treatment for some time.

See also: Allergy; Aneurysm; Autopsy; Cardiomyopathy; Ectopic pregnancy; Embolism; Epilepsy; Haemorrhage; Myocarditis; Subarachnoid haemorrhage; Sudden infant death syndrome; Sudden natural death; Thrombosis

1. For a fuller discussion, see Mason JK 'Coroners from across the Border' (1983) 23 Med Sci Law 271.
2. Brodrick NJL (chairman) Report of the Committee on Death Certification and Coroners (Cmnd 4810) (1971) HMSO, London.

Suffocation

Suffocation is asphyxia by occlusion of the nose and mouth or of the nasopharynx. It is rare as a form of homicide in adults although occasional cases of manslaughter arise due to the misapplication of a gag. Suicidal or accidental suffocation is not uncommon in the mentally deranged who may stuff the mouth with handkerchiefs and the like. Accidental suffocation is a common cause of death in autoerotic sexual asphyxia and may also occur accidentally in children playing with plastic bags over the head[1]; a more sinister variation is the asphyxia which occurs while using plastic bags to assist in solvent abuse ('glue sniffing').

Homicide by suffocation assumes its greatest importance in the case of infants. The application of the hand may be demonstrable at postmortem against the cyanotic congestion of the face induced by a hypoxic death but is, still, difficult to distinguish with certainty from the natural *post mortem* lividity, or hypostasis, which results from death in the prone position — particularly as an infant's body is almost certain to have been moved after death before examination by a doctor. It is, however, extremely doubtful if a normal, unrestrained infant will suffocate in its own bed clothes and the use of perforated pillows to preclude such a possibility is now commonplace.

Evidence of the application of a soft object such as a pillow may be impossible to obtain at autopsy. In years past, the most important differential diagnosis of homicidal suffocation or smothering was accidental overlaying — this must now be extremely rare save in association with severe intoxication on the part of a parent[2]. Today, the alternative, and very much more likely, diagnosis is that of cot death or sudden infant death syndrome (SIDS). Since the cause of the latter is probably a natural cessation of breathing, the *post mortem* signs in both asphyxia and SIDS are likely to be those associated with hypoxia — cyanosis and oedema of the lungs, petechial haemorrhages on the serous surfaces, congestion of the brain and petechial haemorrhages into organs such as the thymus gland. It may, indeed, be impossible to make the distinction at autopsy[3].

See also: Asphyxia; Cot deaths; Hypostasis; Hypoxia; Overlaying; Petechial haemorrhage; Sexual asphyxia; Solvent abuse; Sudden infant death syndrome

1. Toy (Safety) Regulations 1974 (SI 1974/1367).
2. Children and Young Persons Act 1933, s.1(2)(b); Children and Young Persons (Scotland) Act 1937, s.12(2)(b). Both proscribe a person over the age of 16 years being in bed with a child under the age of 3 years when under the influence of drink.
3. Vanezis P 'The role of the pathologist in the investigation of unexpected death in infancy (cot death)' (1981) 21 Med Sci Law 119.

Suicide

Suicide, or intentionally killing oneself, has ceased to be an offence since the passing of the Suicide Act 1961. Deliberate self-destruction is, however, still proscribed by all monotheistic religions.

The true incidence of suicide is difficult to discover. In England and Wales, the coroner is very reluctant to find that a death was due to suicide unless there is obvious evidence to that effect such as a note of intention; the death certificate in Scotland cannot contain a mention of suicide, the Registrar General depending for his statistics on confidential information provided by the Crown Office. There is, however, general agreement that suicide as a whole is commoner in men than in women and that the more violent the method, the more obvious does the sex difference become[1]. Consequently, female suicides outnumber males only in the category of fatal ingestions.

Fatal ingestions comprise approximately 50 per cent of all fatalities which are potentially suicidal[2]. Barbiturates still account for more than half the deaths due to ingestion of Prescription Only drugs although their use in this way is declining. Since the overwhelming proportion of fatal ingestions are due to Prescription Only drugs, many suicides must be iatrogenic in origin; this is, however, an almost inevitable result — those suffering from depression will have seen their practitioner, who must provide the best therapeutic drugs which, in turn, provide the opportunity for suicide. The Edinburgh series[2] indicated that older married women, elderly widowers and single young men are particularly at risk.

Drowning and falling from a height constitute the next most common causes of potentially suicidal death although, clearly, the possibility of a true accident is very high in such events. Hanging is relatively common but the occurrence of deliberate carbon monoxide poisoning has greatly diminished with the increased use of natural gas for cooking and heating. Thus, it never was common in the USA and suicides due to 'gas poisoning' are now virtually confined to the garage. Suicide by shooting is very rare in women.

Parasuicide, or non-fatal deliberate self-harm, shows a rather different distribution from suicide as to age, social class and methods involved; it is discussed under that heading.

Suicide pacts account for less than 2 per cent of all suicides[3]. They may be of the killing/suicide type or double suicides. In the event of the survival of the killer in the former case, the offence is reduced from murder to manslaughter by virtue of the Homicide Act 1957, s.4; the same would apply in practice in Scotland. A survivor from a double suicide would, by contrast, be theoretically guilty of an offence under the Suicide Act 1961, s.2 — although the practical chances of prosecution must be now remote. Williams[4] finds it hard to see what point there is in retaining the legal provision.

British courts have been a trifle inconsistent in correlating failure to prevent suicide with negligence. Substantial damages were awarded to a known suicide risk who sustained injuries due to jumping from a hospital roof while unattended[5]; this contrasted with an earlier case where it was held that patients with known suicidal tendencies could not be kept under constant supervision by the hospital staff[6]. In *Hyde v Tameside Area Health Authority*, the Court of Appeal held that there were strong policy grounds why damages should not be awarded in respect of attempted suicide[7].

See also: Carbon monoxide poisoning; Drowning; Drug overdose; Falls; Hanging; Negligence; Parasuicide; Prescription Only medicines; Suicide Act 1961

1. *See*, for example, Lindelius R 'Trends in suicide in Sweden 1749–1975' (1979) 60 Acta Psychiat Scand 295; Gatter K and Bowen DALl 'A study of suicide autopsies 1957–1977' (1980) 20 Med Sci Law 37.
2. Campbell S and Mason JK 'Fatal ingestions in Edinburgh 1974–78' (1981) 21 Med Sci Law 159.
3. Norton A 'Double suicide' (1984) 288 Br Med J 346.
4. Williams G *Textbook of Criminal Law* (2nd ed, 1983) p.582, Stevens, London.
5. *Selfe v Ilford and District Hospital Management Committee* (1970) 114 SJ 935.
6. *Thorne v Northern Group Hospital Management Committee* (1964) 108 SJ 484.
7. (1981) Times, 16 April, per Lord Denning MR. But policy considerations in general may now be less significant in limiting recovery for foreseeable damage (*McLoughlin v O'Brian* [1982] 2 All ER 298). In the unreported case of *Swiecicki v Camden and Islington Area Health Authority* (1984) 24 Med Sci Law 148, £80,000 were paid for injuries suffered when a woman with postnatal depression fell from a hospital window. *University Hospital Board v Lepine* [1966] SCR 561 is a relevant Canadian case.

Suicide Act 1961

The crime of committing suicide was abrogated by the Suicide Act 1961, s.1. Section 2 of the Act, however, retains the offence of aiding, abetting, counselling or procuring a suicide.

Section 2 of the Suicide Act 1961 has special relevance to doctors who may be asked to assist in the suicide of their patients who are either terminally ill or in intolerable pain. Williams[1] is clearly sympathetic to the concept of 'leaving the pills' for use by the dying patient and distinguishes this from assisting suicide by young people or persuading others to commit suicide. It is, however, difficult to see how the doctor, who must provide some instruction on the toxicity of drugs, can avoid being guilty of counselling and procuring suicide in such circumstances — and the policy of the courts is to consider aiding, abetting, counselling and procuring as a whole. In practice, however, no doctor has been prosecuted under s.2. The law on abetment is generally difficult to apply as the intent must be specific; thus, the general public supply of a booklet advising on suicide cannot be regarded as aiding and abetting under the Act[2].

Neither suicide nor attempted suicide is a crime in Scotland[3]; from this it would appear that there can be no common law art and part offence comparable to s.2 of the 1961 Act.

See also: Euthanasia; Suicide

1. Williams G *Textbook of Criminal Law* (2nd ed, 1983) p.579, Stevens, London.
2. *Attorney General v Able* [1983] 3 WLR 845, [1984] 1 All ER 277. Ash C 'Complicity in suicide' (1982) 132 NLJ 178.
3. Gowers EA (chairman) *Report of the Royal Commission on Capital Punishment* (Cmd 8932) (1953) para.167, HMSO, London.

Superfecundation

Superfecundation is the impregnation by separate acts of coitus of two or more ova discharged at the same ovulation. As with superfetation, it will only be in exceptional circumstances that such an occurrence is distinguishable from the bearing of binovular twins.

See also: Pregnancy; Superfetation

Superfetation

Superfetation is the impregnation of ova produced at different monthly ovulations. Even if it can occur, which is doubtful, it must be rare and, at any event, the condition will be indistinguishable from binovular twinning save in exceptional circumstances. Death of an early fetus *in utero* followed by a further pregnancy before the next menstrual period is, however, a recognisable possibility; the impression will then be given of an abnormally long period of gestation.

See also: Pregnancy

Surgical Shock

Surgical shock is to be distinguished very clearly from the legal concept of shock; the former is a physical condition which may be fatal, the latter is a mental state better referred to as 'nervous shock'.

The essential abnormality in surgical or traumatic shock is the loss of blood volume (hypovolaemia). The causes of this are several — haemorrhage is an obvious cause but fluid may be lost without loss of erythrocytes as in burns or in crushing of the tissues. Plasma loss has the added disadvantage that the blood is concentrated and, therefore, more viscous and inherently more difficult to circulate.

All forms of surgical shock predispose to tissue hypoxia; this, in itself, increases capillary permeability which may lead to further fluid loss — e.g. into the lungs. The condition is thus self-perpetuating and is further exaggerated by progressively poor pulmonary function. The interplay of shock and disseminated intravascular coagulation will also be cumulative and progressive.

The role of bacteria in the production and maintenance of shock is variable. Fluid loss is characteristic of some infections including that by the clostridia which are responsible for gas gangrene and are intimately associated with tissue injury. On the other hand, some organisms — especially those associated with the large bowel — appear to cause shock without manifest infection of the blood. The condition is generally known as endotoxic shock — there was, at one time, almost an epidemic of endotoxic deaths associated with the use of tampons[1], although, in the opinion of many, the diagnosis was often made on circumstantial grounds only.

The basis for fatal surgical shock is heart failure which is clinically associated with hypotension (low blood pressure). The critical pressure is that in the venous return and very severe effects may be present before the arterial blood pressure is significantly reduced. Treatment is a matter of replacement of fluid by blood, and/or electrolyte solutions and/or plasma substitutes with monitoring of the central venous pressure. The amount of fluid needed to be administered is generally much more than is suggested by simple clinical examination. There is, however, one form of shock, associated with bacterial infection, where the cardiac output is apparently normal and the tissues simply fail to take up oxygen; the normal methods of treatment are inadequate and the condition, which is imperfectly understood, has a very high mortality.

It will be seen that, since the basic fault lies in reduced cardiac output, 'shock' may be precipitated centrally within the heart; such 'cardiogenic' shock is characteristic of severe myocardial infarction or of cardiac tamponade.

Hypoxic damage to the tissues may persist after adequate treatment of shock; this is particularly important in the kidneys where the condition of acute renal failure may be established and will require treatment on its own account.

See also: Burns; Cardiac tamponade; Crush injury; Disseminated intravascular coagulation; Gangrene; Hypovolaemia; Hypoxia; Myocardial infarction; Nervous shock; Pulmonary oedema

1. de Saxe MJ et al 'Toxic shock syndrome in Britain' (1982) 284 Br Med J 1641.

Surrogate Motherhood

This is defined as the carrying by a woman of a child in pursuance of an arrangement made before she began to carry the child and made with a view to the child being handed over to, and the parental rights being exercised by, another person or persons[1]. Thus the law makes no distinction between 'surrogate motherhood' resulting from artificial insemination and 'womb leasing' although there are good conceptual reasons for so doing. In the great majority of surrogate motherhoods, the male gamete will be supplied by the husband of the receiving woman. There are a few medical conditions in which such an arrangement might be the optimum treatment for female infertility — e.g. when a woman has a diseased or absent womb or is medically unable to carry a child. Surrogacy may, in such circumstances, provide a reasonable opportunity for the husband to father his own child.

The arguments against surrogacy have been widely canvassed[2]. In addition to those of general morality, they include the difficulties of drawing up and enforcing any contract — e.g. in the event of a change of mind by either party or of indications for an abortion — the legality of any financial involvement in the light of the Adoption Acts and the possible effects on the child on the assumption that there is 'maternal bonding' during pregnancy. Parental rights for the recipient's husband have already been refused[3] and there is no doubt that the practicalities of any surrogacy agreements, no matter how reached, would be heavily biased against the proposed recipients of the child. But it could be argued from this that the difficulties themselves indicated a particular motivation on the part of the prospective parents which could be reflected in an ideal environment for an adopted child[4].

The subject of surrogate motherhood has been dominated by the fear of commercialisation through profit-making agencies which, although probably acceptable in the USA[5], would be antithetic to concepts of medicine in the UK. One case of commercial surrogacy came before the British courts before legislation was passed; it was then held that the commercial aspects were not relevant and, on the principle of the best interests of the child as is applied in wardship cases, care and control was given to the father and his wife[6].

Public anxiety has now dictated the passage of legislation[1]. Under s.2(1), it is an offence for any person to initiate or take part in any negotiations for the making of a surrogacy arrangement on a commercial basis; but no offence is committed by the principals — the surrogate herself or the biological, and intending social, father (s.2(2)). Similarly, the principals do not commit an offence by advertising their needs or availabiltiy but those who publish such an advertisement in any way are guilty of an offence (s.3). Thus, in so far as surrogate motherhood may be a responsible treatment for a minority of cases of infertility, the door is left ajar for the procedure to be conducted either privately or through the medium of officially licensed and non-profit-making agencies who would be responsible for the medical supervision of the process and the ensuing adoption proceedings. The Government have therefore followed, to an extent, the minority report of the Warnock Committee[7].

See also: Adoption; Embryo transfer; Infertility; Wardship proceedings; Womb leasing

1. Surrogacy Arrangements Act 1985.

2. *See*, for example, Winslade WJ 'Surrogate mothers; private right or public wrong?' (1981) 7 J Med Ethics 153; Mady TM 'Surrogate mothers: the legal issues' (1981) 7 Am J Law Med 323; Brophy KM 'A surrogate mother contract to bear a child' (1982) 20 J Fam Law 263; Brahams D 'In-vitro fertilisation and related research' [1983] 2 Lancet 726.

3. *A v C* reported in Parker DC 'Legal aspects of artificial insemination and embryo transfer' (1982) 12 Fam Law 103 following *A v C* (1978) 8 Fam Law 170.

4. For discussion, and approval, of combining surrogacy with adoption, *see* Wright M 'Surrogacy and adoption: problems and possibilities' [1986] Fam Law 109.

5. But *see*, to the contrary, *Doe v Kelley* (1980) 6 Fam LR (BMA) 3011, affd no.50380 (Ct App May 5, 1981).

6. *In re a Baby* (1985) Times, 15 January.

7. Warnock M (chairman) *Report of the Committee of Inquiry into Human Fertilisation and Embryology* (Cmnd 9314) (1984): Expression of Dissent A (HMSO, London). For a similar view, *see* Mason JK and McCall Smith RA *Law and Medical Ethics* (1983) pp.42–46, Butterworths, London. However, at the time of writing, a Surrogacy Arrangements (Amendment) Bill 1986 has been introduced in the House of Lords; under this Bill, it would seem that the only surrogacy arrangements which would not be illegal would be those of a wholly private nature undertaken without medical or other assistance.

Suspended Animation

In very unusual circumstances, the body's metabolic rate may be so reduced that the requirement of individual cells for oxygen is satisfied through the use of oxygen dissolved in the body fluids. In such circumstances, there may be no cardiorespiratory action and, in the event of subsequent recovery of function, the retrospective assumption of suspended animation is made. Hypothermia of the tissues of relatively insidious onset appears to be the overriding requirement for such a unique situation and the appearances will be compounded if the primary respiratory stimulus is inhibited from other causes (e.g. by drug overdose). A close approximation to suspended animation is deliberately induced in the technique of cryosurgery.

Although we believe that some evidence of cardiorespiratory activity — even if demonstrable only by instrumentation — would be discovered in such cases if sought, mistakes are made and a trickle of repetitive reports of elderly parasuicides reviving in the warmth of the mortuary persists, and instructive horror stories of recovery after certification of death from such debilitating diseases as cholera are still told. It is to be noted that hypothermia and drug overdose are two conditions which must be eliminated before a diagnosis of brain stem death is acceptable in the UK.

The most authentic modern instance of genuine suspended animation is, however, that of the young man who stowed away in a nose wheel bay of a trans-Atlantic airliner. He made a complete recovery after nine hours at 8,800 m (29,000 ft) where the alveolar oxygen pressure is about 2.0 kPa (15 mmHg) and the ambient temperature in the nose wheel bay was, at most, −6°C[1].

See also: Brain stem death; Death; Hypothermia

1. Pajares J and Merayo F 'Unique clinical case, both of hypoxia and hypothermia, studied in a 18-year-old aerial stowaway on a flight from Havana to Madrid' (1970) 41 Aerospace Med 1416.

Swab Cases

The leaving by surgeons and nurses of swabs and other medical devices in the abdomens of patients after surgical operations has given rise to a group of actions which are colloquially known as 'swab cases'.

Such cases illustrate very well the occasional need which the courts accept to invoke the doctrine of *res ipsa loquitur* — clearly a mistake has been made but it may be impossible for a plaintiff to identify the negligent act with precision. Thus, in the classic case of *Mahon v Osborne*[1] it was said: 'as it is the task of the surgeon to put the swabs in, so it is his task to take them out. . .and he cannot absolve himself, if a mistake has been made, by saying "I relied on the nurse"'. Since the patient could know nothing of the operating theatre discipline, it was for the surgeon to show that he exercised due care to ensure that the swabs were not left behind. In at least one other case[2], the courts have declined to follow the professional standard test of negligence and have held that it was still possible to follow accepted practice and yet be negligent.

The fact that a foreign body was left in a patient is, today, likely to be accepted as indefensible by insurers; such actions are therefore appropriately settled out of the court in the patient's favour.

See also: Negligence; *Res ipsa loquitur*

1. [1939] 1 All ER 535.
2. *Urry and Urry v Bierer and others* (1955) Times, 16 March; on appeal, (1955) Times, 15 July.

T

Tardieu Spots

'Tardieu spots' is an eponym for petechial haemorrhages, which were first described in asphyxial deaths in infants by the French police surgeon, Auguste Tardieu (1855).

See also: Petechial haemorrhage

Tattoos

Tattooing is the impregnation of the true skin (dermis) with particles or dyes such as carbon, indigo and vermilion. Once inoculated, the particles are very difficult to remove, a property which has been abused in the past as a means of permanent identification of prisoners, etc. Attempts to remove tattoos by, say, laser therapy may cause severe tissue damage in inexpert hands[1].

Tattoos have several forensic implications which may be both direct and indirect. Perhaps their main significance is in identification of the dead, in which circumstance they may be surprisingly permanent; for example, they are often exaggerated in drowned bodies from which the epidermis has peeled and they may well be demonstrated beneath what seems to be excessive charring due to fire. On the other hand, it should be borne in mind that tattoo designs tend to be stereotyped — this may be particularly important in the context of a mass disaster.

As a variation on the theme of identification, tattoos may be sectarian or social in purpose. Thus, homosexual men are said to use specific identifying designs and the same is reported of the drug subculture; in the latter case, however, tattoos may also be used to cover unsightly scars resulting from injection. Highly ornate tattoos may be used in a semi-religious context[2] and as an expression of dignity or rank among many ethnic groups.

Some tattoo processes are conducted under less than satisfactory conditions of hygiene, and transmission of the virus of hepatitis — and possibly that of AIDS — and of the spirochaete of syphilis is quite possible.

The reasons behind the psychological drive to be tattooed are very varied. The process is often painful and it may be an expression of masculinity; there may be a need to support a doubtful proposition — such as undying love — or it may be simply a matter of protest. Because consent to what is, in effect, a form of self-mutilation ought to be that of a mature mind, it is an offence in the UK to tattoo a

551

person under the age of 18[3]. Williams raises doubt as to whether tattooing of adults may not be illegal but finds it impossible to believe that the tattooer can be guilty of an assault[4].

See also: Acquired immune deficiency syndrome; Consent by minors; Hepatitis; Identification

1. *Frempong v The General Medical Council* (1984) 134 NLJ 745.
2. The Japanese experience is interesting. *See* Tsunenaris et al 'How to identify the Yakuza, Japanese racketeers — their sociology, criminology and physical characteristics' (1984) 13 Ann Acad Med Singapore 25.
3. Tattooing of Minors Act 1969, s.1. *See* a previous case, *Burrell v Harmer* [1967] Crim LR 169.
4. *Textbook of Criminal Law* (2nd ed, 1983) pp.571 and 591, Stevens, London.

Terminal Illness

Terminal illness may be defined as illness in which the application of life-sustaining procedures serves only to postpone the moment of death of the patient. Any therapeutic dilemma lies in deciding whether to provide or to withhold such treatment and, at the same time, to sustain maximum comfort — essentially, freedom from pain.

The fully competent patient is an autonomous being who has an absolute right to refuse treatment; whether there is a similar right to demand treatment which is thought to be futile is less clear but common humanity would suggest that such requests should be met unless there are overriding policy considerations to the contrary. Therapeutic decisions in regard to the comatose or demented terminally ill patient must be taken within the general framework of the ordinary/extraordinary treatment test, which includes consideration of the views of close relatives. It is, however, clear that active steps to accelerate the death of the terminally ill patient cannot be condoned — 'if the acts done are intended to kill and do, in fact, kill, it does not matter if the life of the victim is shortened by months or weeks, or even hours or minutes, it is still murder'[1].

Nevertheless, from the same source comes the dictum — 'The doctor. . .is entitled to do all that is proper and necessary to relieve pain and suffering even if the measures he takes may incidentally shorten life'. This would seem to be a clear legal endorsement of the moral principle of double effect, which is firmly based on the implications of intent.

The matter is not, however, entirely straightforward; a senior law lord has said, admittedly in a non-judicial context — 'doing nothing or killing both the pain and the patient who has only a short while to live. . .may be good morals but it is far from clear that it is good law'[2]. The doubt raised may not be of great practical importance as the modern treatment of terminal pain has little adverse effect on life expectancy; nevertheless, it is clear that the matter turns on the good faith of the medical profession.

In view of this, Lord Edmund-Davis has suggested that a doctor might '. . .prefer to proceed within the known protection of the law rather than be left to act in the hope that those charged with law enforcement would turn a blind eye to what in mercy [he] felt compelled to do'[2] and, in fact, several States in the USA have enacted 'allowing to die' legislation[3]. It has been well argued that such statutory control may be counter-productive and operate against the patient's best interests[4]. Certainly, any law must be difficult to apply; the treatment of the terminally ill is so inextricably a matter of medical practice and clinical decision that it is probably better left that way. The growth of the hospice movement is likely to have a profound influence on attitudes.

See also: Double effect; Euthanasia; Hospices; *Mens rea*; Ordinary/Extraordinary treatment

1. Per Devlin J. Quoted in Palmer H 'Dr Adams' trial for murder' [1957] Crim LR 365.
2. Edmund-Davies Lord 'On dying and dying well — legal aspects' (1977) 70 Proc R Soc Med 73.
3. The first being in California (California Health and Safety Code, paras.7185–7195).
4. Lappe M 'Dying while living: a critique of allowing to die legislation' (1978) 4 J Med Ethics 195.

Testamentary Capacity

The making of a valid will requires the testator to have a certain standard of mental capacity at the time the will is made. The will is regarded as invalid and probate will not be granted in the absence of this capacity.

The fact that the will appears superficially to be rational is not of itself sufficient evidence of normality in the testator's mind although it does raise a presumption of sanity. Conversely, the fact that a testator was receiving psychiatric treatment does not necessarily mean that he was unable to make a valid will. The court will consider the question on its merits in each case. Criteria for establishing testamentary capacity were laid down in *Banks v Goodfellow*[1], where the court explained what was meant by the requirement that the testator be of 'sound disposing mind and memory'. It is essential that he should understand that he is making a will, that he has a recollection of the property of which he means to dispose and that he should also recollect the people who are the 'natural object of his bounty', at the same time understanding the way in which it is to be distributed between them.

Largely as a result of the influence of nineteenth century psychiatry, many of the decisions in testamentary capacity invoke the significance of delusions. A delusion has been defined in this context as an irrational belief which cannot be eradicated from the mind of the testator[2]. Such a delusion might affect testamentary capacity if it bears upon a person who is named in the will or who might normally expect to receive some benefit from the testator. The courts have held it to be immaterial when it focuses upon a totally unrelated issue. It might be difficult to distinguish an insane delusion from a merely mistaken or deliberately perverse belief. In *Re Nightingale*[3], for example, the court had to consider whether it was irrational of the testator to believe that his son was trying to kill him when the son had merely rearranged the pillows around his aged father's head. In making such decisions, the courts will usually attempt to allow the testator some room for individual quirkiness before the line between soundness and unsoundness of mind is crossed.

The concept of the lucid interval is similarly stressed. An insane person who appears to experience a period of lucidity may make a will during such a period. In one Canadian case, the testator was described as having had 'good days' and 'bad days'. A codicil made on a 'good day' was upheld by the court[4].

See also: Delusions

1. (1870) LR 5 QB 549.
2. *Dew v Clark and Clark* (1826) 3 Add 79.
3. (1974) 119 SJ 189.
4. *Royal Trust Co v Rampone* (1974) 4 WWR 735.

Further reading
Mellows K *Law of Succession* (4th ed, 1983), p.31 et seq, Butterworths, London.

Thalassaemia

Thalassaemia is that form of haemoglobinopathy which derives from failure of the synthesis of globin.

It occurs in various forms, the delineation of which is beyond the scope of this entry; reports may speak of either alpha- or beta-thalassaemia, of which the latter is by far the more important. The basic feature of beta-thalassaemia is a genetic inability to form adult haemoglobin; the result is that fetal haemoglobin, which is inadequate in the non-placental situation, persists. The condition is genetically determined; the homozygous state is known as thalassaemia major and the hetero-zygous as thalassaemia minor. The former causes a severe anaemic disease with physical deformities and, generally, an early death in the absence of multiple and life-long blood transfusions. Cases of the latter persist with a varying degree of anaemia which is compatible with a good life and which may be symptomless. The beta-thalassaemias are very ethnic dependent and are distributed predominantly along the Mediterranean coast but occur also in a wide band extending through the Middle East to India, Southeast Asia and the East Indies; the condition is therefore very likely to be found in the immigrant population of the UK[1]. The carrier state is recognisable in parents; it may be possible to undertake fetal diagnosis (*see* 'Feto-scopy') if both are found to be carriers.

The main forensic concerns when dealing with a case of thalassaemia minor are those associated with a mild anaemia in general — e.g. special care when undergoing surgical operation. On a social scale, the existence of large numbers of cases of thalassaemia major places an enormous burden on the health services; there is no doubt that antenatal diagnosis and abortion is the most effective way of dealing with the problem in areas where it is prevalent.

See also: Anaemia; Fetoscopy; Genetic disease; Haemoglobinopathy

1. Black J 'Paediatrics among ethnic minorities. Families from the Mediterranean and Aegean' (1985) 290 Br Med J 923.

Threshold Limit Values

The greater part of the art of preventing industrial poisoning consists of maintaining a pure atmosphere. Some escape of poisonous substances is, however, inevitable and the acceptability of contamination is defined in terms of threshold limit values.

The threshold limit value of a substance is the air-borne concentration of that substance to which it is believed nearly all workers may be repeatedly exposed without ill-effects. The concentration may be expressed in weight per volume or in parts per million.

Such a system is to some extent artificial and is a compromise between absolute safety and practicality. Threshold limit values can be compared to speed limits on roads — accidents will occur at speeds below the official limit but transportation might be virtually impossible were the limit to be reduced further. In effect, the threshold limit value in industry is the level thought likely to be injurious if exceeded; all practicable measures must be taken to protect the employees against inhalation of toxic substances if the threshold limit value is exceeded[1]. Practicability in this context refers only to the technical feasibility — cost, for example, does not enter the definition.

See also: Industrial poisoning; Poisoning

1. Factories Act 1961, s.63.

Thrombosis

Thrombosis is the formation of true fibrin clots within the vessels. The conditions for this abnormal circumstance are, firstly, an alteration in the coagulative mechanisms within the blood, secondly, alterations in the inner vessel wall and, thirdly, stasis of the blood. The vascular abnormality within arteries is often provided by atheroma; thrombosis is then facilitated by hypercoagulability and by lowered blood pressure, both of which follow upon trauma. Venous thrombi are of major significance and, in these, the predominant features are hypercoagulability and stasis. Venous thrombi are therefore particularly likely during enforced rest after surgical operations; they will form mainly in the legs and pelvis and steadily increase in size as more clot is laid upon the old. The danger is that the mass of thrombus will break off and become an embolus (*see* 'Pulmonary embolism').

The appearances of *ante mortem* thrombi are typical. The nidus is a collection of platelets with which fibrin mixes; this slows down the blood flow and looser red thrombus forms on top of the platelet aggregation. The end-result is a clot showing laminae of pale and red fibrin thrombi which must be clearly distinguished from *post mortem* clot; this is not laminated and is often divided into a dark red area where the red cells have settled under gravity and a pale fatty area representing the serum component[1].

The presence or absence of *post mortem* thrombi is sometimes of importance in deciding on the mode of death. In general, persons who have died a slow, natural death will show abundant *post mortem* clots. A healthy person, on the other hand, has a greater concentration of circulating fibrinolysins at the time of death and this is further increased during exercise or during periods of emotional stress; it is therefore common to find wholly fluid blood in the bodies of young persons who have died unnatural deaths. This is the probable basis of the now discredited belief that fluid *post mortem* blood is indicative of death from mechanical asphyxia.

The same factors may account for the distribution of thrombi in deaths from coronary insufficiency. Coronary thrombi are common in those persons dying in hospital; they are relatively infrequent in medico-legal cases in which death has been rapid and which are often associated with muscular activity at the time[2].

See also: Atheroma; Coagulation of the blood; Coronary disease; Pulmonary embolism

1. For an easy description, *see* Stalker AL 'Haemorrhage, coagulation and thrombosis' in Mason JK (ed) *The Pathology of Violent Injury* (1978) Chap.18, Edward Arnold, London.
2. *See* Crawford T *Pathology of Ischaemic Heart Disease* (1977) Chap.5, Butterworths, London.

Throttling

Throttling is strangulation by the hands. It may be performed with one or both hands, from the front or from behind. Fingertip abrasions corresponding to these variables will probably be present on the neck but the possibility of changes in grip must be recognised by the pathologist or police surgeon.

The possible modes of death are as described under 'Strangulation' but, in this case, death from vagal inhibition of the heart is even more likely because fracture or dislocation of the laryngeal cartilages is frequent and is a potent cause of sympathetic nerve stimulation.

The diagnosis of death from throttling is made by recognition of the pattern of fingerprints and by the presence of additional abrasions due to the victim's efforts to escape; typical fingernail impressions caused by the assailant's hands may also be seen. Internally, bruising of the muscles of the neck corresponding to the pressure points may be present, as may posterior bruising where the larynx is pressed against the spinal column. The most significant finding is of fracture or dislocation of the laryngeal cartilages. The superior cornua of the thyroid cartilage are most often affected but the greater horns of the hyoid bone may be simultaneously involved due to tension on the thyrohyoid ligament. In practice, it is important that vital reaction in the form of bruising is demonstrated because normal jointing in the bones and cartilages may simulate fracture, poor technique may give rise to fracture during the postmortem dissection and it is not impossible that a fracture may have resulted from a previous incident. Technically, it is useful to drain the area of blood by dissecting the head as a preliminary procedure in the investigation of throttling cases. Fracture is most likely to occur in the calcified cartilages of the elderly, when X-ray confirmation is invaluable as a means of presenting evidence. As in strangulation by ligature, death may be due to venous occlusion, when severe subconjunctival haemorrhages or lesser petechial haemorrhages will be seen. This mode of death is particularly common when the web of the thumb has been used to strangle. Again, however, the length of time needed to kill in this way must be less than would be expected on theoretical grounds.

Acute alcoholism and emotion will exaggerate a sympathetic/vagal reflex. The lover's defence: 'I only clutched her neck in play and she collapsed' may therefore be true[1]. The distinction then rests very much on the degree of injury discovered at postmortem.

See also: Larynx; Petechial haemorrhage; Strangulation; Vagal inhibition of the heart; Vital reaction; X-rays

1. Examples are given in Simpson K (ed) *Taylor's Principles and Practices of Medical Jurisprudence* (12th ed, 1965) p.360, Churchill Livingstone, Edinburgh.

Timing of Death

The estimation of the time interval between death and the examination of the cadaver is far less exact than is commonly supposed. The only period when any semblance of accuracy can be anticipated is in the first 18 hours *post mortem* when the temperature of the body, as measured by rectal or intrahepatic thermometer, provides the best guide.

The dead body produces no heat as it has no metabolism; it will therefore cool until, theoretically, it reaches ambient temperature. The rate of cooling will depend upon the difference between the body and ambient temperatures, and the resultant gradient will be in the form of a curve; but, because some residual enzymatic activity remains and because the partially insulated body core will retain its heat for a time, the curve will be of sigmoid shape with an initial plateau.

Whilst many attempts have been made to explain the cooling of the dead body on scientific principles[1], the fact remains that there are so many uncertain variables in a biological situation as to make it impossible to apply the laws of physics. For example, the body temperature at the time of death is unknown — and some forms of violent death, in particular those associated with asphyxia or with cerebral haemorrhage, may raise the temperature significantly; the isothermic 'plateau' will last for a variable time — it is generally betwen 30 and 60 minutes; the amount of clothing and of the body fat will variably insulate the body and affect the rate of cooling — a clothed body loses heat at about two-thirds the rate of a naked one whilst those bodies with a large surface area as related to body mass (e.g. children and the aged) will always cool faster than will well-built adults; convection currents will significantly affect the rate of cooling; the effect of ambient temperature on the rate of cooling has been noted but the end-result is that the body temperature will equate with the ambient temperature in the same time irrespective of the latter value. As the body temperature approaches ambient temperature the 'curve' flattens out and it is generally agreed that the body temperature is useless as a measure of the *post mortem* interval when it has fallen by 80 per cent of its original excess over the environment. It may, indeed, never reach equilibrium as heat generation by putrefaction may supervene.

Bearing all these difficulties in mind, it is probably reasonable policy to assume that the original body temperature was 37'C and that the cooling rate was 1'C per hour and, then, to make adjustments for conditions in the light of experience. The 'time of death' can then be estimated within a bracket of ± one hour. In practice, many of the variables tend to cancel each other out — for example, a body will be more heavily clothed in a cold atmosphere. If seen within the period of two to eight hours after death, a relatively accurate assessment can be made by taking two temperatures at an interval of one hour; the actual rate at the straightest part of the curve can then be assessed. The body feels cold after some 12 hours but cooling in water may be twice as fast as in air.

Beyond the first 12 hours, the time after death can be approximated by having regard to hypostasis, rigor mortis and the signs of putrefaction, all of which are discussed under separate headings. Some considerable interest has been shown in the biochemical changes in the body fluids, particularly in the vitreous humour of the eye, and these, again, are described under that heading.

Other observations, such as the amount of food in the stomach correlated with the last known meal, have been used; their value in an adult situation is extremely doubtful save in answer to very specific points[2].

See also: Hypostasis; Putrefaction; Rigor mortis; Vitreous humour

1. *See* the classic papers by Marshall TK 'The use of the cooling formula in the study of post mortem body cooling' (1962) 7 J Forens Sci 189 and by Marshall TK and Hoare FE 'The rectal cooling after death and its mathematical expression' (1962) 7 J Forens Sci 56.
2. The confusion engendered in the Canadian case of *R v Truscott* is well described in Polson CJ, Gee DJ and Knight B *The Essentials of Forensic Medicine* (4th ed, 1984) p.33, Pergamon, Oxford.

Torts

The law of torts is that legal area which is concerned with liability for non-contractual civil wrongs. One speaks of a law of *torts* rather than of *tort* because the law in this area consists, for historical reasons, of a number of different wrongs, each of which may have specific rules relating to liability and its requisites. The main torts which will be of medico-legal significance are those of negligence — undoubtedly the most important and rapidly developing form of liability — and of trespass.

The aim of the law of torts is to provide compensation for the plaintiff whose interests have, in some way, been infringed by the act of another. Not all infringements will lead to compensation; for an action to be successful, the defendant's act must either fit into one of the recognised existing categories of tort or must be one which can be considered by the court as providing appropriate grounds for a new action.

The view that the province of the law of torts is steadily contracting with the growth of alternative schemes of compensation is, perhaps, overoptimistic. The advantages of compensation schemes which operate outside the framework of tort law may be considerable but their adoption in the UK and, indeed, in most other countries in the common law world, seems some distance away — it is clearly an area in which old habits die hard[1].

See also: Negligence; Trespass

1. For a discussion of some American plans, *see* Smith R 'Malpractice: a New Zealand solution to an American crisis?' (1985) 291 Br Med J 812.

Toxic Jaundice

Jaundice may derive from toxic insults to the liver of several types — it may, for example, be caused by overdose or repetition of some anaesthetic agents or it may present as an end-stage of alcoholic liver disease. It is customary, however, to reserve the term 'toxic jaundice' for cases which are notifiable to the Health and Safety Executive — that is, jaundice derived from industrial occupation.

This type of jaundice results from liver cell damage following overexposure to hydrocarbons of both aromatic and aliphatic type; absorption is by inhalation but also through contamination of the skin. Aromatic hydrocarbons are only rarely associated with jaundice as a major presenting sign; exposure to trinitrotoluene is the main example. By contrast, toxic jaundice is a common diagnostic sign of poisoning by aliphatic organic compounds which are used principally as cleaning agents or as industrial solvents. Carbon tetrachloride, tetrachlorethane and, especially, dichlorethane are severely damaging to the liver. Tetrachlorethane became notorious in the First World War when it was used to tighten the fabric of aircraft. The extent of toxic jaundice as a whole is fast diminishing as substituted compounds are introduced to industry.

See also: Alcohol; Cirrhosis; Jaundice; Liver disease and injury; Notifiable diseases

Toxicological Analyses

Toxicology is the study of toxic or noxious substances. The law does not distinguish between substances which are poisonous *per se* and those which are poisonous only when taken in excess; the greater part of the modern toxicologist's work consists not of a search for the conventional poisons of the turn of the century but of the analysis of biological materials for the presence of modern medical or paramedical drugs. The difficulties surrounding identification and quantification of drugs in these circumstances are formidable — the drugs will be present in minuscule quantities, they will be contained in biological material which will interfere with the analyses, the drugs may be present in altered form or metabolites, and the material itself may be in poor condition; the accuracy of modern toxicology is a remarkable achievement. Although toxicology may be applied in the clinical situation, we are here concerned more with the investigation of suspicious deaths.

It is convenient to consider the analysis in four stages: isolation — which involves removal of the protein and fat complexes of the biological medium; purification — which is a matter of removing substances similar to that sought; identification; and quantitative assay. The last two are frequently combined in modern laboratory technology.

The methods in common use for identification with or without quantification are spectrometry and chromatography, and these are discussed under separate headings. Some important drugs, including those of the digitalis group, are very difficult to isolate, and relatively new techniques — radioimmunoassay and enzyme multiplied immunoassay — may be used for analyses. The technique depends upon the preparation of antibodies to the drugs which effect an immune reaction, the strength of which can be measured by sophisticated techniques; the tests are not completely specific although they are very effective in clinical work.

Certain practical difficulties always beset the toxicological laboratory. The efficiency of analyses decreases with uncertainty as to what is being sought — the 'drug screen test', which is generally an indication of despair on the part of the pathologist, is equally aggravating and generally unrewarding to the toxicologist. Specimens are often too small for the test to be applied, containers tend to leak and bacterial contamination (which could have been prevented by the use of a suitable preservative) may interfere with, or even falsify, the results (*see* 'Alcohol'). A major concern, especially in criminal cases, is the correct labelling of specimens to ensure continuity of evidence.

An analysis intended for use in the criminal courts is regarded as part of the evidence from the outset. The results are privileged and are not subject to an action in negligence[1].

See also: Alcohol; Chromatography; Immune reaction; Nuclear medicine; Spectrometry

1. *Evans v London Hospital Medical College and others* [1981] 1 All ER 715. For a remarkably similar case and decision in the USA, *see Block v Sacramento Clinical Labs Inc* 182 Cal Rptr 438 (1982).

Transfusion Reactions

The scientific basis of transfusion reactions is described in greater detail under 'Blood transfusion'.

A transfusion reaction due to incompatibility in the ABO blood group system may be limited to a rise in temperature and rigor but, in the event of the recipient's antibodies being particularly strong, the resultant haemolysis of the donor cells may cause serious disease. This will be shown by varying degrees of shock, and the possibility of acute renal failure will be present even if primary treatment is successful.

Clinical manifestations of an incompatible transfusion related to other blood group systems are likely to be relatively benign because the necessary antibody will have been provoked only by previous transfusions. In such a case, the recipient will probably suffer from no more than jaundice; the effects on any similarly incompatible fetus are, however, likely to be very severe (*see* 'Haemolytic disease of the newborn'). All transfusion reactions of the immune type can be prevented by efficient cross-matching of recipient serum and donor cells.

Other non-specific transfusion reactions take the form of feverish illness and are due to so-called 'pyrogens' in the transfused fluid. The nature of these is often indeterminate — they may well be the products of dead bacteria — but, other than in exceptional circumstances, the effects are transient. Very rarely, a reaction results from the release of toxic intracellular electrolytes into the donor plasma; such a cause is directly related to either improper or prolonged storage conditions of the donated blood.

The investigation of a transfusion reaction requires expert analysis of the remaining donor blood and of the blood of the recipient. Since the majority of incompatible transfusions result from clerical or communication errors, a thorough examination of the administrative system is also necessary so that similar mistakes can be prevented in the future.

See also: Blood transfusion; Haemolytic disease of the newborn; Immune reaction; Jaundice; Kidney failure; Surgical shock

Transplantation of Organs

It is particularly tragic if death results not so much from the general process of ageing but from failure of a specific organ in a comparatively young person. The idea of replacing such an organ with one transplanted from another being is extremely attractive.

Aside from the technical expertise required, the first difficulty of transplantation lies in the rejection of the donated organ as a result of a tissue immune reaction. The greater the antigenic dissimilarity, the more intense will be the reaction; hence, in present circumstances, it is not feasible to transplant organs from another animal species to man. Lesser, intraspecies, incompatibilities can, however, be overcome by the use of immunosuppressive drugs which are steadily improving in effectiveness. Even so, the closer the antigenic similarity of recipient and donated organ, the easier and more permanent will be the suppressive effect. Tissue typing is therefore an essential prerequisite of transplantation and involves the use of the HLA (human leucocyte antigenic) system[1].

Donor organs can be obtained from the living or from dead bodies. Since it is not possible to consent to a lethal operation, living donation is limited to that of one of a pair of organs each capable of functioning alone and, in practice, this means kidney transplantation. Such an operation must have a reasonable expectancy of immunological success and is therefore virtually confined to donation from parents or siblings — identical twins being the ideal. Whether parents can properly consent to donation on behalf of their children has been decided in the affirmative in the US courts[2] but donation by minors is prohibited in, for example, Ontario[3]. The Australian Law Reform Commission Draft Bill recommends that minors may donate under stringent conditions, similar to those currently in force in France, but the proposal has met stiff opposition[4]. The point has not been tested in the British courts but there can be little doubt that the procedure would be considered legal if performed in good faith with the consent of the minor and of the parents. Currently, some 10 per cent of transplants in Britain involve living donors.

It is axiomatic that the donor involved in transplant therapy must be free from significant disease; the individual organ must, itself, be viable in that it can still function when it is inserted in the recipient. Thus, the second major difficulty in the process depends upon reducing to a minimum the degenerative changes which occur in the organ during the time it is both warm and anoxic. The superior results from living donation depend to a large extent on the fact that the donor and recipient operations can be performed electively with the latter following the former immediately. The warm anoxic time must, however, be prolonged if cadaver tissue is used; this is not only because there must be an appreciable interval between death and preparation of the operating theatre but also because the conditions of the Human Tissue Act 1961 must be met. Cadaver donations are therefore, at best, suspect and, in the USA at least, are probably unacceptable as not being the best treatment available[5]. The compromise position is provided by the beating heart donor by the use of which fully oxygenated organs can be obtained from the dead body. The acceptibility of the beating heart donor is wholly dependent upon the simultaneous acceptance of brain stem death as an indication of somatic death.

Transplantation of kidneys is therapeutically and economically preferable to renal dialysis and is mainly limited by the shortage of organs. Whether this shortage is due to the terms of the Human Tissue Act 1961, to public apathy or to professional inertia is open to debate[6]. In general, the constraints on the use of scarce resources do not apply in the same way as they do, say, in the case of heart transplants. Moreover, the recipient of a kidney transplant which fails can always return to treatment by dialysis; in the present state of the art, the recipient of a heart or liver transplant must die when that organ fails. As things now stand there is a good case to be made for considering renal transplantation as separate from any other form of organ replacement therapy.

It will be appreciated that the immunosuppression required for successful transplantation is not specific; patients under this treatment are therefore particularly susceptible to infections.

See also: Antigen; Beating heart donor; Brain stem death; Consent to medical treatment; Haemodialysis; Human Tissue Act 1961; Immune reaction; Immunosuppression; Resource allocation

1. This very complicated system is described in fairly simple terms by Batchelor JR 'Tissue matching in relation to organ transplantation' in Camps FE and Lucas BGB (eds) *Gradwohl's Legal Medicine* (3rd ed, 1976) Chap.29, Wright, Bristol.
2. Meyers DW *The Human Body and the Law* (1970) pp.120–125, Aldine, Chicago.
3. *See* Dickens BM *Medico-legal Aspects of Family Law* (1979), p.96, Butterworths, Toronto.
4. *Human Tissue Transplants*, Rep. No.7 (1977). *See also* Kirby MD 'Human tissue transplants: a riposte' [1980] 1 Med J Austral 331.
5. Leading Article 'Brain death' [1975] 1 Br Med J 356.
6. *See*, for example, the series of papers by Kennedy I and Sells RA (1979) 5 J Med Ethics 13, 165 and (1980) 6 J Med Ethics 29.

Trans-sexualism

Trans-sexualism — or the gender dysphoria syndrome — is a conviction that one's gender is wrong; the feeling may be so intense that efforts on the part of the subject to correct the mistake may include submission to extensive and mutilating surgery designed to alter the genitalia and the secondary sex characteristics to those of the opposite sex. The general belief is that the condition is some three times more common in men but this may be a false impression based on the evidence of surgical practice; it is obvious on physiological principles that the fabrication of male genitalia is unlikely to be functionally successful and, accordingly, is less likely to be attempted. There have been strong objections to the simpler 'male to female' operation on the grounds that castration involves an unacceptable maim[1] but it is now generally agreed that sex change surgery is a legitimate form of therapy and it is one which is available under the NHS[2]. Clearly, however, the decision to operate must be made with great care and perhaps even only after a period of trial status[3].

The legal attitude to trans-sexualism has been dominated by *Corbett v Corbett (otherwise Ashley)*[4] in which the sex of a 'converted' male was determined on the three-limbed basis of the chromosomal profile and of the preoperative gonadal complement and genital appearances. Whilst the court was unwilling to ponder on what would be the main consideration in the event that the three tests were not congruent, it was suggested that greater weight would then be given to the preoperative genital condition than to the others — or an assessment of the capacity to fulfil the essential role of a woman in marriage. Psychological and hormonal factors were, accordingly, excluded. It has been emphasised repeatedly that the issue in that case was solely that of a capacity to enter marriage and even this limited approach has been widely criticised by liberal academics[5]; the *Corbett* test has, however, been applied to the Sexual Offences Act 1956[6] and to the Sex Discrimination Act 1975[7]. There is a groundswell towards the acceptance for this unfortunate minority of a marriage union which is based on psychological happiness and it has even been suggested that there is a case for introducing a category of 'indeterminate sex'[8]. In submitting that *Corbett* is wrong in principle, Samuels has said: 'Society ought not to deny these human rights [to choose one's own destiny and gender] in the face of all the evidence'[9]. It is doubtful if public opinion in the UK is yet ready for such a fundamental change in the concepts of marriage and family but there is at least one case in the USA in which the judge could perceive 'no legal barrier, cognisable taboo, or reason grounded in public policy to prevent [a] person's identification at least for the purposes of marriage to the sex generally indicated'[10]. A somewhat similar movement is discernible in the EEC, where a right to respect in relation to privacy and family life has been firmly upheld; a right to trans-sexual marriage may well not be accepted[11].

Attitudes outside marriage are less exacting; for example, there seems to be nothing to stop a person changing his or her sex for the purposes of social security[12]. It seems, however, that legislative action allowing for legal change of sex in certain well-defined circumstances has been taken only in Sweden and in West Germany[13].

See also: Castration; Gender; Maim; Marriage; Sex chromosomes

1. Williams G *Textbook of Criminal Law* (2nd ed, 1983) p.590, Stevens, London.
2. Roth M 'Transsexualism and the sex change operation: a contemporary medicolegal and social problem' (1981) 49 Med-Leg J 5, and subsequent discussion. *See also* Ball JRB 'Thirty years' experience with transsexualism' (1981) 15 Aust & NZ J Psychiat 39.
3. *See* Armstrong CN 'Transsexualism: a medical perspective' (1980) 6 J Med Ethics 90; Lothstein LM 'Sex reassignment surgery — historical, bioethical, and theoretical issues' (1982) 139 Am J Psychiat 417.
4. [1971] P 83.
5. Bailey RJ 'Family law — decree of nullity of marriage of true hermaphrodite who has undergone sex change therapy' (1979) 53 ALJ 659.
6. *R v Tan and others* [1983] 3 WLR 361.
7. *White v British Sugar Corporation* [1977] IRLR 121.
8. This comes from a very searching article: Petit P 'L'ambuiguite de droit face au syndrome transsexuel' (1976) 74 Rev Droit Civ 263. *See also* Kennedy IM 'Transsexualism and single sex marriage' (1973) 2 Anglo-Am LR 112.

9. Samuels A 'Once a man, always a man; once a woman, always a woman — sex change and the law' (1984) 24 Med Sci Law 163.
10. *MT v JT* 355 A 2d 204 (NJ, 1976).
11. *Van Oosterwijck v Belgium* (1980) 3 EHRR 557. The case of *Mark Rees v United Kingdom* (1985) 7 EHRR 429 is currently being considered by the European Court of Human Rights.
12. Note 7 above; *see also* Ormrod R 'Medico-legal aspects of sex determination' (1972) 40 Med-Leg J 78.
13. For discussion, *see* Cremona-Barbaro A 'Medicolegal aspects of transsexualism in Western Europe' (1986) 5 Med Law 89.

Transvestism

Transvestism is wearing the clothes generally regarded as those associated with the opposite sex. Since the wearing of male clothes by women is now fashionable, transvestism, in the sense that it is worthy of a name, is confined to males. It will obviously be a major feature of trans-sexualism and it is a common aberration in cases which come to light as deaths from sexual asphyxia. Most transvestite behaviour is, however, little more than a charade; it is by no means always associated with latent homosexuality and it seems that many women are content to indulge their husband's whims — whims which are expressed theatrically by the female impersonator.

See also: Homosexuality; Sexual asphyxia; Trans-sexualism

Trauma and Disease

Trauma and disease may be related in two ways — either disease may cause injury or injury may cause disease. The latter is of dual relevance: injury may, uncommonly, initiate serious disease and this possibility is discussed under 'Ewing's postulates'; alternatively, and frequently, injury may dictate prolonged immobilisation and, amongst the many possible serious outcomes, hypostatic pneumonia (*see* 'Pneumonia') and pulmonary embolism deserve emphasis. The causation of accidents by disease is, however, of major importance in forensic pathology.

Aside from the academic aspects, the presence of disease causing trauma has practical importance in that the great majority of personal accident insurance policies, which provide a large return for a relatively small premium, include a clause to the effect that death must be due entirely to accident and must occur independently of any natural disease. The pathologist has, therefore, an obligation to resolve such problems.

This is, however, no simple task. In the first place, some significant diseases — in particular, epilepsy — are not normally demonstrable at autopsy. Secondly, it is often not easy to distinguish between natural disease and the results of trauma — a distinction which is particularly important in the interpretation of intracranial haemorrhage. Thirdly, the discovery of disease depends to a large extent on the effort applied (*see*, for example, 'Myocarditis'). And, fourthly, having identified organic disease, the major problem of interpretation still remains — that is, did the process cause or contribute to the accident or was it merely an incidental finding?

The solution of this fundamental problem rests on three main platforms. Firstly, the pathologist must consider the distribution of equivalent disease throughout an equivalent population — that is, what is the probability of a similar finding as a matter of chance? Secondly, there is the quality of the disease — the weight to be given to such variables as the extent and the stage of the disease is essentially a matter of pathological experience. And, thirdly, there is the circumstantial evidence — that is, what was the likelihood of disease provocation in the particular accident under review? This last question is particularly relevant to the day-to-day practice of legal medicine. Some legal authorities hold that the pathologist should make and interpret his findings in ignorance of the history of the event; in our opinion, to do so is to reduce the function of the autopsy to that of a mere technical exercise and to undermine seriously the value of expert medical evidence[1].

The academic importance of such an approach to accidental death scarcely needs emphasis. There can be no scientific evaluation of the role of disease in accident causation in its absence and, of greater importance, there can be no full appreciation of the value of medical screening methods in high risk occupations.

Degenerative disease is to be expected in old age and is clearly important in explaining the high mortality rate from accidents which is found in the elderly. A causative association may be difficult to establish — e.g. the effect of failing eyesight or hearing in a pedestrian road traffic death. In some cases, the causative link may be indirect; an elderly woman may trip, break her femur and die several weeks later from pulmonary embolism — death has, nevertheless, resulted from an accident and is, accordingly, reportable to the appropriate medico-legal authority.

See also: Accidental death; Ewing's postulates; Expert evidence; Intracranial haemorrhage; Myocarditis; Pneumonia; Pulmonary embolism

1. For a review of the principles, *see* Mason JK et al 'Death from coronary disease while at the controls of an aircraft' (1963) 34 Aerospace Med 858. For a practical example, *see* Department of Trade and Industry *Report of the Public Inquiry into the Causes and Circumstances of the accident near Staines on 18th June 1972* (Civil Aviation Aircraft Reports 4/73, 1973) HMSO, London.

Traumatic Asphyxia

Traumatic asphyxia (or crush asphyxia) results from mechanical immobilisation of the respiratory muscles. Characteristically, the autopsy findings are those of very intense congestion with petechial and confluent haemorrhages throughout the body above the diaphragm; there may well be abrasions and bruises corresponding to the primary cause.

Stampeding crowds are a particularly worrying possible source of such deaths and this is a major concern of those responsible for the design and maintenance of stadia[1]. The classic accident producing traumatic asphyxia is that in which the sides of trenches fall upon workers or in which they are overcome by a tip slide. A number of instances are related to automobiles, particularly in garages where a jack may give way or, more commonly, a lorry moves and crushes the mechanic against the garage wall. A surprising number of farm workers die as a result of their tractors falling over and a proportion of these used to die from crushing beneath the vehicle; UK and EEC legislation has now gone some way to preventing such deaths[2].

See also: Asphyxia; Petechial haemorrhage

1. Safety of Sports Grounds Act 1975. *Dougan v Glasgow Rangers' Football Club* (1972, unreported).
2. The Agriculture (Tractor Cabs) Regulations 1974 (SI 1974/2034), r.3. *See also* Directive 77/536/EEC.

Traumatic Subarachnoid Haemorrhage

A degree of diffuse subarachnoid haemorrhage is common following any death involving head injury but it is then little more than an incidental finding or marker of trauma.

The term 'traumatic subarachnoid haemorrhage' should be reserved for that form of the condition which is fatal *per se* and which is clearly related to trauma, particularly to trauma in the region of the upper cervical spine. The mechanism of the injury is obscure but it is assumed that damage to the wall of the vertebral artery as it passes through its foramen in the first cervical vertebra (the atlas bone) results in a leak of blood; this collects in the basal subarachnoid space where an increase of intracranial pressure is particularly dangerous. An actual fracture of the transverse process of the atlas bone is demonstrable, often only with difficulty, in some 50 per cent of cases[1]; the anatomy of the area makes it very difficult to visualise any break in the artery, which is best shown by *post mortem* angiography — but this, in itself, demands considerable foresight on the part of the pathologist and the availability of radiological facilities. Very often, a thorough examination fails to reveal any bleeding point[2].

The mechanism of the injury is quite different from that associated with trauma to the head. Its demonstration may completely alter the reconstruction of events as it can occur from relatively slight force which may well be accidental in origin — e.g. striking the side of a table, bath, etc. Death is rapid and is often complicated by inhalation of gastric contents. A strong relationship with alcohol is reported but this probably only reflects the conditions in which such an injury is likely to occur. An examination of the neck for evidence of internal bruising together with dissection of the cervical spine is essential when a fatal subarachnoid haemorrhage is not obviously associated with pre-existing natural disease. Even so, cases of traumatic subarachnoid haemorrhage may occur in the absence of any cervical injury[3].

The problems of the association between trauma and rupture of a congenital aneurysm are discussed under 'Special sensitivity'.

See also: Angiography; Intracranial haemorrhage; Special sensitivity; Subarachnoid haemorrhage

1. Harland WA, Pitts JF and Watson AA 'Subarachnoid haemorrhage due to upper cervical trauma' (1983) 36 J Clin Path 1335.
2. Simonsen J 'Fatal subarachnoid haemorrhage in relation to minor injuries in Denmark from 1967 to 1981' (1984) 24 Forens Sci Int 57.

3. Coast GC and Gee DJ 'Traumatic subarachnoid haemorrhage: an alternative source' (1984) 37 J Clin Path 1245.

Trespass

The tort of trespass to the person is an intentional interference with the person of another; the common forms of trespass in a medical context are battery and assault. Trespass does not require any touching of the person by the defendant — spitting at another, for example, may constitute trespass. The essence of assault lies in the apprehension of physical danger.

Damages in trespass are awarded in respect of the intrusion on the defendant's integrity. Liability is not confined to foreseeable consequences but includes all loss resulting from the tortious act.

The bringing of actions for trespass in the setting of alleged non-consent to medical treatment has recently attracted disapproval in the English courts[1].

See also: Assault and battery; Battery; Consent to medical treatment; Foreseeability

1. *Hills v Potter and another* [1984] 1 WLR 641. For the relationship between consent and trespass, *see Freeman v Home Office (No.2)* [1984] 2 WLR 802.

Triage

'Triage' is now used as a word to express a military expedient for dealing with multiple casualties. The principle rests on separating the wounded into four categories ranging from those whose slight injuries can be managed by self-care to the extreme of those who cannot be expected to survive even if given extensive treatment and who are, accordingly, managed on a humanitarian basis only[1]. Triage is therefore one solution to the problem of allocation of scarce resources — the resources in this case being medical and surgical manpower.

It is apparent, however, that the practice is ethically acceptable only because the armed forces as a whole are dedicated to a single recognisable objective — to win the battle. It cannot therefore be transmuted to civilian patients other than in those exceptional circumstances in which there is a discernible end-point — e.g. in the management of a major industrial disaster. The term should be reserved for use only in such catastrophic circumstances[2].

See also: Resource allocation

1. Owen-Smith MS *High Velocity Missile Wounds* (1981) Chap.4, Edward Arnold, London.
2. For a philosophical discussion, *see* Bell NK 'Triage in medical practices: an unacceptable model?' (1981) 15F Soc Sci Med 151.

Tuberculosis

Tuberculosis was, up to less than 50 years ago, a major cause of death throughout the world. It is now very rare in developed countries, where many doctors will qualify without having seen a case — the dangers of a missed diagnosis are therefore very real[1].

The causative organism is a very resistant bacterium known as *Mycobacterium tuberculosis*. It occurs in three strains — human, bovine and avian — of which the first two are of human importance. The human strain is transmitted from human to human mainly in the sputum and is typically responsible for pulmonary tuberculosis. The bovine strain is usually passed to the human in cows' milk; it causes disease which is disseminated in the blood and which affects the abdominal cavity, the kidneys, the liver and the lymph nodes, including those of the neck.

The course of tuberculosis is highly destructive of tissue, and vast numbers of bacteria can be coughed up in the sputum and spread as droplets. Death is generally of wasting type but fulminating disease may occur. The relationship of tuberculosis with the pneumoconioses is of major medico-legal importance.

The conquest of tuberculosis was in two distinct phases. Public health measures including testing of dairy herds, pasteurisation of milk, immunisation of children and detection of infective cases using mass radiography of the chest were followed by the discovery of very effective antibiotics. The disease is, however, still present in many developing countries.

Tuberculosis is a prescribed disease for those working in the health care professions and in laboratories. The *Mycobacterium* is designated a Category B pathogen (*see* 'Pathogenic organisms') and a postmortem examination on a patient with open tuberculosis can be a very dangerous procedure — the need must be very considerable to justify continuing with the examination once such disease is discovered by chance in a medico-legal case.

See also: Communicable diseases; Pathogenic organisms; Pneumoconioses; Vaccination

1. Horne N 'Tuberculosis: who should prescribe?' (1983) 286 Br Med J 165.

U

Ultrasound

The use of ultrasound as an alternative to X-ray diagnosis has very great attractions. The inherent dangers of radiation, both to the patient and to the public, are eliminated and structures can be outlined which might otherwise require the use of invasive techniques employing contrast media — for example, ultrasound can identifty gallstones without the need to inject radio-opaque dyes. It is, however, in obstetrics that ultrasound has made its greatest impact and to which this entry is limited. The two major areas in which obstetric ultrasound is of value are in the diagnosis of intrauterine growth retardation and in the disclosure of fetal malformatiohs[1]; the procedure is also an essential preliminary to any intrauterine invasive technique so that the placenta can be properly located.

The diagnosis of intrauterine growth retardation is of little practical value save to indicate to the mother the increased likelihood of perinatal death; the identification of fetal malformations, in addition to indicating the likelihood of death, is intimately associated with genetic counselling as to the management of the pregnancy.

Ultrasound is capable of detecting many malformations — including congenital heart disease — but the identification of such lesions is very time consuming and the occurrence of the defects will be sporadic. Ultrasound screening is therefore only resource effective when applied to the diagnosis of conditions for which abortion under the Abortion Act 1967, s.1(1)(b), might be appropriate and, then, only in populations in which there is a clearly indicated risk. Thus, particular attention is paid to the demonstration of neural tube defects, the likelihood of which may be indicated by the family history or by a positive maternal screening test. The results of ultrasound screening when used in this way are extremely encouraging.

There has been much concern as to whether or not ultrasound is an entirely safe procedure and, since it is a comparative innovation, any late effects are unlikely to be known for some time. It is widely agreed that there are no ill-effects given the current intensities in use — below 20 mW/cm^2. Nevertheless, the existence of a minor uncertainty is another reason for limiting the extent of any routine use of the technique in pregnancy. Recent advances in technique now incorporate invasive uses of ultrasound.

See also: Abortion Act 1967; Genetic counselling; Neural tube defects; X-rays

1. Gough JD 'Ultrasound' in Wald NJ (ed) *Antenatal and Neonatal Screening* (1984) Chap.19, Oxford University Press, Oxford.

Umbilical Cord

The umbilical cord joins the fetus to the placenta and contains veins and the umbilical artery; it constitutes the pathway for oxygenation of the fetus and is also available for intravenous treatment of the fetus and for such measures as exchange transfusion of blood. The cord must be clear to carry blood. Occasionally, it becomes knotted and ineffective, the result being a macerated fetus. It is also possible for the cord to entwine itself around the fetal neck and this may pose a rare problem of distinguishing a natural event from infanticide in which the cord has been used as a means of strangulation. Other medico-legal importance of the umbilical cord is both negative and positive.

On the negative side, the fact that the cord has not been cut does not invalidate a separate existence on the part of the neonate; the state of the cord is irrelevant to an offence under the Infanticide Act 1938. On the other hand, although there is no law on the subject, the morality of both lethal and non-lethal experimentation on the non-viable fetus may be considerably influenced by the presence or absence of an umbilical circulation (*see* 'Fetal experimentation').

Positively, the state of the umbilical stump may be a measure, albeit crude, of a separate existence and one which may be valuable in the presence of putrefaction of a dead neonate. There is a characteristic inflammatory, or 'vital', reaction at the abdominal wall some two days after birth; the cord is shed at about the fifth or sixth day and the umblical scar is healed between ten days and a fortnight after birth.

See also: Fetal experimentation; Infanticide; Maceration; Placenta; Separate existence; Vital reaction

Unborn Child

See 'Fetal rights'.

Unconscious Patient

The ethical and legal arguments surrounding the treatment of the unconscious patient are essentially related to consent. In general, any contravention of ethics is to be justified on the basis of double effect, whilst the legal excuse rests on the doctrine of necessity. The latter was emphasised in the USA, where the doctrine of self-determination is particularly well entrenched, when the liability to the patient of the surgeon who operates without consent was stated to be '. . .true except in cases of emergency when the patient is unconscious and when it is necessary to operate before consent can be obtained'[1].

Even so, this is not an option which should be lightly taken and the greater part of discussion hinges on the restrictions to be placed upon the doctor who is impelled to operate on a patient without consent. There would seem to be no restriction on the premise that the doctor has a duty to act in order to save life or to preserve the health of his patient. Such a duty is dependent upon there being a duty of care which must be regarded as established once a patient is admitted to hospital. Thus, the physician is, we suggest, reacting correctly if he attempts to resuscitate an unconscious case of apparent suicide; notwithstanding the patient's autonomous right to take his own life, the doctor is justified in assuming that, given the chance, the would-be suicide would have changed his mind. Resuscitation of the unconscious patient who is known to be physically or mentally handicapped is a far more difficult area where, in the absence of guidance from competent relatives, the doctor must use the American concept of 'substituted judgement' — or donning the mental mantle of the patient[2]. Much the same principle exists in the Roman law doctrine of *negotiorum gestio* under which it is permissible to assume the management of the affairs of someone who cannot himself do so, on the assumption that he would, if aware of the circumstances, have given a mandate for such interference. The doctrine has not been applied to medical care but it is reasonable to suppose that it would apply in the life-saving situation.

The importance of urgency in negating the need for consent has been demonstrated in the classic Canadian cases of *Marshall v Curry*[3] and *Murray v McMurchy*[4]. Both concerned extension of an operation while the patient was anaesthetised but, in the former, the non-consensual removal of a diseased testis was regarded as justifiable since the health and life of the patient were imperilled whilst, in the latter, the plaintiff succeeded in an action for battery against a surgeon who had sterilised her without consent — it was held that it would not have been unreasonable to postpone the operation until the patient could give an informed consent.

Thus, in the absence of any clear British precedents, it must be assumed that treatment of the unconscious patient is governed by an assumption of what the reasonable man would have consented to in the circumstances. He would not, it is suggested, consent to something which was not essential in the conditions prevailing nor would he consent to treatment which was, at the time, beyond the competence of the doctor and his resources. *Murray v McMurchy* must be very persuasive evidence that the unconscious patient gives no proxy consent to treatment which is unrelated to his primary condition.

See also: Battery; Consent to medical treatment; Double effect; Informed consent; Necessity; Suicide

1. *Schloendorff v Society of the New York Hospital* 105 NE 92 (NY, 1914).
2. *Superintendent of Belchertown State School v Saikewicz* 370 NE 2d 417 (Mass, 1878).
3. [1933] 3 DLR 260.
4. [1949] 2 DLR 422.

Unconscious Plaintiff

Damages for loss of amenities of life constitute an important category of non-pecuniary loss (*see* 'Damages'). This may be straightforward in the case of a plaintiff who has, say, lost a limb and is thereby prevented from enjoying sports but difficulties arise in relation to a plaintiff who is unable, by virtue of brain damage, to appreciate what he has lost. Damages for loss of amenities of life are awarded on an objective basis; lack of knowledge of what has been lost should therefore be immaterial.

The issue arose in the cases of *Wise v Kaye*[1] and *West v Shephard*[2], and the principle established has been reaffirmed more recently by the House of Lords[3]. The majority judgment in *West* rejected the contention that lack of awareness should result in no award under loss of amenities since the deprivation still existed and needed to be compensated. The House of Lords in *Lim Poh Choo* was sensitive to the arguments against this form of compensation in such cases but Lord Scarman pointed out that injustice would result if the court were to change the law, suggesting that the question should be addressed as part of a broader review of the law relating to damages. The Pearson Commission, in fact, recommended that non-pecuniary damages should no longer be recoverable in cases of permanent unconsciousness[4]; the High Court in Australia has taken a critical view of the English rule[5] and has severely limited the damages awarded under this head to an unconscious plaintiff with very restricted prospects of survival[6].

See also: Damages; Persistent vegetative state

1. [1962] 1 QB 638.
2. [1964] AC 326.
3. *Lim Poh Choo v Camden and Islington Area Health Authority* [1979] 3 WLR 44, [1979] 2 All ER 910.
4. Pearson CH (chairman) *Royal Commission on Civil Liability and Compensation for Personal Injury* (Cmnd 7054-1) (1978) para.398, HMSO, London.
5. *Skelton v Collins* (1966) 115 CLR 94.
6. For criticism of the rule, *see* McGregor H *Damages* (14th ed, 1980) p.834, Sweet & Maxwell, London. For Scots law, which is the same as English law on this point, *see Dalgliesh v Glasgow Corporation* 1976 SLT 157.

Unfitness to Plead

The trial of a person accused of a criminal offence may be postponed if his mental state so warrants. Two possibilities exist:

(a) In extreme cases, the Home Secretary may order a mentally disturbed person's detention in hospital if he deems it impracticable to bring him to trial or if the trial is likely to have an injurious effect on his condition[1]. This power is normally exercised only when there would be a 'scandal' if the accused were tried[2].

(b) In the event that the accused is brought to trial and is found to be unfit to plead, he will be detained until his discharge is authorised by the Home Secretary or he recovers an ability to plead[3].

The question of fitness to plead may be raised by the prosecution, the defence or the judge. The matter is then tried before a special jury[4], the onus of proving unfitness resting on the accused if he is the person who has raised the issue[5]. Unfitness must be proved on the balance of probabilities but the onus on the prosecution is to establish unfitness beyond reasonable doubt should they themselves raise the matter. Injustice could result if unfitness were decided before any attention was given to the question of whether or not the accused actually committed the crime and, consequently, the judge may exercise discretion as to the postponement of the fitness issue until after the defence has had the opportunity to challenge the prosecution case[6,7].

The main constituents of fitness to plead to a criminal charge are: an ability to understand the charge; an ability to understand the difference between the guilty and not guilty plea; and the capability to instruct defence counsel and to follow the evidence brought by the prosecution. This has been expressed concisely has having 'sufficient intellect to understand the nature of the proceedings'[8]. A mute defendant who can communicate by signs or by writing will generally be considered fit to plead although deaf mutism may warrant a finding of unfitness[9]. A defendant who claims to be suffering from amnesia in respect of the period during which the offence was committed will not be held to be unfit to plead[10] even though there may be doubts as to whether he can acquaint counsel adequately of all the facts relevant to his defence.

Disposal through a hospital order is, on the face of things, unsatisfactory for the accused because the offence has never been proved against him to the satisfaction of a jury. There is a body of opinion, particularly in the USA, which would abolish the concept and allow everyone to stand trial irrespective of their mental state[11]. The Butler Committee[12] recommended that the term 'unfit to plead' should be replaced by the phrase 'under disability in relation to the trial'. The introduction of the interim hospital order certainly circumvents some of the objections to the concept of 'unfitness'.

In Scots law, the plea of unfitness is known as the plea of insanity in bar of trial.

See also: Amnesia; Hospital orders

1. Mental Health Act 1983, s.48.
2. Smith J and Hogan B *Criminal Law* (5th ed, 1983) p.165, Butterworths, London.
3. Gowers EA (chairman) *Report of the Royal Commission on Capital Punishment* (Cmd 8932) p.76, HMSO, London.
4. Criminal Procedure (Insanity) Act 1964, s.4.
5. *R v Podola* [1959] 3 All ER 418.
6. *R v Robertson* [1968] 3 All ER 557.
7. *R v Webb* [1969] 2 All ER 626.
8. *R v Berry* 1876 1 QBD 447.
9. *R v Sharp* [1960] QB 357, [1958] 1 All ER 62.
10. *R v Podola* (n.5 above); *Russell v HM Adv* 1946 JC 37.
11. Aranella P 'Reflections on current proposals to abolish or reform the insanity defense' (1982) 8 Am J Law Med 271.
12. Butler Lord (chairman) *Report of the Committee on Mentally Abnormal Offenders* (Cmnd 6244) (1975) HMSO, London.

Union of Epiphyses

Centres of ossification form in the epiphyses (ends of long bones) in infancy and adolescence. These joint with the shafts of the bones at varying ages and in relatively constant order during adolescence and young adulthood. A potential method for determining the age of an unrecognisable body or of a skeleton is thus available in this age group.

The range over which such unions may occur in individuals is, however, considerable and, by and large, the union of a given epiphysis will only permit of an estimate of minimum age in the order of two years or more; a similarly inaccurate estimate of maximum age can be made if union has not occurred. As with the appearance of centres of ossification, the more observations which can be made, the closer will be the limits; union of all epiphyses is, however, spread over a remarkably similar age range — between 17 and 25 years — which, again, limits the value of the method. Anthropologists will, however, give extra 'weight' to certain observations.

See also: Age of a body at death; Ossification centres

Unlawful Sexual Intercourse

Unlawful sexual intercourse is nowhere defined but must be taken as meaning intercourse outside marriage. This may be inferred from the wording of the Sexual Offences (Amendment) Act 1976, s.1, which defines rape as unlawful sexual intercourse with a woman who does not consent. Since non-consensual intercourse must always be an offence, the use of the word 'unlawful' is tautologous unless it is taken to exclude intramarital sexual activity[1] — the concept of intramarital rape is discussed under that heading. The use in the statutes of the word 'unlawful' in respect of the various offences of procuration leads to a similar interpretation and there is Scots case law to the point[2].

There are, however, certain statutory circumstances in which it is unlawful to have sexual intercourse and which are defined in the Sexual Offences Act 1956 and in the Sexual Offences (Scotland) Act 1976. Prominent among these is having sexual intercourse with a girl below the age of 13[3]; this is a strict liability offence which carries a potential life sentence upon conviction. A further offence consists of having intercourse with a girl aged between 13 and 16 years. This, again, is a strict liability offence save that it is a defence for a man who has not reached the age of 24, and who has not been charged with a similar offence before, to show that he had reasonable grounds to believe that the girl was aged over 16 years[4]. There have been attempts to extend this concept by attaching importance to the differential age, the purpose being largely to remove teenage sexual experimentation from the list of criminal offences[5]. In the event of a man 'marrying' a girl below the age of 16, it is a defence against a charge of having sexual intercourse unlawfully that he believed the girl to be his wife and had reasonable cause for that belief[6]. It is also unlawful for a man to have intercourse with a mentally handicapped female[7] but, again, it is a defence for the accused to show that he did not know and had no reason to know that the girl was mentally handicapped.

See also: Rape; Sexual intercourse

1. *R v Clarke* [1949] 2 All ER 448.
2. *Henry Watson* (1885) 5 Couper 696.
3. Under s.5 and (S) s.3.
4. Under s.6 and (S) s.4.
5. Notably by the National Council for Civil Liberties *Sexual Offences*, Report No.13 (1976) NCCL, London. Several Australian States have brought in such legislation.
6. Under s.6(2); (S) s.4(2)(a).
7. Sexual Offences Act 1956, s.7 as amended by the Mental Health Act 1959, s.127; Mental Health (Scotland) Act 1984, s.106.

Urine

The urine is made in the kidney and results from the combination of a pressure filtrate of blood, which is formed in the glomeruli, and a selective concentration of that glomerular filtrate which is fashioned in the renal tubules. Thus, the healthy glomeruli preserve the proteins in the plasma while the tubules preserve water and, by specific action, reabsorb and preserve vital substances such as glucose. The urine thus formed is stored in the urinary bladder until it is voided.

Anything which is soluble in the blood and which is not specifically reabsorbed in the kidney will appear in the urine, which may therefore provide a most useful medium in which to seek the presence of circulating drugs and their metabolites. Equally, it will be seen that the urine in the bladder mirrors the blood not as it is at that moment but as to what was the state of the blood throughout the period of storage of urine within the bladder. This is of little significance in normal toxicological work but it becomes important when the precise concentration of a substance at a given time is required to be known — this is the situation classically posed in the estimation of alcohol for the purposes of the amended Road Traffic Act 1972, s.6. It is impossible to take a specimen of glomerular filtrate and, in practice, the bladder will not function unless it contains a reasonable amount of urine which is usually secreted at the rate of approximately 1 ml per minute. The resultant compromise is to void the bladder and to test the next available specimen — usually in about 20 minutes.

A further forensic value of the bladder urine rests on the fact that it is usually sterile and is well protected from bacterial invasion by its thick muscular wall. It does not, therefore, putrefy as rapidly as does the blood and the urine may be the fluid of choice when testing at postmortem dissection for a substance of which the concentration is affected by bacterial contamination. Alcohol is, again, the main focus of interest and there is no doubt that urine, or some other sterile fluid, should be tested for alcohol in parallel with the blood whenever there is a possibility of *post mortem* artefact. Non-sterility of the urine is, however, not uncommon in women and this should be borne in mind when interpreting the analytical results.

See also: Alcohol; Putrefaction; Road Traffic Act 1972; Vitreous humour

V

Vaccination

As described under antigen and antibody, the body can develop specific resistance against foreign invasion in the form of pathogenic organisms. In nature, this process results either from an attack of disease followed by lasting immunity or by a gradual increase in resistance induced by repeated attacks of disease. Immunity can be assured without an overt infection if the primary attack is simulated by the injection or, occasionally, ingestion of the responsible organisms in dead or attenuated form. Such immunity can be revitalised or enhanced by 'booster' doses. This is the process of vaccination.

The procedure is not without its complications or dangers. Thus, an attenuated vaccine may produce minor symptoms of the disease — as in measles. Occasionally, this process may go so far as to be dangerous; thus, if the viable organism can cause convulsions and brain damage, the vaccine itself may do so in susceptible persons and this explains the occasional disasters which are apparently attributable to vaccination against whooping cough. Some vaccines must be grown in a biological substrate and the use of such material may simultaneously immunise the subject against the medium. Thus, early vaccines against rabies resulted sometimes in the production of anti-brain antibodies and an encephalopathy; the problem has been overcome by growing the virus in alternatives to brain tissue. A further danger is that the vaccine may affect a fetus *in utero*. This is specific to vaccines composed of living viruses and, inevitably, is most relevant when the purpose of vaccination is to prevent the actual disease affecting a fetus; such a situation may arise if a woman is inadvertently immunised against German measles in the first three months of her pregnancy.

Any potential danger of immunisation must, however, be weighed against the risks of contracting, and the severity of, the disease to be prevented; the efficiency of the vaccine must also be considered. On an international scale, the major killing disease of smallpox has been virtually eradicated from the world; on an individual basis, few doctors now practising in Britain have ever seen a case of diphtheria. Balancing the benefits and dangers has resulted, in the UK, in the recommendation of routine immunisation against diphtheria, tetanus, whooping cough, poliomyelitis, measles, tuberculosis and German measles[1]. The occurrence of the occasional catastrophe and the difficulty of proving causation has led to the passing of the Vaccine Damage Payments Act 1979 by which a lump sum is payable without proof of negligence to a young person who can be shown to have been severely disabled as a result of vaccination carried out as part of the public health campaign; the sum is also payable if the injury was inflicted before birth. The statutory maximum payment of £20,000 would, however, be regarded as derisory if compared with damages paid following negligence actions in the USA[2].

A major function of vaccination is to prevent the spread of epidemic disease by travellers; several vaccinations are required by international agreement in specified conditions[3] but, in addition, the traveller may wish to protect himself against endemic diseases which are not present in his home country[4].

It has to be added that, as a result of recombinant DNA techniques, the whole process of vaccine production is likely to alter in the near future, with a consequent decrease in many of the potential complications.

See also: Antibody; Antigen; Causation; Genetic engineering; Immune reaction

1. Standing Medical Advisory Committee for the Central Health Services Council *Immunization against Infectious Diseases* (1972) HMSO, London.
2. At the time of writing, the first action for negligence taken in the UK under this head has failed because causation was not proved (1985) *The Times*, 31 August, p.3. Vaccine damage tribunals are now established (Vaccine Damage Payments (Amendment) Regulations 1984 (SI 1984/442)).
3. These include vaccination against yellow fever, plague and cholera.
4. Typhoid fever and poliomyelitis are good examples for UK citizens.

Vagal Inhibition of the Heart

Sudden death due to physiological cessation of the heart beat following an abnormal stimulation of the sympathetic nervous system is a very real entity in forensic medicine. Its mechanism, however, still remains obscure. The most feasible explanation is that an afferent sympathetic stimulus is sent to the brain and an efferent, corrective, stimulus is returned to the viscera via the parasympathetic or vagus nerve. The normal function of the vagus nerve is to slow the heart beat; a markedly abnormal innervation may stop it completely. The result is vagal inhibition of the heart beat which is also known as reflex cardiac arrest.

The essentials for this reflex to occur are that the original stimulus should be sudden and abnormal. A high state of emotional tension will exaggerate the response and any conditions which lower voluntary cerebral control of reflex responses will have a similar effect — these could include, among others, a mild state of alcoholic intoxication, a degree of hypoxia or partial narcosis due to incomplete anaesthesia.

Typical conditions initiating the reflex are discussed under the various headings but include the sudden impact on the nasopharynx of water as in precipitous immersion or of a poorly handled tube during anaesthesia; the violent stretching of the uterine cervix in criminal abortion; or sudden violence to the neck such as by a karate blow or during strangulation.

This mode of death has two major implications in forensic medicine. From the pathologist's point of view, there will be little or no evidence of the primary cause and the mode of death must, generally, be inferred from the circumstances; conversely, the diagnosis should not be made if there *is* no circumstantial evidence. From the criminological aspect, the uncertainty and unexpectedness of reflex death may be sufficient to elide the *mens rea* of murder and to reduce such a charge to one of manslaughter or even to the acceptance of death as an accident. To a lesser extent, the reflex may operate when self-induced stimulation is practised in an emotional setting — it may then be hard to make the distinction between suicide and misadventure. It is not unknown for really frightened people to die in this way from what could be accepted as minimal pain such as the insertion of a needle into the gum.

See also: Anaesthesia; Autonomic nervous system; *Mens rea*

Further reading
The subject is explained in Mason JK *Forensic Medicine for Lawyers* (2nd ed, 1983) (Butterworths, London) at p.13 with frequent specific references in the text.

Vasectomy

Vasectomy, or divison of each vas deferens which connects each testis to the urethra, is a simple method of sterilising the male; the operation can be carried out under local anaesthesia and on an outpatient basis. It is clearly legal — the days of Lord Denning's strictures in *Bravery v Bravery*[1] have long passed — and it is available to NHS patients[2]. The medico-legal difficulty arises in relation to the permanence of the operation. Many men may be concerned lest they remarry[3] and would then prefer to be fertile; they would therefore opt for a reversible operation. The success rate for reversion is unlikely to be better than 25 per cent; moreover, the capacity for reversal is, in general, inversely proportional to the certainty of success in the primary objective — i.e. to make the man sterile at the time. Very few surgeons would therefore agree to operate with a positive view to future reversal.

Even so, the operation is surprisingly fickle and a stringent routine must be followed before a patient is declared to be sterile. An acceptable regimen would be to require two specimens of ejaculate taken two weeks apart at least two months after the operation to be negative; a third specimen should be shown to be negative one month later before a pronouncement is made.

The major British case concerned with failure of sterilisation through vasection is *Thake and another v Maurice*[4]. The action was interesting in that there was no complaint as to the operative technique; the case was originally taken as one of breach of contract. It was held that the failure of the defendant to warn that there was a possibility of natural reversal of a properly performed operation was in breach of that contract; the doctrine of 'informed consent' was held not to bear because the operation itself had been entirely satisfactory. However, on appeal by the surgeon, the majority opinion was that there was no breach, the contract having been only to perform the operation with reasonable skill and care; at the same time, the court held unanimously that the failure to provide a warning amounted to an inadvertent negligent omission in tort. Moreover, whilst the judge of first instance had allowed damages for the unexpected birth of a normal, healthy child[5] — on the grounds that deriving joy from the birth of a child was a virtue which should not go unrewarded —

he had refused damages for the pain and discomfort of pregnancy and delivery, setting these against the happiness of having a child; the Court of Appeal, however, went one stage further and allowed the latter claim.

Thus, the issue of consent-based negligence is still open but, so far as is known, there have been no reported British cases related to negligent *performance* of vasectomy; indeed, such a course may not be possible as no injury results to the subject of the operation[6]. It scarcely needs drawing attention to the fact that, were such an action to be brought, the defendant surgeon might be expected to seek proof of paternity.

See also: Informed consent; Parentage testing; Sterilisation

1. [1954] 1 WLR 1169.
2. National Health Service (Family Planning) Amendment Act 1972.
3. A vasectomy prior to marriage would not be a ground for an annulment.
4. [1985] 2 WLR 215, [1984] 2 All ER 513, QBD; [1986] 1 All ER 497, CA.
5. Despite judicial antipathy on both sides of the Atlantic, a similar decision had been taken many years previously in the USA (*Custodio v Bauer* 251 Cal App 2d 303 (1967)).
6. Argent VP 'Failed female sterilization and the law' (1985) 25 Med Sci Law 136.

Venereal Disease

'Venereal disease' is an unfashionable generic term for disease contracted during or associated with sexual intercourse. Such conditions are now more commonly referred to as sexually transmitted diseases but the term persists in, for example, the Venereal Diseases Act 1917 and the National Health Service (Venereal Diseases) Regulations 1974 (SI 1974/29).

See also: Sexually transmitted diseases

Ventilator Support

The respiratory centre, which is situated in the medulla (in the lower part of the brain stem), may be damaged in the event of head injury or hypoxic insult to the brain. In such circumstances, the respiratory movements can be simulated by cyclical forced ventilation of the lungs — a mechanical and long-term version of the first aid 'kiss of life' manoeuvre.

Ventilator support is, by its very nature, associated with the unconscious subject and is to be distinguished from simple oxygen supplementation of the patient with peripheral cardiopulmonary disease and from respirator support which may be used in the event of paralysis of the respiratory muscles. The common, and most significant, use of ventilator support is in providing a period for diagnosis and assessment of a patient; in such case, the process can be likened to laboratory investigation. As a result of this investigation, the patient may be provided with prolonged support as a therapeutic measure but this inevitably entails withdrawal of support at some time.

Support may be withdrawn because the patient has recovered a capability for spontaneous respiration. At the other end of the scale, withdrawal of support may follow the diagnosis of brain stem death, in which case the physician is merely ceasing to ventilate a corpse. If, however, brain stem death has not been diagnosed, the decision to terminate support can still be taken in the context of the ordinary/ extraordinary treatment test and has been accepted as such in the Scottish courts[1]. The classic case in the USA is *Re Quinlan* where it was held that death as a result of removal from ventilator support would 'not be homicide but rather expiration from existing natural causes'[2]; the *Quinlan* decision seems to have generally been followed in the USA and at least one indictment for murder by doctors has been quashed as a result[3]. It has been suggested, with good reason, that, whereas removal from ventilator care involves only a technical decision reached on the basis of good medical practice, any ethical issues involved in the procedure relate to *admission* for therapeutic purposes[4] — what will be the end-result of reoxygenating a partially damaged brain?

See also: Brain stem death; Head injury; Hypoxia; Ordinary/Extraordinary treatment; Respirator support; Resuscitation

1. *Finlayson v HM Adv* 1978 SLT (Notes) 60. The decision would undoubtedly be followed in England and Wales although the comparable reported case was not quite identical as, in *R v Malcherek, R v Steel* [1981] 1 WLR 690, the diagnosis of brain stem death had been made before treatment was stopped.
2. *Re Quinlan* 355 A 2d 664 (NJ,1976) per Hughes CJ.
3. *Nejdl v Sup Ct Los Angeles Co and the People* 147 Cal App 3d 1006 (1983).
4. Kennedy IM 'Switching off life support machines: the legal implications' [1977] Crim LR 443.

Ventricular Fibrillation

Ventricular fibrillation occurs when the heart ceases to beat rhythmically and the contraction of the ventricles becomes rapid, unco-ordinated and ineffective. The body — and, in particular, the brain and the heart muscle itself — is suddenly starved of oxygen and the result is a precipitous collapse.

The most common cause of ventricular fibrillation is myocardial hypoxia resulting from coronary insufficiency — often of the 'increased demand' type but also occurring when there is frank localised ischaemia due to restrictive disease. Hypoxia of the muscle is particularly important when it is already in a state of hypersensitivity — hence, ventricular fibrillation is a likely cause of death resulting from the combination of anaesthesia and the administration of adrenaline. Ventricular fibrillation may result from an abnormal electric shock or from lightning strike.

Interestingly, ventricular fibrillation can be reversed by the application of a high intensity electric shock; any stimulus may, in fact, serve to convert fibrillation and this is the basis for treatment by either internal or external cardiac massage. Death ensues rapidly in the absence of reversion and is physiological rather than resulting from structural pathological change; thus, the diagnosis at autopsy may have to be inferred rather than be demonstrated through pathological anatomical findings. It is to be noted that reversion always involves a period of cerebral hypoxia; apparently successful treatment of ventricular fibrillation may therefore result in a severely brain damaged individual. The decision to treat may pose a very delicate clinical problem for the doctor.

See also: Anaesthesia; Coronary disease; Hypoxia; Lightning; Myocardial infarction

Viability

Immature fetuses may be born alive, or achieve a separate existence, but be incapable of survival — that is, they may not be viable. Viability is therefore a medical principle and will depend, firstly, upon the condition of the fetus itself and, secondly, on the health care available. Thus, viability is a property related to the individual fetus and a legal difficulty is introduced by the need to generalise as to its meaning. Williams has implied that a viable fetus is one which can be reared in the normal way without intensive care[1] and this may be an acceptable interpretation as to offences against the Infant Life (Preservation) Act 1929. It is, however, less clear in its application to homicide, the possibility of which may arise, particularly, in the case of a late abortion. In practice, failure to treat intensively an abortus which shows signs of life has not been regarded as culpable[2] but there is no obvious reason why coroners should not regard the death of such a fetus as being due to want of attention at birth — for, not being a stillbirth, the fetus is clearly entitled to both a birth certificate and a certificate of cause of death[3]. Obstetricians are thus forced into the unenviable situation of wishing to ensure that the fetus to be aborted is, in fact, dead *in utero* so as to be certain of freedom from prosecution; even then, there is no reason why an offence against the Infant Life (Preservation) Act 1929, s.1, should not have been committed so long as the physician was aware that the child was capable of being born alive — which is all the Act speaks of[4].

The difficulties which can stem from the use of viability as a legal principle have been well shown in the USA. Following the decision in *Roe v Wade*[5] — where the court, whilst unable to define viability other than as a gestational period of between 24 and 28 weeks, accorded rights to the 'viable fetus' — there have been several contentious cases. In what may be an extreme example, the court ordered a woman who appeared to be jeopardising the life of her near-term fetus on religious grounds, to undergo caesarian section[6]. In that particular case, the defect righted itself and the decision was not challenged beyond the State Supreme Court; one can, however, sympathise with the European Commission of Human Rights who firmly declined to attempt a legal definition of 'viability of the fetus'[7].

See also: Abortion; Child destruction; Homicide; Live birth; Separate existence; Stillbirth

1. Williams G *Textbook of Criminal Law* (2nd ed, 1983), p.303, Stevens, London.
2. *R v Hamilton* (1983) *The Times*, 16 September, p.1, is a reported example. The magistrates held that there was insufficient evidence on which to commit to trial on a charge of attempted murder.
3. Lord Wells-Pestell, quoted in Parliamentary Note 'Abortions and disposal of fetuses' [1974] 4 Br Med J 775.
4. It is only in the Abortion Act 1967, s.5(1), that the concept of viability is raised in relation to the 1929 Act. *See* the debate between Tunkel V and Wright G 'Late abortions and the crime of child destruction' [1985] Crim LR 133.

5. 93 S Ct 705 (1973).
6. *Jefferson v Griffin Spalding County Hospital Authority* 274 SE 2d 457 (Ga, 1981).
7. *Paton v United Kingdom* [1981] 3 EHRR 408.

Vicarious Liability

It is a general principle of law that the master is responsible for the faults of his servant. The problem as to the medical profession has been, in the past, the definition of the master/servant relationship. In the UK, the evolution of the law in this field has been both steady and logical[1]. Thus, it was decided in 1947 that a hospital was responsible for its employed staff but not for visiting consultants[2]; later it was held that the hospital was unable to delegate such responsibility[3]. Subsequent decisions extended this responsibility to include part-time or temporary staff, including visiting consultants[4]. There is little doubt that the early indecision was due to the reluctance of the courts to penalise charitable institutions. The coming of the National Health Service, however, simplified the issues and it is now almost universal policy for plaintiffs to sue both the individual they regard as responsible for negligent damage and also the appropriate hospital authority. Any damages awarded are usually divided between the health authority and the doctor's defence society but, as a quid pro quo, membership of a defence society is an essential prerequisite to employment in the NHS.

Scots law lagged behind the developments in England and Wales for some time but, once the NHS was established, a similar wide responsibility was attributed to the hospital administration[5].

The law relating to hospitals in the USA is similarly moving towards general acceptance of what is known there as corporate liabililty. The basis for such policy rests on the increasing public perception of the hospital as the source of quality health care and the implication that a hospital has a direct and independent duty to its patients to exercise reasonable care in granting staff appointments and privileges to physicians; in one successful case against a hospital, seven malpractice suits were pending against a surgeon at the time his appointment was made[6]!

The contract within the British NHS between a general practitioner and the FPC is one for services and involves no master/servant relationship. The practitioner, however, has a vicarious liability for the actions of those he employs, and partners have a liability for things done by each other which are relevant to the practice (*see* 'Partnerships in medicine').

See also: Negligence; Partnerships in medicine

1. Lee RG 'The liability of hospital authorities for the negligence of their staff — a history' (1979) 8 Anglo-Am LR 312.
2. *Collins v Hertfordshire County Council* [1947] 1 All ER 633.
3. *Cassidy v Ministry of Health* [1951] 2 KB 343.
4. *Roe v Minister of Health, Woolley v Same* [1954] 2 QB 66; *Higgins v North Western Metropolitan Hospital Board and Bach* [1954] 1 WLR 411.
5. *McDonald v Glasgow Western Hospitals and Hayward v Board of Management of Royal Infirmary Edinburgh* 1954 SC 453.
6. *Johnson v Misericordia Community Hospital* 294 NW 2d 501 (Wis, 1980).

Viruses

Viruses are self-replicating particles of the basic cellular material, nucleic acid; they may be composed of either deoxyribonucleic acid (DNA) or ribonucleic acid (RNA) but not both, as are bacteria. Such particles are incapable of a free existence and a further criterion of a virus is that it can reproduce itself only within a host cell.

Viruses must therefore alter cells, the usual change being death and, hence, disease of the body. It could be, however, that the cellular change might be one of mutual advantage and the possibility that malignant disease may result from viral infection is very much in the minds of pathologists; certainly, some animal tumours are viral in origin but, as yet, only a few highly specific human tumours can be so regarded — a most important exception may be cancer of the female cervix uteri which is strongly suspected of being, at times, a remote form of sexually transmitted viral disease.

The structure and life style of viruses is such that they are extremely difficult to destroy in the living body — destruction involves coincidental destruction of the host cell whilst their structure is so close to that of life itself that the 'toxic margin' of any potential viricidal drug used would be very small. It is this complexity of treatment, together with the fact that many viruses selectively parasitise the cells of the brain, that accounts for all Category A pathogens being viruses (*see* 'Pathogenic organisms').

On the other hand, the very simplicity of the viral constitution makes them ideal organisms to pre-empt by means of immunisation. Immunity to viruses is likely to be long lasting — we sustain only one attack of chickenpox or German measles in our lives — and a single dose of vaccine against yellow fever allows one to travel in endemic areas for a lifetime; the scourge of smallpox has effectively been eliminated from the world by means of vaccination.

Viruses can, however, cross the placental barrier with ease, and immunisation with living organisms during pregnancy must be undertaken only after careful consideration. Similarly, actual infection during pregnancy must raise questions as to the subsequent management of that pregnancy; the virus of German measles, which is particularly virulent to growing fetal tissues, accounts for a very high proportion of all actions which are brought by the newborn for wrongful or diminished life.

See also: Bacteria; Diminished life; German measles; Malignant disease; Pathogenic organisms; Sexually transmitted diseases; Vaccination; Wrongful life

Vital Reaction

Vital reaction is the natural reaction of the body to trauma of various sorts. Its value in forensic medicine lies in distinguishing *ante mortem* from *post mortem* injuries. The simplest vital reaction is that of capillary dilatation which will be seen as a red area at the periphery of an injury sustained in life if the blood vessels are not ruptured. If rupture has occurred, vital reaction will be seen as external haemorrhage and bruising within the tissues. The appearances often contrast markedly with those of an injury inflicted after death where there is typically a clear line of demarcation between the damaged tissue and the surroundings which appear normal.

The process of repair begins within about four hours of injury and this can be seen microscopically as invasion of the area by the white cells of the blood (the polymorphonuclear cells) which represent the body's immediate defence system. Even before this, subtle biochemical methods can be used to show that the surrounding tissue was active following injury; such methods are, however, of value only in skilled hands and are not available in all laboratories. Nevertheless, simple microscopy will generally show vital changes which develop over days and by means of which the pathologist can often give a fair estimation of the time elapsed between injury and death[1].

See also: Bruises; Burns; Haemorrhage

1. The prototype work done in this field is summarised in Raekallio J 'Histological estimation of the age of injuries' and 'Histochemical and biochemical estimation of the age of injuries' in Perper JA and Wecht CH (eds) *Microscopic Diagnosis in Forensic Pathology* (1980) Chaps.1 and 2, CC Thomas, Springfield IL.

Vitreous Humour

The vitreous humour is the fluid which occupies and maintains the shape of the posterior chamber of the eyeball. Its importance in forensic medicine is, firstly, that the concentration of electrolytes and other substances dissolved in the fluid closely follows that in the blood and, secondly, that the eyes are surprisingly often retained when other parts of the body which might provide fluids for analysis are destroyed; moreover, the fluid is resistant to putrefactive changes.

The vitreous is therefore a favourite site for the analysis of, *inter alia*, the alcoholic content of a cadaver. The concentration of electrolytes in the humour does, however, alter with time after death and attempts have been made to assess the *post mortem* interval in this way, particularly by an assessment of the vitreous potassium[1]. The potassium level certainly rises after death but the scatter of results is such that no reliance can be placed on the analysis of a single specimen as a measure of the *post mortem* interval; moreover, the level in the two eyes may differ. Many other serial estimations have been made on the vitreous humour with varying objectives in mind but it cannot be said that any has stood the test of practical application[2].

See also: Timing of death

1. An early example of this type of study is Hughes WMH 'Levels of potassium in the vitreous humour after death' (1965) 5 Med Sci Law 150.
2. *See*, for example, Coe JI 'Hypothermia: autopsy findings and vitreous glucose' (1984) 29 J Forens Sci 389.

Volenti non fit Injuria

The voluntary assumption of a risk may later exclude a person from claiming damages for injury flowing from that risk. The principle is expressed in the Latin phrase *volenti non fit injuria*. The volenti rule is one of civil law but is analogous to the criminal law defence of consent which is, itself, subject to strong public policy limitations.

The volenti defence may be based on explicit agreement between the parties as where the party assuming the risk gives written or verbal consent, or it may be based on the conduct of the parties. In the latter case, consent to the risk may be implied from the fact that there were actions which indicated this to be so.

The court must be satisfied that the plaintiff was both *sciens* and *volens* — that he knew of the full extent of the risk and that his assumption of it was fully voluntary[1]. In practice, the courts have tended to narrow down the circumstances in which the volenti defence may be claimed successfully. Many plaintiffs have been held not to be *volentes* by virtue of their incomplete apprehension of the risks involved, and the application of a subjective standard in this area is particularly sympathetic to the plaintiff[2]. In the medical context, the volenti defence forms the theoretical basis of the notion that consent legitimates the invasion of physical integrity. Consent to surgery, therefore, renders the patient *volens* as to the operation, provided, of course, that he was aware of what it was to which he gave his consent. This latter requirement raises the vexed question of informed consent, which is discussed separately under that heading.

There are limits to the medical procedures to which a legally effective consent can be given. A patient cannot consent to an operation which is medically unjustified by virtue of its unacceptable riskiness; a volenti defence on the part of a surgeon in such a case would not protect him against a claim for damages by the patient or, in the event of his death, by his family. Sanctions of the criminal law would also be involved here; the removal of a vital organ from a consenting donor would be homicide.

The *volenti* defence is significant in cases involving sports injuries. There are two dimensions to this issue — the question of injury to spectators and that of injury to the participants themselves. Spectators of dangerous sports may be considered, in some circumstances, to assume the risk of injury during the course of the event; whether or not the volenti defence will apply depends upon the nature of the risk and the degree of awareness and acceptance of it[3]. A lesser degree of care is owed by organisers and other players to participants in the event. The fact of participation in the sport means that the player must consent to a certain degree of risk; he accepts, in essence, the normal hazards of the game. Injuries which are received when another player exceeds the permissible limits of conduct within the rules of the game were not, however, necessarily consented to and a *volenti* defence may fail in such cases[4]. Contrariwise, a certain amount of sports violence will fall within the ambit of what is permissible and is therefore implicitly consented to by the fact of participation[5]. Courts have, however, taken a serious view of gratuitous violence on the sports field, particularly when it is encouraged by audiences and goes beyond minor altercations.

See also: Consent to injury; Informed consent; Negligence; Safety of sports grounds; Sports injuries

1. *Nettleship v Weston* [1971] 3 All ER 581.
2. *Smith v Austin Lifts* [1959] 1 WLR 100 (HL; *Dixon v King* [1975] 2 NZLR 357. For discussion of the comprehension of risk, *see* Fleming JG *The Law of Torts* (6th ed, 1983) p.272, Law Book Co, Sydney.
3. Siuskind GE 'Liability for injury to spectators' (1968) 6 Os HLJ 305; *Wilks v Cheltenham Home Guard Motor Cycle and Light Car Club* [1971] 2 All ER 369; *Murray v Harringay*

Arena Ltd [1951] 2 All ER 320 (a 6-year-old plaintiff held to be *volens*, a somewhat unlikely proposition).
4. *Condon v Basi* [1985] 1 WLR 866.
5. *Agar v Canning* (1965) 54 WWR 302.

Vulva

The vulva, or female introitus, is the space bounded externally by the skin and internally by the hymenal orifice; the labia minora and majora form the lateral boundaries. Its medico-legal significance rests on the fact that vulval penetration is sufficient to constitute the *actus reus* of rape and incest. It is therefore important, particularly in the former, for the examining doctor to seek the presence of spermatozoa in the vulva as well as within the vagina.

See also: Incest; Rape

Wardship Proceedings

The wardship jurisdiction of the High Court in respect of children's welfare depends upon the ultimate duty of the Crown to care for those of its minor subjects who need protection. No minor can be made a ward of court except by virtue of a High Court order. The process is rapid, in that a minor becomes a ward of court on the making of an application, and the wardship lasts until the High Court orders its cessation[1]. The High Court can now transfer wardship proceedings to the County Court[2].

Not only are wardship proceedings rapid — a duty judge is available to hear emergency applications — but also the limits of the court's jurisdiction are largely undefined. In taking over the role of parent, the court's first and paramount duty is to the child's welfare and, to this end, the court may take exceptional measures, including ordering non-disclosure of evidence which would be harmful to the child[3]. Anyone, including a local authority, who has an adequate interest can start wardship proceedings and any person below the age of 18 can be made a ward of court; every significant detail of a ward's existence is then subject to the court's approval.

The relationship between wardship and care proceedings is somewhat complex but, whilst, in general, the powers of the court override those of the local authority if the child's welfare is so protected, an application for wardship will not be allowed when the local authority has obtained parental rights over a child nor when it takes the form of a back door appeal against decisions properly taken by the local authority[4]. The local authority may, itself, make application for wardship if it finds its statutory powers inadequate to protect the child; conversely, the court can commit a ward to the care of the local authority if that is the only practical method of taking care of the child[5].

The court may delegate some of its responsibilities in wardship and will appoint the Official Solicitor as guardian ad litem in the rare cases in which the ward needs separate advice and representation. Wardship proceedings are private and the normal rules of evidence do not apply. A child automatically ceases to be a ward of court on reaching the age of 18.

See also: Age of majority; Care proceedings; Guardian ad litem

1. Supreme Court Act 1981, s.41.

2. Matrimonial and Family Proceedings Act 1984, s.38.
3. *Re K (Infants)* [1965] AC 201.
4. *A v Liverpool City Council* [1982] AC 363; *In re W (a minor)* [1985] AC 791; *Re D (a minor)* (1986) Times, 24 March.
5. Family Law Reform Act 1969, s.7.

Whiplash Injury

Whiplash injury results from sudden extension and flexion of the neck. The cervical vertebrae are comparatively resistant to simple flexion; they are, however, highly susceptible to forced flexion from an extended position, which is what constitutes the whiplash injury. Characteristically, the subject, usually the occupant of a car, is struck from behind. As the body as a whole moves forward, the head is subject to inertia and falls back, extending the neck; as the vehicle is then suddenly halted, the head flexes in relation to the torso. The combined forces may cause subluxation of the cervical vertebral joints, leading to persistent pain with, perhaps, secondary effects both on the efferent and afferent nerves. In severe cases, displacement of the vertebrae may lead to arthritic changes and permanent neck stiffness. The onset of symptoms may be delayed and it is advisable always to keep the possibility of late disability in mind in considering any rear-ended motor vehicle accident. The prevention of whiplash injury in cars depends upon the provision of effective head restraints.

Widmark's Factor

Widmark's hypothesis is that alcohol absorbed is distributed uniformly throughout the body water; it follows that the ratio of the concentration of alcohol in the body to the concentration of alcohol in the blood will be given by the ratio of the water content of the body to the water content of the blood. This ratio, the Widmark factor, is variable but is generally assumed to be around 0.6–0.7; the factor for a woman is found to be slightly less than that for a man. Practical experience has shown that a rather low Widmark factor of 0.58 for men which is used in the Tables prepared by the British Medical Association in 1960[1] gives a very fair representation of the facts[2] although others have used rather larger values and have attempted to distinguish between alcohol consumed as beer and that taken as spirits[3].

Widmark's equation for calculating blood alcohol is given by a = bwr/100 where a = grams of alcohol consumed (17 g/pint beer or 9 g/fl oz 40% spirits), b = blood alcohol concentration in mg/100 ml, w = weight in kilograms and r = Widmark's factor. A conversion factor for blood:breath of 2,286:1 is used in the Road Traffic Act 1972, s.12(2) as amended by the Transport Act 1981, Sch.8.

See also: Alcohol; Road Traffic Act 1972

1. British Medical Association *The Relation of Alcohol to Road Accidents* (1960) BMA, London.
2. Mason JK 'Section 10 defence to charges of driving with excess alcohol' (1984) 128 SJ 539.
3. King LA 'Nomograms for relating blood and urine alcohol concentrations with quantity of alcohol consumed' (1983) 23 J Forens Sci Soc 213.

Womb Leasing

The definition of womb leasing is inconsistent. Much confusion is avoided if it is regarded as the, so far, hypothetical state in which a woman accepts a genetically unrelated embryo, conceived *in vitro* or by uterine lavage, for gestation with the ultimate intention of returning the resultant neonate to its genetic parents. The circumstances in which womb leasing could represent an acceptable medical treatment are very rare, being limited to a means of providing parenthood to a woman who could produce ova but could not carry a child — for example, a woman with severe valvular heart disease. Womb leasing is, however, open to abuse in the non-medical setting in such a way as to represent an extension of the Victorian practice of wet nursing; a photographer's model might, for example, resort to womb leasing purely as a way to motherhood without coincident detriment to her income. Whilst some would say that the arguments in favour of allowing surrogate motherhood apply equally to medically indicated womb leasing, others would contend that the potential social evils outweigh any possible medical benefit to such an extent that the latter process should be outlawed.

The Warnock Committee[1] regarded womb leasing as a form of surrogate motherhood. Although that is, indeed, so, it is convenient to separate the two in so far as, whereas surrogate motherhood, as it is generally understood, requires no special technology, womb leasing must, at present, involve expert medical assistance; the two processes are therefore easily distinguishable in legislation.

See also: Embryo transfer; Surrogate motherhood

1. Warnock M (chairman) *Report of the Committee of Inquiry into Human Fertilisation and Embryology* (Cmnd 9314)(1984) HMSO, London.

Wounds

The law in England and Wales relating to wounding is contained in the Offences Against the Person Act 1861, ss.18, 20 and 47. Section 18 defines the offence of maliciously wounding or causing grievous bodily harm with the intention, *inter alia*, of doing some grievous bodily harm for which the potential penalty is imprisonment for life; s.20 specifies the offences of unlawfully and maliciously wounding or inflicting grievous bodily harm; whilst s.47 refers to causing actual bodily harm. A wound must break the whole skin[1] although a break in a mucous membrane continuous with the skin may also constitute a wound[2]. Causing a fracture would therefore not be wounding but rather causing grievous bodily harm; a bruise might constitute actual bodily harm depending on the degree of severity[3]. No such distinctions are made in Scotland, where an injury of any sort serves to aggravate an assault. Wounds are classified as lacerations, which are typically caused by blunt injury, or incised wounds, which result from cutting instruments; if an incision is deeper than it is broad, it becomes a stab wound. Gunshot wounds constitute a separate topic.

Clean wounds repair themselves by a process of capillary growth, which reinstates the blood supply, and by infiltration of the divided tissues by fibroblasts which, ultimately, form a scar. If there is much avascular tissue present — as, say, a blood clot — the process is similar but results in organisation; the avascular material becomes organised into fibrous tissue of varying cellularity and vascularity. Such a wound is very prone to infection before organisation can be accomplished.

See also: Abrasions; Bruises; Fractures; Gunshot injuries; Incised wounds; Lacerations; Scars; Stab wounds

1. *R v M'Loughlin* (1838) 8 C & P 635. Confirmed in *JJC (a minor) v Eisenhower* [1983] 3 WLR 537.
2. *R v Waltham* (1849) 3 Cox CC 442.
3. *R v Jones* [1981] Crim LR 119.

Wrongful Birth

'Wrongful birth' can be defined as the birth of a defective child as a result of antenatal misdiagnosis or of mismanagement of pregnancy. An action under this head is essentially one by the parents and is often taken in negligence against genetic counsellors.

The problem has attracted little notice in the UK although a maternal action was not excluded in the important case of *McKay v Essex Area Health Authority and another*[1]. Heavy damages were, however, agreed in an unreported case in which a mongol child was born following amniocentesis and a normal report; the terms of agreement and the basis of the claim were not disclosed[2]. The finding in the trial court in *Sciuriaga v Powell*[3] (*see* 'Wrongful pregnancy') clearly suggests that such actions could succeed in Britain.

Several US decisions indicate that actions for wrongful birth follow inevitably from a recognition of the 'right to avoid the birth of a defective infant'[4]. It has been pointed out that, in so far as the time which has to be taken for a diagnosis of fetal abnormality may dictate an abortion in the third trimester, this might well be an illegal procedure following the ruling in *Roe v Wade*[5]. There is, however, no doubt that the State's interest in preserving the life of the fetus is minimal in the context of eugenic abortion[6].

See also: Abortion; Amniocentesis; Genetic counselling; Wrongful pregnancy

1. [1982] 2 WLR 890.
2. *Rawnsley v Leeds Area Health Authority* (1981) *The Times*, 17 November, p.2.
3. (1979) 123 SJ 406.
4. *Harbeson v Parke-Davis Inc* 656 P 2d 483 (Wash, 1983). *See also Curlender v Bio-Science Laboratories* 165 Cal Rptr 477 (1980); *Noccash v Burger* 290 SE 2d 825 (Va, 1982).
5. 93 S Ct 705 (1973).
6. *See* Rush CS 'Genetic screening, eugenic abortion and *Roe v Wade*: how viable is *Roe's* viability standard?' (1983) 50 Brook LR 113.

Wrongful Death of the Fetus

It is probable that no action exists in the UK in respect of wrongful death — or death associated with negligence — of the fetus; the fetus which dies *in utero* has no right of action of itself and the most that could be available is a parental action in negligence for medical expenses and for pain and suffering.

Actions for wrongful death have, however, been successful in the USA. In 1981, the Louisiana Supreme Court rejected the argument that parents could not recover for the loss of a child stillborn by virtue of prenatal injuries because children born dead were considered never to have been born; the stillbirth could be regarded as a child and damages awarded for its loss[1]. The Maryland Court of Appeal 'joined the modern trend' in allowing an action for negligence which caused the premature birth and subsequent death of a previable fetus[2]. In that case, the rather unusual plea that the fact that the mother could have aborted her fetus served to mitigate the negligence was considered to be without foundation.

See also: Abortion; Fetal rights

1. *Danos v St Pierre* 402 So 2d 633 (La, 1981).
2. *Group Health Association Inc v Blumenthal* 453 A 2d 1198 (Md, 1983).

Wrongful Life

An action for wrongful life is to be distinguished in that it is pursued on behalf of an infant rather than by his parents. The essence of the claim is that the child, who is deformed, defective or otherwise disadvantaged, avers that his birth ought to have been prevented.

This basis for action was disallowed in the British case of *McKay v Essex Area Health Authority and another*[1] on the grounds that a doctor is under no legal obligation to a fetus to terminate its life; the doctor's duty is to the mother, not to the child, and the fetus has no legal right to die. 'To impose a duty on the doctor [to terminate the life of the fetus] would be to make a further inroad into the sanctity of human life which would be contrary to public policy. It would require that the life of a handicapped child should be regarded not only as of less value than that of a normal child but so much less valuable as not to be worth preserving' (per Stephenson LJ).

The great majority of commentators believe that the Congenital Disabilities (Civil Liability) Act 1976 now precludes an action for wrongful life but the point may yet be tested in the courts; the relevant remarks on the subject in *McKay* can be looked on as obiter.

The progress of wrongful life actions in the USA is interesting. A strong line of judgments has refused such actions, the reasons being largely those of policy or based on the belief that it is impossible to quantify the difference between a defective existence and no existence[2]. There has, however, been a definite shift in recent years. In *Curlender v Bio-Science Laboratories*[3], the California Court rejected the majority of these arguments and allowed the child's cause in full; there was less certainty in *Turpin v Sortini*[4] when a child was allowed to sue for special damages but not for general damages — i.e. the undefinable difference between life and non-life; the same paradox was followed in *Harbeson v Parke-Davis Inc*[5] in the light of the observation that 'it would be illogical to permit the parents only and not the child to recover the costs of the child's own medical care'. This trend has now passed from the Pacific to the Atlantic coast[6].

The movement is therefore best understood as one in favour of allowing actions for diminished life rather than for wrongful life; as such, it is receiving cautious approval from commentators[7].

See also: Abortion; Wrongful birth

1. [1982] 2 WLR 890.
2. For example, *Williams v State of New York* 18 NYS 2d 461 (1966); *Gleitman v Cosgrove* 296 NYS 2d 689 (1967); *Dumer v St Michael's Hospital* 233 NW 2d 372 (1975).
3. 165 Cal Rptr 477 (1980).
4. 182 Cal Rptr 337 (1982).
5. 656 P 2d 483 (1983).
6. *Procanik v Cillo* 478 A 2d 755 (NJ, 1984).
7. For example, Foutz TK '"Wrongful life": the right not to be born' (1980) 54 Tul LR 480; Jones GE and Perry C 'Can claims for "wrongful life" be justified?' (1983) 9 J Med Ethics 162.

Wrongful Pregnancy

Suits for wrongful pregnancy result from failed sterilisation operations either in the wife or in the husband.

Courts on both sides of the Atlantic have been reluctant to award damages under this head on the general grounds that to do so would put pressure on doctors to encourage abortions[1] and that 'the birth of a child is a blessing and a cause for rejoicing'[2]. There is a tendency to a less idealistic approach in the USA[3].

There are, however, many inconsistencies in this attitude, particularly as to its relationship to legal abortion[4], and there has been a recent run of British cases in which the opposite view has prevailed. Thus, in *Sciuriaga v Powell*[5], the trial judge said 'Surely no-one in these days would argue [that damages were not recoverable] if the child was born deformed or diseased. The fact that the child was born healthy cannot give rise to a different conclusion save as to the measure of damages', and this opinion was not challenged on appeal. It was accepted in that case that refusal of abortion beyond the 14th week of gestation was reasonable and this principle was extended in *Emeh v Kensington and Chelsea and Westminster Area Health Authority* when the Court of Appeal, in reversing the policy decision of the lower court, expressed the view that it can never be right to 'declare it unreasonable for a woman to decline to have an abortion in a case where there is no evidence that there are any medical or psychiatric grounds for terminating the particular pregnancy'[6]. Thus, there seems no reason in English law why recovery of damages should not be available for the birth of a healthy child following medical negligence, and this right is unaffected by the refusal to have the pregnancy terminated at any stage.

The arcadian reasoning in *Udale* was overturned in a case involving negligent sterilisation in the male, the negligence lying in failure to warn the patient that nature might reverse the effects of the operation[7]. Peter Pain J held that '[whilst a healthy baby is a lovely creature] every baby has a belly to be filled and body to be clothed. . .The virtue of making the child loved would be unrewarded if compensation for support was irrecoverable'[8]. The Court of Appeal went further in this case and awarded damages for the pain and discomfort of pregnancy.

See also: Negligence; Sterilisation; Wrongful birth

1. *See* Medicolegal 'Damages and the "unwanted child"' (1984) 288 Br Med J 244.
2. *Udale v Bloomsbury Area Health Authority* [1983] 1 WLR 1098 per Jupp J at 1109; *see also Cataford v Moreau* (1978) 114 DLR 3d 585 in which the birth of an eleventh child was held to be a 'general benefit'.
3. A recent example is *Sutkin v Beck* 629 SW 2d 131 (1982) in which the court nevertheless noted that damages resulting from birth of a physically deformed child were recoverable (*see* 'Wrongful birth').
4. *See* Brahams D 'Damages for unplanned babies — a trend to be discouraged?' (1983) 133 NLJ 643.
5. (1979) 123 SJ 406.
6. [1985] 2 WLR 233 per Slade LJ at 243.
7. *Thake and another v Maurice* [1985] 2 WLR 215, [1984] All ER 513, QBD; [1986] 1 All ER 497, CA.
8. It is to be noted that several cases have been settled out of court. *See* Robertson G 'Damages for the birth of a child — some possible policy barriers' (1983) 23 Med Sci Law 2.

X-linked Disease

X-linked diseases are those which are genetically determined and for which the responsible gene is located in the X chromosome. Since an X-linked dominant and harmful gene would be incompatible with survival of the species, the responsible genes are recessive and can be repressed by a normal X chromosome. Females may therefore become unaffected carriers of the disease whilst, save in exceptional circumstances, only males will be overtly affected. Females can acquire the disease only if a carrier mates with an affected male. All females sired by an affected male will be carriers but an affected male cannot pass the disease to his sons.

The common X-linked recessive diseases are haemophilia (types A and B) and Duchenne muscular dystrophy. Statistically speaking, half the males born to a carrier will be affected whilst half the females will continue the carrier line. The disease can thus be prevented by sexing through amniocentesis and termination of the pregnancy in the event of a male fetus being discovered; but this, in current conditions, involves the agonising dilemma of aborting fetuses of which at least 50 per cent are normal. In the future, fetal blood sampling through fetoscopy or DNA studies on cells obtained from the amniotic fluid or chorionic villi (*see* 'Genetic engineering') may ameliorate this difficulty in the case of haemophilia whilst considerable research is being run into the antenatal diagnosis of muscular dystrophy. Elimination of the disease from the population is virtually impossible as, until the abnormal gene can be diagnosed *in utero*, this would entail sterilisation of all carriers. The ethics of such eugenic selection would then require very careful consideration. Genetic counsellors find, in practice, that the concept of X-linked disease is one which causes greatest difficulty to their patients[1].

See also: Amniocentesis; Eugenics; Fetoscopy; Genetic counselling; Genetic disease; Genetic engineering; Sex chromosomes

1. Emery AEH 'The role of the genetic counsellor in the management of genetic disease' in Papadatos CJ and Bartsocas CS (eds) *The Management of Genetic Disorders* (1979) pp.1–11, AR Liss, New York.

X-rays

X-rays form part of the electromagnetic spectrum in the very high frequency range. They are, thus, ionising radiations which are capable of damaging tissue.

The practical value of X-rays in medicine is immense and quite beyond the scope of a limited entry. Their best known use is in visualising fractures or other abnormalities in the dense bony tissues of the body but all tissues are radio-opaque to a greater or lesser degree and soft tissue X-ray of the chest, for example, is an indispensable part of cardiopulmonary medicine — a use which is maximised in the study of the pneumoconioses in which the X-ray findings are used to distinguish *per se* the degree of affection and of disability. The value of X-ray investigation is also greatly enhanced by the use of injection techniques, in which a radio-opaque dye is injected and its distribution and elimination are studied; such procedures are of ever-increasing sophistication and have, for example, revolutionised the management of cardiac disease. In addition to their diagnostic use, X-rays have a useful and relatively non-invasive research function.

The use of X-rays is not, however, without its dangers — in particular to the patient under investigation, to the operator or to the public at large. X-rays have it in common with all ionising radiations that they may so alter the structure of the cell as to stimulate cancerous overgrowth[1]. There is the further possibility that chromosomal alterations in rapidly growing tissues may result in structural disease and that, in so far as X-rays are known to cause mutations, involvement of the sex cells will increase the general incidence of chromosomal disease in the population. Moreover, it is not known whether there is a threshold dose below which X-rays are harmless or whether all exposures have *some* effect. The use of X-rays in certain types of person is therefore limited by good clinical practice — e.g. in their use in pregnant women[2].

Injury to the operator is now controlled by lead screening from the rays themselves and by rigid monitoring of the total radiation dose sustained. The aspect of the diagnostic use of X-rays which is least often considered is its effect on the general level of background radiation to which the population is exposed. By and large, this is proportional to the sophistication of the medical resources available and it must, again, be looked at bearing in mind the possibility of there being no threshold effect.

The upshot is that the use of X-rays must be controlled and that the benefit to a patient is to be balanced against the harm to him and to the environment — in short, a clinical decision is required[3]. (*See* 'Radiology' for further discussion.)

Apparently paradoxically, whilst X-rays may predispose to cancer, they are also used in the treatment of the disease. The difference results from the dose — which is much higher when used in therapy — and from the greater susceptibility to ionising radiation of the malignant cells which are dividing faster than are the normal cells of the body. More elaborate types of radiation are often used now but the principle remains the same.

X-rays have two major uses in forensic pathology: the improvement of the autopsy in violent death — particularly that associated with gunshot or explosive injury — and in the process of identification of severely mutilated bodies. As to the former, the recovery of fragments of bullets or bomb casings is of such forensic importance that X-ray coverage of the dissection is wellnigh essential. The latter is divisible into primary identification — particularly as to the age and sex of the body — and personal identification which involves comparison of *ante mortem* and *post mortem* films. This last has a most useful subdivision as part of dental identification (*see* 'Odontology'). The subject is discussed in detail under 'Identification of the dead'.

See also: Angiography; Cancer; Chromosomal disease; Congenital disease; Explosions; Firearm injuries; Identification of the dead; Ionising radiation; Malignant disease; Mutation; Odontology; Pneumoconioses; Prescribed diseases and occupations; Radiology

1. Blood dyscrasia due to ionising radiation is a prescribed disease.
2. Leading Article 'The ten day rule' [1975] 4 Br Med J 543.
3. Jennett B 'Some medico-legal aspects of the management of acute head injury' [1976] 1 Br Med J 1383.

Z

ZOONOSES

A zoonosis is a disease which, normally, affects animals but which is transmissible to man without morphological change in the causative organism. Such transmission may be direct — as in the passage of the rabies virus in the saliva of a rabid animal; more commonly, an intermediate vector is involved — the transmission of plague, which is a disease of rodents, through the rat flea is a good example. Once established in human hosts, a zoonosis may become epidemic in man — e.g. yellow fever. Occasionally, zoonoses are industrial in nature; leptospirosis, which is spread to man (predominantly miners or sewer workers) by infected rats, is a prescribed disease for the purposes of the Social Security Act 1975.

The main medico-legal importance of zoonoses lies in the fact that preventive action can be taken not only against the intermediate vector but also against the reservoir of infection. This can often be done by regulation and this is particularly effective in an island situation. Thus, the strongest regulations restricting the importation of animals has eliminated rabies from the UK[1] whilst regulations as to the inspection and fumigation of ships have controlled the spread of rat-borne disease from areas in which they are endemic[2].

1. Animal Health Act 1981.
2. International Health Regulations 1969, art.54 as amended.

Journal Abbreviations

A	Atlantic Reporter (USA)
AC	Law Reports, Appeal Cases
ACTR	Australian Capital Territory Reports
ALJ	Australian Law Journal
ALJR	Australian Law Journal Reports
ALR	American Law Reports, Annotated
Acta Psychiat Scand	Acta Psychiatrica Scandinavica
Add	Addams' Ecclesiastical Reports
Advocates Soc J	Advocates Society Journal
Aerospace Med	Aerospace Medicine
All ER	All England Law Reports
Am J Cardiol	American Journal of Cardiology
Am J Comp Law	American Journal of Comparative Law
Am J Dis Child	American Journal of Diseases of Children
Am J Forens Med Path	American Journal of Forensic Medicine and Pathology
Am J Law Med	American Journal of Law and Medicine
Am J Obstet Gynec	American Journal of Obstetrics and Gynecology
Am J Psychiat	American Journal of Psychiatry
Am J Roentgenol	American Journal of Roentgenology
Anglo-Am LR	Anglo-American Law Review
Ann Acad Med Singapore	Annals of the Academy of Medicine, Singapore
Arch Dis Childh	Archives of Disease in Childhood
Arch Environ Hlth	Archives of Environmental Health
Arch Gen Psychiat	Archives of General Psychiatry
Arch Intern Med	Archives of Internal Medicine
Arch Sex Behav	Archives of Sexual Behavior
Aust & NZ J Crim	Australian and New Zealand Journal of Criminology
Aust & NZ J Psychiat	Australian and New Zealand Journal of Psychiatry

Aviat Space Environ Med	Aviation, Space and Environmental Medicine
Biol Psychiat	Biological Psychiatry
BMA News Rev	BMA News Review
Boston ULR	Boston University Law Review
Br J Criminol	British Journal of Criminology, Delinquency and Deviant Social Behaviour
Br Dent J	British Dental Journal
Br J Delinq	British Journal of Delinquency
Br J Hosp Med	British Journal of Hospital Medicine
Br J Psychiat	British Journal of Psychiatry
Br J Surg	British Journal of Surgery
Br Med J	British Medical Journal
Brook LR	Brooklyn Law Review
Bull Am Acad Psychiat Law	Bulletin of the American Academy of Psychiatry and the Law
C & K	Carrington and Kirwan
C & P	Carrington and Payne's Reports, Nisi Prius
CAR	Commonwealth Arbitration Reports
CCC	Canadian Criminal Cases, Annotated
CCLT	Canadian Cases in the Law of Torts
CLJ	Cambridge Law Journal
CLR	Commonwealth Law Reports
CR	Criminal Reports (Canada)
Cal App	California Appeal
Cal LR	California Law Review
Cal Rptr	California Reporter
Cal West LR	California Western Law Review
Camb LJ	Cambridge Law Journal
Can Bar Rev	Canadian Bar Review
Can Med Ass J	Canadian Medical Association Journal
Case West LR	Case Western Law Review
Ch	Law Reports, Chancery Division (since 1890)
ChD	Law Reports, Chancery Division (to 1890)
Cl & Fin	Clark and Finnelly's Reports, House of Lords
Clin Electroenceph	Clinical Electroencephalography
Coke Inst	Coke's Institutes
Col LR	Columbia Law Review
Community Hlth	Community Health
Comp Int LJ Southern Africa	Comparative and International Law Journal of Southern Africa
Conn Med	Connecticut Medicine
Couper	Couper's Justiciary Reports (Scotland)
Cowp	Cowper's Reports, King's Bench
Cox CC	E.W. Cox's Criminal Law Cases
Crim App R	Criminal Appeal Reports
Crim Delinq	Crime and Delinquency
Crim LJ	Criminal Law Journal
Crim LQ	Criminal Law Quarterly

Crim LR	Criminal Law Review
DLR	Dominion Law Reports (Canada)
Dears & B	Dearsly and Bell's Crown Cases Reserved
Den	Denison's Crown Cases Reserved
Dis Nerv Syst	Diseases of the Nervous System
Duke LJ	Duke Law Journal
Dunlop	Dunlop, Court of Session Cases (Scotland) 2nd series
EHRR	European Human Rights Reports
ER	English Reports
Exch	Exchequer Reports
F	Federal Reports (USA)
F & F	Foster and Finlason's Reports, Nisi Prius
Fam	Law Reports, Family Division
Fam Law	Family Law
Fam LQ	Family Law Quarterly
FLR	Family Law Reports
F Supp	Federal Supplement (USA)
Fed Cas	Federal Cases (USA)
Forens Sci	Forensic Science
Forens Sci Int	Forensic Science International
H & C	Hurlstone and Coltman's Reports, Exchequer
HC Debs	House of Commons Debates
ICLQ	International and Comparative Law Quarterly
ICR	a. Industrial Court Reports 1972–74
	b. Industrial Cases Reports 1975–current
IRLR	Industrial Relations Law Reports
Int Arch Occupat Environ Hlth	International Archives of Occupational and Environmental Health
Int J Cancer	International Journal of Cancer
Int J Law Psychiat	International Journal of Law and Psychiatry
Int J Med Law	International Journal of Medicine and the Law
Ir Med J	Irish Medical Journal
Irv	Irvine's Justiciary Reports (Scotland)
JAMA	Journal of the American Medical Association
JC	Court of Justiciary Cases (Scotland)
JP	Justice of the Peace
J Appl Bact	Journal of Applied Bacteriology
J Child Psychol Psychiat	Journal of Child Psychology and Psychiatry
J Clin Path	Journal of Clinical Pathology
J Drug Depend	Journal of Drug Dependence
J Epidem Comm Hlth	Journal of Epidemiology and Community Health
J Fam Law	Journal of Family Law
J Forens Med	Journal of Forensic Medicine
J Forens Sci	Journal of Forensic Sciences

J Forens Sci Soc	Journal of the Forensic Science Society
J Law Soc Scot	Journal of the Law Society of Scotland
J Med Ethics	Journal of Medical Ethics
J Med Genet	Journal of Medical Genetics
J Neurol Neurosurg Psychiat	Journal of Neurology, Neurosurgery and Psychiatry
J Neurosci	Journal of Neuroscience
J Neurosurg	Journal of Neurosurgery
J Philosophy Pub Aff	Journal of Philosophy and Public Affairs
J Roy Coll Gen Pract	Journal of the Royal College of General Practitioners
J Roy Coll Phys Lond	Journal of the Royal College of Physicians of London
J Roy Soc Med	Journal of the Royal Society of Medicine
J Soc Welf Law	Journal of Social Welfare Law
Jur Rev	Juridical Review
KB	Law Reports, King's Bench Division
KIR	Knight's Industrial Reports
LQR	Law Quarterly Review
LR 1 CCR	Law Reports, Crown Cases Reserved, vol. 1
LS	Legal Studies
LT	Law Times
Law Med Hlth Care	Law, Medicine and Health Care
Law Soc Gaz	Law Society Gazette
Leach	Leach's Crown Cases
Lew CC	Lew's Crown Cases on the Northern Circuit
Lloyds Rep	Lloyds List Law Reports
M & R	Manning and Ryland
MLR	Modern Law Review
McGill LJ	McGill Law Journal
Mass	Massachusetts Reports
Med J Austral	Medical Journal of Australia
Med Law	Medicine and Law
Med-Leg J	Medico-Legal Journal
Med Sci Law	Medicine, Science and the Law
Melb ULR	Melbourne University Law Review
Mich LR	Michigan Law Review
Misc	New York Miscellaneous
Miss LR	Missouri Law Review
Monash LR	Monash University Law Review
Mood CC	Moody's Crown Cases Reserved
NE	North Eastern Reporter (USA)
NILQ	Norther Ireland Legal Quarterly
NLJ	New Law Journal
NW	North Western Reporter (USA)
NYS	New York State Reports
NZLJ	New Zealand Law Journal
NZLR	New Zealand Law Reports

New Engl J Med	New England Journal of Medicine
OR	Ontario Reports
Os HLJ	Osgoode Hall Law Journal
P	Pacific Reporter (USA)
P	Law Reports, Probate, Divorce and Admiralty Division (1892–1971)
PD	Law Reports, Probate, Divorce, and Admiralty Division (to 1891)
Prescribers J	Prescribers' Journal
Proc R Soc Ed	Proceedings of the Royal Society of Edinburgh
Proc R Soc Med	Proceedings of the Royal Society of Medicine
Psychiat Med	Psychiatric Medicine
Psycholog Med	Psychological Medicine
Psychosom Med	Psychosomatic Medicine
QB	Law Reports, Queen's Bench Division
Qd R	Queensland Reports
Quart J Med	Quarterly Journal of Medicine
Quart J Studies Alcohol	Quarterly Journal of Studies on Alcohol
R	Rettie, Court of Session Cases, 4th series (Scotland)
RTR	Road Traffic Reports
Rev de Droit	Revue de Droit
Rev Dr Civ	Revue de Droit Civil
Rev Neurol	Revue Neurologique
Rob Eccl	Robertson's Ecclesiastical Reports
Rutgers LR	Rutgers Law Review
SA	South African Law Reports
SALJ	South African Law Journal
SASR	South Australian State Reports
SC	Court of Session Cases (Scotland)
SCCR	Scottish Criminal Case Reports
SCR	Supreme Court Reports (Canada)
SE	South Eastern Reporter (USA)
SJ	Solicitors Journal
SLR	Scottish Law Reporter
SLT	Scots Law Times
S Ct	Supreme Court Reporter (USA)
Scott Med J	Scottish Medical Journal
So	Southern Reporter (USA)
Soc Prob	Social Problems
Soc Sci Med	Social Science and Medicine
Sociol Q	Sociological Quarterly
Sociol Soc Res	Sociology and Social Research
St Tr	State Trials
Stan LR	Stanford Law Review
Surg Gynecol Obstet	Surgery, Gynecology and Obstetrics
TLR	The Times Law Reports

Trans R Soc Trop Med Hyg	Transactions of the Royal Society of Tropical Medicine and Hygiene
Tul LR	Tulane Law Review
US	Reports of Cases in the Supreme Court of the United States of America
USLW	United States Law Week
U Chic LR	University of Chicago Law Review
U Pa LR	University of Pennsylvania Law Review
U Toronto LJ	University of Toronto Law Journal
VR	Victorian Reports
WAR	Western Australian Reports
Wash ULR	Washington University Law Review
White	White's Justiciary Reports (Scotland)
WLR	Weekly Law Reports
WWR	Western Weekly Reports (Canada)
Z Rechtsmed	Zeitschrift für Rechtsmedizin

Statutes and statutory instruments

*The Incest and Related Offences (Scotland) Act 1986 received the Royal Assent as this book was going to press.

List of cases

Thematic index of entries

The purpose of this index is to give the user a general view of the medical and legal topics covered in the encyclopaedia. It is arranged in broad categories within which the subjects are listed, so far as is possible, by progressive association.

Anatomy, Physiology and Pathology

Enzymes, 197
Abdominal cavity, 1
  Stomach, 536
  Liver disease and injury, 331
    Jaundice, 318
    Hepatitis, 264
    Cirrhosis, 104
    Industrial poisoning, 300
  Splenic injury, 528
  Kidney failure, 323
    Urine, 575
    Dialysis, 157
      Haemodialysis, 253
    Transplantation of organs, 561
      Immunosuppression, 289
      Human Tissue Act 1961, 274
  Diabetes, 156
    Insulin, 310
      Hypoglycaemia, 280
Respiratory system, 482
  Larynx, 326
    Hyoid bone, 277
  Lung disease and injury, 334
    Emphysema, 193
    Pulmonary oedema, 454
    Pneumonia, 427
    Pneumoconioses, 426
      Cor pulmonale, 126
    Tuberculosis, 567
  Placenta, 425
    Umbilical cord, 570
Cardiovascular system, 90
  Aorta, 39
    Aneurysm, 34
  Arteries, 41

Atheroma, 48
  Infarction, 303
  Gangrene, 235
Heart disease, 261
  Coronary disease, 126
    Myocardial infarction, 360
    Electrocardiogram, 186
    Ventricular fibrillation, 580
  Cor pulmonale, 126
  Hypertensive disease, 277
    Cardiomyopathy, 89
  Myocarditis, 361
Blood
  Erythrocytes, 199
    Anaemia, 31
    Haemoglobinopathy, 254
      Thalassaemia, 554
      Sickle cell disease, 514
  Blood groups, 64
    Antigen, 38
    Antibody, 37
    Rhesus system, 485
  Blood stains, 66
  Haemorrhage, 255
    Petechial haemorrhage, 419
  Blood transfusion, 67
    Transfusion reactions, 560
    Jehovah's Witnesses, 318
  Plasma, 425
    Electrolytes, 188
    Hypovolaemia, 282
    Surgical shock, 547
  Coagulation of the blood, 105
    Disseminated intravascular coagulation, 166
    Thrombosis, 555
    Embolism, 189
      Pulmonary embolism, 453

Medicine and Professions Allied to Medicine

Medical Treatment and Research

Poisons and Drugs

Death

The Fetus, Neonate and Child

The Family

Subject index